Table of Contents

D1240672

© Robert Frerck/Odyssey/Chicago

*The population figures quoted in this guide are based on
the 1996 estimated US census.*

*Adresses, telephone numbers, opening hours and prices given in this guide
are accurate at the time of publication. We apologize for any inconvenience
resulting from outdated information. Please send us your comments:*

Michelin Travel Publications
Editorial Department, PO Box 19001, Greenville, SC 29602-9001

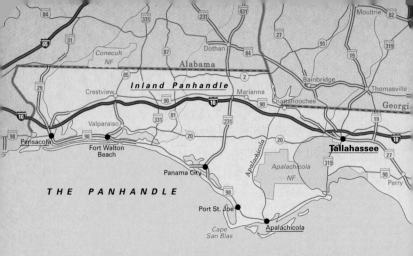

Principal Sights

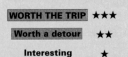

WORTH THE TRIP	★★★
Worth a detour	★★
Interesting	★

Place names in black type indicate the cities and sights
described in this guide *(see Index)*.

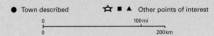

● Town described   ☆ ■ ▲ Other points of interest

| 0 | 100 mi |
| 0 | 200 km |

The Bahamas

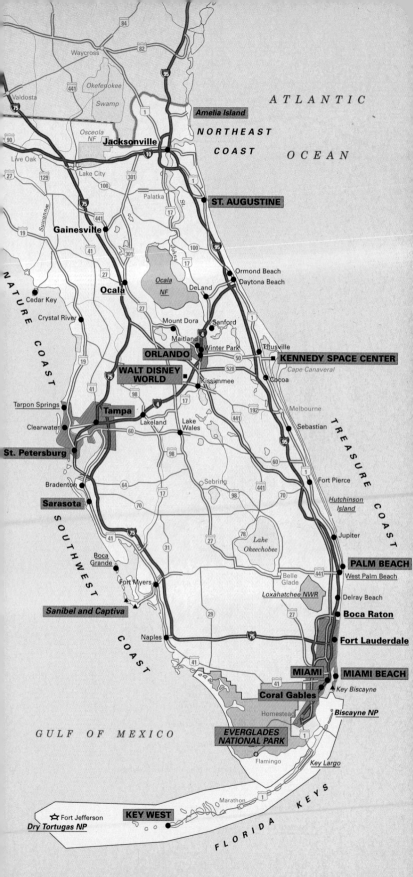

ATLANTIC

NORTHEAST

COAST

OCEAN

Amelia Island

Jacksonville

Osceola NF

Okefenokee Swamp

Valdosta

Live Oak

Lake City

Palatka

ST. AUGUSTINE

Gainesville

Ocala NF

Ormond Beach

Daytona Beach

DeLand

NATURE COAST

Cedar Key

Crystal River

Ocala

Mount Dora

Sanford

Maitland

Winter Park

ORLANDO

Titusville

KENNEDY SPACE CENTER

Cape Canaveral

WALT DISNEY WORLD

Kissimmee

Cocoa

Tarpon Springs

Tampa

Lakeland

Lake Wales

Melbourne

TREASURE COAST

Clearwater

St. Petersburg

Sebastian

Bradenton

Sarasota

Sebring

Fort Pierce

Hutchinson Island

SOUTHWEST

Boca Grande

Lake Okeechobee

Jupiter

PALM BEACH

Fort Myers

Belle Glade

West Palm Beach

Loxahatchee NWR

Delray Beach

Sanibel and Captiva

Boca Raton

Naples

Fort Lauderdale

COAST

MIAMI

MIAMI BEACH

Coral Gables

Key Biscayne

Biscayne NP

Homestead

GULF OF MEXICO

EVERGLADES NATIONAL PARK

Flamingo

Key Largo

Marathon

☆ Fort Jefferson

Dry Tortugas NP

KEY WEST

FLORIDA KEYS

ALABAMA

De Funiak Springs

★★ Florida Caverns SP

The Panhandle

★ Tallahassee

Wakulla Springs SP ★★

Pensacola

Fort Walton Beach

Seaside

Panama City

Port St. Joe

Perry

★ Apalachicola

GULF OF MEXICO

State of Florida

Regional Driving Tours

Coast to Coast:
139 miles – 10 days

East Coast:
385 miles – 15 days

The Keys:
158 miles – 7 days

Nature Coast:
222 miles – 4 days

North Central:
235 miles – 10 days

Panhandle Loop:
429 miles – 7 days

Southwest Coast:
251 miles – 12 days

○   ○   Towns described in this guide (see Index)

   Suggested overnight stop

★★ **Sarasota**   City map in this guide

Treasure Coast   Regional map in this guide

0   100 mi
0   200 km

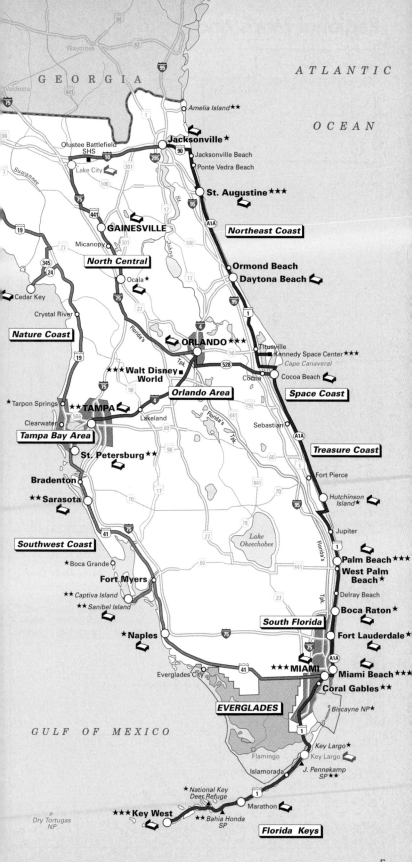

ATLANTIC

OCEAN

GEORGIA

Waycross

Valdosta

Olustee Battlefield SHS

Lake City

Cedar Key

Crystal River

Nature Coast

Tarpon Springs

Clearwater

North Central

GAINESVILLE

Micanopy

Ocala *

Amelia Island ★★

Jacksonville ★

Jacksonville Beach

Ponte Vedra Beach

St. Augustine ★★★

Northeast Coast

Ormond Beach

Daytona Beach

Titusville

Kennedy Space Center ★★★

Cape Canaveral

ORLANDO ★★★

★★★ Walt Disney World

Orlando Area

Cocoa

Cocoa Beach

Space Coast

★★ TAMPA

Lakeland

Tampa Bay Area

Sebastian

Treasure Coast

St. Petersburg ★★

Bradenton

★★ Sarasota

Southwest Coast

Fort Pierce

Hutchinson Island ★

Jupiter

*Boca Grande

Fort Myers

★★ Captiva Island

★★ Sanibel Island

★ Naples

Lake Okeechobee

Palm Beach ★★★

West Palm Beach ★

Delray Beach

Boca Raton ★

Fort Lauderdale

South Florida

★★★ MIAMI

Everglades City

Miami Beach ★★★

Coral Gables ★★

EVERGLADES

Biscayne NP ★

GULF OF MEXICO

Flamingo

Key Largo ★

Key Largo

J. Pennekamp SP ★★

Islamorada

★ National Key Deer Refuge

★★★ Key West

Dry Tortugas NP

Marathon

★★ Bahia Honda SP

Florida Keys

5

Regional Maps and Distance Chart

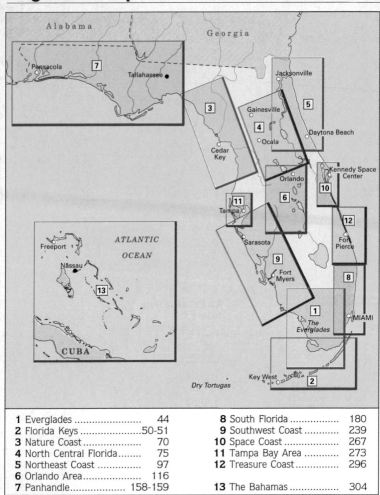

Distances given in miles;
to determine kilometers, multiply by 1.6

	Miami	Orlando	Tampa
Atlanta	674	446	465
Chicago	1388	1160	1179
Dallas	1287	1059	1143
Los Angeles	2760	2532	2531
New York	1291	1095	1142

example: **Miami to Tallahassee** = 485 mi

Cocoa	Daytona Beach	Gainesville	Jacksonville	Key West	Miami	Naples	Orlando	Palm Beach	Panama City	Pensacola	St. Augustine	St. Petersburg	Sarasota	Tallahassee	Tampa
66															
159	98														
156	93	70													
351	412	486	509												
187	255	334	347	157											
226	241	264	319	236	107										
51	54	111	139	390	228	187									
124	193	273	280	229	67	149	166								
386	334	243	265	754	592	481	364	525							
489	434	342	355	857	695	575	467	628	103						
116	54	73	39	469	307	285	111	240	301	404					
143	159	147	220	383	249	143	95	219	370	473	206				
164	183	185	256	345	213	105	129	183	395	498	227	39			
291	237	148	167	642	485	389	257	418	98	188	203	252	285		
122	139	134	198	417	245	156	78	199	360	455	184	22	53	241	

Useful Addresses

VISIT FLORIDA
P. O. Box 1100
Tallahassee FL 32302 ☎ 850-488-5607
or 888-735-2872
www.FLAUSA.com

Florida Association of RV Parks & Campgrounds
1340 Vickers Dr.
Tallahassee FL 32303-3041 ☎ 850-562-7151
www.floridacamping.com

Florida Department of Environmental Protection
Division of Recreation & Parks
3900 Commonwealth Blvd.
Tallahassee FL 32399-3000 ☎ 850-488-9872
www.dep.state.fl.us./parks

Office of Fisheries Management
Mail Station 240
3900 Commonwealth Blvd.
Tallahassee FL 32399-3000 ☎ 850-922-4340

Office of Greenways & Trails
2600 Blair Stone Rd.
Tallahassee FL 32399-2400 ☎ 850-487-4784
www.dep.state.fl.us/gwt

Florida Department of Transportation
605 Suwannee St.
Tallahassee FL 32399 ☎ 850-487-1200

Florida Sports Foundation
2964 Wellington Circle North
Tallahassee FL 32308 ☎ 850-488-3478

US Forest Service
325 John Knox Rd., Suite F100
Tallahassee FL 32303 ☎ 850-942-9300

About This Guide

The guide is organized into 12 regions of
Florida (listed alphabetically) and one section
on the Bahamas. Within these sections, each
Entry Heading is followed by a population
figure, map reference and tourist information
phone number, where applicable. In the text,
useful information such as addresses, recommended visiting times, opening hours,
admission charges and telephone numbers
appears in italics. Several entries contain
digressions, entertaining stops on your
itinerary that are marked by a purple bar
and indicated on maps with the ❶ symbol.
Cross-references to destinations described in
the text appear in SMALL CAPITALS; consult the
Index for the appropriate page number.

Lee Island Coast V8CB

Ocean Drive, Miami Beach - Vladpans, Odyssey/Chicago

Introduction to Florida

Flor. 2

Florida Landscapes

Distinguished by its 1,197-mile coastline—second after Alaska among the 50 states—Florida is surrounded by the sea: the Atlantic Ocean to the east, the Straits of Florida to the south and the Gulf of Mexico to the west. On land, to the north and northwest, lie Georgia and Alabama, whose narrow corridor to the Gulf coast reaches around Florida's extreme northwestern border along the Perdido River. Thanks to the state's peninsular shape, no point is more than 80mi from saltwater. Land elevations vary only slightly—from sea level to a peak of 345ft *(p 11)* in the PANHANDLE. Ranking 22nd in area, the state comprises 59,988sq mi—including 5,991sq mi of water. With an estimated 30,000 lakes, including the nation's third-largest freshwater lake, Lake Okeechobee, Florida claims more lakes than any US state south of Wisconsin. Most of the lakes are natural, with many the result of sinkholes *(p 11)*. In addition, nearly a quarter of the nation's first-magnitude springs (those that discharge 64.6 million gallons or more of water per day) surface in Florida.

Geologic Past

Lacking the telltale exposed strata of eroded mountain outcrops, Florida reveals its geology much less readily than other states. Early efforts at peering into the geological past were mainly a side benefit from deep well borings and other commercial explorations below the land's surface. The evidence amassed by earth scientists over the years has helped sketch a composite portrait of what is probably the youngest region in the continental US—that is, the last to emerge from a primordial, subtropical sea only 10 to 15 million years ago.

Origins – During the late Paleozoic era, Florida was part of the supercontinent Pangea, a C-shaped, crustal conglomerate formed by the earth's colliding major landmasses some 280 million years ago. Straddling the equator, Pangea split along a north-south axis 130 million years later and began to break up into the modern continents of Eurasia, Africa, North and South America, Antarctica and Australia. The Atlantic Ocean was born as the larger continental plates drifted away from the sea's mid-ocean ridge.

Precambrian Florida was one of the many terranes, or smaller crustal pieces, set afloat among the larger continents. Tracking northwards, it was grafted onto the much larger North American plate at a time when a chain of volcanic islands erupted off the mainland and arced into what are now the BAHAMAS.

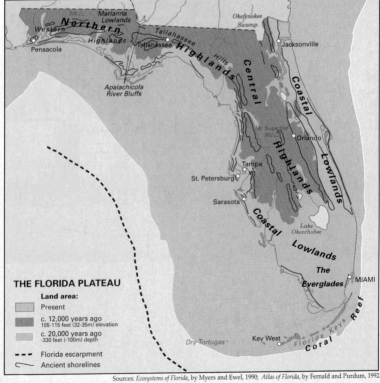

THE FLORIDA PLATEAU

Land area:
- Present
- c. 12,000 years ago
  105-115 feet (32-35m) elevation
- c. 20,000 years ago
  -330 feet (-100m) depth
- - - Florida escarpment
- Ancient shorelines

Sources: *Ecosystems of Florida*, by Myers and Ewel, 1990; *Atlas of Florida*, by Fernald and Purdum, 1992

Over time balmy shallow seas covered this bedrock; while dinosaurs roamed the great landmass to the north, silts and clays washed down from the Appalachian Mountains and fanned out into extensive submarine deltas along Florida's northern shore. To the south, marine shells mixed with microscopic carbonate fragments accumulated in a massive layer of limestone and dolomite. In places 13,000ft to 18,000ft thick, these sedimentary rocks cover much of the Florida Plateau from the Gulf escarpment to the Atlantic Ocean.

During the late Oligocene, the plateau broke the surface of the sea. As Ice Age glaciers locked up more and more of the earth's water, Florida's land area grew—possibly to twice its present-day size. During the early Pleistocene, this part of the continent became a haven for mammoths, mastodons, saber-toothed tigers, sloths and other large mammals retreating overland from the frozen north.

The Florida Plateau Today – As the continental ice sheets melted and re-froze, the sea level rose and fell several times, etching successive terraces into ancient shorelines that are still visible today. Though much the same size, the plateau now lies half submerged again, its edges defining the continental shelf which surrounds Florida at some 300ft below the sea. Deepwater harbors on the Gulf side result from a pronounced westward dip of the plateau that continues to this day: the plateau's surface rises about 6ft at MIAMI, and it tilts downward about 30ft at PENSACOLA.

Regional Landscapes *Map p 10*

For the most part a flat terrain with sandy and clay soils, Florida holds within its boundaries an astonishing diversity of landscapes, each exhibiting its own distinct characteristics. From hardwood forests to freshwater marshes, from coastal dunes and barrier islands to tropical coral reefs, the Sunshine State promises great variety to travelers of both highway and foot path.

Northern Highlands – Encompassing much of the Panhandle between the Alabama state line and the Withlacoochee River, this hilly area of forests and rivers unrolls as a 250mi long and 30mi wide band from west to east. Florida's natural apex—at 345ft, not even as high as some of the state's urban skyscrapers—stands 25mi north of De Funiak Springs in Walton County near the Alabama border. Encased by scrub and high pine as well as temperate hardwood forests, Florida's principal rivers course through this sparsely populated, largely rural region. The state's largest springs also originate here.

Ranging from the Perdido River to the Apalachicola River, the **Western Highlands** form a south-sloping complex dissected by narrow stream valleys with steep bluffs. An open overstory of longleaf pines and deciduous oaks above a ground cover of perennial grasses characterizes the vegetation of this region. The life cycle of long-leaf pine is indelibly linked to fire. Lightning-sparked blazes foster seed germination and enhance pine forest regeneration.

Encompassing most of the upstream drainage basins of the Chipola and Choctawhatchee Rivers, the **Marianna Lowlands** may have been the first area of Florida to emerge from the sea. Composed of Eocene sedimentary rocks, the rolling landscape wedged into this corner of the 10 features numerous springs, scattered limestone outcrops, and countless sinkholes, lakes and ponds.

One of the state's unusual geographical features, **sinkholes** occur when the limestone foundation erodes under topsoil, leaving a bowl-shaped depression in the earth. Whereas a solution sinkhole forms gradually, a collapse sinkhole happens suddenly when an underground cavern caves in. Sinks often result from either drought or heavy rain—both of which can weaken the underlying limestone structure. Many become basins for swamps, ponds or lakes.

Just to the east of the Marianna Lowlands, the **Tallahassee Hills** stretch 100mi from the Apalachicola River to the Withlacoochee River. This region of gentle rises and forested valleys slopes upward to form a 300ft-high plateau west of Tallahassee near the Georgia border. Its fertile clay soils nourish hardwood forests (cypress, live oak, magnolia and hickory) more extensive than those found anywhere else in the state.

One of Florida's most remarkable geological formations can be found on this area's western border. The **Apalachicola River Bluffs**, a series of steep bluffs and ravines, line the eastern

■ **Sinkholes**

In 1981 a 300ft-wide sink opened up in Winter Park, engulfing six vehicles, a house and parts of two streets. The largest sink on record in Florida, it measures 100ft deep. (It's no wonder that sinkhole insurance has become a popular financial instrument in the state!) Between 400 and 4,000 new sinkholes develop in Florida every year, most less than 20ft wide.

shore of the Apalachicola River in Gadsden and Liberty counties. Parts of this river system, which rose in the Appalachian Mountains during the early Cenozoic era, have been above sea level for as long as 24 million years. Forests along these bluffs shelter the native Torreya trees. Now near extinction, *Torreya taxifolia* is preserved in Torreya State Park *(p 160)*.

Central Highlands – The green spine of Florida runs down the middle of the peninsula from the southernmost reaches of the Okefenokee Swamp (which dips across the Georgia border into northeast Florida) for 250mi to Lake Okeechobee. Though the northern section bulges to 60mi in width, the region tapers to a point in the south, where it converges with the EVERGLADES and the Coastal Lowlands. Characterized by longitudinal ridges and upland plains and valleys, this region boasts thousands of lakes.

The world's heaviest concentration of **citrus trees** flourishes along a 100mi-long ridge (1mi to 25mi wide and 240ft high) from Leesburg to Sebring. "The Ridge," acclaimed science writer John McPhee notes, "is the Florida Divide, the peninsular watershed, and, to hear Floridians describe it, the world's most stupendous mountain range after the Himalayas and the Andes...." This infamous ridge reaches its pinnacle at 302ft Mount Sugarloaf.

Northern reaches of the Central Highlands also claim a high concentration of natural **springs**. The combination of warm climate, heavy humidity, abundant decayed vegetation and a thick limestone bedrock makes north Florida ideal terrain for spring formation. South of Lake Okeechobee, where the limestone peters out, no springs exist. Bubbling up from the Floridan Aquifer *(p 14)*, these clear pools provide soothing, therapeutic waters for thousands of visitors each year.

Coastal Lowlands – Harboring nearly all the state's major commercial, industrial and resort areas, the flat, low-lying areas rimming the peninsula spread inland as much as 60mi in some places and include the Florida Keys and the Everglades. Dominated by pastureland and extensive farming, the region's interior contrasts sharply with its glittering margins, where the state's environment-based tourism and recreational activities are focused. Florida's fine quartz and calcium carbonate (shell fragments) sand make dazzling white beaches. The oldest, finest—and purest quartz—sand, washed over the eons to a powdery texture, can be found on Florida's west coast near SARASOTA and along the Panhandle coast *(p 162)*.

Beach in Northwest Florida

Blessed with a gentle climate and warm Gulf and Atlantic waters, the state's coastal areas encompass a variety of natural environments. **Estuaries**, the most productive marine habitat in Florida, line nearly the entire coast where freshwater mingles with saltwater. These shallow-water communities are vital for the development of a tremendous number of marine organisms. Another nursery for fish and shellfish, **mangrove swamps** edge the southeast and southwest coasts. More than 200 different types of fish and 180 bird species find habitat here, as do the endangered American crocodile and the Florida manatee. Wind-blown **dunes** and their backdrop of **maritime forest** harbor sea oats and 22 other native plant species, as well as hosts of shorebirds.

Along both the Atlantic and Gulf coasts, strings of narrow, elongated sandy spits form protective **barrier islands** sheltering the mainland's many inlets, bays and estuaries. In addition to the periodic damage caused by hurricanes and violent winter storms, their ecological survival is severely tested by coastal development.

The Everglades – Considered a separate ecosystem, the broad expanse of the Everglades is covered by a shallow, slow-moving river that flows southward from Lake Okeechobee to the Florida Bay. Freshwater marshes, saw grass prairies, swamps and hardwood hammocks cover this depression. The youngest part of Florida, the area south of Lake Okeechobee emerged from the sea upon built-up layers of live coral clinging to submerged oolitic limestone. With the eventual formation of sand dunes that sealed out the ocean, a new freshwater basin filled with marine plant life and eventually became the peat- and boglands that served as the forerunner to the Everglades—a territory unlike any other in the world.

Scattered along the southern end of the Everglades, small rocky hammocks—designated as **South Florida Rockland**—give rare shelter to pines and broad-leaved tropical plants among barren limestone outcrops.

Tropical Coral Reefs – Vital to Florida's economy, **coral reefs** extend in a 150mi-long curve from near Miami to the Dry Tortugas, 65mi west of KEY WEST. Commercial and recreational fishing industries depend on the reef ecosystems, as do diving and snorkeling enthusiasts. Found nowhere else in the continental US, these spectacular underwater worlds are composed of calcified limestone secreted by invertebrate coral polyps. The formations began forming some 7,000 years ago. Colorful fans, coral branches and plumes on the reef create intricate forests inhabited by diverse communities of tropical fish, sponges, spiny lobsters and other exotic sea creatures, making the Keys one of the world's most popular diving destinations.

Balancing Act – With one of the fastest growing populations in the country, Florida faces the likelihood of ever-greater loss of its wildlife, native vegetation and natural resources. Coral reefs and other marine environments contend with oil drilling and contamination; wetlands are lost to drainage, filling and development; and upland forests and flatwoods are reduced by logging and conversion to citrus groves. In response, state and private organizations have begun to buy more and more land to be set aside for conservation and recreation. Public awareness of the importance of these environments has also helped strike a balance between nature and man. Programs like the state-funded Preservation 2000, which commands a $300 million annual budget for purchasing environmentally sensitive land, offer Florida a fighting chance of preserving for future residents and visitors a few wild landscapes washed by balmy breezes and timeless subtropical seas.

Climate

Considered by many its most important natural resource, Florida's climate generally remains pleasant from January to December, drawing tourists year-round. Conditions vary from tropical in the KEYS and subtropical in the central region to temperate in the PANHANDLE. Positioned at a more southerly latitude than any US state except Hawaii, Florida claims the country's highest average year-round temperatures, with Key West ranking as the hottest city in the nation at an average of 77.4°F. The warm Gulf Stream, which flows around the Florida Straits and north up the Atlantic coast from the tropics, tempers the prevailing easterly wind that blows over the peninsula.

More than half the average annual rainfall of 52in a year falls between the beginning of June and the end of September (the month when most hurricanes occur). These hot, humid summers bring hordes of mosquitoes to the forests and marshes. Winter, the main tourist season, enjoys mild and relatively dry weather—especially in central and south Florida. The Panhandle suffers a more continental winter, with a higher frequency of freezing temperatures. Snowfall is almost nonexistent, though several inches—a dusting of which reached as far south as MIAMI BEACH—were recorded in the north part of the state in 1977.

The combination of moist air and sun-heated land and water surfaces in Florida provides ideal conditions for the formation of **thunderstorms**. In fact, the state experiences more thunderstorms than anywhere in the world except east Africa. On summer days, hot air rises over the peninsula. When it meets with damp air from the Gulf and the Atlantic, converging airstreams force air upward, where it condenses into towering thunderheads. Parts of south Florida have more than 90 storms a year; FORT MYERS leads the state with an annual average of 100 days with lightning.

Hurricanes – Florida also lies in the path of intense tropical cyclones spawned in the Atlantic, the Caribbean or the Gulf of Mexico. Most common in August and September when weak low-pressure systems develop over warm water, hurricanes can measure upwards of 500mi in diameter and contain winds of up to 200mph (a tropical depression officially becomes a hurricane once its winds reach a speed of 74mph). These doughnut-shaped storms commonly churn across the Atlantic coast between Cape Canaveral and the Keys (a corridor popularly known as "hurricane alley"), though in recent decades the Panhandle has received a significant share of these storms as well. An average of one hurricane a year, usually of low or moderate intensity, strikes Florida. Several devastating storms have hit in this century: A hurricane in 1926 scored a direct hit on MIAMI, causing the worst city damage in history; two years later, another storm took some 2,000 lives when floodwaters breached levees around Lake Okeechobee; the Labor Day hurricane of 1935—holding the record for the highest sustained winds and storm tide—struck the Keys and ripped into the Gulf, killing more than 400 people. More recently, Hurricane Andrew mowed an 8mi swath across south

Miami-Dade County in 1992, leaving in its wake 85 dead, 10,000 injured, and $30 billion in damage. In early October 1995, Hurricane Opal—the 15th named storm of that season—pummeled the Panhandle coast, racking up over $2 billion worth of damage and washing away some of the area's famous dunes.

On the positive side, Florida's epic storms invigorate its natural environment. High winds often distribute plant seeds over a wide expanse. The combination of winds and heavy rains stirs up sediments and nutrients on the bottoms of bays and backwaters. When hurricanes level forests and other protective ground cover, sun-loving plants and small animals quickly exploit the newly available niches, thus generating a whole new cycle of life.

Water Resources

Floridians have one of the highest per capita rates of water use in the country, thanks to the seemingly inexhaustible reserves of the **Floridan Aquifer**, the state's largest and only artesian aquifer (characterized by water that is forced up through cracks in non-porous rock by hydrostatic pressure). Called "Florida's rain barrel," the Floridan underlies the entire state and varies in depth up to 2,000ft in the areas surrounding Jacksonville and Orlando. Along with the shallower **Biscayne Aquifer**, which serves southeast Florida, the Floridan provides nearly 90 percent of the state's water for drinking, recreation, irrigation and waste disposal. These layers of porous limestone serve as underground reservoirs that give Florida more groundwater than any other state. Water levels are replenished by an abundant annual rainfall—the greatest amount falling in the extreme northwest and southeast corners of the state.

One of the largest sources of surface water in the state, **Lake Okeechobee** (Seminole for "big water") supplies south Florida's cities and farms, as well as the EVERGLADES. At 700sq mi it ranks as the state's largest lake. After Okeechobee inundated nearby farming communities as a result of hurricanes in 1926 and 1928, the US Army Corps of Engineers began taming the lake with a new system of canals, dikes, pumping stations and spillways. Now its waters can be manipulated to control flooding of surrounding fields and towns. With an ever-increasing population in south Florida, Lake Okeechobee today lies at the heart of many complex land-use controversies, which pit environmentalists against the area's farmers.

Flora

Dubbed by Ponce de León "Isle of Flowers" (for the Spanish *Pascua florida* Eastertime feast), Florida boasts an abundance of lush vegetation. Early botanists catalogued over 3,000 types of indigenous flowering plants, from tiny orchids to showy magnolias. To this total thousands of tropical and subtropical plants have been added over the years. Positioned between 24°30'N and 30°N latitude—the same latitude as Egypt—Florida juts southward from the temperate zone into warm tropical seas. This location produces a unique inversion: temperate zone plants bloom in winter and the tropical varieties flower in summer. Furthermore, Florida's regional climatic variations contribute to the great diversity of native botanical species found in the state, from the high pine forests of the northwest to the saw grass marshes of the Everglades. The state's vegetation is generally distributed among seven habitats—hammocks, pinelands, flatwoods, scrublands, swamps, savannas and salt marshes. Together they contain about half the tree species north of Mexico.

Sabal Palm

Hammocks and Flatwoods – Occurring in the north and central regions, **hardwood hammocks** are raised islands of hardwoods and broad-leaved shrubs surrounded by prairie or pine forest. They harbor fertile soil that nourishes oaks, hickories, beeches, magnolias, cabbage palms and others, often swathed in Spanish moss or vines of rattan or wild grape. From the tree farms of slash and loblolly to the wild-growing longleaf of the uplands and the scrub pine of flat sandy areas, the state's many species of pine constitute Florida's most common tree.

Flatwoods containing boggy soil are found all over Florida and contain a number of blooms, including 64 kinds of terrestrial **orchids**. Found in the central peninsula and along the coastal dunes, **scrublands** are characterized by thick stands of evergreen live oaks, saw palmetto and blackjack. Much of this land has been converted to vast groves of oranges and grapefruit. The savannas, or grasslands, in central Florida support a variety of marine grasses, including turtle, eel and manatee grasses.

A Profusion of Palms – Symbol of a luxuriant lifestyle, the **palm** also proliferates in Florida, which claims several hundred species—more than any other state. The cabbage or **Sabal palm**, one of only 15 native palms, is Florida's official state tree and flourishes throughout the state; early settlers harvested its crunchy edible bud, which was said to taste like cabbage. Among other notable natives, the tall royal palm graces many prominent boulevards and the low-lying palmetto forms dense thickets in the flatlands, varying in color from light green to grayish blue. The coconut palm massed lavishly in south Florida until an outbreak of lethal yellowing disease in the 1970s, when more than five million palms around Miami were destroyed. Many of the coconut palms were replaced by the hybrid Maypan and the coconut-bearing Malayan Dwarf.

The Marvelous Mangrove – The only known trees that can survive in saltwater, mangroves have received much attention in recent decades, rising in status from developers' nuisance to coastal guardian. **Red mangroves** *(Rhizophora mangle)* thrive in the tidal zones; **black mangroves** *(Avicennia germinans)*, distinguished by short finger-like aerating branches called pneumatophores that project above the soil, are found slightly more inland. **White mangroves** *(Laguncularia racemosa)* generally grow at the highest elevations. All have the ability to withstand the saltwater of wind spray and high tide. Their cage-like root systems can stabilize a shoreline better than a seawall, as well as providing sanctuary for hundreds of species of fish. The most well-known of the three Florida varieties, the red mangrove grows near the water on reddish aerial roots that absorb oxygen and freshwater and filter out salt. (Indians dubbed the red mangroves "walking trees," because the above-ground roots look like legs wading out into the water.) Black and white mangroves excrete salt by means of glands on the surface of their leaves.

Natives and Exotics – Among the 350 different types of trees found in Florida are the thick, coppery **gumbo-limbo** and the **manchineel**, one of the continent's most poisonous plants (often mistaken for poisonwood or poison sumac). Manchineel trees grow in swamps and produce a sap so toxic that even water dripping from their leaves can irritate the skin. A type of ficus native to the Sunshine State, the **strangler fig** wraps around its host (often a Sabal palm) and eventually kills it. The deciduous **bald cypress**, commonly found in Florida swamps, is named for its leafless winter appearance.

Over the years, **exotic plants** have been introduced to Florida, threatening the survival of many native species. Parks and conservation areas have implemented programs to rid their locales of such imported exotics, which now constitute 27 percent of all the plant species in the state. Trees such as the Brazilian pepper, imported for shade and ornamentation, have spread from backyards to wilderness, crowding out indigenous vegetation. Likewise, the Australian pine provides wonderful shade but also prevents anything from growing underneath its dense branches. The fire-resistant **Melaleuca** (also called the tea tree or cajeput), native to Australia and New Guinea, was planted in the Everglades in the 1930s to help dry up the wetlands; since then this uncontrollable pest has conquered tremendous acreage. Dade County now prohibits the planting or sale of any of these three species.

Fauna

Florida's gentle winters and warm sunshine support a bursting variety of animal life, including some 100 species of mammals and more than 400 species and subspecies of birds. While an increasing human population continues to reduce the available territory for wildlife, an ardent segment has arisen to ensure that in the next century Florida will carry on its ark with as many wild creatures as possible.

If you visit the Florida coast, you're likely to see bottle-nosed **dolphins**—a perennial favorite with visitors and residents—frolicking offshore. These sleek mammals frequent the shallow waters of the Gulf of Mexico as well as the Atlantic. Once hunted almost to extinction, **alligators** *(p 42)* have enjoyed a renaissance in Florida and now number more than a million. Though often viewed as menacing, the giant reptiles help control populations of snakes and small mammals.

Perhaps the most easily observed animals, dozens of species of waterbirds make permanent or part-time homes in Florida. Of the species more likely to be found in Florida than anywhere else, the long-necked **anhinga** *(p 43)* is known for its skill in spearing fish with its beak. Bird-watchers may also add **roseate spoonbills** to their must-see lists; sometimes mistaken for flamingoes, spoonbills are shorter and are characterized by the flat, spoon-shaped beaks for which they are named. They flock in pink clouds over the wildlife refuges on SANIBEL and Merritt islands. Another rare find, the **purple gallinule** frequents marshy waterways in the Everglades. This small bird is recognizable by its bright purple and blue feathers. The **brown pelican** makes a graceful sight skimming along the Atlantic and Gulf coasts. The pelicans' prevalence in Florida is misleading: Outside the state they are rare, their numbers diminished by pesticides.

Florida provides haven to more than 67 species of threatened or endangered animals. Prominent on the endangered list are the reclusive **Florida panther** *(p 43)*, the West Indian **manatee** *(p 71)*, the diminutive **Key deer** *(p 55)*, the **wood stork**, a wading bird once prevalent in mangrove and cypress swamps, and the Florida **sandhill crane**, another long-legged wader. The five kinds of **sea turtles** *(p 298)* that nest in Florida are all either endangered or threatened; and the aggressive **American crocodile** *(p 42)*, nearly extinct in the US, lives only in southern Florida.

While the high number of endangered species may seem to indicate a losing battle, Florida has actually made progress in slowing, and sometimes reversing, the decline of some animals. For instance, leatherback turtles, for the first time in a decade, have recently begun nesting as far north as St. Augustine and Jacksonville. Conservation organizations, wildlife hospitals, state parks and concerned citizens all appear determined to provide for Florida's wild kingdom for many years to come.

History

Prehistoric and Native Floridians

Prehistoric peoples probably inhabited the area of North America that now includes Florida as early as 10,000 BC. While it has long been thought that Ice Age nomads filtered southeast after crossing the Bering land bridge from Siberia into Alaska between 20,000 and 15,000 BC, there is now speculation that those who reached the Florida peninsula may have come instead from Central and South America through the Antilles. The earliest Indians here were hunter-gatherers whose diet included the meat of saber-toothed tigers, mastodons, bison and other Pleistocene animals. (Divers in northern Florida rivers often discover fluted stone spearheads, known as Clovis or Suwannee points, used by prehistoric hunters.)

The first semipermanent settlements began to spring up along Florida's waterways around 5000 BC. Evidence of this can be found in ancient **midden mounds**—or trash heaps—containing the discarded shells of shellfish, which had become increasingly important to the Indians' diet. Agriculture, including the cultivation of squash, beans and corn introduced from South America or Mexico, began when the population became more sedentary around 1000 BC. Archaeologists have also found some 14,000 **burial mounds** throughout the state (many lost to modern development). In these mysterious mounds, thought to reflect the influence of the Hopewell cultures of Illinois and Ohio, the bodies of chiefs or religious leaders were found resting face-up toward the sun. Other important tribal figures were buried face-down above them. By the Christian era, some of the ceremonial sites had developed into large complexes comprising several individual mounds connected by an intricate system of canals and roadways.

By the time European explorers visited the Florida peninsula in the 16C, the native population numbered an estimated 100,000. There were six main groups: the **Timucua** (occupying northeast Florida as far south as present-day Cape Canaveral); the **Apalachee** (Panhandle), the **Ais** (central and southeast coast), the **Tequesta** (southeast coast), **Tocobaga** (Tampa Bay area) and the **Calusa** (southwest region). Developing

Timucuan Indians Taking Crops to Granary, drawing by Jacques Le Moyne (16C)

St. Augustine Historical Society

independently, each group maintained a separate culture with specific social orders and sophisticated religious and political institutions. The northern Indians subsisted by farming, while those south of the Everglades generally hunted game and fished for seafood.

Within 250 years of European colonization, intertribal wars, Spanish slave raids and European-imported diseases such as smallpox, influenza and measles had decimated most of the Indian population. The few hundred remaining Timucua and Apalachee left Florida for Cuba with the Spanish in 1763. Today the only remaining traces of Florida's earliest native cultures are archaeological.

First Spanish Period 1513-1763

European explorers and fortune hunters began making forays into the Caribbean and Florida Straits in the 15C. Soon after Christopher Columbus discovered Hispaniola in 1492, Italian-born cartographer **Giovanni Caboto** (also known as John Cabot), commissioned by England's King Henry VIII, ventured into the New World to chart his findings. Although there is no specific record of it, Cabot and his son Sebastian probably sighted the Florida peninsula in 1497 or 1498. At least three European maps made between 1502 and 1511 indicate that others soon followed. Accounts that early explorers encountered Spanish-speaking Indians on the Florida peninsula support the theory that Spanish slave hunters from the West Indies had been there as well.

In 1513, explorer **Juan Ponce de León**, awarded with a Spanish patent to colonize any lands he found, made the first recorded—and officially sanctioned—landfall. De León, who was looking for the island of Bimini, went ashore somewhere between present-day St. Augustine and the St. Johns River in early April. He gave the name *La Florida* to an area that covers most of the present-day Southeast, west to the Mississippi River and north into the Carolinas. When de León returned to the southwest coast in 1521 he was fatally wounded in an Indian attack; he then sailed to Cuba where he died within a few weeks.

Subsequent Spanish colonization attempts also failed miserably. **Pánfilo de Narváez** set sail from Spain in 1527 with a patent to settle Florida—a reward from Emperor Charles V for de Narváez' service in the Spanish conquest of Cuba. In 1528 de Narváez landed in Tampa Bay, and with over half his cadre of 400 men, marched north by foot to Apalachee in search of gold, sending his ships up the coast to wait for him. When the men reached the coast, they found no ships so they set out for Mexico in several crude boats. De Narváez and all but 80 of his men subsequently met their end in a storm off the coast of Texas. Accomplished conquistador **Hernando de Soto's** legendary three-year search (1539-41) for riches in the New World also proved disastrous. After trekking several thousand miles with his 600 men—throughout central and northern Florida and as far west as present-day Oklahoma—de Soto died from fever. The remaining dispirited fortune-hunters—some 300 survivors—eventually found their way back to Spain. Next to try his luck, wealthy Spanish viceroy **Tristán de Luna** followed de Soto in 1559. Plagued by storms, hunger and dissension among his soldiers, de Luna was forced to abandoned his effort to establish a settlement at Pensacola Bay.

Finding plenty of trouble but none of the anticipated riches, Spain (already importing gold and silver from Mexico and Peru) temporarily lost interest in colonizing *La Florida*. The peninsula's strategic location on the Florida Straits, however, was vital to protecting the country's Caribbean trade routes from pirates. In 1562, a French expedition led by the ardent Calvinist **Jean Ribault** *(p 96)* entered the St. Johns River in search of a site for a Huguenot colony. When Ribault's fledgling settlement completed building Fort Caroline near the river's mouth in 1565, an alarmed Spain moved to reclaim her hold. Accordingly, later that year **Pedro Menéndez de Avilés** sailed into the Florida Straits and founded ST. AUGUSTINE (to be the first permanent European settlement in Florida). He then massacred the French at Fort Caroline. At least one important legacy survives the French defeat: the published drawings *(p 16)* and descriptions of the native population by French illustrator **Jacques Le Moyne** remain one of the most detailed accounts of early Florida history.

The Mission Chains – Although Spain retained her power in Florida for the next two centuries, the region attracted few independent settlers outside the military and the Catholic Church. Besides two garrisons at Pensacola and St. Augustine, the Spanish presence consisted of about 100 missions. Begun in 1565, the first of two chains led north from St. Augustine along the coast of present-day Georgia and South Carolina. A second string, built from the early 1600s to 1704, stretched west across the Panhandle to the Apalachee Bay region. At its center stood powerful San Luis de Talimali *(p 175)*, built in 1656 near present-day TALLAHASSEE, which included a church, a convent for the friars, cemetery, council and block houses, as well as an Apalachee Indian village and ball field. The missions functioned primarily as a strategic defensive system, designed to convert, centralize—and thus control—the Indians, who were coerced into labor and defense of the Spanish frontier. Ultimately the system failed, succumbing to both internal power struggles among the Franciscan friars and to external attack. By the early years of the 18C, most missions had been burned in raids—supported by defecting Indians— led by British soldiers from the English colony of South Carolina. Remaining structures, fashioned from perishable wooden frames roofed with palm thatch, quickly deteriorated, and soon all traces of the missions had disappeared.

British Period 1763-1783

The 1763 **Treaty of Paris** ending the Seven Years War between England and France marked a decisive turning point in Florida history. Under its provisions, the Spanish colony was ceded to Britain in exchange for Havana, Cuba, which England had captured the previous year. Florida was then split into two parts. East Florida, with a capital at St. Augustine, included the peninsula and the Panhandle as far as the Apalachicola River. West Florida, with PENSACOLA as its capital, was bounded on the north by the present state line, and on the west by the Mississippi River. By British charter in 1764, Florida gained a section between the Mississippi and Chattahoochee Rivers extending north to present-day cities of Jackson, Mississippi, and Montgomery, Alabama.

In contrast to Spain, Britain attempted a self-supporting colony. Sugar, rice, indigo and cotton plantations were established along the St. Johns River. Export subsidies and generous land grants drew Protestant settlers from Great Britain as well as Tory sympathizers who left Georgia and South Carolina after the Revolution. The new population also included a 1768 colony of some 2,000 Greeks, Italians and Minorcans at New Smyrna, about 75mi south of St. Augustine. By the mid-18C, a number of different loosely organized Indian groups (later known as the Creek Confederacy), pushed by settlers out of Georgia, Alabama and South Carolina, had also begun to filter into northern Florida. From the Creeks, two main nations, the Hitchiti-speaking **Miccosukee** and the Muskogee-speaking **Seminoles**, emerged.

Second Spanish Period 1784-1821

British occupation of Florida was to last only 20 years. With Britain's forces engaged in Revolutionary War battles farther north, Spain (participating in the war indirectly as a French ally) took advantage of Florida's weakened defenses and captured Pensacola in 1781. Under the **Second Treaty of Paris** (1783) ending the Revolution, the remainder of Florida reverted to Spanish control—excluding the northern section added above the Panhandle in 1764. By about 1800, Seminole villages were scattered from Apalachicola east to the St. Johns River and from south Georgia down to the Caloosahatchee River. During the War of 1812, violence erupted repeatedly between white settlers and Indians, who were resented for harboring runaway slaves and controlling valuable land. In 1814, a battle with the Upper Creeks at Horseshoe Bend ended in Indian defeat and a treaty opening 20 million acres of Creek land to US settlement. From 1817 to 1818, General Andrew Jackson led a special US command against the Seminoles, initiating a series of raids later known as the **First Seminole War** and attacking several Spanish settlements.

By this time it was clear that Spain could neither govern nor police its increasingly turbulent territory effectively. Its power thus diminished, Spain negotiated the **Adams-Onís Treaty** in 1819. This agreement transferred the land east of the Mississippi to the US and formalized the boundaries of present-day Florida with the Panhandle terminating at the Perdido River. The treaty was ratified in 1821 and the two Floridas were handed over to General Andrew Jackson in Pensacola on July 17.

Early Settlement and the Seminole Wars

In 1822 President Monroe unified the two Floridas into a single territory with two counties: Escambia and St. Johns. Two years later, the first Territorial governor, William P. DuVal, named Tallahassee as the capital. In the new US Territory, the government recognized all land grants made before 1818, pending fulfillment of the original terms. Congress also granted the right of pre-emption to settlers, allowing squatters to remain if they purchased 80 acres of land at $1.25 an acre. With the area now open to settlers, tensions mounted over the Indian presence.

In the 1820s, the US government attempted to contain the native population on a single tract of land in central Florida. When this failed, Jackson, now president, signed the **Indian Removal Act** in 1830, in hopes of resolving Indian conflicts once and for all by relocating eastern tribes to a designated area west of the Mississippi River. This law specified that the Indians must consent to moving, that they would be paid for their land and they would hold perpetual title to their new territories in the west. The Seminoles demonstrated the greatest resistance to this infamous forced exodus, known as the **Trail of Tears**. In 1832 a small group (unauthorized by their leaders) signed the **Treaty of Payne's Landing**, requiring the Indians to relinquish their land and relocate to a reservation in Arkansas (now Oklahoma). At the end of a three-year grace period, however, not a single Seminole had left.

US troops arrived in 1835 to enforce the treaty. In December Seminoles ambushed the command of Major Francis Dade near Bushnell *(p 67)*, precipitating the **Second Seminole War**. The leader of the Seminole resistance was **Osceola**. Still remembered for his cunning and courage, this great man met a bitter end. In late 1837, he was tricked into entering a US army camp near St. Augustine. There under a flag of truce, he was imprisoned and transferred to Fort Moultrie in Charleston, South Carolina, where he died in 1838. The Seminole Wars ended in 1842, when at least 3,000 Indians and blacks were sent to Oklahoma. For every two Indians removed, one white soldier was killed; the cost to the federal government was $20 million. Eluding capture, several hundred Seminoles melted into the Everglades.

In 1845 Florida was admitted to the Union as the 27th state. Indian rights remained unresolved, as Floridians kept pressing the US government for total removal of the Seminoles from the state. Increasing incursions of the white man into Indian reservation land eventually led to the **Third Seminole War** of 1855-58, an inconclusive series of swamp skirmishes that ended with the surrender of Seminole chief Billy Bowlegs and never resulted in a formal treaty with the US government.

Osceola (c.1837) Portrait by John Rogers Vinton

St. Augustine Historical Society

The Plantation Belt – During early statehood, settlement centered primarily between the Suwannee and Apalachicola Rivers in an area called Middle Florida, where pioneers and cattle drivers established small farms. The dark, sandy loam there also proved excellent for **cotton** cultivation and hundreds of plantations flourished by 1850, building a cotton economy comparable to that of antebellum Georgia. (In 1834 the first railroad incorporated in Florida connected the cotton market of Tallahassee to the port of St. Marks. It was built for the express purpose of shipping cotton to textile mills in New England and overseas.) Eventually, this plantation belt spread southeastward, encompassing Alachua and Marion counties by 1860. Aside from cotton, timber, turpentine and sugarcane were common plantation products. Sugarcane plantations were concentrated along the St. Johns and Manatee Rivers.

While plantation size varied from 1,000 to 5,000 acres, wealth was measured not by acreage but by the number of slaves one owned. "Planters" were defined as those who owned 20 or more slaves. The number of planters who owned 30 or more slaves doubled between 1850 and 1860. This elite group set the local political, economic and social tone.

The Steamboat Age – The riverboat industry was critical to Florida's economic development and settlement. The first steamboat service was offered in 1827 on the Apalachicola River. This, with the Chattahoochee and Flint Rivers, formed an important cotton outlet. Lumber, then a major export item, was also ferried via steamer. During the Second Seminole War, the government chartered 40 steamboats to transport troops and supplies. By 1848 service from Jacksonville connected Palatka and Enterprise on the St. Johns River. With the steamers came Florida's first winter tourists, a major portion of whom were northerners whose doctors had recommended a sunny clime to cure their ailments. Commenting on this phenomenon, one Floridian of the time noted: "We live on sweet potatoes and consumptive Yankees, [and] we sell atmosphere." Sick and healthy passengers alike slept in elegantly furnished staterooms and dined on fine food, while the exotic foliage, Spanish moss and alligators sighted on the banks of the dark, winding waterways delivered the promised trappings of a wilderness adventure.

Civil War and Reconstruction

A steady flow of settlers and the sound plantation economy increased Florida's population of 34,700 in 1830 to 140,400 in 1860. Almost half of them were "non-white." To protect its one-sided economy, which relied heavily on slave labor, the state seceded from the Union in 1861 and became an important supplier of beef, cotton and salt to the Confederacy. The major Civil War clash on Florida soil was the 1864 battle of Olustee (p 90) near Lake City; there on February 20, Confederate troops drove back the Union soldiers and preserved supply lines to Georgia. A second important victory occurred the next year, when Tallahassee—the only southern capital to escape capture—was successfully defended in the Battle of Natural Bridge (p 170).

The war put the state into near bankruptcy, but reconstruction brought new investors from the north, ready to finance business, land speculation, transportation and tourism. Sharecroppers and tenant farmers, including freed blacks, took over the plantations. Cotton, timber and cattle sales helped boost the economy. In the late 1860s, some 6,000 Cubans immigrated to Florida at the start of Cuba's Ten Years' War of Independence (1868-78), establishing KEY WEST as a major cigar-making center. Soon thereafter, the commercial sponge market, established in Key West in 1849, moved its hub north after new beds were discovered off TARPON SPRINGS in the 1870s. And the commercial citrus industry increased and thrived—until two terrible freezes in the winter of 1894-95 obliterated about 90 percent of the crop.

The Railroad Boom – Florida's late 19C growth was closely linked to its rapid railroad development, spurred by the state's 1881 sale of four million acres of swamp and over-flow land in central Florida to Philadelphia entrepreneur **Hamilton Disston** *(p 115)*. Most importantly, this sale provided funds to clear the titles of state-owned land from earlier railroad promotions and opened the way for subsidies and land grants to new railroad builders. The undisputed leaders in the field—and in Florida development—remain two of the most colorful figures in the state's history: railroad tycoons **Henry Bradley Plant** *(p 279)* and **Henry Morrison Flagler** *(p 104)*. Plant consolidated and expanded numerous existing short lines and extended track to Tampa in 1884 to create an important link to northern markets. The Plant system merged with the Atlantic Coast Line in 1902 to complete a network of about 2,250mi of track originating in Richmond, Virginia. Flagler concentrated on the **Florida East Coast Railway** (FEC), extending it from Jacksonville to St. Augustine in 1886 and subsequently to Palm Beach (1894), Miami (1896) and Key West (1912). As the railway system expanded to link Florida to the rail lines crossing the US, it also spurred the state's winter production of fruit and vegetables.

Extravagant hotels strategically placed at each new railhead, such as the sprawling Ponce de Leon *(p 109)* in St. Augustine, the Royal Poinciana in Palm Beach (the dining room seated 1,600), and Miami's Royal Palm (with its circular six-hole golf course) became fashionable resort destinations for the northern social set in the late 19C.

© CAMERA GRAPHICS

Bathing Beach at the Breakers Hotel, Palm Beach (c.1928)

20C Development

The early 20C was Florida's gilded age, a brief period of glamour, extravagance and no income or inheritance tax. Millionaire industrialists luxuriated in fabulous villas, while movie stars arrived from Hollywood to make films in Jacksonville, then a leading motion-picture production center. The economy had benefited from the 1898 **Spanish-American War**, when embarkation camps for American troops were located in Tampa, Miami and Jacksonville. After the US won its bid to gain Cuban independence from Spain, many soldiers returned to Florida with their families. For the first time, good roads—the Florida Road Department was established in 1915—and the affordable Model T automobile made vacations accessible to people who could not afford luxury hotels. Modest, family-operated motels and tourist courts sprouted on the Florida roadside. By the 1920s "tin-can tourist camps," filled with Tin Lizzies outfitted as campers, had appeared in every major Florida city.

Dozens of land speculators, including Carl Fisher *(p 221)* in MIAMI BEACH and George Merrick *(p 204)* in CORAL GABLES, not only peddled Spanish bungalows, but also a new lifestyle and a rosy future in the "Empire of the Sun." From 1920-25, the state grew four times faster than any other. As real-estate agent and self-proclaimed con-man Wilson Mizner (younger brother of architect Addison Mizner, *p 228)* assessed the situation: "Right up to January 1926, it was only necessary to point carelessly to a mudhole and tell a client that there was his future. He could not deny it, and even the salesman was in deadly fear that he spoke the truth."

Unfortunately, the bust was just as rapid as the boom. The real-estate crash came in 1926 on the heels of over-speculation and a destructive hurricane that beheaded palm trees, leveled cheaper construction and stopped new building in its tracks. A ruinous Mediterranean fruit fly invasion in 1929 devastated the citrus industry. And the onset of the national Depression that same year only confirmed what Floridians already knew.

Effects of World War II – Despite the lean years, Florida's population had grown to around two million by 1940. This number was supplemented by another three million tourists annually. World War II stimulated the economy with defense-related industry, road-building, and new and revitalized naval bases. After the war, servicemen who trained on the beaches of Daytona, Miami and St. Petersburg returned to find jobs or enroll in Florida colleges under the GI bill. The economy diversified. Frozen citrus juice concentrates became a major industry by 1950. The same year, the US inaugurated a long-range, missile-testing program at Cape Canaveral, followed by a new space satellite program eight years later.

After World War II, a strong Florida government made a concerted effort to bring corporate industry to the state. In addition, millions of people began to vacation here as the two-week paid vacation became standard. To accommodate them, more new hotels appeared in Greater Miami between 1945 and 1954 than in all the other US states combined. In 1958 the first US domestic jet service, from New York to Miami, opened the way for more. Highway travel increased, too, and with it small attractions—featuring everything from alligators to mermaids—mushroomed along the Florida roadside. These private businesses were the forerunners of modern corporate-run theme parks, including the ever-expanding Disney empire. Today, some 40 million visitors come to Florida each year.

During the same period, Florida hosted another growing population: foreign refugees. Most notably, the 1959 Cuban Revolution sent waves of exiles into Dade County in that year and again in 1961. Between 1965 and 1973, a series of Cuban government-controlled airlifts—that came to be known as "Freedom Flights"—carried thousands more refugees to Florida. In 1980 the Cuban government again allowed emigration. This time, more than 125,000 residents of the port of Mariel, among them criminals released from Cuban prisons, landed on Miami's shores. The number of Cubans in Florida climbed to about 670,000 in 1990, infusing the state's culture with a strong Latin flavor.

Contemporary Florida

Only a few decades ago, Florida was seen as a region of infinite potential. "So many of Florida's resources are as yet undeveloped, so much wealth lies hidden in her soil, so great an area of wilderness beauty is yet to be discovered and appreciated," boasted a 1930 promotional booklet. Many would argue that during the next half-century, those same resources were not only overdeveloped, but exhausted. The boom cycles, transportation advancements and population influxes that define Florida history also brought the inevitable housing complexes, strip malls, high-rise beach developments and traffic jams—making it difficult to believe that the peninsula was a beckoning frontier as recently as the early 20C. The state's proximity to South America means that much of the illegal drug trade entering the US filters through Florida. And immigration remains a sensitive subject, as the influx of Cuban exiles, Haitians, Nicaraguans, Jamaicans, Vietnamese, Cambodians and many other groups continues. Another type of immigrant—northern retirees—has also made an indelible mark on the Florida landscape, boosting the economy yet crowding roads and towns.

Florida's resources still abound, however, and in recent decades a trend toward preserving them has been emerging. Begun in 1981, the award-winning planned town of Seaside (p 162) on the Panhandle has become an international model of environmentally sensitive contextual design. A proposal to remove some of the man-made locks and spillways in the EVERGLADES in an effort to restore the natural water flow is being implemented. Politically active Seminole Indians are working to revive and preserve their cultural traditions. To be sure, any economy so dependent on tourism will always struggle to maintain the delicate balance between modern development and conservation of the land and people that constitute its natural resources.

Time Line

12,000-8,000 BC	First migration of prehistoric Indians to the Florida peninsula.
5000 BC	First semipermanent Native American settlements in Florida.
1492	Christopher Columbus lands in the region of the present-day Bahamas.
1513	Spanish explorer **Juan Ponce de León** lands in the area of present-day St. Augustine and names the land "*La Florida.*"
1521	Ponce de León returns to the southwestern coast of the Florida peninsula and attempts to establish a colony.
1528	Explorer **Pánfilo de Narváez** goes ashore at Tampa Bay and marches to Apalachee in search of gold.
1539-1541	Conquistador **Hernando de Soto** explores the Florida interior, trekking north and west into the continent.
1559	Spanish nobleman **Tristán de Luna** attempts to establish a settlement at Pensacola Bay.
1562	French Protestant **Jean Ribault** starts a Huguenot colony on the banks of the St. Johns River.
1565	**Pedro Menéndez de Avilés** founds *San Augustin*, the first permanent European settlement in America.

Juan Ponce de León   Hernando de Soto   Pedro Menéndez de Avilés

Courtesy of St. Augustine Historical Society

1565-1705	Spain founds about 100 **missions** in two chains stretching north and west from St. Augustine.
1586	Sir Francis Drake sacks St. Augustine.
1672	Work begins on the **Castillo de San Marcos** at St. Augustine, the first stone fort built by the Spanish in Florida.
1702	British colonel James Moore destroys St. Augustine but fails to capture the Castillo de San Marcos. Britain begins attacks on Spanish missions two years later.
1719	French soldiers capture Pensacola but soon return the colony to Spain. France occupies the Gulf Coast west of Pensacola.
1720s	First migration of Creek groups—later called the Seminoles and **Miccosukee**—from Georgia into Florida.
1740	The British military invades Florida from Georgia.
1763	**Treaty of Paris** ends the Seven Years War (1756-63) between Britain and France. Britain gains Florida from Spain and splits the region into two provinces divided by the Apalachicola River.
1768	Minorcan, Italian and Greek colonists establish a colony at New Smyrna.
1781	Spanish capture Pensacola from the British.
1783	The **Second Treaty of Paris** ends the American Revolution. Florida returns to Spanish control.
1814	Driven from their land in Alabama, homeless Creeks migrate to Florida, doubling that territory's Indian population.
1817-1818	General Andrew Jackson initiates a series of raids against the Seminoles, later known as the **First Seminole War**.
1818	US gains Pensacola and pushes for Spanish withdrawal from the region.
1821	Spain gains the Texas territory and relinquishes Florida to the US under the terms of the **Adams-Onís Treaty**. Jackson is elected the first governor of the two Florida colonies.
1822	President Monroe unifies East and West Florida into one territory and settlement begins. Jacksonville is founded.
1824	Tallahassee is chosen as the state capital. Key West becomes a US naval station.

1827	The first steamboat service is established on the Apalachicola River.
1830	President Andrew Jackson signs the **Indian Removal Act** authorizing the relocation of eastern tribes to an area west of the Mississippi River.
1831	First cigar factory is built in Key West.
1832	US claims Seminole lands in Florida under the **Treaty of Payne's Landing**.
1834	Florida's first railroad, the mule-drawn Tallahassee-St. Mark's line, is incorporated.
1835-1842	US military forces and Florida Indians clash in the **Second Seminole War**. Some 4,000 Indians and blacks are relocated to Arkansas and Kissimmee area is opened to white settlement.
1837	Seminole leader **Osceola** is imprisoned under a flag of truce at a St. Augustine army base.
1838	Osceola dies at age 34 in a South Carolina dungeon. First Constitutional Convention held in St. Joseph (Port St. Joe).
1841	Yellow fever epidemic hits the Panhandle.
1845	Florida becomes the 27th US state under President John Tyler. William D. Moseley is elected the first governor.
1849	The first commercial sponge market opens in Key West.
1851	Dr. John Gorrie patents the process of making ice artificially.
1855	Under Florida's **Internal Improvement Act**, undeveloped Florida land is made available to investors.
1855-1858	Billy Bowlegs—the last chief under whom all Seminoles were united—leads the Indian resistance in the **Third Seminole War**.
1860	The first east-west Florida railroad, linking Cedar Key with Fernandina, is completed.
1861	Florida secedes from the Union.
1864	Confederate troops win the **Battle of Olustee** near Lake City, Florida, preserving interior supply lines to Georgia.
1865	Florida militia repulse Union forces at **Natural Bridge**, saving Tallahassee from capture.
1868	New Florida constitution is adopted.
1875	The city of Orlando is incorporated.
1881	Philadelphia industrialist **Hamilton Disston** buys four million acres of land in central Florida and begins the first private land development in the state.
1883	The first all-black high school is founded in Jacksonville.
1884	**Henry Plant** completes a rail line into Tampa.
1885	**Henry Flagler** begins building a rail line between Jacksonville and St. Augustine and establishes the Florida East Coast Railway.
1886	Fire destroys the entire commercial district of Key West. Labor disputes cause the cigar industry to relocate from Key West to Tampa.
1894-1895	Winter freezes destroy citrus crops in central and north Florida and force the citrus industry to move south.
1896	In April, Flagler extends railroad to Miami; three months later, the City of Miami is incorporated.
1898	Embarkation camps for American troops are established in Tampa, Miami and Jacksonville during the **Spanish-American War**.
1901	Fire destroys most of Jacksonville, gutting more than 2,000 buildings.
1906	Drainage of the Everglades begins, spearheaded by Florida governor Napoleon Bonaparte Broward.
1912	Flagler's **Overseas Railroad** from Homestead to Key West is completed.
1914	First regularly scheduled commercial airline flight is made by pilot Tony Jannus between St. Petersburg and Tampa.
1917-1918	World War I soldiers and aviators train in Florida.
1926	Miami takes a direct hit from a deadly September hurricane.
1927	Pan American Airways inaugurates commercial service with a flight from Key West to Havana, Cuba.
1928	The Tamiami Trail (US-41) across the Everglades is opened.
1929	A Mediterranean fruit-fly infestation destroys citrus crops in 20 central Florida counties.
1935	A devastating Labor Day hurricane batters Key West, destroying the Overseas Railroad.
1941-1945	Defense-related industry boosts the Florida economy during **World War II**.
1947	University of Florida opens to female students. President Harry S Truman dedicates **Everglades National Park**.
1950	Frozen citrus concentrates become a major Florida business. US inaugurates long-range missile-testing program at Cape Canaveral.

Overseas Railroad (c.1920)

1954	The Sunshine Skyway bridge connects St. Petersburg with Manatee County to the south.
1955	Florida legislature authorizes the construction of a turnpike to run the length of the state.
1958	Newly formed National Aeronautics and Space Administration (NASA) begins operations at Cape Canaveral and launches first US satellite.
1959	The first regularly scheduled domestic air flights begin between New York and Miami.
1959-1962	Thousands of refugees flee Cuba for Florida to escape Fidel Castro's communist regime.
1961	NASA launches the first American astronaut, Alan Shepard, into space from Cape Canaveral.
1962	The first black students are admitted to undergraduate schools at Florida State University and the University of Florida.
1964	Race riots break out in Jacksonville and St. Augustine.
1969	On July 16, the first manned moon launch lifts off from Cape Kennedy.
1971	Walt Disney World opens near Orlando.
1972	Miami Beach hosts the Democratic and Republican national conventions.
1973	Freedom flights from Cuba to Miami end after bringing over 250,000 refugees to the US.
1979	The Miami Beach Art Deco district is designated a National Register Historic District.
1980	Some 125,000 Cuban refugees land in Key West. Riots erupt in Miami after four white policeman are acquitted in the beating death of a black man.
1981	On April 12, the Kennedy Space Center launches the first space shuttle, *Columbia*.
1983	A Christmas freeze strikes central Florida citrus groves; losses exceed $1 billion.
1986	Space shuttle *Challenger* explodes shortly after take-off from Cape Canaveral, killing all eight crew members aboard.
1989	Serial killer Theodore Bundy—who confessed to 31 murders in nine states—is executed in Florida's electric chair.
1990	Senator Gwen Margolis, a Democrat from Miami Beach, is elected first woman President of the Florida Senate.
1992	**Hurricane Andrew** smashes into Dade County on August 24, sending 80,000 citizens into shelters.
1993	President Clinton names Janet Reno, State Attorney of Dade County, as US Attorney General. Nine foreign tourists are murdered in Florida within 12 months.
1994	Florida Legislature passes the **Everglades Forever Act**, authorizing removal of agricultural pollutants from the area's waters.
1995	Hurricane Opal wreaks havoc along the Panhandle coast in October.
1996	Vice President Al Gore announces a comprehensive seven-year plan to restore the Everglades ecosystem in south Florida.
1998	Environmental advocate **Marjory Stoneman Douglas**, champion of the Everglades, dies at the age of 108. Major grass fires ravage northeast Florida, forcing 70,000 residents to evacuate their homes.

Economy

By the time Florida became part of the United States in 1821, it already had a thriving plantation economy in the northern part of the state, where most of the people lived. After the Civil War, new and diverse industries sprang up: timber, citrus, shipping, cattle and cigar-making helped establish Florida's importance in the national marketplace. Once the railroads linked the state with the rest of the country in the late 19C, Florida's economy began to blossom. Speculative land sales rocketed in the 1920s, but ended just as suddenly several years later. The subsequent downturn in real estate activity, followed by the Depression, slowed the state's growth until after World War II. Since then Florida's population has expanded rapidly, with retirees and young families fueling a healthy economy that varies from high-tech electronics and finance to agriculture and fishing.

Industry – Florida's **service** industries as a whole account for about 80 percent of the gross state product. Leading this list are community and personal services, such as health care and tourist-related enterprises. About 30 percent of the state's employees work in this sector, earning one-quarter of the gross revenues.

Economists forecast that with Florida's aging population, **health care** will be one of the fastest growing industries in the next decade. The second biggest service industry, **retail** generates over 12 percent of the state's revenue in some of the country's largest department stores, malls, car dealerships, service stations and grocery stores. Enlisting about 15 percent of all workers, **government** extends its hand into schools, hospitals and the military.

Another big wedge of the service pie belongs to **finance and real estate**. Real estate in particular has mushroomed with the state's population growth, and now employs more than double the national average. Although Miami has recently topped Jacksonville as the state's leading financial center, Jacksonville still reigns as the insurance king, with several major insurance company headquarters located there. Transportation and foreign trade round out the service sector, with the latter expected to be one of Florida's hottest industries in upcoming years.

Highlighting the transportation field, **air travel** helps make large-scale tourism possible, while **trucks** transport most of the state's industrial and agricultural products. And some 15 deepwater **ports** serve Florida's international clients, with TAMPA doing the largest volume of business.

Entertainment, now a subset of the service industry, has in the last 15 years made exciting moves: Universal and Disney-MGM have opened studios in Orlando. Motion picture, television, commercial and music video productions have injected more than $220 million into the local economy. In 1992 alone, Florida hosted 27 feature film productions and 21,000 commercial and music ventures.

Because of Florida's distance from major US cities, **manufacturing** has traditionally taken a back seat to tourism and other service industries. With only 10 percent of the gross state product, manufacturing plays a small role here. Yet, since the beginning of the space program in the late 1950s, **high-technology** products have become a staple of the state's economy. National firms have opened branches here for the manufacture of communications devices, x-ray equipment, semiconductors and other computer components. Florida also engages in a sizable **food production** business that includes canned fruit juice, canned fruits and packaged vegetables. The **construction industry** has fluctuated with speculation based on the availability of loans as well as the predicted need of new housing. After peaking in 1973, new construction plummeted with the mid-'70s recession; in 1994 the housing starts again began to rise.

Natural Resources – With Florida's waters claiming more than 700 species of fish, the **commercial fishing** industry nets the state more than $200 million a year, led by catches of shrimp, lobster, crab and snapper. Other important local species include grouper, swordfish, tuna and mullet. Ten percent of the total US shrimp harvest comes from Florida, and the state's Gulf estuaries—particularly off Apalachicola and the Big Bend coast—produce about 6 percent of the US oyster catch. Unfortunately, overfishing, foreign competition and contamination have caused a recent decline in the shellfish haul, and Florida has made some attempts at aquaculture to provide a more reliable harvest. Forests cover about half of Florida's total land area, or almost 16 million acres. The north part of the state is the most densely timbered—commercial forests occupy 75 percent of the northwest region. Since the early 19C, **forestry** has held a significant place in the state's economy. In the years before the Civil War, hardwoods were cut for lumber and pines were tapped for turpentine and rosin used in shipbuilding. By the 1920s the **turpentine industry** had already peaked, but pulp mills were on the rise. Between 1889 and 1933, more than one billion board feet were sawed every year in Florida's great virgin forests before a division of forestry was established to manage this precious resource. Slash pine today ranks as the top commercial tree; common hardwoods include magnolia, black tupelo and oak. Among valued trees harvested almost to extinction are pecky cypress (a porous wood, resistant to termites and rotting) and Dade County pine, both popular local building materials during the early 20C.

Heading the list of mineral deposits, **phosphate** was discovered in the southwest part of the state in 1881. Florida now produces 80 percent of the country's phosphate—an essential ingredient in fertilizer. Florida also leads the nation in production of rutile and zircon, heavy minerals found in ancient beach deposits and used in ceramics, metals and chemicals. Found in greater quantities here than in any other state, **peat** is prized as a soil conditioner. Florida also boasts extensive amounts of **limestone** (its most prevalent mineral). All of Florida's mining operations combined account for less than one-half of one percent of the gross state product.

Citrus Fruit Sorted for Shipping

Robert Torrez/Tony Stone Images

Agriculture – Leading the southeastern US in farm sales, Florida produces a variety of fruits, vegetables and nursery plants that it transports fresh to northern markets in the winter and spring. **Citrus fruits**, first introduced to Florida around 1570, outpace all Florida's other agricultural products, with oranges claiming over three-quarters of the total citrus sales. Florida variably leads the nation in orange and grapefruit production, and supplies the vast majority of its orange juice. (Hard freezes in the 1980s destroyed thousands of acres of citrus groves in central Florida, forcing the state to import juice concentrate from Brazil.) Among Florida's many popular varieties of citrus are Valencia oranges (the world's most ubiquitous juice orange), Temple oranges, and Duncan grapefruit (its white flesh is considered the most flavorful).

While it is the single biggest crop, citrus makes up only a third of the state's total crop sales. Florida stands as the nation's top producer of **sugarcane**. Sugar plantations of the late 18C and early 19C were largely destroyed during the Seminole Wars, but the industry held on until finally receiving a big boost when US trade relations with Cuba soured in 1961. Now Florida produces nearly half the country's sugar, primarily in the area just south of Lake Okeechobee.

Only California beats out Florida in total production and value of fresh **vegetables**. Major local crops include tomatoes, sweet corn, green peppers, snap beans and cucumbers. The state's dairy and beef industries generate a quarter of its total farm income, making Florida the largest cattle state east of the Mississippi.

Tourism – From the time railroads linked Florida's grand east coast resorts in the late 19C, visitors have been flocking to the Sunshine State to escape the cold winters of more northern climes. With the widespread use of automobiles and the increase in small-scale tourist facilities, more people could afford an excursion to Florida. After World War II, the advent of indoor air-conditioning made south Florida a year-round destination. Now more than 40 million people visit the state annually, lured by clear subtropical seas, white-sand beaches and world-class tourist attractions. The opening of WALT DISNEY WORLD in 1971 outside ORLANDO meant a greater distribution of tourists among the non-coastal areas; the Orlando area now attracts some 34 million tourists annually.

Visitors spend a total of $32 billion a year and generate work for 719,000 Floridians— about 12 percent of the state's jobs. Employing people in travel, restaurants, hotels, retail stores and recreational facilities, tourism continues to be the state's top economic resource. Winter remains the busiest tourist season, while spring lures hordes of vacationing college students to DAYTONA BEACH and PANAMA CITY. Summertime brings auto-touring families to beaches and theme parks, but autumn sees the fewest visitors—only 75 percent of the winter numbers. Among foreign travelers to Florida, Canada chips in more than two million—about the same number as the European countries combined.

Economy 2000 – While Florida was weakened like the rest of the country by the recession of the early 1990s, it has been among the quickest to recover. Economists caution, however, that slow and steady will be watchwords for economic growth through the rest of this century. Lower interest rates have meant less income for dividend-receiving retirees, which translates to less cash flow and fewer new jobs. With a decrease in population growth and expected cuts in space and defense spending, job and income growth rates will likely be the slowest over the next 15 years of any similar period since 1930— but they are still predicted to exceed the national average. One sector of the economy that forecasters claim could outperform tourism in the next decade is **international trade**. Florida's proximity to Latin American and Caribbean markets coupled with its international ports and modern airports give the state an edge in this burgeoning field.

As for regional growth, look for Orlando to lead in population increase and housing starts. Southeast Florida, the most populous region, will likely maintain a healthy economic climate. Smaller areas on the move include NAPLES, FORT WALTON BEACH, Panama City, OCALA, FORT MYERS, FORT PIERCE and Port St. Lucie.

Architecture

For a relatively young state, Florida claims a remarkably rich and diverse heritage of building traditions incorporating the practical, the outrageous, the witty—and the bizarre—in equal measure. Ever since 17C Spanish colonization, a strong Mediterranean current has run through the architectural landscape here. The tropical terrain and climate also influenced early design and continue to do so today as a new generation of architects begins to discover and re-invent the past.

Native Structures – The traditional dwelling of the Miccosukee and Seminole tribes is the **chickee**, an open-air shelter framed with rot-resistant cypress poles and thatched with palmetto fronds. Well-adapted to the swampy glades where the tribes hid their camps, the practical structures featured a platform floor of split logs or sawn boards elevated about 3ft off the ground to provide protection from snakes, alligators and flood tides. A compound comprised several individual chickees for sleeping, cooking, communal eating and religious rites.

Seminole Chickee

Early Spanish Building – Although Dominican and Franciscan friars were the true founders of Spanish colonial architecture in Florida, scant archaeological traces remain of some 100 wooden mission compounds established here beginning in 1565. The oldest extant Spanish-built edifice in Florida is the 1695 Castillo de San Marcos *(p 106)* in St. Augustine. The massive structure of quarried **coquina** (native shellstone) is considered the best surviving example of a type of European fortress introduced after gunpowder was invented in the late Middle Ages.

Most early Spanish colonial houses were simple one-story, two-room palmetto-thatched shelters built of wood planks or coquina blocks and rough **tabby** plaster—made of oyster shells and lime. Only the more substantial two-story 18C coquina structures have survived. Following Spanish tradition, the houses in Florida's two Spanish garrisons, St. Augustine and Pensacola, fronted directly onto the street and were part of private, walled compounds entered by a gate. Loggias, or galleries, captured cooling summer breezes and the low winter sun. The glass-paned double-hung windows (replacing earlier wood *rejas*, or open window grills), hipped roofs, dormers and clapboard upper stories seen on many 18C St. Augustine houses were probably introduced by the British during the 1763-83 occupation.

19th Century – The term "Cracker" is believed to have originated with the whip-cracking cattle drivers who began crossing into Florida in the early 19C. The first so-called **Cracker houses** of the Panhandle and central Florida regions were log cabins of several standard types: single-pen (one room), **saddlebag** (two rooms and a central chimney) or **dogtrot** (two rooms and a central breezeway). Such structures were raised off the damp ground on blocks made of limestone, heart pine or rot-resistant cedar. Florida's pioneer houses took on a number of interesting variations after the **balloon frame** (a system of framing a wooden building by nailing together lightweight wood studs), was invented in the 1830s and began to replace the more expensive and labor-intensive pegged-timber frame throughout the US. A typical balloon-frame Cracker house is the 1.5-story farmhouse, with vertical board-and-batten siding and a pitched roof (often of inexpensive sheet metal) sloping over a broad porch. The **four-square** Cracker house, named for the shape of its floor plan, incorporates a porch and hipped roof (four slopes), often vented with a rooftop cupola designed to draw warm air up and out of the interior. **Shotgun** houses served as cheap housing for laborers along the Gulf Coast in south Florida's early Bahamian settlements. This narrow one-room-wide structure with a long row of back-to-back rooms is thought to be an African form that evolved on

Dogtrot Cracker Dwelling

Haitian sugar plantations. It was said that if a shotgun were fired through the front door, the load would pass straight through the line of rooms and out the back door. Built from the 1830s to 1920s, the **Conch house** of Key West is named for the Bahamian islanders—colloquially known as "Conchs"—who settled in the Keys in the 19C. The earliest Conch houses were framed by ships' carpenters using a pegged-and-braced timber system borrowed from shipbuilding, but most of those remaining are balloon-frame structures. The one- or two-story clapboard Conch house is usually raised on stone or brick piers and topped by a peaked roof (shingled or tin) with the gable end facing front; louvered blinds at the doors and windows block the heat of the fierce tropical sun.

The first **plantation houses** built after Florida became a US territory in 1821 were unpretentious two-story, wood-frame structures. In the antebellum years these were replaced by imposing **Greek Revival** mansions fronted by columned two-story porches. Dating from the late 19C, when many citrus and railroad fortunes were made, elaborate **Queen Anne** houses—featuring asymmetrical facades, turrets, ample verandahs, recessed balconies, gingerbread trim, spindles, turned railings and decorated gables—may be found throughout the state. Look also for the charming white board-and-batten Carpenter Gothic churches from the same period, distinguished by their pointed-arch windows.

Early 20th Century – The early 20C building boom coincided with the rise of the **Mediterranean Revival** style, which borrowed loosely from medieval Moorish and Spanish architecture. The style became popular after California featured a Spanish-style pavilion at the widely publicized California-Pacific Exposition in 1915. Although other period revivals were also fashionable at the time, the Mediterranean mode caught on especially well in California and Florida where Spanish roots were strong. Pastel colored stucco walls, red-clay roof tiles, arcaded loggias, towers, arched windows and ornate wrought-iron detailing not only suited Florida's tropical landscape, but also "…express[ed] the spirit of a land dedicated to long, carefree vacations," as a 1925 issue of *House Beautiful* described it. The style became the unifying design theme for dozens of Florida's boomera developments, including Carl Fisher's MIAMI BEACH, George Merrick's model suburb CORAL GABLES, and Addison Mizner's 1,600-acre architectural playground, BOCA RATON. Indeed, many society architects, among them Mizner, Carrère and Hastings and Walter DeGarmo (Florida's first registered architect) made their names with commissions for the luxurious Mediterranean Revival villas that still dominate Florida's early seaside resorts.

Resort Hotels – Perhaps the most distinctive symbols of Florida's heyday are the great resort hotels of the pre-Depression era. The tradition of extravagant hospitality catering to affluent northerners started in the late 19C. The friendly rivalry of railroad magnates Henry Bradley Plant and Henry Morrison Flagler extended to gigantic (and often unprofitable) hotels located at each major railhead. The first was Flagler's 1889 Ponce de Leon Hotel in St. Augustine (now Flagler College; *p 109*), designed by Thomas Hastings (later a partner in the prestigious New York firm of Carrère and Hastings). Plant countered with the 500-room brick, minaret-crowned Tampa Bay Hotel *(p 282)* in 1891. Subsequent hotels were built of less costly wood, and consequently most of these were later claimed by

fire. Plant's multi-gabled, 600-room Belleview Hotel, opened near Clearwater in 1897, may be the sole survivor.

A second wave of posh resorts reached its peak in the 1920s. By this time, the Mediterranean Revival style was considered the apex of architectural design, and most of these enormous structures were built of masonry, adorned with decorative tiles, stone carvings, frescoes and woodwork. While many of the hotels fell into disrepair after the economic crash of 1926, a recent restoration movement has returned a few choice examples to their original luster. St. Petersburg boasts both the **Vinoy Park** *(p 276)*, restored in 1992, and Henry du Pont's **Don CeSar** *(p 279)*, a five-story pink stucco confection with belvedere towers and red clay roof tiles. Others include the majestic Coral Gables **Biltmore Hotel** *(p 206)*, the Palm Beach **Breakers Hotel** *(p 229)*, and Mizner's **Cloister Inn** in Boca Raton. Originally built as a 100-room hotel, the Cloister now forms the east wing of the Boca Raton Resort & Club *(p 183)*.

© Susan Russell

The Biltmore Hotel, Coral Gables

Art Deco Hotels, Miami Beach

Modern Movements – The first widely popular style in the US to purposely break with traditional historical revivals, **Art Deco** transformed hundreds of gas stations, diners, theaters, homes, hotels, motel courts and storefronts across the US into eye-catching streamlined designs between the late 1920s and into the 1940s. An offshoot of the **International Style** with its simple forms and austere surfaces, Deco adopted the sleek lines, cubic massing and new materials of the technology-oriented modernist aesthetic that was emerging in Europe after World War I. At a time when they were trying to bury memories of the recent war and Depression, Americans welcomed the fresh contemporary look of Art Deco buildings. Rather than reject ornament, as pure modernists did, Florida's Deco designers embraced fanciful decoration wholeheart-edly—in particular exotic motifs (palmettos, chevrons and ziggurats) inspired by ancient Egyptian, Aztec and Mayan design.

A later phase of Art Deco, called **Streamline Moderne**, took on an even more futuristic look. Beginning in the 1930s, buildings were stripped of surface decoration and angular elevations were smoothed with rounded corners, horizontal bands ("speed lines") and porthole windows inspired by contemporary streamlined trains, planes and ocean liners. New mass-produced materials—steel, chrome, glass block and concrete block—made it possible to build fast and cheaply. This proved a plus for developers of post-war boom towns like Miami Beach, which now boasts the largest and best-preserved concentration of Art Deco and Streamline Moderne buildings in the world. By the 1950s, Florida was better known for its glitzy resort architecture, most notably **Morris Lapidus'** stupendous movie-set Miami Beach hotels, such as The Fontainebleau *(p 227)* and the Eden Roc. More recently, however, renowned modern architects have helped make metropolitan skylines here as sophisticated as any in the US. Downtown Miami boasts landmarks by I.M. Pei (International Place, 1985), Skidmore, Owings & Merrill (First Union Financial Center, 1984) and John Burgee and Philip Johnson (Miami-Dade Cultural Center, 1982; *p 200*). Florida's best-known architectural firm, Miami's **Arquitectonica International**, features witty, brash designs incorporating both high-tech and historical references rendered in bold geometry and bright colors. Their work—described by critics as "beach blanket Bauhaus"—includes the exuberant Miracle Center Mall in Coral Gables as well as three extravagant luxury apartment towers erected during Miami's "Mondo-Condo" building boom of the early 1980s: the Palace *(p 202)*, the 21-story Atlantis *(p 202)*, and the Imperial *(p 202)*.

The most notable example of the **post-Modern** movement (which emphasizes human scale, historical references and the relationship of a building to its neighbors) is found in the Panhandle coast town of **Seaside** *(p 162)*. Following the lead of developer Robert S. Davis, Miami architects Elizabeth Plater-Zyberk and Andres Duany created the master plan for this model beach community in 1981. The nostalgic pastel wood-frame buildings intentionally recall Florida's 19C Cracker houses and reflect a new and growing appreciation for the state's early vernacular architecture. More recent build-ings have taken on postmodern lines while adhering to a strict building code.

More recently, the development of WALT DISNEY WORLD has added "entertainment archi-tecture" to Florida's mélange of styles. Resembling larger-than-life cartoons, the Dolphin and Swan hotels (1990, Michael Graves) near Epcot Center illustrate the Disney sense of whimsy: each is crowned with a pair of its namesake animals. Also near Orlando, the Team Disney building (1991, Arata Isozaki) presents a riveting cluster of bright geometric shapes that create intriguing optical illusions.

The Arts

Though most visitors venture to Florida for its resorts and outdoor recreation, they may be surprised to find that the state claims a growing number of artists and cultural exhibitions, as well as more than 30 museums of fine art. Indeed, vibrant arts scenes now exist within Miami, Sarasota, Tampa and other smaller cities. And with the recent population explosion of Caribbean immigrants, the Miami area has become a cradle for innovations in Latin and West Indian music.

Visual Arts – A number of 19C painters visited Florida and captured its sun-drenched landscapes on canvas. Among them were Boston artist **William Morris Hunt** (1824-1879), who sought Florida's subtropical climate in 1873 as a balm for his jangled nerves; British painter **Thomas Moran** (1837-1926), who chose Fort George Island *(p 000)* to illustrate an issue of *Scribner's Monthly;* **Martin Johnson Heade** (1819-1904), a Pennsylvanian from the Luminist school who favored Florida's salt marshes; and George Inness, Jr. (1854-1926), who wintered and painted in TARPON SPRINGS.

Honoring those who have made significant contributions in the state, the Florida **Artists Hall of Fame** recognizes several nationally and internationally famous artists, including artist **Robert Rauschenberg**, a modern experimental painter who has lived off and on in Florida for many years. The abstract expressionist creations of **Hiram Williams**, a University of Florida faculty member, have earned him a national reputation. Also at the University of Florida, surrealist photographer **Jerry Uelsmann** has exerted a widespread influence on his field.

West Palm Beach's **Norton Museum of Art** and Winter Park's **Charles Hosmer Morse Museum of American Art** are among museums with fine collections of art by Floridians.

Sunset, Tropical Marshes (c.1880) by Martin Johnson Heade

Performing Arts – Florida's performing arts have also blossomed in the last few decades. Since the founding of the **Greater Miami Opera** in 1941, six more companies have sprung up around the state. Florida now offers some 35 theater companies as well as 33 professional dance groups, including the **Miami City Ballet**, which has been performing classical and modern dance in south Florida since the mid-1970s.

Most of Florida's major cities have professional symphony orchestras, and numerous regional and university music ensembles present frequent concerts. The **Florida West Coast Symphony** performs for audiences in Bradenton and Sarasota. Florida's official teaching festival, the **Sarasota Music Festival** takes place every June, attracting talented young professionals from around the world. Young musicians (age 21 to 30) also fill the ranks of the Miami Beach-based **New World Symphony**. Moving up the coast, the **Florida Philharmonic Orchestra** plays in Fort Lauderdale and southeast Florida, while the **Jacksonville Symphony Orchestra** entertains music-lovers farther north.

Fueled by the success of singer **Gloria Estefan** and her producer-husband Emilio, Miami Beach has become the national capital for the Latin music boom. The Estefans' new Sony Building in the Art Deco Historic District *(p 222)* has full music- and video-production facilities. Another longtime Florida resident is singer-songwriter **Jimmy Buffett**, whose vagabond-sailor persona has beguiled an international following.

Film and Television – Famous for its theme parks that celebrate film and TV, Florida has carved out a solid niche for itself in the **movie industry**. After years of providing the jungle backdrop for such early films (1940s and 1950s) as the Tarzan series and

Creature From the Black Lagoon, Florida welcomed Universal and Disney-MGM studios in the late 1980s. Operating as both theme parks and actual production facilities, these two Orlando operations add to the smaller studios in Miami to create an attractive milieu for filmmaking. Recent big-budget pictures filmed in Florida include *True Lies*, *The Specialist* and *The Bird Cage*. Over the years, the state has also hosted a number of television series, including *Flipper*, *Miami Vice*, *SeaQuest*, *Sins of the City* and several Latin soap operas.

Folk Arts – Ethnic and regional **folk arts** are kept alive through numerous festivals, apprenticeships, and grants. The annual Florida Folk Festival, held each May at the **Stephen Foster State Folk Culture Center** in White Springs, illustrates regional folklife through music, dancing and farm crafts. Namesake of the Folk Culture Center, Pennsylvania-born composer **Stephen Collins Foster** (1826-1864) immortalized Florida's Suwannee River in his 1851 song *Old Folks At Home*. In 1935 this folk tune was officially designated as the state song.

Ranking second (after New York) in state appropriations for the arts, Florida hands out $22 million every year in grant awards to artists, many of whom preserve the traditions of folklife maintained in the state's numerous ethnic groups. **Cubans** in Key West, Miami and Tampa's Ybor City make woodcarvings and *guyaberas*—light shirts decorated with pleating and embroidery. Caribbean transplants continue a rich maritime craft tradition with handmade boats, sails and fishing gear. **Greeks**, who have maintained a vibrant presence in TARPON SPRINGS since the early 1900s, bring their own nautical arts to modern Florida, along with sponge diving, Greek folk dance, colorful embroidery and music.

South Florida is also home to tribes of **Seminole** and **Miccosukee** Indians, who still craft bracelets, bead necklaces, palmetto-fiber dolls, painted wood tomahawks, pine-needle

Charles Hosmer Morse Museum of American Art

and sweet-grass baskets, and dazzling calico clothing. The latter boasts colorful patchwork designs suggesting lightning, arrows, diamonds and other symbols. These Native American wares are plied in reservation gift shops and at arts fairs in the Everglades' Miccosukee Indian Village *(p 44)* and Ah-Tha-Thi-Ki Museum *(p 192)*.

People

Four out of five Floridians are not native to the state. As a group, residents of Florida have in common the identity of "newcomer" more than anything else, and beyond that identity lies a hodgepodge of races, ages, origins and attitudes that sometimes sits uneasily side-by-side in this growing state. Yet along with their status as newcomers, Floridians as a whole share a sense of hope. Some come here seeking new job opportunities and others political freedom; but all come looking for a piece of the American good life, a place in the sun.

Florida's phenomenal growth has outstripped most of the country: In 1900 the state ranked 33rd in population; by 1960 it had risen to 10th. With more than 13 million people, it now ranks as the fourth largest state in the nation. And the population has redistributed itself as the south Florida wilderness has yielded to the dreams of pioneers and developers. In 1900 north Florida held 66 percent of the population,

Miccosukee Indian Child in Traditional Dress

compared to 5 percent in south Florida. Today the north has shrunk to 20 percent, while the south carries 37 percent—with one-third of the entire state living on the 65mi strip from Miami to West Palm Beach known as the Gold Coast.

Early Minorities – One of the smallest ethnic groups, the **Seminoles** are themselves relatively new to Florida. They coalesced from various southeastern tribes and moved into Florida in the 18C to escape harassment by white settlers. Though most were relocated to Oklahoma in the mid-19C, about 2,000 Seminoles still live and maintain elements of their culture on reservations in and around the Everglades. The percentage of **African-Americans** has decreased from 44 percent of the population in 1900 to about 13 percent in 1990; in recent decades, their population has shifted heavily from the rural north to the urban Gold Coast.

North and South – If some Floridians consider the label "Cracker" a slur, most proudly acknowledge it as an ethnic identity that extols the frontier virtues of independence and self-reliance. The term—probably deriving from the snapping noise of whips used by early Florida cowboys—refers loosely to descendants of native white Floridians who owned small farms or ranches in the north part of the state. Whereas the peninsula has funneled in Yankees from the northeast over the past 50 years, north Florida has retained the flavor and drawl of neighbors Georgia and Alabama. The north, with its large concentration of military retirees, takes conservative political stances, while the south, claiming a high number of Jews and northeasterners, tends toward a more liberal outlook.

Old and New – Add to this complex mélange senior citizens, Hispanics and numerous smaller groups, and the portrait of Florida becomes even richer and more difficult to delineate. Since the end of World War II, the elderly have pushed in from less hospitable climes, until Florida now claims a higher percentage of **seniors** than any other state. This group has made southwest Florida one of the fastest growing areas in the country. Another large number of retirees, known as "snowbirds," migrate to Florida for the winter, then return home in the spring.

The most influential new group of arrivals to Florida, **Hispanics** have swirled up from Cuba and other places south with the frequency of tropical storms ever since the Cuban revolution in 1959. From that time to this, more than 750,000 people from the Caribbean have moved to Florida, giving the state one of the largest populations of Hispanics in the country. About 72 percent live on the Gold Coast, imparting their lively language and customs to the Miami region.

Over the Hill – Florida's population explosion may finally see some relief in the next decade. As the over-65 age group dwindles, fewer retirees will move to the Sunshine State. Of course, along with slower growth and less crowding comes a less robust economy. The Gold Coast area, already near capacity, suffered in the early 1990s from a high crime rate brought on, in part, by a heated mixture of diverse people jostling for the promised good life. Other areas of Florida stand ready to usher in the next wave of arrivals, from wherever they may come, and residents and visitors alike will have the chance to witness a state in the exciting process of defining itself.

Literature

Long after gaining statehood Florida remained a largely untamed frontier. The sense of mystery and raw natural beauty of the unfamiliar landscape lured both adventurers and romantics—writers among them—and have proved enduring themes in the region's literature.

Early Voices – Naturalists were among the first visitors to chronicle Florida and its native inhabitants. Appointed "Royal Botanist of the Floridas" by King George III, **John Bartram** (1699-1777) traveled from Philadelphia into the tropical wilderness in 1765-66, documenting unknown species of flora and fauna in *A Description of East Florida* (1769). His son William Bartram followed with *Travels Through North and South Carolina, Georgia, East and West Florida* in 1791.

During the 19C, magazine fiction and travel stories constituted a major body of Florida writing. In the 1830s and 1840s, the monthlies *Knickerbocker* and *Graham's* published Florida adventure tales by such popular figures as **Washington Irving** and **James Fenimore Cooper**. In 1897, **Stephen Crane** (1871-1900), author of *The Red Badge of Courage* (1896) and a brief resident of JACKSONVILLE, wrote *The Open Boat*. This dramatic story was based on a shipwreck he survived off New Smyrna Beach on his way to Cuba to fight in the Spanish-American War.

Contemporary travel guides were pivotal in bringing settlers and tourists to Florida. Among the classics now coveted by collectors are *Florida for Tourists, Invalids, and Settlers* (1881) by George Barbour (a phenomenal best-seller in its day) and *Florida: Its Scenery, Climate, and History* (1875) by the acclaimed southern poet, **Sydney Lanier** (1842-1881).

One of the many travelers who returned to Florida to live was author **Harriet Beecher Stowe** (1811-1896), who spent winters in Mandarin, just outside Jacksonville, from 1868 to 1884. Her widely read *Palmetto Leaves* (1873) celebrated the beauty of the St. Johns River and attracted hundreds of curious travelers to the area.

Black Voices – Black writers have also helped shape the state's literary tradition. Jacksonville native **James Weldon Johnson** (1871-1938) was the author of several books, poems and songs. His works include *Autobiography of an Ex-Colored Man* (1912) and *Lift Every Voice and Sing*, which has been called the black national anthem. Eatonville's master story-teller **Zora Neale Hurston** (1901-1960) is acclaimed for fiction and essays that celebrate black culture and bespeak the honest values of rural southern life. They include the autobiographical *Dust Tracks On A Road* (1942) and *Their Eyes Were Watching God* (1937), considered one of the first black feminist novels of this century.

20C – Remaining unspoiled well into the 20C, the rugged beauty of backwoods Florida captivated many northern transplants, including **Marjorie Kinnan Rawlings** (1896-1953). Rawlings settled in the hamlet of Cross Creek *(p 79)* in 1928, and shaped many of her novels and stories around characters and settings inspired by her rural surroundings. The 1938 classic *The Yearling*—the story of a young boy and his pet deer in the Big Scrub (now Ocala National Forest)—won a Pulitzer Prize in 1939. Other Florida-inspired Rawlings titles include *South Moon Under* (1933) and *Cross Creek* (1942). A longtime resident of COCONUT GROVE, **Marjory Stoneman Douglas** (1890-1998) arrived in Miami in 1915 and became one of the state's first environmentalists. Her 1947 volume, *The Everglades: River of Grass*, remains an eloquent warning against the exploitation of this imperiled natural resource. During the 1930s and 1940s, novelist **Hervey Allen** (1889-1949) and America's Poet Laureate, **Robert Frost** (1874-1963), taught at the University of Miami's Winter Institute of Literature.

Call of the Keys – Key West also proved a magnet for writers. **Wallace Stevens** (1879-1955), who frequented the island on his yearly travels south from Connecticut, touted the tropical lushness of South Florida in his poetry anthology, *Harmonium* (1923). **Ernest Hemingway** *(p 64)*, Florida's favorite literary son, spent most of the 1930s in Key West. Among the many works he wrote there, *To Have and Have Not* (1937) evokes the dignity and despair of the Depression-era life in the then-hard-bitten fishing village. Cultivated during his Key West years, Hemingway's fascination with the physical and intellectual challenge of deep-sea fishing was later reflected in *The Old Man and the Sea* (1952). Poet **Elizabeth Bishop** (1911-1979) made Key West her home in the late 1930s and early 1940s. Among the plays **Tennessee Williams** (1911-1983) wrote in his Duncan Street studio were *The Rose Tattoo* (1950) and *Night of the Iguana* (1961). Other well-known literary figures attracted to Key West include Thornton Wilder—who penned *The Matchmaker* there in 1954—poet and playwright Archibald MacLeish, humorist S.J. Perelman, and poet Richard Wilbur. Contemporary Key West writers include Philip Caputo, Ralph Ellison and Thomas McGuane (whose 1978 novel *Panama* is set in Key West).

Elsewhere in Florida, mystery writer and former Sarasota resident **John D. MacDonald** (1916-1986), author of *Condominium* (1977) and *The Lonely Silver Rain* (1985), used Florida's Gold Coast as the backdrop for the exploits of his fictional private eye, Travis McGee. Kurt Vonnegut, Gore Vidal and Alison Lurie number among the other novelists, short-story writers and essayists drawn to the Sunshine State, which continues to inspire literary themes ranging from ecological and social concerns to pure adventure.

Recreation

World-famous for over a century, Florida's glorious **beaches** continue to top the heap of the state's recreational venues. With their fine white sand, rolling dunes and gentle clear blue surf, these beaches attract hordes of sun-worshippers and swimmers. SANIBEL ISLAND and other Gulf coast beaches offer **shelling** unparalleled anywhere in the country, and over the past several years, 15 Florida beaches have ranked among the top 20 in the nation in an annual independent survey. Variously rated for their beauty, water and air temperatures, sand softness, water clarity and solitude, beaches that have been awarded the highest marks include those at Florida's St. George Island State Park *(p 156)*, Grayton Beach State Recreation Area *(p 162)*, and Caladesi Island State Park *(p 274)*. St. Joseph Peninsula State Park *(p 168)*.

© Al Messerschmidt

Windsurfing in Biscayne Bay

In and On the Water – Water sports of all types abound along both coasts, with **surfing** concentrated on the Atlantic side and **sailing** and **windsurfing** on the calmer Gulf. Florida manufactures more pleasure boats than any other state in the country; many of them are used for **waterskiing** or for taking fishing parties out to cast for such deep-sea denizens as mackerel, marlin, bonefish, sailfish and tarpon. Inland, the state's numerous rivers, lakes and springs provide ample opportunity for freshwater **fishing**, as well as **canoeing** through primeval swamplands. The Florida Canoe Trail *(p 335)* system boasts 950mi of designated routes along 36 rivers and waterways.

Snorkelers don fins and mask along both coasts to explore ancient wrecks and exotic fish. For sheer underwater beauty, **scuba divers** head to the coral reef that stretches off the shores of the Florida Keys. Divers also plunge into the mysterious underwater caves located in many of Florida's crystal-clear springs, where they encounter such creatures as American eels and blind crayfish.

Back On Land – Florida claims over 1,000 **golf courses**, more than any state in the union, and most of which are open to the public. Another year-round sport, **tennis** is played throughout the state; many hotels and resorts offer vacation packages that include tennis lessons with resident pros. A significant number of tourists also escape to Florida to take advantage of its many **spas**, which promise rest for the weary and rejuvenation for the aged.

Backcountry in the Everglades and the Panhandle attract **campers** to vast acreages of national and state parks. And **hiking** is becoming a more and more popular activity, with over 2,300mi of developed trails in the state. In the years ahead, state officials hope to link the **Florida National Scenic Trail** *(p 82)* with the Appalachian Trail, thus extending the latter from Georgia to the Everglades. The Florida trail currently traverses some 1,000mi through swampland, scrub and hardwood forest. And agencies plan to add more footpaths to the Lake Okeechobee area and to convert the state's old railroad beds into bike trails.

Spectator Sports – Among the many spectator sports in the state, **jai alai** is perhaps the most uniquely Floridian. Originating in the Basque region of Spain and imported from Cuba, the world's fastest game is played on six *frontons* (176ft courts) throughout Florida, including America's oldest, the 1926 Miami Jai-Alai Fronton. Players hurl *pelotas* (balls) against curved walls at speeds of 170mph or more and catch them in *cestas* (baskets) attached to their arms. Spectators may wager on games.

Auto racing, which started on the beach near DAYTONA in 1902, continues on the Daytona International Speedway *(p 88)* with the famous Daytona 500 and other events. Racing fans can also watch greyhounds or horses run on tracks throughout the state. Miami's Hialeah Park (1925) remains one of the most popular venues for horse racing in Florida. **Professional sports** teams *(p 333)* bring some of the country's top athletes to Florida. Since 1901 the state has been a favorite location for major league **baseball spring training camps**. Twenty teams train here and hold exhibition games, while several minor league clubs provide summertime ballpark excitement.

Culinary Traditions

Taking advantage of the bounty of its offshore waters, its year-round growing season and the influence of its Latin and Caribbean immigrants, the Sunshine State offers a crazy-quilt of cuisines that varies regionally from north to south. Whether your tastes run to "down-home" cooking or haute cuisine, you can find it in Florida.

Specialty of the House at Joe's Stone Crab

Cracker Cooking – Saltpork, cornmeal, molasses and turnip greens were staples in the diets of Florida's early settlers. Known as "Crackers"—supposedly for the sound of the cattle ranchers' whips—these pioneers hunted squirrel, deer and raccoon to add to their tables. Freshwater fish, caught in local rivers and springs, was pan-fried. And the ubiquitous Sabal palm *(p 15)* was harvested for its edible bud, said to taste like raw cabbage. Called "swamp cabbage" by the settlers, this same delicacy is known today by the more elegant appellation "hearts of palm."

In the Panhandle and northeastern regions, dishes still echo this early style of cooking, replete with the southern accents of neighbors Georgia and Alabama. Steamed Apalachicola Bay oysters, broiled amberjack (a mild, flaky white fish), fried catfish or Gulf shrimp, hush puppies (small balls of deep-fried cornmeal dough) and grits (a

---

■ **On the Wild Side: Florida's Exotic Fruits**

South Florida's subtropical climate nurtures a plethora of little-known fruits from around the world. What follows is a sampling of Florida's exotic bounty.

Carambola – Each slice of the yellow-green, ridged carambola forms a star, thus its more popular moniker, star fruit. Hailing from East India, the crunchy carambola has a fresh, slightly acidic flavor that enhances desserts and salads.

Kumquat – Eaten raw, this Chinese quail-egg-size citrus fruit tastes tart and its rind bitter. Chefs recommend poaching kumquats in sugar syrup to render them more palatable.

Lychee – Another China native, resembling a small red ball with knobby skin, the lychee grew in Florida as early as 1886. Its honeyed, fragrant white flesh is often served for dessert in Chinese restaurants.

Mango – The dark, oval fruit has been cultivated in tropical East Asia for over 6,000 years. Florida growers stagger ripening times so mango-lovers can enjoy this peachy treat for as long as five months a year.

Passion Fruit – Encased in a hard, bitter-tasting, yellow or purple shell, the juicy edible pulp of the passion fruit is studded with tiny black seeds. The South American native caught on as a commercial fruit in the 1980s.

Plantain – This jumbo cousin of the banana originated in Africa. Rarely eaten raw, plantains—an essential ingredient in Cuban cuisine—are usually served fried, boiled or baked.

Sapodilla – Fans of the egg-shaped, brown-skinned sapodilla claim it tastes like a pear infused with maple syrup. This fruit grows wild in parts of Mexico and Central America.

Ugli Fruit – A cross between a tangerine and a grapefruit, the ugli is named for its unappealing thick yellow-green skin. Despite its appearance, this pear-shaped native of Jamaica boasts a sought-after, tart-sweet flavor.

bland gruel made from ground white corn) constitute typical northern fish-house fare. A menu in these restaurants might also include fried alligator and frog legs, as well as spicy Cajun creations such as the thick seafood stew called gumbo, and jambalaya, a hearty variety of meats and shellfish cooked together with rice.

Tropical Melting Pot – South Florida cooking takes its cues from the fresh vegetables, exotic fruits, and the bountiful numbers of commercial fish harvested in the state. Here you can sample smoked mullet and freshly caught grouper, pompano, snapper and mahimahi—all often paired with tropical fruit salsas. Succulent stone crab claws *(p 226)*, chewy conch fritters (made from the mollusk found inside Florida's state shell) and clawless spiny lobster constitute some of the state's unique shellfish dishes. Although renowned for its citrus fruit—over 20 varieties are grown here—Florida has added exotics *(p 37)* such as passion fruit, papaya, mango and carambola to its expanding list of produce. In addition Florida claims the small, yellowish, bracingly tart key limes used in making **key lime pie**. A simple mixture of egg yolks, sweetened condensed milk and key lime juice in a graham-cracker crust, the state's famed dessert is served topped with either whipped cream or fluffy meringue.

Ever-evolving Florida cuisine is generously peppered with foreign flavors. Cubans have introduced plantains (a cousin to the banana), yuca (a mild-tasting root vegetable) and boniato (a nutty Cuban sweet potato) to grocery stores. And such dishes as black beans and rice, *arroz con pollo* (chicken with yellow rice) and *ropa vieja* (Spanish for "old clothes"), shredded beef dressed with tomatoes, peppers, onions, garlic and white wine, appear as entrees on many restaurant menus. Miamians have even come to favor the strong, dark *café Cubano* now available throughout the city. Nicaraguans, Peruvians, Haitians and other ethnic groups have also influenced Florida's culinary scene. One of the best-known Nicaraguan contributions is *tres leches* (three-milks cake), a dessert made with a mixture of fresh milk, evaporated milk and sweetened condensed milk.

Everglades

River of Grass – Uniphoto Picture Agency

Renowned throughout the world, the vast "river of grass" known as the Everglades covers the southern end of the Florida peninsula in a subtropical wetland that is home to hosts of rare birds, mammals and reptiles. The 50mi-wide sheet of moving water stretching from Lake Okeechobee to the Florida Bay began to form during the last Ice Age, when a shallow tropical sea intermittently covered the area, creating the limestone bedrock that now underlies it. Waters draining from the Kissimmee Basin to the north gradually inundated the land. This slow-moving river—averaging 6in in depth and losing only 2in of elevation for every mile it slopes down toward the Gulf of Mexico—gives rise to diverse ecosystems: coastal and saw grass prairies, mangrove swamps, tree islands, pinelands, hardwood hammocks and coastal estuaries. All of these communities depend upon the seasonal rhythm of the flow of water feeding them. Heavy rains nourish the area during the wet season, from May to October, while the landscape becomes increasingly parched during the dry winter months.

Calusa Indians were the first known people to inhabit what they called Pa-hay-okee, or "Grassy Waters." Archaeological evidence indicates that the Calusa lived in these coastal areas for as long as 2,000 years, disappearing from southern Florida only after the arrival of the Spanish in the 16C.

Small bands of Miccosukee and Seminoles took refuge in the Glades in the mid-19C, to escape the Seminole Wars and to avoid being sent west to reservations by the federal government. The remaining Indians developed a subsistence culture here and were virtually the area's sole inhabitants until the late 19C. At that time a few intrepid white settlers braved the heat and mosquitoes to settle along the coastal periphery of the Everglades.

Animals and plants in the Everglades today belong to a complex, interdependent cycle of water, fire, grasses and soils that has been interrupted in recent decades by the human manipulation of water flow. During floods too much water is channeled into the Everglades from urban and agricultural areas to the north; during droughts not enough water is allowed to flow south to the Gulf. Recent legislation seeks to address the increasingly complicated demands of this unique ecosystem in the dawn of a new century.

When to Go

The best time to visit is in **winter** (the dry season, Nov–mid-Apr), when daytime temperatures range from 60°-80°F, mosquitoes are tolerable, and wildlife is easier to spot. The busiest week is Dec 25–Jan 1. Make lodging and tour reservations several months in advance. Although the park is less crowded in **summer** (the wet season, May–Oct), temperatures often soar to 95°F and the hot, humid weather brings clouds of mosquitoes and other biting insects. Insect repellent is recommended year-round. During the wet season, flooding can cause closing of some park facilities, roads and trails.

Getting There

By Air – **Miami International Airport** (MIA): closest commercial airport, 34mi north of Homestead *(map p 44)*. Shuttle service to Homestead: Super Shuttle *(24/hr service; one-way $41 first passenger, $12 second passenger)*, for reservations ☎ 871-2000; The Airporter *(3 times daily; one-way $20)*, for reservations ☎ 852-3413 or 800-830-3413. Rental car agencies *(p 323)* located at airport.

By Car – There are two entrances to Everglades National Park: to reach the southern terminus at Flamingo, take Route 9336 east then south from Florida City *(directions from Miami p 40)*. US-41 cuts through the northern part of the park.

By Bus – Four trips daily between Miami and Homestead. Greyhound/Trailways bus station: 5 N.E. 3rd St., Homestead ☎ 800-231-2222.

General Information

Visitor Information – **Park Headquarters**, 40001 State Rd. 9336, Homestead FL 33034 ☎ 242-7700. The park is open daily year-round. Entrance fee is $10/vehicle; ⚠ ♿. **Ernest F. Coe Visitor Center**: 11mi southwest of Homestead on Rte. 9336 *(open daily 8am–5pm)* ☎ 242-7700. Additional visitor centers: **Royal Palm** on US-41 *(open daily 8am–4:15pm)* ☎ 242-7700; **Flamingo** at terminus of Rte. 9336 *(open daily 8am–5pm)* ☎ 941-695-2945; **Shark Valley** on US-41 *(open daily 8:30am–5:15pm; $8/vehicle)* ☎ 221-8776 and **Gulf Coast** in Everglades City *(open daily 7:30am–5pm)* ☎ 941-695-3311. Rangers lead wildlife walks, canoe trips and evening programs; for schedules check the park newspaper or visitor centers. **Everglades Area Chamber of Commerce**, PO Box 130, Everglades City FL 34139 ☎ 941-695-3941 or 800-941-6355, provides information on local lodging, gas stations and recreation.

Accommodations – *(p 324)* Flamingo Lodge, Marina & Outpost Resort facilities include motel, cottages ($89–$135), full-service marina, houseboat rental (Oct–May; 2-7 days $475–$1,375, fully equipped) and restaurant. Reservations: #1 Flamingo Lodge Hwy., Flamingo FL 33034-6798 ☎ 941-695-3101 or 800-600-3813. Everglades City, Homestead and Florida City offer hotels, motels, campgrounds and RV parks. *Rates quoted are average prices for a double room in high season (lower in summer).*

Tours – Narrated tours (reservations suggested) leaving from Flamingo: **Bald Eagle Florida Bay cruise** departs from marina *(Nov–Apr daily 10am–sunset; rest of the year daily 2:30pm; round-trip 1hr 30min; commentary; $10)*. **Pelican Backcountry cruise** departs from the marina *(Nov–Apr daily 10:15am–3:30pm; rest of the year daily noon & 4:30pm; round-trip 2hrs; commentary; $16)*; the *Everglades Queen* departs from the marina for a backcountry tour *(year-round Wed–Mon; twice daily; round-trip 3hrs; commentary; $32)*. Also available at Flamingo Lodge are canoe *($22/half day, $32–$50/day)*, skiff *($65/half day, $155/day)*, kayak *($27/half day, $60/day)* and bicycle rentals *($8/half day, $17/day)*, as well as charter fishing with experienced guides. Schooner *Windfall* departs from marina and sails the Florida Bay; reservations ☎ 941-695-3101. Shark Valley tram tours, see p 44.

Sports and Recreation – **Camping** at Long Pine Key, Flamingo and Chekika *(mid-Dec–mid-Apr; $14/camp site; group rate for 15-20 people $28/camp site; rest of the year free)*. **Backcountry** is accessible by boat, canoe and on foot only. A permit ($10-$30) is required for all overnight trips. A Florida **fishing** license *(p 331)*, available at local bait and tackle shops, is required for fresh- and saltwater fishing. Seven **canoe** trails thread the southern park region. Rental canoes are available at Nine-Mile Pond and Westlake through TW Recreational Services, Inc. ☎ 941-695-3101. Boat tours of Ten Thousand Islands, see p 45. Canoe the **Wilderness Waterway** *(p 45)* with North American Canoe Tours *(Nov–Apr; day trip $40-$60/person; 4 or 7 days $450–$800/person; reservations required)* ☎ 941-695-4666. Sea kayak tours *(Dec–Jan, 4 day minimum, $500-$875/person; reservations required)* by Wilderness Southeast ☎ 912-897-5108. Eight **hiking** trails fan out from Flamingo *(p 41)*; for maps and trail information, contact Park Headquarters.

EVERGLADES NATIONAL PARK★★★

Map of Principal Sights p 3 – Map p 44
Tourist Information ☎ 305-242-7700

One of only a few American parks that enjoys UNESCO status as a World Heritage Site and falls within an International Biosphere Reserve, the 1.5-million-acre Everglades National Park, attracts birding enthusiasts, canoeists, fishermen and those who simply want to drink in the spectacle of an aquatic wilderness that remains unique in the world.

Historical Notes

Ecosystem in Jeopardy – The timeless rhythm of the Everglades was seriously compromised in the early 20C, when **Napoleon Broward** *(p 186)*, a Florida gubernatorial candidate, proposed draining the soggy area to provide water for agriculture and land for urban development. Broward won the election and in the following decades, water was diverted from the Glades through some 1,400mi of man-made canals that drain the Everglades' water for farmland and suburban drinking water.

Though early grassroots conservationists protested the desecration, their efforts generally proved ineffective. In 1916, however, the first Everglades preserve—the roughly 2,000-acre **Royal Palm State Park**—was established, thanks in large part to the efforts of the Florida Federation of Women's Clubs. Even so, development also rolled on. In 1928 the **Tamiami Trail** (US-41) was completed, cutting through the heart of the Everglades and blocking the water's southerly flow. Today these "grassy waters" lie mostly in private hands.

Preserving Pa-hay-okee – The establishment of the park in 1947 stemmed the tide of development that threatened to destroy this fragile ecosystem. About the same time, *The Everglades: River of Grass* appeared. This popular work by late Florida journalist **Marjory Stoneman Douglas** explained the need to protect the Glades, at the same time extolling the beauty of "their vast glittering openness ... the racing free saltness and sweetness of their massive winds, under the dazzling blue heights of space." Douglas remained in the forefront of the ongoing fight to preserve the Everglades and return their natural flow of water until her death in 1998 at the age of 108.

Since the park's establishment, its boundaries have been increased several times, most recently with the 1989 **East Everglades Expansion Act**, which added an additional 107,600 acres to the park. Now the third largest national park in the continental US after Death Valley and Yellowstone, the area still suffers from its proximity to major farming and urban centers that introduce toxins—such as the 200 annual tons of phosphates from agricultural fertilizers and pesticides—into this wilderness. The Everglades ecosystem also has natural enemies. Exotic plants—like the fire-resistant Australian Melaleuca tree, one acre of which sucks up the area's precious water at a rate of 2,100gal per hour—that have been introduced into the Glades threaten to overtake native vegetation, thus upsetting the delicate ecological balance.

Florida's Legislature began removing agricultural and other pollutants from the area's waters following the passage of the **Everglades Forever Act** in 1994; two years later, the federal government announced a comprehensive seven-year plan to restore the Everglades ecosystem. Construction projects to reestablish water flow are ongoing. Balancing human needs against natural ones continues to be problematic, but fortunately policy makers now acknowledge Douglas' contention that "there are no other Everglades in the World."

Whitewater Bay, Southern Everglades

SOUTHERN EVERGLADES *1 day*

While you can see the highlights in a day, to best experience and understand the Everglades you must spend some time hiking its trails and boating on its waters. Sights in the southern part of the national park are organized as a driving tour, going from north to south.

From Miami, take Florida's Turnpike (I-75) south until it dead-ends at Florida City. Turn right on Rte. 1 south to Palm Dr. (Rte. 9336). Follow Rte. 9336 1.7mi and turn left on 192nd Ave. Continue 2mi to 376th St. S.W. Turn right and follow the road 5.6mi to park entrance. Route 9336 then continues 38mi to its terminus in Flamingo.

Ernest F. Coe Visitor Center – *Just inside park entrance on right. Open year-round daily 8am–5pm.* ✕ & 🅿 *www.nps.gov/ever* ☎ *305-242-7700.* The new Coe Visitor Center, named for one of the park's early champions, was dedicated in 1996 to replace a previous visitor center destroyed by Hurricane Andrew. Its hipped, metal roof

Everglades Regulations

▲ Water-skiing is prohibited.

▲ Firearms and hunting are prohibited.

▲ Smoking on trails is not permitted.

▲ Pets are not allowed on trails.

▲ All vehicles must stay on designated roads; off-road vehicles are not permitted.

▲ Reduce speed in marked wildlife areas.

Safety Tips

■ Exercise extreme care when burning campfires, permitted in fire rings in campground area only.

■ Do not disturb or feed wildlife.

■ When hiking, advise someone of your itinerary.

■ Owing to abundant wildlife in freshwater ponds and poor underwater visibility, swimming is not encouraged.

■ Watch for sudden weather changes, especially when boating, that can produce heavy thunderstorms with dangerous lightning and high winds.

■ Always wear a sunscreen and protective clothing.

and wood siding enable it to blend inconspicuously into the natural environment. Exhibits and films educate visitors not only on the Everglades, but also on the environmental crises confronting the greater South Florida ecosystem. An information desk provides details on recreational activities within the national park; administrative offices are located in an adjacent building.

Continue 2mi on Rte. 9336 and turn left at the sign for Royal Palm visitor center and the popular Gumbo Limbo and Anhinga Trails.

★★**Anhinga Trail** – *.5mi. Begins at rear of visitor center. Ranger-led walks and lectures are held here several times daily (first-come, first-served).* One of the park's most popular areas, this trail begins as a wide paved path, which follows a portion of the Old Ingraham Highway. A boardwalk then leads across Taylor Slough (pronounced "slew"), a shallow, slow-moving river that channels through a marsh dense with willow thickets and punctuated by a palm hammock. Alligators, turtles and myriad birds congregate here, particularly in the dry winter months.

★**Gumbo Limbo Trail** – *.4mi.* This trail weaves through the luxuriant vegetation of historic Paradise Key Hammock, the area that formed the original **Royal Palm State Park** *(p 39).* A typical tropical island of hardwood trees, Paradise Key supports a rich variety of ferns, lianas, orchids, royal palms and, of course, gumbo-limbo trees. The latter is known in Florida as the "tourist tree" because its red, peeling bark resembles sunburned skin.

Return to Rte. 9336 and continue 4.4mi.

Pinelands Trail – *.3mi.* A paved trail here circles through a rocky, drier landscape that supports one of the few existing forests of **Florida slash pine**, also known as Dade County pine. Highly prized for its durability, slash pine was extensively logged earlier in this century. That, and the suppression of forest fires, which allow the fire-resistant pine to compete with hardwoods, has led to the demise of the pine forests that once covered much of southern Florida. Only a total of 20,000 acres of slash pine remain, making this species the continent's most endangered member of the pine family.

Continue 6.3mi to the turn-off for Pa-hay-okee Overlook.

★★**Pa-hay-okee Overlook** – This elevated platform provides a sweeping **view**★★ of the Everglades' seemingly endless saw grass prairie, interrupted only by sporadic islands of trees. Saw grass *(Cladium jamaicense)*, part of the sedge family, is by far the most dominant flora in the Everglades. Though its long blades are razor-sharp, its soft roots are edible.

Return to Rte. 9336 and drive 7mi; turn right at sign for Mahogany Hammock.

Mahogany Hammock – *.3mi.* Tunneling through a lush display of ferns and mahogany trees, the boardwalk trail passes the largest known mahogany tree in the country. Unfortunately, this landmark was damaged by Hurricane Donna in 1960 and again by Hurricane Andrew in 1992.

Return to Rte. 9336 and continue 11.3mi; turn right to parking area for West Lake.

★**Mangrove Trail** – *.3mi.* Follow the boardwalk here along the edge of West Lake across a watery mangrove swamp. The dense concentration of mangroves, with their complex tangle of roots and branches, typifies Florida's coastal areas, where freshwater and saltwater mix. Three types of mangroves *(p 15)* grow in the Everglades: red, distinguished by their reddish arcing roots; black, whose bases are surrounded by spiky breathing tubes called pneumatophores; and white, generally found on drier ground.

Continue 3.6mi.

Mrazek Pond – Right beside the road, this watering hole is popular with birders. At dawn and dusk, waterbirds such as grebes, herons, egrets, ibis and roseate spoonbills congregate here to feast on fish and shellfish.

Continue 3.5 mi to Flamingo.

Flamingo – *Located at the southern terminus of Rte. 9336 (38mi from park entrance).* A small outpost overlooking Florida Bay serves as the hub of visitor services in the southern Everglades, providing the only food and accommodations in this part of the park. The **visitor center** *(open year-round daily 8am–5pm;* ⚠ ✕ ♿ ▯ ☎ *941-695-2945)* houses a small display area with natural history exhibits. The adjacent marina serves as the boarding point for a variety of **Wilderness Cruises**★★ *(p 38)* that tour the backcountry canals and the open waters of Florida Bay. Cruise guides point out wildlife and natural features of the landscape.

Man-made **Eco Pond**★ *(.9mi west of visitor center)* is a bird-watcher's paradise, particularly at dawn and dusk, when flocks of waterfowl and wading birds gather to feed. The **observation platform** provides an excellent vantage point. *Bring binoculars.*

NORTHERN EVERGLADES *1 day*

Completed in 1928, the Tamiami Trail (US-41) cuts across the Everglades, linking Miami with Naples on the west coast. Land along this strip of swampland and saw grass prairie is maintained under the jurisdictions of Everglades National Park, neighboring Big Cypress National Preserve and the South Florida Water Management District. The main entrance into the national park along this route is at Shark Valley.

★★**Shark Valley** – *30mi west of Miami, entrance on south side of US-41. Open year-round daily 8am–5pm. $8/vehicle. www.nps.gov/ever* ♿ ▯ ☎ *305-221-8776. Maps and detailed park information are available at the kiosk adjacent to the parking lot.* Named for the shallow, slow-flowing slough that empties into the

American Alligator

© Lynn M. Stone

A Haven for Wildlife

One of the major wetlands left on this continent, the Everglades supports some 600 species of animals—including 350 types of birds, 60 species of mosquitoes and 26 kinds of snakes—some of which are found nowhere else in the world. The southern Everglades, in fact, is the only place in the world where you'll find both alligators and crocodiles. Birds provide the greatest spectacle in the park, with herons, egrets, ibis, cranes and other waterbirds almost always within sight. Bald eagles and ospreys nest here, and white pelicans—largest birds on the continent, with a wingspan of 9ft—winter here. The following creatures number among those that make their home in the Glades.

American Alligator *(Alligator mississippiensis)* – Once a species with a poor prognosis for survival, the alligator *(p 41)* has made a strong comeback and is routinely seen gliding silently through freshwater channels and marshes. Reaching lengths of up to 16ft, male alligators rank as the largest reptiles on the continent. Mating occurs in the spring, after which the female will build a nest and deposit up to 80 eggs. Incubation requires between 9 and 10 weeks. For these cold-blooded reptiles, the sex of the hatchlings is determined by the temperature at which the egg incubates: temperatures below 87°F will produce females; temperatures above 89°F will yield males. The young are black with yellow bands; adults are black. Efficient predators, gators also contribute to the survival of other animals. As the dry season approaches, the reptiles dig out "gator holes," depressions that fill with underground water and help sustain many kinds of animals during the dry months.

American Crocodile *(Crocodylus acutus)* – Cousin to the alligator, the endangered American crocodile has been reduced to a few hundred animals, concentrated in the salty mangrove inlets in the southern part of Everglades National Park and in Crocodile Lake National Wildlife Refuge *(p 51)* on the northern end of Key Largo. Crocodiles can be distinguished from alligators by their lighter gray-green coloring, long pointed snout, and the lower incisors that protrude from

either side of their jaw when their mouth is closed. On land, these reptiles move with an agile swaying motion, enabling them to reach speeds of 15mph. Generally considered more aggressive than the alligator, American crocs tend to avoid humans, unless molested or protecting their young.

Anhinga *(Anhinga anhinga)* – This long-necked denizen of the Everglades has become its symbol, often spotted in trees with its black wings outstretched. Lacking the oil covering that other birds have on their wings, the anhinga must air dry its wings in order to fly again after it has emerged from a feeding foray. To obtain food, the anhinga dives underwater and spears fish with its pointed bill. When swimming, only the bird's sinuous neck is exposed above the water; thus it is sometimes called the "snakebird."

Florida Panther *(Felis concolor coryl)* – Experts believe that only 30 of these big tawny brown cats *(p 45)*—designated Florida's state animal—still roam the state's wetlands, the only habitat left for them in the eastern US. The panther's birthrate of two to four kittens every other spring has been diminished by infertility caused by mercury-contaminated prey. Once widespread, these members of the cougar family have been squeezed down to the tip of the peninsula, mostly into the protected lands of Big Cypress Swamp *(p 45)* and Everglades National Park. Secretive and difficult to spot, adults stand about 2ft high and weigh between 60 and 130 pounds.

Snail Kite *(Rostrhamus sociabilis plumbeus)* – This small, shy, gray-brown hawk survives exclusively on Pomacea, or apple, snails. With its curved beak, it extracts the snail from its shell. While snail kites are common in some parts of Central and South America, in North America these endangered birds are found only in central and southern Florida. Draining the Everglades has killed the kite's main source of food; it is estimated that fewer than 900 snail kites remain in Florida.

brackish—and shark-infested—Shark River to the southwest. Shark Valley is actually a basin that lies a few feet lower than the rest of the Everglades. The waters that drain this valley flow into the Gulf of Mexico.

★**Tram Tour** – *Ticket booth is located adjacent to the parking lot. Tours depart from thatched-roof structure Dec–Apr daily 9am–4pm. Rest of the year daily 9am–3pm. 2hrs round-trip. Commentary. Reservations suggested Dec–Apr. $9.* ♿ 🅿 *($8) Shark Valley Tram Tours* ☎ *305-221-8455. Bike rentals also available. Bring water on tram.* The 15mi loop road here—part of which was constructed by early oil prospectors—cuts through open fields of grassy wetland. The easiest way to traverse this route is via the park's open-air trams. Along the way, park naturalists pause to point out some of the local denizens: snail kites, egrets, herons, alligators and gar fish, to name a few. At the halfway point, the tram stops at a concrete **observation tower**, so visitors can glimpse the expansive landscape.

Miccosukee Indian Village – *.5mi west of Shark Valley entrance, on south side of US-41. Open year-round daily 9am–5pm. $5 (includes optional guided tour). Airboat rides (30min) $7.* ✕ ♿ 🅿 *www.miccosukee.com* ☎ *305-223-8380.* Since the mid-19C Miccosukee Indians have inhabited the Everglades. Originally a part of the Creek Confederation, this tribe shares some similarities with the Seminoles but remains a distinct group with its own language and traditions. Now numbering some 500 people, the Miccosukee are concentrated in the northern Everglades, where they maintain a residential enclave and attempt to preserve their traditional native culture.

Miccosukee Indian Village, a commercial venture, re-creates a traditional settlement of chickees—palm-thatched, open-sided structures once used as shelters. Natives demonstrate crafts such as beadwork and the bright patchwork for which the Miccosukee are renowned. A **museum** displays reproductions of traditional clothing,

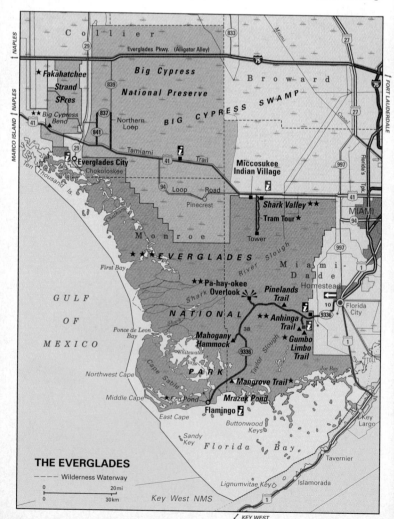

THE EVERGLADES

- - - - Wilderness Waterway

0   20mi
0   30km

tools and basketry, as well as historic photographs. In the village's **alligator arena**, wrestlers demonstrate the bare-handed way in which Miccosukee hunters once captured alligators *(11am & 12:30pm, 1:30pm, 3pm, 4:30pm)*. Since meat spoils so quickly in the tepid subtropical climate, the animals had to be kept alive until the Indians were ready to eat them. Thus it was necessary to subdue the alligator and tie its feet before bringing it back to the village to await the tribe's next meal.

Everglades City – *4mi south of US-41 on Rte. 29.* Established in the 1920s as a headquarters site for the building of the Tamiami Trail, Everglades City now serves as an access point to the watery domain of the northwestern Everglades. The town's most famous institution remains the **Rod and Gun Club** *(200 Waterside Dr.).* Serving as a fishing and hunting club since the late 19C, this structure originally served as the residence of one of the area's first settlers, W.S. Allen. The rambling white frame Victorian, with its rich interior paneling, gained world renown in the 1930s as one of the most exclusive sports clubs in the nation. Then owned by **Barron Collier** *(p 250)*, the land speculator largely responsible for the building of the Tamiami Trail, the club played host to a number of dignitaries. It now operates as an inn.

★★**Cruises of the Ten Thousand Islands** – *Cruises depart from the ranger station on Rte. 29 (from US-41, take Rte. 29 south 4mi to traffic circle; stay on Rte. 29—3/4 turn around circle—and continue .5mi to Everglades National Park Gulf Coast Visitor Center on right) year-round daily 9am–5pm. Round-trip 1hr 45min. Commentary. $13. Everglades National Park Boat Tours* ✗ ⅋ ▯ ☎ *941-695-2591.* Park-sponsored tours offer a look at the marine world of Chokoloskee Bay. Countless small islets here are covered collectively with one of the largest mangrove forests in the world. During the cruise you may see dolphins, manatees and numerous waterbirds, including ospreys, herons, and, if you're very lucky, nesting bald eagles.

Historic Smallwood Store – *360 Mamie St. From Everglades City, continue south onRte. 293.3mi onto Chokoloskee Island; turn right on Smallwood Dr. and left on Mamie St.; follow Mamie to end. Open Dec–Apr daily 10am–5pm, rest of the year daily 10am–4pm. Closed major holidays. $2.50. www.florida-everglades;com/chokol/smallw.htm* ☎ *941-695-2989.* Perched at the edge of Chokoloskee Bay, this weathered wooden structure functioned as a trading post and general store from 1906 to 1982. Named for C.S. "Ted" Smallwood, the Collier County pioneer who founded it, the store now functions as a museum. It displays turn-of-the-century wares—90 percent of which are original to the store—and recalls the atmosphere of an earlier era in southern Florida.

Wilderness Waterway – A paradise for boaters and canoeists, this watery inland course twists 99mi through protected rivers and bays, from Flamingo to Everglades City. Markers designate the waterway, and campsites (some furnished with chickee shelters) punctuate the route. *National Park Service permits are required for overnight camping; course takes 6-8hrs by motorboat and 8-10 days by canoe. Pick up permit (no more than 24hrs before start of trip) and maps at the ranger station in Flamingo* ☎ *941-695-2945 or Gulf Coast Visitor Center (p 38),* ☎ *941-695-3311.*

© Lynn M. Stone

Florida Panther

Big Cypress National Preserve – *Accessible from US-41 and I-75. Open daily year-round.* ⌂ ⅋ *ww.nps.gov/bicy* ☎ *941-695-4111.* Contiguous to the northern Everglades, the 728,000-acre preserve protects a portion of the 2,400sq mi **Big Cypress Swamp**, a rich variegated wetland covered with forests of bald cypress trees. Few giant cypress still stand, having been heavily logged earlier in this century, and much of the terrain is now covered with dwarf cypress and saw grass prairie. In the 1960s, developers hatched plans to drain the vast swamp and build on its lands. In 1974 however, the government—recognizing that this area was a critical link in south Florida's wetlands wilderness—established a 500,000-acre preserve. An additional 200,000 acres have been added since. A major habitat for much of the same wildlife found in the Everglades, Big Cypress is particularly favored by dwindling numbers of the endangered Florida panther *(p 43)*.

Visit – The **Oasis Visitor Center** *(19mi west of Shark Valley on US-41; open year-round daily 8:30am–4:30pm; closed Dec 25;* ▢ ☎ *941-695-4111)* shows a 15min movie on the geology, flora and fauna of Big Cypress. Behind the center, the **Florida National Scenic Trail** *(p 82)* leads 21mi into the heart of the preserve. A 26mi loop road *(Rte. 94 from Forty Mile Bend to Monroe Station)* circles through haunting cypress swamps in the southern part of the preserve.

An unpaved **northern loop** *(16.5mi)* begins at Route 839 and travels through wide-open saw grass prairie *(follow Turner River Rd./Rte. 839 north 7.3mi; turn left on Rte. 837 to Birdon Rd./Rte. 841, which leads back to US-41.*

★**Fakahatchee Strand State Preserve** – *Open year-round daily dawn–dusk.* ☎ *941-695-4593. Big Cypress Bend trail parking located 7mi west of Rte. 29; look for a brown park sign on right.* Adjacent to Big Cypress National Preserve, Fakahatchee features a 20mi-long and 3- to 5mi-wide swamp forest containing a dense and exotic mix of vegetation. Its flora includes the largest stand of native **royal palm** in the US, as well as the greatest concentration and diversity of **orchids** *(different species can be seen blooming year-round)*; 15 species of bromeliads; and a variety of epiphytes, or air plants. A boardwalk *(1mi round-trip)* at **Big Cypress Bend**★★ leads through an eerily beautiful virgin cypress forest, ending at a primeval swamp frequented by alligators. *Bring mosquito repellent.*

■ Rap on Reptiles

- Sluggish-looking alligators can sprint at speeds nearing 15mph for distances of 50 yards.

- There are six types of poisonous snakes in Florida: Pygmy Rattlesnake *(Sistrurus miliarius barbouri)*; Eastern Diamondback Rattlesnake *(Crotalus adamanteus)*; Canebrake Rattler *(Crotalus horridus articaudatus)*; Coral Snake *(Micrurus fulvius)*; Florida Cottonmouth, a.k.a. Water Moccasin *(Agkistrodon piscivorus conanti)*; and Southern Copperhead *(Agkistrodon contortrix contortrix)*.

- Alligators have been clocked swimming at speeds of 14 knots, or 16mph.

- The small dark lizards you see everywhere in Florida are Cuban Brown Anoles *(Anolis sagrei sagrei)*, a species introduced into the state from the West Indies. Its lesser-seen relative, the Green Anole *(Anolis carolinensis)*, is a Florida native.

- Alligators' jaws can crush their prey with 3,000 pounds of pressure per square inch!

- Rattlesnakes and other pit vipers grow new fangs on the average of one set every three months.

The Keys

Seven-Mile Bridge – David Ball, Tony Stone Images

Curving southwest 220mi from Biscayne Bay to the Dry Tortugas, the thousand-some islands and islets that compose the Florida Keys scribe a narrow archipelago separating the waters of the Atlantic from Florida Bay and, farther south, the Gulf of Mexico. Not far from the bustle of MIAMI some 50mi north, the Keys maintain a laid-back atmosphere throughout, though the character of the individual islands varies. The upper and middle Keys serve as a jumping-off point for sportfishermen, divers, snorkelers and wildlife enthusiasts interested in the wealth of marine life on the offshore **coral reef**. The lower Keys are dominated by the town of Key West, an internationally renowned destination with its own distinctive flavor.

With the exception of the northernmost sand islands, the Keys consist of the remains of coral reefs that began forming as early as 10 to 15 million years ago, when the area was covered by a shallow sea. Until the 20C, most of these "chaotic fragments of coral reef, limestone, and mangrove swamps," as one early writer called the Keys, supported only a small, scattered population of Indians and, later, indomitable fishermen and farmers. In the 1800s, the islands were a less than hospitable place, owing to the plague of mosquitoes that blackened the sides of homes and forced residents to burn perpetual smudge pots. In these early days, boats were the only means of transportation between the Keys.

Then in 1904, railroad magnate **Henry Flagler** *(p 104)* launched plans to extend his Florida East Coast Railway south from Miami to Key West. Although the construction of "Flagler's Folly," as the **Overseas Railroad** was popularly known, was thwarted from the beginning by hurricanes, Flagler persisted; in 1912 the first train pulled into Key West. At the end of the train's maiden voyage in January, Flagler—who had just turned 82—proclaimed, "Now I can die in peace." The following year he passed away. For 23 years Flagler's railroad provided transportation to the Keys. Disaster struck in September 1935, when a killer hurricane destroyed the line. Flagler's successors at the FEC decided not to rebuild the line that had never been a money-maker.

In 1938 the current **Overseas Highway** was completed along the former railroad bed. Crossing 43 bridge/causeways (only one of them over land), this southernmost stretch of US-1 offers fine views of the Atlantic to the east and the shallow, aquamarine waters of Florida Bay to the west.

When to Go

The months from December through April are considered high season; afternoon temperatures range from 73°F to 79°F. The rest of the year they run 75°F to 85°F; annual average temperature is 77.4°F. Rainfall is considerably less than on the mainland and falls in brief thunderstorms during summer afternoons.

Getting There

By Air – **Marathon Airport** (information: ☎ 743-2155) and **Key West Airport** (information ☎ 296-5439; *p 58)* are serviced by most domestic airlines as well as charters. Rental car agencies *(p 323)* are located at both airports. International flights connect through Miami International Airport *(p 198).*

By Car – Small green mile-marker (MM) posts, sometimes difficult to spot, are used to delineate locations of sites along US-1 (Overseas Highway) giving distances from Key West. The Mile-Marker system begins in Florida City (MM 127), on the mainland, and crosses a causeway to Key Largo (MM 110). From here it drops down through the Keys to its terminus in Key West (MM 0). Most of the route is two-lane, and traffic can be heavy, particularly in the high season (mid-Dec–mid-May) and on weekends. Allow 3hrs for the drive. The best places along US-1 to find lodging, restaurants and other amenities (marinas, recreational facilities) are: Key Largo (MM 110-87), Islamorada (MM 86-66), Marathon (MM 65-40), Big Pine Key (MM 39-9) and Key West (MM 0).

By Bus – Greyhound/Trailways **bus** makes scheduled stops in Key Largo, Islamorada, Marathon, Big Pine Key, Ramrod Key and Key West. For further information ☎ 800-410-KEYS or 800-231-2222.

By Boat – **Intracoastal Waterway** allows travel by boat from Miami into Florida Bay.

Visitor Information

	MM	Hours of operation	☎
Key Largo Chamber of Commerce 105950 Overseas Hwy. Key Largo FL 33037	106	daily 9am–6pm	451-1414 or 800-822-1088
Islamorada Chamber of Commerce PO Box 915, Islamorada FL 33036	82.5	Mon–Fri 9am–5pm, weekends 9am–2pm	664-4503 or 800-322-5397
Marathon Chamber of Commerce 12222 Overseas Hwy., Marathon FL 33050	53.5	daily 9am–5pm	743-5417 or 800-842-9580
Lower Keys Chamber of Commerce PO Box 430511, Big Pine Key FL 33043	31	Mon–Fri 9am–5pm, Sat 9am–3pm	872-2411 or 800-872-3722
Greater Key West Chamber of Commerce Mallory Square, Key West FL 33041		daily 8:30am–5pm	294-2587 or 800-527-8539

These organizations provide additional information regarding shopping, entertainment, festivals (p 318) and recreation.

Accommodations – *(p 324)* Area visitors' guides including lodging directories are available (free) from area Chambers of Commerce *(above).* Accommodations include hotels, motels and resorts ($95-$250). Reservation service: Welcome Center of Florida Keys ☎ 296-4444 or 800-352-8538; AAAccommodation Center ☎ 800-732-2006. Apartment and condo rentals are available through local property management groups. **Camping** and **RV parks** are located throughout the Keys and offer full hookups, and in some cases, beaches, freshwater pools, marinas and rental boats. KOA Kampground at Fiesta Key ☎ 664-4922 and Sugarloaf Key ☎ 745-3549; America Outdoors Camper Resort, Key Largo ☎ 852-8054. A different way of exploring the Keys is to rent a houseboat ($950-$1,375/weekend; $1,495-$2,300/week fully equipped; advance reservations required). Smilin Island Houseboat Rental, Key Largo ☎ 451-1930; Houseboat Vacations, Islamorada ☎664-4009. *Rates quoted are average prices per night for a double room and are subject to seasonal variations.*

Sports and Recreation – Visitors can enjoy many activities including sailing, snorkeling, fishing, scuba diving and boating. **Diving** in the Florida Keys is best from March–July. Dive shops rent equipment and offer day trips and package deals as well as instruction. Outfitters' boats that include a captain and mate leave daily year-round *(round-trip 4hrs; advance reservations strongly recommended; divers can bring their own equipment):* Marina Del Mar (MM 100), Key Largo ☎ 451-4107 or 800-451-DIVE; Sea Dwellers Dive Shop (MM 100), Key Largo ☎ 451-3640 or 800-451-3640; Halls Diving Center (MM 48), Marathon ☎ 743-5929 or 800-331-4255; Strike Zone Charters (MM 29.5), Big Pine Key ☎ 872-9863 or 800-654-9560; Looe Key Reef Resort (MM 27.5), Ramrod Key ☎ 872-2215.

Scuba and **snorkel cruises**: Theater of the Sea *(p 53)*, MM 84.5, Islamorada *(year-round daily 8:30am and 1pm; round-trip 4hrs; commentary; purchase tickets in advance at Theater of the Sea; $49.95 including equipment rental)* ☎ 664-2431; Underseas Inc., MM 30.5, Big Pine Key *(depart from Dive Shop year-round daily 9am & 1pm; round-trip 4hrs; commentary; reservations required; $25-$40; $55 including equipment rental)* ☎ 872-2700 or 800-446-5663.

To explore the **backcountry**—Key West National Wildlife Refuge and the Great White Heron National Wildlife Refuge—visitors should engage a reputable guide. Area **golf** courses: Stock Island (MM 5) ☎ 294-5232; Key Colony Beach (MM 53.5), Marathon ☎ 289-1533.

Kids Meet a Dolphin at Pennekamp State Park

Dolphin encounter sites – Visitors participate in a marine orientation seminar *(30min–3hrs 30min, depending on facility)* followed by a swim *(30min)* with Atlantic bottlenose dolphins. Participants must be at least 10 years old, be good swimmers in deep water and be experienced in the use of mask and fins. Reservations should be made 4-8 weeks in advance. Prices range from $85–$100/person.

Dolphin Research Center *(p 55)*, MM 59, Marathon ☎ 289-1121.

Dolphin Adventure at Theater of the Sea *(p 55)*, MM 84.5, Islamorada ☎ 664-2431.

Dolphins Plus MM 100.5, Key Largo www.pennekamp.com/dolphins-plus ☎ 305-451-1993.

Sportfishing Tournaments

Season	Tournament	☎
late March	Islamorada All-Tackle Spring Bonefish Tournament	852-1694
late Apr–early May	Texaco Key West Classic	294-4042
Apr–Nov	Key West and Lower Keys Fishing Tournament	745-3332
June	Women's World Invitational Tarpon Fly Championship Tournament	664-2080
late June	TNT/Golden Fly Invitational Tarpon Championship	664-2080
late Sept	Little Palm Island Grand Slam	664-2002
mid-Oct	Sloppy Joe's/Galleon Marina Fish Roundup	296-7182
late Nov	WCA Light Tackle Sailfish Tournament, Marathon	743-6139
late Nov	Marathon Small Boat Billfish Tournament	743-6139
Dec–May	Metropolitan South Florida Fishing Tournament Mini-Met	376-3698

KEY LARGO★

Map of Principal Sights p 3 – Map p 51
Tourist Information ☎ 305-451-1414 or 800-822-1088 (US & Canada)

Called *Cayo Largo*, or "Long Island," by 16C Spanish explorers, Key Largo is the first and largest in this chain of coral rock isles. The real beauty of this island, which spans 26mi in length but only one mile at its widest point, lies along its shoreline and underneath its crystal blue waters. Immediately to the east lies the vast windswept Atlantic Ocean; to the west, the calm shallow Florida Bay serves as a nursery for birds and marine life. Mangrove swamps and tropical hammocks envelop the island's shores, where turtles, crocodiles and great white herons reside. The commercial strip of US-1 runs down the spine of Key Largo, taking in the small community of Tavernier.

Historical Notes

From Pirates To Promoters – It wasn't until the early 19C that Key Largo saw its first settlers: pirates who preyed on the ships that wrecked on the perilous coral reef offshore. When the government opened the area to homesteading in the 1870s, pioneers arrived to try farming, sowing pineapples and coconuts in the area's rich organic soil. When Henry Flagler's railroad pulled into Key Largo in 1906, settlements such as Rock Harbor—as Key Largo was originally called—were already established on the island. Believing that the train would give them greater access to markets for their produce, farmers longed for the tracks to reach Key West. The completed railroad, however, proved to be their undoing. Key West soon outstripped Rock Harbor and Planter (now Tavernier) as a produce shipping center. Gradually these towns faltered, further hindered by exhausted soil and damage done by the 1935 hurricane *(p 13)*.

During the 1920s, ferries brought visitors to the local taverns that operated freely despite Prohibition. Although US-1 was completed between the mainland and Key Largo in 1938, the island did not see its first boom until after World War II. In the

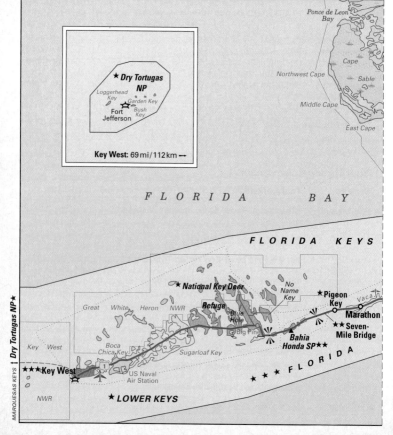

1950s, 49 new subdivisions were laid out. During this period, land speculators purchased 1,500 acres around Rock Harbor and planned a bustling city for 100,000 people. Real-estate promoters also petitioned to rename the town for the popular 1948 movie *Key Largo*, after scenes from the film were shot here.

Fortunately, the Nature Conservancy and the Fish and Wildlife Service rescued some of the land from development when they bought it in 1979 to form the **Crocodile Lake National Wildlife Refuge** *(not open to the public)*. Here along Card Sound Road, some 500 crocodiles—the largest concentration of these reptiles in North America—dwell in 6,686 acres of mangrove swamp and upland jungle.

Preserving the Reef – The coral reef that lies off Key Largo forms part of the **Florida Reef Tract★★★**, the largest living coral reef system in North American waters and third largest barrier reef in the world (after Australia's Great Barrier Reef and the Belize Barrier Reef off Central America). Lying several miles off the Keys in shallow Atlantic waters, the reef protects nearly 200mi of coastline from Fowey Rock (south of Miami) to the Dry Tortugas. The reef, which descends to depths of near 80ft, consists of calcium carbonate (limestone) secreted over thousands of years by colonies of small, soft-bodied coral polyps (members of the coelenterate phylum) and associated organisms.

This fragile reef system, including coral reefs, seagrass meadows and mangrove forests, is protected by the expansive **Florida Keys National Marine Sanctuary**, which protects the waters surrounding the Keys from Biscayne National Park to the Dry Tortugas, encompassing the former Key Largo National Marine Sanctuary as well. The sanctuary provides mooring buoys at various dive sites to prevent boaters from anchoring on the reef.

In order to remain healthy, coral requires water of a certain salinity, temperature and clarity. Over the years, pollution, overharvesting and careless use have adversely affected the Florida Reef. Fortunately, a comprehensive management plan and water-quality protection program developed for the newer Keys sanctuary should help reverse the destructive trend and restore this national treasure to full health.

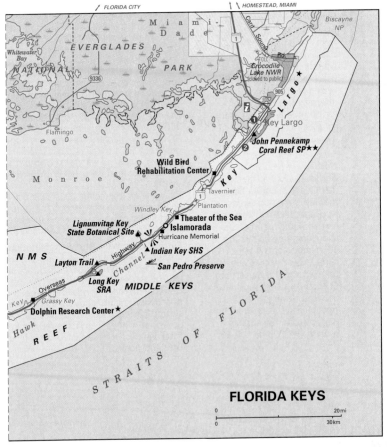

FLORIDA KEYS

Snorkeling off Key Largo

SIGHTS *1 day*

** **John Pennekamp Coral Reef State Park** – *MM 102.5. Open year-round daily 8am–dusk. $4/vehicle; 50¢ per person.* ⚠ *(reservations suggested)* ✕ ♿ Ⓟ *www.dep.state.fl.us/parks* ☎ *305-451-1202.* Stretching along Key Largo's coastline and reaching 3mi into the ocean, America's first underwater park encompasses a dazzling kaleidoscope of vivid coral and sea creatures. Established in 1960, the park is named for the *Miami Herald* associate editor who lobbied to preserve the reef and was instrumental in creating EVERGLADES NATIONAL PARK.

Informative displays relating to the reef and its marine life in the **visitor center** *(open year-round daily 8am–5pm)* provide an excellent introduction to the undersea world offshore. Of the 150 species of tropical fish that feed here, the most colorful and conspicuous are angelfish, parrot fish, triggerfish and snapper. A profusion of sea fans, whips, plumes and sponges cling to the coral. Since 96 percent of the park lies underwater, snorkeling and scuba diving are the best ways to experience this site. You can also take a glass-bottom boat tour of the reef, or rent a variety of water craft *(tours depart from the marina year-round daily 9:15am, 12:15pm & 3pm; round-trip 2hrs 30min; commentary; reservations suggested; $15; for tours and equipment rental: Coral Reef Park Company www.dep.state.fl.us/ parks* ☎ *305-451-1621).*

Near the visitor center, a small rocky beach edges a shallow lagoon for swimming and snorkeling, and several nature trails wind through tropical hammocks.

Florida Keys Wild Bird Rehabilitation Center – *MM 93.6 in Tavernier. Open year-round daily dawn–dusk.* ♿ Ⓟ ☎ *305-852-4486.* At this bird recovery center alongside Florida Bay, wooden boardwalks wind above a mangrove swamp past spacious enclosures where dozens of winged waterbirds recuperate from injuries, most inflicted by fishing lines and hooks.

❶ Caribbean Club
Map p 51. MM 103. ✕ Scenes from the Bogart-Bacall film classic *Key Largo* (1948) were filmed in this local beach bar. The deck on the west side of the building offers a ringside seat for viewing the Keys' legendary sunsets.

❷ African Queen
Map p 51. MM 100 at Holiday Inn Key Largo Resort. Docked at the marina adjoining the hotel is the 30ft steam-powered workboat (c.1912) that carried Katherine Hepburn and Humphrey Bogart in the 1951 movie of the same name. Now restored and privately owned, the *African Queen* is available for cruises between November and May *(minimum 15 people; 2-3 day advance reservations required* ☎ *305-451-4655).*

© Stephen Frink/Tony Stone Images

MIDDLE KEYS

Map pp 50-51
Tourist Information ☎ 305-664-4503 or 305-743-5417

Less developed than Key Largo, the Middle Keys reach from MM 85 to MM 45. Sport-fishermen favor these islands—especially Islamorada—casting their waters for such deep-sea trophies as sailfish, tarpon, marlin and bonefish. Below MM 80, US-1 crosses a series of viaducts, causeways and bridges connecting myriad individual islands. Driving through them, however, you'll have less a sense of separate bodies of land than an overall impression of water, as sweeping **views**★★★ of the cerulean Atlantic Ocean and Florida Bay fan out on either side of the road. Development returns briefly with the roadside shopping plazas, motels and eateries in Marathon. Just past Marathon at the south end of Vaca Key, Seven-Mile Bridge spans the distance to the Lower Keys.

SIGHTS *1 day*

South of Key Largo, you'll pass through the hamlets of Tavernier and Plantation. Just past Plantation (MM 85), you'll come to Windley Key.

Theater of the Sea – **Kids** *Windley Key, MM 84.5. Open year-round daily 9:30am–4pm. Reservations required for special programs. $15.75.* ⑤ ▣ ☎ *305-664-2431.* This four-acre marine park, second oldest in the US after St. Augustine's Marineland *(p 113)*, was established in 1945 in an old railroad quarry. Its small, open-air pools house sharks, turtles and fish. At two larger lagoons, visitors are invited to participate in shows featuring dolphins and sea lions. Continuous guided tours through the park explain the behavior and biology of different animals. The park also offers a swim-with-the-dolphins program *(p 49)*.

Islamorada – *MM 84-80.* Early Spanish explorers named this place *islas moradas* ("purple islands"), because of the profusion of violet sea snails *(Janthina janthina)* they found here. Islamorada ("EYE-la-ma-RAH-da") is noted for **charter fishing** and hosts a number of sportfishing tournaments *(p 49)*. Seafood restaurants and small motels line US-1 here. At MM 81.7, a roadside **Hurricane Memorial** *(east side of highway)* of local limestone marks the mass grave of the 400-some people killed in the 1935 hurricane.

Layton Trail – *Long Key, MM 68, trailhead marked by Long Key Fishing Club historic marker on right side of US-1.* Administered by the Long Key State Recreation Area *(below)*, this dirt path *(.25mi)* tunnels through a low-hanging, dense tangle of tropical vegetation at the edge of Florida Bay. Botanical labels identify species that include gumbo-limbo, wild lime, coffee, poisonwood and Jamaica dogwood.

Long Key State Recreation Area – *Long Key, MM 67.5. Open year-round daily 8am–dusk. $3.25/vehicle and 50ô/person.* ⚠ ⑤ ☎ *305-664-4815.* The shorelines of the 965-acre park touch both ocean and bay waters and offer swimming, snorkeling, fishing and camping. The **Golden Orb Trail** *(1mi)* begins as a boardwalk across a mangrove creek, where a low observation platform allows views of the lush treetops. It then crosses a narrow beach habitat and enters a shady tropical hammock.

★**Dolphin Research Center** – **Kids** *Grassy Key, MM 59. Open year-round daily 9am–4pm. Closed Jan 1, Thanksgiving Day, Dec 25. $12.50.* ⑤ ▣ *www. dolphins.org* ☎ *305-289-1121.* Combining research with public education and entertainment, the Dolphin Research Center maintains a population of roughly 15 dolphins in holding pens in Florida Bay. Visitors watch trainers work with several groups of dolphins as guides explain dolphin behavior, socialization and physiology. The facility has been used in the filming of several dolphin movies, including the 1960s classic, *Flipper.* They also offer a swim-with-the-dolphins program *(reservations required; p 49)*.

Marathon – *MM 50 on Vaca Key.* Commercial and administrative hub for the Middle Keys, Marathon began as a base camp for laborers on Flagler's Florida East Coast Railway. The town's name derives from those early days, when crews stationed here engaged in a "marathon" effort to complete the rail to Key West before Flagler's death. After the camp was abandoned, the settlement languished until the 1950s, when a Detroit developer planned Marathon's first subdivisions.

Tropical Crane Point Hammock – *MM 50 in Marathon. Open year-round Mon–Sat 9am–5pm, Sun noon–5pm. Closed major holidays. $7.50.* ▣ *www.thefloridakeys.com/marathon/museum.htm* ☎ *305-743-9100.* Trails that wind through 63 acres of tropical forest connect a **Museum of Natural History**, the adjoining **Florida Keys Children's Museum** **Kids** and **The Adderly Village Historic Site**. Displays in the yellow stucco natural-history museum limn local flora and fauna, including marine life on the coral reef and collections of native tree snails and butterflies, as well as Middle Keys history. At the Children's Museum, youngsters visit habitats for iguanas, hawks and scorpions. Restoration work is ongoing at Adderly Village, a site pioneered in 1903; currently open for visits are George Adderly's Bahamian Conch house, a reconstructed outdoor kitchen and culinary gardens.

★**Pigeon Key** – *MM 45 on Knight Key. Visit by tram tour; departs from Pigeon Key Visitor Center, on the east side of US-1; turn left just before Seven-Mile Bridge. Trams depart year-round daily every hour on the hour 9am–5pm. Not operating*

Thanksgiving Day & Dec 25. Round-trip 2hrs; visitors can remain on Pigeon Key and return later. Commentary. $7.50. ✷ 🅿 ☎ *305-289-0025.* From the visitor center, housed in a pastel-blue railroad car, a shuttle takes you across a 2.2mi span of the **Old Seven-Mile Bridge** to the former railroad work camp on Pigeon Key *(you may also walk across bridge, but no private vehicles are allowed)*. Completed in 1912, the Old Seven-Mile Bridge formed a vital link in the rail line. It was laid on 546 concrete foundation piers anchored in bedrock as deep as 28ft underwater. A cluster of modest, turn-of-the-century houses on the four-acre islet is all that remains of the residences once inhabited by construction and maintenance crews who helped build the bridge. In Pigeon Key's heyday the village was home to some 410 people. Tour guides explain life here during that time and take visitors through one of the unfurnished houses. Pigeon Key is also the site of a **shark research facility** operated by Sarasota's Mote Marine Laboratory *(p 260)*. The former section-gang quarters now houses a "wet lab" of marine specimens.

★★**Seven-Mile Bridge** – *MM 47-40, from Knight Key to Little Duck Key*. Considered an engineering masterpiece, this sweeping bridge ranks as the longest segmental bridge in the world. Its 288 135ft-long sections link the Middle and Lower Keys. Completed in 1982 to replace Flagler's concrete and steel marvel, the new span is both wider and higher than the Old Seven-Mile Bridge *(above)*, providing a 65ft clearance for vessels to pass underneath. Its heights afford expansive **views**★★ of the open ocean.

OFFSHORE EXCURSIONS *Map p 51*

Lignumvitae Key State Botanical Site – *3hrs. Accessible by boat only; departs from Robbie's Marina MM 77.5 year-round Thu–Mon 9:30am & 1:30pm. Round-trip 1hr 30min. Commentary. Reservations suggested. $15.* 🅿 *Robbie's Rent-a-Boat www.robbies.com* ☎ *305-664-4196 or 664-9814. Mosquitoes can be extremely dense; wear clothing that covers your arms and legs and bring insect repellent.* A rare **virgin forest**★ covers much of this 280-acre Florida Bay island with lignumvitae, gumbo-limbo, strangler fig and other flora characteristic of a tropical hammock. The modest **Matheson House** (1919), made of coral rock, served as a care-taker's home when the island was owned by William Matheson, a wealthy resident of Key Biscayne who brought yachting entourages to the island.

Indian Key State Historic Site – *1.5hrs. Accessible by boat only; departs from Robbie's Marina MM 77.5 year-round Thu–Mon 8:30am & 12:30pm. Round-trip 1hr 30min. Commentary. Reservations suggested. $15.* 🅿 *Robbie's Rent-a-Boat www.robbies.com* ☎ *305-664-4196 or 664-9814.* Now uninhabited, the 11-acre island off the east coast of Lower Matecumbe Key played a critical role in the history of the Keys, thanks to a New Yorker named **Jacob Housman**. In the 1830s Housman arrived in Florida and became involved in Key West's lucrative wrecking business. Seeking autonomy from local laws there, he came north and established a small salvaging town on Indian Key. In 1836 Housman convinced local authorities to create Dade County, appointing his town as the county seat. (Indian Key is now part of Monroe County.) Unfortunately, Housman's ambitious little community was short-lived—Seminole Indians attacked and burned it in 1840.
Dirt lanes of the former 19C village still grid the island, but little else remains save a few crumbling foundations and a re-creation of the tombstone that marked Housman's grave. An observation platform affords a panorama of the island and surrounding waters. Offshore breezes sweep the island, keeping it blessedly free of mosquitoes.

San Pedro Underwater Archaeological Preserve – *2hrs. 1.25 nautical miles south of Indian Key. Accessible via private boat only. For rental, contact Robbie's Rent-a-Boat* ☎ *305-664-4196.* Located in 18ft of water on a sand bottom, the remains of the *San Pedro*, a Dutch-built merchant vessel that sank in July 1733, are now protected as an underwater archaeological preserve. The ship was part of a 21-vessel convoy sailing from Havana to Spain. Caught in a hurricane off the Keys on Friday the 13th, all but one vessel in the flotilla was lost in the storm. Salvaging at the wreck sites went on for years; in recent decades, the *San Pedro* has been rediscovered and more of its treasure recovered. Popular with divers and snorkelers, the *San Pedro* site contains a mound of ballast stones and attracts a colorful array of marine life.

LOWER KEYS★

Map p 50
Tourist Information ☎ 305-872-2411

Scrub and slash pine characterize this handful of wooded islands extending from MM45 to the outskirts of Key West at MM 5. Their low, wet land and its surrounding waters provide refuge for a variety of wildlife, including the great white heron and the diminutive Key deer. For sun worshippers, Bahia Honda boasts one of the few sand beaches in the Keys; for those who prefer to be underwater, the unusually clear waters of the reef at **Looe Key**, a parcel of the Florida Keys National Marine Sanctuary *(7mi offshore in the Atlantic;* ☎ *305-292-0311)*, constitute a diver's paradise.

SIGHTS *1/2 day*

Once across the Seven-Mile Bridge, you enter Bahia Honda Key.

★★ Bahia Honda State Park – *Bahia Honda Key. MM 36.8. Open year-round daily 8am–dusk. $4/vehicle.* ⚠ 🅿 ☎ *305-872-2353.* Named by the Spanish for its "Deep Bay," Bahia Honda Key encompasses one of the largest stretches of rare sand **beach**⚌⚌ in the chain. (The Keys owe their lack of high surf and sandy beaches to the existence of the reef. It serves as an offshore barrier, breaking the impact of Atlantic waves—and the sands they would carry—before they reach shore.) This popular park covers 524 acres and includes a lagoon, mangrove forest and a tropical hardwood hammock. Stroll through these diverse communities on the **Silver Palm Trail** *(.25mi)*, where you'll glimpse such unique West Indian specimens as yellow satinwood and Jamaica morning glory. At the southern tip of the park, you can walk out on a segment of the original **Bahia Honda Bridge**, erected for Flagler's railroad and later remodeled for the Overseas Highway. Owing to the depth of the water here, this bridge was both the highest and the hardest to build. From its vantage point high over the ocean, stretch lovely **views★** of stately palms swaying above tranquil turquoise water.

★ National Key Deer Refuge – *MM 30.5, on Big Pine Key. Open year-round daily dawn–dusk.* ♿ 🅿 *www.gorp.com/gorp/ resource/usnwr/flnatio.htm* ☎ *305-872-2239.* This refuge protects the unique **Key deer** *(Odocoileus virginianus clavium)*, which is found only in the lower Florida Keys. Smallest of all North American deer, members of this subspecies of Virginia white-tailed deer, measure about 2ft high at the shoulder and weigh from 50 to 100lbs. How the deer came to occupy the Keys is unknown, but it is believed that they migrated here from the mainland thousands of years ago. Uncontrolled hunting and land development reduced the number of deer to less than 50 in the 1940s. The refuge was established in 1954 to protect these animals. Since then, the Key deer population has grown and stabilized; currently some 300 diminutive deer inhabit Big Pine Key.

Visit – *1.5 hrs. At MM 30.5, turn right onto Key Deer Blvd. (Rte. 940) and follow it .3mi to the refuge office, located in shopping center on right. To see the refuge itself, continue 3mi west on Key Deer Blvd. The 30mph speed limit is strictly enforced; keep alert for deer crossing the road.* Two trails within the refuge provide good opportunities for **deer sightings★★**, particularly at dawn and dusk, when the shy animals come out to feed. At **Blue Hole** *(west side of Key Deer Blvd., 1.25mi north of intersection with Watson Blvd.)*, you may see deer drinking in this old rock quarry now filled with water. The pond is also home to alligators, turtles and sunfish. The **Jack C. Watson Nature Trail** *(continue .3mi north on Key Blvd.)* weaves .6mi through a thicket of slash pines and palms, a favorite Key Deer habitat.

A short drive across less populous **No Name Key** *(turn east on Watson Blvd., which dead ends at Ave. B; turn left and cross bridge; road dead-ends at east end of No Name Key)* often rewards visitors with views of tiny deer feeding on the sides of the road.

Key Deer

KEY WEST★★★

Population 25,339
Map of Principal Sights p 3 – Map p 60
Tourist Information ☎ 305-294-2587 or 800-527-8539 (US & Canada)

Pirates, wreckers, writers, US presidents and Cuban freedom fighters have at one time all found a haven on this small island at the southernmost tip of the continent. Closer to Havana than Miami, Key West cultivates an atmosphere of sublime laissez-faire that encourages an eclectic mix of residents, from old-time "conch" families (descended from the island's original settlers) to a more recently arrived gay community. Key West is undeniably commercial, yet it possesses a charm and a long-standing independent spirit that still appeals to writers and artists, as well as to the droves of tourists who come here each year.

Historical Notes

Early Prosperity – When Spanish explorer Ponce de León arrived here in 1513, he claimed the island for Spain and named it *Cayo Hueso*, ("Island of Bones"), apparently owing to the abundance of Indian bones he found there. (The English later transformed *Cayo Hueso* into Key West.) Through the 18C the island remained largely the domain of the Calusa and Ais Indians and of roving pirate bands, neither of whom cared that the island technically passed back and forth between Spanish and British control. In 1822, with Florida firmly a US territory, Key West became permanently American and a customs house was established. Soon thereafter, **Commodore David Porter** was sent to rid the area of pirates. Although Porter's aggressive "Mosquito Fleet" performed admirably against the brigands, his men were unable to stand against the mosquitoes themselves, which periodically ravaged the area with yellow fever.

In the late 1820s Key West became the headquarters for a lucrative enterprise called **wrecking**. Dauntless wreckers salvaged goods from the many ships that ran aground on the Florida reef. Though reviled by outsiders as scavengers, wreckers were licensed by the federal government and described by a visiting New York journalist as "decent men of good common sense." The great heyday of wrecking lasted until mid-century, when better navigational guides made shipping safer. By then, however, a new industry, **cigar-making**, had begun. By 1889 the combined revenues from the fishing, sponging, wrecking and cigar-making industries had made Key West the wealthiest town per capita in the country.

During the Civil War, Key West became a town divided. While the population overwhelmingly sided with the Confederacy, Union troops had early on occupied Fort Taylor to ensure that this strategic stronghold stayed in Yankee hands. Though the military used Key West as a staging point from which to control ship traffic through the Florida Straits, the island saw no serious action.

Following the war, the town's incipient cigar-making business boomed, as Cuban cigar barons, disaffected with Spanish control of Cuba, moved here and opened factories. In their wake came Cuban workers and revolutionaries. By 1890 the town ranked as the largest cigar-manufacturing city in the world, and was a hotbed of Cuban revolutionary activity.

Tragedy struck in 1886 when a fire broke out in the San Carlos Club (now the San Carlos Institute) on Duval Street. The blaze burned unchecked for 12 hours—the town's one fire truck was in New York being repaired—and ravaged 50 acres of the wooden town. Despite the damage done to wooden structures, Key Westers quickly rebuilt their town in the same vulnerable material.

The cigar business began to fade after the fire destroyed many of the largest factories and local manufacturers were lured away to TAMPA, but the business of revolution continued. In the 1890s, Cuban liberator **José Martí** (1853-1895) headquartered himself in Key West. In 1898, the *USS Maine* departed Key West for Havana and exploded there, precipitating the short-lived **Spanish-American War**.

Key West continued to prosper into the early 20C with a diverse economy. In 1912 Henry Flagler's Overseas Railroad reached its terminus in Key West, finally connecting the island with the rest of the continent. The deluxe **Casa Marina** hotel *(now the Marriott Casa Marina; 1500 Reynolds St.)*, designed by the eminent New York firm Carrère and Hastings and equipped with a hurricane-proof reinforced concrete exterior, opened in Key West nine years later.

From Last Resort to Chic Resort – The Depression years saw Key West lapse into desuetude, its homes unpainted and its population poor. The town apparently maintained its charm nonetheless, for in 1931 author **Ernest Hemingway** *(p 64)*—destined to become Key West's most celebrated son—bought a house here, beginning a literary tradition that continues to this day. In addition to "Papa" Hemingway, the town has been home to writers John Dos Passos, Tennessee Williams, Elizabeth Bishop, Robert Frost, Philip Caputo, John Ciardi, James Merrill, Thomas McGuane, Wallace Stevens, Ralph Ellison and John Hersey, among others. *The Key West Literary Seminar sponsors a weekly Writer's Walk through Old Town (p 58)*. In mid-century **President Harry Truman** also became enamored of Key West, escaping to his Little White House *(p 59)* on the Navy base there.

In 1934, $5 million in debt and with 80 percent of its population on welfare, Key West declared bankruptcy. Florida Governor David Sholtz finally called in the Federal Emergency Relief Administration and organized a local volunteer effort to spruce up the island. The successful program transformed the shabby town into an attractive tourist destination. Their victory, however, was to be short-lived: On Labor Day 1935, a violent hurricane destroyed the railroad to Key West. The town languished for three years before the **Overseas Highway** was completed on the old rail bed, making Key West more accessible to travelers than ever before.

In 1980 the Mariel boatlift brought thousands of Cuban refugees into Key West, and though most dispersed, the town still maintains a palpable Cuban presence. In 1982 locals staged their own mini-revolution in reaction to a US Border Patrol roadblock set up to check all outbound vehicles for guns, illegal aliens and drugs. A group of outraged Conchs, as native Key Westers call themselves (after the mollusk that thrives in local waters and whose meat provided the mainstay of the settlers' diet), declared Key West a sovereign state, the **Conch Republic**. Happily, the "revolution" soon subsided and Key West rejoined the Union.

In the past several decades, the island has undergone a slow transformation from renegade outpost to fashionable resort. The town's overtly commercial main stem, 14-block-long **Duval Street**, is named for William Pope DuVal, the first governor of the Florida Territory. Amid the eateries, bars and boutiques that line the north end of Duval, Key West still cultivates its eccentricity. By night, live music fills the streets, spilling out of bars frequented over the years by such notables as authors Ernest Hemingway and Truman Capote, and singer-songwriter Jimmy Buffett.

Some of the old-time Conch families continue to make their living as fishermen or by operating charter fishing boats. However, they are outnumbered now by outsiders who have moved here for the climate, the desultory lifestyle, or the literary, historic and artistic ambiance. To many new arrivals, President Truman's sentiments about Key West still ring true: "This place is what I'd hoped it would be and was almost sure it wouldn't be."

Key West Architecture – The 200-square-block area of **Old Town**★★ designated a National Historic District ranks as one of the largest on the National Register, boasting more than 3,000 significant historic structures. Diverse 19C and early 20C architectural styles found here range from gracious Neoclassical homes to gingerbread-trimmed Victorians, to Caribbean-influenced "Conch cottages."

Owing to the New England background of many of the 19C seafarers who settled here, much of Key West's architecture follows the Classical Revival style. Among the indigenous features added to this style to adapt it to a subtropical climate, the "eyebrow" is unique. This West Indian element consists of eaves that partly overhang second-story windows, thus resembling a brow over squinting eyes. Like an awning, the "eyebrow" blocks out direct sunlight, thus keeping the house cool. Among the 50-some **eyebrow houses** extant in Key West are the homes at 401 and 525 Frances Street, 643 William Street and 1211 Southard Street.

Bahamian features, such as wide, breeze-catching verandahs, also figure in the architectural mix. Due to a lack of trees on the island, some early settlers from the Bahamas actually dismantled their homes and floated them to Key West. A couple of classic examples of imported **Bahama Houses** still stand.

The many simple vernacular buildings found throughout the city are locally known as **Conch houses**. While these take varied forms, in general they are wood frame, devoid of ornamentation, and only a story or two high with a porch across the front. Distinguishing features are the front porch (running full-height on two-story houses) and widow's walk, which may be borrowed from the New England houses seen by Key West seafarers. The narrow, single-story **shotgun house**, a variation on this style, is only one room wide, with a roofline that runs perpendicular to the street. Many of these plain dwellings were built by cigar-makers for their workers. A good sampling of Conch cottages can be found in the 600 and 700 blocks of Elizabeth Street. You'll also find a number of elegant Queen Anne structures on the island, among them the George Patterson House *(p 61)* and the Southernmost House *(p 65)*.

OLD TOWN WALKING TOUR *1/2 day. 1.5mi. Map p 60.*

Begin at the intersection of Duval and Front Sts. (northwest end of Duval St.).

Ornate brickwork and balcony of the striking **First Union Bank** building on the far corner *(422 Front St.)* reflect the origins of the Cuban cigar manufacturers who financed its construction in 1891.

Continue west 2 blocks on Front St.; turn right on David Wolkowsky St.

Mallory Square – *Behind Mallory Market on Front St.* Overlooking Key West Harbor, this former warehouse area is named for Stephen Mallory, Florida's fourth US senator and son of one of the island's oldest families. It now harbors souvenir vendors, craft shops and eateries, and its adjacent dock provides a berth for the large cruise ships that call at Key West. Don't miss the sunset-watching ritual held every evening *(weather permitting)* on **Mallory Square Dock** *(behind Mallory Square;*

PRACTICAL INFORMATION ....

Getting There

By Air – **Key West Airport** (EYW): serviced by most domestic airlines as well as charters; information ☎ 296-5439. Transportation to Old Town by taxi *($5–$15)* and hotel courtesy shuttles. Rental car agencies *(p 323)* are located at airport.

Getting Around

Local **bus service** travels two routes *(Mon–Fri 6am–10:30pm, weekends 9:15am–6:30; 75¢)*. For schedules and route information ☎ 292-8160. The best way to get around Old Town Key West is on foot as most attractions are within easy walking distance of each other. Another good means of transportation is bicycle or scooter: Adventure Scooter & Bike Rental ☎ 293-9933; Bicycle Center ☎ 294-4556; Caribbean Scooter Rental ☎ 293-9971. Daily rentals average $4–$10 for a bike and $23–$35 for a scooter.

Taxi service: Friendly Cab ☎ 292-0000; Maxi Taxi ☎ 296-2222. Gas prices are higher in Key West than on the mainland. Parking is limited in Old Town area; public parking lots average 75¢/hr; Mallory Square parking garage: $2/hr.

General Information

Visitor Information – **Greater Key West Chamber of Commerce**, 402 Wall St., Key West FL 33040 *(open year-round Mon–Fri 8:30am–6pm, weekends 8:30am–5pm)*, ☎ 294-2587 or 800-527-8539. *This organization provides additional information regarding lodging, shopping, entertainment, festivals (p 318) and recreation.*

Accommodations – *(p 324)* A variety of lodgings from large hotels and resorts ($95–$250) to small motels ($65–$125) are offered. Most accommodations in Old Town Key West are guest houses and bed-and-breakfast inns ($49–$275). Reservation service: Welcome Center of Florida Keys ☎ 296-4444 or 800-352-8538. Youth Hostel ($17–$20) ☎ 296-5719. Camping and RV park: Boyd's Key West Campground ☎ 294-1465. *Rates quoted are average prices per night for a double room and are subject to seasonal variations.*

Sightseeing – Conch Train Tour *(departs from Mallory Square or Roosevelt Blvd. year-round daily 9am–4:30pm; round-trip 1hr 30min; $15; commentary; ⚹)* ☎ 294-5161. Old Town Trolley Tour *(departs from various locations year-round daily 9am–4:30pm; round-trip 1hr 30min; $16; commentary; free reboarding)* ☎ 296-6688. Key West Writer's Walk *(departs from Heritage House Museum Dec–May Sat 10:30am, from Hemingway House Sun 10:30am; 1hr; $10; purchase tickets from Heritage House Museum)* ☎ 293-9291.

Entertainment – Consult the arts and entertainment section in the *Key West Citizen* (Friday), *Travelhost* and *See Florida Keys* (available free at hotels and restaurants) for schedule of cultural events and addresses of principal theaters. Tennessee Williams Fine Arts Center: Broadway shows, concerts, jazz ☎ 296-1520; Red Barn Theater: plays ☎ 296-9911; Waterfront Playhouse: plays, musicals ☎ 294-5015.

Useful Numbers   ☎

Police/Ambulance/Fire	911
Police (non-emergency) Key West	294-2511
Florida Highway Patrol	289-2300
US Coast Guard Boating and Safety Hotline	743-6388
Visitor Assistance Program (multilingual)	*(Florida only)* 800-771-KEYS
Weather	294-1122

Conch Train Tour on Duval Street

follow Fitzpatrick St. through parking lot to dock). Here, locals and visitors gather to view the spectacular Key West **sunset**★★, described by John James Audubon *(below)* as "a blaze of refulgent glory (that) streams through the portals of the west." During the winter tourist season *(late Nov–late Mar)*, awaiting sunset becomes a fête of sorts, with mimes, jugglers, fire-eaters, and even trained cats entertaining audiences along the dock.

★**Shipwreck Historeum** – *1 Whitehead St. in Mallory Square. Visit by guided tour (45min) only, year-round daily 9:45am–6pm. $8.* ✗ *www.trolleytours.com/keywest/-shipwreck.htm* ☎ *305-292-8990.* The feel of a 19C dockside warehouse is re-created here. Following a 14min video portraying the early wreckers of Key West, actors recount the thrills and dangers of the wrecking business. After the performance, visitors can roam the two floors of exhibits of items salvaged from the 1856 wreck of the square-rigged packet *Isaac Allerton.* From the second floor, climb up the lookout tower—a replica of many built in Key West in the days preceding lighthouses—for a 360° **view**★ of the island.

Key West Aquarium – 🄺🄸🄳 *Facing Shipwreck Historeum on Wall St. Open year-round daily 10am–6pm. $8.* ♿ *www.historictours.com* ☎ *305-296-2051.* Wall tanks here display a variety of denizens from local waters, such as pufferfish, grouper, angelfish and spiny lobsters. A touch tank allows visitors tactile encounters with starfish, conchs, anemones and other touchable sea creatures. At the rear of the building, a large **shark pen** harbors the gliding forms of a variety of sharks. Rays and barracudas occupy an outside pool.

Return to Front St. and continue west past the intersection with Whitehead St.

Recognizable by its distinctive arched bays, the old **Coast Guard Building** *(219 Front St.),* served as the first naval storehouse in 1856. The town's oldest government edifice and the oldest masonry building in the Keys now holds the shops of Clinton Square Market. Adjacent to the Coast Guard Building, the imposing red-brick, Romanesque Revival **US Customs House/Post Office** (1891) is currently being renovated to house the Key West Museum of Art and History *(p 000),* which hopes to move to its new quarters by 2001.

A **Civil War memorial (1)** honoring Union soldiers occupies the small greensward called Clinton Place *(Greene and Whitehead Sts.).*

Cross Front onto Greene St.

★**Mel Fisher Maritime Heritage Society** – *200 Greene St., in raised brick plaza diagonally across from Customs House. Open year-round daily 9:30am–5pm. $6.50.* ♿ 🄿 *($2/hr)* ☎ *305-294-2633.* Housed in a former Navy building, the museum recounts the story of treasure-hunter Mel Fisher's discovery of the Spanish galleon *Señora Nuestra de Atocha,* a Spanish galleon that sank in the Florida Straits in 1622. The don of modern treasure hunters, Mel Fisher spent 16 years and lost a son in his unswerving pursuit of the Spanish wreck. In 1985 Fisher's crew found their prize on the ocean floor, the total spoils valued at more than $400 million. A 22min video details the 1985 discovery of *Atocha's* mother lode; displays on the first floor feature some of the fabulous gold, silver, gems and other artifacts recovered from the dive site. The second floor is devoted to special exhibitions and traveling shows.

Cross Whitehead St.

★**Audubon House** – *205 Whitehead St., across from Mel Fisher's museum. Open year-round daily 9:30am–5:30pm. $7.50.* ♿ *www.audubonhouse.com* ☎ *305-294-2116.* Captain William Geiger built this gracious Neoclassical home in the 1840s. Its restoration by Key West native Mitchell Wolfson in 1960 sparked the island's preservation movement. Wolfson dedicated the house to America's premiere ornithologist, **John James Audubon**, who visited Key West in 1832 while working on his authoritative volume *Birds of America.* Decorated in 19C period furnishings, the house is notable for its fine collection of 28 original **Audubon engravings**★ and for its lovely tropical **garden**.

Continue one block south on Whitehead St.

A plaque identifies **Kelly's Caribbean Bar & Grill (A)** *(corner of Whitehead and Caroline Sts.)* as Airways or Pigeon House, because it hosted the first corporate offices of Pan American Airways. In October 1927, the airline launched the first commercial flight from Key West to Havana, made by a Fokker Tri-motor F-7. The name "Pigeon House" derives from the fact that Pan Am sent carrier pigeons along in earlier flights to carry messages should an emergency occur en route. The pigeons actually roosted in this building (moved from its original location at the north end of Duval Street), now owned by actress **Kelly McGillis**.

Cross Whitehead and enter the gates to the Truman Annex, a 44-acre private condominium development on the grounds of the former naval station. Continue for one block and turn left on Front St.

★★**Harry S Truman Little White House Museum** – *111 Front St. in Truman Annex. Entrance on right just past the corner of Front St. Visit by guided tour (35min) only, year-round daily 9am–5pm. $7.50.* ♿ ☎ *305-294-9911.* This large, unpretentious white clapboard home, the favorite retreat of America's 33rd President,

Harry S Truman (1884-1972), gives a rare glimpse of the personality and private life of the man the press called "an uncommon common man." Originally built in 1890 as a duplex to house the commandant and paymaster of Key West's naval station, the unadorned home, with its wooden jalousies, was first visited by Truman in 1946 when his physician persuaded him that he needed a respite from official duties. Prior to Truman, Thomas Edison had lived here while working on his depth charge for the Navy during World War I.

Truman found the casual atmosphere and warm climate of Key West relaxing. Over his next seven years in office, he spent 175 days of "working vacations" at his "Little White House." While here, he ran the country from the desk that still sits

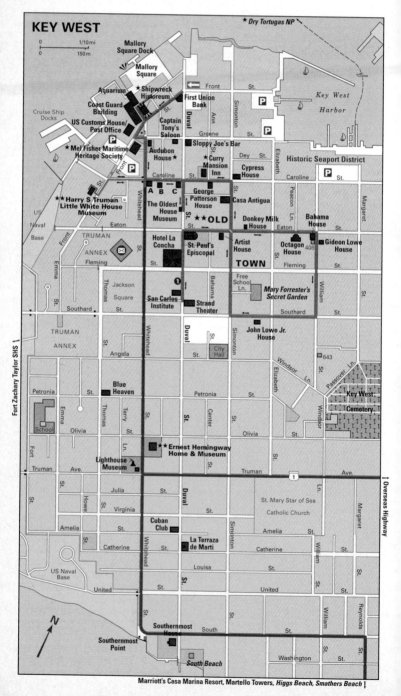

in a corner of the living room. Indeed, Truman came to relish his time in Key West, declaring it his favorite place in the world—aside from his boyhood home, a farm near Independence, Missouri.

Guided tours of the house begin with a 10min video detailing the time Truman spent here. The house is furnished much the way it was during the Truman era, with most of the pieces chosen by Miami decorator Haygood Lassiter in 1948. Truman's personal **desk** can be seen in his bedroom upstairs.

Return to Kelly's at the corner of Whitehead and Caroline Sts., and continue east on Caroline.

★**Jessie Porter's Heritage House and Robert Frost Cottage (B)** – *410 Caroline St. Visit by guided tour (30min) only, daily Mid-Sept–May 10am–4:45pm. Rest of the year daily 10am–4pm. Closed Jan 1, two weeks in Sept, Thanksgiving Day & Dec 25. $6.* & ☎ *305-296-3573.* Much of Key West's 19C and 20C history is embedded in this pastel-green Classical Revival Conch mansion. Built c.1834 by Captain George Carey, the house was purchased and restored by local chatelaine Jessie Porter Newton in 1934. A fifth-generation Key Wester and granddaughter of Dr. Joseph Porter *(below)*, Miss Jessie, as she was known, figured prominently in local literary and preservationist circles. Her home's eclectic furnishings reflect her travels to Europe and the mid-20C island lifestyle of the literati. Many items from Miss Jessie's collection of antiques and museum-quality artifacts were gifts from local ships' captains who brought them back from the South Pacific, Malaysia and the Orient.

In the rear garden sits tiny **Robert Frost Cottage** *(not open to the public)* where the poet spent 15 winters between 1945 and 1960. While in the garden, visitors listen to a recorded reading of Frost's poem, *The Gift Outright*, which was read at President John F. Kennedy's inauguration.

Continue to the corner of Caroline and Duval Sts.

The stately 1838 **Joseph Porter House (C)** *(429 Caroline St.)*, now an art gallery, belonged to the prominent Porter family for eight generations. Extensively remodeled after Dr. Joseph Porter (Jessie's grandfather) and his wife took possession of it in 1896, the house today represents a mélange of Second Empire, Victorian and Italianate elements. Dr. Porter—born here in 1847—was later named the state's first public health officer and recognized as one of the country's foremost authorities on sanitation and yellow fever.

Turn right on Duval St. and walk half a block.

The Oldest House Museum – *322 Duval St. Open year-round daily 10am–4pm. $4.* & ☎ *305-294-9501.* Considered the oldest house in Key West, this small, two-story clapboard residence—formerly known as The Wrecker's Museum—was built c.1829 on Whitehead Street, then moved here in 1832. Its 19C furnishings, which include fine Meissen tea and chocolate pots, reflect the comfortable lifestyle of wrecker Captain Francis Watlington, who lived here until the late 1800s. Spacious grounds in the rear hold a cookhouse and pavilion with further exhibits relating to the wrecking industry.

Return to Caroline St., turn right and walk east for half a block.

★**Curry Mansion Inn** – *511 Caroline St. Open year-round daily 10am–5pm. $5.* ▣ *www.currymansion.com* ☎ *305-294-5349.* William Curry, a self-made millionaire and mayor of Key West, built the rear of this rambling, white Victorian mansion before his death in 1896. His son Milton greatly expanded the house at the turn of the century, adding elaborate reception rooms and bedrooms to the front. Now an inn, the mansion retains its Belle-Époque grandeur. Visitors can take a self-guided tour of the house, which offers the only publicly accessible **widow's walk** *(third floor)* in Key West. After your tour, relax on the wide, shady verandah.

Built around 1889, the elegant white frame **George Patterson House** *(across from Curry Mansion at 522 Caroline St.; not open to the public)* features gables, porches and galleries adorned by delicate spindlework—all characteristic elements of the Queen Anne style.

Continue to the corner of Caroline and Simonton Sts.

Distinctive for its unpainted, weathered cypress exterior, the 1887 **Cypress House** *(601 Caroline St.)* was originally owned by the Kemp family, Bahamians who are credited with introducing the sponge industry to Key West. The low facade and simple lines of this private inn typify Bahamian architecture.

Turn right on Simonton St. and continue half a block.

Casa Antigua – *314 Simonton St. Courtyard garden open Nov–May daily 10am–6pm. Rest of the year daily 11am–7pm. Closed Thanksgiving Day & Dec 25. $2.* & ☎ *305-296-3887.* The first incarnation of this square, beige Mediterranean Revival structure with brown balconies was the Trev-Mor Hotel, one of the island's earliest hotels (1919). The first floor held the Trevor and Morris Ford dealership (note the garages at street level). Ernest Hemingway spent several weeks in an apartment here on his first trip to Key West in 1928; while there he worked on his novel *A Farewell to Arms*. Extensively rebuilt after a fire in 1975, the building now houses a Caribbean crafts shop and boasts a tropical garden out back.

Walk half a block up Simonton to Eaton St., then left on Eaton for half a block.

Donkey Milk House – *613 Eaton St. Open daily 10am–5pm. $5.* 🅿 ☎ *305-296-1866.* Visitors to this Neoclassical house can glimpse a recently restored Key West home, complete with interior details such as an 1890 hand-painted Italian ceiling and a black walnut staircase. The 1866 structure acquired its unusual name from the donkey-drawn milk carts that pulled into the alleyway behind it in the mid-19C. In 1886 it was home to Peter A. ("Dynamite") Williams, the US marshal famous for halting a fire that same year by using dynamite to divert the flames. The present owner has furnished the house with his own collection of antiques.

Continue east on Eaton St. and cross Elizabeth St.

One of Old Town's best known homes, the unique **Octagon House** *(712 Eaton St.),* was built in 1885 by Richard Peacon, who opened Key West's first supermarket. Renovated by acclaimed interior designer Angelo Donghia in the 1970s, the house was also briefly owned by clothing designer Calvin Klein.

Continue on Eaton St. to the corner of William St.

Bahama House – *730 Eaton St. Not open to the public.* Originally constructed on the island of Abaco, this symmetrical white pine structure was disassembled and brought to Key West by schooner in 1847 as the home of Bahamian shipbuilder John Bartlum. Its wide airy verandahs on both stories, louvered windows and doors, and low-ceilinged interior rooms typify Bahamian architecture. Exterior siding incorporates boards of different widths. Note these same features on the house next door *(408 William St.),* which was transported from Green Turtle Cay.

Turn right on William St.

Note the temple form of the c.1866 **Gideon Lowe House** *(409 William St.),* a fine example of the Classical Revival style.

Walk two blocks south on William to Southard St. and turn right. Continue west 1.5 blocks.

Built of heart pine and Honduran mahogany, the 1855 **John Lowe, Jr. House** *(620 Southard St.)* was constructed with wooden pegs, mortise-and-tenon joints and square timbers. The second story was added later, creating a Classical Revival house tempered by Bahamian influences. Its widow's walk—one of the few remaining on the island—was once used to sight downed ships offshore by the house's first owner, wrecker John Lowe, Jr.

Continue to intersection of Simonton St. and turn right; walk one-half block north and turn right on Free School Ln. to a small gate at its end.

Nancy Forrester's Secret Garden – *1 Free School Ln. Open year-round daily 10am–5pm. $6.* ☎ *305-294-0015.* Owner-artist Nancy Forrester has devoted more than a quarter-century to creating her personal one-acre tropical oasis amidst the hubbub of downtown Key West, opening it to the public only in 1994. Today the lush botanical garden enamors nature lovers who wander its winding paths among ferns, heliconias and orchids, beneath a canopy of century-old hardwood trees—Spanish limes, sapodillas, gumbo-limbos—and a collection of rare palms. Forrester herself, a licensed minister, conducts weddings in the garden's secluded glades.

Return to Simonton St. and turn right. Continue 1.5 blocks north and turn left on Eaton St.

Key West surgeon Thomas Osgood Otto built the lavender Queen Anne **Artist House** *(534 Eaton St.),* which is distinguished by its octagonal turret. Now a guest house, the two-story 1887 structure features wraparound verandahs ornamented with slender balusters and delicate corner brackets.

Continue west to corner of Eaton and Duval St.

St. Paul's Episcopal Church – *401 Duval St. Open year-round Mon–Sat 9am–5pm, Sun 7am–5pm.* ♿ ☎ *305-296-5142.* Oldest church in the Florida diocese, St. Paul's was established in 1832. The current white Spanish Colonial building (1919) with its imposing belltower, is the fourth church on the site. Vaulted wooden ceilings inside are designed to resemble inverted ships' hulls.

Turn left and walk south on Duval St.

Since its opening in 1926, Duval Street's highest landmark building has been **Hotel La Concha** *(no. 430).* The six-story, pink concrete hotel (now operated by Holiday Inn) has housed such luminaries as Tennessee Williams, who wrote *Summer and Smoke* here in the mid-1940s. Late in the afternoon, stop by the hotel's rooftop bar, **Top of La Concha**, for a drink and a panoramic **view** of the island and its surrounding waters.

Cross Fleming St. to the 500 block of Duval St.

Duval Street

San Carlos Institute – *516 Duval St. Open year-round Tue–Sun 11am–6pm. Closed Jan 1, Easter Sunday, Dec 25. $3 contribution requested.* ⚬ ☎ *305-294-3887.* This imposing Spanish Colonial structure was built in 1924 (to replace the previous wooden building that was destroyed by the 1919 hurricane), but its roots date back to 1871. Founded as a social club and school by Cuban exiles during the Ten Years' War, the San Carlos Institute was named after the Seminario San Carlos, a famed learning center in Cuba where Father Felix Varela planted the seeds of Cuba's independence movement (a bronze likeness of the priest stands in the lobby of the Key West site). The nonprofit institute quickly became the hub of social and revolutionary activity for Cubans in Key West.

> **① Margaritaville Cafe**
>
> *Map p 60. 500 Duval St.* ✗ ☎ *305-292-1435.* This popular cafe and its adjacent souvenir shop is owned by singer Jimmy Buffett, who got his start playing in Key West bars. Treat yourself to a "cheeseburger in paradise" or go next door, where you can purchase a variety of items inspired by Buffett's song lyrics, including his famous "lost shaker of salt."

The present institute building, the third on this site, serves as school, museum, library, art gallery and theater. It contains two floors of exhibits relating to Cuba's fight for independence from Spain. Displays on the ground floor focus on **José Martí**, organizer of the second effort for Cuban independence, who often spoke at the Institute. Descriptive panels in several rooms upstairs detail Cuban history and presence in Florida. Interior walls of the restored building are lined with bright blue majolica tiles that were imported from Spain; floors incorporate checkered Cuban mosaics.

Across the street from the San Carlos Institute, note the pastel ornamented facade of the former **Strand Theater** *(527 Duval St.)*, a 1930 movie palace restored in 1993. It now houses Ripley's Believe It or Not Odditorium.

A half-dozen blocks up Duval Street are two additional sites that relate to Cuban history. The **Cuban Club** *(1108 Duval)* is a two-story, white frame replica (1989) of the Key West headquarters of *Sociedad Cuba*, established in 1900 to offer education, medical care and social activities to the Cuban émigré community. Fire destroyed the original building in 1983; the present incarnation, which incorporates the original columns, turrets and facade pediment, houses shops and condominium units.

Nearby, **La Terraza de Martí** (locally known as "La-te-da") restaurant *(1125 Duval St.)* occupies the former home (1892) of cigar manufacturer Teodoro Pérez. From its second-floor balcony, the leader of the Cuban Revolutionary party, José Martí, frequently exhorted his countrymen to action.

ADDITIONAL SIGHTS *1/2 day. Map p 50.*

Fort Zachary Taylor State Historic Site – *Enter through gatehouse to Truman Annex at the west end of Southard St. Open year-round daily 8am–dusk. $4.50/vehicle and 50¢/person.* ⚹ ☎ *305-292-6713.* Remains of the three-story, trapezoidal 19C brick fort started in 1845 (and never completed) form the centerpiece of this 87-acre park overlooking the Atlantic Ocean. During the Civil War, some

800 soldiers were quartered here, but they saw no significant action. Today you can walk along vestiges of the fort's 5ft-thick battlements, and visit the small **museum** that showcases artillery once employed here. Nearby, a pleasant wooded grove edges a narrow (and somewhat rocky) Atlantic **beach**, with opportunities for swimming, fishing and snorkeling.

★★Ernest Hemingway Home & Museum – *907 Whitehead St. Open year-round daily 9am–5pm. $6.50.* ▣ ☎ *305-294-1136.* Half-hidden amid lush vegetation, the gracious yellow stucco house enjoys renown as the place where Key West's legendary figure, novelist Ernest Hemingway, spent his most productive years.

Hemingway and Trophy (c.1935)

Hemingway Collection, J.F. Kennedy Library, Boston

The Making of "Papa" – **Ernest Hemingway** (1889-1961) first visited Key West in 1928 with his second wife, Pauline. He had already achieved literary fame with the 1926 publication of *The Sun Also Rises*, and was returning to the US after years of living in Europe. After a brief stay in Cuba, the couple arrived in Key West, where a new Ford was to have been waiting for them to drive north. However, shipment of the car was delayed, giving the Hemingways time to become acquainted with the island Hemingway dubbed "the St. Tropez of the poor."

For three subsequent winters they returned here, then in 1931 purchased a large but run-down home, which Pauline described at the time as a "miserable wreck." They renovated the house and Hemingway lived there until his marriage ended in 1939; Pauline remained in the house and continued to be a prominent member of Key West society until her death in 1951.

It was during his Key West years that Hemingway cultivated his machismo "Papa" image, spending his days writing, fishing and drinking with a coterie of locals he called the "Key West Mob." His legend continues to infuse many corners of the island and is the impetus behind the annual **Hemingway Days** festival. Held in conjunction with the writer's birthday (July 21), the week-long event features look-alike contests, arm wrestling and several other "Papa"-like activities.

Visit – *1hr.* Built by wealthy wrecker and merchant Asa Tift in 1851, this one-of-a-kind house is made of coral rock mined on the property and covered with stucco. Tift brought the French Colonial-style cast-iron pillars, verandahs and balusters from New Orleans. Full-length, double-paned arched windows open like doors to catch island breezes. Sparsely decorated rooms contain period pieces, some of which belonged to the family. In Hemingway's bedroom, notice the **ceramic cat** made for "Papa" by Pablo Picasso.

A wooden catwalk once connected the master bedroom to Hemingway's **studio★**, a pleasant room above the carriage house where he wrote such classics as *Death in the Afternoon, For Whom the Bell Tolls* and *To Have and Have Not*. (The character of Freddy in the latter novel is modeled after Joe Russell, the late owner of Sloppy Joe's Bar.) The attractive grounds contain a large **swimming pool**—the first one built on the island. Commissioned by Pauline in the 1930s while Hemingway was off covering the Spanish Civil War, the $20,000 pool infuriated "Papa" when he returned. He reportedly railed at Pauline, declaring that she had spent his last cent, and threw a penny on the ground to emphasize his point. His wife had the coin embedded in the cement by the pool where it remains to this day.

The legions of six-toed cats that roam the grounds are said to be descended from felines once owned by Hemingway himself. Over the years, however, bloodlines have thinned and today their fabled lineage is dubious at best.

Other Hemingway landmarks include **Sloppy Joe's Bar** *(201 Duval St.),* a cavernous local pub that was "Papa's" favorite hangout. **Captain Tony's Saloon** *(428 Greene St.)* housed the original Sloppy Joe's bar from 1933 to 1937. Hemingway attended cockfights and boxing matches in the two-story, blue clapboard Conch cottage called **Blue Heaven** *(729 Thomas St.).* A former brothel, it now contains a cafe and artists' studios.

Key West Lighthouse Museum – *938 Whitehead St., across from Hemingway House. Open year-round daily 9:30am–4:30pm. Closed Dec 25. $6.* 🅿 ☎ *305-294-0012.* Built in 1846 and decommissioned in 1969, the crisp, white-brick lighthouse now offers a sweeping **view** of the island from atop its 90ft tower. A **lightkeeper's quarters** on the grounds, panelled in gleaming Dade County pine, displays lighthouse lenses, military artifacts and period rooms re-creating the lifestyle of early 20C light keepers.

Key West Cemetery – *Margaret St. and Passover Ln. Guided tour (1hr 30min) sponsored by the Historic Florida Keys Foundation year-round daily. $10. Reservations required.* ♿ ☎ *305-292-6718.* Monuments to Key West's past can be found among the cemetery's more than 35,000 headstones, which date back to 1847 when the earlier cemetery near the south coast was washed out by a hurricane. A bronze sailor surveys the marble markers commemorating seamen who lost their lives in the 1898 sinking of the *USS Maine.* Another plot contains an arch inscribed *A Los Martires de Cuba* ("to the Cuban Martyrs"), for those who died in the 1868-78 insurrection against Spain.

East Martello Museum and Gallery – *3501 S. Roosevelt Blvd. Open year-round daily 9:30am–4:30pm. Closed Dec 25. $6.* 🅿 *www.keywestkeywest.com/historic.htm* ☎ *305-296-1702.* The names of this brick tower and its counterpart, West Martello Tower *(below)*, derive from a type of impregnable cylindrical tower first built in Corsica in the Middle Ages. Begun in 1862 as back-up fortifications to the nearby Union stronghold, Fort Zachary Taylor *(p 63),* the East Martello Tower was never completed. Yellow fever, labor strikes and wartime exigencies delayed the work, and in 1873 building ceased on the unfinished battlements.

Today, remains of the East tower house the **Key West Art & Historical Society★**. Historical exhibits range from ancient Indians through the sinking of the *USS Maine* to local 20C literary figures (including seven Pulitzer Prize winners, Ernest Hemingway and Tennessee Williams among them). The art gallery hosts special exhibits, notably, the "junkyard sculpture" of late Key West folk artist **Stanley Papio**; folk art by local Cuban painter **Mario Sanchez**; and the famous **portrait of Hemingway** by WPA artist Erik Smith.

Broad, man-made **Smathers Beach**—the largest on the island—stretches for 2mi along South Roosevelt Boulevard.

West Martello Tower – *White St. and Atlantic Blvd., on Higgs Memorial Beach. Open year-round Tue–Sat 9:30am–3pm. Closed major holidays.* ♿ 🅿 ☎ *305-294-3210.* Companion to East Martello Tower, this Civil War citadel served as a lookout tower during the Spanish-American War. Its brick ruins are now edged in tropical plantings maintained by the Key West Garden Club.

Adjacent to the tower, **Higgs Beach** (also called Monroe County Beach) is another popular local spot on the Atlantic for swimming and sunbathing.

Southernmost House – *1400 Duval St. Not open to the public.* This rambling, cream-colored brick Queen Anne manse with pale green trim (built in 1899 by Judge J. Vining Harris) claims to be the southernmost house in the continental US. Anchoring the south end of Duval Street, the elegant structure exemplifies the Queen Anne style in Key West: Its variation of color, shape, texture and embellishment have been modified to suit both local tastes and climate.

■ A Key to Limes

When you think of a lime, you probably picture a dark green, seedless Persian lime, a hybrid of the fruit that originated in Southeast Asia. Limes were introduced to the western Mediterranean region by returning crusaders in the 12C and 13C. Christopher Columbus brought limes on his second voyage (1493) to the New World, where the tree rapidly took root throughout the Caribbean and spread to Florida and Central America. Before Hurricane Andrew hit in 1992, 90 percent of the limes grown in the US were from Florida.

Florida's signature dessert, key lime pie, depends on the biting acerbic juice of key limes. This small, yellowish, seed-filled citrus fruit can be found growing on thorny trees in backyards throughout the Keys.

Small **South Beach** lies across from the house. Around the corner *(west end of South St.),* a large red, black and yellow buoy marks what it claims is the **Southernmost Point** in the lower 48 states. (In fact, the true southernmost point extends from a restricted naval base just to the west.) In front of the buoy, sidewalk vendors hawk a variety of "southernmost" seashells and trinkets.

EXCURSION *Map p 50*

*★***Dry Tortugas National Park** – *1/2 day. 69mi southwest of Key West. Accessible only by plane or boat. Open year-round dawn–dusk.* △ ☎ *305-242-7700. No concessions available on the island.* **Plane** *departs from Key West International Airport year-round daily. One-way 40min; half day $159/person, full day $275/person, camping trip $299/person. Picnic coolers, soft drinks and snorkel equipment provided. Advance reservations required, payment by credit card or travelers checks.* ▣ *Seaplanes of Key West, Inc. www.conch.net/~seaplane.com* ☎ *305-294-0709 or 800-950-2359.* **Boat** *departs from Land's End Marina mid-Dec–Sept daily 8am, returns to Key West by 7pm. Rest of the year Mon, Wed, Fri & Sat 8am, returns to Key West by 7pm. One-way 3hrs. Commentary. Reservations recommended. $85 incl. breakfast and lunch.* &. ▣ *($5) www.yankeefleet.com* ☎ *305-294-7009 or 800-634-0939.*

Encompassing 100sq mi in the Gulf of Mexico, the park protects the small cluster of reef islands called the Dry Tortugas, west of the Florida Keys. One of these, 10-acre Garden Key, is the site of **Fort Jefferson**, the largest coastal stronghold built by the US in the 19C. Sitting in the middle of a windswept nowhere, this vast brick fort echoes with its own past. Park waters offer good opportunities for wreck-diving, snorkeling and fishing *(information available from visitor center at fort).*

A Strategic Site – Spanish explorer Ponce de León named these islands *Las Tortugas* ("The Turtles") when he explored them in 1513. (The anglicized addition of the word "Dry" refers to the islands' lack of fresh water.) They remained Spanish possessions until Florida came under US control in 1821. Recognizing the importance the Tortugas could play in keeping shipping channels open between the Atlantic and the Gulf of Mexico, American military strategists recommended locating a fort here; construction of Fort Jefferson began in 1846.

Sixteen million bricks were used to form the perimeter walls, which measure 50ft high and 8ft thick. The weight of the structure eventually caused the walls of the ill-fated fort to sink into its unstable base of sand. By the time the Civil War broke out, the brick hexagon was only two-thirds completed.

Though soldiers never fired at an enemy from Fort Jefferson, it did serve as a prison for Union deserters during the Civil War. In 1865 **Dr. Samuel Mudd** was interned here as a co-conspirator in President Lincoln's assassination. (Mudd unwittingly set the broken leg of Lincoln's fleeing assassin, John Wilkes Booth, without realizing Booth's identity.) During a yellow fever epidemic in 1867, Mudd unstintingly treated the prison's victims of the disease. His efforts won him a pardon from President Andrew Johnson and he was released in early 1869. Yellow fever struck the citadel again in the early 1870s, and four years later it was finally abandoned. Proclaimed a national monument in 1935, the fort was changed to national park status in 1992 in order to protect the nearby coral reef and the shipwrecks that are now popular dive sites.

Visit – Inside the visitor orientation area, a 10min film details the fort's history. Parade grounds inside the walls hold remnants of a cavernous magazine, soldiers' barracks and officers' quarters. A self-guided walk leads through the arched case-mates and up onto the battlement wall, where a lighthouse, no longer functioning, still stands. From this vantage point, there's a lovely **view★★** of the fort and nearby Bush and Loggerhead Keys. (The former supports a boisterous colony of terns.) The top of the surrounding moat also serves as a walking path, and a palm-fringed white-sand snorkeling **beach** lies on the island's west side.

Fort Jefferson

Great Blue Heron – © Lynn M. Stone

The section of Gulf Coast stretching from the Suwannee River, near Florida's PAN-HANDLE, down to Hernando County, above TAMPA, is often called the "real Florida" because so much of the area has remained undeveloped. While ancient burial grounds indicate the region was inhabited as early as 500 BC by Indians of the Dept-ford culture, this coast remained a wilderness well into the 18C, when Spanish soldiers made an occasional appearance.

In 1835 a quiet woodland setting near Bushnell saw a skirmish that helped precipi-tate the Second Seminole War. On December 28, **Major Francis Dade** and a command of some 100 soldiers were en route from Fort Brooke (Tampa) to provide relief units to Fort King (Ocala) when they were ambushed by Seminole Indians. Dade and most of his men were killed. Today the **Dade Battlefield State Historic Site** *(off Rte. 301, 1mi south of Bushnell; open year-round daily 8am–dusk;$2/vehicle;* ♿*)* commemorates this battle with an annual reenactment the last weekend in December *(for information* ☎ *352-793-4781).*

After the US government began forcing Seminoles out of Florida to Oklahoma reser-vations in the 1830s, white settlers established inland plantations, growing sugar cane and Sea Island cotton. During the Civil War, several salt furnaces operated along the Gulf Coast supplying salt to the Confederate army. These plants were considered so important to the war effort that workers were exempted from military duty. Following the war, homesteaders began to arrive. Eventually commercial fishing and lumber industries thrived as fish caught in local waters were transported to whole-sale dealers in Cedar Key by sailing sloop, and cedar trees were harvested and shipped to Crystal River and Cedar Key to be carved into pencils. A few of the Gulf settle-ments began attracting northern visitors to large hotels and sportsmen's lodges. Visitors arrived in Ocala by train, then made the final journey to the coast by horse and buggy.

The area's quiet, natural beauty—which captivated landscape artists Winslow Homer and George Inness in the late 19C—still entices visitors today. While the main north-south artery, US-19/98, can be as congested as any Florida highway, a turn west will invariably lead to an unspoiled coastal hamlet such as Suwannee, Yankeetown or Pine Island. An abundance of wildlife, including alligators, manatees *(p 71)*, armadillos and bald eagles, makes its home in and around the region's wetlands, hammocks and crystal-clear, spring-fed rivers. Area restaurants are widely known for local seafood delicacies, including redfish, Gulf shrimp, oysters and stone crab.

CEDAR KEY

Population 849
Map of Principal Sights p 3 – Map p 70
Tourist Information ☎ 352-543-5600

Occupying Way Key, the largest (about 1.5mi long) in a cluster of low-lying islands 3mi off the mainland (and the only one linked by bridge), this historic Gulf Coast town supports a mix of commercial fishermen, artists and weekenders, many of them from Tallahassee and Gainesville. The pace is slow in the down-home hamlet of tin-roofed porches and weathered piers with views of bayou and bay. Most activity centers along the three-block stretch of Second (Main) Street and the "Big Dock" *(off A and C Sts.)*, lined with gift shops and seafood restaurants. **Cedar Keys National Wildlife Refuge**, a group of 12 beach-rimmed islets—nesting areas for pelicans, ospreys, white ibis and hun-dreds of other species of birds—lies 5mi offshore *(open daily year-round; ☎ 352-543-5600; boat trips depart from City Marina year-round daily 11am–dusk; round-trip 1hr 30min; commentary; $10; ▣ Island Hopper ☎ 352-543-5904).*

Historical Notes – Occupied sporadically by Spanish soldiers and traders during the 18C, *Las Islas Sabinas* (the Cedar Islands) became a major shipping center in the 1840s for cotton, sugar, tobacco and turpentine ferried out from inland plantations (the mainland road was not opened until 1886). The 1860 completion of the first trans-Florida railroad, linking Cedar Key on the Gulf with FERNANDINA BEACH on the east coast, put the town on the map, and the islands served as a Confederate supply depot during the Civil War until they were blockaded by Union troops.

Real boom times came in the 1870s and 1880s when a commercial seafood industry thrived and regular steamer service operated to New Orleans, Tampa, Key West and Havana, Cuba; many of the hip-roofed tabby buildings on Second Street are former hotels and saloons dating from this era. Lumbering was also a mainstay until an 1896 hurri-cane destroyed two sawmills where cedar (lightweight and easy to cut without splitting)

Cedar Key Dock at Sunrise

© Ian Adams/Dembinsky Photo Assoc.

was processed for northern pencil manufacturers. At about the same time, ships began bypassing Cedar Key for deeper harbors. The ensuing economic decline lasted well into the 20C. Even today, there are fewer than 700 year-round residents and more than half the houses are owned by out-of-towners. Tourism is on the rise, however, and the seafood industry is regenerating, thanks to new small-scale aquatic breeding farms for clams and oysters, whose once-flourishing beds were exhausted in the 1930s.

SIGHTS *2hrs*

Cedar Key Historical Society Museum – *6092nd St., at Rte. 24. Open daily Nov–Apr Mon–Sat 11am–5pm, Sun 2pm–5pm. Rest of the year daily Mon–Thu 2pm–5pm, Fri & Sat 11am–5pm, Sun 2pm–5pm. $1.* ♿ ☏ *352-543-5549.* A picturesque two-story tabby structure, built in 1871 as one of the first private residences on the island, houses the small but comprehensive museum. Highlighted by an extensive collection of **19C photographs**, displays focus on Cedar Key's history as a major US sponge exchange and center for commercial oystering, fishing and turtling. There are also artifacts from the Eagle Pencil Co. and Eberhart Faber sawmills once located here, along with beautifully crafted brushes and brooms from a local palm-fiber factory that operated in the area from 1910 to 1952.

Cedar Key State Museum – *1710 Museum Dr. (1.5mi from town center). Open year-round Thu–Mon 9am–5pm. Closed Jan 1 & Dec 25. $1.* ♿ 🅿 ☏ *352-543-5350.* Opened in 1962, this one-story brick museum contains a remarkable collection of **Florida shells** and glassware assembled by the late St. Clair Whitman, a local resident and self-taught naturalist. Additional exhibits trace Cedar Key history through Indian and other artifacts. Outside stands Whitman's late-19C red-shingled Victorian home, which was moved from its original site on Goose Cove and awaits restoration.

EXCURSION

Manatee Springs State Park – *1/2 day. 34mi north near Chiefland. Take Rte. 24 east for 9mi; turn left on Rte. 345. At Chiefland, take US-19/98 north to Rte. 320 west and follow to park entrance. Open year-round daily 8am–dusk. $3.25/vehicle. Canoe rental Memorial Day–Labor Day daily 9am–4pm. Rest of the year weekends only. $5 first hour, $4 each additional hour.* △ ✗ ♿ 🅿 ☏ *904-493-6072.* Feeding into a sparkling run, Manatee Springs forms the centerpiece of this 2,000-acre nature preserve. An area for swimming is roped off at the crystal-clear headwaters. Nearby, a boardwalk *(.25mi)* zigzags alongside the run, passing through a swamp lush with cypress, gum, ash and maple trees. Along with bald eagles and various wading birds, it's not unusual to spot alligators and an occasional wintering manatee along the walk, which ends at an **observation deck** on the Suwannee River.

Manatee Springs State Park

CRYSTAL RIVER

Population 4,200
Map of Principal Sights p 3 – Map below
Tourist Information ☎ 352-795-3149

The 7mi waterway that gives Crystal River its name was known until the mid-19C as "Weewahiiaca," from two Creek words meaning "clear water." Of the 30 natural springs feeding the river, 28 form headwaters at **Kings Bay**, considered one of the county's most important **manatee sanctuaries★**, harboring some 200 of the gentle sea cows each winter. A premier area for boating, fishing, scuba diving, snorkeling and underwater photography, Kings Bay also forms the focal point of **Crystal River National Wildlife Refuge** which encompasses nine small, undeveloped bay islands *(accessible by boat only; for information check with local dive operators or refuge office, open year-round Mon–Fri 7:30am–4pm; www.gorp.com/gorp/resource/us-nwr/fl-cryst.htm ☎ 352-563-2088)*.

As the only area in Florida where people may swim and interact directly with manatees, Kings Bay is exceedingly popular with nature lovers. Numerous local dive shops offer boat, snorkeling and scuba rentals, along with guided boat tours of the river and bay. *Best time to see manatees is from January through March. Recreational water-use regulations—including strict boat speed limits—are enforced to protect the manatees.*

SIGHT *1/2 day*

Crystal River State Archaeological Site – *3400 N. Museum Point Rd., 2mi north of town center. Open year-round daily 8am–dusk. $2/vehicle.* ♿ ☎ *352-795-3817.* It is believed that this 14-acre prehistoric ceremonial site was established by Indians of the Deptford Culture (500 BC to AD 300), who lived in small villages on nearby islands and came to the mainland to bury their dead. They were followed by members of the Weedon Island culture, who used the site from about AD 300 to 1300. Why they left is a mystery.

At the entrance, a **visitor center** *(open year-round daily 9am–5pm)* houses an impressive display of ancient arrowheads and tools and offers a 10min interpretive video. Outside, a path (.5mi) leads past two midden mounds made of discarded oyster shells, three burial mounds and two temple mounds. Along the trail, you will pass two mysterious **ceremonial stones**, or stelae, more commonly associated with Central American groups and rare to North America. The stones were placed here around AD 440, possibly as markers for the summer and winter solstice.

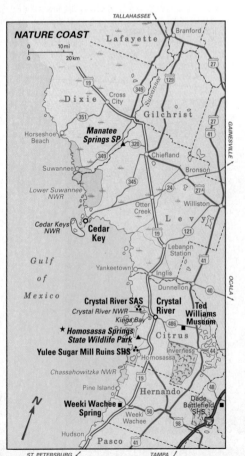

EXCURSIONS

★ **Homosassa Springs State Wildlife Park** – *3hrs. 7mi south in Homosassa. Take US-19/98 south to Rte. 490; turn right on Rte. 490 and follow signs to park at 9225 W. Fishbowl Dr. Open year-round daily 9am–5:30pm. $7.95.* ✕ ♿ 🅿 *www.citrusdirectory.com/hsswp ☎ 352-628-2311. Visitors can park on Rte. 19 and take an interpretive boat ride (30min; commentary) along Pepper Creek. Parking is also available on Fishbowl Dr. across*

Manatees at Crystal River

© Mark J. Thomas/Dembinsky Photo Assoc.

■ Florida's Gentle Giant

With its clumsy, gray-brown, sausage-shaped body, gentle nature and doleful expression, the West Indian manatee *(Trichechus manatus)* is one of the most beloved members of Florida's extensive and varied family of wildlife. This curious beast is a marine mammal, but is unrelated to the whale, seal or dolphin. Its closest relative is, in fact, the elephant, although the manatee's two front flippers contain the same bones (arranged differently) as the human hand. Manatees use their undulating tails to propel themselves forward; flippers function as rudders. Females normally begin breeding when they're about seven years of age. After a 13-month gestation period, a cow typically gives birth to one calf; a newborn manatee weighs about 66 pounds.

The herbivorous manatee has earned the sobriquet "sea cow" owing to its habit of browsing on aquatic vegetation—consuming as much as 100 pounds per day. On such a diet, an adult manatee can measure up to 13ft long and weigh more than 3,000 pounds. Manatees frequent rivers, estuaries, bays and canals. While these animals once flourished, it is estimated that only about 2,000 of them survive in the US. All now reside in the southeast, traveling to the Carolinas and Louisiana in summer, and spending winter in Florida's warm spring-fed rivers, which maintain a constant temperature of 72°F-74°F. (Manatees cannot survive for extended periods in water colder than 68°F.)

Manatees have no natural enemies, but development of the state's coastal areas has diminished feeding grounds, forcing the slow-moving mammals into boating areas where they often become tangled in fishing lines and injured or killed in collisions. Indeed, boat strikes currently rank as the leading human-related cause of manatee mortality in Florida. In 1973 manatees were listed as an endangered species; to further protect them, the entire State of Florida was established as a manatee sanctuary in 1978.

Among the best spots for viewing manatees in their natural habitat are Homosassa Springs State Wildlife Park *(p 70)*, Kings Bay *(p 70)* and Blue Spring State Park *(p 74)*. Manatee season officially runs from November 15 to March 15, but the best viewing time is generally from January through March. To adopt a manatee, contact Save the Manatee Club ☎ 800-432-5646; funds go toward education, research and lobbying efforts.

from the park entrance. This 45ft-deep natural spring forming the headwaters of the Homosassa River provides a **sanctuary for rehabilitating manatees** scheduled for release back to the wild after recovering from boating accidents. Those too seriously injured to survive in the wild are allowed to stay here. An underwater observatory permits a close-hand look at the manatees, paddling lazily through schools of speckled trout, redfish, jack crevalle and snook. The 155-acre park is also a refuge for injured and orphaned bobcats, Florida black bear, the endangered American crocodile, alligators, river otters and birds of prey. Be sure to catch one of the manatee programs *(three times daily)* and educational animal and reptile encounters *(twice daily).*

Yulee Sugar Mill Ruins State Historic Site – *1hr. 10mi southwest on Rte. 490 in Homosassa. Open year-round daily 8am–dusk.* ☎ *352-795-3817.* Partially restored limestone ruins survive as the last remnant of a 5,100-acre sugar plantation, called Margarita, owned by **David Levy Yulee**. Founder of the first trans-Florida railroad *(p 68)*, Yulee was later elected the first US senator from Florida. The mill began operation in 1851 and supplied sugar and its by-product, molasses, to Confederate troops during the Civil War. In 1864 Union troops burned the plantation, but the mill was spared; the cast-iron boiler, steam engine and processing kettles remain intact.

Ted Williams Museum and Hitters Hall of Fame – *1hr. 11mi east near Hernando. Take Rte. 486 east toward Hernando; museum is located 3.5mi west of Hernando at the entrance to Villages of Citrus Hills, 2455 N. Citrus Hills Blvd. Open year-round Tue–Sun 10am–4pm. Closed Easter Sunday, Thanksgiving Day, Dec 25. $3.* ⚐ 🅿 ☎ *352-527-6566.* The extensive collection of photos, uniforms, equipment and memorabilia housed here pays tribute to baseball great **Ted Williams** (b. 1918), who played for the Boston Red Sox between 1939 and 1960 before retiring and moving to Florida to pursue his other love: fishing. During his illustrious career, the left-fielder batted .344 (the sixth-highest average in history) while stroking 521 home runs. His single-season .406 average in 1941—one of six years he won a batting title—has not been surpassed since. The diamond-shaped museum, dedicated in 1994, includes life-size dugouts and a ticket booth. A theater complete with bleacher seats shows a 20min film of Williams discussing his choice of the top 20 hitters of all time. These players, including Babe Ruth, Lou Gehrig, Joe DiMaggio, Ty Cobb, Willie Mays and Mickey Mantle, are honored in the Hall of Fame.

Weeki Wachee Spring – 🄺🄸🄳 *3hrs. 21mi south at the intersection of Rte. 50 and US-19 in Weeki Wachee. Open year-round daily 9:30am–5:30pm. $16.95.* ✕ ⚐ 🅿 *www.silversprings.com* ☎ *352-596-2062.* Designed around a freshwater spring, the multi-theme park is best known for an underwater theater where local "mermaids" have performed in the crystal-clear water since 1946. In addition to an exotic bird show, a wilderness river cruise *(30min)* and a petting zoo, the park operates one of the largest raptor rehabilitation centers in Florida. Successful graduates include eagles, hawks, falcons and vultures that swoop and dive daily in the Birds of Prey show.

Visitors can swim in Weeki Wachee Springs at **Buccaneer Bay**, the only natural spring water park in the state *(open Mar–Sept daily 10am–5pm; $12.95;* ✕⚐ 🅿 *www.silversprings.com* ☎ *352-596-2062).* Three water slides, bumper boats, a beach, lagoon, rope swings and a volleyball court provide hours of entertainment.

North Central Florida

A magnet for biking, fishing and canoeing enthusiasts, this largely rural area—running across the peninsula from Alachua, Marion and Lake counties in the west to Volusia and Seminole counties in the east—is one of remarkable natural beauty. A gently rolling terrain of open pasture and shady back roads distinguishes the region, which is perhaps best known for its darkly mysterious rivers, freshwater springs, complex strings of lakes (the Tsala Apopka chain alone contains seven) and the 430,000-acre **Ocala National Forest** *(p 82)*.

Before white settlers arrived in the mid-19C, Timucuan and then Seminole Indians made their homes here. Many of the lakes and rivers (Withlacoochee and Ocklawaha, for example) retain their Seminole names. During the period of British occupation (1763-83), the St. Johns River in the east was the site of several sugar-cane and indigo plantations. After the Civil War, settlers began taking advantage of the Armed Occupation Act, which provided free 160-acre tracts of land to homesteaders in Florida. Before the development of the railroad in the 1870s and 1880s, most early settlers were farmers who grew citrus and raised cattle.

With a strategic location on the St. Johns River, Sanford became an important supply center for the central Florida interior, receiving goods by paddle wheeler from Jacksonville. Steamboats also ferried supplies down the Silver River to Silver Springs, from where they were transported to surrounding settlements by wagon.

By the 1870s, commercial citrus cultivation accounted for myriad small boom towns that appeared across central Florida, shipping produce through Gainesville and Ocala. Although the great freeze of 1894-95 spelled doom for many small outposts, well-preserved Victorian architecture in McIntosh, Windsor, Waldo and Mount Dora still recalls the glory days. In 1889 phosphate mining became a mainstay of the Ocala area until World War I cut off the predominantly European market. Agriculture supported the eastern counties, where cool lake breezes and good soil conditions proved ideal for commercial nurseries and vegetable farms.

While retirees and tourism now bolster the area's economy, central Florida continues to earn most of its revenue from agriculture, boosted by light manufacturing. Although the citrus industry was hit hard again by bad freezes in the early 1980s, citrus remains an important local crop. Tiny mom-and-pop fruit stands abound on back roads; be sure to stop for a jar of homemade marmalade or orange-blossom honey.

DeLAND

Population 18,607
Map of Principal Sights p 3 – Map p 75
Tourist Information ☎ 904-734-4331 or 800-749-4350 (US & Canada)

Envisioning an "Athens of Florida," New York manufacturer Henry A. DeLand founded this pleasant inland town in 1876 and started DeLand Academy seven years later. Renamed **Stetson University** in honor of DeLand's friend, Philadelphia haberdasher John B. Stetson, the school boasts several notable buildings including **DeLand Hall** *(Woodland Blvd. and Minnesota Ave.)*, built in 1884, and the stately 1910 **President's House** *(west side of Woodland Blvd. at Michigan Ave.)*. Another noteworthy resident, Chinese horticulturist Lue Gim Gong, developed successful new varieties of the orange and grapefruit in the late 19C.

SIGHTS *1/2 day*

Driving-tour brochures pointing out the town's historic structures may be obtained at the Chamber of Commerce Welcome Center, 336 N. Woodland Blvd. (at Michigan Ave.; ☎ 904-734-4331).

Gillespie Museum of Minerals – *234 E. Michigan Ave. at Amelia Ave. Open year-round Mon–Fri 9am–noon & 1pm–4pm. Closed during Stetson University holidays. Contribution requested.* 🅿 ☎ *904-822-7330*. Originally owned by Mr. and Mrs. Thomas Gillespie of St. Augustine, the group of 30,000 gems, rocks and fossils owned by the museum makes up one of the largest private **mineral collections★** in the world. Some 10,000 specimens fill cases in the ground floor rooms of this house on the edge of the Stetson University campus. The Gillespies donated their sizable mineral collection to the university in 1958. Treasures representing a dazzling variety of finds from around the globe include a 130-pound chunk of translucent Brazilian topaz, a remarkable group of fluorescent specimens, spikes thought to have been formed by lightning, and iron meteorites.

Henry A. DeLand House – *137 W. Michigan Ave. Open year-round Tue–Sat noon–4pm. Closed major holidays. Contribution requested.* ♿ 🅿 *www.volusia.com/delandhouse* ☎ *904-734-7029*. Now headquarters of the West Volusia Historical Society, this 1886 residence was built by the town's first attorney, George Hamlin. John Stetson later purchased the house for university faculty housing, which it remained until it was donated to the city in 1988. In the early 20C, the second story and Greek Revival facade were added to this 1.5-story structure. Decorated with 19C furnishings, the house boasts a unique bow-bay window in the south parlor, as well as its original pine woodwork, staircase and floors.

© Mark J. Barrett

Boating at Blue Spring State Park

EXCURSIONS

★ **Blue Spring State Park** – *1/2 day. 3.5mi southwest near Orange City. Take US-17/92 south to W. French Ave.; turn right and continue 3mi - to park. Open year-round daily 8am–dusk. $4/vehicle.* ⚠ ♿ 🅿 *www.dep.state.fl.us/parks/* ☎ *904-775-3663*. This park is best known as a haven for **manatees** *(p 71)*, which congregate in Blue Spring from November through March. An observation platform is located on a short boardwalk trail *(.3mi)*, which leads along the spring run through a stretch of dense hammock to the spring headwaters, a popular swimming and snorkeling spot. A pontoon boat ride *(2hrs)* around Hontoon Island *(p 76)* leaves twice a day from the dock at the bottom of the spring run.

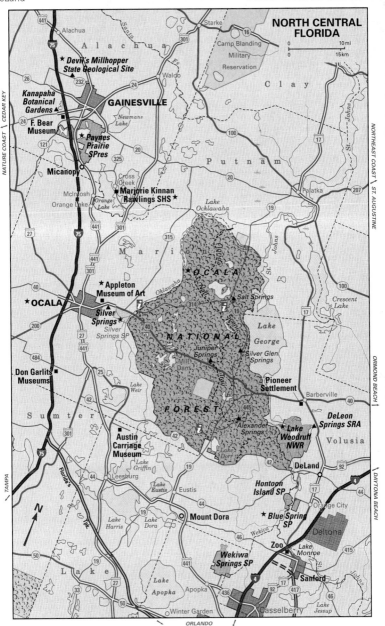

Visitors may picnic by the tin-roofed, wood-frame **Thursby House**, built in 1872 atop a Timucuan shell mound by an early settler. Louis Thursby operated a steamboat landing at Blue Spring, once an important mail and shipping stop on the busy St. Johns River route. *The restored interior of Thursby House is open the last weekend of January during the park's Manatee Festival (visit by 30min guided tour 9am–4:30pm only).*

★**Lake Woodruff National Wildlife Refuge** – *2hrs. 6mi north of DeLand. Take US-17 north and turn left (west) on Retta St. Turn left (south) on Grand Ave. and right (west) on Mud Lake Rd. and follow to end. The only way to explore the refuge is by foot; comfortable walking shoes and a sun hat are recommended. Open year-round daily dawn–dusk.* 🅿 ☏ *904-985-4673.* A cool canopy of gum and hickory trees shrouds the one-lane sand track leading into this lovely wildlife preserve. Administered by the US Fish and Wildlife Service, the refuge encompasses some 19,500 acres of lake, timbered swamp and freshwater marshes dotted by island hammocks and three man-made impoundments. In these areas, water levels are kept high in the warm weather to foster plant and animal life, then lowered in cool months to provide easier feeding for migrating fowl and wading birds. Bird-watchers may spot more than 200 species, including bald eagles, ospreys and wood storks. The refuge is also ideal for fishing, canoeing, bicycling, photography and hiking *(trails and distances are marked on a map at the entrance)*.

Hontoon Island State Park – *2hrs. 6mi southwest of DeLand. Take Rte. 44 west and turn left on Old New York Ave./Rte. 4110; follow this 2mi and turn left on Hontoon Rd./Rte. 4125 and follow 4mi to park. Open year-round daily 8am–dusk. $2/vehicle.* ⚠ ♿ *www.dep.state.fl.us/parks/* ☎ *904-736-5309.* Tucked between the St. Johns and Hontoon Dead Rivers, this bucolic 1,650-acre island park is accessible only by private boat or by the free passenger ferry that makes the run regularly *(departs from River Ridge Road year-round daily 8am–dusk; one-way 3min; ♿ 🅿).* On the island, an 80ft observation tower offers an excellent river **view**, and a nature trail *(3mi round-trip)* leads to midden mounds made by Timucuan Indians, the island's earliest inhabitants.

De Leon Springs State Recreation Area – *2hrs. 8mi north in De Leon Springs. Take US-17 north 6mi; turn left on Ponce De Leon Blvd. and follow it 1mi to park: 601 Ponce De Leon Blvd., at Burt Parks Rd. Open year-round daily 8am–dusk. $3.25/vehicle.* ✕ ♿ 🅿 ☎ *904-985-4212.* Stately live oaks shade the pleasant picnic grounds of the 603-acre recreation area located on the former site of Timucuan burial grounds and a 16C Spanish sugar plantation. Visitors may hike the 5mi nature trail, swim in Ponce de Leon spring—now enclosed by a concrete wall to form a large circular pool—or explore adjacent Spring Garden Creek by paddleboat or kayak. The 3mi run into Lake Woodruff Wildlife Refuge *(p 75)* is a popular canoe trip *(rentals available at the concession)*. A renovated 19C sugar mill next to the spring offers grill-your-own pancakes made from flour milled on the premises *(open year-round Mon–Fri 9am–4pm, weekends and holidays 8am–4pm; closed Thanksgiving Day & Dec 25)*.

Pioneer Settlement for the Creative Arts – 🅺🅸🅳🆂 *1.5hrs. 15mi north in Barberville. Take US-17 north to intersection of Rte. 40; turn left and continue 1 block to museum at 1776 Lightfoot Ln. Visit by guided tour (1hr) only, year-round Mon–Fri 9am–3pm, Sat 9am–1pm. Closed major holidays. $2.50.* ♿ 🅿 ☎ *904-749-2959.* In 1975 a group of art teachers rescued an abandoned 1919 school building and transformed it into a folk museum. Relying on donations and craft sales, they have, over 20 years, built an institution that draws several hundred schoolchildren a day. Guides at this unpretentious living-history attraction demonstrate uses of turn-of-the-century household and farm implements, and allow visitors to try their hand at such pioneer crafts as weaving and candle-making.

Cypress Trees

GAINESVILLE

Population 87,295
Map of Principal Sights p 3 – Map below
Tourist Information ☎ 352-374-5231

A friendly college-town atmosphere pervades Gainesville, home to the University of Florida. The busy 2,000-acre campus lies primarily to the west of US-441, the main north-south thoroughfare. The historic downtown area, Courthouse Square and quiet residential streets lined with loblolly pines and live oaks occupy the east side of town.

Historical Notes – Gainesville was laid out in 1853 as the new seat of Alachua County, replacing Newnansville farther north. A product of Florida's developing railroad system, the town was deliberately given a strategic position on the planned trans-Florida rail line from Fernandina to Cedar Key. Some say the name Gainesville (originally spelled without the final "E") came from a campaign to *gain* enough votes from the reluctant Newnansville citizens to support the new location; others argue the town was named for **Edmund Gaines**, a prominent US general who fought in the Seminole Wars.

In the late 19C, Gainesville thrived as a shipping center for citrus, strawberries, phosphate and lumber. Local revenues now depend on the university and the manufacture of archery equipment. Despite the inevitable suburban sprawl, some 700 buildings are preserved in five historic districts. Notable among the turn-of-the century structures in the **Northeast Historic District** is **Thomas Center** *(302 N.E. 6th Ave.)*. Built in 1910, the elegant Mediterranean Revival-style home was remodeled as a hotel in 1928 and is now a cultural center featuring changing art exhibits *(open year-round Mon–Fri 8am–5pm, weekends 1pm–4pm; closed major holidays;* ♿ 🅿 ☎ *352-334-5064)*.

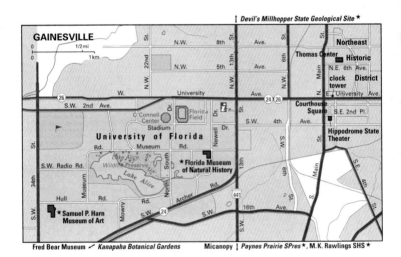

SIGHTS *1 day. Map above.*

Courthouse Square – *S.E. 1st St. and University Ave.* Brick-paved streets, wide boulevards and early 20C commercial buildings—some housing pleasant outdoor cafes—help maintain the character of Gainesville's old downtown. A local landmark, the **clock tower** *(northeast corner of E. University Ave. and N.E. 1st St.)* contains the original clock from the second (1885) Gainesville courthouse, demolished in 1959. The grand Beaux-Arts style 1909 Post Office building *(25 S.E. 2nd Pl.)* fronted by a two-story Corinthian portico, is now home to the **Hippodrome State Theater**.

University of Florida – *S.W. 13th St. between University Ave. and S.W. Archer Rd. It is difficult to navigate the busy UF campus without a map and parking information, available at the Main Entrance Information Booth, US-441 (S.W. 13th St.) and S.W. 2nd Ave.* Located on 2,000 acres, this is Florida's oldest and largest university, consolidated in 1906 from several state educational facilities (including Florida Agricultural College in Lake City). The university admitted only men until 1947, when about 600 women joined the student body of 9,000. Today, with 40,000 students, 16 colleges and four graduate schools, the University of Florida ranks among the country's 10 largest universities. The campus includes several early 20C Collegiate-Gothic-style buildings (now part of a historic district), a teaching hospital, an 84,000-seat football stadium (the Gators are a perennial national title contender), two museums and the 81-acre Lake Alice Wildlife Preserve.

★**Samuel P. Harn Museum of Art** – *S.W. 34th St. and Hull Rd., on University of Florida campus. Open year-round Tue–Fri 11am–5pm, Sat 10am–5pm, Sun 1pm–5pm. Closed major holidays.* ⚫ 🅿 *www.arts.ufl.edu/harn* ☎ *352-392-9826.* Opened in 1990, the Harn Museum is the state's first major art museum on a college campus. Some 35,000 objects assembled at the University of Florida over the last several decades—previously stored in attics and closets—are now consolidated in the striking 62,000sq ft post-Modern building, distinguished by roof pyramids and a dramatic three-story glass atrium. Periodic shows draw on the permanent collection, which includes strong holdings in **early 20C American art**, with works by such figurative artists as John Marin, Paul Sample and Leon Krull; **tribal art** of West Africa and Papua New Guinea; Asian sculpture and painting; and pre-Columbian pottery. The museum also features exhibits by contemporary artists—both established and emerging—and presents some 20 traveling shows a year, often with experimental themes.

★**Florida Museum of Natural History** – *Museum Rd. at Newell Dr. on University of Florida campus. Park on southwest corner at Police Dept. Open year-round Mon–Sat 10am–5pm, Sun & holidays 1pm–5pm. Closed Thanksgiving Day & Dec 25. Contribution requested.* ✗ ⚫ 🅿 *www.flmnh.ufl.edu* ☎ *352-846-2000.* This official state repository for Florida's natural history collection houses the museum's departments of Natural Sciences and Anthropology and the largest **research collection**★ of fossil and modern invertebrates, vertebrates and plants in the South. Emphasis is on Florida and Caribbean natural history. Displays on **Florida environments** explore the ecosystems of a coral reef, savannah, and temperate and tropical hammock. There is also a full-size limestone cave and replica of a Mayan palace (AD 800). Glass-topped drawers and wall cases in the **Object Gallery** offer a close-up view of skeletons, rocks, minerals and fossils.

★**Devil's Millhopper State Geological Site** – *4732 Millhopper Rd., off N.W. 53rd Ave./Rte. 232. Open year-round daily 9am–5pm. $2/vehicle. Ranger-led walks offered Sat 10 am.* ☎ *352-955-2008. Insect repellent recommended.* Stop at visitor center for a 5min orientation video; then take the winding staircase to the bottom of the dramatic **sinkhole** known as Devil's Millhopper, after an Indian legend that told of the devil hurling human bodies into its depths. Here, watered by burbling falls and supported by cool, below-grade temperatures, thrives plant life similar to that of Appalachia. Mosses and liverworts hold moisture, allowing larger plants to grow. Among these, needle palms—rare for northern Florida—grow here because the sinkhole rarely experiences freezing temperatures.
Measuring 120ft deep and 500ft wide, this depression was probably formed in two stages. Sinkholes are created as rainwater seeping into limestone substrata forms an underground cavern; eventually the cavern roof collapses, leaving a deep cavity. The first collapse of Devil's Millhopper occurred as many as 14,000 years ago and the second about 1,000 years ago, resulting in a funnel-like shape similar to that of a corn hopper (a device used to feed corn into a grist mill).

Fred Bear Museum – *Fred Bear Dr., just west of I-75 off S.W. Archer Rd/Rte. 24. Open year-round daily 10am–6pm. Closed Jan 1, Easter Sunday, Thanksgiving Day, Dec 25. $4.* ⚫ 🅿 ☎ *352-376-2411.* A tribute to its namesake, the late bowhunter and founder of Bear Archery, the museum presents a large collection of archery artifacts as well as Bear's trophies. A variety of mounted beasts, including grizzly bears, moose and tigers, lines the walls of the second-floor gallery. The self-guided tour includes taped explanations of how Bear and others bagged some of these trophies. You can glimpse the production area of Bear Archery products through windows along one side of the second floor.

Kanapaha Botanical Gardens – *4700 S.W. 58 Dr. Off S.W. Archer Rd./Rte. 24, 1.5 west of I-75. Summer months offer the best color. Open year-round Mon–Tue & Fri 9am–5pm, Wed & weekends 9am–dusk. Closed Dec 25. $3.* ⚫ 🅿 *www.hammock.ifas.ufl.edu.kanapaha* ☎ *352-372-4981.* There is a lighthearted, almost wild feeling to this 62-acre garden maintained by the North Florida Botanical Society. Visitors may wander at leisure along a 1.5mi paved walkway that dips in and out of fern cobbles and palm hammocks, passing through flower beds, an herb garden and an occasional vine-draped trellis. Florida's largest collection of **bamboo** species is found here (some plants grow 2in/hour during the spring season). A water lily pond nestles in a cove of Lake Kanapaha.

EXCURSIONS

★**Paynes Prairie State Preserve** – *1.5hrs. 10mi south on US-441 in Micanopy. Open year-round daily 8am–dusk. $3.25/vehicle.* △ ⚫ 🅿 *www.afn.org/~pprairie* ☎ *352-466-3397.* Named for King Payne, an 18C Seminole leader, Paynes Prairie ranks as one of Florida's most important natural sites. This irregularly shaped basin, measuring 8.5mi at its widest point, was formed as the terrain settled over a sinking limestone bed that periodically fills with water. A glass-fronted **visitor center**

(2mi from the entrance at the end of Park Dr.) and nearby observation tower *(follow short path in front of visitor center)* both offer a sweeping **view** over **Paynes Prairie**, now a marsh where wild Spanish horses (reintroduced in 1985) roam freely. During a dry spell in the late 1600s, the prairie was the site of the largest cattle ranch in Spanish Florida. In the late 19C, the area became a lake with a busy steamboat route until the water drained abruptly, leaving one boat stranded. The 22,000-acre preserve today boasts a rich cross-section of Florida habitats, including swamps, ponds, pine flatwoods and hammocks woven with over 25mi of hiking trails. Sandhill crane, bald eagles and other wildlife winter here.

Micanopy – *1hr. 10mi south on US-441. Most shops are open daily 10am–5pm; some shops are open weekends only.* An antiques center with a sleepy, unspoiled air, the tiny village was founded in 1821 as the first permanent white settlement in what is now Alachua County. The town was first called Wanton but was renamed in 1834 after Micanopy, a powerful Seminole chief who once ruled this territory. Enormous live oaks shade the main street, Cholokka Boulevard; shops, housed in early 20C commercial buildings, overflow with vintage china, collectibles, clothing and books. The **Micanopy Historical Society Museum** *(Cholokka Blvd. and Bay St; open year-round Wed & Fri–Sun 1pm–4pm; $2;* ♿ ▯ *www.co.alachua.fl.us/~acvacb* ☎ *352-466-3200)* explains the town's past through historical photographs and artifacts.

★ **Marjorie Kinnan Rawlings State Historic Site** – *2hrs. 17mi south in Cross Creek. Take Rte. 20 east 9mi to Rte. 325; follow Rte. 325 south 8mi to Cross Creek. Site is just south of town on right. Grounds open year-round 9am–5pm.* ♿ *Visit house by guided tour (45min) only, Oct–Jul Thu–Sun 10am–4pm (every hour, limited to 10 people). Closed Jan 1, Thanksgiving Day, Dec 25. $3.* ▯ ☎ *352-466-3672.* Well-known for her affectionate portrayals of life in backwoods Florida, author Marjorie Kinnan Rawlings (1896-1953) owned this rambling Cracker-style house and 72-acre grounds from 1928 until her death. Among the many original furnishings is the writing table, on the front porch, where Rawlings wrote her Pulitzer Prize-winning book, *The Yearling* (1938), and *Cross Creek* (1942). Both novels were later made into popular films. The house sits in a citrus grove dominated by a magnificent magnolia tree. Just across the road, a leaf-carpeted path makes a short loop *(.25mi)* through a hardwood hammock of wild palms, oaks, sweet gums, hickories and hollies.

MOUNT DORA

Population 8,766
Map of Principal Sights p 3 – Map p 75
Tourist Information ☎ 352-383-2165

This charming town sits 184ft above sea level on one of the highest points in Florida (thus qualifying it as a "mount"). Ancient live oaks, turn-of-the-century homes and picturesque views of Lake Dora make it an ideal place for a peaceful weekend getaway. Once a prosperous citrus center, Mount Dora was settled in the 1870s and originally called Royellou, after an early postmaster's three children, Roy, Ellen and Lou Tremain. By the late 19C it was a popular haven for wintering northerners who settled into rambling Victorian hotels such as the recently renovated 1883 **Lakeside Inn** *(100 N. Alexander St.)* for the season. The town experienced its heyday in the 1920s, then fell into obscurity. In recent years, however, downtown has been restored and tourists have rediscovered this sleepy enclave, which lies about 30mi northwest of ORLANDO and 40mi southeast of Ocala. Along Fifth Avenue and Donnelly Street, you can easily while away a half-day browsing in quaint craft and **antiques shops** and snacking in tearooms and cafes.

Local festivals occur throughout the year, including the popular **Mount Dora Bicycle Festival**, which takes place the third weekend of October, and an annual art show the first weekend in February. The IceHouse Theatre *(1100 N. Unser St.)* presents plays and musicals from September to May.

SIGHTS *1/2 day*

The Chamber of Commerce, located in the old train depot *(341 N. Alexander St.)*, offers maps for a self-guided 7mi scenic driving tour and a 3mi walking tour of the historic downtown. A highlight of the latter is the turreted 1893 Queen Anne-style **Donnelly House**, now a Masonic Lodge *(Donnelly St. between 5th and 6th Aves.; not open to the public).* Note its ornate fretwork.

Royellou Museum – *450 Royellou Ln. between 4th and 5th Aves. Open Oct–Apr Thu & weekends 12:30–3pm, Fri 11am–3pm. Rest of the year Fri–Sat 10am–2pm, Sun noon–3pm.* ♿ ☎ *352-383-0006.* Tucked into a small back alley parallel to

Donnelly Street, this tiny local history museum uses the city's former jail building (1923) for its odd assemblage of memorabilia, including historic photographs and two old jail cells.

Palm Island Park – *Intersection of Tremain St. and Liberty Ave.* A surprisingly lovely haven of 12 acres of wetland hammock skirts Lake Dora. It features a boardwalk nature trail *(.3mi)* where you might glimpse alligators, otters, bald eagles and ospreys.

EXCURSIONS

Wekiwa Springs State Park – *1.5hrs. 12mi southeast in Apopka. Take US-441 south to Apopka; stay on Main St. through center of town and turn left on Rte. 436. Turn left on Wekiwa Springs Rd. and follow it to park entrance. Open year-round daily 8am–dusk. $3.25/vehicle.* ⚠ ♿ 🅿 *www.dep.state.fl.us/parks ☎ 407-884-2008. Canoe rentals $14 (2hrs), $25 (day); ☎ 407-880-4110.* The centerpiece of this 6,900-acre park is Wekiwa Spring, which pumps 42 million gallons of water a day into the 15mi-long Wekiva River. Recreational activities include swimming in the spring and hiking 13.5mi of wooded nature trails. Canoeists will enjoy the trip up the Rock Springs Run *(7.5mi)*, which leads out of the spring. Look for midden mounds left by the Timucuan Indians, who made their homes along the riverbanks from 3000 BC to AD 800.

OCALA★

Population 44,975

Map of Principal Sights p 3 – Map p 75

Tourist Information ☎ 352-629-8051

Centered in the rolling green countryside of Marion County, Ocala is synonymous with horses. The "Lexington of the South," as it has been dubbed, contains some 400 farms for Arabians, Clydesdales, thoroughbreds and quarter horses, and ranks high as a training and breeding center. Each February the city hosts the **Horses In The Sunshine International Show** that features hunting and jumping competitions. Agriculture and a booming cattle industry (the largest in Florida), along with a constant influx of northern retirees, make Marion one of the fastest-growing counties in America.

Historical Notes

No traces remain of the Timucuan settlement of Ocali (meaning "water's edge"), believed to have been located near Silver Springs *(p 81)*. Hernando de Soto reportedly found 600 houses there when he passed through in 1539, but not, to his disappointment, the gold, silver and pearls rumored by the Spanish to be stockpiled in Timucuan towns.

A US military outpost known as Fort King was established here in 1827 and served as headquarters for central Florida during the Seminole Wars. Settlers arrived in the 1840s, and by the late 19C Ocala had become a major shipping center for phosphate and citrus fruits. A number of Victorian and Queen Anne-style houses from that era are preserved in the 55-block **Ocala Historic District** *(centered around Fort King St. between Watula Ave. and 13th St.)*.

A natural pastureland owing to the underlying limestone aquifer that waters it, Marion County is now home to some 450, or 75 percent, of Florida's thoroughbred breeding and training facilities. These have produced 37 North American champions and five Kentucky Derby winners. *For a view of the countryside farms, resplendent in rolling pasture and magnificent live oaks, drive south of the city on S.W. 27th Ave. (Rte. 475A) or S.E. 3rd Ave. (Rte. 475). For information about public tours of area thoroughbred farms or to watch training sessions, call Lorna Hagemeyer's Farm Tours ☎ 352-351-5524.*

SIGHTS *1 1/2 days*

★**Appleton Museum of Art** – *4333 N.E. Silver Springs Blvd. Open year-round Tue–Sat 10am–4:30pm, Sun 1pm–5pm. Closed major holidays. $5.* ♿ 🅿 *www.fsu.edu/~svad/Appleton/AppletonMuseum.htm ☎ 352-236-7100.* A dramatic axial sculpture fountain enlivens the approach to this elegant two-story neoclassical structure clad in travertine marble. In 1986 Chicago industrialist Arthur I. Appleton (owner of a thoroughbred breeding and training facility in Ocala) donated funds to build the museum on 44 acres of land donated by the city of Ocala. Today the museum, land and art collection are jointly owned by the Florida State University Foundation and the Central Florida Community College Foundation. First-floor galleries frame a central courtyard and feature Classical and Egyptian antiquities, West African sculpture, pre-Columbian pottery, and an extensive display of **Asian art**, including lovely jades, porcelains and Tibetan bronzes. The upper level

Silver Springs

Glass-Bottom Boat Tour of Silver Springs

is devoted primarily to 18C and 19C English and European painting and decorative arts. The museum also mounts several temporary shows throughout the year. A new wing houses traveling exhibitions, an interactive video classroom, art library and workshop.

★**Silver Springs** – Kids *5656 E. Silver Springs Blvd./Rte. 40 (1.5mi east of Appleton Museum). Open year-round daily 9am–5:30pm. $29.95 (includes all rides and shows).* ✗ ♿ ▯ ($3) ⅲⅲ *www.silversprings.com* ☎ *352-236-2121 or 800-234-7458 (US and Canada).* A subtropical hammock surrounding some 150 natural springs at the head of the Silver River sets the scene for this 450-acre multitheme nature park. Together the waters form the largest **artesian spring** *(p 14)* in the world, producing about 5,000 gallons per second (which would fill an Olympic-size swimming pool in two minutes). Timucuan Indians, who believed the 100,000-year-old spring held mystical powers, worshipped the sparkling aqua waters as the "shrine of the water gods." Exotic palm trees, live oaks dripping with Spanish moss, and a substantial alligator population also fascinated 19C visitors. They began arriving by steamboat on the tourist route from Palatka, 46mi northeast, as early as the 1860s—making Silver Springs the oldest attraction in Florida.

Visit – *1/2 day. Expect waiting time for boat rides and Jeep Safari. Snack bars are located throughout the park.* Springside Mall, located to the left of the main entrance, offers several eateries and an array of gift shops. Just past Springside Mall, **A Touch of Garlits** showcases a group of antique autos owned by champion drag racer Don Garlits *(p 82).*

Glass-Bottom Boat Rides – *25 min.* These vessels provide an amazingly clear view of the underwater world of the main spring, including several caverns (the deepest is 81ft) that contain fossilized bones of Pleistocene animals. Waters here are so pure (98 percent) and transparent that they have long been the setting for film and television; six of the original Tarzan movies, parts of the James Bond film *Moonraker* (1979) and the movie *The Abyss* (1989), and underwater scenes for more than 100 episodes of the *Sea Hunt* television show were all shot at the springs.

Lost River Voyage – *25min.* Cruise on a quiet electric boat down the subtropical Silver River, said to look much as it did when the Spanish arrived in the 16C. Boats stop at an animal rehabilitation post, where Silver Springs' staff oversees a program for eagles and other birds and animals found sick or injured in the wild.

Jeep Safari – *15min.* Climb into zebra-striped Jeeps for a ride through a 35-acre natural habitat site. Here, some 60 species of birds and animals roam free, including vultures, egrets, armadillos, rhesus monkeys and Amazonian two-toed sloths (which eat, sleep, mate and give birth while upside down). Next to Jeep Safari, visitors can feed giraffes, llamas, pygmy goats and baby deer at **Doolittle's Petting Zoo**.

Cypress Island – A wooded five-acre island plaza here hangs above a natural marsh. Enclosures along the boardwalk trail hold alligators, crocodiles, flamingos and giant tortoises. Be sure to see the three animal shows offered several times a day *("Creature Feature" 11:50am, 1:50pm & 3:50pm; "Amazing Pets" 11:25am, 1:25pm & 3:25pm; "Reptiles of the World" 11am, 1pm & 3pm).* From Cypress Island, you can catch the **Jungle Cruise** *(30min)* down the Fort King Waterway past an open-air zoo of exotic animals.

Adjoining Silver Springs, **Wild Waters** 🚻, a six-acre water park *(on Rte. 40)* features a 45,000-gallon wave pool, eight flumes with water sleds and a miniature golf course *(open Mar–Sept daily Sat–Thu 10am–5pm, Fri 10am–7pm; $19.95;* ✕♿ 🅿 ☎ *352-236-2121).*

Discovery Science Center – 🚻 *50 S. Magnolia Ave. Open year-round Tue–Fri 9am–4pm, Sat 10am–4pm. Closed major holidays. $3.50.* ♿ 🅿 ☎ *352-620-2555.* While the center's focus is on children, visitors of any age can easily become caught up in interactive exhibits designed to explain such scientific phenomena as light, sound, gravity, motion and space. Perhaps most intriguing are the **holusions**, images formed by random patterns that trick the eye into seeing a three-dimensional image.

EXCURSIONS

Don Garlits' Museums – *1.5hrs. 10mi south of city center. Take Exit 67 off I-75 and go east on Rte. 484; take first right on Rte. 457A. Museum entrance is on right at 13700 S.W. 16th Ave. Open year-round daily 9am–5pm. Closed Dec 25. $7.50; $10 combination ticket.* ♿ 🅿 *www.garlits.com* ☎ *352-245-8661.* Champion drag racer and Marion County resident "Big Daddy" Don Garlits—the first to break 200mph—founded this museum in 1976. Drag racing is a one-on-one, quarter-mile competition in which drivers accelerate custom dragsters from a dead stop and race in a straight line; it differs from stock-car competitions, where drivers race on a circular track using autos that are custom-built to resemble street models. (Stock cars originally were built entirely from stock parts). The plain, single-story building is packed with trophies, vintage gas tanks and an excellent collection of antique autos and engines with mind-boggling capacities for torque and horsepower. Garlits' first dragster (1954)—a car so ugly that *Hot Rod Magazine* wouldn't even print a picture of it—is housed here, as is "Swamp Rat I," his first world-record-setting dragster, and many of the 33 subsequent models in that series. Prized stock cars and dragsters complete the displays. In an adjacent museum building *(same hours as above; $5)* a collection of some 100 classic automobiles, including many Fords from the 1930s and '40s, is exhibited.

★**Ocala National Forest** – *1/2 day. 11mi east of Ocala. (Enter at Highway 40 Visitor Center, 10863 E. Rte. 40; 6mi east of Silver Springs). Open year-round daily 9am–5pm. Closed Dec 25.* ⚠ 🅿 *www.fs.fed.us* ☎ *352-625-7470. Two additional visitor centers serve the forest: Salt Springs to the north (14100 N. Rte. 19); and Pittman to the south (45621 Rte. 19) near Lake Dorr. Each offers maps, forest-related exhibits and a bookstore.* Established in 1908, Ocala National Forest is the oldest national forest east of the Mississippi. Locally known as "Big Scrub" for its predominance of scrub pine, the forest encompasses some 430,000 acres of wetlands, timber, scrub, hiking trails and freshwater lakes and springs. It stretches about 60mi from southern Marion County up to Lake Ocklawaha. To the west lies the Ocklawaha River; the St. Johns River and Lake George mark the eastern boundary. A replica of a Cracker homestead is located at the Mill Dam Recreational Site *(7mi from Forest Visitor Center; turn left on Forest Rd. 79 off Rte. 40 near Mill Dam; open year-round daily 8am–8pm; $2;* 🅿 *[$1]).* Several half-mile nature trails thread through the forest.

Freshwater Springs – Some of central Florida's most beautiful natural springs grace the park. Picturesque **Juniper Springs** *(17mi east of visitor center on Rte. 40; open year-round daily 8am–8pm; $3;* ⚠ 🅿 ☎ *352-625-3147; canoe rental* ☎ *352-625-2808)* features a palm-fringed swimming area, enclosed in the 1930s by the Civilian Conservation Corps, and a short nature trail through subtropical foliage and past bubbling spring "boils." The 7mi trip down Juniper Creek through the Juniper Prairie Wilderness is a particularly popular canoe run. Clear waters draw boaters, snorkelers and scuba divers to **Alexander Springs** *(10mi southeast of Juniper Springs on Rte. 445; open year-round daily 8am–8pm; $3;* ⚠ 🅿 ☎ *352-669-7495; canoe rental* ☎ *352-669-3522).* The combination of freshwater and saltwater flowing into the headspring at **Salt Springs** *(junction of Rte. 19 and Rte. 314; open year-round daily 8am–8pm; $2;* ⚠ 🅿 ☎ *352-685-2048; canoe rental* ☎ *352-685-2255)* creates differences in salinity at different depths, causing objects viewed underwater to appear unusually distorted. Popular with snorkelers, **Silver Glen Springs** is surrounded by ancient Indian shell mounds *(8mi north of junction of Rte. 19 and Rte. 40; open year-round daily 8am–8pm; $3;* 🅿 ☎ *352-685-3990; canoe rental* ☎ *352-685-3990).*

Florida National Scenic Trail – *Within the forest, primary access points to the trail are the Clearwater Lake Recreation Area (Rte. 42), Alexander Springs (Rte. 445), Farles Lake (Forest Rd. 595-1), Juniper Springs (Rte. 40), Hopkins Prairie (Forest Rd. 88-C near Lake Kerr), Lake Delancy (Forest Rd. 75-2) and the Rodman Recreation Area on Lake Ocklawaha. Both day and overnight hikes are permitted.*

Florida Trail Association, www.florida-trail.org/~fta ☎ 904-378-8823. Offering more than 300mi of hiking in Florida, this is one of eight National Scenic Trails in the country and will eventually run the length of the state (more than 1,000mi are currently completed, but only 300mi are open for public use). A 67mi stretch of the scenic trail threads through Ocala National Forest. The north/south route, marked by orange-colored blazes, winds through scrub pine, live oak and juniper stands; skirts lakes and springs; and traverses cypress and gum swamps via well-maintained boardwalks.

Austin Carriage Museum – *23mi southeast of Ocala. Take US-441 south 13mi to Rte. 42; go east 4mi to Weirsdale, south 2mi on Rte. 25, then east 1.4mi to museum entrance at 3000 Marion County Rd. Visit by guided tour (90min) only, Mon-Fri 1pm–4pm. Sat by appointment. $12. ♿ 🅿 www.continentalacres.com/ ☎ 352-750-5500.* Tucked away on the 265-acre Continental Acres Equine Resort at the edge of Ocala National Forest is the largest private collection of antique horse-drawn carriages in the South. More than 75 of them from the late 19C and early 20C have been restored to near-mint condition with tufted velvet and leather upholstery, shiny brass ornaments and working lamps. They include a Tour Neau Sociable, one of only three models of this US-made pleasure carriage still intact; a hunting carriage with a dog compartment; a medicine carriage; and a US mail cart. One c.1890 carriage was used by MGM Studios in 1930s movies. Resort owner Gloria Austin has driven many of the carriages in international competitions.

★ **Marjorie Kinnan Rawlings State Historic Site** – *2hrs. 20mi north in Cross Creek; 4.5mi west of US-301 on Rte. 325.* *Description p 79.*

SANFORD

Population 35,559

Map of Principal Sights p 3 – Map p 75

Tourist Information ☎ 407-322-2212

This historic 13sq mi town on the south shore of Lake Monroe traces its beginnings to 1837, when Fort Mellon was established here during the Second Seminole War. Originally called Mellonville, the neighboring settlement was the navigational head for the steamboats that began running to and from Jacksonville on the north-flowing St. Johns River in the 1840s. In 1870 **Henry Shelton Sanford**, a distinguished lawyer and US diplomat from Connecticut, purchased 12,548 acres and platted a formal town, selling lots from land offices both here and in London, England. Using Swedish labor from the nearby settlement of New Upsala, Sanford also established an experimental 145-acre grove on Lake Mary. With the help of a Swedish botanist, he cultivated 30,000 exotic trees from South America and Africa and more than 140 varieties of citrus. Although the freeze of 1894-95 ruined the grove, Sanford is credited with introducing the now-famous **Valencia orange** to Florida, along with many packing and shipping innovations still used in the citrus industry today.

Incorporated as Sanford in 1877, the town prospered as a winter resort and became a major shipping center for vegetables in the early 20C—earning it the sobriquet "Celery City" in the 1940s. Today the seat of Seminole County is perhaps best known as the southern terminus of Amtrak's Auto Train *(p 322)*.

SIGHTS *1/2 day*

A self-guided walking tour of the **historic downtown** leads visitors past Victorian store-fronts and turn-of-the century houses in a roughly four-square-block area *(map available for $2 at the Greater Sanford Chamber of Commerce, located at 400 E. 1st St.)*. A drive north or south on US-17/92 offers a lovely view of **Lake Monroe**, which is surprisingly undeveloped (look for alligators along the lake's banks in the early morning before traffic picks up).

Sanford Museum – *520 E. 1st St. Open year-round Tue–Fri 11am–4pm, Sat 1pm–4pm. Closed major holidays. ♿ 🅿 ☎ 407-302-1000.* Early photographs, paintings and maps displayed in the four galleries of this Spanish Revival-style building document Sanford's glory days as a river port in the late 1880s and highlight the achievements of founding father **Henry Shelton Sanford** (1823-1891). Among the oldest historical artifacts showcased is a Timucuan log canoe dating back to around AD 800. A re-creation of the elegant wood-paneled library (designed by noted 19C architect Richard Morris Hunt) from Sanford's Victorian home in Derby, Connecticut, fills one gallery. The handsome room contains sculptures, furniture and a collection of books (in seven languages) that belonged to Sanford, who was appointed as a diplomat to the royal court of Belgium by President Abraham Lincoln.

Central Florida Zoological Park – 🧒 *3755 N. US-17/92; 3mi north of town center; take Exit 52 off I-4. Open year-round daily 9am–5pm. Closed Thanksgiving Day & Dec 25. $7.* ✕ ♿ 🅿 ☎ *407-323-4450.* Set in a 109-acre nature preserve, this 21-acre zoo features wildlife from around the world. A wooden boardwalk leads visitors on a leisurely stroll past open-air exhibits and outdoor habitats, taking a .25mi detour through a hammock wetland dense with palms, live oaks and cypress trees. Many exotic felines, including the black leopard, Florida cougar, caracal and jaguarundi (otter cat), are highlights. There are also primates and exotic birds such as the kookaburra and tawny frogmouth, alligators and American crocodiles, and an indoor herpetarium where an especially beady-eyed collection of lizards and snakes stare out from lifelike dioramas. Animal feedings and elephant demonstrations are scheduled on weekends and holidays.

Florida State Archives

The Fred K. DeBary sailing the Upper St. Johns River (1887)

▪ Cruising the St. Johns River

One way to enjoy Florida's largest river is to cruise its waters as the state's early tourists did. On such a relaxing journey you may see alligators sunning on the banks as you pass bucolic riverside ranches. Watch for ospreys, great blue herons and bald eagles along the way. Listed below are two cruises that leave from Sanford.

Rivership Romance *departs from Monroe Harbour Marina (433 N. Palmetto Ave.) year-round daily 11am. Round-trip 3hrs and 4hrs. $35-$45, lunch included. Dinner cruises Fri & Sat 7:30pm. Round-trip 3hrs 30min. $50, dinner included. Commentary. Reservations required. Schedules on holidays vary.* ♿ 🅿 *Romance Inc. www.rivershipromance.com* ☎ *407-321-5091 or 800-423-7401.*

St. Johns River Cruises *depart from Sanford Boatworks Marina (4255 Peninsula Point) year-round Tue–Sun 11am & 1:30pm. Round-trip 2hrs. $12. Commentary. Reservations required.* ✕ ♿ 🅿 *For schedule and reservations, call St. Johns River Cruises* ☎ *407-330-1612.*

Northeast Coast

Jacksonville Skyline – Ken Biggs, Tony Stone Images

Though motorists once raced through this corner on their way south, more and more travelers are discovering the myriad charms of the 125mi strand from Fernandina Beach to Daytona Beach. Long heralded for historic St. Augustine and boisterous Daytona Beach, northeast Florida also claims its own sea islands (the southern part of Georgia's famous chain). The city limits of Jacksonville take in the greatest area of any US city.

Though Spanish sailor-explorer **Ponce de León** landed in northeast Florida in 1513 and "claimed" it for Spain, such bravado amounted to little more than planting a flag on the moon. Real ownership required permanent settlement, and this was not achieved until St. Augustine was founded in 1565, preceding Jamestown, Virginia, by 42 years. The 600 original settlers barely held on under the onslaught of diseases, hurricanes and attacks by Indians and English mariners. To defend themselves they constructed a massive fort, Castillo de San Marcos *(p 106)*, which now draws hundreds of thousands of visitors annually.

Except for a brief British occupation (1763-83), St. Augustine remained Spanish for the next 254 years until Spain handed Florida over to the US in 1819. Jacksonville was founded soon afterward, 30mi north on the banks of the St. Johns River, and rose to prominence as a port and tourist town. By the end of the 19C, however, Jacksonville's days as Florida's premier destination were over, thanks largely to Henry Flagler's Florida East Coast Railway, which opened up St. Augustine and other sunny spots further south. In modern times, Jacksonville has carried the banner of industry and commerce while St. Augustine has perfected its image as a bastion of history. One of the greatest magnets for tourists in this region, particularly during the frenzy of Spring Break, is the relative newcomer, Daytona Beach.

Travelers to Jacksonville today will find a modern, skyscraping metropolis that beckons with art museums, a landscaped Riverwalk and nearby gorgeous beaches. Scars of drug-associated crime are evident in the downtown area, but city leaders have initiated bold new revitalization projects, including the acquisition of a professional football team, the Jacksonville Jaguars. St. Augustine, on the other hand, cossets tourists at almost every turn with red-tile roofs, quaint courtyards of 17C coquina buildings, quiet lanes lined by mossy trees, and charming B&Bs. To the south, fast-growing Flagler County still maintains an undiscovered feel while offering several worthwhile attractions along A1A.

DAYTONA BEACH

Population 65,203
Map of Principal Sights p 3 – Map below
Tourist Information ☎ 904-255-0415 or 800-854-1234 (US & Canada)

Gateway to a 23mi stretch of hard, wide **beach**≙≙, this sun-worshippers' sanctuary is widely known for its car races and Spring Break crowds. From February to April, streets, beaches and motels teem with racers, motorcyclists, racing fans and college students. During the rest of the year, the town reverts to a quieter, more family-oriented atmosphere, and visitors in need of a day off from the beach can find a number of cultural attractions highlighting the area's prehistoric and pioneer past.

Historical Notes

The Plantation Era – In the late 18C and early 19C, three successive waves of planters settled in the area and then left. Plantations of indigo, rice and sugar cane ultimately failed—first due to raids during the second Spanish occupation (1783-1819), later because the brutal Second Seminole War (1835-1842) demoralized even the most prosperous landowners.

Developer Mathias Day of Ohio came here in 1871 looking for a place to build a community of wide streets and big lots. He chose the site of an abandoned plantation along the Halifax River and laid out the town of Daytona. The arrival of the railroad in the 1880s, and the subsequent influx of wealthy vacationers 12mi north in Ormond Beach, launched the Daytona area. However, it was a later vehicle that altered the city's course and provided its most distinguishing feature.

Speed City – Automobile racing, which began here in 1902, continued on the beaches until the late 1950s when a new track was built to protect drivers and ever-increasing crowds. Early racers, including Barney Oldfield, Sir Malcolm Campbell and Sir Henry

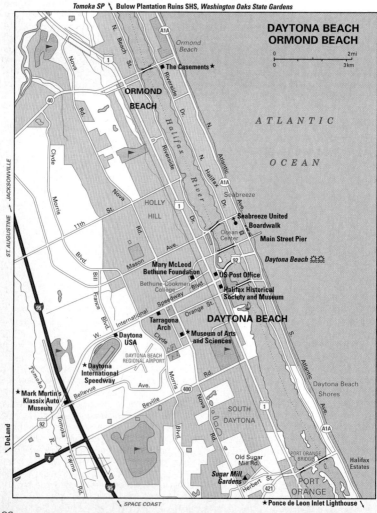

Daytona Beach

Seagrave, regularly set speed records on the beach; speeds leapt from 57mph in 1902 to an incredible 275mph in 1935. Several major formula and stock-car races are now held at the **Daytona International Speedway**, including the famous **Daytona 500** in February. March brings thousands of rumbling motorcycles for Bike Week *(p 89)*, followed by flocks of students for the annual rite of Spring Break. The tradition of driving on the beach continues to the present day. *For a $5 fee, motorists may cruise a designated stretch of the 23mi strand—driving no more than 10mph—or they may park, set up an umbrella and join the suntan set, which clusters around Main Street Pier (below) and the Boardwalk amusement area.*

The introduction of I-95 and its major arteries in the early 1970s pulled much of the town's commerce west, away from the historic center. By the late 1970s the downtown had deteriorated, and in 1982 redevelopment projects began. The city's efforts paid off six years later when downtown Daytona Beach was designated a Historic District on the National Register of Historic Places. Today eight million annual visitors make tourism the town's dominant industry. More than 300 motels, most of them lining A1A (which runs along the barrier island separated from the mainland by the Atlantic Intracoastal Waterway), cater to beachgoers and racing fans.

SIGHTS *1 day. Map p 86.*
Start your tour at the ocean and work your way west.

Boardwalk and Main Street Pier – Kids Boardwalk extends 3 blocks north from Main St. to Ora St. ☎ *904-238-1212.* Focal point of beach activities, the Boardwalk is actually a 20ft-wide concrete walkway outfitted with benches and pay telescopes. WPA workers constructed the promenade—originally called the Boardwalk—and the 4,500-seat coquina-rock bandshell between 1936 and 1938. The 1,000ft-long pier dates from 1925, when it replaced the 1900 original that was destroyed by fire. Tourists young and old gravitate to this area in all seasons, encountering a seaside bazaar of video arcades and fishing rentals, as well as the popular Space Needle and sky lift rides *(mid-May–Sept daily 11am–midnight; rest of the year daily 11am–9pm; $1; ✕).* The sprawling stepped structure built in 1989 to house the Marriott (now the Adam's Mark Daytona Beach Resort) dominates the skyline near the pier.

Halifax Historical Society and Museum – *252 S. Beach St. (3 blocks south of US-92). Open year-round Tue–Sat 10am–4pm. Closed major holidays. $3.* ♿ ▯ *www.halifaxhistorical.org* ☎ *904-255-6976.* Jacksonville architect W.B. Talley designed the Beaux Arts-style Merchants Bank building in 1910. Inside, a 1938 model of the Boardwalk scaled to 15ft, and murals of such local landmarks as the Bulow Plantation *(p 101)* and the Ponce de Leon Inlet Lighthouse *(p 89)* provide a look at local history. Noted Florida landscape artist Don J. Emery, who designed the 1926 Spanish-style **Tarragona Arch** *(W. International Speedway Blvd. and Tarragona Way),* and his son painted the murals in 1947. The museum also keeps Indian artifacts and memorabilia from pioneers and early automobile racers, as well as photographs, archives and an extensive collection of 19C postcards.

United States Post Office – *220 N. Beach St. Open year-round Mon–Fri 8am–5pm, Sat 9am–noon. Closed major holidays.* ♿ 🅿 ☎ *904-253-5166.* Like the Boardwalk, this building resulted from President Franklin Roosevelt's post-Depression WPA projects. In 1932 local architect Harry M. Griffin designed the Spanish Renaissance-style post office, which features a terra-cotta roof sloping gently to a line of gargoyles. Griffin also designed the Mission-style **Seabreeze United Church** in 1930 *(501 N. Wild Olive Ave.).*

★ **Museum of Arts and Sciences** – *1040 Museum Blvd. (off Nova Rd., .7mi south of US-92/W. International Speedway Blvd.). Open year-round Tue–Fri 9am–4pm, weekends noon–5pm. Closed major holidays. $4.* ♿ 🅿 *www.moas.org* ☎ *904-255-0285.* Located on the 60-acre Tuscawilla Preserve, the museum offers a number of fine permanent exhibits, including collections of pre-Castro Cuban art, American paintings and decorative art, and African ritual pieces. Furniture, portraiture and landscape paintings from the colonial period to the turn of the century are found in the **American wing**★★. On display are Chippendale chairs (c.1780), a Hepplewhite desk (c.1800), paintings by Albert Durand and Gilbert Stuart, silver, pewter and glasswork.

A gift of former Cuban President Fulgencio Batista, the fine **Cuban art** collection chronicles life in Cuba from 1759 to 1959. Enlarged 19C photographs of towns and landscapes enhance the artwork. The gallery devoted to **African art** presents 165 masks, totems and other objects from 30 different cultures.

The sciences are represented by a prehistory wing that showcases a marvelous 150,000yr-old **giant ground sloth skeleton**★. Found several miles south of the museum in 1975, the 13ft-tall sloth is the most complete fossil skeleton of its genus ever found in North America. Almost all the bones on display are authentic, except for the skull (the original is used for research). Temporary exhibits and an outdoor display of modern sculpture round out the museum's holdings. Guided tours of **Gamble Place**, a restored Cracker bungalow on the Spruce Creek Environmental Preserve, are available by appointment through the museum.

Mary McLeod Bethune Foundation – *640 Mary McLeod Bethune Blvd. (on the campus of Bethune-Cookman College). Open Sept–June Mon–Fri 9am–4pm. Rest of the year and weekends by appointment only.* 🅿 *www.bethune.cookman.edu* ☎ *904-255-1401.* Educator **Mary McLeod Bethune** (1875-1955), daughter of a freed slave, lived in this two-story white clapboard house from 1914 to 1955. She established Florida's first black girls' school here in 1904 and later became an advisor to five US presidents and served in FDR's administration. The house was the state's first site to honor an African American. Bethune's furnishings, awards, letters and other mementos are displayed inside.

★ **Daytona USA** – *1801 W. International Speedway Blvd. (1mi east of I-95). Open daily Jan–Aug 9am–10pm. Rest of the year daily 9am–7pm. Closed Dec 25. $12.* ✂ ♿ 🅿 *www.daytonausa.com* ☎ *904-254-2700.* Built in 1959 to move auto racing off the beach, **Daytona International Speedway** hosts eight major annual car and motorcycle races in February, March, July and October. The rest of the year was fairly quiet until this interactive motor-sports center replaced the former visitor center in July 1996. Visitors now can computer-design and video-test their own NASCAR stock cars, change a race car's tires in a timed pit-stop competition, broadcast a race finish from a sound booth and interview famous racers like Jeff Gordon and Dale Jarrett via laser-disc technology. A 14min movie, *The Daytona 500*, puts viewers in the midst of the adrenaline-pumped highlight of the speedway's race year—traveling at a simulated 190mph. Half-hour guided **speedway tours** take visitors to the pits, the infield (jammed with campers during race events) and around the 2.5mi track, with its 31° banked turns *(weather and track schedule permitting)*. Adventurous entrants in the Richard Petty Driving Experience, named for one of NASCAR racing's all-time champions, are treated to a high-speed, three-lap stock-car ride around the Daytona track.

★ **Mark Martin's Klassix Auto Museum** – *2909 W. International Speedway Blvd. Turn left on Tomoka Farms Rd. (first light west of I-95 overpass); take first left on Bellevue Ave. and immediate left into museum. Open year-round daily 9am–6pm. $8.50.* ♿ 🅿 *www.klassix-auto.com* ☎ *904-252-3800.* This classic-car-lover's dream, which opened in early 1994 and now boasts Mark Martin, a leading NASCAR racer, as a backer, makes a convincing case for the glamour of sports cars. Relive the 1950s in a life-size diner with carhops, a drive-in theater and a vintage garage. The second floor, comprising nearly half of the facility's 54,000sq ft space, is devoted to Corvettes—from their inception in 1953 to the present. Other displays include cars used in *Days of Thunder* (filmed in the area in 1990) and vintage motorcycles. Eighty-two cars worth $13 million and 45 motorcycles are set amid neon signs, videos presenting a streamlined history of racing, and period music. All this, plus a real ice-cream parlor, makes the Klassix Auto Museum a fun stop even for non-enthusiasts.

■Bike Week

Each year in early March some 350,000 bikers roll into Daytona Beach on their Harleys and Hondas for 10 days of races, swap meets and parties, known collectively as Bike Week. Festivities culminate with the **Daytona 200**, a superbike championship race first run in 1942 on Daytona's wide sands. Today the International Speedway *(p 88)* hosts the event, which attracts motorcycle-racing fans from around the world. For information about accommodations and events, call the Daytona Beach Area Convention and Visitors Bureau *(☎ 800-854-1234)* and ask for the *Bike Week Pocket Guide.*

EXCURSIONS *Map p 86*

Sugar Mill Gardens – *1hr. 5mi south in Port Orange. Take US-1 south and continue 5mi south of US-92. Turn right (west) on Herbert St. (1 block north of Rte. 421/Old Dunlawton Rd.); follow Herbert St. 1mi and turn right on Old Sugar Mill Rd. Garden entrance on left. Open year-round daily dawn–dusk.* ♿ ▯ ☎ *904-226-9446.* Ruins of a 19C sugar plantation are preserved in the 12-acre county park. Started by Patrick Dean of the Bahamas, the mill was partially destroyed—and Dean was slain—by Indians in 1836 during the Second Seminole War. During the mill's heyday, juice was extracted from sugar cane by crushing it between steam-powered rollers. This process yielded sticky brown sugar and its liquid by-product, molasses. A pleasant trail completely shaded by live oaks leads to the ruins along informal gardens and past concrete prehistoric beasts—the remains of a dinosaur park that operated here in the 1950s.

★**Ponce de Leon Inlet Lighthouse** – *1hr. 11mi south of US-92 in Ponce Inlet. Take A1A (which becomes Atlantic Ave.) south to Beach St. Turn right on Beach, continue .3mi to Peninsula Ave. and turn left; lighthouse is .2mi farther on left. Open May–Aug daily 10am–9pm. Rest of the year daily 10am–5pm. Closed Dec 25. $4.* ▯ *www.ponceinlet.org ☎ 904-761-1821.* First lit in 1887, this 175ft red beacon never missed a night of operation until 1970, when expenses forced the government to move to a nearby Coast Guard Station. Restoration began in 1972 and the light was re-lit 10 years later. Today visitors here will find one of the most complete restored light stations in Florida. Several keepers' cottages and outbuildings now display a wealth of nautical memorabilia, maps, photographs and model ships. A new lens exhibit building contains an 1860 first-order Fresnel lens retired from the Cape Canaveral Lighthouse. Visitors may climb the 203 steps inside the original light tower for a breathtaking 360-degree **view**★ of the ocean and inland waterway.

DeLand – *1/2 day. 20mi west of Daytona. Description p 74.*

Daytona Beach Pier

JACKSONVILLE★

Population 679,792

Map of Principal Sights p 3 – Map pp 94-95

Tourist Information ☎ 904-798-9102 or 800-733-2668 (US & Canada)

The largest city—in terms of area—in the US extends over 840sq mi in Florida's north-eastern corner, anchored by the north-flowing St. Johns River. An artery of trade and transportation coursing through the heart of downtown, the river brought the city into being, pumped life into it and sculpted its shape and its destiny. Today it rolls past Jacksonville's finest offerings: pristine beaches, museums of art and science, glass-sheathed high-rise office towers, charming historic neighborhoods, a zoo and a newly developed waterfront.

Historical Notes

'Place of Cows Crossing' – It was almost inevitable that a city would grow up here, around the narrowest place in the St. Johns River. The spot proved an opportune location to traverse the river, and native villagers built huts nearby, swimming their cattle across and naming the place Wacca Pilatka or "place of cows crossing." By the early 1770s, British colonists had established a tiny settlement and ferry landing on the river's north bank, calling it Cowford. The little community soon spread to the south bank and served travelers on the Kings Road, a thoroughfare extending from the St. Marys River (near today's Florida-Georgia border) to St. Augustine.

Spotting the area's potential for growth once Florida passed into American hands, a local landowner named Isaiah D. Hart convinced his neighbors—most of whom had received their land in grants from the Spanish government—to part with some of their acreage. On this land Jacksonville was founded in June 1822. The first residents named their city to honor General Andrew Jackson, then provisional governor of Florida.

Despite its promising beginnings, Jacksonville struggled to survive its first decades. A hard freeze, followed by the onset of the Second Seminole War in 1835, slowed trade and settlement to a trickle. Though the city regained some momentum through the 1840s, a devastating fire and an outbreak of yellow fever in the 1850s further deterred growth. The city was sacked repeatedly by both Union and Confederate forces during the Civil War. In fact, the most decisive battle fought in Florida took place some 45mi west of Jacksonville in Olustee. Here in February 1864, some 5,000 Confederate troops defeated Union forces marching inland from Jacksonville and seeking to cut Confederate supply lines. Volunteers reenact that skirmish each February at **Olustee Battlefield State Historic Site** (off US-90, 14mi east of Lake City; open year-round daily 8am–5pm; closed major holidays; 🅿 ☎ 904-758-0400).

Despite these setbacks, Jacksonville flourished in the second half of the 19C. Citrus fruits from groves along the St. Johns River were shipped to market by steamboat, and lumber and naval stores industries grew and thrived. Residential communities developed on former plantation lands in the areas surrounding downtown. The city was linked by rail to Savannah in 1881, and grand wooden hostelries were constructed to accommodate an ever-increasing annual influx of wealthy visitors, whisked here by rail and steamboat from their homes in the north. One such visitor was noted author **Harriet Beecher Stowe** (p 33), who in 1867 purchased a home just south of Jacksonville in the community of Mandarin.

The city's heyday as a tourist destination came to an end in the late 1880s with the development of the Florida East Coast Railway, which engendered growth of more popular resort areas further south in St. Augustine and PALM BEACH. In 1888 a second deadly epidemic of yellow fever swept the population, forcing the temporary evacuation of the entire city. Nevertheless, the area's viability as a port grew as a system of jetties and dredging projects—at the mouth of the St. Johns River—later opened the waterway to deep-draft cargo vessels.

The Great Fire – On the afternoon of May 3, 1901, a fire broke out at the Cleveland Fibre Factory near downtown. A deadly gusting wind carried sparks to the dry wood and pitch rooftops of nearby buildings, and within an hour the city had erupted in flames. The conflagration consumed most of downtown Jacksonville and many residential areas. The worst disaster in Jacksonville's history, the fire nevertheless provided the city with an opportunity to transform itself. Architects and artisans flocked here, and a new downtown rose quickly from the ashes. Newspaperman H.L. Mencken, who had covered the fire for the Baltimore Morning Herald, reported that Jacksonville's population more than doubled in the decade following the fire.

By 1910 the city had become the winter headquarters of the fledgling motion-picture industry, as movie studios based in New York and Chicago set up shop to escape frigid northern temperatures. Several studios established themselves in Jacksonville year-round, and such popular stars as comic actor Oliver Hardy began their careers here. By 1920, however, Hollywood had bypassed Jacksonville as the center of the American motion-picture industry.

Other industry prospered and the city's population grew. From 1921 to 1954, four bridges were erected across the St. Johns River, replacing the slower ferry operations that had linked the north and south banks since Jacksonville's earliest days. The advent of World War II increased the tempo of industry, most notably at the numerous shipyards along the river.

Through the second half of the 20C, Jacksonville assumed the proportions of a modern metropolis. The **Port of Jacksonville**, extending along the banks of the St. Johns River between its main facilities at Talleyrand Docks and Blount Island, took its place among the Southeast's most important deepwater ports; Florida's three principal rail systems— CSX, Norfolk Southern and Florida East Coast—established headquarters here. High-rise buildings, most notably the **Gulf Life Tower** (1967; now Riverplace Tower) and **Independent Square** (1975; now Barnett Tower), rose along the downtown skyline.

Jacksonville Today – Thanks to a 1968 referendum that merged the governments of Jacksonville and Duval County, Jacksonville now ranks as the largest metropolitan region (in terms of area) in the US. In recent decades, many sections of the city have fallen victim to serious urban blight; public and private efforts to grapple with the problem have set numerous revitalization projects in motion. One example is the transformation of the old Union Station passenger terminal into the **Prime F. Osborn Convention Center**. The 1993 decision of the National Football League to locate a professional franchise in Jacksonville sparked expansion and improvements to the **Jacksonville Municipal Stadium** (formerly known as the Gator Bowl) and surrounding areas; the Jacksonville Jaguars played their first regular-season home game in September 1995.

Practical Information .... Area Code: 904

Getting There – **Jacksonville International Airport** (JIA): 10mi north of city; information ☏ 741-4902. Transportation to downtown via taxi *($22)*. Rental car agencies *(p 323)* located at airport. Amtrak **train** station: 3570 Clifford Ln. ☏ 800-872-7245. Greyhound/Trailways **bus** station: 10 N. Pearl St. ☏ 800-231-2222.

Getting Around – Local **bus service**: Jacksonville Transit Authority (JTA) *(year-round daily; 60¢ to city, $1.10 to beaches);* schedules and route information ☏ 630-3100. **Skyway Express** monorail travels between the Convention Center, Jefferson St., Hemming Plaza, Omni Hotel, San Marco and Florida Community College Jacksonville; *(year-round Mon–Thu 6:30am–7:30pm, Fri 6:30am–10pm & Sat 10am–10pm; every 4min; 25¢; ▣).* **Water taxi** departs from docks at Riverwalk and Jacksonville Landing *(year-round Sun–Thu 9am–11pm, Fri & Sat 9:30am–10pm; runs continuously; one-way 10min; $2; ঙ ▣)* Bass Marine Taxi ☏ 730 -8685. Downtown metered parking: 50¢/hr.

Visitor Information – **Jacksonville and the Beaches Convention and Visitors Bureau**, 201 E. Adams St., Jacksonville 32202 *(open year-round Mon–Fri 8am–5pm)* ☏ 798-9111 or 800-733-2668 (US and Canada). **Visitors Center**, 2 Independent Dr. in Jacksonville Landing *(open Mon–Sat 10am–8pm, Sun 12:30–5:30pm)* ঙ ☏ 791-4305. *This organization provides additional information regarding shopping, entertainment, festivals (p 318) and recreation.*

Accommodations – *(p 324)* Area visitors' guide including lodging directory available (free) from Jacksonville and the Beaches Convention and Visitors Bureau *(above).* Accommodations range from hotels ($80-$150) to motels ($35-$75) and bed-and-breakfast inns ($70-$185). Campgrounds and RV parks are also available in the area. *Rates quoted are average prices per night for a double room and are subject to seasonal variations.*

Sightseeing – By **riverboat cruise** *(round-trip 2hr 30min; commentary; lunch $22; dinner $33).* For schedules and reservations, call River Cruises ☏ 396-2333. Narrated evening **city walking tour** *(1hr; $6)* offered by Sideline Tours; for schedule and reservations ☏ 278-9409.

Shopping – Shops of Historic Avondale *(p 93)*, designer boutiques, antiques, restaurants; Jacksonville Landing *(p 92)*, specialty shops, restaurants, entertainment ☏ 353-1188; Avenue Mall (department stores, 110 specialty stores, eateries) ☏ 363-3060.

Entertainment – Consult the arts and entertainment section of *The Times-Union* (Friday) and *Travelhost* publication for schedules of cultural events. Florida Theatre *(p 92)*: Jacksonville Symphony Orchestra, Broadway shows, plays ☏ 355-2787; Theatre Jacksonville: drama, comedy and musicals ☏ 396-4425. Times-Union Center for the Performing Arts; for ticket and event information ☏ 633-6110. Free concerts at Jacksonville Landing, Center Courtyard ☏ 353-1188. For arts and sporting events tickets: **Ticketmaster** ☏ 353-3309.

Sports and Recreation – The area's miles of **beaches** offer swimming, surfing, boating and fishing. Boat rentals available at area marinas. **Spectator sports:** Jacksonville Jaguars (NFL) at Municipal Stadium ☏ 633-2000. Jacksonville Suns at Wolfson Baseball Park ☏ 358-2846. Many area **golf** clubs welcome visitors: Champions Club at Julington Creek ☏ 287-4653; Mill Cove Golf Club ☏ 646-4653; Jacksonville Beach Golf Course ☏ 247-6184. **Fishing**: Jacksonville Beach Fishing Pier *(daily 6am–9pm, until 10pm during summer months; $4; ✕ ঙ)* ☏ 246-6001.

DOWNTOWN *1 1/2 days. Map pp 94-95.*

Downtown Jacksonville's most popular gathering spots ramble along both banks of the St. Johns River as it wends its way through the city en route to the ocean. Shopping, entertainment and office facilities crowd the north side; the south bank offers chances to stroll along a boardwalk or browse through a museum. Privately operated water taxis *(p 91)* cruise across the river throughout the day, allowing visitors access to both banks without the annoying task of reparking the car. Water taxis also provide transportation to the stadium on game weekends.

North of the River

★**Jacksonville Landing** – *2 Independent Dr.* ☎ *904-353-1188.* This brightly lit, two-level, horseshoe-shaped building twinkles at the feet of the north bank's office towers. Completed in 1987 as part of the downtown's revitalization, Jacksonville Landing is one of the signature "festival marketplaces" developed by Rouse Corporation (creators of Boston's Faneuil Hall and Miami's Bayside Marketplace; *p 201*). It tempts shoppers with upscale boutiques and eateries.

After shopping, stroll the broad concrete walkways bordering the river for views of the opposite bank. When completed, the walkway will extend a full mile west to the **Cummer Museum** *(p 93)*, thereby creating a pedestrian link between the cultural center and the skyscrapers of downtown.

Jacksonville Landing

Jack Elka

Florida Theatre – *128 E. Forsyth St. Performances year-round. Access during non-performance times by appointment only.* ♿ *Box Office www.ftjax.com* ☎ *904-355-2787.* This historic Mediterranean Revival building (1927) is a survivor of America's era of opulent movie palaces. The theater closed as a movie house in 1980, but was renovated and reopened in 1983 as a performing-arts center hosting concerts, lectures and films. The lobby whimsically recreates a Moorish courtyard by night, with side balconies and deep blue ceilings.

★**Riverside/Avondale Historic District** – *Bounded by the St. Johns River on the south and by I-10 and I-95 on the north.* Jacksonville's showcase neighborhood of gracious historic homes offers a pleasant diversion, particularly for architecture buffs. A drive through the district's tree-shaded streets reveals a plethora of architectural styles that resulted from reconstruction in the wake of the 1901 fire. Mediterranean Revival, Art Deco, Queen Anne, Colonial Revival, Georgian Revival, Shingle, Tudor Revival, Prairie and Bungalow styles are represented. The largest and most grandiose manses occupy lots closest to the river.

Plantations flourished in this area immediately west of the river until the late 1800s, when a handful of profit-minded Yankees purchased large tracts of agricultural land, subdividing and selling them as residential plots to moneyed winter visitors. In the 1920s, another group of investors carved out a second exclusive neighborhood within Riverside's boundaries. Named **Avondale**, the community boasted a wealth of two-story Mediterranean Revival homes. Throughout subsequent decades, Avondale developed its own identity distinct from Riverside, and the two enjoyed a long heyday as Jacksonville's most desirable addresses. The entire area was placed on the National Register of Historic Places in 1985.

Visit – *1hr.* Riverside Avenue between Memorial Park and Van Wert Street is the backbone of the historic area; streets between here and the river retain the most elegant, best-preserved homes. **Memorial Park** *(1600 block of Riverside Ave.)*, recently rehabilitated and now a focal point for community events, was designed by Frederick Law Olmsted to commemorate Florida's World War I veterans. Nearby **Five Points** *(intersection of Park, Margaret and Lomax Sts.)* offers upscale shopping and dining in an eclectic, if run-down, historic setting.

Drive down **St. Johns Avenue** for a beautiful passage beneath canopies of enormous live oak trees. Some of the largest, most elaborate mansions survive along this broad thoroughfare. The avenue passes through the **Shops of Historic Avondale** *(St. Johns Ave. at Ingleside)*, a charming assemblage of quaint boutiques and upscale restaurants established in the 1920s.

Well worth a look is the looming **Riverside Baptist Church★** *(intersection of Park and King Sts.)*, a massive Mediterranean Revival edifice conceived by celebrated Florida architect Addison Mizner *(p 228)*.

★★Cummer Museum of Art and Gardens – *829 Riverside Ave., at Post St. Open year-round Tue & Thu 10am–9pm; Wed, Fri & Sat 10am–5pm; Sun noon–5pm. Closed major holidays. $5.* 🅿 *www.cummer.org* ☎ *904-356-6857.* This elegant museum houses a modest, but broad collection of European and American art and decorative arts. With its remarkable **riverfront setting** and its outstanding interactive arts education center, the Cummer boasts a reputation as one of Florida's best small art museums.

Following their marriage in 1897, Jacksonville residents Arthur and Ninah Cummer began construction of a grand Tudor Revival residence on the vast Riverside estate that belonged to Cummer's father, lumber baron Wellington W. Cummer. Indulging her passions for art and horticulture, Ninah planted formal gardens on the grounds fronting the river and decorated the house with works of fine art. Through her travels, she eventually acquired more than 65 paintings, tapestries and objets d'art. After Ninah's death in 1958, the house and art treasures were converted to a museum, as her will stipulated.

In the 1960s, the Cummer home was demolished and a new museum structure erected on the site. The original Italian and English formal gardens were retained, as was the mahogany-paneled Tudor Room. Through acquisitions and gifts in the years since Mrs. Cummer's death, the collection has expanded to more than 3,800 works.

Visit – *2hrs. Begin in the concourse gallery to the left of the entrance foyer.* Galleries are arrayed around an open courtyard so that by proceeding clockwise, visitors witness a progression of works from classical antiquity to the 20C. Two galleries facing the garden *(nos. 5 and 6)* are reserved for temporary exhibits.

After viewing pre-Columbian, Egyptian and ancient Roman artifacts in the concourse gallery, proceed through galleries 1 to 4 to see oil and tempera Gothic and Renaissance panels, and Renaissance, Baroque and Mannerist oil paintings. Highlights include *Madonna and Child* (c.1400) by Antonio Gaddi, woodcuts by Albrecht Dürer, and works by Cranach the Elder, Giorgio Vasari, Salomon van Ruysdael and Peter Paul Rubens.

The Wark collection of **early Meissen porcelain★★** occupies gallery 7 *(across the courtyard)*. Donated to the Cummer in 1965, the collection includes some 750 pieces of tableware dating from 1710-50, the first 40 years of European porcelain production. During this period, the factory in Meissen, Germany, was the first and only manufacturer of true, hard-paste white porcelain outside China. Don't miss the two complete 18C tea services, one owned by Marie, the last Queen of Hannover; and a dinner service owned by Elizabeth, Empress of Russia.

American art appears in galleries 8 and 9; paintings by Winslow Homer, Benjamin West, Gilbert Stuart and George Inness figure among the fine landscapes and portraits on view. A luminous trio of works by William-Adolphe Bouguereau highlights 19C European paintings in gallery 10, while gallery 11 offers selections from European and American Impressionism and contemporary art.

Horoldt Saucer, Meissen (c.1725)

Cummer Museum, Jacksonville

From the main galleries, the concourse gallery leads to **Art Connections** ★ **Kids**, the art education center where colorful, free-standing displays interpret art history, technique, composition, color and materials, using specific works from the Cummer collection as examples.

Formal Italian and English **gardens** behind the museum offer pergola-shaded paths among meticulously maintained greens and hedges, statuary and reflecting pools. Beyond the grounds rolls the St. Johns River.

South of the River

Riverwalk – The broad expanse of boardwalk extending 1.2mi along the south bank across from downtown draws joggers, strollers and noontime lunchers by day, meanderers by evening, and fun-loving revelers throughout the year during several annual festivals. The walk offers some of the best views of the river and the north bank, with Jacksonville Landing framed by gleaming office towers. Lovers of shipping and maritime lore will enjoy stopping in the **Jacksonville Maritime Museum (M¹)**, a small collection of artifacts presenting the city's maritime history (*1015 Museum Cir., Unit #2, at foot of Main St. Bridge; open year-round Mon–Sat 10:30am–3:30pm, Sun 1pm–5pm; closed Easter Sunday, Thanksgiving Day, Dec 25; & ▣ www.jaxmarmus.com ☎ 904-398-9011*). The **Jacksonville Historical Center (M²)** likewise presents the city's past from pioneer days to the present through artifacts, photographs and panel displays (*on Museum Cir., next door to Maritime Museum; open year-round daily noon–5pm; & ☎ 904-398-4301*).

Just west of the Main Street bridge lies Friendship Park, established in 1965; the geyser-like **fountain** at its center shoots jets of water high into the air.

★ **Museum of Science and History and Planetarium** – **Kids** *1025 Museum Cir. Open year-round Mon–Fri 10am–5pm, Sat 10am–6pm, Sun 1pm–6pm. Closed major holidays. $6. & ▣ www.jacksonvillemuseum.com ☎ 904-396-7062.* History is adventure and science is fun at this intriguing, hands-on museum housed in an attractive complex near the foot of Main Street Bridge. Here you can explore natural and physical sciences, regional natural history and North Florida's past through permanent and changing exhibits designed to appeal to all ages.

The first floor is devoted to science, its interactive stations revealing mysteries of chemistry, physics and biology. The outstanding **Atlantic Tails** exhibit studies threatened marine mammals inhabiting northeast Florida waters: whales, dolphins and manatees. **The Living World** houses a live-animal collection of creatures from water, land and air, while the conservation-oriented **Hixon Courtyard** displays a lush, landscaped floral garden. There's also an exhibit on bats.

Highlighting the museum's upper-level permanent displays is its new history exhibit, **Currents of Time: A History of Jacksonville and Northeast Florida**. Time travelers begin their journey around 12,000 BC. They trace the ancient culture of the riverine Timucuan Indians, follow early European exploration and settlement, and see Jacksonville destroyed by the great fire of 1901 but recover to become a thriving modern city by the turn of the 21C. Another installation is devoted to the **Maple Leaf**, a Civil War steamship sunk by a Confederate beer-keg "torpedo" in April 1864 in the St. Johns River off Mandarin Point. Preserved within the airless mud of the river bottom, the *Maple Leaf* harbors a priceless trove of artifacts.

The Alexander Brest Planetarium boasts a state-of-the-art sound system. Multimedia shows are held daily (*fee included in admission price; check at ticket office for show times*).

The Jacksonville Museum of Contemporary Art – *4160 Boulevard Center Dr. Open year-round Tue–Fri 10am–4pm (Thu 9pm), weekends 1pm–5pm. Closed major holidays. $3. & ▣ ☎ 904-398-8336.* Contemporary pieces and works by local and Florida artists highlight the offerings of this regional museum. Founded in 1924 as

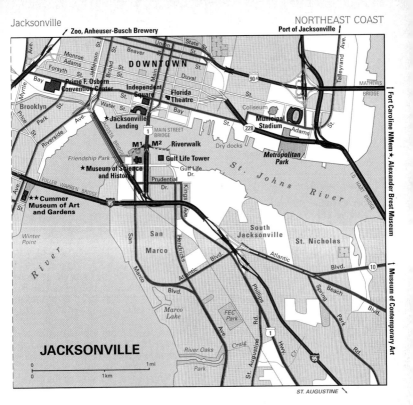

the Fine Arts Society, the museum is Jacksonville's oldest visual arts organization. A significant collection of pre-Columbian artifacts highlights the 1,500-piece permanent holdings, which also include works by Alexander Calder, Ellsworth Kelley and Helen Frankenthaler. A majority of exhibition space, however, is devoted to traveling shows, presentations drawn from the permanent collections, and temporary exhibits presenting works by local and regional artists. Some 15 shows are mounted annually, each for a period of six to eight weeks.

ADDITIONAL SIGHTS *1 day. Map p 97.*

Jacksonville Zoological Gardens – 🧒 *8605 Zoo Pkwy. From downtown, drive north on I-95 to Hecksher Dr./Exit 124. Turn right and continue .5mi to zoo. Open year-round daily 9am–5pm. Closed Thanksgiving Day and Dec 25. $6.50.* ✕ ⅋ 🅿 *www.jaxzoo.org ☎ 904-757-4463.* With more than 750 reptiles, birds and mammals thriving on a 73-acre site along the north bank of the Trout River, the Jacksonville Zoo ranks as a recognized leader in programs for botanical and zoological conservation; more than six endangered species have been successfully bred here in the recent years.

A special highlight is the **African veldt**, where a boardwalk leads out across a 16-acre grassy enclosure, home to lions, ostriches, gazelles and other animals commonly found on the Serengeti Plain. The **Seronera Overlook** puts visitors face-to-face with elephants keeping cool in a 275,000gal pool; the adjacent reptile house displays a collection of venomous snakes. At the new **Great Apes of the World** exhibit, only a thin pane of Plexiglas separates viewers from western lowland gorillas, chimpanzees and other large primates.

In the petting zoo at **Okavango Village**, kids encounter pygmy goats, miniature horses and other domestic animals of southern Africa. The village itself re-creates a fishing community in southwest Africa's Okavango River region. Footsore visitors can hop aboard the **Okavango Railroad** for a 1.3mi chug around a selection of the zoo's exhibits *(operates every half-hour; round-trip 30min; $5)*. Future zoo plans call for completion of a Florida Wetlands exhibit by early 1999 and a Land of the Maya display of Latin American animals by the end of that year.

Anheuser-Busch Brewery – *111 Busch Dr. From downtown Jacksonville, drive north on I-95 to Busch Ave. east/Exit 125 and follow signs. Open year-round Mon–Sat 9am–4pm. Closed major holidays.* ⅋ 🅿 *www.budweisertours.com ☎ 904-696-8373.* Fresh, yeasty aromas fill the air at this massive brewery north of downtown. Inside, a self-guided tour introduces the brewing and bottling processes and tells the long and colorful company history. In business since 1852, Anheuser-Busch Companies, Inc., operates numerous popular Florida theme parks, including SeaWorld *(p 131)*, Cypress Gardens *(p 120)* and Busch Gardens *(p 287)*.

Alexander Brest Museum – *2800 University Blvd. N., on the campus of Jacksonville University. Use north entrance to campus and bear left; follow signs to museum. Open year-round Mon–Fri 9am–5pm, Sat noon–5pm. Closed during Jacksonville University holidays.* ♿ 🅿 ☎ *904-744-3950.* A modest yet significant collection of decorative arts and pre-Columbian artifacts occupies four galleries of the university's Phillips Fine Arts Building. Most of the collection was acquired by Jacksonville engineer and businessman Alexander Brest, whose construction firm built much of the city's early road network. Be sure to see the **Tiffany and Steuben glass** and selected pieces of **Boehm porcelain** and intricately carved European and 17C-19C oriental **ivories**.

The small, wood-frame **cottage** just behind the Phillips building was occupied during the mid-1880s by English composer **Frederick Delius**, who settled in nearby Solano Grove while trying to establish himself as an orange grower. The cottage was moved here from Solano Grove in 1961.

★**Fort Caroline National Memorial** – *12713 Fort Caroline Rd. 13mi from downtown via Rte. 10A/115 east. Turn left (north) on Monument Rd. and follow signs to park. Open year-round daily 9am–5pm. Closed Dec 25.* ♿ 🅿 ☎ *904-641-7155.* This tiny, replicated fort on the south bank of the St. Johns River has a somber tale to tell. The fate of Fort Caroline mirrors the fate of 16C French attempts to gain sovereignty in the New World.

Historical Notes – Fort Caroline was established in 1564 by a band of some 300 Huguenots who arrived from France under the command of René de Laudonnière. Also on board was **Jacques Le Moyne**, a French artist assigned to document the expedition. The ships halted at the mouth of the St. Johns River and erected a triangular wooden fort some 5mi upriver.

Colonists were ill-prepared to forge a life in the New World, and starvation was rampant that spring of 1565. Disheartened, the French were preparing to abandon the colony when Huguenot mariner **Jean Ribault** arrived with a fleet of fresh supply ships from France.

Ribault brought disturbing news: The Spanish king had been alerted to the French presence at Fort Caroline and was sending an armada under the command of Pedro Menéndez de Avilés to attack the settlement. The Spanish arrived at the mouth of the St. Johns River shortly after Ribault, but the confrontation there proved inconclusive. Determined to attack the Spanish before they could return, Ribault set sail with most of his soldiers, only to be swept far south of his goal by hurricane winds. After establishing a beachhead at ST. AUGUSTINE, Menéndez marched north to Fort Caroline and slaughtered the French, sparing only the women and children. The 50-some men who escaped over the walls of the fort—de Laudonnière and Le Moyne among them—boarded two ships in the river and returned to France. Menéndez quickly garrisoned Fort Caroline and returned to St. Augustine.

The Spanish hastened to forestall Ribault and his men, who had been seen making their way up the coast on foot in two separate columns. Eventually they met a party of Frenchmen stranded on a riverbank about 18mi south of St. Augustine. Unarmed and starving, the French surrendered. Menéndez ordered them bound and ferried across the river; on the opposite bank, his soldiers fell on the prisoners with swords and bayonets. The second French column, Ribault among them, were similarly dispatched when they arrived several days later. Thereafter, the inlet, beach and river were known by the name *matanzas* (Spanish for "place of slaughters").

Fort Caroline (renamed San Matéo) remained a Spanish stronghold until 1568, when Dominique de Gourgues, a Catholic Frenchman on a mission of revenge, burned the fort to the ground, killing all of its occupants before he returned to France. The Spanish rebuilt the fort, only to abandon it the following year.

Visit – *1hr. Insect repellent strongly recommended.* Begin at the visitor center, where a short video recounts the story of Fort Caroline and of the French attempts to establish a stronghold in the New World. Artifacts on display include period weapons, tools, armor, navigational instruments and Timucuan Indian artifacts.

From the visitor center, a short path leads to the reconstructed fort. The present version, erected in 1964, is based on the drawings of the artist Le Moyne, and is estimated to be about two-thirds the size of the original. The actual site of Fort Caroline is believed to have been on a river plain that was eroded away by tides after the river channel was dredged and deepened in the 1880s.

A monument to Jean Ribault marks a scenic overlook on the St. Johns River, .5mi east of the park entrance.

THE BEACHES *1 day. Map p 97.*

Naval Station Mayport – *On Mayport Rd., 15mi from downtown. Take Atlantic Blvd. (Rte. 10) east to Mayport Rd. (A1A) and turn left; follow signs to entrance gate.* Commissioned in 1942, this bustling 3,409-acre military base at the mouth of the St. Johns River ranks among the largest naval installations in the US. Mayport is home base to five squadrons of Light Airborne Multipurpose System

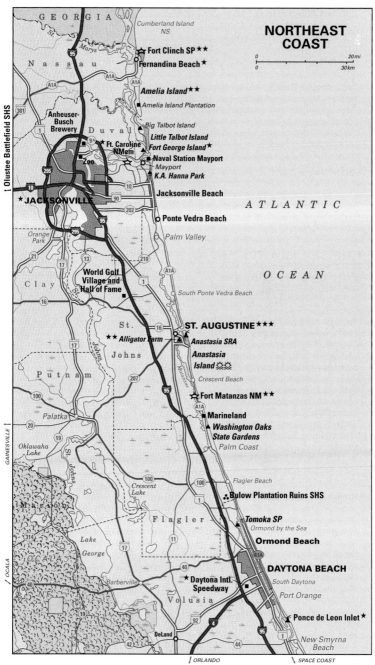

Mark III helicopters and 23 ships, including destroyers, frigates, guided-missile cruisers and an aircraft carrier. Through Mayport's weekend Visit **Ship** program, one vessel is made accessible for guided tours *(vessels change weekly; visit by 1 hr guided tour only, year-round Sat 10am–4pm, Sun 1pm–4pm;* ☎ *904-270-6289).* A red-brick lighthouse, erected in 1859, also stands on the property *(not open to the public).*

The historic fishing village of **Mayport** *(west of naval base via A1A)* offers rough charm in its narrow streets, shrimping vessels and "shrimp shacks" that serve up bounteous portions of fresh crustaceans. A1A crosses the St. Johns River via car ferry from Mayport landing to Fort George Island *(operates year-round daily 6:20am–10:15pm every half hour; one-way 10min; $2.50/car and driver one-way, 50¢/person one-way; St. Johns River Ferry Service* ♿ ☎ *904-241-9969).*

Kathryn Abbey Hanna Park – *500 Wonderwood Dr.; on A1A, south of Mayport Naval Station. Open year-round daily 8am–dusk. 50¢.* ⚠ ♿ 🅿 ☎ *904-249-4700.* A distinctly sylvan atmosphere lures visitors to this 450-acre oceanfront park. Named in memory of Florida historian and educator Kathryn Abbey Hanna, the park boasts a splendid white-sand **beach** minus the intrusive urban backdrop. Scenic hiking and biking trails lace the park.

Jacksonville Beach – *East of downtown via Rte. 90/Beach Blvd.* The bustling seaside community directly east of Jacksonville serves up traditional beach-town fare: swimwear and souvenir shops, high-rise hotels, fast-food restaurants and a broad, busy thoroughfare paralleling the coastline. A concrete boardwalk edges the beachfront between Fourth Avenue and the lifeguard station, offering vistas of horizontal sun worshippers who flock here on clear days, especially during weekends. At Fifth Avenue South, a long fishing pier juts into the ocean.

Ponte Vedra Beach – *From A1A south, bear left on Ponte Vedra Blvd.* Ranging along the coast south of Jacksonville Beach, this wealthy residential and resort community is home to some of the nation's most prestigious professional tennis organizations. From its headquarters in Ponte Vedra Beach, the Association of Tennis Professionals oversees some 87 tournaments on six continents; the Tournament Players Club is also located here.

THE SEA ISLANDS *1 day. Map p 97.*

★Fort George Island

20mi northeast of Jacksonville. From downtown take I-95 7mi north to Exit 124 (Heckscher Dr. east). Continue east 15mi to Fort George Rd. and turn left.

Though the lushly attractive sea island bordering the St. Johns River to the north holds secrets and stories dating from every phase of Florida's human history, Fort George Island bears relatively few marks of its long occupation. Timucuan Indians had lived here for as many as 3,500 years before the French—and later the Spanish—laid claim to Florida. Mission San Juan del Puerto (for which the St. Johns River was named) was founded in 1587 by Spanish monks, and it is thought that a fort established by British General James Oglethorpe was located near the center of the island, although no traces remain.

During the first half of the 19C, the island flourished as a profitable plantation. Today, Fort George Island seems to be making a return to the wilderness. Timucuan shell middens lie concealed beneath dense overgrowth; the elegant Sabal palms lining the avenue to Kingsley Plantation are nearly dwarfed by surrounding evergreens, and tall stands of pampas grass flourish on the fairways of the deserted Ribault Club, once an exclusive golf resort. The plantation, along with Fort Caroline *(p 96)*, lies on land protected by the 46,000-acre Timucuan Ecological and Historical Preserve.

★**Kingsley Plantation** – *11676 Palmetto Ave. From Fort George Rd. turn left onto unpaved Palmetto Ave. and continue 2mi to plantation. Open year-round daily 9am–5pm. Closed Dec 25.* 🅿 ☎ *904-251-3537.* The oldest remaining plantation house in Florida, and the best-preserved example of the plantation system that flourished in Florida's Territorial Period, lies at the end of a peaceful road through the forest canopy. Kingsley Plantation originally formed part of a land grant given by the king of Spain to John McQueen, who in the 1790s erected the stately plantation house that sits today near the edge of a peaceful marsh. The property was sold in 1804 and again in 1817—this time to Zephaniah Kingsley, a wealthy landowner and a member of the Florida Territory's Second Legislative Council. Convinced that the viability of Florida's plantations depended on the institution of slavery, Kingsley advocated lenient treatment of slaves, believing that such an attitude would perpetuate the slave system. A maverick for his time, Kingsley himself married an African woman, and acknowledged and provided for her and their four children. The plantation, one of Florida's most important producers of Sea Island cotton, was sold in 1839 to Kingsley's nephew and passed through several hands before being acquired by the state in 1955.

Visit – *1hr. Insect repellent highly recommended. Ranger information desk located at the main house.* Begin at the **main house**, where interpretive displays examine the Sea Island cotton industry and the life of Zephaniah Kingsley and his nephew, Kingsley Beatty Gibbs. Displays in the adjacent kitchen building recall the life of slaves at Kingsley Plantation. Ruins of 23 of the original 32 slave cabins—built of tabby, a compound of lime, sand and shells—stand in a semicircle near the entrance to the plantation site.

If you stay on Fort George Road instead of turning off for the plantation, **Fort George Island State Cultural Site** *(open daily year-round;* ♿ ☎ *904-251-2320)* offers a 4.4mi loop drive around the island with 28 numbered signposts marking points of historic interest *(self-guided tour booklets available at the Old Ribault Club, 1.5mi from entrance on right).*

Little Talbot Island *Just east of Fort George Island via A1A.*

Sheltering Fort George Island from the Atlantic's force, this 2,500-acre barrier island has remained free of development save for the facilities of **Little Talbot Island State Park**. Occupying the entire island, the park offers miles of pristine, white-sand beaches�& as well as a hiking trail (4.1mi) through live oaks and hollies in the hardwood hammock on the island's west side *(open year-round daily 8am–dusk; $3.25/vehicle;* ⅚ 🅿 ☎ *904-251-2320).*

On neighboring **Big Talbot Island** *(just northwest of Little Talbot Island via A1A),* large sections of the hammock are developed as private residences.

★★Amelia Island *42mi northeast of Jacksonville via A1A.*

Vacationers flock to this 13.5mi strip of barrier island occupying Florida's northeasternmost corner. Named for its beauty by General James Oglethorpe after Princess Amelia (daughter of King George II of England), the island is situated just across the St. Marys River from Georgia's Cumberland Island. Virgin beaches, salt marshes and hardwood forests attract nature lovers, while golf courses, championship tennis facilities and the resort amenities of the exclusive **Amelia Island Plantation** and **The Ritz-Carlton, Amelia Island** lure more sybaritic visitors. In the town of Fernandina Beach you'll find boutiques, specialty shops and an impressive array of Victorian houses within the 50-block Centre Street Historic District. Despite its popularity, the island feels but sparsely inhabited throughout the year.

★**Fernandina Beach** *– On the north end of Amelia Island. Follow A1A north and turn left on Atlantic Ave., which becomes Centre St.* Named for Ferdinand, consort to Queen Isabella of Spain, the town of Fernandina was established in the late 18C amid the marshes on the far northeastern end of Amelia Island. The town thrived as a port due to its location on the border between Spanish Florida and the US; smugglers routed their clandestine goods through here when Thomas Jefferson's Embargo Act of 1807 closed US ports to foreign shipping.

Fernandina's destiny changed forever with the arrival of Senator **David Yulee** (1810-1886; *p 72*) who had advocated Florida's entry into the Union in 1845 partly as a means of acquiring federal lands for a cross-state railroad. By 1853 Yulee was president of the Florida Railroad Company, formed to build the first cross-state railroad from Fernandina to CEDAR KEY on the Gulf of Mexico. When Fernandina's swampy location presented difficulties, Yulee persuaded residents to move the town south to its present location, where trade goods could be more easily transferred from rail car to cargo steamer.

Following the Civil War, Fernandina experienced a "Golden Age" of growth as shipping increased and tourists came to enjoy Florida's salubrious climate. Luxury hotels appeared, as did an abundance of elegant Victorian homes on the quiet avenues off Centre Street *(below)*. The development and application of fishing techniques around the turn of the century, including use of the offshore trawl, led Fernandina to proclaim itself the "birthplace of the modern shrimping industry."

The **Old Fernandina Depot** (1899) now houses the Chamber of Commerce, where walking-tour maps of the historic district are available *(102 Centre St., open year-round Sun–Fri 9am–5pm;* ⅚ 🅿 ☎ *904-261-3248).*

★**Centre Street Historic District** *– Along Centre St. between 11th St. and Front St., bounded on the north and south by Escambia and Elm Sts.* Specialty stores and late-19C facades draw droves of visitors to the cobbled sidewalks of historic Centre Street. Fernandina's principal east-west artery dead-ends at the waterfront overlooking the Amelia River. The street lies at the heart of a 50-square-block

Bailey House

area designated as a National Historic District for its outstanding collection of more than 450 structures built between 1873 and 1900, including excellent examples of Queen Anne and Italianate styles.

The heaviest concentrations of historic buildings lie along North Sixth and South Seventh streets, and along Centre Street itself. Most prominent is the red-brick **Nassau County Courthouse** *(Centre St. at 5th St.)*, an eye-catching Victorian structure built in 1891. Don't miss the **Tabby House** *(northwest corner of 7th and Ash Sts.)*, built in 1885 of tabby and Portland cement, the only house of its type in Fernandina. The 1895 **Bailey House** *(opposite the Tabby House)* sports the towers, asymmetric plan and fish-scale exterior paneling typical of the Queen Anne style. **Fairbanks House** *(corner of S. 7th and Cedar Sts.)*, a stunning Italianate home, was built by local newspaper editor George Fairbanks in 1885 as a surprise for his wife. Local legend holds that Mrs. Fairbanks hated the house, which thereafter became known as "Fairbanks' Folly." Both the Bailey and Fairbanks houses are now bed-and-breakfast inns. Also worth seeing is eclectic **Villa las Palmas** *(315 Alachua St.)*, a beautiful cedar-shingled residence that dates from 1910.

Amelia Island Museum of History – *233 S. 3rd St., 3 blocks south of Centre St. Visit by guided tour (1hr 15min) only, year-round Mon–Sat 11am & 2pm. $3. Library and 2nd floor open year-round Mon–Fri 10am–5pm. Closed major holidays.* ◫ ☎ *904-261-7378.* Lovingly refurbished, the former Nassau County Jail building today guards the history of Amelia Island. A departure from traditional museums, this "oral-history museum" features unlabeled artifacts, maps and displays. Background information is provided by docents who regale visitors with the story of Amelia Island, from the time of Native American habitation to the early 20C. Tours proceed at a leisurely pace through display rooms; a reference room stocked with historical information, maps and architectural documents is available to visitors. The museum also operates architectural and historical walking tours of sections of Fernandina Beach and Centre Street *(2hr guided walking tour departs from Old Depot at the foot of Centre St. year-round Mon–Sat; reservations required; $10).*

★★ **Fort Clinch State Park** – *2601 Atlantic Ave. Park entrance on north side of Atlantic Ave., just west of A1A. Park open year-round daily 8am–dusk. $3.25/vehicle.* ⚠️◫ *Fort open year-round daily 9am–5pm. $1.* ⚠️◫ ☎ *904-277-7274.* A handsome, well-preserved Civil War-era brick fort protects the northern tip of Amelia Island. Separated from Georgia only by the slow-moving waters of the St. Marys River, Fort Clinch was established in the late 1840s to protect Cumberland Sound, the gateway to Fernandina Harbor. The fort was named for General Duncan Lamont Clinch, a hero of the early Seminole Wars.

Work on the fort proceeded so slowly that it was incomplete and unfortified when the Civil War began in 1861. Confederate troops took Fort Clinch quickly and easily, installing gun batteries but suspending construction. The following year, the Georgia and South Carolina sea islands fell into Union hands, leaving Florida in isolation; the Confederates quickly withdrew.

By the time Fort Clinch neared completion in the late 1860s, it already was obsolete, its brick and masonry walls vulnerable to the high-velocity, heavier shot launched by newly invented rifle-barreled cannons. The federal government deactivated the fort in 1867, maintaining it without a garrison except for a brief time during the Spanish-American War. In the 1930s, the Florida park system purchased the property and engaged the Civilian Conservation Corps to construct roads and other facilities. Fort Clinch opened in 1938 as one of Florida's first state parks.

Visit – *1hr.* Displays in the visitor center outline US government defense systems prior to the 1840s, and detail the construction and armament of Fort Clinch. From the center, a short lime-rock path leads to the fort itself, its massive pentagonal walls interrupted only by a wooden drawbridge. Visitors are free to wander about the impressive four-acre interior, exploring rooms, bomb-proof shelters and officers' quarters, or to climb the ramparts for a view of Cumberland Island across the St. Marys River. Rangers in period dress offer daily living-history demonstrations, illustrating the life of soldiers billeted here. The park also offers beach access, fishing and nature trails.

ORMOND BEACH

Population 32,266
Map of Principal Sights p 3 – Map p 86
Tourist Information ☎ 904-677-3454

A seamless continuation of Daytona Beach, this small beach community was born when **Captain James Ormond**, a Scotsman from the Bahamas, built a 2,000-acre sugar plantation just north of here in 1815. The settlement began prospering when Henry Flagler brought his Florida East Coast Railway through in 1888. That same year he bought and expanded the Ormond Hotel (1875), which became a palatial establishment catering to wealthy winter vacationers.

Two of these early guests, automakers Alexander Winton and R.E. Olds (founder of Oldsmobile), decided in 1902 to race their cars on the wide, hard-packed sand of the beach. This spontaneous race (declared a tie) started the one-on-one, quarter-mile competition now known as drag racing. Many of the hotel's guests—with such names as Vanderbilt, Gould and Rockefeller—became patrons of the racers. In 1904 Henry Ford raced here, but slept in his car because he could not afford to stay at the Ormond. The hotel was razed in 1992; a condominium now stands in its place *(east side of Halifax River, just north of Ormond Bridge).* Today Ormond Beach welcomes more than 100,000 tourists each year.

SIGHTS *1/2 day. Map p 86.*

★**The Casements** – *25 Riverside Dr. (at Granada Blvd., just southeast of Ormond Bridge). Open year-round Mon–Thu 9am–9pm, Fri 9am–5pm, Sat 9am–noon. Closed major holidays.* ♿ ▯ ☎ *904-676-3216.* Now a cultural and civic center, this gracious 1912 mansion named for its many casement windows was the winter home of oil tycoon **John D. Rockefeller** (1839-1937) from 1918 until his death. Rockefeller entertained various celebrities here, including Will Rogers, Harvey Firestone and racer Sir Malcolm Campbell. In the decades after Rockefeller's death, the house went through several incarnations, becoming a women's junior college, a retirement home and an apartment hotel. Vandals partially destroyed it in the early 1970s, after which the city bought the house for $500,000 and began to restore it.

Tours *(Mon–Fri 10am–2:30pm)* take visitors through the second-floor Rockefeller room, which contains the tycoon's grand mirror and desk. The third floor houses a collection of Boy Scout memorabilia. From here, an octagonal stained-glass skylight casts a beam down to the first floor. A two-acre grassy garden across the street offers fine views of the river. The Casements also presents a full schedule of lectures, concerts and exhibits.

Tomoka State Park – *2099 N. Beach St. Open year-round daily 8am–dusk. $3.25/vehicle.* △ ♿ ▯ ☎ *904-676-4050.* Situated on a peninsula separating the Tomoka and Halifax Rivers, this park was the site of Nocoroco, a Timucuan village discovered by Spanish explorers in 1605. The area became part of an indigo plantation in the 18C. Now a peaceful preserve shaded by live oaks and watered by tidal creeks, the park boasts a tribute to its cultural heritage: a 40ft **outdoor monument**, entitled *The Legend of Tomokie*, by New York artist Fred Dana Marsh *(1.1mi from park entrance).* The visitor center contains other works by Marsh, who moved to Ormond Beach in the 1920s.

EXCURSIONS *Map p 97*

Bulow Plantation Ruins State Historic Site – *1hr. 12mi north in Bunnell. From Rte. 40, take US-1 (Old Dixie Hwy.) north 10.3mi to Old Kings Rd.; turn right and continue 2.5mi to park entrance on right. Follow one-lane Plantation Rd. 1mi to Bulow Creek. Ruins are located .5mi to left via road or nature trail. Open year-round daily 9am–5pm. $2/vehicle.* ▯ ☎ *904-517-2084.* Beside a tidal creek, Major Charles Bulow carved a plantation out of the wilderness in 1821 and planted it with sugar cane, rice, cotton and indigo. He died soon thereafter, leaving the property to his son John, who with the help of 200 slaves built a sugar mill. The Seminoles burned the plantation houses and mill in 1836 during the Second Seminole War. Today mossy stone **ruins** rear up from a ghostly forest that has repossessed the cleared fields. A glassed-in interpretive station beside the ruins limns the fascinating history of the plantation and its tragic destruction.

Washington Oaks State Gardens – *2hrs. 25mi north in Palm Coast. From Rte. 40, take A1A north to park entrance on left at 6400 N. Ocean Shore Blvd. Open year-round daily 8am–dusk. $3.25/vehicle.* ▯ ☎ *904-446-6780.* Spreading from the Matanzas River to the Atlantic Ocean, this 400-acre preserve displays horticultural beauty along a fairly undeveloped stretch of coast. A surveyor named George Washington, relative of the first US president, married the daughter of the plantation's original owner. In 1936 the gardens and groves were bought by Owen Young, chairman of the board of General Electric, whose widow donated the property to the State of Florida in 1964.

Paths thread the formal gardens that highlight the park, passing reflecting pools, camellias, azaleas and roses. Visitors can obtain good views of the tranquil Matanzas River and the tidal marsh from the Indian shell mound in the rose garden, or from the small interpretive center. Across A1A, a boardwalk leads to the **beach**. *Swimmers should beware of submerged rocks.*

ST. AUGUSTINE***

Population 12,167
Map of Principal Sights p 3 – Map p 103
Tourist Information ☎ 904-829-1711 or 800-653-2489 (US & Canada)

The oldest continuously occupied European settlement in the US lies on Florida's east coast, 33mi south of Jacksonville. Situated on a finger of land extending south from the mainland, between the Matanzas River on the east and the San Sebastián River on the west, historic St. Augustine mingles humble, one-story 18C structures with architectural showpieces from the 19C, cheek-by-jowl with 20C tourist attractions. The city's distinctive, time-burnished flavor is captured in narrow, cobbled lanes bordered by red-roofed buildings of pale coquina, many of them survivors of the 18C.

Historical Notes

European Tug of War – On September 8, 1565, five Spanish ships commanded by **Pedro Menéndez de Avilés** dropped anchor near the present-day harbor of St. Augustine. Menéndez' mission as *adelantado*, or lord, of Spanish Florida (a title conferred upon him by King Philip II of Spain) was to rid the territory of "heretical" French Huguenots who claimed it as their own, and to establish two cities as footholds of the Spanish empire. Menéndez had sighted the harbor several days earlier, en route from Puerto Rico to confront the Huguenot forces of Jean Ribault at Fort Caroline (p 96).

After a fruitless skirmish near the St. Johns River, the Spanish ships fell back, landing here near the Timucuan village of Seloy. About 600 settlers unloaded their belongings onto the marshy coast and set about building a fort between the Matanzas and San Sebastián rivers. The new colony was named St. Augustine in honor of the patron saint of Avilés, Menéndez' hometown. Menéndez himself eventually set sail for Havana after slaughtering Jean Ribault and his followers at the mouth of the river thereafter called Matanzas (Spanish for "place of slaughters") to commemorate the bloody event.

St. Augustine's first European residents were plagued by problems from the outset. Although Florida's strategic importance near the shipping lanes between Europe and the Caribbean was undeniable, Spain was slow to dispatch supplies, manpower and money to the colonists. Ill-equipped to raise or procure food in the new land, settlers plundered the stored harvests of the Indians. In retaliation, the natives drove colonists from their homes to the dubious shelter of their flimsy wooden fort.

In 1586, English raider **Francis Drake** paid a brief but devastating visit to St. Augustine, destroying crops and buildings, chopping down orange trees and sailing off with money earmarked for soldiers' salaries. Though Menéndez had established the seat of Spanish government farther north at the coastal settlement of Santa Elena, Indian hostilities forced the abandonment of that village, and in 1587 St. Augustine became the capital of Spanish Florida.

Subsequent years brought a measure of peace between the natives and the Spanish, in concert with the success of Franciscan missionary efforts among the Timucuans. Beginning in 1573, a chain of some 100 missions grew slowly northward along the coast from flourishing Nombre de Dios (p 112) in St. Augustine, westward to the Apalachee Province near present-day TALLAHASSEE. By the early 18C, the missions had disappeared, victims of British raids and deterioration by the elements.

During the first half of the 17C, epidemics of measles, yellow fever and smallpox took their toll on the Indians, whose immune systems were unable to withstand white man's diseases. Although the Indian threat was thus reduced, Spain's tenuous foothold in the New World was further beleaguered by new French and English settlements along the coastline to the north. The European challenge to Spain's sovereignty grew imminent in 1670 when England founded the Carolina colony, with its capital at Charles Town some 275mi north. Consequently, St. Augustine's governor began construction on a massive stone fort, Castillo de San Marcos (p 106).

Vast deposits of **coquina**, a stone created by the sedimentation of seashells, had been discovered on nearby Anastasia Island; the water-soaked stone was soft, but it hardened as it dried, proving to be an ideal material with which to build a permanent fortification. Rising ever higher above Matanzas Bay, the Castillo's walls gave the town a new air of solidity and strength during the waning years of the 17C. A relaxation of restrictions on the use of coquina for other-than-official construction enabled townspeople to replace their rotting wooden residences with more substantial dwellings of coquina blocks.

In 1702 in the wake of new alliances between the French and Spanish in Europe, **James Moore**, governor of the Carolina colony, made plans to invade St. Augustine before it could be fortified by the French. As the settlers gathered their meager supplies and took refuge in the partially completed Castillo, two separate forces of British soldiers moved on the city by land and by sea. A state of siege existed for nearly two months while the British tried unsuccessfully to penetrate the fortress walls. Upon arrival of Spanish reinforcements from Cuba, Moore's troops gave up, burning most of the buildings before they retreated. In the years following Moore's withdrawal, a line of earthworks and other barriers rose north of town, spanning the peninsula from the bay to the San Sebastián River. Earthen defenses proved crucial when, a year after war was declared between England and Spain in 1739, the forces of British General **James Oglethorpe** marched on St. Augustine. Oglethorpe, who had founded a settlement at the Savannah River in 1733 with

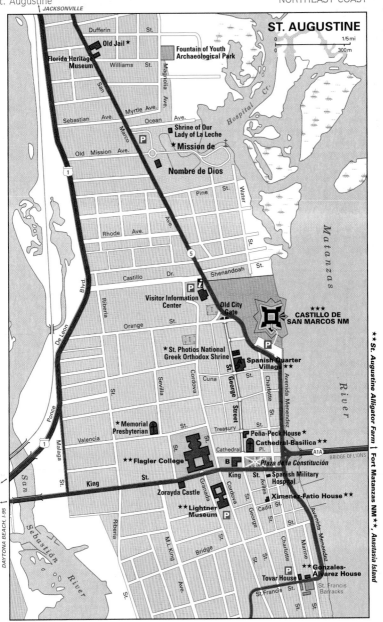

plans to further infiltrate Spanish territory, established camps on Anastasia Island and in the forests north of town. Again residents took refuge in the Castillo amid a hail of shells from British guns; once more, help arrived from Cuba, soon forcing Oglethorpe's retreat.

Although St. Augustine prospered for two decades after Oglethorpe's attack, peace did not come until hostilities ended between England and Spain in 1763. By the terms of the **Treaty of Paris**, Spain relinquished possession of Florida to England in exchange for Cuba, which had been captured by the British earlier in the course of the conflict. By the stroke of a pen, the British had finally taken St. Augustine.

British St. Augustine – Terms of the treaty permitted residents of Spanish Florida to remain, but most chose to leave rather than swear loyalty to the British Crown. After entrusting the sale and disposition of their property to agents, nearly 3,000 Spanish citizens sailed from Florida to reestablish themselves in Cuba and the West Indies.

British soldiers and settlers who arrived in St. Augustine found the vacant city rather primitive for all its nearly 200 years of existence. Fires, floods, hurricanes, disease, overdependence on aid from Spain, and conflicts with native and foreign powers had all prevented true development. The first British governor, General James Grant, turned his attention to the exploitation of Florida's fertile soil, something the Spanish had never undertaken. Pursuing a program of plantation development, Grant conferred huge land grants upon wealthy British citizens. These slaveowners put their laborers to work clearing forests, draining swamplands and planting export crops such as rice and indigo. The British settlers founded public schools and erected many new buildings, including a Masonic lodge. New roads connected St. Augustine with outlying plantations and other British colonies to the north.

Although rebel activity began to increase throughout British North America in the mid-18C, St. Augustine was never central to either British or rebel strategy during the American Revolution. The city instead became a training ground for forces preparing to defend Florida. Mercantile activity reached a fever pitch to supply the war effort. St. Augustine's ranks swelled with Loyalist refugees from Savannah and Charleston, as well as British troops and captured rebels.

In 1783 the British governor received word that Florida was to be transferred back to Spain under the terms of the new Treaty of Paris, by which Great Britain formally acknowledged American independence. British residents thus made plans to evacuate the city.

Second Spanish Period and Americanization – Despite the new Spanish governor's efforts to repopulate St. Augustine with Spanish residents, only a handful of those who had evacuated 20 years earlier chose to return. During the second Spanish period, St. Augustine was peopled by a cosmopolitan hodgepodge of Spanish, English, American, Minorcan, Italian, Greek, Swiss, German, French and Scottish settlers. Slaves and free blacks—attracted to St. Augustine by Spain's liberal policies—added to the town's ethnic mix, as did Seminole Indians. Though most British residents chose to leave in 1784, a substantial number remained, most of them landowners who elected to swear allegiance to Spain rather than abandon their plantations. The naval-stores industry developed as residents exploited outlying pine forests for export products, but the Spanish were, as before, unable to maintain economic independence. As trade with the American states to the north increased, St. Augustine's Spanish culture declined.

As Spanish power lessened through the first part of the 19C, the American states to the north grew more populous and their residents became hungrier for territory. Upon ratification of an 1819 treaty by which Spain ceded Florida to the US, the American flag rose over the Castillo, which was renamed Fort Marion.

Americans arriving in St. Augustine found the city in shambles, its Spanish residents having neglected repairs and improvements once Americanization became certain. Despite an epidemic of yellow fever in late 1821 and the transfer of Florida's territorial capital to Tallahassee in 1824, the city's population increased. Soldiers billeted to defend America's new territory during the Second Seminole War arrived in droves, along with new residents and winter visitors eager to enjoy Florida's climate.

The Civil War effectively stemmed the flow of tourists to St. Augustine. Considered a military backwater, the city languished through the 1860s. The end of the war brought an improved rail line to the city from the St. Johns River, but it was the resumption of the tourist trade—and the arrival of one tourist in particular—that spurred St. Augustine's economic recovery after the war.

Henry M. Flagler (c.1905)

The Flagler Era – The son of an itinerant Presbyterian minister, **Henry Morrison Flagler** (1830-1913) was born in Hopewell, New York, into a family of four children. At the age of 14, sick of school, young Henry set out to Ohio to make his fortune. There he landed a job in a general store for $5 a month, and soon developed a knack for salesmanship. Eventually, Henry tried his hand in the grain and salt industries before entering into partnership in 1867 with his friend, wealthy industrialist John D. Rockefeller. Their oil refinery, incorporated in 1870 as Standard Oil Company, established the massive fortunes of these two influential men.

Flagler visited Florida in 1877 on the advice of doctors treating his invalid wife, Mary; their cure for her chronic respiratory ailment was an extended winter holiday in a warm climate. Widowed by

Henry Morrison Flagler Museum Archives

1883, Flagler returned to Florida to honeymoon in St. Augustine with his second wife—Mary's former nurse, Ida Alice Shourds. On that visit, the businessman shrewdly observed that while St. Augustine's agreeable climate drew crowds of wealthy winter visitors, the city offered poor amenities and few amusements. Two years later, Flagler had hatched a plan to erect a large luxury hotel and make other improvements to the city's infrastructure—all in the interest of transforming St. Augustine into an elegant resort city rivaling France's Riviera. Part of his plan involved erecting a bridge over the St. Johns River to the north, purchasing and improving the railway leading from the bridge to St. Augustine, and thus linking the city for the first time with the populous centers of the Eastern seaboard.

Flagler's massive **Ponce de Leon Hotel** *(p 109)* and its second, less elegant counterpart, the Hotel Alcazar *(p 110)*, attracted throngs of winter visitors to St. Augustine. By 1889 he had purchased the Casa Monica Hotel, another large property next to Hotel Alcazar; this triumvirate of grand hotels was the basis of St. Augustine's brief heyday as Florida's premier resort destination. The former oil magnate eventually acquired and consolidated several additional rail lines to form the Florida East Coast Railway, extending south from DAYTONA to MIAMI via PALM BEACH. Flagler, whose second wife lapsed into incurable insanity, divorced and married a third time and spent the rest of his life developing resort areas in south Florida. Upon his death in 1913, his remains were returned to St. Augustine and interred at Memorial Presbyterian Church *(p 110)*.

Practical Information.. Area Code: 904

Getting There – **Jacksonville International Airport** (JIA): 52mi north of St. Augustine via US-1; information ☏ 741-4902. Transportation to St. Augustine *(advance reservations required)*: East Coast Transportation *($70/1-3 people)* ☏ 246-3741, or Dial-a-Ride *($55/1-2 people)* ☏ 829-0880. Rental car agencies *(p 323)* located at airport. Nearest Amtrak **train** station in Palatka ☏ 800-872-7245. Greyhound/Trailways **bus** station: 1000 Malaga St. ☏ 800-231-2222.

Getting Around – Visitors are encouraged to park in the Visitor Information Center parking lot. Parking regulations are strictly enforced; yellow curbs indicate no-parking zones.

Visitor Information – **St. Johns County Visitors and Convention Bureau**, 88 Riberia St., Suite 250, St. Augustine 32084 ☏ 829-1711 or 800-653-2489 (US and Canada). **City of St. Augustine Visitors Information Center**, 10 Castillo Dr., near San Marco Ave. *(open Apr–May daily 8:30am–6:30pm; Jun–Labor Day daily 8am–7pm, early Sept–Oct daily 8:30am–6:30pm; rest of the year daily 8:30am–5:30pm; ✕ ⅃ ▣ [$3])* ☏ 825-1000. *The above organizations provide additional information regarding shopping, entertainment, festivals (p 318) and recreation.*

Accommodations – *(p 324)* Area visitors' lodging directory available (free) from St. Johns County Visitors and Convention Bureau *(above)*. Accommodations range from hotels ($55–$100) to moderate motels ($40–$55) and bed-and-breakfast inns ($50–$275). KOA **campground**: St. Augustine Beach ☏ 471-3113; RV and camping at Indian Forest Campground ☏ 824-3574. *Rates quoted are average prices per night for a double room and are subject to seasonal variations.*

Sightseeing – Narrated **trolley tours** of historical district offer on-and-off privileges *(depart from Old Jail complex year-round daily 8:30am–5pm; every 15-20min; call for schedule and admission fees)* ☏ 829-3800. Sightseeing **trains** depart from eight different stations and stop at attractions, shops and restaurants; tickets valid for three consecutive days *(depart from 170 San Marco Ave. and seven other stations year-round daily 8:30am–5pm; every 15-20min; $12; package tours from $22–$62; ⅃)* ☏ 829-6545. Guided **walking tours** of Old St. Augustine *(year-round daily 8pm; $5)*. Ancient CityTours ☏ 797-5604. **Horse-drawn carriage tours** *(year-round daily 8:30am–dusk; round-trip 1hr; $15 with a $50 minimum)* by Colee's Sightseeing Carriage Tours ☏ 829-2818. Scenic **cruises** leave from Municipal Marina *(year-round daily 11am–4:30pm, extended hours during summer months, additional cruises mid-May–mid-Oct; round-trip 1hr 15min; $9.50; ⅃ ▣)* ☏ 824-1806.

Sports and Recreation – St. Augustine Beach pier and the lighthouse pier offer excellent **fishing**; bait and tackle shop at 442 Ocean Vista Ave. Some area **golf** clubs welcome visitors: St. Augustine Shores Golf Club ☏ 794-GOLF; St. Johns County Golf Course ☏ 825-4900. **Shopping**: St. George Street in the historic district ☏ 829-1711; Lightner Antique Mall ☏ 824-2874; St. Augustine Outlet Center (more than 90 factory outlet stores) ☏ 825-1555.

By the turn of the century, Flagler's dream of an American Riviera at St. Augustine had fizzled, but the city had begun to rely on tourism as its economic mainstay, capitalizing on its long history and miles of unspoiled beaches. Museums, casinos and other attractions sprouted up, both in town and on Anastasia Island, and national recognition of St. Augustine's historical importance sparked research, preservation and restoration throughout the 20C.

The Oldest City – Today the moniker "America's Oldest City" attracts nearly two million visitors annually to St. Augustine. Many of the city's historic structures have been purchased by organizations or individuals to be operated as tourist attractions, occasionally at some sacrifice of authenticity. In recent years, a cornucopia of private collections have also been established as museums and appear throughout the city's historic areas. Though the apparent credo, "The older it is, the better it is," has resulted in an overabundance of sights with the word "oldest" in their titles, several—such as the Oldest House *(p 111)*, the Oldest Wooden Schoolhouse *(14 St. George St.)* and the Oldest Store Museum *(4 Artillery Ln.)*—are well worth a peek for their depictions of various periods in St. Augustine's long and tumultuous history.

SIGHTS *4 days. Map p 103.*

Begin your visit at the large, modern **Visitors Information Center** *(p 105)*, where knowledgeable staff will answer questions, make reservations and offer discount tickets to most of St. Augustine's attractions. This is also a good place to obtain tickets for any of the privately owned **sightseeing trains** *(p 105)* that tour the city throughout the day, stopping at points of interest. A small theater here screens *Dream of Empire*, a 50-minute dramatization of the founding and settling of St. Augustine *($3; admission included in parking fee)*.

Castillo and St. George Street Areas

Following a visit to the Castillo, a slow meander down **St. George Street** offers the best exposure to St. Augustine past and present. This backbone of the old city manages to retain its historic flavor despite a plethora of gift shops, craft boutiques, restaurants and other commercial establishments catering to the tourist trade. Many of these occupy restored 18C buildings. St. George Street is closed to vehicular traffic between the Old City Gate *(north end of St. George St. at intersection with Orange St.)* and the **Plaza de la Constitución** *(bounded by St. George, King and Charlotte Sts. and Cathedral Pl.)*, a broad plaza laid out as a parade ground by Governor Mendez de Canzo about 1600.

★★★**Castillo de San Marcos National Monument** – *1 Castillo Dr. S. at Orange St. Open year-round daily 8am–4:45pm. Closed Dec 25. $4. Cannon firings mid-May–Labor Day weekends 11am & 1:30pm, 2:30pm, 3:30pm; rest of the year once a month. Living-history reenactments throughout the year; call for schedules.* P *www.nps.gov/casa* ☎ *904-829-6506.* Defender of St. Augustine since the beginning of the 18C, the oldest masonry fort in the US stolidly overlooks Matanzas Bay at the northern boundary of the old city. The Castillo withstood every enemy attack that beset it and today ranks among the best-preserved examples of Spanish colonial fortifications in the New World.

Castillo de San Marcos

A Fortress of Stone – Until the mid-17C, the Spanish defense system in St. Augustine relied on a series of rickety wooden stockades that were poorly manned and vulnerable to termites, rot and enemy fire. The increasing threat from English, Dutch and French forces, coupled with a devastating pirate raid in 1668 that left the town a smoldering ruin, convinced Spanish officials in Madrid that St. Augustine needed a permanent stone fortification. Money and manpower were provided, and by 1671 rafts had begun ferrying blocks of coquina to the site from deep quarry pits on Anastasia Island.

Construction continued fitfully through the end of the 17C, but by 1695 the fort was largely complete. Four-sided, with pointed triangular bastions at each corner, the structure boasted 12ft-thick outer walls broken only by an iron portcullis. The outwardly sloping lower walls were designed to counter artillery fire. A massive wooden drawbridge traversed a broad moat. During the 19C, barrel-vaulted rooms were added in the space between the inner and outer walls. A coquina gatehouse was erected beyond the drawbridge, and an earthen embankment, or glacis, rose outside the moat.

By 1702 the fort had proven its worth, sheltering St. Augustine's residents within its walls as the troops of English General James Moore sacked the town. A more serious threat loomed in 1740, when English warships under the command of General James Oglethorpe appeared in the harbor. England saw the Spanish fort as a threat to land it claimed in Georgia, and for 27 days the warships bombarded the Castillo. Their cannonballs sank into the soft coquina walls, however, and did little damage.

The Castillo was handed over to British authority on July 21, 1763, the day possession of Florida was transferred from Spain to Great Britain. Renamed Fort St. Mark and fortified against siege during the American Revolution, the structure was recovered by Spain at the close of the war. In 1821 the Spanish flag was lowered here for the last time as Spain ceded Florida to the United States. The Castillo, renamed Fort Marion after Revolutionary War commander Francis Marion (the legendary "Swamp Fox"), served as a military prison until the early 20C. In 1924 it was designated a national monument.

Visit – *1.5hrs.* Begin by attending one of the ranger talks or audiovisual programs held several times daily in one of the barrel-vaulted storage rooms surrounding the interior courtyard *(10am, 11am, 2pm & 3pm; 20-30min)*. Other rooms contain displays describing various periods of the fort's history. Don't miss the excellent presentation of ordnance used at the fort; from this display, you must stoop to enter a low passageway leading to the powder magazine deep in the northeast bastion. A long stairway ascends to the **gundeck**, outfitted with some of the Castillo's original cannons and mortars. A panoramic **view** from here demonstrates the ease with which sentries could monitor an intruder's approach.

Old City Gate – *North end of St. George St.* This handsome pair of coquina pillars supported a gate that served as the only entrance to the city through the Cubo Line, a wood-and-earthwork fortification erected after Gen. James Moore attacked it in 1702. The wall extended from the Castillo to the San Sebastián River. The present coquina structures were built in 1808.

★**St. Photios National Greek Orthodox Shrine** – *41 St. George St. Open year-round daily 9am–5pm. Closed Easter Sunday & Dec 25.* & ☎ *904-829-8205.* The only national shrine of the Greek Orthodox Archdiocese of North and South America occupies Avero House, an unassuming white historic residence on the east side of bustling St. George Street. Dedicated in 1971 to the first Greek settlers in the New World, the shrine honors St. Photios, the Ecumenical Patriarch of the Greek Orthodox Church. In 1768 Andrew Turnbull, a London physician interested in the settling of Florida, enlisted nearly 2,000 Greeks, Minorcans, Corsicans and Italians to leave their troubled homelands for a stab at life in the New World. When living conditions at their New Smyrna colony (75mi south of St. Augustine) became unbearable, the surviving settlers fled north in 1777 and established a center for worship in the former Avero residence. The building passed through several owners before the Greek Orthodox Church purchased it in 1966. It was restored in 1982.

Exhibits in the display area tell the story of New Smyrna colony and the role of its survivors in the development of St. Augustine. In the serene shrine chapel, glimmering candles illuminate 30 **frescoes**, designed and executed in the Byzantine style by George Filippakis. Highlighted in gold leaf, the frescoes depict Christian saints and scenes from the life of Christ.

★★**Spanish Quarter Village** – *33 St. George St. Open year-round daily 9am–5pm. Closed Dec 25. $6 includes all sights in the Spanish Quarter.* ☎ *904-825-6830.* Behind a low wall fronting St. George Street, the heart of colonial St. Augustine beats on in a living-history museum dedicated to re-creating the 18C city. Within, eight structures have been rebuilt according to historical and archaeological research sponsored by the Historic St. Augustine Preservation Board. After entering through Florencia House, visitors are free to meander about the grassy "streets" of St. Augustine c.1740. The dwellings of a foot soldier, an artillery sergeant and a cavalryman emphasize variations in wealth, rank and status of soldiers based at the Castillo. A sweating smithy works his craft in the restored **blacksmith shop**, while costumed interpreters demonstrate spinning, carpentry, basketry and other daily activities of 18C life, highlighting the struggle to feed, clothe, house and otherwise provide for the residents of the new city.

★ **De Mesa-Sanchez House (A)** – *Visit by guided tour (20min) only, year-round daily 10am–5pm. Closed Dec 25.* ♿ ☎ *904-825-6830.* One of the city's fine restored historic residences, this handsome structure began as a one-room coquina dwelling built to house the family of Antonio de Mesa, a shoreguard stationed at the Castillo during the first Spanish period. Guides in period dress recount the house's long history of changes and additions over the ensuing decades, during which it served as a residence, boarding house, barber shop, store and restaurant. The house appears today as it might have in the 18C. Of special interest is a large display of kitchen tools; these cleverly devised implements bear witness to the ingenuity of St. Augustine's early residents.

★ **Peña-Peck House** – *143 St. George St. Visit by guided tour (30min) only, year-round Mon–Sat 10am–4:30pm, Sun noon–4pm. Closed major holidays. $2.50.* ☎ *904-829-5064.* Erected in the 1740s as the official residence of Spanish St. Augustine's royal treasurer, this gracious two-story edifice began as a simple, U-shaped building similar to those found throughout the city during the first Spanish period. It was renovated during the late 1830s by Dr. Seth Peck, a New Englander, for use as a medical office; a second story was added to accommodate the doctor's family.

The house remained in the Peck family until 1931, when ownership was willed to the city by Anna Gardner Burt, granddaughter of Seth Peck. Today members of the Women's Exchange offer guided tours of the house, which is partly furnished with Peck family heirlooms transported from New England in the 1830s.

★★ **Cathedral-Basilica of St. Augustine** – *North side of Plaza de la Constitución. Open year-round daily 9am–5pm.* ♿ ☎ *904-824-2806.* The scalloped facade and tower gracing the north side of the Plaza de la Constitución mark the home of the parish of St. Augustine. This parish is considered to have been founded in 1565 at the first Mass said upon the landing of Pedro Menéndez de Avilés, and therefore ranks as the oldest Catholic parish in the nation.

The British later burned the beleaguered church and monastery at St. Augustine. The parish church was abandoned and relocated numerous times throughout the 18C. Not until 1793 did diocesan authorities commission a permanent structure of coquina north of the plaza. An 1887 fire destroyed all but the walls and facade of this church. Noted architect James Renwick—who was visiting St. Augustine at the time of the fire—aided in the reconstruction, enlarging the structure and adding a transept and a bell tower. Additional renovations and modifications to the facade were effected in the 1960s, and the cathedral was designated a Minor Basilica in 1976.

Inside, massive decorated timbers support the lofty ceiling above floors of colorful Cuban tile. A large, ornamental reredos of gold and white wood—incorporating the marble altar table from the original church—highlights the sanctuary.

★ **Government House Museum (B)** – *48 King St. Open year-round daily 9am–5pm. Closed Dec 25. $3.* ♿ ☎ *904-825-5079.* Despite the fact that portions of the walls and original foundations of this stately, two-story masonry edifice have overlooked the Plaza de la Constitución since the late 16C, Government House has retained its official purpose throughout nearly 400 years of existence.

The first construction on the site appeared in 1599 as part of a program to extend and rebuild the city in the wake of a fire and a hurricane. St. Augustine's Governor Gonzalo Méndez de Canzo stipulated that a parade ground be laid out and surrounded by various governmental buildings, among them his own wooden residence. Méndez' house subsequently became the official governor's residence and a center of administrative activities. A crumbling hulk by 1687, it was rebuilt of more durable coquina, but succumbed to fire during the British attack on St. Augustine in 1702. Rebuilt by 1713, it was renovated by the Spanish government in 1759 and again in the late 18C. After 1821 the US government used the structure as a courthouse, post office and civil services building; in 1936 the Post Office Department began restoring the edifice to its 1764 appearance. Today Government House serves as a museum and headquarters of the Historic St. Augustine Preservation Board.

Visit – *1hr.* Inside, a small museum provides a comprehensive look at the development of St. Augustine. Colorful displays describe the cultural collage of settlers during the various periods of history and present aspects of life in the new settlement, including commerce, social structure, architecture and entertainment.

King Street Area

★★Flagler College – *74 King St. Open May–Aug daily 10am–4pm. Rest of the year daily 10am–3:30pm.* ♿ *www.flagler.edu* ☎ *904-829-6481.* Formerly the Ponce de Leon Hotel, this grand edifice was the cornerstone of Henry Flagler's master plan to transform St. Augustine (and with it, much of Florida) into an American resort destination. The striking Spanish Renaissance building today houses the residence facilities, dining room and lecture halls of Flagler College.

Cast in Concrete – At the time of Flagler's first visit to St. Augustine in the winter of 1876-77, wealthy visitors lodged mainly in large, multi-story hotels built of flammable pitch-pine lumber. Flagler determined that his Ponce de Leon Hotel would be a grand, permanent structure, designed and constructed to withstand the passage of time while reflecting St. Augustine's Spanish architectural heritage. Villa Zorayda *(p 110)* offered the model: cast-in-place concrete construction. Flagler promptly hired Thomas Hastings and John M. Carrère, an inexperienced team of young architects (Flagler's friendship with Hastings' father may have influenced his choice) who later went on to an illustrious career, designing the New York Public Library and one of the US Senate office buildings in Washington, DC. Working alongside Carrère and Hastings were Bernard Maybeck (then in the early stages of his career) and Louis Comfort Tiffany. The interior decoration of the Ponce de Leon was Tiffany's first major commission.

The hotel's architects created a vast pile of a building, lavishly embellished with Medieval, Moorish, Mediterranean and Victorian elements; its Renaissance overtones are the most prominent. The structure's twin bell towers were then, and remain today, the most distinctive features of St. Augustine's skyline. Terra-cotta ornamentation abundantly adorns the gray concrete walls and palm trees flourish on the grounds.

In January 1888, without fanfare or celebration, the Hotel Ponce de Leon opened its doors for business. The nation's first major building employing poured-concrete construction, it rivaled in luxury and elegance the fashionable hotels of the day. Guests feasted on sumptuous meals prepared by New York chefs. They luxuriated in elegant rooms and common areas decorated with Austrian crystal chandeliers crafted by Tiffany and dramatic murals painted by American artist George W. Maynard.

The Ponce de Leon fared well for only a few years; economic downturns and competition from Palm Beach and other resort areas to the south curtailed the flow of vacationers, although business boomed for short periods in the early 20C. During World War II, the building was temporarily leased to the US Coast Guard for use as a training facility. It reopened after the war but its days as a resort hotel were numbered. In 1967 the Ponce de Leon ceased operation and the building was converted into a private liberal-arts college. Today students of Flagler College attend classes in the former hotel common areas and eat their meals in the elegant dining room, amid the glow of light through Tiffany's leaded-glass windows.

Visit – *Interior accessible by guided tour (30min) only.* A handsome bronze statue of Henry Flagler stands before the arched main entrance leading into a graceful, arcaded courtyard. Tours begin in the Main Hall beneath an 84ft rotunda richly decorated with gold leaf and Maynard murals. The oak wainscoting, leaded-glass windows and whimsical, lion's-head light fixtures in the dining room are all original. Some of the most prominent figures of the early 20C, including presidents Warren Harding, Theodore Roosevelt and William McKinley, sat in these dining-room chairs.

© Ian Adams/Dembinsky Photo Assoc.

Flagler College

★★Lightner Museum – *75 King St., across from Flagler College. Open year-round daily 9am–5pm. Closed Dec 25. $6.* ✗ ⛾ 🅿 ☎ *904-824-2874.* Across King Street from Flagler College, echoing its Spanish flavor, rises the massive bulk of Flagler's former Hotel Alcazar (1888). Today the corridors and rooms where guests once trod house a diverse assortment of decorative arts and collectibles, including an astonishing array of art glass.

The Hotel Alcazar – Henry Flagler commissioned the Hotel Alcazar as a comfortable, yet less luxurious (and more affordable) alternative to the Ponce de Leon Hotel, and to provide the latter's guests with some diversion in the way of shopping and entertainment. Designed by Carrère and Hastings, the poured-concrete structure boasted a quadrangle of shops and a casino annex with a large swimming pool, ballroom, bowling alley, billiards room and a gymnasium and spa—including Russian (dry) and Turkish (steam) baths.

To Flagler's surprise, guests preferred the relaxed atmosphere of the Alcazar to the more formal Ponce de Leon, and the hotel soon outstripped its neighbor in popularity. The same economic factors that slowed business at the Ponce de Leon also proved the Alcazar's undoing, however. The hotel closed its doors for good in 1937. In 1946, empty and forlorn, the building was purchased by Otto C. Lightner, a Chicago editor and publisher of *Hobbies* magazine. Following his own credo that "everyone can be a collector of something," Lightner had amassed (largely from once-wealthy Chicago estates dismantled during the Depression) a rather indiscriminate collection of objects and decorative arts. By 1947 the vast assemblage had been installed in the corridors of the Hotel Alcazar. Financial difficulties plagued operations throughout the 20C, but efforts of local citizens kept the museum alive; today it occupies the former spa and gymnasium. The casino and ballroom have been restored to their original condition; an antiques mall and café occupy the drained basin of the swimming pool.

First level – Sciences, both natural and human, are the focus of exhibits here; weights and scales, mineral collections and drafting tools are presented as if in a Victorian-era exhibition hall. Don't miss the beautiful steam engine created entirely of blown glass. Antique instruments, including an orchestrion, a nickelodeon and phonographs, occupy the music room, and everyday late-19C objects are displayed in a special section outfitted as a Victorian village.

Second level – The main baths section houses the showpiece of the museum: Lightner's extensive collection of **art glass★★**. From Bohemian to Bristol to spatter and spangle, the handsomely displayed pieces are grouped largely according to type, style and manufacturer, thus offering a fascinating and beautiful trip through the world of art glass. Displays feature works by Louis Comfort Tiffany, as well as Wedgwood, Meissen, majolica and lusterware glass and porcelain.

Third level – Intricately carved 19C furniture from India, samplers stitched in the 18C, and an Art Nouveau parlor suite number among the pieces in Lightner's decorative arts collection.

★Memorial Presbyterian Church – *36 Sevilla St. Open year-round Mon–Sat 9am–4:30pm, Sun noon–4:30pm. Closed Easter Sunday, Thanksgiving Day, Dec 25. $1.* ⛾ 🅿 ☎ *904-829-6451.* This lavishly appointed Renaissance-style edifice was commissioned by Flagler to commemorate his daughter, Jennie Louise Benedict, who died of complications from childbirth in 1889. Designed by Carrère and Hastings, the church was completed in less than a year by construction crews working around the clock. Lancet-shaped stained-glass windows illuminate the mahogany and marble-embellished sanctuary, adjoining the **mausoleum** where Mrs. Benedict, Flagler and his first wife, Mary Harkness, are interred.

Zorayda Castle – *83 King St. Open year-round daily 9am–5pm. Closed Dec 25. $5.* ⛾ 🅿 ☎ *904-824-3097.* A glimpse of Moorish Spain in downtown St. Augustine, this compact, two-story concrete "castle," with its contrasting plain and richly ornamented surfaces, scalloped archways and square corner tower, was a radical departure from the city's primarily wood and coquina construction when it was built in 1883. Boston entrepreneur Franklin W. Smith commissioned Villa Zorayda, as he called it, in a fit of admiration for the Alhambra in Granada, Spain; the building was intended to replicate a wing of that 12C castle at one-tenth scale. St. Augustine's first poured-concrete structure, the villa served as the inspiration for Flagler's Ponce de Leon Hotel.

In 1913, former Egyptian consul Abraham Mussallem purchased the structure, housing there his collection of Egyptian and Middle Eastern furnishings and decorative arts. They are now displayed by Mussallem's descendants, who operate the villa as a tourist attraction.

South of the Plaza

Spanish Military Hospital – *Aviles St., just off the Plaza de la Constitución. Open year-round daily 10am–4pm. Closed Dec 25. $2* ☎ *904-825-6808.* Erected originally as a stable, the simple, rose-colored building is a reconstruction of the apothecary wing of St. Augustine's military hospital as it might have appeared during the late 18C. The building was acquired by the Spanish government in 1791 and served as the city's main hospital after 1818. Razed in 1880, it was reconstructed in 1967 by the Historic St. Augustine Preservation Board, which now operates it as a museum in conjunction with the Spanish Quarter Village *(p 107)*. Inside, a bed-filled ward and several side rooms paint a picture of medical care in the late 18C, from the bundles of herbs drying slowly for use in medicines to the frighteningly rudimentary surgical implements of the day. Copies of the c.1790 *reglamentos*—rules governing the operation of hospitals and the educational requirements of doctors and apothecaries—are posted on the walls.

★★**Ximenez-Fatio House** – *20 Aviles St. Visit by guided tour only, year-round Mon & Thu–Sat 11am–4pm, Sun 1pm–4pm.* ☎ *904-829-3575.* This attractive, two-story coquina residence offers a fascinating look at the way early St. Augustine buildings were expanded and adapted for various uses throughout the city's long history. For most of the 19C the house was owned by women and operated as a boarding house, one of the few means by which independent women could respectably support themselves during that period. The structure was built in 1798 by Spanish merchant Andrés Ximenez as his residence and general store. The property passed to Ximenez' heirs at his death; it was eventually acquired by an American woman who added a second floor and balcony to the warehouse wings and converted the ground floor into bedrooms for use as a boarding house. Under a later owner, the establishment thrived as St. Augustine's most popular inn from the mid-19C to the late 19C, when competition from Henry Flagler's hotels slowed business.

Visit – *1hr.* Today the house is restored to reflect the period between 1830 and 1850; individual rooms are charmingly appointed as if to accommodate various 19C boarders, including an itinerant artist, a soldier, a family and an elderly woman. Research commissioned by the National Society of the Colonial Dames of America (current owners of the property) authenticates the paint color and other decorative treatments. Objects unearthed in archaeological digs at the site are displayed throughout the house.

★★**Gonzalez-Alvarez House (The Oldest House)** – *14 St. Francis St. (between Charlotte and Marine Sts.). Visit by guided tour (40min) only, year-round daily 9am–5pm. Closed Dec 25. $5.* ⬛ *www.oldcity.com/oldhouse* ☎ *904-824-2872.* This handsome National Historic Landmark dwelling on the north side of St. Francis Street is thought to be St. Augustine's oldest extant residential structure. With each room furnished as it would have been by its various inhabitants, the house offers a fascinating look at the progress of St. Augustine from Spanish colony to British outpost to American city.

Initially a flat-roofed, rectangular coquina dwelling with tabby floors, the house was built in the early 18C for Tomás Gonzalez y Hernandez, a settler from the Canary Islands. A second story, fireplace and balcony were added during the British period by Joseph and Mary Peavett, who operated it as a tavern. The Geronimo Alvarez family acquired the house in 1790 and it passed through various generations of that clan before being sold in 1882. During the late 19C, the house's various owners added embellishments typical of the day, including interior paneling and a two-story corner tower. In 1918 the house was purchased by the St. Augustine Historical Society, whose members restored the structure to its 18C appearance.

Visit – The gloomy lower level, with its rugged tabby floors and exposed coquina walls, describes the spartan lifestyle of the Gonzalez family, while the upstairs reveals the relative comfort enjoyed by the Peavetts and the Alvarez family. The mosquito-netted, four-poster bed and porcelain pitcher and washbowl in the upstairs bedroom date from Florida's territorial period.

Tovar House – *Adjacent to the Gonzalez-Alvarez House; same hours as above.* Formerly the residence of José Tovar, this building was purchased along with the Gonzalez-Alvarez House in 1918 by the St. Augustine Historical Society. Today its rooms house the **Museum of Florida's Army★**, with displays tracing the history of the army in the region. Costumed mannequins, replicated flags, muster rolls and text describing the military climate of each period illustrate life for soldiers in Florida from 1565 to the present.

San Marco Avenue

Fountain of Youth Archaeological Park – *155 Magnolia Ave. Open year-round daily 9am–5pm. Closed Dec 25. $4.75.* ♿ ☎ *904-829-3168.* Visitors who are fearless of the drawbacks of eternal youth can drink from the small spring at this privately owned park, although the waters of St. Augustine's "Fountain of Youth" are as devoid of supernatural powers—and more sulfurous—as any water in this part of Florida. While stories proclaiming this spot as the landing site of Ponce de León in his search for the fantastical fountain are the stuff of legend, the importance of the **archaeological site** here is unquestioned. In recent decades, teams of researchers from the Smithsonian Institution in Washington, DC, and the University of Florida have uncovered artifacts and building foundations that indicate Pedro Menéndez de Avilés' presence here, as well as the probable location of the Timucuan village of Seloy, home to the Indians who welcomed Menéndez in 1565.

Graves of Indian skeletons positioned for Christian burial indicate the proximity of the Mission de Nombre de Dios. Today a small enclosure painted with murals stands over the plot containing the reinterred bones. A similar structure houses the spring.

★**Mission de Nombre de Dios** – *San Marco Ave. at Old Mission Ave. Open year-round Mon–Fri 8am–5pm, weekends 9am–5pm. Closed Dec 25 & during church services.* ▣ ☎ *904-824-3045.* A 208ft stainless-steel cross marks the approximate spot where Pedro Menéndez de Avilés and his men came ashore to take possession of Florida for Philip II of Spain in 1565. Menéndez' chaplain marked the event by saying Mass, thus establishing the Mission de Nombre de Dios, the first Catholic mission in the US. Nothing remains today of the original structures. The gleaming cross, erected in 1966 to commemorate the 400th anniversary of the founding of St. Augustine, looms above the placid salt marsh bordering a peaceful forest of cypress and palm trees. Paths meander about the site leading to a tranquil, ivy-covered chapel housing the **Shrine of Our Lady of La Leche**, originally erected here in 1613 by Spanish settlers. The present chapel is the fourth to stand on the site.

★**Old Jail** – *167 San Marco Ave. Open year-round daily 8:30am–5pm. Closed Easter Sunday & Dec 24-25. $4.25.* ✗▣ ☎ *904-829-3800.* The large, dark-red Victorian building situated north of downtown is a handsome edifice with a somber history. Erected in 1892 to serve as the St. Johns County Jail and sheriff's residence, the building was largely funded by Henry Flagler, who was eager to see the previous jail relocated from near the entrance to his Ponce de Leon Hotel. In 1953 a larger jail facility was constructed north of town and this building began to be operated as a tourist attraction. Now smartly restored and appointed with period furnishings, the Old Jail clearly depicts the extent to which the lives of the sheriff and his family revolved around the care of the prisoners.

Guided tours explore the bedrooms, living room, office and kitchen of the sheriff's residence. In the kitchen, the sheriff's wife cooked two meals a day for all the prisoners, transporting the food via dumbwaiter to the second floor for the jailers to serve. The jailhouse itself is divided into separate sections for white, black and female prisoners and those requiring maximum security. The walls bear handcuffs, shackles and a collection of antique handguns used in crimes. Out back stand the gallows used to mete out punishment before the turn of the century.

Florida Heritage Museum – *167 San Marco Ave., adjacent to the Old Jail. Same hours as Old Jail (above). $4.25.* ♿ ☎ *904-829-3800.* Florida and St. Augustine history is glossed over here in three small rooms through displays of objects of everyday life. The broad permanent collection includes early coins, weapons and furniture from the first Spanish period, as well as dolls, toys, quilts and Civil War artifacts. Particularly noteworthy is an exhibit on Henry Flagler that traces the Flagler family's genealogy and features a model of the Florida East Coast Railway.

Anastasia Island *Map p 97*

★★**St. Augustine Alligator Farm** – 🧒 *A1A, 1mi south of the Bridge of Lions. Open mid-Jun–Aug daily 9am–6pm. Rest of the year daily 9am–5pm. $11.95.* ♿ ▣ ☎ *904-824-3337.* Founded in 1893, this alligator farm may have been Florida's earliest animal park. Two entrepreneurial St. Augustinians with financial interests in the mule-drawn tram line leading from downtown to present-day St. Augustine Beach founded the attraction at the tram terminus to encourage ridership. By 1910 it was an established attraction and a linchpin of St. Augustine's efforts to promote tourism. The property was relocated 2mi north to its present site in 1922 after storms razed the wooden buildings; the present Mediterranean-style entrance structure dates from 1937.

Visit – *2hrs.* Some 2,500 crocodilians reside at the Alligator Farm in landscaped habitats, swamps and animal displays traversed by attractive boardwalks. Plan to attend one of the excellent nature talks presented hourly in the reptile theater, where knowledgeable lecturers present examples of Florida wildlife, including snakes and alligators. Visitors sometimes wonder if the 84 alligators sunning themselves in the **main pen** are alive; languorous by nature, they tend to remain immobile for long periods. A special indoor exhibit, **Gomek Forever★**, pays homage to a 1,700-pound saltwater crocodile from New Guinea who was the park's star resident from 1990 until his death in 1997. Now mounted, Gomek consumed 100 pounds of nutria and chicken a week during the warm season (most crocodilians don't eat in cold weather). Don't miss the **Land of Crocodiles★**, Alligator Farm's outstanding—and rare—collection of all 22 species of crocodilians. Its inhabitants hail from every tropical area of the world. The attraction also showcases many species of wildlife from Africa, South America and Asia, including macaws and other exotic birds. The wading bird rookery is home to egrets, herons and wood storks during the nesting season.

St. Augustine Lighthouse and Museum – *81 Lighthouse Ave. Take A1A south and turn left on Old Beach Rd., across from the Alligator Farm. Open late May–Labor Day Mon–Thu 9am–7pm, Fri–Sun 9am–8pm. Rest of the year daily 9am–5pm. Closed Easter Sunday, Thanksgiving Day, Dec 25. $4.* ▣ *www.stauglight.com* ☎ *904-829-0745.* This brick-and-iron lighthouse, distinctively painted with a black-

and-white spiral, has illuminated the northern point of Anastasia Island since 1874. The current structure replaced an earlier wood-and-coquina light tower that toppled into the ocean. A panoramic **view** awaits those who brave the 219-stair climb to the top, where the original, first-order Fresnel lens boasts a beam distance of 19 nautical miles. The adjacent brick **lightkeeper's residence**, a handsome Victorian structure gutted by fire in 1970 but rebuilt in 1988 and refurbished to its period appearance. Displays recount the demanding lives of the keepers—who maintained and operated the light until its automation in 1955—and of their wives and children.

Anastasia State Recreation Area – *A1A, just south of Lighthouse Museum. Open year-round daily 8am–dusk. $3.25/vehicle.* △ 🅿 ☎ *904-461-2033.* Devotees of sun and sand flock to the broad, lovely **beach**≈≈ edging this 1,492-acre state park for some of the area's finest fishing, swimming and sunning. A protected saltwater lagoon provides excellent canoeing and windsurfing. The park's boundaries encompass dunes, salt marshes, scrublands and hammock as well as the quarries from which blocks of coquina were taken to construct Castillo de San Marcos *(p 106)*.

EXCURSIONS *Map p 97*

World Golf Village and Hall of Fame – *12mi north via I-95, exit 95-A. Open year-round daily 10am–6pm. $9 Hall of Fame; $6 IMAX; $13.50 combination ticket.* ⚔ ♿ 🅿 *www.wgv.com* ☎ *904-940-4123.*
Opened in May 1998, this facility's centerpiece is the **World Golf Hall of Fame**, a two-story, 75,000sq ft museum that pays tribute to the greatest male and female golfers of past and present, both American and international. Crystal busts display the likenesses of 73 athletes (through 1998); visitors watch video highlights of the golfers' careers at computer stations. Elsewhere, the museum inspires even non-avid golfers with 18 interactive exhibits. Visitors can play an 1880s-style putting green with hickory-shafted putters; have their swings computer-analyzed; or watch highlights of golf's greatest moments in a mini-theater.
Spread across 450 acres between St. Augustine and Jacksonville, the $250 million World Golf Village also includes a major resort hotel with two 18-hole golf courses and a 300-seat IMAX theater currently developing the first-ever IMAX golf film.

★★**Fort Matanzas National Monument** – *2hrs. 15mi south via A1A. Monument is located on Matanzas River just south of Crescent Beach. Open year-round daily 8:30am–5:30pm. Closed Dec 25.* 🅿 *www.nps.gov/foma* ☎ *904-471-0116.* A 300-acre park here preserves a coquina watchtower erected in 1742 to defend Matanzas Inlet. The site's significance goes beyond the historic watchtower, however. In 1565 some 250 French Huguenot soldiers and settlers were slaughtered here by the forces of Pedro Menéndez de Avilés, thereby changing the course of Florida's history.
Soldiers in a wooden tower had maintained watch over Matanzas Inlet since 1569. If approaching ships were sighted, a runner carried the news to St. Augustine. The 1740 siege of the Castillo de San Marcos *(p 106)* brought home to the Spanish the potential for British invasion, and the need for an armed fortification here at the "back door" to St. Augustine. Piers were sunk into the marshy soil of a small barrier island at the inlet's mouth, and the coquina structure soon arose.

Visit – In the visitor center, a short film describes the turbulent history and modern restoration of Fort Matanzas. From a nearby landing, board a ferry for the trip across the Matanzas River to the fort itself. Stairs and ladders lead up to the gun balcony, from which you can explore the soldiers' and officers' quarters and the upper balcony. Back on the mainland, a pretty nature trail leads among bayberry, live oak, saw palmetto, Spanish bayonet and red cedar trees to a plaque commemorating the site of the massacre.

Marineland – 🅺🅸🅳🆂 *2hrs. 18mi south via A1A at 9507 Ocean Shore Blvd. Open year-round daily 9am–5:30pm. Closed Dec 25. $14.95.* △⚔ 🅿 ☎ *904-460-1275.* Marineland enjoys an **oceanfront setting** straddling highway A1A with the Matanzas River on one side and nearly 4,000ft of beachfront on the other. The park was originally conceived as an underwater film studio by a group that sought footage of marine life. Founders included Cornelius Vanderbilt Whitney, great-grandson of transportation magnate Cornelius Vanderbilt, and Ilia Tolstoy, grandson of acclaimed Russian author Leo Tolstoy. Opened in 1938, the studio was an object of local interest and quickly became a tourist attraction. Techniques for photographing dolphin behavior, recording dolphin sounds and maintaining marine life in a man-made environment were pioneered here.

Visit – *Check schedules at entrance for times of shows and underwater oceanarium feedings.* Most of the park's 3,000 resident sea dwellers swim and play in two massive oceanariums and in smaller aquariums on the ocean side of the park. Dolphins swim right up to visitors at the **Top Deck** of the circular oceanarium, also the site of jumping dolphin shows. Dolphins-in-training perform throughout the day at the Dolphin Stadium. Be sure to check out **Wonders of the Spring**, a 35,000gal freshwater aquarium featuring largemouth bass and other native Florida species.

Orlando Area

One of the most popular tourist destinations in the US, the Orlando area in central Florida attracts nearly 34 million visitors annually. Best known as the home of Walt Disney World, the region also boasts the elaborate theme parks of Universal Studios, SeaWorld and a number of major corporate headquarters. The city of Orlando itself, the state's largest inland city, serves as the region's hub. Though superhighways lined with chain hotels, resort complexes, eateries and discount shopping malls now web the flat, lake-pocked subtropical landscape of this growing region, historic neighborhoods still grace the older portions of cities and towns.

As you move southwest farther into the interior, the land becomes less developed and more devoted to agriculture. The towns of Lakeland and Lake Wales sit at the heart of the state's citrus-growing region and offer a quieter, more nostalgic atmosphere, as well as a subtle change in terrain. At the southern end of the state's north-south-running Central Highlands *(p 12)*, this area occupies a gently rolling landscape. Iron Mountain, just north of Lake Wales, is one of the peninsula's highest points at 298ft. Central Florida experienced its first influx of settlers—largely north Florida cattlemen who were attracted to the area's lush grasslands—after the end of the Second Seminole War in 1842. Forty years later, towns mushroomed along the line of Henry Plant's **South Florida Railway** *(p 20)*. Railroad access encouraged tourism and other economic

ventures, including lumbering and a healthy naval stores industry that produced turpentine, pitch and rosin from the sap of the locally abundant longleaf pines. After a
killing frost in the 1890s, citrus farmers from the northern part of the state migrated
south to join the growers already in this area, and the citrus industry burgeoned.

In contrast to the wealthy winter visitors who arrived by train in the early 1900s, mid-
century tourists were middle-class families traveling by car. The ever-growing pace of
tourism increased exponentially in the early 1970s with the opening of Walt Disney
World 20mi southwest of Orlando. The corridor stretching between the two and south
to Kissimmee quickly became a commercial mecca, while the area southwest of
Kissimmee has managed to maintain its traditional base in the citrus economy. Today
Orlando and its environs rank among the fastest growing metropolitan areas in the US.

KISSIMMEE

Population 36,510
Map of Principal Sights p 3 – Map p 116
Tourist Information ☎ 407-847-5000

Two distinct personalities characterize the city of Kissimmee. A placid residential community spreading along the shores of 29sq mi Lake Tohopekaliga quietly reflects the
town's historic role as a center of Florida's cattle industry. Less than a mile away, visitors throng the glittering length of US-192, which extends between downtown and
Walt Disney World giving rise to Kissimmee's moniker "the Gateway to Disney."

Historical Notes

Cattle Country – Given the neon glitz of US-192, it's easy to overlook the fact that
tourism was not always Kissimmee's economic mainstay. For centuries before the first
tourist attraction was opened, central Florida's marshy prairies, interspersed with
stands of virgin timber, proved ideal pastures for livestock. Spanish and Indian cattle
drives passed through the Kissimmee River valley in the period prior to the US takeover
of Florida, but the area was not permanently occupied until American cowmen settled
here in the 1840s.

In 1855 the General Assembly created the **Internal Improvement Fund**, charged with selling
bonds to investors and distributing state lands to private corporations to assist in the
construction of railroads and other infrastructure. These lands were acquired when
the federal government ceded the nation's swamp and overflowed lands to the states
for drainage and reclamation, and to promote internal improvements. Florida eventually found itself with 16 million acres to manage.

The Civil War interrupted development. By the late 1860s Florida was without railroads or profits and was accruing a large debt. With bondholders clamoring for some
return on their investments, plans were afoot to force the Internal Improvement Board
to sell its lands.

Hamilton Disston and His Dredges – Into the fray stepped **Hamilton Disston** (1844-
1896), a wealthy Pennsylvania industrialist whose family had amassed a fortune in the
tool-making industry. Convinced that Central Florida's marshes would prove perfect for
agricultural development once drained, Disston purchased—for 25 cents an acre—some
four million acres in the swampy Kissimmee, Caloosahatchee and Peace River valleys.
This 1881 sale enabled the Internal Improvement Fund to pay off its bondholders and
saved the state from bankruptcy. Disston rapidly established the Disston Land Company
at Allendale, a tiny settlement that he renamed Kissimmee. Then he set about dredging
a series of canals linking various lakes in the region, among them Tohopekaliga, East
Tohopekaliga, Cypress, Hatchineha and Kissimmee. Disston's dredges straightened and
deepened the Kissimmee River south to Lake Okeechobee and linked that great lake to
the upper Caloosahatchee River some 30mi to the west.

Orange groves, sugar plantations and lumber camps soon flourished in the former
swamplands, and steamboats loaded with cargo and passengers chugged through the
new canal systems. The South Florida Railway landed its terminus at Kissimmee and
the town rapidly developed as a center for shipbuilding, agriculture and transportation. Demand for beef throughout the first half of the 20C fueled the regional cattle
industry and Kissimmee thrived as a placid agricultural center.

Gateway to Disney – The opening of Disney World in 1971 foretold Kissimmee's
metamorphosis from a farm community to a tourist center. US-192 rapidly became a
lively corridor of attractions and amenities designed to accommodate the floods of
Disney-bound visitors. As Kissimmee's population boomed, cattle ranchers retreated
south to less populous areas.

Today some 4.5 million tourists annually flock to the putt-putt golf courses, water
parks, go-cart tracks, motels, shopping centers and amusement parks that line both
sides of US-192. In the evening, crowds fill "dinner shows," where meals match the
theme of the accompanying live entertainment; themes run the gamut from medieval
England to the Old West to gangland Chicago.

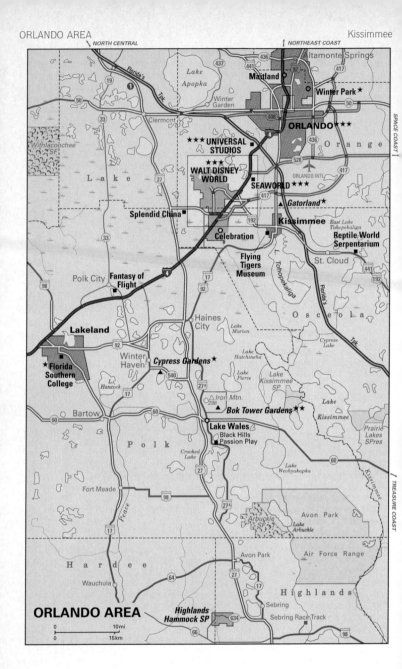

ORLANDO AREA

0   10mi
0   15km

Although development pushes inexorably eastward toward the town of St. Cloud, Kissimmee's old commercial area appears as it might have in the days before Disney. Placid Lakefront Park extends along the northern shore of **Lake Tohopekaliga** a few blocks from downtown. A stroll along **Broadway Avenue** *(south of US-192 via Main St.)* reveals charming storefronts that are reminiscent of Kissimmee's late-19C days as a cattle town.

SIGHTS *1 day. Map above.*

Flying Tigers Warbird Restoration Air Museum – *231 Hoagland Blvd. From US-192 turn south on Hoagland Blvd. and follow signs. Open year-round Mon–Sat 9am–6pm, Sun 9am–5:30pm. $8.* ♿ 🅿 *www.warbirdmuseum.com* ☎ *407-933-1942.* Less a museum than the active workshop of an organization devoted to the restoration and reconstruction of vintage World War II aircraft, this facility sits on the grounds of Kissimmee's small regional airport. Since 1972, when the organization's founder began restoring American "warbirds" to flying condition, Flying

Tigers has returned some 24 planes to the air. Guided tours explore the storage hangars for an up-close look at the 28 beautifully restored aircraft, and the workshops for glimpses of those under restoration. Planes commonly on view include a Boeing B-17, a P-51 Mustang, an A-4 Skyhawk and a Russian MIG 21. Planes are occasionally flight-tested *(call for schedule)* and the museum also offers warbird and biplane rides.

A World of Orchids – *Map p 137. 2501 Old Lake Wilson Rd. From I-4 take Exit 25B west and proceed west 2mi on US-192; turn left on Old Lake Wilson Rd. (Rte. 545) and continue 1mi. Open year-round daily 9:30am–5:30pm. Closed Jan 1, July 4, Thanksgiving Day, Dec 25. $8.95.* ♿ 🅿 ☎ *407-396-1887.* The tropical conservatory, landscaped with waterfalls and winding paths, contains an ever-changing rainbow of bright flowering orchids from around the world. Hundreds of species flourish here, including several rare ones. In the adjoining gift shop, visitors can purchase orchids that have been propagated in the site's own laboratory.

Splendid China – *3000 Splendid China Blvd. From I-4 take Exit 25B west and proceed west 3mi on US-192. Open year-round daily 9:30am–7pm. Closing times vary with season. $28.88.* ✗ ♿ 🅿 *www.floridasplendidchina.com* ☎ *407-397-8803.* Laid out on a sprawling, 76-acre site just west of the entrance to Disney World, Splendid China departs from the traditional rides-and-attractions theme parks that abound in the immediate vicinity. Intended to offer the visitor a "10,000-mile journey through 5,000 years of Chinese history and culture," the park presents some 60 scale replicas of China's architectural and natural wonders in a landscaped setting. The handcrafted **replicas★**, executed at scales ranging from 1:3 to 1:15, were created using techniques and materials authentic to the original periods of construction. Chinese actors, dancers and acrobats bring to life the "Mysterious Kingdom of the Orient" *(nightly 6pm except Mon)*, while snow tigers and other creatures are the focus of an intriguing animal show *(twice daily except Wed)*.

EXCURSIONS *Map p 116*

★**Gatorland** – 🧒 *2hrs. 6mi north of Kissimmee at 14501 Orange Blossom Tr. (US-17/92/441). Open year-round daily 9am–dusk. $13.95.* ✗ ♿ 🅿 *www.gatorland.com* ☎ *407-855-5496.* What this alligator-oriented animal park lacks in technological magic, it makes up for with the charm common to 1950s-era theme parks. Founded in 1949 as a combination alligator farm and amusement park, Gatorland today continues both traditions, selling 1,000 alligators annually for their meat and skins, and entertaining visitors with gator jumping and gator-wrestling demonstrations.

Gaping alligator jaws "swallow" visitors at the entrance to the gift shop. Within the park, wooden boardwalks and platforms intersect above holding ponds where gators swim. For a quick orientation, take a narrated chug around the park on the Gatorland Express *(10min)*; guides offer informative lectures on the biology of the resident crocodilians. From the three-level wooden **observation tower**, views extend over the park and its 10-acre bird sanctuary and breeding marsh. Plan to attend any or all of the three live shows held regularly throughout the day, particularly Gatorland's trademark "**Gator Jumparoo**" during which full-grown alligators lunge 4ft out of the water to snag pieces of chicken dangled by handlers.

At the southern end of the park, a swinging rope bridge leads to a short boardwalk stroll through the lush cypress swamp forming the northern head of the Kissimmee chain of lakes, which flows from here to the EVERGLADES, 175mi south.

Reptile World Serpentarium – *30min. 12mi east of Kissimmee at 5705 E. Irlo Bronson Memorial Hwy. (US-192). Open Oct–Aug Tue–Sun 9am–5:30pm. Closed Thanksgiving Day & Dec 25. $4.55.* ♿ ☎ *407-892-6905.* Part snake zoo, part cottage industry, the long white stucco building shelters a small but broad collection of snakes and reptiles from around the world and facilities of a commercial purveyor of snake venom. The interior display area houses more than 60 different types of snakes and other reptiles including mambas and cobras lying in placid repose, with placards describing their native habitats, eating habits, behaviors and other aspects of natural history. Visitors to the serpentarium also have a unique opportunity to witness the thrice-daily "milking" of poisonous snakes for their venom, which is processed for use in research and production of antivenin.

★**Cypress Gardens** – 🧒 *Description p 120. 34mi south of Kissimmee. From US-192 take I-4 west 10mi to US-27 south; continue 18mi. Exit at Cypress Gardens Blvd.*

LAKELAND

Population 73,157
Map of Principal Sights p 3 – Map p 116
Tourist Information ☎ 941-688-8551

Named for the dozens of lakes dotting the metropolitan area, this prosperous small city benefits from its location at the heart of Florida's citrus-producing region. Abraham Godwin Munn, a Kentucky entrepreneur and winter resident of Florida, catalyzed Lakeland's development in 1881. Won over by the region's pleasant winter climate, Munn purchased—sight unseen—about 1,000 acres of land in south Florida from the Internal Improvement Fund *(p 115)*, including 80 acres of present-day Lakeland. By 1883 squatters had formed a fledgling settlement around Lake Wire, site of a work camp established to lay the rails of Henry Plant's railroad linking Tampa and Kissimmee. Munn induced the railroad to create a stop at Lake Wire by constructing an elaborate railway station at his own expense, and the town of Lakeland quickly took shape. By 1885 the arrival of two more rail lines assured Lakeland's future as a transportation hub. Streets radiated out from Munn Park, an attractive square located next to the station.

The region's fertile soils yielded strawberries and citrus fruits (the Marsh seedless grapefruit was developed here) and mounds of powdery phosphate from area mines traveled out by rail to fertilizer manufacturers. In 1904, after a roaring fire consumed much of the downtown area, a collection of masonry and brick structures arose in the triangle between Lakes Wire, Mirror and Morton. Today many of these historic commercial buildings house antique shops in the **Munn Park Historic District**. Pleasantly landscaped with brick walkways, benches and flower beds, **Munn Park** *(bounded by Kentucky Ave., Main St., Tennessee Ave. and Cedar St.)* serves as a community gathering place. Agriculture and mining remain important contributors to Lakeland's economy: nearly a quarter of all US citrus fruit is grown and packed in the immediate vicinity.

SIGHTS *1/2 day*

Polk Museum of Art – *800 E. Palmetto St. Open year-round Tue–Fri 9am–5pm, Sat 10am–5pm, Sun 1pm–5pm. Closed major holidays.* ☎ *941-688-7743.* Situated next to the public library near picturesque Lake Morton is a contemporary red-brick hodgepodge of right angles and cylinders. This striking building houses this excellent small museum, which marries a growing permanent collection and a thriving agenda of educational and community outreach programs. The permanent collection emphasizes contemporary works by artists living and working in Florida, including Robert Rauschenberg and James Rosenquist. Also on display are a permanent exhibit of pre-Columbian artifacts from Central and South America and rotating collections of Georgian silver, European decorative arts, Japanese ceramics and Korean pottery. High-caliber temporary shows change every two months.

★**Florida Southern College** – *Bounded by Johnson St., McDonald St., Ingraham Ave. and Lake Hollingsworth Dr. Visitor parking entrance on Johnson St. Visitor center located at 111 Lake Hollingsworth Dr. Open Tue–Fri 11am–4pm, Sat 10am–2pm, Sun 2pm–4pm. Closed major holidays and college vacations.* ▣ ☎ *941-680-4116.* The campus of this small Methodist college boasts the largest collection in a single location of buildings designed by **Frank Lloyd Wright** (1867-1959). Though Wright's eight structures bear the marks of decades of wear and tear typical of academic buildings, lovers of his work will nevertheless recognize the innovative designs and aesthetic genius that mark the creations of the father of modern American architecture.

In 1938, seeking to reverse an alarmingly decreased enrollment in the wake of the Great Depression, college president Dr. Ludd Spivey approached the celebrated architect with the proposal that he create a great education temple in Florida. Upon visiting the open verdant site, Wright pronounced it one of the most beautiful spots on earth and readily accepted the commission. His grandiose plan, which he dramatically dubbed "A Child of the Sun," entailed some 18 new buildings and landscape features (one has since been dismantled; the remainder were never built).

Executed in materials native to the region, buildings incorporate the intricately juxtaposed, rounded and geometric forms characteristic of Wright's organic architecture. His designs meld gracefully with the gently rolling land, closely hugging its slopes or soaring skyward to elevate the structures above the low-lying terrain. Standouts include the **Annie Pfeiffer Chapel**, its central worship space crowned by an open tower revealing stepped-pyramid forms; and the smaller **Danforth Chapel**, whose exterior rooflines attest to Wright's fascination with Japanese architecture.

EXCURSION

Fantasy of Flight – *14mi east of Lakeland at 1400 Broadway Blvd. (Rte-559), Polk City. From I-4 turn north at exit 21 and follow signs. Open daily 9am–5pm. $15.95.* ✗ ৬ 🅿 ☎ *941-984-3500.* This $30 million museum has a special appeal for vintage aircraft buffs. It displays some 30 historic aircraft, mainly dating from 1930 to 1945; they include a B-17 Flying Fortress (in a full-scale reenactment of a World War II bombing mission), a B-24 Liberator, a British Spitfire, a Short Sunderland (said to be the world's last airworthy civilian four-engine flying boat), and a replica of Charles Lindbergh's *Spirit of St. Louis.* In the "Fightertown" arcade, interactive flight simulators enable kids of all ages to engage the enemy in aerial dogfights over the Pacific. Outside, hot-air balloon and ultralight flights are offered from two private grass runways extending across 300 acres.

LAKE WALES

Population 9,930
Map of Principal Sights p 3 – Map p 116
Tourist Information ☎ 941-676-3445

This tranquil community surrounding Lake Wailes is located in the southern portion of the Lake Wales Ridge, a narrow spine of low, sandy hills extending 200mi from Ocala into Highlands County. The ridge encompasses some of peninsular Florida's highest elevations.

Historical Notes

The discrepancy between the spelling of the lake's and the town's names occurred in 1913. It seems that the town's founders felt that Wailes sounded too much like wailing, so they dropped the "i" from the name to avoid any negative connotations. Land of the present-day city was part of an 180,000-acre tract purchased in 1905 by the Sessoms Company, a Jacksonville investment firm with an interest in the region's virgin stands of longleaf yellow pine trees. Pine sap, once distilled into rosin, pitch and turpentine, was a key ingredient in manufactured products such as soap, ink, paint and shoe polish. In 1911, shortly after the Atlantic Coast Line railroad passed through on its route from Lakeland to Haines City, a group of four investors acquired 5,000 acres from the Sessoms Company and platted them for development. Active promotion campaigns quickly lured residents. By the end of the 1920s a prosperous business district defined the downtown area.

Today several original brick and masonry commercial structures from that period form the core of a charming National Register **historic district** where time seems to stand still. In the rose-colored **Lake Wales Museum and Cultural Center**, formerly the Atlantic Coast Line depot (1927), the Lake Wales Historical Society mounts temporary thematic exhibits drawn from a permanent collection of costumes, photographs, textiles and local artifacts *(325 S. Scenic Hwy.; open year-round Mon–Fri 9am–5pm, Sat 10am–4pm; closed major holidays;* ৬ 🅿 *www.cityoflakewales.com* ☎ *941-678-4209).*

Lake Wales is also the winter home of the **Black Hills Passion Play**, originally staged in Lünen, Germany, in 1242 and moved to the Black Hills of South Dakota in 1932 *(Passion Play amphitheater 1.5mi south of downtown on S. Scenic Hwy./US-27A; mid-Feb–mid-Apr Tue, Thu, Fri & Sun; for schedule and tickets* ☎ *941-676-1495 or 800-622-8383).*

SIGHT *1/2 day*

★★ Bok Tower Gardens – 1151 Tower Blvd., 3mi north of downtown. Take US-27 to Burns Ave. (Rte. 17A) and follow signs. Open year-round daily 8am–5pm. $4. ✗ ৬ 🅿 *www.boktowergardens.org* ☎ *941-676-1408.* When American editor, author and philanthropist Edward Bok was a young boy, his grandmother bade him and his brother, "Wherever your lives may be cast, make you the world a bit better or more beautiful because you have lived in it." Many years later, Bok completed his contribution: a 130-acre botanical garden conceived as a sanctuary for plants, animals and people.

Born in The Netherlands, **Edward William Bok** (1863-1930) moved with his family to Brooklyn at age 6. Early in his career he held positions with Henry Holt and Charles Scribner's Sons publishing companies. In 1886 Bok founded the Bok Syndicate Press and later served as editor of *Ladies Home Journal.* During his 30-year tenure the magazine achieved phenomenal popularity, becoming the first in the world to garner one million subscribers. In 1920 his autobiography, *The Americanization of Edward Bok,* won a Pulitzer Prize.

In 1923 Bok decided to create a nature sanctuary as a gift to the American people. He invited Frederick Law Olmsted, Jr., son of the famed creator of New York City's Central Park, to transform a sandy, pine-covered site atop Iron Mountain into a botanical haven. The park was dedicated in 1929 at ceremonies led by President Calvin Coolidge.

Gardens – Begin at the **visitor center** *(follow signs from parking area)*, where you may view displays on the history of the gardens and a film tour of the interior of Bok Tower. From here, meander along bark-mulched paths amid lush stands of live oaks, conifers, palm trees and ferns. Ever-changing splashes of color are painted seasonally on this green canvas by an abundance of flowering plants, among them bright azaleas *(in bloom Dec–Mar)* and camellias *(in bloom Nov–Mar)*. **Window by the Pond**, a small wooden hut fitted with a large plate-glass window, welcomes visitors to sit and watch the play of life unfolding in a freshwater pond. The marble **excedra**, a monumental semicircular conversation seat, marks the 298ft summit of Iron Mountain, considered the highest point in peninsular Florida.

★★**Tower** – *Interior not open to the public.* Encircled by a placid moat, the beautiful 205ft tower of pink-and-gray-streaked Georgia marble and buff-colored coquina quarried near ST. AUGUSTINE is the focal point of the gardens. Designed by Philadelphia architect Milton B. Medary, the Gothic Revival shaft unifies, rather than dominates, the surrounding landscape. Four-sided at the base and octagonal above 150ft, the tower is embellished with turquoise and brown earthenware tiles, masterfully carved sculptures and friezes, and intricately wrought ironwork. The graceful edifice is affectionately known as the "Singing Tower" for its **carillon** of 57 chromatically pitched bronze bells, designed in England and operated by hammers from a keyboard located on the sixth level. Installed in 1929 and most recently updated in 1979, the carillon marks every half hour with its harmonious strains. Carillon recitals, live or recorded, are staged daily by the resident carillonneur.

Pinewood – *Visit by guided tour (50min) only, mid-Sept–mid-May Tue & Thu 11am & 1pm, Sun 1pm & 1:30pm. $5.* ⚐ ☎ *941-676-1408.* This elegant estate nestled on the broad slope of Iron Mountain was erected in 1931 as the winter home of Bethlehem Steel executive Charles Austin Buck. Landscape architect William Lyman Phillips, an associate in the Olmsted Brothers firm, and architect Charles Wait together conceived a Mediterranean Revival design that harmonizes both formal and natural gardens with tile roofs, terraces and softly shaded stucco walls. Detailed woodwork and Cuban tiles adorn the luxurious interior, which is furnished with part of the original collection of 17C, 18C and 19C French, Italian and Spanish antiques. Formal gardens incorporate citrus allées that terminate in circular plantings of trees—elements common in Italian Renaissance garden design. The property was acquired by Bok Tower Gardens in 1970.

EXCURSIONS

★**Cypress Gardens** – ▨ *1/2 day. 12mi northwest in the town of Cypress Gardens. Take Rte. 27 north and turn left (west) on Rte. 540; continue 4.5mi to gardens' entrance on left. Open year-round daily 9:30am–5:30pm. Closing times vary with season. $30.95.* ✗ ⚐ ▣ *www.cypressgardens.com* ☎ *941-324-2111 or 800-282-2123.* Rides and live-performance shows take a back seat to spectacular floral displays at this botanical wonderland of a theme park. Spilling down a sloping site in a former cypress swamp, Cypress Gardens proclaims itself Florida's first, and longest continually operating, theme park.

Cypress Gardens was born in the mid-1930s when Midwest businessman Dick Pope and his wife Julie, longtime winter visitors to Florida, purchased 16 acres on Lake Eloise, one of a series of eight interconnected lakes known in Polk County as the "Chain of Lakes." The Popes hired laborers to dig a network of canals and transformed the virgin swampland into a tropical garden park that opened to the public in January 1936.

Over the years the gardens have been expanded, consistently achieving ever-more-extravagant feats of floral wizardry. Today some 8,000 plant varieties from 90 countries are displayed in different areas of the park, which mounts four annual flower festivals and other themed celebrations throughout the year. Cypress Gardens is now owned by Busch Entertainment Corporation, which also owns SeaWorld in ORLANDO and Busch Gardens in TAMPA.

★**Botanic Gardens** – A slow meander through a network of fragrant, shaded pathways near the water's edge offers a glimpse of the park's lush original gardens. Fresh lake breezes fan colorful blooms of gardenias, bougainvillea, hibiscus and palm in the French and oriental gardens. The path circles up to a quaint white gazebo that serves as a popular site for weddings. Photogenic floral vistas abound. Visitors who prefer to ride can float through the gardens on a boat cruise along cypress-draped canals *(boats depart continuously throughout the day from the landing near the main entrance; $3.50).*

Southern Crossroads – This charming, antebellum-themed area features live-performance ice, magic and comedy shows, a couple of museum-quality displays and other attractions. Not to be missed is **Wings of Wonder★**, a 5,500sq ft glass conservatory housing more than 1,000 colorful butterflies; the graceful creatures flit free and light on lovely, nectar-bearing flowers to the accompanying music of an indoor waterfall. Visitors can sniff herbs, vegetables, fruits and roses in the **Plantation**

Gardens, dedicated to the cultivation of plants known to thrive in the southern US. **Cypress Roots** displays Cypress Gardens' history, including celebrity photographs, antebellum wardrobes and memorabilia from early water-skiing competitions. Train buffs won't want to miss **Cypress Junction**, a remarkable and elaborate model railroad exhibit. Panoramic aerial **views** of the park and points beyond await riders of **Island in the Sky**, a revolving platform that rises 153ft on its huge steel arm. Children will enjoy the junior-size rides and games assembled at Carousel Cove.

Nature's Way – Beyond Southern Crossroads lies this area, focused around **Nature's Boardwalk**, a small complex of shoreside habitat areas for deer, wallabies, capybaras and other creatures, and the **Birdwalk Aviary**, where friendly tropical birds and munjac deer freely interact with visitors. **Nature's Arena** hosts raptor and reptile shows. Also within this area are an **Antique Radio Museum**, featuring an outstanding collection of early sets (complete with golden-era radio programs), and the **Florida Historical Railway Garden**, highlighted by scale re-creations of many of the state's best-known historic buildings.

** **Water-Ski Shows** – *(1-3 shows daily; 25min; check park brochure for show times).* In 1943 a group of local water-skiers gathered to entertain a troop of 500 military servicemen enjoying a day of leave at the park. That first performance spawned Cypress Gardens' trademark water-ski shows, executed by a resident team of 56 champion skiers. Watch them perform stunts such as mid-air somersaults and a four-tier human pyramid in front of the double-grandstand lakeside stadium. Night shows are also presented during annual flower festivals.

Highlands Hammock State Park – *1/2 day. 40mi south in Sebring. Take US-27 south and exit at Rte. 634 west; continue 3mi to park entrance at 5931 Hammock Rd. Open year-round daily 8am–dusk. $3.25/vehicle.* ⚠ 🅿 ☎ *941-386-6094.* One of Florida's four original state parks, this 4,694-acre site preserves one of the state's few remaining large virgin hammocks and other diverse plant communities. Biking and hiking trails pass beneath leafy canopies of hardwood trees; most paths are linked by a paved loop leading from the camping and recreation areas to the undeveloped sections of the park. From the western bend of the loop extends the **Cypress Swamp Trail★** *(.75mi)*, where lofty cypress trees and feathery ferns draw sustenance from the rich humus soil and tannin-brown pools of the floodplain embracing Charlie Bowlegs Creek. Displays in the state of Florida's Civilian Conservation Corps Museum *(across from Bailey's Camp Store in the picnic area)* commemorate the corps of men who built Florida's state parks and much of its infrastructure during the 1930s and 40s.

Water-Ski Stunts at Cypress Gardens

MAITLAND

Population 8,834
Map of Principal Sights p 3 – Map p 116
Tourist Information ☎ 407-644-0741

Set in an agricultural area studded by numerous lakes—14 within the city limits—
Maitland is graced with the quiet atmosphere of a small town located just 10mi from
ORLANDO. First known to the Seminoles as Fumechiliga ("Place of the Muskmelons"),
modern Maitland takes its name from the supply depot and way station established
here in 1838 for soldiers traveling between larger forts at Orlando and Sanford.

Historical Notes

Settlers trickled into the area after the Second Seminole War ended in 1842. One of
the first was James Hill, who came from Alabama in 1872 and planted the seeds of
Maitland's first orange grove. With the burgeoning citrus industry came the problem
of how to ship the fruit to markets along the East Coast, a dilemma solved in 1880
when the South Florida Railway extended its line to Maitland. Incorporated five years
later, the town boasted an ice factory, two livery stables and a citrus-packing house
by the turn of the century.
Citrus crops thrived in the area's mild climate and rich soil, leading to a banner year of
production in 1926. In the years following the stock-market crash, local landowners
discouraged new business from changing Maitland's tranquil face; thus incoming industries set up shop in nearby WINTER PARK and Orlando. Unfortunately, city fathers could
only stay development so long. Rapid growth accompanied the gearing-up of the US
space program in the 1950s, swelling Maitland's population and resulting in the sale
and development of former citrus groves. The city continued to mushroom in the 1960s
and '70s as Disney's presence brought still more people into the area. Today Maitland
welcomes both new industry and visitors. With its many lakes and a thriving arts community, this hamlet provides a pleasant respite from the theme-park frenzy of Orlando.

SIGHTS *1/2 day*

Historic Waterhouse Residence – *820 Lake Lily Dr., off Rte. 17/92 (Orlando
Ave.). Visit by guided tour (40min) only, year-round Thu–Sun noon–4pm. Closed
major holidays. Contributions requested.* 🅿 ☎ *407-644-2451.* This two-story
yellow Victorian home overlooking Lake Lily was built in 1884 by Maitland pioneer
William Waterhouse, who moved here from New York and helped secure the city's
charter in 1885. Constructed of Florida heart pine, the house boasts board-and-
batten paneling and an Eastlake-style staircase hand-carved by Waterhouse, who
was a builder by trade. The guided tour, conducted by members of the Maitland
Historical Society (who restored the house in 1992), gives visitors a glimpse into
the lives of a middle-class Florida family at the turn of the century. Behind the
house sits the one-room **Waterhouse Carpentry Shop**, where the former owner once
plied his trade. Antique carpentry tools—some belonging to Waterhouse—are on
display in this small workshop.

Maitland Art Center – *231 W. Packwood Ave., off Rte. 17/92 (Orlando Ave.).
Open year-round Mon–Fri 9am–4:30pm, weekends noon–4:30pm. Closed major
holidays. Contribution requested.* ♿ 🅿 ☎ *407-539-2181.* Artist and architect Jules
André Smith (1880-1959) built the stucco and cast-concrete **complex★** (1937) that
is listed on the National Register of Historic Places. Often hailed for its architecture, the center's buildings enclose a central courtyard and feature more than
200 fanciful cement carvings echoing a Mayan and Aztec motif. Changing exhibits
of both established and emerging contemporary artists rotate through several small
galleries inside the main building, and artists still work in the adjoining studios that
Smith designed. The center also offers a program of lectures, demonstrations and
classes throughout the year.

Maitland Historical Museum – *221 W. Packwood Ave. Visit by guided tour
(30min) only, year-round Thu–Sun noon–4pm. Closed major holidays. Contribution requested.* 🅿 ☎ *407-644-1364.* Located next door to the Art Center, this
small collection of historical photographs, artifacts and Victoriana presents Maitland's past. It includes a roomful of old telephones and related equipment, housed
in an addition in back of the building. This collection bills itself as the **Telephone
Museum**, in honor of the town's first telephone exchange, established in 1910.

Florida Audubon Society Center for Birds of Prey – *1101 Audubon Way, off S.
Lake Sybelia Dr. Open year-round Tue–Sun 10am–4pm. Closed major holidays. $5.*
🅿 *www.audubon.usf.edu* ☎ *407-644-0190.* The southeast's leading facility for
the rescue and rehabilitation of injured and orphaned raptors provides temporary
or permanent homes for 20 species of birds, including ospreys, bald eagles and
the threatened crested caracara. A walk-through aviary gives visitors a look at birds
disabled by gunshots, power lines, car collisions and other hazards. More than
500 birds are brought here every year for an average stay of three months. After
they recover, the birds are returned to the wild by the Florida Audubon Society.

ORLANDO★★★

Population 173,902
Map of Principal Sights p 3 – Map p 116
Tourist Information ☎ 407-363-5871

Once a sleepy orange-producing area, the sprawling metropolitan Orlando region now ranks as one of the nation's fastest-growing cities, as well as a tourist mecca attracting 34 million visitors annually. While the rapidly expanding southwestern corridor is filled with outlet malls, hotels, restaurants and entertainment complexes, the older, lake-dotted downtown area, with its historic architecture, retains the charm of early 20C Florida.

Historical Notes

A County Called Mosquito – In 1824 swampy Mosquito County stretched southward from St. Augustine and westward to Alachua County, encompassing the 2,558sq mi of land that today defines the Orlando metropolitan area. Mosquito County's population numbered some 700 settlers when the Second Seminole War broke out near Ocala in 1835. In order to protect the area's pioneers during this tumultuous period, the US government established several forts in the county. One of these, **Fort Gatlin**, was built in 1838 near the favored meeting place of local Seminole leaders.

After the hostilities ended in 1842, Congress lured settlers back into the area with the **Armed Occupation Act**. A wave of white pioneers responded to the government's offer, receiving 160 acres of land with the agreement that they would live on the frontier for five years and maintain their own defense. (Troops were finally withdrawn from the fort in 1849.) The settlement that arose in the wilderness around Fort Gatlin formed the nucleus of the future city of Orlando.

As in much of central Florida, cattle and cotton reigned as the major money-makers in those early decades. By the 1860s, the area known as Orange County (Mosquito County was subdivided into three separate counties shortly after Florida achieved statehood in 1845) was prized for its cotton, considered to be some of the finest in the South. The embryonic town of Orlando occupied part of a vast cotton plantation; Orlando was not incorporated as a city until 1875.

Citrus intruded as a major crop in the 1880s when the new South Florida Railway gave local growers access to wider markets. In spite of two disastrous freezes in the winter of 1894-95 that ruined crops and financially destroyed many growers, Orlando rebounded into a thriving agricultural town by the early 20C. Its economy was rooted in agriculture through the first half of the century until, in the early 1960s, a man named Disney forever changed the face of the city.

The Dawn of Disney – In 1965, having clandestinely purchased almost 30,000 acres in Orange and Osceola Counties, **Walt Disney** (p 134), animated-film wizard and creator of California's Disneyland, announced his plans to build a new theme park outside Orlando. Overnight, land values in the area skyrocketed; throughout the remainder of the decade, development engulfed the communities southwest of the city along the I-4 corridor. Walt Disney World opened to great fanfare in 1971. SeaWorld followed two years later, and Universal Studios Florida joined the local theme-park ranks in 1990.

In the 25 years since, the population of metropolitan Orlando has tripled. The area currently ranks as one of the top commercial tourist destinations in the world. Service-oriented development has produced endless outlet malls, restaurants and entertainment facilities; the Orlando metro area now boasts the largest concentration of hotel rooms in the US. This development has, in turn, created more jobs: The service sector alone saw a nearly 138 percent increase in employment within the last decade. Local industry has burgeoned with the addition of a number of large corporations—AT&T, Westinghouse and the American Automobile Association among them—to old-timers Tupperware and Lockheed Martin. And Hollywood has moved east, with both Universal and MGM-Disney studios filming dozens of movies and television shows in Orlando.

Judging by these indicators—coupled with Walt Disney World's continual expansion of its realm and Universal Studios' plans to triple the size of its complex—demographic and financial forecasters predict that Orlando will continue to be one of the country's fastest-growing areas well into the next century.

DOWNTOWN *1 day. Map p 126.*

Since Orlando's incorporation in 1875, this area has been the city's administrative hub. Though it fell victim to the decay that afflicted most downtown areas in mid-century, it has been revitalized in the last two decades, becoming a lively night spot popular both with residents and travelers. An eight-square-block core of downtown, centered around Orange Avenue and encompassing Church Street Station and Exchange, is designated the **Orlando Downtown Historic District**.

Practical Information... Area Code: 407

Getting There – **Orlando International Airport** (MCO): 7mi south of city; information booth *(open daily 7am–11pm; multilingual service)* ☎ 825-2352. Transportation to downtown: limo *($30)*; taxi *($25)*; 24hr-shuttle vans *($12–$21)* provided by Transtar ☎ 825-3187 or Mears ☎ 839-1570; public transportation *(Bus #11; Mon–Sat 4:45am–10:45pm Sun 5:45am–6:45pm. Bus #51; Mon–Sat 5:15am–9pm Sun 6:25am–6:25pm)*; and hotel courtesy shuttles. Rental car agencies *(p 323)* located at airport. Amtrak **train** station: 1400 Sligh Blvd., Orlando, and 150 W. Morse Blvd., Winter Park ☎ 800-872-7245. Greyhound/Trailways **bus** station: 555 N. John Young Parkway ☎ 800-231-2222.

Getting Around – Local **bus service**: Lynx *(year-round daily; 85¢; transfers 10¢)* schedule and route information ☎ 841-8240. The Beeline (Rte. 528), East-West Expressway and Central Florida GreeneWay are toll roads. Downtown shuttle service Lymno *(Mon–Thu 7am–10:30pm, Fri 7am–midnight, Sat 10am–midnight, Sun 10am–10pm; every 5min)*.
I-Ride trolley system services the International Drive area *(daily 7am–midnight; every 15 minutes; 75¢ each way)*; www.iridetrolley.com ☎ 354-5656. Metered downtown street parking *(75¢/hr)*; average rate for parking garages *($1/hr, $7/day)*. Parking information ☎ 246-2154.

Visitor Information – **Orlando/Orange County Convention and Visitors Bureau**, 6700 Forum Dr., Suite 100, Orlando FL 32821; **Official Visitor Center**, 8723 International Dr., Suite 101 *(open year-round daily 8am–7pm, closed Dec 25)* ☎ 363-5872. To obtain the Orlando Magicard *(free)*, which offers savings on accommodations, attractions, dining and shopping: ☎ 800-551-0181 (US and Canada). *The above organizations provide additional information regarding shopping, entertainment, festivals (p 318) and recreation.*

Accommodations – *(p 324)* Area visitors' guide including lodging directory available *(free)* from Orlando/Orange County Convention and Visitors Bureau *(above)*. Many hotels offer transportation to Disney parks and Universal Studios. For information on accommodations within Disney parks, see *p 135*. Hotel reservation service ☎ 800-950-0232 (US and Canada). **Central Reservation Service** ☎ 339-4116 operates 24hr courtesy phones at airport. Accommodations range from luxury hotels ($150-$400) to motels ($55-$125) and condominiums. **Youth Hostel**: Orlando/Kissimmee Resort ($14-$19/person; $30-$57/family) ☎ 396-8282. Campgrounds and RV parks available in area. *Rates quoted are average prices per night for a double room and are subject to seasonal variations.*

Entertainment – Consult the arts and entertainment section of *The Orlando Sentinel* (Friday), *Travelhost* and *See Orlando* publications for schedules of cultural events, attractions and restaurant information. Bob Carr Performing Arts Center: Orlando Opera Company, ballet, Broadway performances ☎ 849-2577; Orlando Arena: sporting events, rock concerts, circus ☎ 849-2020. Citrus Bowl Stadium: rock concerts, sporting events ☎ 849-2000. For arts and sporting-events tickets: **Ticketmaster** ☎ 839-3900.

Sports and Recreation – **Spectator sports**: Orlando Magic basketball (NBA), Orlando Arena ☎ 896-2442; Seminole Greyhound Park ☎ 699-4510; Orlando-Seminole Jai Alai Fronton ☎ 339-6221. Many area **golf** clubs allow non-members. Captain's Choice Golf Services, Inc. books tee times and offers transportation to most local courses; for reservations ☎ 352-1102. Public courses: International Golf Club ☎ 39-6909; Casselberry ☎ 699-9310; Orange Lake Country Club offers golf and water sports ☎ 239-0000. **Shopping**: Belz Factory Outlet World, International Dr. (over 150 stores) ☎ 354-0126; Church Street Exchange; Park Avenue, Winter Park.

Several residential historic districts surround downtown. The **Lake Cherokee District** *(south edge of downtown)* and the **Eola Heights District** *(northeast of downtown)* feature fine examples of Mediterranean, Colonial, Classical and Tudor Revival homes, as well as Art Deco structures, bungalows and substantial Victorians built between 1875 and 1930.

★**Orange Avenue** – Old Orlando's main business thoroughfare holds an eclectic mix of architecture that reflects the city's past and present. Anchoring the south end of the avenue, the classically inspired, domed **City Hall** (1992) is fronted by an expansive fountained plaza. Off the interior lobby, the **Terrace Gallery** displays changing exhibits devoted to the works of regional artists *(open year-round Mon–Fri 8am–9pm, weekends & holidays noon–5pm; closed Thanksgiving Day & Dec 25;* ✕ ⧉ ▣ ☎ *407-246-3146)*.

A block north, in the shadow of the SunTrust Center tower, is the old **First National Bank Building (A)** *(corner of Orange and Church Sts.).* Now part of Valencia Community College, the 1930 structure combines Classical Revival composition with Art Deco details. **McCrory Five & Dime** *(corner of Orange and Pine Sts.)* was once the largest McCrory store in the south, but now contains a game arcade. Its streamlined, horizontal lines exemplify the 1930s Art Moderne style. Several blocks away *(nos. 37-39 Magnolia Ave.),* the Queen Anne-style **Rogers Building** (c.1906) boasts a rare facade of pressed zinc panels. The nearby 1927 **Orange County Courthouse** *(Magnolia Ave. and Washington St.)* is presently being renovated to house The Orange County Historical Museum *(p 127),* which hopes to move into these new quarters by 2000. At the north end of downtown rises the **Barnett Bank Center** *(formerly the duPont Center; Orange Ave. and Livingston St.),* a lofty, three-towered high rise topped by silver spires. Completed in 1987, the building displays works of art, including Renoir's *Washerwoman,* in its public courtyard and lobby areas.

Church Street Station

★Church Street Station and Exchange – 🄺 129 W. Church St. Open year-round Sun–Thu 11am–1am, Fri–Sat 11am–2am. ✕ ⚕ 🄿 *($5) www.churchstreetstation.com* ☎ *407-422-2434.* This entertainment and shopping complex, begun in the 1970s, served as the rejuvenating force behind the area's redevelopment. Now downtown Orlando's main attraction, the complex features brick-paved walkways, re-created storefront facades and lavish Victorian interiors. Church Street Station comprises restaurants and themed showrooms, featuring live music and dancing to country-and-western, contemporary rock, classic rock and Dixieland jazz music *(year-round; hours vary; $17.95).*
Largely a shopping emporium, the Exchange is scattered with bars and eateries. The old brick **Orlando Railroad Depot (B)** (1887-90), which now houses offices, typifies late Victorian railroad design in its domed cupola and eyebrow roofline *(p 57)* covering dormer windows. On the tracks beside it sits "**Old Duke**," a 1912 Baldwin steam locomotive.

Lake Eola Park – *Central Blvd. and Rosalind Ave.* Downtown's best place for a pleasant stroll or a quiet break, the city's most popular park offers a band shell for concerts, paddleboats, a playground and a cafe. Attractive landscaping rims the lake, as does a pathway for walking, jogging and skating. Numerous benches provide good spots to view the city skyline and the lake's fountain, which is illuminated at night.

Additional Sights Near Downtown *Map p 126*

★Orlando Museum of Art – *2416 N. Mills Ave., in Loch Haven Park. From downtown, take I-4 east to Exit 43 (Princeton St.); turn right on Princeton. Park entrance is on Princeton, between Orange and Mills Aves. Open year-round Tue–Sat 9am–5pm, Sun noon–5pm. Closed major holidays. $4.* ⚕ 🄿 *www.omart.org* ☎ *407-896-4231.* Formed as a small local art center in 1924, the museum has expanded in step with

125

the city's growing population. A 1997 renovation, in fact, doubled the size of its gallery space. The heart of the permanent collection here is rotated in four large contemporary galleries. More than 600 works of **19C and 20C American art** include paintings by John Singer Sargent, George Inness, Georgia O'Keeffe, Maurice Prendergast and Gene Davis. Pre-Columbian cultures are represented by Western Mexican, Peruvian and Costa Rican pottery, jade, stone and textile artifacts dating from 1200 BC to AD 1521. An excellent African collection, supplemented by an ongoing series of temporary exhibits, features Yoruba beadwork, Asante statuary and Benin metalwork. Traveling exhibits occupy several additional small galleries. Youngsters will enjoy the hands-on "Art Encounter" 🚼 sponsored by Walt Disney World Co.

★**Orlando Science Center** – 🚼 *777 E. Princeton St., in Loch Haven Park. Open year-round Mon–Thu 9am–5pm, Fri–Sat 9am–9pm, Sun noon–5pm. Closed Thanksgiving Day & Dec 25. $9.50; additional charge for theaters.* 🍴 & 🅿 *www.osc.org* ☎ *407-514-2000.* This beautiful new, $48.8 million museum—a cylindrical building with a four-story central atrium—opened in February 1997 with interactive exhibits that educate and entertain children and adults alike. There are five principal display areas: On Level 1 (the ground floor), NatureWorks features lifelike dioramas of Florida ecosystems, including cypress and mangrove swamps (with real turtles and baby alligators) and a coral reef. Level 2 is dominated by Science City, whose interactive displays relate to mathematics, physical sciences and engineering, among them a power station and a suspension bridge. On Level 3, Cosmic Tourist instructs visitors in geology and astronomy. Level 4 features BodyZone, which demonstrates how our various anatomical systems rely on one another for total health, as well as Tech Works, an expansive exhibit that emphasizes applied technologies, especially computer simulation and laser optics.

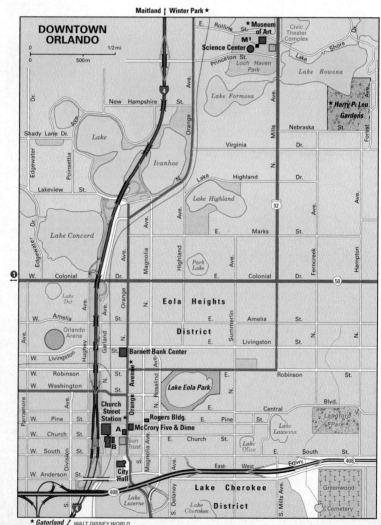

The center's two theaters—the 310-seat **Dr. Phillips CineDome** for large-format films and planetarium shows, and the 250-seat **Darden Adventure Theater** for live performances and science demonstrations—are complemented by the rooftop **Crosby Observatory** *(open Fri & Sat, weather permitting)*, which houses Florida's largest refractor telescope and sends live video feeds to the CineDome and classrooms. With 207,000sq ft of floor space, the Science Center is among the first in the country to tailor its exhibits and programs to mandated public-school science and math curricula requirements.

Orange County Historical Society and Museum (M¹) – *812 E. Rollins Ave., between the Science Center and Museum of Art in Loch Haven Park. Open year-round Mon–Sat 9am–5pm, Sun noon–5pm. Closed major holidays. $4.* ♿ 🅿 ☎ *407-897-6350.* This two-story museum presents regional artifacts ranging from prehistoric stone tools to mid-19C pioneer and Victorian furnishings to an early 20C print shop. Behind the museum stands **Fire Station #3**, Orange County's oldest standing firehouse (1927): The brick structure holds Orlando's original fleet of American LaFrance fire trucks, as well as 19C and 20C fire-fighting equipment. (This museum is scheduled to move by 2000 to the former Orange County Courthouse at Washington Street and Magnolia Avenue in downtown Orlando.)

> **① Lakeridge Winery & Vineyards**
>
> *Map p 116. 20mi west in Clermont. Take the East-West Expressway west to Florida's Turnpike; head north on turnpike to Exit 285 (Rte. 50 west). Follow Rte. 50 west to US-27 and go north 5.5mi to vineyard. Open year-round daily 10am–5pm. Closed Jan 1, Easter Sunday, Thanksgiving Day, Dec 25.* ♿ 🅿 ☎ *904-394-8627.* One of only three Florida wineries, Lakeridge was established in 1989. About 34 acres of native muscadine and Florida hybrid bunch grapes grow in the well-drained soil, where European varieties cannot survive. A guided tour includes a 14min introductory video and a view of the winery and bottling room from a second-story deck. At the end of the tour, visitors can taste the vineyard's wines. Grapes are harvested in early July and August.

★**Harry P. Leu Gardens** – *1920 N. Forest Ave. From Loch Haven Park, follow Princeton St. to Mills Ave. Turn right on Mills, then left on Virginia Dr., which becomes Forest Ave. Purchase tickets in the Garden House. Open Nov–Mar daily 9am–5pm. Rest of the year Mon–Sat 9am–8pm, Sun 9am–6pm. Closed Dec 25. $4.* ♿ 🅿 *www.ci.orlando.fl.us/departments/leugardens/index.html* ☎ *407-246-2620.* Orlando businessman and exotic plant collector Harry P. Leu donated his home and 50-acre botanical reserve to the city in 1961. Situated along the southern shore of Lake Rowena, the gardens are renowned for their **camellia collection**★ featuring more than 2,000 specimens, a number of which are rare or historic *(in peak bloom from Jan–mid-Feb)*. More than 1,000 roses representing 250 varieties color the largest formal **rose garden** in the state *(in bloom from Mar–Jan)*. Some 2mi of sidewalk meander past plantings that include cacti and succulents (in the xerophyte garden) and 40 different species of palms. A small conservatory devoted to orchids, ferns and bromeliads stands near the southeast corner of the garden.

Built as a modest farmhouse in 1888, the two-story white frame **Leu House Museum** was enlarged by its subsequent owners—including the Leu family, who lived here from 1936 to 1961. Furnishings reflect the early 20C *(visit by 30min guided tour only, Mon–Sat 10am–3:30pm, Sun 1pm–3:30pm; free with admission to gardens)*. The gracious white-columned Garden House, opened in 1995, holds a gift shop, classrooms and meeting and banquet space.

EXCURSION

★**Gatorland** – 🅺🄸🄳🄸 *Description p 117. 13mi south of downtown Orlando. Take I-4 west to Exit 26; follow Rte. 536 east 2mi, then take the Central Florida Greene Way (Rte. 417) north 6mi; turn right on Orange Blossom Tr. (US17/92/441); Gatorland is on left .5mi south of the GreeneWay, at 14501 Orange Blossom Tr.*

★★★UNIVERSAL STUDIOS ESCAPE *Map p 116*

Universal Studios was taking its first giant steps toward head-on-head competition with Walt Disney World as this edition went to press. Formerly a single theme park and working movie studio, the fantasy broker is expanding its focus (and its name) with an impressive new theme park, **Universal Studios Islands of Adventure** *(p 130)* scheduled to open in summer 1999. "Islands" will be linked to **Universal Studios Florida** (the original park) with an upscale dining, entertainment and shopping complex, **Universal Studios CityWalk** *(p 131)*, set to begin opening in late 1998. Also in the development stages are several resort hotels, including the first-ever Hard Rock Hotel, and more studio production space, nearly tripling the size of the pre-existing Universal Studios.

★★★Universal Studios Florida *Map p 116*

The original 444-acre theme park and working studio (with nine soundstages), Universal Studios Florida ranks as the largest motion picture and television facility outside Hollywood. Intended as a place where visitors can "ride the movies," the park's attractions are based on popular films and television shows.

Universal Goes East – Universal Studios Florida continues the tradition begun in 1915 by the studio's Hollywood founder, **Carl Laemmle**, who encouraged paying visitors to stop by and watch movies being made. A joint venture between MCA Recreation Services Group and the Rank Organisation, the park opened in 1990. The Orlando site was chosen for its climate and established tourist base, and for its appeal to movie and television talent. Director Steven Spielberg, as creative consultant, carefully designed the Florida site as an "integrated production and entertainment facility." Since streets frequently double as movie sets, you may see a shoot as you tour the park. You can also visit soundstages where such television shows as the Nickelodeon Network's *Keenan and Kel, Clarissa Explains It All* and *The Mystery Files of Shelby Woo,* as well as *Waterboy,* a 1998 movie starring Adam Sandler, have been filmed.

Practical Information – Taking in all the shows and rides requires 1.5 very full days, in part owing to this park's long lines. Arrive 30min to 1hr prior to opening time. As soon as the gates open, head for Twister (Universal's newest attraction), Terminator 23-D, Back to the Future and JAWS; then visit E.T. Adventure, FUN-tastic World of Hanna-Barbera, and Kongfrontation. Plan to see shows during midday, when ride lines are longest. Check Preview of Today's Rides and Shows for scheduled times. The park often closes with the **Dynamite Nights Stunt Spectacular**, a boat chase spangled by special effects, which roars around the Universal lagoon. The VIP Studio Tour gives visitors priority entrance to leading attractions *(daily 10am & noon; 5hrs; 72hr advance reservations required; $110, includes park admission; for reservations Mon–Fri 9am–6pm ☎ 407-363-8295).*

Visit *1 day*

Kids *1000 Universal Studios Plaza. Follow I-4 to Exit 29 (Sand Lake Rd.); turn right on Sand Lake Rd. and take next right on Turkey Lake Rd. Studio entrance is less than 2mi on right. Open year-round Mon–Fri 9am–6pm, weekends 9am–7pm. Open until 10pm during Easter week and Jul–Aug, until midnight mid-Oct to Halloween. Rest of the year closing times may vary. Adult $44.52, children 3-12 years $36.04; 2-day pass: adult $65.72, children 3-12 years $55.12.* ✗ ⚕ 🅿 ⅢⅢ *www.usf.com ☎ 407-363-8000.*
Chrome and glass-block shops and eateries line the **Front Lot**, where such celebrity look-alikes as Mae West, Lucille Ball, Ricky Ricardo and Charlie Chaplin may put in an appearance. Universal's reproduction of **Hollywood** angles off to the right, where palms sway above such legendary landmarks as the Beverly Wilshire Hotel and Schwab's soda fountain. Among replicas of the exclusive shop fronts of Rodeo Drive lies **Lucy, A Tribute**, a gallery devoted to Lucille Ball memorabilia and clips from the *I Love Lucy* show. **The Gory Gruesome & Grotesque Horror Make-up Show** treats audiences to a view of comically inclined make-up artists who demonstrate the tricks of their trade, while in the Pantages Theatre on Hollywood Boulevard is another makeup display that changes according to what Universal film is currently "hot." **AT&T at the Movies** is an interactive arcade where visitors can touch the technology of moviemaking.

Terminator 23-D: Battle Across Time – Arnold's back–with a vengeance–in this sequel to the popular Schwarzenegger film *Terminator 2: The Final Judgment.* Your senses will thrill to the close encounters and pyrotechnics in this show, presented both in live action and as a 3-D movie. At $23 million, the 12min film—directed by James Cameron whose credits include the 1998 hit, *Titanic*—is said to be the most expensive action movie ever shot, minute for minute.

At the far end of the park's eight-acre lagoon, Hollywood gives way to **Expo Center**. Modern facades here, with flags representing the 1984 Olympics in Los Angeles, hold some of the park's most successful attractions.

E.T. Adventure – The magic of director Steven Spielberg's spectacularly popular film is captured both in this ride and its waiting area, where visitors are guaranteed to spend a good bit of time. Long lines weave through a dark, dreamy Northwest forest, scented with evergreens. E.T. has returned to Earth to obtain our assistance in healing his Green Planet, which has fallen ill. Riders hop aboard bicycles that carry them and the unforgettable extraterrestrial on an airborne adventure above an American cityscape and on to E.T.'s beloved home.

Fievel's Playland – Another tribute to a Spielberg character, this whimsical playground is based on the antics of Fievel the mouse (from the animated film *An American Tail*). Nets for climbing, tubes for exploring, and watery slides for getting wet make up this miniature world.

A Day in the Park with Barney – Colorful sets with top-flight stage effects complement songs by the purple dinosaur of PBS fame and his friends, Baby Bop and B.J. A new human character, the endearingly kooky Mr. Peekaboo, adds to the fun. After exiting the theater-in-the-round, the audience enters "Barney's Backyard," an educational play area.

Animal Actors Stage – Performances on this outdoor stage feature look-alikes for such canine and equine stars as Lassie, Benji and Mr. Ed. *Check park brochure for show times.*

Back To The Future: The Ride – In Universal's most popular ride, you'll heed the taped plea of Doc Brown (actor Christopher Lloyd) to help save the universe from evil villain Biff Tannen. Board a Time Vehicle for a white-knuckle flight into the Ice Age, where you'll thunder over glacial fields and free-fall into a flaming volcano. Multisensory special effects enhance the experience.

Wild, Wild, Wild West Stunt Show – Commandeering the stage of this amphitheater, the Hopper (as in Clod) family ham it up with their fancy shootin' and stuntsmanship. *Check park brochure for show times.*

At the east end of the lagoon, small, weathered clapboard facades and street vendors re-create the New England seaside atmosphere of **Amity**, fictional setting of the 1975 movie hit *Jaws*.

JAWS – On a cruise through the waters around Amity, passengers find themselves virtually in the maw of that infamous and indestructible Great White. Boat pilots, however, have a few tricks up their sleeves, and after some spectacular fiery clashes, all are returned safely to shore.

Along the north edge of the Lagoon, Amity melds into **San Francisco**. The old Ghirardelli chocolate factory and trolley tracks running through the street leave no doubt that you've entered that city's famous Fisherman's Wharf area.

Earthquake – The attraction begins with a behind-the-scenes look at how Charlton Heston made the movie *Earthquake* in 1974. Visitors then board a San Francisco subway for a truly ground-breaking trip, in which the earth shakes and cataclysm follows.

Beetlejuice's Rock 'n' Roll Graveyard Revue – In this camp musical revue emceed by the incorrigible Beetlejuice, Dracula, Frankenstein and his bride, and other movie monsters stomp through rock-'n-roll classics. *Check park brochure for show times.*

The streets of **New York** capture the romantic, if somewhat decrepit, charms of the brownstones, parks and billboards of the Big Apple. At various intervals, the **Blues Brothers** stage their own outdoor show on Delancey Street. *Check park brochure for show times.*

Kongfrontation – After winding through a New York subway station complete with graffiti-splattered walls, passengers board cable cars for a trip above the city streets. But with the great Kong on the loose, they're guaranteed a primate confrontation or two.

Twister! Ride It Out – An adaptation of the 1996 movie of the same name, Twister! subjects visitors to the fury of a large tornado as it rages through a rural town on the Great Plains, right down to tanker fires, broken water mains and a flying cow, just 20ft away.

The **Production** section is more devoted to the art of television and filmmaking than any other portion of the park. **Stage 54 (Production Central)** features props and sets from a recent major Universal film or television show, actually re-creating some of the film's most dramatic scenes. Six warehouse-style buildings contain working sound stages, while the centrally located **Bone Yard** features such classic movie props as the dorsal fin sported by the great white shark in *Jaws*.

Hercules and Xena: Wizards of the Screen – Fans of the two TV series starring Kevin Sorbo and Lucy Lawless get a glimpse of the way acting, sound and general production come together to create a combined episode of the popular fantasy shows. Audience volunteers go shoulder-to-shoulder into battle with their screen heroes and otherwise assist in making the magic work.

Alfred Hitchcock: The Art of Movie Making – In a multimedia theater, the audience watches 3-D film clips of Hitchcock thrillers, as the master of suspense explains his methods. Volunteers get a chance to play some of the more memorable roles in Hitchcock's 1960 film *Psycho*.

Flintstones Characters and Friends

The FUNtastic World of Hanna-Barbera – Belying its childlike cartoon theme, this ranks as one of the park's most action-packed rides. A theater audience strapped into rollicking seats takes a simulated zoom through cartoonland, visiting the Flintstones, the Jetsons, Yogi Bear and a host of other Hanna-Barbera familiars along the way. The exit leads into a hands-on playroom filled with cartoon whimsy. *For those interested in the cartoon but not the motion, stationary seats are located at the front of the theater.*

The **Green Slime Geyser** located on Nickelodeon Way periodically erupts in an ooze of the gooey green mixture featured in several of the Nickelodeon Network's television series.

Nickelodeon Studios Tour – *Tours operate continuously 9am–closing; first-come, first-served;* &. The tour gives visitors a look at the two soundstages where 80 percent of the acclaimed Nickelodeon shows (aimed at pre- and early teens) are taped. You stand a good chance of observing a taping in session here. Even when the cameras aren't rolling, a guide explains the process of putting a show together and takes visitors past soundstages, make-up and hair departments, and dressing rooms of the show's young stars.

Universal Studios Islands of Adventure

With producer-director Steven Spielberg as creative consultant, "Islands" is destined to be acclaimed as a triumph of imagination. Summer 1999 is the target date for its grand opening, although its gateway area, Port of Entry, is scheduled to open in October 1998 to whet the appetites of theme-park lovers.

With its unique and eclectic architecture representing a variety of world harbor cultures, **Port of Entry** is projected mainly as a shopping and dining area. Island-Hopper Cruises will depart from here for the five unique islands that will comprise the bulk of the park. **Seuss Landing** will feature the whimsical characters of child-literature favorite Theodor "Dr. Seuss" Geisel. **Toon Lagoon** will bring to life classic cartoon characters. Realistic dinosaurs will stalk visitors at **Jurassic Park**, while high-tech thrill rides will be the main attractions of **The Lost Continent** and **Marvel Super Hero Island**.

Universal Studios CityWalk

Scheduled to open gradually between December 1998 and March 1999, this is designed as a two-tiered, 30-acre promenade of individually themed entertainment venues wrapped around a four-acre harbor. It will link the main entrances of Universal Studios Florida and Islands of Adventure, which then will be accessible only through CityWalk. Highlights will include jazz, rock and reggae nightclubs, a New Orleans-style bar and restaurant, and a production center for E! Entertainment Television.

★★★SEAWORLD ADVENTURE PARK ORLANDO Map p 137

Kids *7007 Sea World Dr. (International Dr.). From downtown, follow I-4 west to Exit 28, then follow signs to SeaWorld. Open Apr–Sept daily 9am–10pm. Rest of the year daily 9am–7pm. Extended hours during spring break and Christmas week. $42.* ✗ఈ �ⵁℍℍ *www.seaworld.com* ☎ *407-351-3600 or 800-432-1178.*

This 200-acre commercial marine zoological park mixes entertainment and education in its many animal shows, touch pools and aquariums. Opened in 1973, the park is one of four SeaWorlds nationwide. Together these parks, now owned by Anheuser-Busch, support the world's largest collection of marine life. In addition to its public attractions, SeaWorld actively pursues research and breeding programs, and has successfully bred five orcas (killer whales). The Beached Animal Rescue and Rehabilitation Program has assisted hundreds of wild animals in distress, including manatees, dolphins and whales.

Practical Information – Along with the park's rides, Journey to Atlantis and Wild Arctic, many of SeaWorld's most popular attractions are shows, whose schedules are listed in the map of the park you receive when you purchase your ticket. Head for Atlantis first, then to Wild Arctic, and plan the rest of your visit around show times, as other attractions are relatively accessible throughout the day. Orca shows in Shamu Stadium are the most popular. As is the case with most Orlando attractions, the busiest periods are during summer, Christmas and spring vacations.

Three different behind-the-scenes guided educational tours, ranging from 45min to 60min, explain the park's animal care, training and research facilities, including its Arctic and deep-sea divisions. Purchase tickets *($5)* at the Information Center when you enter the park.

Visit *1 day*

Roughly elliptical, SeaWorld is a maze of walkways with a large lagoon dominating its southern half. Most of the pools and aquariums lie on the north, or entrance, side of the lagoon. **Marine Mammal Shows** *(25min)* are repeated several times daily *(check park brochure for show times).*

Enter through a new six-acre gateway area with a 55ft lighthouse at its heart. The tower, painted with a stylized image of Shamu, the park's trademark orca, stands atop rocks in a million-gallon harbor, surrounded by sailing ships and stone sea lions. Its beacon guides nighttime visitors back to their vehicles. Adjacent ticket and guest-relations counters, restaurants and gift shops all have taken on a pleasant harbor-town ambience.

Just beyond the gateway is the **Tropical Reef**, a man-made coral reef (no real coral is used in the park, because it can't survive in an artificial environment) into which are set some three dozen small aquarium tanks representing a wide variety of marine habitats and sea creatures, such as moray eels and chambered nautiluses. Behind the building is a **Tidal Pool** where visitors may touch and examine sea anemones, sea cucumbers and other marine mammals while posing questions to a naturalist. To the right of the tropical reef, a short walkway leads to the **Dolphin Nursery**, where young marine mammals are nurtured. South Seas dancers perform by the lagoon in the **Luau Terrace** room four times each afternoon *(check park brochure for show times)* and at a Hawaiian-style dinner show; a beachfront stage that once was home to the hula is scheduled to host a bird show.

Key West at SeaWorld – Moving clockwise from the gateway, a short walk brings you to this quirky village, which re-creates the spirit of Florida's furthest resort outpost in its shops and cafes. It even has a resident band playing Jimmy Buffett and Beach Boys music. Attractions include **Stingray Lagoon**, where visitors can touch the broad flat fish as they swim by; **Turtle Point**, which introduces several endangered species; and **Dolphin Cove**, where viewers can participate in feeding the marine mammals.

Key West Dolphin Stadium – Watch dolphins leap 18ft above the water and execute full flips and triple twists for fish rewards during the five-time-daily "Key West Dolphin Fest." These graceful mammals further demonstrate their learning skills as trainers dance with them and ski around the pool—each foot on the nose of a dolphin. *Those seated in the first few rows may get wet.* The stadium is also home to the **Dolphin Interaction Program** (DIP), whose participants pay $148 to undergo 90min of early-morning education before swimming with highly intelligent bottlenose dolphins under the supervision of experienced trainers.

Manatees: The Last Generation? – Manatees here share a re-created Florida wetland with great blue herons and wood storks. On a lower level visitors may peer into the pool and view the slow-moving sea cows from an underwater vantage point. A film explains the plight of these endangered creatures in the wild and current efforts to save them.

SeaWorld also operates an ongoing manatee release program, in which orphaned or injured manatees are released into the wild at the rate of about six per year (orphans are released at the age of five or six).

Journey to Atlantis – You're guaranteed to get wet—very wet—at SeaWorld's newest attraction and its first true thrill ride. As the story goes, the mythical lost city of Atlantis has mysteriously risen from the floor of the Aegean Sea, and you're one of the first explorers. Your eight-passenger Greek fishing boat is actually a high-speed roller coaster that carries you through dark and misty passageways haunted by evil sirens, down a nearly vertical 60ft waterfall and around a pair of S-curves into another free-falling plunge.

Continue clockwise (south) from Atlantis, which is at SeaWorld's northeastern corner.

Penguin Encounter – Step on the beltway for a ride past a frosty 28°F setting where puffins, murres and several species of penguins—including chinstrap, gentoo, rockhopper and king—reside. Through a glass-sided observation pool you can view the graceful swimming of these flightless birds.

Pacific Point Preserve – Rocky shoals of an open-air pool capture the atmosphere of the Pacific coast. Harbor and fur seals bob in the waters, sea lions lounge on rocks, and a symphony of sounds is always in progress.

Sea Lion & Otter Stadium – Sea lions Clyde and Seamore, the Abbott and Costello of the pinniped family, star as stranded buccaneers in "Clyde and Seamore Take Pirate Island." After a clever otter steals a pirate's treasure map, he enlists the help of the dynamic duo in recovering the scaly wealth. A walrus co-stars in the 25min show, presented five times daily.

Stroll west from the stadium to the SeaWorld Theater. The Sky Tower is immediately to its south.

SeaWorld Theater – The 25min show presented here five times each day has little or nothing to do with the sea, but it's a family favorite. "Pets on Stage" features the talents of 12 dogs and 18 cats—nearly all of whom were rescued from animal shelters—as well as birds, rats, three pot-bellied pigs and a one-horse stampede.

Sky Tower – For those who want a bird's-eye **view** of SeaWorld, this tower lifts passengers in a rotating chamber to the top of a 400ft shaft for a view of Orlando area attractions *($3)*. A footbridge crosses the central lagoon to attractions on its far side.

Return to your clockwise course around the lagoon.

Terrors of the Deep – At the entrance to this memorable attraction, a small outdoor pool houses several varieties of sharks and rays. Inside, visitors walk through an acrylic archway that tunnels through a 660,000gal aquarium while a spectacular array of fish swim by on all sides. The tank's B-shaped contours were specifically designed to accommodate the swimming patterns of sharks, five different species of which glide through these waters. Smaller tanks contain beautiful but deadly lionfish, sinister barracuda and other denizens, making this the largest collection of "dangerous sea creatures" in the world.

Nautilus Theater – SeaWorld's excellent Cirque de la Mer ("Circus of the Sea") presents a 25min musical adaptation of "The Flight of the Condor," a traditional South American story. Narrated by renowned Peruvian comedian Cesar Aedo, the show blends music and dance, athletic and aerobatic feats with dramatic special effects. Shows are presented four times daily.

Immediately south at the **Anheuser-Busch Hospitality Center** guests are offered free samples of the company's famous beers. A brief film, *The Color of Life*, recounts the company's role in conservation. Brawny horses that serve as the Busch mascots are tethered in the adjacent **Clydesdale Hamlet**. A festive eight-horse hitch of Clydesdales parades around the park, weather permitting, twice a day *(except Fridays; check at Clydesdale Hamlet for times; Hospitality Center closes 1hr prior to the rest of the park).*

Shamu's Happy Harbor – This fanciful playground is geared to the under-10 crowd and others who enjoy water mazes, squirting fountains, air bounces and other energetic pastimes.

Shamu Stadium – SeaWorld's signature attraction, this water show, staged in a five-million-gallon tank, stars the renowned five-ton orca Shamu, along with his protégés, Baby Shamu and Baby Namu. Guided by their trainers, the trio leaps and twirls to music in a wholesome water ballet that is simultaneously captured on an immense ShamuVision© screen. Trainers also enter the water to ride the orcas and demonstrate some truly remarkable feats.

In the latest 30min show, **The Shamu Adventure**, animal expert Jack Hanna introduces the audience to Alaska's Glacier Bay, the fiords of Norway and the sub-antarctic Crozet Islands of the south Indian Ocean. Video footage of whales in their natural habitats points up behavior that is then mimicked in SeaWorld by Shamu and off-spring. An original score and a live appearance by bald eagles make this *(offered three times daily)* one of the best Shamu shows yet.

The last performance of the evening incorporates a light show, **Shamu Rocks America**, followed by a fireworks display *(check park brochure for show times)*. *The first 14 rows are designated the "splash zone" with good reason. If you don't wish to get doused with icy salt water, or if you have expensive camera or video equipment, seek seats higher up in the stadium. For the best seats, arrive 15-30min prior to show time during peak seasons.*

Just in front of the stadium, you can see whales swimming and interacting with trainers between shows in the 1.7-million-gallon pool at **Shamu: Close Up!** This research facility fosters study of killer whale behavior as well as sponsoring a successful breeding program.

Wild Arctic – A virtual-reality helicopter ride takes passengers on a northern adventure, pitching and rolling over a crevassed landscape above caribou, polar bears and narwhals. After narrowly escaping an avalanche, you disembark at a mock-up of an arctic research station, featuring above- and below-water views of beluga whales as well as polar bears, walruses and harbor seals. Here visitors learn how station scientists while away the long frozen days monitoring whale creaks, whistles and clicks. *Visitors who don't want to suffer the pitching and reeling of the helicopter ride can travel to Base Station Wild Arctic by simulated cross-country ski tour.*

Atlantis Bayside Stadium – The 3,800-seat water stadium, on the southwest shore of the SeaWorld lagoon, is home to a 30min stunt show, **The Intensity Games**. Taking advantage of a craze for "extreme" sports, it features a 20-member team of world-class water skiers. Speed, strength, stamina, danger and the "big air" athleticism of world-class gymnastics are part of this fine show, offered three times daily. Look for long-distance jumping, high-speed barefoot skiing and aerial acrobatics *(check park brochure for show times)*.

Orca Show at Shamu Stadium

WALT DISNEY WORLD★★★

Map of Principal Sights p 3 – Map p 137
Tourist Information ☎ 407-824-4321

Truly a microcosm unto itself, this immense 29,900-acre (47sq mi) complex—about twice the size of Manhattan Island—lies 20mi southwest of Orlando and compasses four extensive theme parks (Magic Kingdom, Epcot, Disney's Animal Kingdom and Disney-MGM Studios), 27 separate resort hotels with more than 25,000 rooms, 12 nightclubs, three water parks, six 18-hole golf courses, a 200-acre sports complex, numerous lakes, a zoological park and much more. First opened in 1971 with the Magic Kingdom, Walt Disney World continues to grow, combining in its attractions the romantic nostalgia of the mid-20C Disney vision with the fast-paced technology of the present.

Historical Notes

The Story Behind the Dream – Born and raised in the Midwest, **Walter Elias Disney** (1901-1966) showed early signs of a keen imagination and an aptitude for drawing— talents that would catapult him to success. By the age of 21 he had already established an animation studio in Kansas City. When that failed, he headed for Hollywood.

The Disney Brothers Studios, established by Walt and his brother Roy in 1923, scored its first popular success in 1928 with *Steamboat Willie*. With characteristic Disney inventiveness, the film, starring a mouse named Mickey, combined animation and the new technology of sound. That creativity carried through to a series of successes in the 1930s and early 1940s. Disney's first full-length animated film, *Snow White* (1937), met with instant success.

In the early 1950s, his film interests well-established, Disney again let his imagination rove. Disillusioned with the tawdriness of existing amusement parks, he began planning his own in Anaheim, California. Disneyland, which opened in July 1955, was destined to change the face of global amusement. Owing to its phenomenal popularity, Disney launched plans to open a second theme park. He wanted to acquire a far larger tract that could be buffered from the sort of commercial development that had sprung up around the 180-acre Anaheim site. His new park would create a Disney-styled world where visitors could eat, sleep and enjoy his entertainment.

Disney's New Kingdom – Walt Disney chose central Florida as the site of his new park in the mid-1960s, presumably because land was inexpensive, the climate was good, and growth was anticipated in the area. Keeping his identity a secret, Disney bought almost 30,000 acres of land at less than $200 an acre. He then presented the Reedy Creek Improvement District Act to the Florida legislature. When it passed, the bill designated Disney's tract a self-governing municipality.

Disney envisioned his Florida property as an **Experimental Prototype Community of Tomorrow** (Epcot)—a place that would function both as a model for future communities and highlight the creativity behind American industry. He also included a Magic Kingdom like Anaheim's in the plans; that segment was to open first. As building began, however, Disney was diagnosed with cancer; the 65-year-old cartoonist died in 1966. In deference to his brother, Roy Disney changed the name of the Florida complex from Disney World to Walt Disney World, keeping Walt's concept for the park more or less intact. In 1971 Magic Kingdom opened, followed in 1982 by Epcot. Seven years later, Walt Disney World added Disney-MGM Studios, a combination working film studio and theme park celebrating the magic of the movies. Disney's Animal Kingdom opened to the public in spring 1998.

The immensely popular Disney concept has also been exported abroad. In 1983 Tokyo Disneyland opened, followed in 1993 by Disneyland Paris *(see Michelin Green Guide to Disneyland Paris)*. Orlando's Walt Disney World, however, remains the largest Disney complex and the most visited theme park in the world.

The Shape of Attractions to Come – Walt Disney's realm is ever-changing. Early 1996 saw the start-up of the Disney Institute, a program that offers a variety of learning vacations designed for adults and families with children *(for information, call* ☎ *800-496-6337)*. Later that year the **Walt Disney World Speedway** hosted its first Indy 200 race, and the corporation opened a replica of a 1930s-era Atlantic-coast **Board-Walk**, complete with shops, restaurants, nightclubs and a hotel. Completed in 1997 were **Disney's Wide World of Sports**, a 200-acre complex with a 5,000-seat baseball stadium and facilities for 30 other amateur and professional sports, and the **Richard Petty Driving Experience**, a 145mph test-track adventure. The 500-acre Animal Kingdom opened in 1998, as did **Downtown Disney West Side**, a dining-and-nightlife complex. The company even launched a brand-new Disney Cruise Line based at Port Canaveral, on the Atlantic coast.

Lots are selling fast at **Celebration**, a $100 million planned community under construction 15mi south of Magic Kingdom by the Disney conglomerate. The first residents occupied their homes in summer 1996. Eventually to cover 4,900 acres, Celebration embodies Disney's vision of the turn-of-the-century American small town. When completed, the community will include its own school, health-care facility and business district.

When to Go

Walt Disney World is busiest during the summer, Christmas and spring holidays. The least crowded period falls between Thanksgiving and December 25, followed by September and October, then January. Mondays, Tuesdays and Wednesdays—except during holiday seasons—are the busiest days of the week at Magic Kingdom. Tuesdays and Wednesdays are more crowded at Epcot; attendance at Disney-MGM Studios is heaviest on Thursdays and Fridays. Sunday morning tends to be least crowded at all three parks. Due to constant updating and maintenance, some rides and eating facilities may be closed. During the summer months (late May–late Sept), temperatures range from 85°-95°F during the day, and from 68°-75°F at night. Humidity is high and afternoon thundershowers are frequent. The rest of the year, temperatures average from 75°-82°F during the day, and dip between 52°-65°F at night. Lightweight, comfortable clothing, a hat and sunscreen are suggested.

Planning your Visit – Each of the four theme parks requires at least a full day, from opening to closing time. For a more leisurely visit, take two days to see both Epcot and Magic Kingdom—particularly if you are traveling with young children. On the day of your visit, arrive at the park when ticket booths open, usually one hour before the scheduled opening time. With your ticket, you will receive a Walt Disney World guide, detailed map and show schedule that lists times for performances, parades and all other entertainment. Visitors staying at Walt Disney World properties can enter the parks at 7:30am on selected days (Magic Kingdom: Mon, Thu & Sat; Epcot: Tue & Fri; Disney-MGM Studios: Wed & Sun). For up-to-date schedules, call ☎ 824-4321 or Guest Relations, or access their Web site at www.disneyworld.com. All **guided tours** are limited to 15-20 people; prices are in addition to park entrance fees; advance reservations are required ☎ WDW-TOUR (939-8687). For information on special events in celebration of the **millennium** in 2000: ☎ 824-4321.

Getting There

By Air – Orlando International Airport (MCO): 28mi northeast of Walt Disney World; information booth *(open daily 7am–11pm)* ☎ 825-2352. Shuttle service to Walt Disney World *(departs from baggage claim area year-round daily every 15-20min; $14/one-way, child $10)* Mears Motor Shuttle ☎ 839-1570. Limo and taxi service also available. Rental car agencies *(p 323)* located at the airport. If driving from Orlando airport, take the Beeline Expressway, Route 528 west *(toll)*, then continue on I-4 west to parks.

By Car – Walt Disney World is located 20mi southwest of downtown Orlando. Take I-4 west to Exit 26B for best access to Epcot, Typhoon Lagoon, Downtown Disney, River Country and Discovery Island. For the most direct route to Disney's Animal Kingdom, Wide World of Sports, Disney-MGM Studios and the Magic Kingdom, take Exit 25B (Route 192 west) and follow signs to the various parks. Trams shuttle visitors to the main gates from pick-up areas throughout the sprawling parking lots. Note the section and row where you park; it's easy to lose track of your vehicle.

By Train or Bus – Nearest Amtrak station: 1400 Sligh St., Orlando *(24mi from park)* ☎ 800-872-7245. Greyhound/Trailways station: 555 N. McGruder Blvd., Orlando (26mi from park), and 16 N. Orlando Ave., Kissimmee *(12mi from park)* ☎ 800-231-2222.

General Information

Accommodations – *(p 324)* The vast Walt Disney World complex offers over 25,000 rooms at 27 properties that include resort hotels, villas, condominiums, cabins and campgrounds. Rates vary depending on location, type of hotel and season; rates are lower during early Jan–mid-Feb, mid-Apr–mid-Jun and Sept–mid-Dec. Children under 18 stay free in rooms with parents. In-room baby-sitting service is available. KinderCare center accepts 1- to 4yr-old children. For all reservations ☎ W-DISNEY (934-7639), dial *88 from specially marked phones, or visit the Guest Relations booths at individual parks.

Outside the Disney Complex – Numerous lodging facilities lie within easy reach (5-10min) of the main entrances. Accommodations range from luxury hotels ($220–$350) to moderate hotels ($90–$220) and budget motels ($49–$65). Many offer free shuttle service to Disney attractions. Make reservations three to five months in advance—especially for summer and holiday stays. Information on area accommodations available from the **Orlando/Orange County Convention and Visitors Bureau** *(p 124)*. *Rates quoted are average prices per night for a double room and are subject to seasonal variation.*

Visitor Information – For general information and to request a free Vacation Guide, contact Walt Disney World Guest Information, PO Box 10040, Lake Buena Vista FL 32830-0040; www.disneyworld.com. ☎ 824-4321. All Walt Disney World attractions are accessible to visitors with disabilities. All attractions are free for children under 3. **Parking:** $5. Same-day **reentry** is permitted with a valid ticket and hand stamp. Proper dress is required at all times. Baby strollers and wheelchair rentals available in limited quantities *($5)*. For most visitor services (foreign language maps, information for guests with disabilities, baby facilities, lost and found, storage lockers, banking facilities, camera centers, Disney character greeting information), contact Guest Relations at individual parks: City Hall, Main Street USA at Magic Kingdom; near Gift Stop at Epcot; Hollywood Boulevard at Disney-MGM Studios; next to Creature Comfort at Animal Kingdom. For **lost children**, check the lost children's logbooks at Baby Care Centers or contact Guest Relations. For **medical emergencies**, contact the First Aid Centers near Guest Relations.

Admission Fees

	Adults	Children
All attractions are free for children under 3		*(ages 3-9)*
One-day/One park ticket	$42	$34
4-day Value Pass (1 day at each park)	$149	$119
5-day World-Hopper (unlimited admission to all 4 parks)	$189	$151
All-In-One (unlimited admission to all 4 parks plus 6-day admission to all attractions)	$249	$199
Annual Passport (unlimited admission to all 4 parks)	$299	$254
Premium Annual Pass (unlimited admission to all attractions)	$399	$339

Getting Around – Monorail trains, buses, ferry boats and water taxi (all free) link all attractions including hotels and resorts throughout the complex. Buses operate approximately every 20min. starting 1hr prior to park opening until closing. Routes painted in RED are direct routes after 4pm. The only exceptions: Service to Magic Kingdom, Epcot, Disney-MGM Studios from Disney's Old Key West Resort and the Disney Institute operates on scheduled pick-up times between noon and 6pm. Service to Disney's Blizzard Beach Water Park operates on a schedule with up to a 35min. interval between buses on some routes.

Eating – A wide selection of eateries punctuates the complex. Sidewalk stalls sell fresh fruit, hot dogs, ice cream and snacks; cafeterias and carryout stands accommodate diners on the run; more expensive restaurants *(lunch $14.95-$21.95/person, child $6.99; dinner $16.95–$47/person, child $7.95-$9.55)* mirror the theme of the parks in which they are located. Make reservations early in the day by contacting Guest Relations. Crowds and lines are heaviest at peak dining hours *(11:30am–2pm and 6–8pm)*. Dining at any of the Disney Resort hotels and dinner shows is open to the public; for reservations ☎ 939-3463.

Sports and Entertainment – Enjoy a round of golf on one of Disney's six championship courses *($45–$150; for tee times* ☎ *824-2270)*. Other recreational opportunities available to the general public and Disney Resort guests include tennis, boating, fishing, health club, swimming, waterskiing and horseback riding. **Youth Education Series** programs focus on nature, art, culture, ecology; ☎ 939-2223. A variety of live-performance stage shows are presented in the parks throughout the day. All operate on a first-come, first-served basis. For times, check the show schedule brochure; each park prints its own entertainment schedule. **Disney Character Breakfast** served daily at various resort hotels and at Magic Kingdom, Epcot. Reservations can be made 60 days in advance ☎ 939-3463. A wedding on a private island can be arranged for parties of up to 250 guests: **Disney Fairy Tale Weddings** ☎ 828-3400.

Disney by Night – During the summer months and on holidays, visitors are treated nightly to an extravaganza of lights, lasers and fireworks at the three original parks. SpectroMagic, a stellar parade of lighted floats, makes its way down Main Street USA twice each evening; while Fantasy in the Sky fireworks transform the Magic Kingdom into a wonderland to the tune of "When You Wish upon a Star." IllumiNations held around the lagoon at Epcot showcases a breathtaking display of lasers, fountains, music and fireworks. The new Fantasmic! laser-and-water display at Disney-MGM Studios is also spectacular. Consult entertainment schedules for locations and times.

Useful Numbers ☎

Emergency	911
Hotel and Dinner Show Reservations	934-7639
Walt Disney Resort Information	824-4321
Resort Dining and Recreation	939-3463
Magic Kingdom Lost and Found (same day)	824-4521
Epcot Center Lost and Found (same day)	560-6105
Disney-MGM Studios Lost and Found (same day)	560-3764
Animal Kingdom Lost and Found (same day)	938-2265
Central Lost and Found	824-4245

★★★ MAGIC KINGDOM *2 days. Map below.*

🚗 *Take I-4 west to Exit 25B (US-192 west). Turn right on World Dr. and follow signs to entrance of park straight ahead. Open year-round daily 9am–7pm, until midnight from mid-Jun–early Aug, 2 weeks at Easter, Thanksgiving weekend and Christmas week; until 10pm during President's Week (3rd week of Feb) and school spring breaks.* 🏛.

This Florida version of the Magic Kingdom lacks some of the old-fashioned attractions and sentimental appeal preserved in the original California Disneyland. Roughly square, the 100-acre Florida park includes seven areas that radiate out from the Central Plaza in front of Cinderella Castle. Shops, eateries, attractions and costumed "cast members" (ride attendants, shopkeepers and other staff) in each area echo the dominant theme of their "land."

Magic Kingdom is the most popular—and thus crowded—of the four parks, and the most time-consuming to access. After taking a shuttle across the parking lot to the **Ticket and Transportation Center**, you board either a monorail train or a replica paddlewheeler that crosses the Seven Seas Lagoon. Thrill rides—Space Mountain, ExtraTERRORestrial Alien Encounter, Splash Mountain and Big Thunder Mountain—along with Pirates of the Caribbean tend to attract the greatest crowds; head for them first.

A guided walking tour, "Keys to the Kingdom," explains the park's history and technology and takes in several rides, as well as the Diamond Horseshoe Saloon Revue *(departs from City Hall daily 9:30am & 10am, except during holidays; 4hrs; 16 years or older; $45; reservations required; ☎ 939-8687).*

Main Street, USA

Tidy Victorian storefronts holding commercial shops re-create the milieu of an early 19C town. In designing Main Street, USA, Walt Disney used a film device called forced perspective: upper stories of buildings are not as high as lower ones, giving the buildings a taller appearance. Adding to the atmosphere, a horse-drawn trolley, antique fire engine, omnibus, "horseless carriages" and jitneys carry passengers between the Town Square and Central Plaza. Minstrels often stroll the street, and the cartoon-character-filled **Disney's Magical Moments Parade** wends its way down Main Street every afternoon, highlighting recent animated film successes *(check park brochure for show times).* During evenings in peak periods (summer and

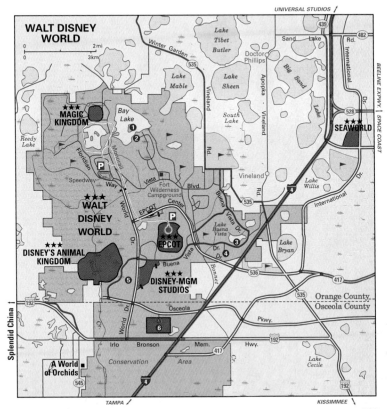

137

① Discovery Island

Kids *Map p 137. Located in Bay Lake, adjacent to the Magic Kingdom. Accessible by boat from the Magic Kingdom, and by bus then boat from Fort Wilderness. Open mid-Mar–Jun daily 9:30am–6pm, Jul–Aug daily 9:30am–7pm, Sept–late Feb daily 10am–5pm. $12.67, $6.89 children ages 3-9.* & 🅿. ☎ *407-824-4321.* A lovely respite from the fast-paced attractions of the theme parks, this 11-acre zoo lies on an island in Bay Lake. A 1mi trail winds through lush tropical palms and ferns, past enclosures housing some 100 species of animals. Colorful toucans, macaws, scarlet ibis and flamingos are featured here, as are swans, hornbills and herons. The island is also home to captive alligators, lemurs and threatened Gala-pagos tortoises. Professional trainers and naturalists stage animal programs periodically throughout the day *(check Discovery Island brochure for times).*

② River Country

Kids *Map p 137. Adjacent to Bay Lake. Take I-4 west to Exit 25B (US-92 west). Turn right on World Dr. and follow signs to park. Open early Nov–Jun daily 10am–5pm, Jul–early Sept daily 9am–8pm. $16.91, $13.25 children ages 3-9.* 🚻 ☎ *407-824-4321.* Bathing-suit clad visitors slip and slide down rapids, through flumes and around a boulder-strewn "river" in Disney's six-acre answer to the local swim-ming hole.

Christmas holidays), the **SpectroMagic** parade fills the street with a dazzling spectacle of Disney characters. This is often followed by **Fantasy in the Sky**, featuring a flying Tinkerbell and a fireworks display *(check park brochure for show times).*

Walt Disney World Railroad – Passen-gers can board steam trains that circle the park, stopping at Frontierland and Mickey's Starland. Purchased from the Mexican government, the trains were formerly used to haul sugarcane and tropical fruit.

Main Street Cinema – Six small screens in an arcade-style room continually show black-and-white Disney animated classics from the 1920s and 1930s. The main at-traction here is the film *Mickey's Big Break*, a light-hearted story about Mickey's Hollywood discovery.

Tomorrowland

Bowing to the age of technology, Walt Disney World in the mid 1990s undertook a major overhaul of the Tomorrowland attractions, many of which had been sadly outdated. Rather than attempt to predict the future, Disney has opted to create a "fantasy future city," recapturing the fu-turistic visions of the 1920s and 30s.

ExtraTERRORestrial Alien En-counter – Queue up early for a truly spine-tingling 18min in this sci-fi sce-nario designed with the help of special-effects guru George Lucas. Inside the Interplanetary Convention Center you'll meet a maniacal corporation executive from another planet who attempts to demonstrate his new technique of inter-galactic teleportation. But the experi-ment goes awry, and a hideous alien space creature is mistakenly material-ized. The ensuing blitz of sound, light and other special effects in the darkened theater treat the audience to a terrify-ingly realistic encounter with a carnivo-rous monster. *Expect long lines.*

Timekeeper – Guided by a madcap robot (whose voice is supplied by comedian Robin Williams), spectators at this en-grossing CircleVision 360 film *(15min)* journey through time from the age of dinosaurs to the future. Along the way you'll meet such historical figures as Mozart, Leonardo da Vinci and H.G. Wells, as the camera swoops through breathtaking scenery from around the world.

Astro Orbiter – Pilot your own orbiter through swirling planets around Tomorrow-land's colorful central spire. Although popular with the younger set, the updated ride affords adults good views of the Magic Kingdom.

Galaxy Search – On the open-air Galaxy Palace Theater stage, silver-suited cone-head and larger-than-life cartoon characters perform to classic rock music with space-theme lyrics in a 22min song-and-dance revue.

Carousel of Progress – Housed in a round building, the revolving theater circles four stages where life-size Audio-Animatronics© characters portray the evolution of life in an American home, from the pre-electric 19C to the computerized end of the 20C.

Buzz Lightyear's Space Ranger Spin – Due to open in fall 1998, this "interac-tive space fantasy" will team visitors with the character from *Toy Story* in defending Earth's battery supply against the evil Emperor Zurg. As combatants fire infrared lasers, targets will spring to animated life.

Space Mountain – Since it opened in 1975, this roller coaster enclosed in a futuristic mountain has been one of Disney's most popular rides. Not for the faint-of-heart, Space Mountain hurtles passengers through near-darkness, plunging them into sudden, atmospheric comet showers and past faintly twinkling stars. *Expect long lines.*

Tomorrowland Speedway – Young and old motorists alike take the wheel of these small sports cars and maneuver them along a gently curving raceway—inset with an iron track to keep things on course. *Children must be 52in tall to drive.*

Tomorrowland Transit Authority – Hop aboard this overhead tram for a bird's-eye view of the "city of the future" as imagined by early science-fiction visionaries.

Skyway to Fantasyland – Cable gondolas gliding 60ft above the ground offer views of Mickey's Starland and the storybook rooftops of Fantasyland.

Mickey's Toontown Fair

Retaining bits and pieces of Mickey's Starland, which it has replaced, Toontown Fair occupies a relatively quiet, three-acre corner of the Kingdom. Scaled to visitors under age 10 (and their parents), the whimsical village is built of pastel-shaded, round-edged buildings with a sort of gingerbread appeal. For kids who want to meet their favorite Disney characters, this is the best place.

Toontown Hall of Fame – In effect a big Disney store with the ambience of an old-fashioned country fair tent, the Hall of Fame boasts "character greeting locations" where Goofy and Pluto, for instance, shake hands, scrawl their autographs and pose for photos all day long.

Mickey's Country House – A stroll through Mickey's cozy home gives visitors a look at the lifestyle of Disney's greatest celebrity, including a peek at his grocery list. Displayed are plaques and trophies of his years of success. A corridor leads to a soundstage and theater; Mickey himself (now in his 70s, but with a seemingly direct line to the Fountain of Youth) holds court backstage, signing autographs for admirers (except during parade times).

Minnie's Country House – Opposite Mickey's house, of course, is Minnie's quaint pink palace. It reflects a traditional role for "the fairer sex" where even the appliances seem to smile and giggle. Across the lane are **Donald Duck's Boat**, the *Miss Daisy*, which lures youngsters to climb through its tunnels and up its stairs; and an unthreatening roller coaster, **The Barnstormer at Goofy's Wiseacre Farm.**

Fantasyland

With the fairy-tale air of an old European village, the original Fantasyland in California was Walt Disney's personal favorite. While this version lacks some of the quaintness of the original, it still ranks as the most popular area in all Walt Disney World. Adults with a taste for whimsy are captivated by its old-fashioned magic, as are young children who have seen the Disney classics through rerelease and on videotape. Live shows are held periodically at the **Castle Forecourt Stage** and at **Fantasyland Pavilion.** Merlin the Wizard also appears in front of Cinderella's Carousel for a **Sword in the Stone** presentation *(check park brochure for show times)*.
For a quick trip from fantasy to future, visitors can ride the **Skyway to Tomorrowland**, the return portion of the Skyway to Fantasyland *(above)*.

Cinderella Castle – Of all the castles in Disney theme parks worldwide, this 189ft-high Gothic extravaganza, ornamented with its turrets, towers, gold spires and leaded-glass windows, is the largest. It was inspired by one of the 19C castles built in Bavaria by King Ludwig II. Though the interior is not an attraction but a restaurant, the arched entrance through the castle gate is inlaid with detailed mosaics depicting the rags-to-riches story of Cinderella.

Cinderella's Golden Carousel – Many of the mounts on this merry-go-round are hand-painted antiques. A band organ plays Disney tunes as horses gallop beneath a canopy painted with scenes from the Disney movie *Cinderella*.

Legend of the Lion King – In this 15min condensation of the popular animated film, life-size stick puppets mouth lines prerecorded by the original voice talents of James Earl Jones, Jeremy Irons and others.

It's a Small World – This cross-cultural fantasy was conceived for the 1964 World's Fair and embodies an idealized view of international brotherhood. Boarding small boats, visitors float past 500 Audio-Animatronics© children and animals representing nearly 100 nations, all singing the repetitive theme song.

Dumbo, the Flying Elephant – Longtime favorite with small visitors, the carnival-style ride allows passengers to make their individual Dumbos soar up and down by manipulating a knob in front of the seat.

Mad Tea Party – This updated version of the old teacup favorite looks like a modern tilt-a-whirl with cup-and-saucer conveyances. Passengers control the amount of spin by turning a wheel in the center of each cup.

Ariel's Grotto – A cast member dressed as *The Little Mermaid* poses for photos in a concrete sea cave as little girls line up with their dads to await their turns. Little boys are more amused tip-toeing around an unpredictably spouting fountain outside the cave.

Disney Animated Classics – Fantasyland lauds Disney's early celluloid successes with several enclosed or "dark" rides. Based on animated feature films, these rides whisk visitors past Audio-Animatronics© figures and scenes that unfold the movie's plot.
In **Mr. Toad's Wild Ride**, jaunty vintage sports cars whoosh passengers from England's picturesque countryside into London's foggy back streets, where surprises lurk around every corner. **Snow White's Adventures** takes visitors from the Seven Dwarfs' cozy cottage to an encounter with the Wicked Queen and on to a happy ending. Riders aboard the pirate-ship gondolas of **Peter Pan's Flight** float out of the Darling children's bedroom above a charming, fiber-optic version of nighttime London. Soon after, passengers are plunged into Never Never Land, where Captain Hook, Smee and the Lost Boys await in their galleons.

Tips for Visiting Walt Disney World

■ See popular attractions early, during a parade or late in the day.

■ Eat lunch or dinner during non-peak hours (before 11:30am or after 2pm and from 4pm–6pm or after 8pm).

■ Choose a restaurant that takes reservations, or try one of the many Walt Disney World resort restaurants.

■ See a show or browse in the shops in the afternoon when many rides have long lines.

■ Best places to see the fireworks at Epcot: Matsu No Ma lounge in the Japan pavilion; the patio of the Rose & Crown in the United Kingdom pavilion; and Cantina de San Angel in the Mexico pavilion.

Liberty Square

A celebration of America, Liberty Square re-creates a brick and clapboard colonial town set around a central square. Cast from the same mold as the revered original, a Liberty Bell sits in the center of the square. The 130-year-old live oak designated as the site's "liberty tree" was discovered on the Disney property and carefully transplanted to this location.

Haunted Mansion – Hosts of ghosts and ghouls spook the creepy mansion that looms ominously along the shore of the Rivers of America. From the "stretchroom," where heights and dimensions are not what they appear, visitors board small black "doom buggies" for a spine-tingling trip among holographic images and haunting, if humorous, special effects. *Expect long lines.*

Hall of Presidents – This impressive multimedia production begins with an unabashedly patriotic film on the history of the Constitution, then blossoms into an Audio-Animatronics© tour de force in which all 42 US Presidents appear on stage for a roll call and, of course, a few speeches.

Liberty Belle Riverboat – A three-decker, gingerbread-trimmed sternwheeler, the *Liberty Belle*, plies the Rivers of America, past Audio-Animatronics© animals, an old-time trapper, and an Indian village. Just down the riverfront, visitors also can board the **Mike Fink Keelboats**, smaller, two-story boats such as the *Gullywhumper* that ply the same circuit as the sternwheeler.

Frontierland

The Old West lives on in the wooden walkways, country stores, and saloon of this frontier town. On many afternoons, gunslingers take to the rooftops for a rambunctious shoot-out. The **Diamond Horseshoe Saloon Revue**, a dance hall-style show, is performed several times daily in the Golden Horseshoe Saloon at the edge of Liberty Square. At **Country Bear Jamboree**, a winsome troupe of Audio-Animatronics© "Bear-itones" sing, tell jokes and generally delight crowds with their down-home performances *(check park brochure for show times)*.

Splash Mountain – Riders board dark dugouts for a languid float through swamps and bayous inside Splash Mountain, as Br'er Rabbit, Br'er Fox and other characters from the 1946 Disney classic *Song of the South* serenade passing boats. At the mountaintop awaits one of the biggest thrills in the Magic Kingdom: a 52ft flume that hurls dugouts down a 47-degree slope to a monstrous soaking splash. *Expect long lines.*

Big Thunder Mountain Railroad – This runaway train pulls out of an old mining town, then gathers steam as it roller-coasters through and around a red-rock mountain, negotiates a terrain of hoodoos, caves and canyons, and even plunges down through a dark, rickety mine shaft.

Tom Sawyer Island – Log rafts carry energetic explorers across the Rivers of America to Tom's island, where they can wander through Injun Joe's cave, the stockaded Fort Sam Clemens, a swinging footbridge, a tree house and more.

© The Walt Disney Company

Big Thunder Mountain Railroad

Adventureland

An eclectic mix of Polynesian, Moorish, French Colonial and Spanish Colonial architecture establishes an exotic atmosphere here. Adding its own authentic tones, a steel-drum band, **J.P. and the Silver Stars**, gives performances in the Caribbean Plaza throughout the day *(check park brochure for show times)*. The **Adventureland Challenge** is a shop-to-shop treasure hunt, offered six times a day, which rewards successful seekers of a lost idol by sending them to the front of any line in the Magic Kingdom.

Enchanted Tiki Room – The 10min show presented here—"Under New Management"—introduces brash birds Iago (from Disney's *Aladdin*) and Zazu (from *The Lion King*) as the new landlords of the Tiki Room. When they offend the resident tiki gods, however, they find themselves in big trouble. A cast of Audio-Animatronics© birds and orchids hold their own in this funny fantastical show that blends several choreographed musical numbers.

Swiss Family Tree House – Visitors can climb through the sprawling, 80ft artificial banyan tree (refurbished in 1998) that re-creates the arboreal home of the indefatigable Swiss Family Robinson. This famous family originated in the 19C novel of Johann David Wyss, and was later immortalized in a Disney film.

Pirates of the Caribbean – Considered among the most popular amusement park rides ever created, this piratical adventure embodies the spirit of Disney at its best. Boarding boats, visitors weave through a darkened swamp before entering a Caribbean village raided by pirates. There the crafts drift past a series of sets peopled by lifelike buccaneers, pigs, parrots and more. (Disney designers used their own faces as models for the pirates' features.) *Expect long lines.*

Jungle Cruise – Passengers on this nostalgic Disney favorite float down a jungle river that combines features of Africa, Asia and South America. Beware of mechanized crocodiles, hippos and elephants that pop up along the way past ruins overgrown with lush foliage. Boat pilots spice up the trip with pun-laced dialogue. Nearby, you'll find **Shrunken Ned's Junior Jungle Boats**, a remote-controlled attraction.

★★★ EPCOT *2 days. Map p 137.*

🔟 *Take I-4 west to Exit 26B; go west on Epcot Center Dr. and follow signs to park entrance on left. Open year-round daily 9am–9pm, until midnight from mid-Jun–early Aug); until 10pm during third week of Feb), school spring breaks, 2 weeks at Easter, Thanksgiving weekend and Christmas week. World Showcase open daily 11am–9pm (10pm during summer months).* ▥.

The daunting 260-acre Epcot is divided into two distinct areas: Future World, housing pavilions devoted to technology and ingenuity, and World Showcase, where the culture and architecture of 11 nations are represented. Walt Disney envisioned Epcot as a model community of the future, but he died 16 years before its 1982 opening and his initial plans were somewhat altered. No dome encloses the Future World complex, but the area does celebrate American industry and serves as a "showcase for new ideas" as Disney intended. The Land and Living Seas pavilions function as working research centers as well as attractions. In order to maintain its innovative character, Future World is ever-updating and revamping its exhibits.

Make a beeline for the newest attractions and rides, which draw the heaviest crowds. Guides leading the "Hidden Treasures of World Showcase" tour explain the derivation of Epcot's architecture, as well as behind-the-scenes operations *(departs from East Showcase Tue; 2hrs; 16 years or older; $35).* A similar horticultural tour called "Gardens of the World," is also offered *(departs from Tour Gardens Tue & Thu; 3hrs; 16 years or older; $45; reservations required; ☎ 939-8687).*

Future World

Eight large pavilions here encircle the 180ft-high faceted geosphere *(below)* that has come to symbolize Epcot. The 16-million-pound structure is supported by pylons sunk 100ft into the ground. Sponsored by major American corporations, pavilions here house rides, interactive display areas and films, all saluting humankind's ingenious technological achievements.

Spaceship Earth – Spiral up 18 stories in a time machine vehicle inside Epcot's giant landmark sphere, where you'll ride past animated scenes depicting the history of human communication from prehistoric tribes to present-day technology. On the way down, you'll have a "satellite's view" of Earth. Back on the ground, take a film-simulated "ride" along the information highway and explore an ever-changing floorful of interactive simulations and video games that illustrate state-of-the-art communications technology in the **Global Neighborhood**.

Innoventions – Two facing crescent-shaped buildings behind Spaceship Earth showcase some of the world's newest inventions. Virtual keyboards, computer chips that learn, and a virtual reality tour of St. Peter's Basilica in Rome are just some of the ideas presented at **Innoventions West**. Across the plaza at **Innoventions East**, you'll find the latest developments in "smart-home" technology, auto design and the information superhighway. Most of the displays are interactive, entertaining even as they educate.

The Living Seas – Essentially a 5.7-million-gallon aquarium, this old-fashioned crowd-pleaser, with waves lapping its exterior, begins with a short film on the sea, then proceeds to the **Caribbean Coral Reef Ride**, a tram that moves through an acrylic cylinder in the world's largest man-made saltwater aquarium. After the ride, visitors board an elevator down to **Sea Base Alpha**, a prototype undersea research facility. Here you'll learn about ocean ecosystems and watch an array of marine life, including dolphins, sharks and manatees, cavort in large modular tanks.

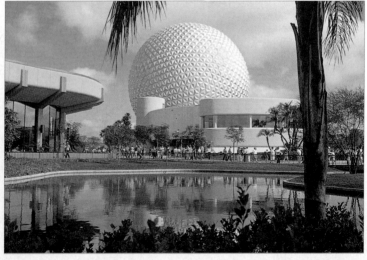

© The Walt Disney Company

Spaceship Earth

The Land – Setting the tone for the ecological theme of this enormous working greenhouse, a plaque outside the entrance contains a quote by the late, renowned scientist René Dubos, who called the earth "a garden to be cultivated." Inside, the **Living With the Land** boat ride transports visitors, accompanied by a live narrator, through a simulated rain forest, desert and prairie before emerging into the pavilion's greenhouse gardens. Here scientists experiment on a variety of herbs, vegetables and other plants to perfect growing methods and to develop new hybrids. Horticulture enthusiasts may wish to take the **Harvest Tour**, a 45min guided walk through the greenhouses. *Sign up for tours outside "Food Rocks" on the first floor.*

In the **Harvest Theater**, characters from Disney's 1994 animated film *The Lion King* act out an environmental fable entitled *The Circle of Life*. Audio-Animatronics© bands, such as The Peach Boys and Pita Gabriel, sing the praises of good nutrition in the musical **Food Rocks** show *(15min)*. An extensive food court occupies much of the interior of this building.

Journey Into Imagination – Inside lopsided glass pyramids, visitors are guided by an Audio-Animatronics© red-bearded professor named Dream-finder and his sidekick, Figment, on a fantastic journey through the potential of human imagination. At journey's end, riders can exercise their own imaginations in **Image Works**, an interactive treasure house of high-tech gizmos—ranging from an electronic symphony and paintbrush to electronic Stepping Stones, which play music and create light when you step on them. Next door in the Imagination Institute, you'll don 3-D glasses to watch the rollicking, laugh-packed adventure film **Honey, I Shrunk the Audience** *(20min)*.

Wonders of Life – Fun-loving and informative films, multimedia shows and interactive exhibits in **Fitness Playground** explain and explore health and the human body inside this geodesic dome. The popular **Body Wars** ride reigns as one of Epcot's few thrillers. In a flight simulator, passengers are "shot" into the human body for a mad dash through the circulatory system. **The Making of Me**, starring comedian Martin Short, is an entertaining and sensitive film on human reproduction. In the multimedia presentation **Cranium Command** *(15min)*, Buzzy, an Audio-Animatronics© robot, appears against a film backdrop that traces a day in the life of a 12yr-old boy. Different parts of the brain are played by a number of popular comedians, including former *Saturday Night Live* cast members.

Universe of Energy – Here a pyramidal roof winks with 80,000 photovoltaic cells that produce solar energy to power the ride within. **Ellen's Energy Adventure**, starring comedienne Ellen DeGeneres, is a multidimensional journey that explores where

③ Downtown Disney

Map p 137. Take I-4 west to Exit 27. Turn north onto Vineland Rd.; left at first light on Hotel Plaza Blvd. Entrance to Marketplace at intersection of Hotel Plaza Blvd. and Buena Vista Dr.; Pleasure Island and West Side extend west along Buena Vista Dr. ✗ ♿ ▯ ☎ *407-824-4321.* This shopping and entertainment district on the southern shore of Lake Buena Vista is the most adult-oriented of any Disney attraction. Parents and children browse the shops of Marketplace by daylight, but after the sun goes down, the restaurants, nightclubs and theaters of Pleasure Island and West Side take center stage.

Marketplace – *Open 9:30am–11pm; free admission.* This complex boasts an overwhelming assemblage of Disney character collectibles, along with resort wear and arts and crafts. Eateries cater to families on the go. At the new LEGO Imagination Center, visitors of all ages are awed by gargantuan, detailed structures built from the tiny plastic Danish bricks.

Pleasure Island – *Open 10:30am–2am; free admission during day; after 7pm admission ($18.95) restricted to those 18yrs or older unless accompanied by a parent.* Seven nightclubs and a commercial theater offer late-night entertainment in a "warehouse" setting, ranging from rock 'n roll, country-and-western, rhythm-and-blues, jazz and comedy to a fireworks display that ends each evening. At the Adventurers Club, "members" parody a British travelers' fraternity.

West Side – *Open 10:30am–2am; free admission.* At 66 acres the largest of the three Downtown Disney areas, West Side includes two restaurant-nightclubs, Bongo's Cuban Cafe and the House of Blues; a Cirque du Soleil theater; a five-story interactive "virtual-reality" entertainment center called DisneyQuest, and a 24-plex cinema. At the entrance stands the globe-shaped, celebrity-owned Planet Hollywood restaurant.

© The Walt Disney Company

Honey, I Shrunk the Audience

energy has come from and where it may be going. Ellen dreams she's a contestant on the "Jeopardy!" game show. Unfortunately, every question deals with energy, a subject about which she knows little or nothing. Visitors come along (slowly traveling in banks of theater seats) as Bill Nye, the Science Guy, takes Ellen on a trip back through time—*all* the way back, to the Big Bang—to explain the origin of fossil fuels. They get a fright in the Jurassic era where they're confronted by life-like Audio-Animatronics© **dinosaurs,** but they have the good fortune to witness primitive man's discovery of fire. By the time they return to the late 20C, everyone has a greater grasp of the world's current energy needs.

Horizons – Board suspended train cars for a journey through past and present visions of the future. The trip begins with an Audio-Animatronics© version of Jules Verne and his bullet rocket and progresses through re-creations of science-fiction film robots from the 1930s and '40s to 21C options for living and working—including an agricultural complex in a once-arid desert and a floating city in the Pacific Ocean.

World Showcase

The 1.3mi promenade at World Showcase circles a 40-acre lagoon and passes the pavilions of 11 different countries. Each pavilion—staffed by nationals of the country it represents—reflects the architecture, foods, crafts, costumes and traditions of that culture. Live performers are often on hand to play music or demonstrate other artistic endeavors specific to their native land. Some pavilions also feature rides or films.

A variety of live stage shows are held at **America Gardens Theatre by the Shore** *(in front of the United States pavilion).* In the evenings, World Showcase lagoon and pavilions become the setting for **IllumiNations,** an extravaganza of laser lights, music, fountains, and fireworks *(check park brochure for show times).*

Mexico – Both the dynamism of current-day Mexico and the dignity of its past are evident here. A lush tropical garden leads the way to a small-scale reproduction of a Mayan pyramid, housing a gallery of **pre-Columbian artifacts.** Beyond the gallery lies a colorful colonial plaza, where vendors sell typical Mexican wares and dark lighting gives the scene an appealing nighttime atmosphere. At the far edge of the plaza runs **El Rio del Tiempo.** Passengers on this boat ride drift down the River of Time through a history of Mexico, from smoking volcanoes to the modern landscapes of Mexico City.

Norway – Norway re-creates a small cobblestone plaza lined with a mix of traditional and medieval architectural styles. One-room **Stave Church,** a replica of a 12C house of worship, contains small changing exhibits on Norwegian topics. **Maelstrom,** the pavilion's major attraction, plunges riders through treacherous northern seas.

China – The red and gold opulence of Beijing's Temple of Heaven (replicated at half size) overlooks a Chinese garden here, where koi shimmer through a pond crossed by elegant walkways. The interior of the temple houses a serenely ornamented Hall of Prayer for Good Harvest; a **museum** that features changing exhibits of Chinese art; and a CircleVision 360 Theater, where the vastness of China is portrayed in the film **Wonders of China: Land of Beauty, Land of Time.** A narrow street angling off from the temple is fronted by the facade of a home, school and shops.

Germany – A facade modeled after the Eltz and Stahleck Castles backdrops cobblestone St. Georgesplatz, a square named for its prominent statue of St. George and the Dragon. Small buildings reflecting a romantic mix of turreted German village architecture surround the plaza, and a traditional glockenspiel chimes the hour. Buildings contain shops and a capacious *biergarten*-style restaurant whose popular dinner show serves up oom-pah entertainment. East of the pavilion, an outdoor model railway re-creates Germany's "Romantic Road" between Füssen and Würzburg.

Italy – A certain desultory elegance permeates this plaza, where reproductions—the elaborate Doge's Palace, and a brick campanile topped with a sculpted angel—re-create Venice's Piazza San Marco. Antiqued facades, an open-air market, and a Bernini-inspired fountain *(rear of plaza)* add to the *dolce vita* atmosphere. Classical musicians often perform here. Facing the pavilion, on the lakefront, is a Venetian gondola landing missing only the gondolier.

American Adventure – Prominently situated at the midpoint of World Showcase, a five-story brick building serves as the host pavilion. Several major colonial landmarks inspire its architecture: Independence Hall in Philadelphia, Boston's Old State House and Thomas Jefferson's Monticello in Charlottesville, Virginia. The highlight here is **The American Adventure**, a state-of-the-art multimedia show *(25min)* narrated by startlingly lifelike Audio-Animatronics© versions of Ben Franklin and Mark Twain. The pair comment sagaciously on the show's retrospective of great moments and figures in American history.

Japan – Landscaped with peaceful water and rock gardens and perfectly placed evergreens, this pavilion captures the contemplative serenity of traditional Japan. Its prominent bright blue, five-story pagoda is based on the 8C Horyuji Temple in Nara. At the rear, a re-creation of an 18C feudal castle houses changing exhibits of **Japanese art**. Visitors can purchase an array of Japanese items in Mitsukoshi Department Store, a venerable mercantile institution dating to the 17C, housed in a reproduction of Kyoto's 8C Gosho Imperial Palace. World Showcase Lagoon is perfectly framed by the pavilion's red torii, a Japanese gateway commonly built at the entrance to a Shinto shrine.

Morocco – Elaborate tilework and carving crafted by Moroccan artisans under the patronage of the King of Morocco create a faithful and detailed representation of the sights, smells and sounds of this North African country. Fronted by a replica of Marrakech's famous Koutoubia Minaret, the pavilion is divided into a new and old medina, or city. Beyond the fountain of the new city's plaza lies the **Royal Gallery**, which houses changing displays of Moroccan art in its exquisitely ornamented interior. The narrow, exotic casbah opens onto a formal Moroccan restaurant and a bevy of shops.

France – Capturing the romantic atmosphere of turn-of-the-century Paris, the main street is lined with mansard-roofed buildings. Even the Eiffel Tower stands here, at one-tenth its actual size. A second street re-creates a provincial village scene, complete with shops and an authentic French restaurant. A 17C parterre garden is a nice place to sip a glass of imported wine. As an added treat, the whole of France fills five screens in the film **Impressions de France** *(20min)*, a compelling scenic tour of the country. Lest you forget this is Disney, however, the Hunchback of Nôtre Dame and Esmeralda, his love, occasionally sign autographs here.

United Kingdom – Hundreds of years of British architecture—from a 15C brick home to the 16C thatched-roof cottage of Anne Hathaway (Shakespeare's wife) to a 19C English garden—are represented along a brick-paved street. Specialty shops and a pub that serves British-brewed ales complete the scene. You may find Beatles impersonators regaling listeners with Fab Four hits from the pub's courtyard.

Canada – Celebrating Canada's cultural diversity, the pavilion features a model of a 19C French château-style hotel, totem poles and a longhouse, as well as a log trading post. Landscapes here vary from a replica of Victoria's famous Butchart Gardens to a re-created Rocky Mountain gorge. In the CircleVision 360 theater, the film **O Canada!** surrounds the audience in spectacular scenery.

★★★DISNEY'S ANIMAL KINGDOM *Map p 137*

Take I-4 west to Exit 25B. Go west on US-192, right (north) on World Dr. and left (west) on Osceola Pkwy., then follow signs to parking plaza. Open year-round daily 7am–8pm.

Disney's newest theme park, which opened in spring 1998 to worldwide hoopla, is devoted to the natural world: animals living and extinct, as well as creatures of the imagination. Geographically the largest park, Animal Kingdom has placed

> **4 Typhoon Lagoon**
>
> Map p 137. Take I-4 west to Exit 26B. Go west on Epcot Center Dr. and turn right on Buena Vista Dr. Follow signs to park entrance on right. Open Jan–Jun daily 10am–5pm, Jul–Aug daily 9am–8pm, Sept–early Nov daily 10am–5pm. $28.51, $21.73 children ages 3-9. ☎ 407-824-4321. Four times the size of River Country, Typhoon Lagoon claims to be "the ultimate water park." Water slides, rapids and snorkeling compete here with the site's highlight: an immense wave pool pounded by 4ft surf.

1,000 animals (of 200 species) and four million plants (of 3,000 species) on more than 500 acres of land. Whimsy meets stark reality here, as visitors can move from colorful pageants to a re-created African savannah, from sophisticated rides and exhibits to primitive native villages, and even watch veterinary surgeons at work in the operating room. No matter that dinosaurs graze, dragons lurk and many animals and insects speak—this is Disney at its best.

Although animal-rights activists have expressed concern for the welfare of park denizens, Animal Kingdom delivers an unabashedly conservationist message. Visitors can meet with animal behavior experts, monitor animal-care facilities and learn about the depletion of world rainforests and grasslands. Mock research stations offer a glimpse of field observation procedures.

Visit *1 day*

Animal Kingdom extends in four directions from its hub, the **Tree of Life**, in the heart of Safari Village. The two most popular attractions, Kilimanjaro Safaris and Countdown to Extinction, are at opposite ends of the park; head first to one or the other to beat the crowds. Of the live shows, "Festival of the Lion King" is most popular but has the largest arena. You'll also find long lines for the 3-D film **It's Tough to Be a Bug** beneath the Tree of Life.

As you head toward Safari Village from Animal Kingdom's main gateway, you'll first pass through **The Oasis**, a lush botanical garden whose grottoes are inhabited by brightly colored macaws, miniature deer, iguanas, tree kangaroos and other unusual animals. Safari Village occupies a man-made riverine island; footbridges link it to the other segments of the park. If you think of The Oasis as being at 6 o'clock from this axis, you will find DinoLand U.S.A. at 4 o'clock, Camp Minnie-Mickey at 8 o'clock, Africa at 10 o'clock and Asia at 2 o'clock. The Conservation Station is reached by train from Africa.

Various shows, parades and musical performances are scheduled throughout the day in Animal Kingdom. You can obtain a schedule along with the park map you're given at the entrance.

Safari Village

Fashioned as a tropical artists' colony, Safari Village is home to roving world musicians, puppeteers and storytellers as well as resident experts in fine arts and crafts. Twice each day, its painters, sculptors, basketmakers, weavers, stained-glass artisans, papier-mâché makers and costume designers have their work displayed during **The March of the Animals** pageant *(check park brochure for times)*. The vivid artwork contributes to fanciful animal costumes, from termites to tigers, for 55 dancers, musicians and acrobats who prance and bounce through the village.

The Tree of Life – This park centerpiece is a giant (145ft) man-made tree of unidentifiable classification, into whose 50ft-wide trunk and 8,000 branches are intricately carved 325 images of mammals, birds, reptiles, amphibians and insects. Adapted from Disney's animated feature *The Lion King*, it celebrates all creatures in the song "The Circle of Life." The tree is visible from points throughout the park. At its foot, birds and small animals revel in pools and meadow-like plots.

It's Tough to Be a Bug – *8min.* A delightful cast of animated insects and arachnids—crickets, beetles, bees, ants, spiders and the like—express the harsh "reality" of their lives in a 430-seat theater beneath the "roots" of the Tree of Life. Meanwhile, the audience, wearing 3-D glasses, experiences such special effects as termite sneezes (you'll get wet), stinkbug emissions (they stink!) and a cloud of pesticide (actually fog). The short film is said to be tied to the upcoming release of a new Disney movie, *A Bug's Life. Expect long lines.*

Discovery River Boats – These Adventureland-style boats ply the waterway between here and Asia, albeit without the same level of Audio-Animatronics© fauna of their Magic Kingdom counterparts. Nevertheless, voyagers do encounter steaming geysers, the lair of a fire-breathing dragon and a 30ft iguanodon browsing on marsh grasses. Narrators carry exotic birds, reptiles, tarantulas and the like aboard the boats to exhibit to keep passengers' interest from flagging.

Camp Minnie-Mickey

Resembling an Adirondack summer camp with its pine-and-oak buildings and picnic shelters, this is the perfect place for younger children to interact with favorite Disney characters. "Green rooms"—jungle and forest canopies—act as greeting areas where Mickey Mouse and friends, Winnie the Pooh, and characters from *The Lion King* and *The Jungle Book* sign autographs for their visitors. There are two live-performance venues *(check park brochure for show times)*.

Festival of the Lion King – *30 min.* This splashy show presents 50 performers in bright African tribal garb or animal costumes, singing, dancing and doing aerial acrobatics on (or above) four giant rolling stages to melodies like "Hakuna Matata" and "The Circle of Life." Toward the end of the show, Simba (the Lion King) himself, assisted by Pumba (the warthog) and Timon (the meerkat), leads the audience in a chorus of "The Lion Sleeps Tonight." The show is held in a hexagonal open-sided, roofed pavilion with seating for 1,000.

Grandma Willow's Grove – *12min.* "Colors of the Wind, Friends from the American Forest" is the name of the musical presented in this amphitheater, named for its resident talking tree. Guided by the ancient willow's wisdom, Indian maiden Pocahontas (another animated Disney star) learns the only animal that can save all the forests and their inhabitants is— you guessed it—man himself.

Africa

While Disney excels at homogenizing exotic cultures, real or imagined, the river port of **Harambe** may be its best effort yet. Minus such Third World unpleasantries as noxious odors and life-threatening diseases, greedy merchants and hostile governments, Harambe is a sufficiently authentic representation of a coastal Kenyan community as to bring tears of homesickness to the eyes of East Africa-born Disney employees. Shop owners peddle their wares from marketplace stalls; elsewhere, white-coral walls and reed-thatched roofs typify the Arab-influenced Swahili architecture.

5 Blizzard Beach

Kids *Map p 137. Just west of World Dr., adjacent to Disney's All-Star Resorts. Take I-4 west to Exit 25B. Turn right on World Dr.; then left on Buena Vista Dr. and follow signs. Open mid-Feb–May daily 10am–5pm, Jun–Aug daily 9am–8pm, Sept–Oct daily 10am–7pm, Nov–late Dec daily 10am–5pm. $28.51, $21.73 children ages 3-9.* ☎ 407-824-4321. This star in the constellation of Disney attractions entertains visitors with slides and rides in a tropical lagoon framed by snow-capped mountains! At Blizzard Beach you can ride tubes down a twisting series of falls, race on mats down an eight-lane sluiceway, and experience a 120ft drop at 55mph on Summit Plummet. *Arrive early to avoid long lines, which can last an hour or more for a 20-second slide. Towels and lockers are available for rent.*

Kilimanjaro Safaris – The staging point for these "backcountry" journeys, Animal Kingdom's leading attraction is at the far end of Harambe village. The entrance line winds through a warehouse of safari gear in the shadow of a giant baobab tree. Open-sided all-terrain trucks carry 32 passengers at a time down a rutted and twisting dirt road, across river fords and through tropical forests, to the grasslands of the Serengeti Plain. Assisted by a bush pilot-game warden (who flies ahead as a wildlife spotter), travelers look for rhinoceroses, elephants, lions, cheetahs, zebras, giraffes, baboons, various gazelles and antelopes, and other residents of the savannah.

These animals are all real but much of the rest of the journey is fantasy. Baobabs and 20ft termite hills are made of concrete. A rickety suspension bridge is geared to collapse just as visitors cross it. The airborne navigator exists only on tape, and the insidious ivory poachers he requests help in capturing are another wonder of Audio-Animatronics©. *Expect long lines.*

Blizzard Beach

Gorilla Falls Exploration Trail – This self-guided trail through a bamboo jungle affords close-up views (through crystal-clear acrylic windows) of two troops of lowland gorillas, some of whom seem to thrive on the attention; several hippopotamuses, easily viewed swimming underwater from a bi-level viewing area; and nearly three dozen species of exotic birds beneath a canopy of trees in an enclosed aviary. A re-created wildlife research station includes maps and computerized exhibits, as well as a display of the cutaway burrows of rare naked mole rats, a creature that never sees the light of day.

Conservation Station

An off-the-beaten-path facility, this is Disney's best statement of eco-consciousness. In addition to animal-care facilities (which visitors can monitor through surveillance cameras) and a children's petting zoo ("The Affection Section"), there are interactive demonstrations and high-tech exhibits—hosted by such famous naturalists as chimpanzee expert Jane Goodall—of animal behavior and of conservation work being performed around the world. One particularly poignant "exhibit" in a darkened sound booth warns of the destruction of the planet's rainforests.

Still more fascinating is a window on an operating room where veterinarians perform surgical procedures on park animals: The chief veterinarian has the appropriately unlikely name of Dr. Peregrine Wolff.

To reach Conservation Station, visitors must board the Wildlife Express—a 19C, colonial-style, narrow-gauge steam train—from Harambe's East African Depot. From the depot at Conservation Station, it's a 100yd walk through a jungle of lush vegetation to the central building.

Asia

This quadrant is a work in progress: Its principal attractions aren't scheduled to open until 1999; as of this writing, it offers only a Discovery River Boat dock and an open-air amphitheater. When completed, it will center around a rural Asian village set amid rainforest vegetation. The **Maharajah Jungle Trek** will depart from here, winding past decaying temple ruins and perhaps glimpsing Bengal tigers, Komodo dragons, and other animals roaming freely without apparent barriers from guests or from one another. **Tiger Rapids Run** will combine a whitewater thrill ride with an environmental theme.

Flights of Wonder – The avian talents of falcons, macaws, ibis and other birds are featured in this free-flying show at the Caravan Stage. The story line features a treasure-seeking youth and a wise, if mythological, phoenix.

DinoLand U.S.A.

This theme area has the greatest appeal to the elementary-school set. It is constructed to resemble a research camp from which a paleontological dig is taking place. As the story goes, scientists and hip grad students (none of whom visitors ever see, of course) moved into this abandoned fishing village when dinosaur bones were discovered nearby. Their supposed discoveries are shown at the **Fossil Preparation Lab** (now exhibiting bones of a 50ft Tyrannosaurus rex, largest ever found, as they are cleaned and studied by staff from The Field Museum in Chicago) and in a bone museum called **Dinosaur Jubilee** where casts of authentic dinosaur skeletons are displayed.

Meanwhile, research notes from DinoLand's pseudo-paleontologists accompany displays along the **Cretaceous Trail**. You'll find plants (cycads, palms, ferns) and animals (turtles, lizards, beetles) that survived the calamity, 65 million years ago, believed to have ended the age of dinosaurs. You may even spot a nest of fossilized dinosaur eggs. Nearby is **The Boneyard**, a playground of slides, rope bridges, tunnels and caves that mimics a fossil park.

Countdown to Extinction – Visitors who board a 12-passenger "Time Rover" are sent by a deranged scientist (Dr. Grant Seeker) back to late Cretaceous times to bring home a living dinosaur, just before an asteroid threatening all life strikes the planet. Along their tilting, twisting, bumpy route, they dodge nine different species of Audio-Animatronics© dinosaurs and plunge through total darkness before narrowly escaping meteoric disaster and returning home, mission accomplished.

Journey into Jungle Book – *30min.* Seemingly out of place in DinoLand, this entertaining musical show at Theater in the Wild, is inspired by Disney's animated treatment of the 19C Rudyard Kipling novel. Musical numbers follows man-child Mowgli through his jungle adventures with a cast of curious Indian animals. A highlight is a rendition of "Bare Necessities" by Baloo, the bungling bear.

★★★DISNEY-MGM STUDIOS *Map p 137*

Kids *Take I-4 west to Exit 26B. Go west on Epcot Center Dr. and turn left on Buena Vista Dr. Follow signs to studio entrance on left. Alternate access via Exit 25B (US-192 west): Turn right on World Dr. and follow signs to entrance on right. Open year-round daily 9am–7pm, until 10pm or midnight from mid-Jun–early-Aug and holidays.* ▓.

This theme park/studio celebrates the magic of filmmaking, from animation and stuntsmanship to adventure and romance. Art Deco architecture throughout the 154-acre site re-creates the look of Hollywood in its 1930s and '40s heyday. Sophisticated techniques coupled with a playful, fun-loving style characterize the attractions, which include rides, film performances and live shows—often with audience volunteers—that provide behind-the-scenes explanations of moviemaking. As a working studio, Disney-MGM produces scores of television shows and Disney animated films.

Visit *1 day*

The least crowded of the four parks, this one also has a more compact design that makes visiting easy. If you would like to see a live taping, check at the **Production Information Window** just inside the entrance gate to see when shows are scheduled. Audience tickets are available on a first-come, first-served basis. As in all the parks, thrill rides and newest attractions tend to have the longest lines; experience Tower of Terror and Star Tours first.

Lined with palm trees and sleek, low-slung Art Deco-style buildings filled with commercial shops, **Hollywood Boulevard** opens onto a central plaza by a lush red-and-gold, pagoda-roofed replica of Mann's Chinese Theater in Los Angeles. The latter's forecourt is set with footprints of famous film and Disney stars.

The Boulevard is the scene of the daily **Mulan Parade**, which shows off the music, magic and characters of Disney's summer 1998 release, *Mulan*, about a Chinese girl who saves her father's life by disguising herself as a man and joining the army in his place. A new 25min evening show, **Fantasmic!**, complete with Disney music, animation and special laser effects, is due to open in fall 1998 in a new 6,900-seat amphitheater.

Two new attractions are scheduled for 1999: **Copperfield Magic Underground,** a venture of magician David Copperfield, promises to treat diners in a 500-seat restaurant to grand illusions. The 360-degree twists and turns of the high-speed **Rock 'n' Roller Coaster** will be amplified by a synchronized rock soundtrack resonating from speakers in each vehicle.

The Great Movie Ride – *22min.* Housed in the model of Mann's Chinese Theater, this ride takes you on an unforgettable trip through the great movie classics. A tram with a live guide moves you through a multimedia show that includes everything from clips of classic Disney films, to an Audio-Animatronics© Gene Kelly "singin' in the rain," to a gangster or western shoot-out where you're caught in the crossfire between the real and the imaginary.

Sunset Boulevard – For a glimpse of the glamorous Hollywood of the 1930s, walk down this palm-lined street set with its Mediterranean Revival facades, antique autos, fruit vendors in Depression-era garb, and the swing music of Glenn Miller playing from hidden speakers. You may even be caught in the middle of an impromptu street skit. At a neon-lit movie palace, Mickey and other Disney characters sign autographs and pose for photographs.

Beauty and the Beast – Live on Stage – A rousing live stage version *(20min)* of the Disney motion picture features lip-synching cups and pots as well as a costumed chorus singing and dancing their way through the film's highlights *(check park brochure for show times).*

The Twilight Zone Tower of Terror – At the end of Sunset Boulevard looms the wonderfully decayed Hollywood Tower Hotel where guests enter a world of illusion. Incorporating part of an episode from the popular television series *The Twilight Zone* (1959-1965), this 10min thrill ride transports visitors back in time to a stormy night when a group of guests mysteriously disappeared from the hotel. Laser technology and convincing architectural details—cobblestone walkways, vine-covered trellises and iron gates—enhance the effects. The ride culminates in a 13-story plunge in the old service elevator.

Voyage of The Little Mermaid – *17min.* This musical stage show is based on the 1989 Disney animated hit *The Little Mermaid.* Special effects, such as the dark and misty undersea feel of the theater, enhance the experience.

Disney-MGM Studios Backlot Tour – *35min.* Boarding a tram, visitors snake through back lots and boneyards of the working studio, past a prop and costume warehouse and a street lined with the facades of homes used in motion pictures

149

Twilight Zone Tower of Terror

and television shows. The tour takes in George of the Jungle's treehouse and The American Film Institute Showcase before it climaxes in **Catastrophe Canyon**, where it seems the whole show could be derailed by a deluge.

Backstage Pass – *30min*. A behind-the-scenes walking tour past soundstages and postproduction suites is led by a guide who explains the inner workings of film-making. It includes visits to the prop room where costumes and set pieces used in 1996's live-action *101 Dalmatians* are stored, and to a working film set for an upcoming Touchstone production. Top-name actors sometimes appear on the set.

The Magic of Disney Animation – Visitors on this informative yet marvelously whimsical walking tour of a **working animation studio** get a rare glimpse of what Disney does best. Beginning in a gallery that displays Disney's Oscar trophies and animated cels from Disney classics, the tour introduces animation with a short film featuring news anchor Walter Cronkite and comedian Robin Williams as pre-taped guides. Visitors then walk through viewing galleries above the studio, where they can observe various stages of the animation process being applied to an upcoming Disney movie. The tour ends with a 10min film that highlights scenes from Disney's animated hits.

Along **New York Street**, building facades use forced perspective to fool the eye into believing that the skyscraping vista of the Empire State Building and other towers are looming large at the end of the street. Several musical and theatrical shows are presented here.

Backlot Theater – *32min*. The presentation here changes annually to feature Disney's latest animated movie. Recently playing was "Disney's The Hunchback of Notre Dame: A Musical Adventure." Lively gypsies give the hit movie a live-action spin with elaborate stage sets, puppetry and special effects. This is followed by a lively, gee-whiz documentary in which actors, musicians and artists explain the incredible labor of assembling several hundred thousand drawings into one feature-length film.

"Honey, I Shrunk the Kids" Movie Set Adventure – Youngsters are dwarfed by enormous blades of grass and insects in the fantastical playground, where everything is made to be climbed on, slid through and touched.

"Goosebumps" Fright Show – Based upon author R.L. Stine's best-selling juvenile mystery series, this outdoor stage act serves up spooky fun five times daily.

Jim Henson's Muppet© Vision 3D – *25min.* After visiting a reproduction of the Muppet set, visitors watch a funny film featuring the late Henson's winsome stars and some startlingly realistic 3-D and other special effects.

Star Tours – *10min.* This popular, futuristic thrill ride was jointly conceived by Walt Disney "Imagineers" and Star Wars creator George Lucas. Led by Star Wars droids C3PO and R2D 2, travelers board a StarSpeeder for a voyage to the Moon of Endor. Through the large "window" in their craft, space travelers experience excellent special effects during their simulated high-speed voyage.

Indiana Jones Epic Stunt Spectacular – *30min.* Re-creating scenes from the adventure-packed Indiana Jones movies, a riveting and humorous show is staged in this 2,200-seat, open-air amphitheater. Members of the audience are chosen to participate as extras, while the cast and crew enact awesome stunts—complete with a variety of pyrotechnics—and the show's host explains the techniques behind them.

6 Disney's Wide World of Sports

Map p 137. Take I-4 west to Exit 25B. Turn right on World Dr., right again on Osceola Pkwy. at first interchange, and follow signs. Open daily 10am–5pm. $8, $6.75 children ages 3-9. ☎ *407-824-4321.* This 200-acre complex has professional-caliber facilities for more than 30 competitive sports, including baseball, basketball, bicycle racing, soccer, tennis and track-and-field. Numerous championship amateur and pro events are scheduled here; the Atlanta Braves major-league baseball team make their spring-training home at the complex's 9,500-seat stadium. A permanent fixture is **The NFL Experience** Kids, a National Football League-sponsored skill test in passing, kicking and receiving for armchair quarterbacks. There are also sports-themed restaurants and stores.

ABC Sound Studio: One Saturday Morning – In this comical and informative look at the way sound is added to film, audience volunteers take positions behind wind-blowing, door-creaking and other devices on a Foley stage (named after the man who created most of the sound equipment). From here they add head bonks, face splats and other audio effects for the Saturday morning "101 Dalmatians" cartoon show—with some hilarious results.

SuperStar Television – Here you may get a chance to star in everything from *I Love Lucy* to *Cheers* to *Home Improvement*, or even make a guest appearance on *The Tonight Show*. Through a split-screen technique, volunteers appear to be part of the shows. In all, 28 audience members are cast in classic series six times daily.

Fringing Echo Lake, **Lakeside Circle** is replete with such "California Crazy" architecture as an ice-cream booth in the shape of Gertie—a dinosaur derived from a 1914 cartoon by Windsor McKay—and a Spanish galleon housing a restaurant. Palms edge the lake and a cheerful fountain festoons its center.

Michelin's Green Guide to Florida brings you the best of the natural and cultural attractions in the Sunshine State from the bustle of Miami to the spectacular white-sand beaches of the Gulf coast. In this guide you'll find a host of features including:

- *A selection of nearly 1,000 points of interest throughout the state*
- *Over 40 detailed city and regional maps*
- *Insightful essays highlighting Florida's history, geography and artistic heritage.*
- *Detailed walking and driving tours*

WINTER PARK★

Population 23,247
Map of Principal Sights p 3 – Map p 116
Tourist Information ☏ 407-644-8281

Both Winter Park and its leading institution, Rollins College, were founded in 1885 by affluent Congregationalists from New England. The town, set on one of six connected lakes, supported a logging industry during the late 19C. After timber was harvested along the shoreline, it was pulled by boat to waterside sawmills. (A series of shady canals built along natural streams to connect the lakes in 1894 still serves recreational watercraft today and draws many visitors onto the water with the **Winter Park Scenic Boat Tour**; *east end of Morse Blvd; $6;* ☏ *407-644-4056*). With its temperate climate and beautiful scenery, the growing settlement attracted many winter residents who built substantial landscaped estates overlooking Lake Osceola. (For a good landside view of these privately owned homes, drive along Alabama or Interlachen Avenues.) The main downtown artery is **Park Avenue**, lined with attractive cafes, antique shops and elegant specialty boutiques, as well as some familiar high-end chain stores. Be sure to explore the passageways between store fronts, which lead to small flower-filled courtyards. The south end of Park Avenue terminates at the entrance to Rollins College at Holt Avenue.

SIGHTS *1/2 day*

★**Charles Hosmer Morse Museum of American Art** – *445 Park Ave. N. Open year-round Tue–Sat 9:30am–4pm. Sun 1pm–4pm. Closed major holidays. $3.* ♿ 🅿 ☏ *407-645-5311.* An extensive group of works from the studios of artist **Louis Comfort Tiffany** (1848-1933) forms the centerpiece of this 4,000-piece collection of late 19C and early 20C American and European paintings, decorative and graphic arts, American Art Pottery, Art Nouveau jewelry and Arts and Crafts furniture. Founder Jeannette McKean named the museum after her industrialist grandfather, who retired in Winter Park. First shown at a Rollins College gallery in 1942, the Morse collection moved in 1995 to its present 7,800sq ft quarters, specifically designed to showcase large window panels and architectural elements.

Framed by two marble columns with capitals of Favrile glass daffodils from Tiffany's Long Island mansion, the 20ft-high **Tiffany window gallery** displays the exquisite **leaded windows**★ that Tiffany designed for the 1893 World's Columbian Exposition in Chicago. Holdings also include the stunning **Magnolia Window** from the Tiffany family's New York City mansion, as well as glass panels by William Morris, Frank Lloyd Wright and John Lafarge. Among the other beautifully preserved **Tiffany pieces** that occupy the majority of the museum's 15 galleries are lamps, vases, jewelry, blown glass and pottery.

Rollins College – *1000 Holt Ave. at the south end of Park Ave. Grounds open to the public.* A private, four-year coeducational liberal arts college of 1,425 undergraduate students, Rollins was founded in 1895 and ranks as the oldest recognized

Wistaria Panel (c.1910) by Louis Comfort Tiffany

college in the state. A stroll through the serene palm-studded, 67-acre campus—on the shores of Lake Virginia two blocks from downtown Winter Park—is a pleasure. Notice the **Walk of Fame** at the entrance *(north of Holt Ave.)*, lined with stones from the homes and birthplaces of some 500 luminaries (including Helen Keller, Theodore Roosevelt and Martin Luther King, Jr.). Inside the lobby of **Crummer Hall**, which houses the graduate business school, you'll see two 1929 **Tiffany medallion windows** on display. Originally designed for a church in St. Louis, Missouri, these panels depict scenes from the life of Christ.

★ **Knowles Memorial Chapel** – *Holt Ave. Open Sept–May Mon–Fri 8:30am–5pm. Rest of the year and weekends by appointment only.* ♿ *www.rollins.edu* ☎ *407-646-2115.* This church ranks among the most distinguished of the many early 20C Mediterranean Revival buildings on campus. With its creamy stucco walls and red-tiled roof, the structure boasts an ornate tiered bell tower and carved door tympanum depicting a Franciscan monk flanked by Spanish conquistadors and Florida Indians. This impressive building was designed in 1932 by **Ralph Adams Cram** (1863-1942), one of America's most highly acclaimed ecclesiastical architects, whose work also includes the Cathedral of St. John the Divine in New York City. Inside, note the stained-glass rose and chancel windows (representing St. Augustine of Hippo and St. Francis of Assisi) and the 16C Brussels tapestry, based on a Raphael cartoon portraying the stoning of St. Stephen, that hangs over the tower entrance. An annual Bach Festival takes place here each February.

Cornell Fine Arts Museum – *West end of Holt Ave.; parking in the adjacent lot. Open year-round Tue–Fri 10am–5pm, weekends 1pm–5pm. Closed major holidays.* ♿ 🅿 *www.rollins.edu/cfam/index.html* ☎ *407-646-2526.* Fronted by a tile-roofed, Spanish-style portico, the single-story Mediterranean Revival building houses three galleries and hosts six to eight traveling exhibits a year. Shows drawn from the museum's own permanent collection of some 6,000 objects—including American painting, European painting from the Renaissance to the 20C, bronzes, sculpture, prints, decorative arts and glass are featured from June to September. During the summer months, the museum displays objects from its private collection. Films, concerts and lectures are scheduled regularly.

Albin Polasek Galleries – *633 Osceola Ave. Open Sept–Jun Wed–Sat 10am–4pm, Sun 1pm–4pm. Closed major holidays.* ♿ 🅿 ☎ *407-647-6294.* The Mediterranean Revival-style villa of Albin Polasek (1875-1965) now showcases about 200 paintings and sculptures by the Czech-American artist. Born in Moravia, where he trained as a woodcarver, Polasek came to America in 1901 and was named head of the sculpture department of the Art Institute of Chicago in 1916. He moved to Winter Park in 1950. The stone, terra-cotta and bronze pieces displayed in Polasek's studios, private chapel and three-acre gardens include versions of the artist's monumental religious and classical sculptures commissioned for churches and parks throughout the US.

Charles Hosmer Morse Museum of American Art

The Panhandle

Gulf Islands National Seashore – A Blake Gardner

Squeezed between Georgia, Alabama and the Gulf of Mexico, the Panhandle shoots 200mi westward from the Florida peninsula in a band 30mi to 100mi wide. This region lies far enough north to trumpet a summer tourist season and far enough west to be in a different time zone from the rest of Florida (Central Time Zone begins at the Apalachicola River, 45mi west of Tallahassee). Here you'll find rolling hills clad with pines and hardwoods, as well as the state's highest point (345ft) tucked up against Alabama. In personality the Panhandle more closely resembles its Deep South neighbors, Georgia and Alabama, than it does Florida's fast-paced Atlantic coast.

For 10,000 years mound-building tribes lived in the region and took a good living from the sea. Spanish explorers gained a toehold here in 1559, when **Don Tristán de Luna** established a short-lived settlement at Pensacola, six years before the founding of ST. AUGUSTINE. Spain failed to rediscover northwest Florida until the late 17C, then until the mid-18C jockeyed with France for control of Pensacola Bay. Settlement as far west as Panama City waited upon British rule in the late 18C. From 1783 to 1819, Spain again held the Florida territory, finally deciding to sell out to the US. Soon thereafter, Tallahassee sprang to life as the seat of Florida government.

Throughout the 19C, the Panhandle's deepwater ports exported the bounty of the region's waters and forests. Inland plantations grew cotton and sugar; pine forests hummed with sawmills; and the Gulf yielded remarkable numbers of fish. More recently, large military installations like Eglin Air Force Base and the Pensacola Naval Air Station have pumped money into the region, and a burgeoning tourist trade has lined the coast from Pensacola to Panama City with fine resorts and retirement homes. Fortunately, the **Gulf Islands National Seashore** *(p 167)* protects large chunks of wild beach and dune environment.

Visitors to the Panhandle today are rewarded with gorgeous beaches, an emerald sea teeming with fish, well-preserved historic towns and true Southern hospitality. Although the area's renowned white-sand beaches took a pounding in October 1995 from Hurricane Opal—the worst storm to hit this coast in 30 years—most of the dunes, beaches, smaller coast roads and beachfront accommodations were restored within a year thereafter.

APALACHICOLA ★

Population 2,834
Map of Principal Sights p 2 – Map p 159
Tourist information ☎ 850-653-9419

Occupying the tip of a spit of land where the Apalachicola River empties into the Gulf of Mexico, Apalachicola (a Creek word meaning "land beyond") prides itself on being a serene little fishing community, with abundant greenery and well-preserved ante-bellum and Victorian homes.

Historical Notes

Once the third busiest port on the Gulf—eclipsed only by New Orleans, Louisiana, and Mobile, Alabama—Apalachicola's access to waterways made it the ideal destination for the crops of wealthy north Florida and south Georgia cotton planters during the 1830s and 1840s. Once there, the fiber was sold to a factor, or cotton broker, and shipped to New York, Boston or major ports in Europe. A number of prosperous cotton brokers built impressive homes, some of which still grace Apalachicola's quiet streets. Indeed, the tiny town, organized in 1831, was such a thriving center of commerce that it even boasted French and Belgian consulates.
After the Civil War, trees took up where cotton left off, with several local cypress mills producing large quantities of lumber for export. Again a number of extravagant homes went up, constructed by prosperous lumber barons eager to show off their new affluence. By the 1920s, however, the rails had replaced shipping as the country's major means of transportation; Apalachicola, a port with no railroad, sank into quiet obscurity. Apalachicola's location on an estuary to the Gulf of Mexico has long dictated its economy; fishing and oystering remain the town's major industries. Indeed, the Apalachicola basin boasts one of the country's largest oyster nurseries. Although severely damaged by Hurricane Kate in 1985, the oyster beds have since recovered, producing more than three-fourths of Florida's annual crop—about 1,500 tons of oyster meat—as well as more than half of its shellfish. Within the last decade, tourists have begun to discover the excellent deep-sea fishing and laid-back lifestyle in this formerly isolated section of Florida, a factor which has helped to diversify the economy of the once single-industry town.

SIGHTS *1/2 day*

★**Historic Downtown** – *Walking-tour maps are available at the Chamber of Commerce (57 Market St.).* Water Street served as Apalachicola's commercial hub in the 1830s, and vestiges of the past can still be seen today. Although in disrepair, the best example of a surviving **cotton warehouse** stands at the corner of Water Street and Avenue E. During its heyday, Apalachicola boasted 43 of these impressive red-brick structures, all three stories tall with granite posts and lintels decorating the facade on the ground floor. Here cotton was compressed and readied for shipment. Just up the street *(corner of Ave. E and Commerce St.; also unrestored)*, is the city's **Sponge Exchange** (c.1838), where harvested sponges were cleaned and sold. Although the town's sponge trade never approached that of TARPON SPRINGS, the industry employed more than 10 percent of the town's population at its zenith.
One of the city's best examples of Greek Revival antebellum architecture is the white porticoed **Raney House** *(128 Market St.)* built by merchant David Raney in 1838. The restored Victorian **Gibson Inn** *(corner of Ave. C and Market St.)*, whose wide wraparound verandah commands a view of the bay, still entertains visitors as it has done for 90 years. A number of other early homes, like those along Chestnut Street (Avenue E), represent various architectural styles, including Greek Revival and Victorian *(homes are not open to the public, but are indicated on the walking-tour map)*.

John Gorrie State Museum – *6th St. & Ave. D. Open year-round Thu–Mon 9am–5pm. Closed Jan 1, Thanksgiving Day, Dec 25. $1.* ♿ 🅿 ☎ *850-653-9347.* Exhibits in this small one-room structure chronicle the career of Apalachicola physician **John Gorrie** (1803-1855), inventor of an artificial refrigeration process. Gorrie's invention resulted from the 1841 yellow fever epidemic that wiped out 10 percent of Tallahassee's population. He was looking for a new way to cool his feverish patients' rooms (other than natural ice imported from northern states) when he devised the machine. The museum contains a replica of the apparatus, which used cool air to chill brine; the cold brine was then used to freeze fresh water. (The actual patented model resides in the National Museum of American History at the Smithsonian Institution in Washington, DC.) Gorrie is buried directly across Sixth Street on a plot of land known as Gorrie Square.

Trinity Episcopal Church – *6th St. and Ave. D, at Gorrie Square. Open year-round Mon–Fri 8am–noon, weekends 8am–5pm.* ♿ ☎ *904-653-9550.* Organized in 1835, Trinity is one of the oldest churches in North Florida. Dr. Gorrie *(above)* was among its founders. The white pine Greek Revival church was built in 1839 in upstate New York, then taken apart and shipped piece-by-piece to Apalachicola, where congregation members re-assembled the structure using wooden pegs. Inside, note the original organ and pews (c.1840), as well as the unusual hand-stenciled ceiling.

155

Chestnut Street Cemetery – *Between 6th and 8th Sts. on Ave. E.* Laden with moss-draped live oaks, the picturesque old burial ground dates to before 1831. It contains the graves of numerous yellow fever victims; several Confederate soldiers, seven of whom fought at Gettysburg as part of the Florida Brigade; shipwrecked sailors; and ordinary citizens. Noted botanist Alvin Wentworth Chapman, who moved to Apalachicola to study Southern flora, is also buried here.

Lafayette Park – *West end of Ave. A, where it becomes Walnut St.* This lovely, shaded park, replete with gnarled oaks and azaleas, is perched on a high bluff overlooking Apalachicola Bay. Brick walkways crisscross the landscape, leading to a replica turn-of-the-century gazebo in the center. A boardwalk on the south end leads down to an overlook offering an expansive view of the bay. A marker at the overlook identifies the estuary as one of world's most productive oyster beds.

EXCURSIONS *Map p 159*

⌂**St. George Island** – *1/2 day. 6mi east of Apalachicola. Take US-98 east 4mi to Eastpoint. Turn right on causeway and follow it to island.* This relatively undeveloped barrier island, for many years accessible only by private boat, retains a rich history as a pirate's hideout, Indian campground and playground for turn-of-the-century vacationers. Its forests provided a resource for the early turpentine industry; scars can still be seen on some of the island's slash pines. Twenty-five miles long, it is the largest of three barrier islands off the coast of Franklin County—and the only one connected by causeway to the mainland.

Although a few hardy souls lived on the island year-round, there was little here until 1965. It was then that completion of the causeway spurred the construction of vacation homes, concentrated in the middle and west end of the island. The east and west (Cape St. George) ends are preserved as state lands. Today St. George Island and its lovely white-sand beaches are popular with locals as a weekend getaway spot. With the exception of a few restaurants, an inn, a motel and family-owned grocery stores, there is little commercial activity.

Two additional barrier islands guard the Franklin County coastline, protecting the mainland from high winds and hurricanes: Isle de Chien or **Dog Island** to the east of Apalachicola *(accessible only by private boat;* △ ☎ *850-653-8808)*, and **St. Vincent Island**, 9mi west *(permit required to visit; www. fws.gov/r4eao/nwrsvn.html* ☎ *850-653-8808)*. In 1948 two millionaire brothers purchased St. Vincent Island and populated it with exotic animals. Now owned by the US Fish and Wildlife Service, its unspoiled shores provide sanctuary for a number of endangered plant and animal species, as well as more than 180 species of birds.

★★**Dr. Julian G. Bruce St. George Island State Park** – *1/2 day. 7mi east on St. George Island. Take US-98 east 4mi to Eastpoint and turn right on causeway road; turn left on Rte. 300 and follow it to park entrance. Open year-round daily 8am–dusk. Closed during hurricanes. $4/vehicle.* △ ♿ ☐ ☎ *850-927-2111.* High dunes dotted with sea oats and sparkling white **beaches**⌂ characterize this island park, which encompasses more than 1,900 acres and 9mi of pristine shoreline on St. George's east end. It's one of five Florida beaches ranked in *USA Today* as being among the top 10 in the US (the other five are in Hawaii). Largely uninhabited until the late 19C, St. George Island sacrificed significant acreage of its pine forests to the turpentine industry. Although the land was acquired in 1963, the park was not opened to the public until 1980. Boardwalks and hiking trails thread the salt marshes, pine forests and oak hammocks, where migratory birds, osprey, snowy plovers and diamondback terrapins number among the abundant wildlife that finds habitat here. Bay and Gulf waters abound with flounder, redfish, sea trout and shellfish. Although pleasant in all seasons, the park is at its best in the early spring and late fall when there is a respite from the intense summer heat.

FORT WALTON BEACH

Population 21,933
Map of Principal Sights p 2 – Map p 158
Tourist information ☎ 850-244-8191

Located on the Gulf coast some 40mi east of Pensacola, this beach town began as a Confederate installation in 1861. Walton Guards (named for George Walton, acting governor of territorial Florida and son of a signer of the Declaration of Independence) garrisoned the fort, which saw little action and was abandoned when the Confederates left Pensacola to fight farther north. After the war, some of the original guards returned to the area to homestead. One of these settlers, John Thomas Brooks, founded Brooks Landing at the old Indian mound where the guards had camped. Fort Walton Beach grew from this settlement.

Eglin Air Force Base, one of the world's largest air bases, began in the early 1930s as a golf course owned by wealthy innkeeper James Plew. In 1934 Plew donated 4,160 acres of land to the government for a bombing and gunnery range. Today the 720sq mi base boasts unique testing facilities and ranges, and ranks as the county's leading source of revenue.

With New Deal funding in the 1940s came roads connecting the mainland to Santa Rosa Island *(map p 158)*, and an accompanying leap in population. From a count of 90 in 1940, the area has swelled to more than 85,000 people. Tourism generates the most revenue after Eglin Air Force Base, adding more than 2.5 million annual visitors, who savor the quartz sand beaches and sumptuous seafood.

SIGHTS *1/2 day*

Gulfarium – ▨ *1010 Miracle Strip Pkwy. (1mi east of town on US-98). Open mid-May–mid-Sept daily 9am–6pm. Rest of the year daily 9am–4pm. Closed Thanksgiving Day, Dec 25. $14. ⚲ ▯ www.gulfarium.org ☎ 904-243-9046.* For 40 years this marine-life attraction has entertained and educated area beach enthusiasts. Trained dolphins leap 20ft into the air and perform other amazing stunts. In one large glass tank, scuba divers handle sharks, stingrays and moray eels. Other exhibits feature sea lions, tropical birds and fish. From various vantage points in this facility you can behold the beach and pier, where wild dolphins often show themselves. Gulfarium also rescues stranded turtles and birds, and it has begun a new research program in conjunction with the University of West Florida that uses dolphins to coax responses from autistic children.

Indian Temple Mound Museum – *139 Miracle Strip Pkwy. (US-98). Open Jun–Aug Mon–Sat 9am–4:45pm, Sun 1pm–4pm. Rest of the year Mon–Fri 11am–4pm, Sat 9am–4pm. Closed major holidays. $2.01 ▯ ☎ 850-833-9595.* Visitors to the area may be surprised to find a 15ft-high earth mound rising from the otherwise flat commercial strip of Fort Walton Beach. Indians built the mound as a political and ceremonial center about 600 years ago. A replica log-and-thatch temple tops the mound and tall moss-draped trees shade it. The adjacent long, low building houses a collection of Indian artifacts found within a 40mi radius of the mound. In addition to authentic pottery, bone and stone tools, and spear points, the museum presents beautifully made replicas of ancient Indian crafts, as well as hands-on Indian tools.

Air Force Armament Museum – *6mi north of US-98, on Rte. 85 (east side) just past interchange with Rte. 189. Open year-round daily 9:30am–4:30pm. Closed Jan 1, Thanksgiving Day, Dec 25. ⚲ ▯ www.eglin.af.mil/sponsor/museum.htm ☎ 850-882-4062.* Dedicated to the display of Air Force weapons, this spacious facility satisfies civilians' curiosity about the world's most advanced defense system. Outside stand more than 20 aircraft and missiles including a B-17, B-52, SR-71 Blackbird, and Mace and Hound-dog missiles. Two floors of indoor exhibits chronicle air weaponry from World War I to Desert Storm. Among the highlights are the **Weapons Display Vault**, with its impressive glass cases full of antique and modern guns; a sobering POW exhibit; and an innocent-looking replica of "Fat Man"—the atom bomb that exploded over Nagasaki in 1945, instantly annihilating 45,000 people.

EXCURSION *Map p 158*

Fred Gannon Rocky Bayou State Recreation Area – *1hr. 16mi northeast in Niceville. From US-98 in Fort Walton Beach, take Rte. 85 north 12mi to Rte. 20. Go east on Rte. 203mi to park. Open year-round daily 8am–dusk. $2/vehicle. △ ⚲ ☎ 850-833-9144.* For a non-beach nature outing, try this secluded little park nestled against an arm of the Choctawhatchee Bay. Named for an Air Force colonel who helped establish the park in the mid-1960s, Rocky Bayou encompasses 357 acres of sand pine forest with hiking trails and campsites. Anglers may try their luck with both freshwater and saltwater fish. The former frequent Rocky Creek; the latter inhabit the bay.

INLAND PANHANDLE★

Map of Principal Sights p 2 – Map pp 158-159
Tourist information ☎ 850-892-3191

A little-known region of the state, the inland Panhandle has been left in the dust of progressive Florida. As more and more visitors discover the quiet beauty of the Gulf coast, many are also heading off to explore the backroads of northwest Florida. From anywhere on the Panhandle beaches, you're never more than an hour or two from the border of Alabama or Georgia. Like these two Deep South neighbors, the inland Panhandle was tamed by large plantation owners. Cotton, sugar and tobacco were shipped from Georgia and Alabama down through Florida on the Apalachicola River to the Gulf of Mexico. Interspersed among the plantations were, and still are, backwaters of poor whites and blacks existing on the murky edges of civilization.
Visitors to the Panhandle today will notice a world of difference between the sprawling coastal cities, with their more transient military- and tourism-related populations, and the small, sparsely populated inland towns that have changed little over the past decades. Farming and forestry support the economy of this region, where some of

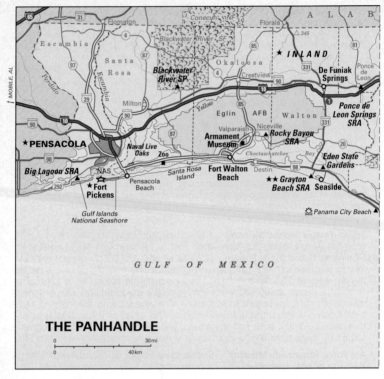

THE PANHANDLE

```
0              30mi
0          40km
```

Florida's more unique geological features—hills, cliffs, sinkholes, caverns—are found. Uncrowded state parks feature clean rivers for boating and fishing, beautiful forests brimming with wildlife, and unspoiled wetlands. Just west of the state's capital, **Apalachicola National Forest** extends through parts of Leon, Liberty and Wakulla counties.

SIGHTS *1 day. Sights are organized from west to east.*

Blackwater River State Park – *7720 Bridge Rd., Holt. Take Exit 10 off I-10, and follow Rte. 87 north to US-90. Take US-90 east 5.6mi to sign; turn left and go 3mi to park. Open year-round daily 8am–dusk. $2.* ⚠ ♿ 🅿 ☎ *850-983-5363.* This 590-acre park centers around a 2mi stretch of the Blackwater River, a tannin-stained, sandy-bottomed river with inviting white sandbars. Part of the designated **Florida Canoe Trail** *(p 335),* the river slides past forests of oak, red maple and tupelo intermingling with meadows of wire grass and gallberry. Denizens of the park include white-tailed deer, turkeys and bobcats. A short hiking trail meanders through the park.

De Funiak Springs – *80mi east of Pensacola. Take Exit 13 off I-10 and turn left (north) on Rte. 331; turn right at the second traffic light on Live Oak St., which dead-ends at Circle Dr.* Named in 1882 for the chief engineer on the Louisville & Nashville Railroad, this former train station became, within a few years, a town of wealth and elegance when the New York Chautauqua association chose it as the winter home for its cultural and educational symposia. Though the Chautauqua programs officially ended in 1928, De Funiak Springs continues to host annual cultural activities, and many graceful turn-of-the-century homes attest to the halcyon period of the town's history.

★ **Circle Drive** – *The Walton County Chamber of Commerce (Circle Dr. and West Ave., next door to library) offers brochures outlining a walking or driving tour around Circle Drive.* Rimming the town's spring-fed lake, this 1mi loop proceeds beneath ancient live oaks and magnolias and passes house after house of historical and architectural note. Built in 1886, the **Walton-De Funiak Library** *(100 Circle Dr.)* contains a small collection of swords and other weaponry dating as far back as AD 1100. When Frederick De Funiak, the town's namesake, ignored a request for a donation to the library, the Ladies' Library Association removed his name from the sign over the entrance. To this day the sign reads simply, "Library." Next door, the white wooden **Chautauqua Hall of Brotherhood** houses the Walton County Chamber of Commerce. Across the street, **St. Agatha's Episcopal Church** (1896) boasts beautifully preserved stained-glass windows. The light blue, three-story Victorian at no. 219, with its fanciful trim and twin turrets, ranks among the most lovely of the private homes here, as does the 1904 **Tharpe House** *(no. 307),* with its large double verandahs. Note also the home at no. 402 (1907), with its magnificent balconied portico; and the c.1885 "Dream Cottage" *(no. 506)* built for Wallace Bruce, former US ambassador to Scotland.

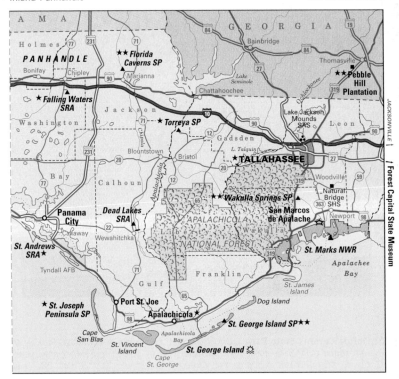

Ponce de Leon Springs State Recreation Area – *On Rte. 181A, Ponce de Leon. Take Exit 15 off I-10; follow Rte. 81 north and turn right on US-90. Park is .5mi south of US-90. Open year-round daily 8am–dusk. $2/vehicle.* 🚻 ☎ *850-836-4281.* A rock-and-concrete pool, built around a spring flowing with transparent emerald-green water, forms the centerpiece of this site, named for the explorer associated with the legendary fountain of youth. The refreshing 68°F water is just right for swimming on a hot day. Twenty developed acres of the 443-acre park also offer picnic facilities and two walking trails *(.4mi each)* winding through a floodplain forest of moss-draped cypresses. Fishermen cast the creeks for largemouth bass, catfish, chain pickerel and panfish.

★**Falling Waters State Recreation Area** –
Off Rte. 77 south of Chipley. Take Exit 18 off I-10 and follow Rte. 77 south 1mi; turn left on Rte. 77A and continue 1mi to park. Open year-round daily 8am–dusk. $3.25/vehicle. ⚠ 🚻 ☎ *904-638-6130.* Here you'll see one of the state's most remarkable geological features: a rare stream-fed **waterfall** that plunges into a 100ft-deep sinkhole. A wooden platform provides a good vantage point for peering into the abyss; where the water ends up remains a mystery. A short boardwalk trail encircles several other sinkholes, all formed long ago by the seepage of rainwater into the ground's porous limestone. Over the years, the area's natural resources have been tapped several times: the famous waterfall powered a grist mill during the Civil War; a legal whiskey distillery operated here around 1880; and in 1919, wildcatters drilled down 3,900ft trying to find oil.

Three short nature trails *(.8mi total)* wind past these sites and through a hardwood hammock and a pine forest flecked with wildflowers.

❶ Chautauqua Winery

Map p 158. Intersection of I-10 and US-331. Guided tour (20min) available. Open year-round Mon–Sat 9am–5pm, Sun noon–5pm. Closed Jul 4, Thanksgiving Day, Dec 24-25. ♿ 🚻 ☎ *904-892-5887.* Established in the mid-1980s, this regionally famous winery has won numerous awards for its sweet wines made from local muscadine grapes. The vineyards (located 12mi north) annually produce 400,000 pounds of grapes, which are made into wine on the hill overlooking the busy interstate. Stop by to watch a 4min video on the wine-making process, view the stainless-steel fermenting tanks through a glass booth, and enjoy free samples.

A. Blake Gardner

Bottomlands of Torreya State Park

★★Florida Caverns State Park – *On Rte. 166, 2.6mi north of Marianna. Park open year-round daily 8am–dusk. $3.25/vehicle. Visit by guided tour (1hr) only, year-round daily 9:30am–4:30pm. $4. Closed Thanksgiving Day & Dec 25.* ⚠ ⓟ ☏ *850-482-9598.* Limestone caves (featuring Florida's only touring cavern) show off a remarkable variety of subterranean architecture comparable to some of the largest caves in the country. These caverns formed 40 to 60 million years ago when the level of an underground stream dropped, leaving a cavity in the earth. Bizarre formations result from slow drips of acidic water into the cave. Tours start off slowly with a 15min movie in the **visitor center**, but then move to a nearby cave, made accessible to the public by the Civilian Conservation Corps in 1937. Lights illuminate stalagmites (that grow from the floor), stalactites (that hang from the ceiling), soda straws, columns, rimstones, flowstones and draperies. *Guides request that you not touch the formations, since oil from skin can damage the fragile decorations that took tens of thousands of years to form.*

★Torreya State Park – *Off Rte. 12 in Rock Bluff, 13mi north of Bristol. Take Exit 25 south off I-10; follow Rte. 12 11mi south; turn right on Rte. 1641 and continue 7mi to park. Open year-round daily 8am–dusk. $2/vehicle.* ⚠ ⓟ ☏ *850-643-2674.* The 150ft-high **bluffs** here afford lovely views of the lazy Apalachicola River and the thick forests beyond. Torreya trees—a rare species of conifer *(Torreya taxifolia)*—grow only on these bluffs. A 7mi loop trail threads through the forest and along the ridge. Perched at the edge of the bluff, the two-story white clapboard **Gregory House**, built in 1849 by planter Jason Gregory, affords visitors a glimpse of plantation life on the river. Daily tours describe the period antiques inside as well as recounting local history *(visit by 1hr guided tour only, year-round Mon–Fri 10am, weekends & major holidays 10am, 2pm & 4pm; $1).* From the front lawn, the **river view** glows with a luminous beauty, especially in the golden light of an autumn sunset.

PANAMA CITY

Population 35,986
Map of Principal Sights p 2 – Map p 159
Tourist Information ☏ 850-233-6503 or 800-722-3224 (US & Canada)

Bordered on three sides by bays, Panama City ranks second to Pensacola as the Panhandle's leading port. Although Spanish sailors explored the area in the early 16C, it was the English who established a permanent village here in 1765. These days visitors ignore the no-nonsense industrial corridors of the city and head directly for **Panama City Beach**⚏, a 20mi stretch of sugar-white sand bordering turquoise Gulf water.
Along both sides of the main drag, stretching for mile after mile, are resorts, high-rise condominiums, inexpensive motels, hot-dog and soft ice-cream stands, water parks, and the outrageous architecture of numerous miniature golf courses. Ramshackle joints

stand side-by-side with spanking new shops and eateries. One old warhorse, Miracle Strip Amusement Park *(12000 Front Beach Rd.)* has attracted thrill-seekers for more than 30 years; it was re-landscaped, with new shows and rides, in 1995.

Despite the building boom that has altered the face of Panama City Beach in recent decades, much natural beauty remains. Popular area sports include golfing, snorkeling, diving and game fishing.

SIGHTS *1 day*

★**St. Andrews State Recreation Area** – *4607 State Park Ln. (east end of Panama City Beach). Open year-round daily 8am–dusk. $4/vehicle.* △& 🅿 ☎ *850-233-5140.* A lovely refuge of fine sand beaches and freshwater marsh, pine flatwoods and sand pine scrub, this park occupies land on either side of the entrance channel to St. Andrews Bay. Fishing piers and jetties extend into Grand Lagoon and the Gulf of Mexico, where flounder, trout, dolphin, bluefish, bonito, redfish and Spanish mackerel abound. Jetties form protected pools perfect for swimming and snorkeling.

A nature trail *(.6mi)* traipses past a reconstructed Cracker turpentine still, a two-story wood-and-brick structure typifying those that operated in Bay County into the 1930s. Charts and diagrams outline the distillation process.

☂☂ **Shell Island** – *Accessible by boat only. Departs Jetty Dive Store, St. Andrews State Recreation Area Feb–Oct daily 9am–5pm (on the half-hour). One-way 5min. Commentary. $7.50 (snorkeling $16.95).* 🅿 *Captain Blacks* ☎ *904-233-0197. Shell Island has no facilities of any kind, nor any shade; plan accordingly.* Created in the 1930s by the dredging of the channel, this unspoiled barrier island measures 7mi long and .5mi wide. Most of the island is owned by the park, with Tyndall Air Force Base and a few private owners holding the remainder. Here visitors will discover a gorgeous strand of aquamarine water and squeaky white sand, backed by a scrub-covered dune ridge. For best shell finds, walk away from the tip of the island, where visitors tend to cluster, and wade a few feet into the surf.

Gulf World Aquarium – 🄺🄸🄳 *15412 US-98A. Open Feb–Apr daily 9am–3pm. May–Sept daily 9am–7pm. Hours vary during Thanksgiving weekend and Christmas week. $14.88.* & 🅿 ☎ *850-234-5271.* This popular marine entertainment complex features a 2.5hr cycle of shows that repeats throughout the day. You can choose among performing parrots, scuba demonstrations, sea lion and dolphin acrobatics, and a shark feeding. Visitors may also pet dolphins enclosed in small tanks, as well as stingrays that have had their barbs removed.

Museum of Man in the Sea – *17314 Back Beach Rd. (on US-98, .25mi west of Rte. 79). Open year-round daily 9am–5pm. Closed Jan 1, Thanksgiving Day, Dec 25. $5.* & 🅿 *www.iod.ycg.org* ☎ *850-235-4101.* Recognizable by its outdoor display of large submersibles, or deep-sea exploration vehicles, this small facility traces the history of diving. Run by the Institute of Diving, the museum offers chronologically arranged exhibits, starting with dioramas of 17C divers who salvaged wrecked vessels using diving bells. Among other displays are diving suits, fish tanks, and artifacts from the Union transport ship *Maple Leaf*, which sank near Jacksonville in 1864. Photographs and videos explain the work of underwater archaeologists on wrecks off the Florida coast, including the *Maple Leaf*, the *Urca de Lima* (1715) and the *Atocha* (1622).

Junior Museum of Bay County – 🄺🄸🄳 *1731 N. Jenks Ave. (between 15th and 23rd Sts.). Open year-round Mon–Fri 9am–4:30pm, Sat 10am–4pm. Closed major holidays.* & 🅿 ☎ *904-769-6128.* Science exhibits, a costume room and fish tanks provide a good diversion for children. The **pioneer farmstead** out back includes a gristmill, smokehouse, barn, corncrib and an 1887 log house with pioneer furnishings. Most of the buildings were moved here from Jackson and Holmes Counties, on the Alabama border. Adjacent to the farmstead stands a diesel locomotive that hauled freight and passengers between Panama City and Dothan, Alabama, in the 1940s. A boardwalk nature trail across from the museum traverses a hardwood swamp.

EXCURSIONS

Eden State Gardens – *2hrs. 32mi northwest in Point Washington. From Panama City, take US-98 west 31mi to Rte. C-395. Go north 1mi to park entrance. Gardens open year-round daily 8am–dusk. $2/vehicle.* & 🅿 ☎ *850-231-4214.* Though the formal gardens have suffered neglect with the recent cuts in state funding, the house and its grounds are well worth a visit. Built of yellow heart-pine by lumberman William Henry Wesley in 1895, the stately Greek Revival **house** features wraparound porches on two levels *(visit by 45min guided tour only, year-round Thu–Mon 9am–4pm; $1.50).* House tours inventory the large collection of antiques—especially Louis XVI furniture—amassed by Eden's final private owner, New York journalist Lois Maxon. Pieces include an 1820 carved rosewood canopy bed, a Chippendale mahogany bedside table, English chandeliers and a Louis XVI mirror. A sloping lawn surrounds the house, providing a field for the rich play of afternoon shadows that fall from ancient live oaks hung with scrims of Spanish moss. Visitors may picnic at the old 20C lumber mill site on picturesque Tucker Bayou.

Seaside – *1hr. 35mi west of Panama City on US-98A.* Located off US-98 midway between Panama City Beach and Fort Walton Beach, the tiny town of Seaside reflects the nostalgic vision of developer **Robert S. Davis**, who remembered the area in simpler times. His award-winning planned community, platted in 1981 by Miami architects Andres Duany and Elizabeth Plater-Zyberk, boasts more than 300 cottages, shops and restaurants huddled together on 80 acres in Easter-egg pastels. Plans call for another 100 homes to be added by the millennium. Drawing from Florida's vernacular architecture, elements such as picket fences, widow's walks, latticework balconies, fanciful parapets, and steep-pitched roofs with deep overhangs conform to Davis' architectural guidelines. Although owners are free to hire their own architects, the community's building code requires they use only pre-World War II materials (i.e., tin roofs and wood siding).

Seaside

The resulting variety of frame vernacular designs suggests a beach town of KEY WEST ilk, but the newness of the place lends it the aura of a Hollywood set. Indeed, as "Seahaven," it was the focus of the popular 1998 movie, *The Truman Show.* (Star Jim Carrey's Natchez Street "home" is known locally as the Truman House.) To maintain the community atmosphere, only residents and guests may drive on the brick side streets. Seaside has been featured in *Architectural Digest* and has won accolades from several organizations, the American Institute of Architects and Progressive Architecture among them.

** **Grayton Beach State Recreation Area** – *1/2 day. 1.5mi west of Seaside on Rte. 30A. Open year-round daily 8am–dusk. $3.25/vehicle.* ⏇⏇ ☎ *850-231-4210.* This small park harbors a gorgeous 1mi strand of shoreline that has been rated one of the country's top 10 beaches by the University of Maryland's Laboratory for Coastal Research. Minimal development, low numbers of people and insects, clear aquamarine waters and high dunes account for the high rating. Though not as wide as some area beaches, Grayton offers plenty of room for exploring or just swimming and sunning. A lovely nature loop *(1mi)* penetrates a tunnel of dwarf live oaks and emerges out past the dunes and pine flats on a trail lined with wild daisies, goldenrod and saw palmetto.

■ **Panhandle Beaches**

What makes the Panhandle coast beaches so white? According to Stephen Leatherman, director of the International Hurricane Center in Miami and a recognized expert on beaches, quartz is responsible for the color and texture of these sands. Whereas most beaches contain multiple minerals, the Panhandle's shores are composed of nearly pure quartz. Eons ago, sediments eroded from the Appalachian Mountains and washed down to the Gulf of Mexico. Waves pummeled these sediments, grinding up the minerals and eventually washing most of them away, leaving quartz to color the sands. The Panhandle's beaches stay so sparkling white because the area's rivers flow over limestone on their way into the Gulf; since limestone does not produce sediment, no impurities are introduced into the pristine sand.

PENSACOLA★

Hugging the western shore of Pensacola Bay and well protected by Santa Rosa Island and Perdido Key, this coveted seaport on the Panhandle's west end has been fought over many times in its long and colorful history. Five nations have laid claim to Pensacola since its founding in 1698, the town passing back and forth between them 13 times. Like its western neighbors Mobile and New Orleans, this southern city preserves its rich past in historic districts that showcase architectural styles from Creole to ornate Victorian. And its barrier islands, minutes away, lure sunseekers to the warm, uncrowded beaches of the Gulf of Mexico.

Historical Notes

City of Five Flags – Although Spanish conquistadors visited Pensacola Bay as early as 1516, the first permanent settlement here was not established until 1698. For the next several decades, the Spanish and French played tug of war with Pensacola until a hurricane in 1761 destroyed half the town. Soon thereafter, the British took their turn with the port, laying out orderly streets and expanding the town. In 18 years of British occupation, Pensacola grew more than it had in the first 65 years of its existence. The British envisioned a booming center of trade between America, Mexico and the West Indies.

In 1781, while England was busy fighting the American colonists, Spain recaptured Pensacola. The conquerors rechristened the English streets with such names as Salamanca, Alcaniz and Tarragona—names they still bear today. When the British and Americans went to war again in 1812, Spain let the British use Pensacola as a base from which to incite Indians to fight the Americans. Andrew Jackson stormed into town in 1814 and ran the Brits off, and in 1821 Spain finally ceded Pensacola to the US as part of the Florida purchase.

Three months before the first shots of the Civil War rang out, Confederates seized forts at Pensacola. Union forces entrenched themselves at Fort Pickens (p 168), the largest of four area forts, and in October 1861 exchanged fire with the Confederates across the bay. By 1862 southern troops had conceded Pensacola. Since then only the flag of the United States has flown over the "City of Five Flags."

Practical information .... Area Code: 850

Getting There – **Pensacola Regional Airport** (PNS): 3mi northeast of city; domestic flights ☎ 435-1746. Transportation to downtown: taxi *($9)* and hotel courtesy shuttles. Rental car agencies *(p 323)* located at airport. Amtrak **train** station: 980 E. Heinberg St. ☎ 800-872-7245. Greyhound/Trailways **bus** station: 505 W. Burgess Rd. ☎ 800-231-2222.

Getting Around – Local **bus service**: Escambia County Transit System ☎ 595-3228. Downtown historic district is best explored on foot. Downtown metered parking available *(25¢/hr)*.

Visitor Information – **Pensacola Convention and Visitor Center**, 1401 E. Gregory St., Pensacola FL 32501 *(open year-round daily 8am–5pm)* ☎ 434-1234 or 800-874-1234 (US and Canada); **Pensacola Beach Visitor Center**, 735 Pensacola Beach Blvd. *(open year-round daily 9am–5pm)* ☎ 932-1500 or 800-635-4803. *These organizations provide additional information regarding shopping, entertainment, festivals (p 318) and recreation.*

Accommodations – *(p 324)* Area visitors' guide including lodging directory available (free) from Pensacola Convention and visitor Center *(above)*. Accommodations offered include hotels ($65-$100), motels ($58-$80) and condominiums (rates lower in winter). Campgrounds and RV Parks are also available. Coastal **camping**: Big Lagoon State Park ☎ 492-1595; Fort Pickens, Gulf Islands National Seashore ☎ 934-2622. *Rates quoted are average prices per night for a double room and are subject to seasonal variations.*

Shopping – Palafox Historic District *(p 165)*.

Entertainment – Consult the arts and entertainment section of the *Pensacola News Journal* (Friday) for schedules of cultural events. Pensacola Civic Center: concerts, shows and sporting events ☎ 432-0800. Saenger Theatre: Broadway shows, plays and symphony concerts ☎ 444-7686; for advance tickets, call Ticketmaster ☎ 434-7444.

Sports and Recreation – Hidden Creek Golf *(open to public)* ☎ 939-4604. Pensacola Greyhound Track *(year-round)* ☎ 455-8595. Canoeing trips: *(4mi-11mi)* Adventures Unlimited ☎ 623-6197.

A Modern Port – Today Pensacola remains the Panhandle's leading port. Though a 1980s building boom added some new faces to the cityscape, Pensacola's skyline is still a low, gentle sweep to the wharves, where tall cranes toil among freighters. Opened in 1914, the **Pensacola Naval Air Station** to the southwest has become a prominent contributor to Pensacola's economy. At the other end of town, the University of West Florida lends a youthful vibrancy, and a new airport, completed in 1990, has welcomed more than two million business travelers and vacationers, many of whom find time to slip off to nearby Pensacola Beach and the Gulf Islands National Seashore on Santa Rosa Island and Perdido Key.

DOWNTOWN *3 days. Map below.*

⭐**Seville Historic District** – Concentrated between Tarragona and Florida Blanca Streets on the west and east and between Garden and Main Streets to the north and south, Seville is the oldest of the three contiguous historic districts. Through here run streets platted by British surveyor Elias Durnford in 1765 and later renamed by the Spanish. The restored quarter is brimming with frame vernacular, Victorian and Creole homes, many converted to law offices, restaurants and shops, and others open to the public. *Tickets for Historic Pensacola Village – permitting entry to nine houses and museums—may be purchased at the reconstructed* Tivoli House *(205 E. Zaragoza St.), which acts as a visitor center, or at the T.T. Wentworth, Jr. Florida State Museum (330 S. Jefferson St.). Village open year-round Tue–Sat 10am–4pm. Closed major holidays. $6.* 🅿 *www.pcola.com/hpv.html* ☎ *850-595-5985. Ticket price includes admission to Lavalle House and Dorr House; tours depart from Tivoli House. Also included is admission to the museums of Commerce and Industry, the Wentworth Museum, the Julee Cottage and the Quina House.*

Museum of Commerce – *Tarragona and Zaragoza Sts. Open year-round Tue–Sat 10am–4pm. Closed major holidays.* Contained in this masonry warehouse is a turn-of-the-century streetscape, complete with wooden sidewalks, dim street lamps, walk-in barbershop, leather and harness shop, music store and others.

Museum of Industry – *200 E. Zaragoza St. (across from Museum of Commerce). Open year-round Tue–Sat 10am–4pm. Closed major holidays.* A late 19C warehouse showcases the industries that fueled Pensacola's early growth—brick making,

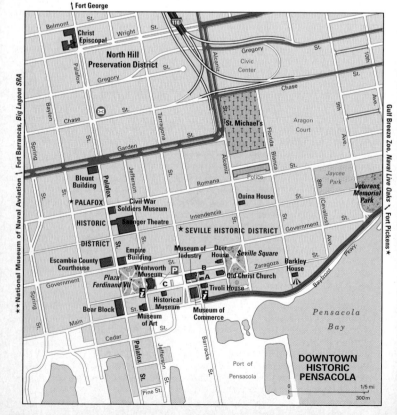

forestry, shipping and fishing. Clay from local bluffs was fired into bricks used for forts and other buildings. Huge forests of pine, oak, cedar and cypress were harvested for lumber, as well as rosin, pitch and turpentine. And the sea yielded such bountiful catches that the area was once known as the "red snapper capital of the world." Among the informative exhibits here are a replica brick kiln, machinery from a lumber mill, and an old wooden fishing boat.

Julee Cottage (A) – *210 E. Zaragoza St. (next door to Museum of Industry). Open year-round Tue–Sat 10am–4pm. Closed major holidays.* Built between 1803 and 1808, this saltbox dwelling is one of the oldest extant houses in the city. Owned by Julee Panton, a free black woman, the house originally sat five blocks to the west. Much of the original cypress framework has been lost, but some ceiling timbers and pegged framing remain. Descriptive panels in the modern interior trace the role of black Americans in the area's history.

Lavalle House (B) – *205 E. Church St. (across courtyard from Julee Cottage). Visit by guided tour (1hr) only, year-round Tue–Sat 11:30am & 1:30pm. Closed major holidays.* The 1805 French Creole home was built by brick maker and builder Charles Lavalle. Brick pillars elevated the house and windows on all sides, thus allowing cross ventilation. Bright interior and exterior color schemes typify the Creole style. Inside, where four rooms display 1820s furnishings, the ochre and yellow walls mimic the colors of local clays.

Old Christ Church – *Adams and Zaragoza Sts. Not open to the public.* This lovely red-brick church, built in the style of Sir Christopher Wren in 1832, currently is undergoing restoration. The Union army used it as a barracks and hospital; it subsequently served as a public library and was home for several years to the Pensacola Historical Museum. The church sits opposite lovely **Seville Square**, a park with overhanging live oaks, where the Spanish built a fortified outpost in the 1750s.

Dorr House – *Church and Adams Sts., across from Old Christ Church. Visit by guided tour (1hr) only, year-round Tue–Sat 11:30am & 1:30pm. Closed major holidays.* An example of gracious living in the 19C, this 1871 Greek Revival home was built by Clara Barkley Dorr, widow of lumber tycoon Eben Dorr and daughter of merchant George Barkley. The restrained elegance of the pale yellow exterior gives way to a more luxurious style within. Big bay windows with lace curtains and the unusual **jib windows**—the lower halves of which open out like doors—lend a light, airy feel to the house. Heart-pine floors, sliding pocket doors separating living from dining room, and a roomy kitchen bespeak the residents' refined lifestyle. Period antiques grace the rooms.

Quina House – *204 S. Alcaniz St. (one block north of Seville Square). Open year-round Tue–Sat 10am–4pm. Closed major holidays.* This simple wood-frame cottage was built in the early 1800s by Italian native Desiderio Quina in the Creole style. Slaves constructed the 1.5-story house on brick piers, using native pine, cypress and oak. The separate kitchen building was later attached to the rear of the main house. Interior appointments include an 1840 mahogany-laminated buffet, a maple wood bed, finger-pine kitchen floors, and a mid-19C Chinese Chippendale cabinet.

Barkley House – *Florida Blanca and Zaragoza Sts. Open year-round Tue–Sat 10am–4pm. Closed major holidays.* Wealthy Pensacola merchant George Barkley erected the grand bayfront house in the 1820s for his wife, and here they raised nine children. The wide gallery porch and dormer windows represent Creole architectural influences, while the central-hall floor plan borrows from American tradition. Sometimes called a "high house" because of its elevated first floor, the home commands a splendid **view** of Pensacola Bay.

St. Michael's Cemetery – *Alcaniz and Chase Sts.* Established on land deeded as burial ground by the King of Spain in 1806, this plot contains many noteworthy examples of monumental sculpture. Early town settlers, as well as priests, political leaders, and slaves are buried here. Among the nearly 3,000 graves are many raised tombs, similar to those found in New Orleans.

★**Palafox Historic District** – Just west of the Seville Historic District *(along Palafox St. from Garden St. to Pine St.)*, the commercial spine of Pensacola since the late 19C. **Palafox Street** retains the look of earlier days. Though fires and hurricanes have destroyed some of the old buildings, many remain intact and others have been restored. The 1907 Beaux Arts-style **Blount Building** *(Garden and Palafox Sts.)* boasts impressive terra-cotta arches and copper cornices. One block south, the Spanish Baroque **Saenger Theatre** (1925) was the venue for vaudeville acts and Hollywood features; it now offers Broadway plays and concerts. Continuing south on Palafox, you encounter the massive **Escambia County Courthouse** *(at Government St.)*, a Renaissance Revival structure dating from 1887. And just across the street (east side) looms the 10-story **Empire Building** (1909), also known as Seville Tower.

On the other side of Government Street lies a peaceful park of live oaks and magnolias, **Plaza Ferdinand VII**. Its central location has made the plaza a site of important events: Spanish Governor Callava handed over West Florida to Andrew Jackson here in 1821. Across Palafox Street, the colorful ironwork balconies and ornate arches of the two-story **Bear Block** (1892) once ornamented the wholesale grocery of Lewis Bear Company. South of Main Street, toward the wharves, was the haunt of sailors, longshoremen and streetwalkers.

Civil War Soldiers Museum – *108 S. Palafox Pl. Open year-round Tue–Sat 10am–4:30pm. Closed Jan 1, Thanksgiving Day, Dec 25. $5. &* *www.cwmuseum.org ☎ 850-469-1900.* A wonderful variety of artifacts, maps, documents, paintings and photographs here retell the story of the Civil War's major campaigns. Life-size dioramas portray the gore of a Confederate field hospital and the austerity of a Union camp. A short film *(23min)* recounts the Civil War history of Pensacola.

T.T. Wentworth, Jr. Florida State Museum – *330 S. Jefferson St. Open Jun–Aug Tue–Sun 10am–4pm, rest of the year Tue–Sat 10am–4pm. Closed major holidays. $6 admission ticket also includes Historic Pensacola Village. & www.pcola.com/hpv.html ☎ 850-595-5985.* Completed in 1908 as the City Hall, this substantial Renaissance Revival building features a triple-arched entrance, four red-tiled towers and a second-story arcade. The first two floors house the eclectic collection of local realtor Theodore Thomas Wentworth, who started collecting in 1906 at age 8. Among the grab bag of items found here are mounted animals, antlers, license plates, old radios and antique Coke machines. A hands-on area 🖼 for children occupies the third floor.

In the plaza behind the museum, visitors may view the **Colonial Archaeological Trail (C)** an in-progress excavation that has unearthed evidence of Spanish, British and American forts built between 1752 and 1821 *(visit during daylight hours; site is not lit at night).*

Pensacola Historical Museum – *115 E. Zaragoza St. Open Apr–Sept Mon–Sat 9am–4:30pm. Rest of the year Mon–Sat 10am–4:30pm. Closed major holidays. $1. & ☎ 850-433-1559.* Lodged in the Arbona Building (c.1882), this informative museum—operated since 1960 by the Pensacola Historical Society—provides an overview of Pensacola's complex past. Exhibits are organized by a quartet of themes, each presented more or less chronologically: native Indian presence, multicultural influence, maritime past and military heritage. The two-story, red-brick building was erected by Spanish immigrant Eugene Arbona, who operated a saloon here. (His family lived on the second floor.)

Pensacola Museum of Art – *407 S. Jefferson St., 1 block south of T.T. Wentworth Museum. Open year-round Tue–Fri 10am–5pm, Sat 10am–4pm. Closed major holidays. $2. & www.artsnwfl.org/pma ☎ 850-432-6247.* This yellow stucco Mediterranean Revival structure (1908) served as the city jail until the 1950s. Iron cell gates now close on classrooms of young art students. The museum's permanent collection of Steuben and Tiffany glass pieces, and 20C American works on paper is augmented by 18 traveling exhibitions annually.

ADDITIONAL SIGHTS

Veterans Memorial Park – *9th Ave. and Bayfront Pkwy. Open daily year-round. & ☎ 850-433-8200.* Set between a housing project and beautiful Pensacola Bay, this serenely manicured little park possesses a 256ft black granite wall with the engraved names of all 58,217 Americans who died in the Vietnam War. A small-scale replica of the Vietnam Veterans' Memorial in Washington, DC, the memorial is accompanied by a computer that provides data about the veterans and helps friends and relatives locate their loved ones' names on the wall.

North Hill Preservation District – *Bordered by Blount, Cervantes, Palafox and A Streets.* Just northwest of the Palafox Historic District lies the 50-block North Hill neighborhood, a gathering of Victorian homes built at the turn of the century for Pensacola's upper middle class. Architectural styles represent Queen Anne, Neoclassical, Mediterranean Revival and Tudor Revival styles. Many of the houses along Palafox Street have been converted into law offices and other businesses. Massive Spanish Colonial-style **Christ Episcopal Church** (1902) squats at Palafox and Wright Streets. It boasts a copper dome rising 64ft and stained glass taken from the Old Christ Church *(p 165)* on Seville Square. The corner of Palafox and LaRua Streets was the site of **Fort George**, the largest of three forts built by the British in 1778. A small park here displays a re-created section of the battlement. One block north in Lee Square, the oblong park in the middle of Palafox, a 50ft-high **obelisk** honors the Confederacy.

★★**National Museum of Naval Aviation** – *Located at the US Naval Air Station, 8.5mi from downtown. Take US-98 west (which becomes Navy Blvd./Rte. 295). Stay on Rte. 295 south and follow signs to museum. Open year-round daily 9am–5pm. Closed Jan 1, Thanksgiving Day, Dec 25. ⚔ & 🅿 www.naval-air.org ☎ 850-452-3604.* More than 100 aircraft and nearly 300,000sq ft of exhibit space make this one of the largest air and space museums in the world. Among the many

Pensacola Convention & Visitor Center

Blue Angels' A-4 Skyhawks

highlights of this innovative attraction are a sleek fleet of the Blue Angels' A-4 Sky-hawks suspended in diamond formation in a seven-story glass-and-steel atrium *(above)*; a full-scale replica World War II aircraft carrier equipped with such fighters as the Corsair, Hellcat and Avenger; a replica World War II airship; hands-on trainer cockpits; a Stearman biplane flown by President George Bush; and a flight simulator *($3)*. Videos, flight gear and outdoor displays supplement the aircraft.
A 1996 expansion added an IMAX theater *($4.50)*, presenting the museum's signature film, *The Magic of Flight.* In the new entrance hall is the striking **Spirit of Naval Aviation Monument**, representing pilots in flight gear from five conflicts since the First World War. A Flight Adventure Deck, with interactive displays targeting aerospace education, opened in 1998.

Fort Barrancas – *Located on US Naval Air Station, 8.5mi from downtown. Take Garden St./US-98 west (which becomes Navy Blvd./Rte. 295). Stay on Rte. 295 south and follow signs to fort. Open Apr–Oct daily 9:30am–5pm. Rest of the year daily 10:30am–4pm. Closed Dec 25.* ☐ *www.nps.gov/guis/* ☎ *850-934-2600.* One of four forts built in the first half of the 19C to protect Pensacola Bay—all now administered by **Gulf Islands National Seashore** *(below)*—Fort Barrancas perches on a bluff (or *barranca* in Spanish) providing a fine view of the bay and barrier islands. The Spanish recognized the strategic importance of this location and built a fortification here in 1698. The present fort was constructed by some 60 slaves between 1839 and 1844. Only during the Civil War did the fort see any fighting, and then briefly. Until 1947 the fort was used for artillery training. Visitors may take a self-guided tour through cavernous gallery passageways; note the arched brickwork. Another fort, the **Advanced Redoubt** *(.2mi north on Taylor Rd.)*, was built to protect the navy yard from an inland invasion. The self-guided tour here takes you from the point of view of an attacker—over parapets, around a dry moat, up to the drawbridge—to show how suicidal an attempted assault would be. Prickly sand spurs now constitute the fort's main defense. *Wear high-top shoes.*

EXCURSIONS   *Map p 158*

Naval Live Oaks – *1hr. 1801 Gulf Breeze Pkwy. 8mi southeast via US-98. Cross Three-Mile Bridge into Gulf Breeze (6mi from downtown) and head east 2mi. Open Apr–Oct daily 8:30am–5pm. Rest of the year daily 8:30am–4:30pm. Closed Dec 25.* ♿ ☐ *www.nps.gov/guis/* ☎ *850-934-2600.* Headquarters for the **Gulf Islands National Seashore**, this 1,300-acre preserve encompasses land set aside by President John Quincy Adams in 1829 as a federal tree farm to supply timber for warships. Dense, disease-resistant live oaks that thrived in coastal areas were ideal for building ships. Displays in the visitor center demonstrate methods and materials of early shipbuilding, and interpretive trails meander to Pensacola Bay and Santa Rosa Sound through a peaceful forest of pines and namesake majestic live oaks bearded with Spanish moss. The national seashore, which stretches sporadically westward 150mi from Fort Walton Beach, Florida, to Gulfport, Mississippi, includes several beach parks—among them Rosamond Johnson Beach on Perdido Key, southwest of Pensacola, and Santa Rosa Island Beach to the southeast—as well as forts Pickens and Barrancas, the Advanced Redoubt and battery ruins on Perdido Key.

Big Lagoon State Recreation Area – *1hr. 13mi southwest at intersection of Rtes. 293 and 292A. Take US-98 west to Gulf Beach Hwy. (Rte. 292). Turn south on Rte. 293 and follow signs. Open year-round daily 8am–dusk. $3.25/vehicle.* ⚿ ✕ ♿ 🅿 ☎ *850-492-1595.* Spreading on 698 acres alongside Big Lagoon, this aromatic haven of pines and evergreen oaks, saw palmetto and rosemary harbors a wealth of mammals and waterbirds. Trails lead back along a tidal marsh and out to the lagoon. The park road curves through a pine forest open to views of the water and ends 2.5mi later at a boardwalk punctuated by picnic pavilions. A short walk takes you to a 30ft observation tower that affords excellent **views** of Perdido Key, the Gulf and lagoon, and herons wading in the sun-dappled shallows.

★**Fort Pickens** – *2hrs. 17.6mi southwest on Santa Rosa Island. Cross Three-Mile Bridge into Gulf Breeze and continue on Rte. 399 to Santa Rosa Island. Turn right (west) on Fort Pickens Rd. and follow it 9mi to fort on western tip of island. Open Apr–Oct daily 9:30am–5pm. Rest of the year daily 8:30am–4pm. Closed Dec 25. $6/vehicle.* ⚿ ♿ 🅿 *www.nps.gov/guis/* ☎ *850-934-2600.* Largest of a quartet of forts erected to defend Pensacola Bay and the navy yard, this colossal feat of slave labor took 21.5 million bricks and five years to build. Fort Pickens was a triumph of coastal defense when it was built in 1834, yet ironically had become obsolete by the 1860s. During the Civil War—the only war in which the bastion was directly involved—new technology such as rifled cannon and armored warships rendered a brick fort defenseless. Modern visitors will discover both the original fort and the changes it underwent during its 118 years of service: a dynamited wall, a concrete gun battery (1898) dividing the parade ground, a filled-in moat, and quarters that once housed Apache prisoner **Geronimo**.
A parcel of Gulf Islands National Seashore, Fort Pickens also boasts a visitor center, museum and auditorium, large campground, fishing pier and two self-guided nature trails.

Gulf Breeze Zoo – 🄺🄸🄳🅂 *2hrs. 17.3mi east in Gulf Breeze. Take US-98 11.3mi east of Gulf Breeze to 5701 Gulf Breeze Hwy. (entrance on south side). Open May–Aug daily 9am–6pm. Rest of the year daily 9am–5pm. Closed Thanksgiving Day & Dec 25. $9.75.* ✕ ♿ 🅿 *www.the-zoo.com* ☎ *850-932-2229.* Among more than 700 animals are representatives of several endangered species, including gibbons, ring-tailed lemurs and scimitar-horned oryx. The **lowland gorilla enclosure** and the petting zoo rate as perennial favorites, as does the 20min train ride through a 30-acre open range that provides a home for more than 100 animals. Elephant shows and rides round out the zoo's offerings.

PORT ST. JOE

Population 4,150
Map of Principal Sights p 2 – Map p 159
Tourist Information ☎ 850-227-1223

The 33mi separating this area from Panama City seem like as many years. Its remoteness from centers of tourism has earned this sleepy shore the promotional moniker, "Florida's Forgotten Coast." If you approach Port St. Joe on US-98, the paper mill (west side of town), one of the area's largest employers, breaks the lovely views of palm- and pine-lined St. Joseph Bay and distant **Cape San Blas**. The site of the state's first constitutional convention, this pleasant little town boasts a deepwater port and a scallop-rich bay. Angling into the Gulf of Mexico, the cape flashes a jewel of a state park for those who make the 20mi drive from Port St. Joe. Popular area sports include skin diving, charter fishing and swimming in the Gulf waters.

SIGHT *1hr*

Constitution Convention State Museum – *200 Allen Memorial Way; .5mi north of US-98. Open year-round Thu–Mon 9am–5pm. Closed Jan 1, Thanksgiving Day, Dec 25. $1.* ♿ 🅿 ☎ *850-229-8029.* The informative little museum commemorates Florida's first constitutional convention. On this site in late 1838, delegates from the territory's counties met to draft a state constitution. St. Joseph (as Port St. Joe was called) was then a booming town; a yellow fever epidemic and a hurricane in the early 1840s nearly wiped it off the map. Exhibits detail area and state history, and a replica convention meeting room features automated mannequins who deliver a 3min program.

EXCURSIONS

★**St. Joseph Peninsula State Park** – *1/2 day. 20mi southwest of Port St. Joe. Take US-98 east and bear right on Rte. 30A; continue 7mi and turn right on Rte. 30ᶠ. Follow Rte. 30ᶠ 8mi to park entrance. Open year-round daily 8am–dusk. $3.25/vehicle.* ⚿ ☎ *850-227-1327.* Occupying the end of a narrow peninsula, this gorgeous 2,516-acre park offers 8mi of white sand **beach** on the Gulf of Mexico

and another 8mi along St. Joseph Bay. It was ranked in 1998 in *USA Today* as
the nation's third best beach, after two in Hawaii. Indians once gathered shellfish
from the bay's shallow water. During World War II, US Army forces trained here.
Now these pristine beaches and quiet forests attract fishermen, campers and
beach-lovers. Bird-watchers have recorded more than 200 species, including
endangered peregrine falcons. In the fall, Monarch butterflies stop here during
their migration south to Mexico.

Dead Lakes State Recreation Area – *2hrs. 25mi northeast in Wewahitchka.
Follow Rte. 71 north through Wewahitchka; continue 2mi north to park entrance
(east side). Open year-round daily 8am–dusk. $2/vehicle.* ⚠ 🄿 ☎ *850-639-2702.*
A natural lake, formed when the Apalachicola and Chipola Rivers flooded 12,000
acres of cypress swamp, is preserved here. Dead trees give the lake an eerie aspect
but do not deter anglers, who find the lake alive with freshwater fish. Two short
trails wind through a swamp and a longleaf pine woodland.

TALLAHASSEE★

Population 136,812
Map of Principal Sights p 2 – Map p 159
Tourist Information: ☎ 850-413-9200 or 800-628-2866 (US & Canada)

Set amid gently rolling hills, some 12mi from the Georgia state line and 20mi from the
Gulf of Mexico, Florida's capital city was named for the Seminole Indian word meaning
"old fields." Despite Tallahassee's urban growth in recent decades, its moss-draped live
oaks, abundant azaleas and gracious old homes still bespeak the charm of the Old South.

Historical Notes

From Mounds to Missions – Members of the Mississippian culture peopled the shores
of Lake Jackson as early as AD 1000. Evidence of their existence survives in three earth
temple mounds at **Lake Jackson Mounds State Archaeological Site** *(1313 Crowder Rd.; open
year-round daily 8am–dusk; $2/vehicle;* 🄿 ☎ *850-922-6007).* By the time the first
European explorers had arrived in the 16C, the area was dominated by the Apalachee,
an agricultural Mississippian tribe with established villages throughout northwest Florida.
In the mid-1500s, the Spanish were setting out to explore the rich new land discovered by Juan Ponce de León in 1513. Seven years later, Pánfilo de Narváez led an
unsuccessful gold-seeking expedition to Apalachee country; and Hernando de Soto celebrated the first Christmas Mass in the New World near the site of Tallahassee's
present-day downtown in 1539. Although no exhibit commemorates it, the **Hernando
de Soto State Archaeological Site** *(1022 DeSoto Park Dr.)* marks the spot where de Soto
and his men camped during the winter of 1539-40.
Deterred by Apalachee hostility, Spaniards did not return to the area for almost 100
years. When they did, they came in the form of Franciscan friars who were generally
accepted by the Indians. By 1675 the Franciscans had constructed seven missions in the
environs of the modern capital. The most important of these, **San Luis de Talimali**, eventually served as the provincial seat for more than 40 Apalachee villages. Missions endured
until the 18C, when most were destroyed by British soldiers and Seminoles during Queen
Anne's War (1702-1713). Apalachees who were not killed in the conflict fled to other
areas, opening the way for bands of Seminoles to migrate into the region from Georgia.

Birth of a Capital – Under Spanish rule, Florida was divided into two provinces, with
capitals at Pensacola and St. Augustine. However, more than 400mi separated the
settlements, which were connected only by a series of rough Indian and Spanish trails.
After the US acquired Florida from Spain in 1821, territorial officials appointed two
commissioners to find a suitable spot for the permanent seat of government between
the Ochlockonee and Suwannee Rivers. In the fall of 1823, the commissioners chose
a "high, rolling, and well-watered" site halfway between the two existing capital cities.
That halfway point was Tallahassee.
Officially proclaimed Florida's capital in March 1824, Tallahassee soon welcomed its
first settlers, who began constructing log cabins to house the Legislative Council.
Shortly afterward, Congress granted land for a capitol, and Tallahassee was laid out
with the Capitol Square at its center and four additional public squares surrounding
it. By 1825 Tallahassee, a typical "small courthouse town," consisted of more than
50 homes, a school, a church and several shops. Settlers began work on a two-story
capitol in 1826, but financial difficulties ensued and it was never finished. Thirteen
years later, Congress appropriated $20,000 and a brick and mortar edifice was com-
pleted in 1845, the year Florida gained statehood.
Most early settlers were entrepreneurs, merchants or cotton planters who usurped
the Indians' land. As they did so, relations with the Seminoles deteriorated and a series
of hostilities continued off and on until 1858, after which time most of the Indians
were relocated. When the Civil War broke out, Tallahassee reigned as the largest and
most prosperous town in Central Florida, with much of its success attributable to the

cotton industry. Its population had bloomed to almost 2,000 and it had become an important trade center, connected by Florida's first railroad to the port of St. Marks, 16mi to the south.

The Civil War gave the city another distinction: It became the only Confederate capital east of the Mississippi to remain uncaptured. In March 1865 Union troops launched an assault, only to be repulsed by the local militia at Natural Bridge, 14mi south of the city. Victory was short-lived; two months later the war ended, and the Stars and Stripes once again waved over Tallahassee. Today a monument at **Natural Bridge State Historic Site** commemorates the battle *(Natural Bridge Rd., off Rte. 363, 6mi east of Woodville; open year-round daily 8am–dusk; reenactment of Civil War battle held in Mar;* 🅿 ☎ *850-922-6007).*

Tallahassee Today – Until Florida's recent growth spurt, Tallahassee was considered a sleepy southern city. Even the presence of two universities, Florida State University and Florida Agricultural and Mechanical University, did not alter its image. In the 35 years following the Civil War, the town's population increased by only 1,000, and as late as 1947 it numbered just 22,000. Florida's growth exploded in the 1970s and '80s, and Tallahassee and Leon County's population increased by an astounding 370 percent. As Florida's population spiraled, state government was forced to expand to provide services for newcomers.

Agriculture still plays a part in the area's economy, but the days of King Cotton are long gone. Tallahassee today is primarily a center of government, which (including the universities) employs more than 40 percent of the local workforce. Although it shares hot, humid summers with South Florida, in culture and lifestyle Tallahassee remains worlds away from the glitz of trendy metropolitan centers in the southern part of the state. Family-oriented outdoor recreational activities and sports events predominate as entertainment in this ever-growing city, where the state's most important decisions are made.

Practical information .... Area Code: 850

Getting There – **Tallahassee Regional Airport** (TLH): 5mi southwest of city; domestic flights ☎ 891-7800. Transportation to downtown: taxi *($12)* and hotel courtesy shuttles. Rental car agencies *(p 323)* located at airport. Amtrak **train** station: 918 1/2 Railroad Ave. ☎ 800-872-7245. Greyhound/Trailways **bus** station: 112 W. Tennessee St. ☎ 800-231-2222.

Getting Around – Walking-tour maps of downtown historic districts available (free) from Tallahassee Area Convention and Visitor Bureau, PO Box 1369, Tallahassee FL 32302 ☎ 413-9200. Local **bus service**: Taltran *($1; free transfers)*. Free transportation around downtown on **Old Town Trolley Tour** *(year-round Mon–Fri 7am–6pm; every 10min)* ☎ 891-5200. Metered parking available downtown *(25¢/hr)*.

Visitor Information – **Tallahassee Area Visitor Information Center**, New Capitol Building, West Plaza Level, N. Duval St., Tallahassee FL 32302 *(open year-round Mon–Fri 8am–5pm; weekends 9am–3pm)* ☎ 413-9200; **Tallahassee Chamber of Commerce**, 100 N. Duval St., Tallahassee FL 32302 *(Mon–Fri 8am–5pm)* ☎ 224-8116. *These organizations provide additional information regarding shopping, entertainment, festivals (p 318) and recreation.*

Accommodations – *(p 324)* Area visitors' guide including lodging directory available (free) from Tallahassee Area Visitor Information Center *(above)*. Accommodations offered include hotels ($65-$100) and motels ($45-$70). Rustic and RV **camping**: Tallahassee East KOA Kampground ☎ 997-3890. *Rates quoted are average prices per night for a double room and are subject to seasonal variations.*

Entertainment – Consult the arts and entertainment section of the *Tallahassee Democrat* (Friday) for schedules of cultural events. Florida State University: year-round concerts, recitals and opera; for schedules and ticket information ☎ 644-4774. Tallahassee Symphony Orchestra ☎ 644-6500 .

Sports and Recreation – Florida State University athletic events ☎ 644-1830; Florida A&M University athletic events ☎ 599-3141; Tallahassee Tiger Sharks professional ice hockey, home games *(Oct–Apr)* ☎ 224-4625. Seminole Golf Course *(open to public)*; ☎ 644-2582. Whippoorwill Sportsman's Lodge offers fishing, boating and camping ☎ 875-2605. You can go crabbing, hiking, fishing and bird-watching at St. Marks National Wildlife Refuge *(p 178)* ☎ 925-6121. Wakulla Springs State Park *(p 176)* features nature trails and river cruises ☎ 922-3633. Gulf beaches are located about 70mi south of Tallahassee. **Shopping**: Historic downtown *(E. Park Ave. and the Capitol)*; the town of Havana *(on US-27, 12mi north of city)* is known for its antique shops.

DOWNTOWN *2 1/2 days. Map p 172.*

A walking-tour guide to Tallahassee's historic downtown is available from the visitor center (first floor of new Capitol building).

Downtown Tallahassee sprouted up around a four-block quadrant bounded by Capitol Square on the south, Adams and Monroe Streets on the east and west, and Park Avenue on the north. The 200ft clearing designed to protect the city from Indian attack now contains a seven-block-long linear park. The quarter took on hints of its present appearance in 1843 after a fire decimated the wooden frontier buildings in the business district. When the town was rebuilt, fireproof brick structures replaced the flimsier wooden ones.

Although the central downtown area still lies within its original boundaries, most of the major commercial activity has moved to suburban malls. A focal point of the modern downtown is **Adams Street Commons**, a block-long, brick-paved section of Adams Street *(between Pensacola St. and College Ave.)*. This serpentine thoroughfare, lined with restaurants and offices, creates a pleasant lunchtime retreat for local business people. The two-story brick building with ornamental ironwork on the northeast corner of Pensacola and Adams Streets was formerly **Gallie's Hall** (c.1874), the city's first opera house.

★**Capitol Complex** – *400 S. Monroe St., at Apalachee Pkwy.* Crowning Tallahassee's downtown, as it has since the town's founding, is the Capitol Complex. The restored 1845 Capitol and the modern 1978 Capitol juxtaposed here symbolize Florida's evolution over the past century and a half.

★**Old Capitol** – *Open year-round Mon–Fri 9am–4:30pm, Sat 10am–4:30pm, Sun & holidays noon–4:30pm. Closed Thanksgiving Day & Dec 25.* ▣ *www.dos.state.fl.us/dhr/museum* ☎ *850-487-1902.* "Like a jewel worn by the new (capitol)," as one architect described it, this white stucco Neoclassical building, with its elegant columned portico and gray-trimmed pediment, ornaments the plain concrete structure that rises behind it. Constructed near the site of three crude log cabins that held the state's first legislative meeting in 1824, the original Capitol has undergone several major transformations over the years. In 1902 the copper dome was added; subsequent alterations (1923, 1936, 1947) doubled the building's usable space and added four new wings. When the Florida Legislature approved plans for a new Capitol in 1969, controversy began swirling about what to do with the old one. Preservation advocates finally won the battle to keep the Old Capitol and agreed in 1979 to restore the building to its 1902 incarnation, a process which required demolishing 80 percent of the structure. Frank P. Milburn's 1902 design features a handsome lantern-crowned dome and bas-reliefs of the state seal on the front and back pediments. Red-striped window awnings again shade the interior from the fierce summer sun as they did at the turn of the century. Inside, a grand central staircase divides the rotunda, which is topped with a multicolored **art-glass interior dome**.

Although it still contains a few state offices, the painstakingly restored Old Capitol has served as a museum since 1982. A self-guided tour directs visitors to the **Old Supreme Court Chamber★** and to early-20C governor William Jennings' office suite on the first floor. The second floor features the former **House and Senate Chambers**. Historical exhibits, including a collection of reproductions of the state's Constitutions, fill several rooms between the chambers.

Capitol Complex

Directly across Monroe Street from the Old Capitol, the twin marble columns of the **Vietnam Memorial** *(corner of Apalachee Pkwy. and S. Monroe St.)* honor more than 300,000 Floridians who served in the Vietnam War.

New Capitol – *Open year-round Mon–Fri 8am–5pm. Closed major holidays.* ✗🅑 ☎ *850-413-9200.* This imposing white concrete, 22-story tower, flanked by two domed four-story wings, looms 307ft above the original Capitol. Built by Edward Durell Stone (architect of the Kennedy Center in Washington, DC) in 1978 to provide needed space for governmental chambers and state offices, the New Capitol ranks as Tallahassee's tallest building. Guided tours *(45min; Mon–Fri 9am–3pm on the hour, weekends 10am & 2pm)* are offered by the **Tallahassee Area Visitor Information Center** *(first floor, West Plaza entrance on Duval St.);* they take in the Heritage Chapel, which features a striking blue altarpiece illustrating the Creation; the **House of Representatives and Senate chambers** *(open to the public when Legislature is in session, each Feb and Mar),* which anchor the building at either end; and the rotunda containing the marble and bronze Great Seal of Florida. Atop the skyscraper's 22nd floor, an observation deck affords unique sweeping **views★** of the city and its surroundings. Original artwork, including a pair of murals portraying symbols of the state's environment *(Plaza level),* and a permanent collection of paintings by Florida artists *(outside the House Chamber),* are displayed throughout the building.

Union Bank Building– *219 Apalachee Pkwy., at Calhoun St. Open year-round Mon–Fri 9am–4pm.* 🅑 ☎ *850-599-3020.* This exquisite little edifice (c.1841), the oldest surviving bank building in Florida, housed one of Tallahassee's first banks. Union Bank lasted just two years before its 1843 failure, which has been variously attributed to a poor cotton crop, the Seminole Wars and financial mismanagement.

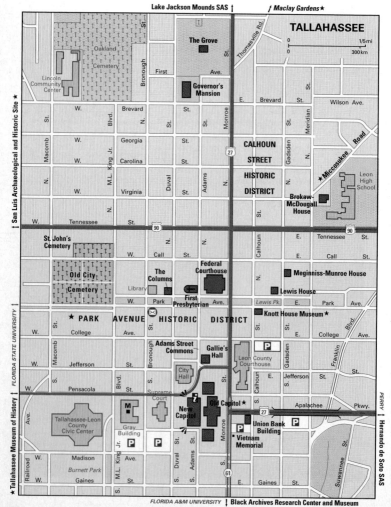

Originally located on South Adams Street, the blue stucco structure, marked by three fanlights on the facade, saw incarnations as a bank for freed slaves, a shoe factory and a dance studio before being moved to its present location in 1971. Restored to its 1841 appearance and furnished with period antiques, the bank opened to the public as a museum in 1984. Today it houses an overflow collection from the Black Archives Research Center *(p 174).*

★**Park Avenue Historic District** – *District runs along a seven-block section of Park Ave. bounded by Macomb St., Meridian Rd. and Call St.* In 1830 this mixed-use neighborhood, now composed of commercial, residential and religious structures and bisected by parks, formed the northern boundary of Tallahassee. As prosperous settlers built large homes along the clearing's edge, a series of greenswards grew up in the street's median. Adjoining downtown and lined with elegant homes, Park Avenue—whose name was changed from McCarthy Street in 1905 at the request of one of the district's wealthy matrons—became a prestigious address. Although the Greek Revival style predominates, a number of other types of architecture are represented, including Victorian and Classical Revival. Anchored on the west by the city's two oldest cemeteries, the district spreads eastward to the vernacular 1854 **Meginniss-Munroe House** *(125 N. Gadsden St.),* now the LeMoyne Art Foundation, a local gallery that hosts traveling art exhibits.

Lewis House – *316 E. Park Ave. Open year-round Mon–Fri 10am–3pm. Closed one week in September and major holidays.* ♿ 🅿 *www.fccmh.org ☎ 850-224-6048.* The 2.5-story, Southern vernacular frame house (c.1845) with its turret bay window was built for Charles Dyke, a well-known Florida editor. From 1850 to 1993 it remained in the hands of the Benjamin C. Lewis family, whose members included prominent Tallahassee bankers. It currently houses the headquarters of the Florida Council for Community Mental Health. The recently restored taupe exterior is enlivened by bright teal window frames. Eastlake-style oak paneling and decorative spoolwork adorn the conference room and various fireplace mantels inside the house; coffered ceilings cover the front and back parlors.

★**Knott House Museum** – *301 E. Park Ave. Visit by guided tour (1hr) only, mid-Aug–mid-Jul Wed–Fri 1pm–4pm, Sat 10am–4pm. Closed Jan 1, Thanksgiving Day, Dec 24-25.* ♿ *www.dos.state.fl.us ☎ 850-922-2459.* In the waning months of the Civil War, this two-story, white wood Classical Revival residence (c.1843) served as the headquarters of Union General Edward McCook, who read the **Emancipation Proclamation** from its front steps on May 20, 1865. It was home to former state treasurer William Knott and his family from 1928 to 1985, and earned the sobriquet, "The House That Rhymes," because of Mrs. Knott's propensity to write poems that she attached with satin ribbons to pieces of furniture and objets d'art. Now a museum, the house has been restored to its appearance in 1928—the year the Knotts added the imposing portico. Rooms are furnished with an eclectic group of Knott family Victorian antiques. A hand-carved mahogany staircase leads to the second floor, where one of the bedrooms has been converted into a gallery for local history exhibits. Outside the kitchen, a restored garden blooms in summer with prize-winning daylilies.

Federal Courthouse – *110 W. Park Ave., at corner of Monroe St. Open year-round Mon–Fri 8:30am–5pm. Closed major holidays* ♿. Dedicated in 1939 by US Treasury Secretary Henry Morganthau, the imposing Georgia marble Classical Revival courthouse (1936, Eric Kebbon) is notable as Tallahassee's most significant Works Progress Administration (WPA) project. The building, which once served as the city's post office, contains murals depicting milestones in Florida history. A $20 million annex was completed in 1998.

First Presbyterian Church – *110 N. Adams St. To view the sanctuary, inquire in church office next door.* ♿ 🅿 ☎ *850-222-4504.* This prim, white Greek Revival church (1838) reigns as the oldest sanctuary in continuous use in Florida. The structure, which provided early settlers refuge from Indian attacks, has undergone four renovations over the years; the most recent one was completed in 1986. White paneling and wainscoting and a simple wooden communion table decorate the austere interior.

The Columns – *100 N. Duval St. Open to the public only as offices of the Tallahassee Chamber of Commerce.* Tallahassee's oldest home within the original city limits was built by banker William "Money" Williams in 1830. This stately brick Greek Revival structure, with its two-story pedimented entrance portico, served as Williams' Bank of Florida office as well as his home. Moved from its original site across the street in 1975, The Columns now houses the Tallahassee Chamber of Commerce. The building's interior still contains its original heart-pine floors, door facings and windows; the exterior was recently restored to its turn-of-the-century appearance.

Old City Cemetery – *Entrance on M.L. King, Jr. Blvd. between Park Ave. and Call Sts. Walking-tour brochure available at entrance. Open year-round daily 8am–dusk.* ☎ *850-222-7100.* Live oaks, azaleas and camellias dot the landscape of

Tallahassee's oldest public cemetery, authorized in 1829 by the Territorial Legislative Council and acquired by the city in 1840. Markers ranging from flat marble slabs to elaborate carved monuments in the 11-acre plot bear witness to the city's earliest history. Slaves, free men, Confederate and Union soldiers, and victims of the 1841 yellow fever epidemic are among those buried here.

St. John's Cemetery – *Entrance on Call St. between Macomb and M.L. King, Jr. Blvd. Open daily year-round 9am–dusk. Contribution requested.* & ☎ 850-222-2636. Adjacent to the Old City Cemetery and graced by native flowers, palmettos and oaks, this graveyard was established in 1840 to serve parishioners of St. John's Episcopal Church. Twin stone obelisks mark the graves of Prince Achille Murat *(p 175)*, nephew of Napoleon Bonaparte, and his wife, Princess Catherine. Two former Florida governors, David S. Walker (1865-1868) and William Bloxham (1881-1885; 1897-1901), are also interred here.

Calhoun Street Historic District – *District lies along and adjacent to Calhoun St., bounded by Tennessee, Georgia and Meridian Sts.* This area was laid out in 1827 as the "North Addition" to the city. Called "Gold Dust Street" in the mid-19C because it counted so many prominent Tallahassee citizens among its residents, Calhoun Street still boasts a number of elegant town homes from the period. Greek Revival, Victorian and Bungalow are among the architectural styles represented. The only home open to the public in this district is the **Brokaw-McDougall House** *(329 N. Meridian; open year-round Mon–Fri 9am–1pm; closed major holidays;* & ▣ ☎ *850-891-3900)*. Graced with an elegant portico and crowned by an Italianate cupola, this two-story ochre frame structure (c.1856) originally belonged to a livery stable owner. The second floor now houses offices of the Historic Tallahassee Preservation Board, but visitors are welcome to walk through first-floor rooms to appreciate the 14ft ceilings and period furnishings. Outside, gravel paths lace restored formal 19C gardens that were first laid out in the early 1850s.

Florida Governor's Mansion – *700 N. Adams St., 1mi north of Capitol Complex. Visit by guided tour (45min) only, Mar–mid-May Mon, Wed & Fri 10am–noon.* ▣ ☎ *850-488-4661*. Patterned after the Hermitage—Andrew Jackson's antebellum home near Nashville, Tennessee—this red-brick Neoclassical residence (Wyeth, King and Johnson) has housed Florida's governors since 1957, when it was built on the same site as the 1907 mansion. Jackson's home was considered an appropriate model because of his position as first territorial governor of the state. A beveled-glass window inscribed with the state seal crowns the front door; six Corinthian columns flank the entrance.

Tours take visitors through the state dining room, reception room, guest bedroom, Florida Room and garden. Inside, dentil crown molding and Italian marble floors distinguish the entrance hall, and 18C English antiques furnish the public rooms. Note also several original paintings on loan from the John and Mable Ringling collection *(p 256)* including two Audubon prints, and an Austrian brass clock (c.1820) presented to a Tallahassee family by the Marquis de Lafayette's nephew. In the dining room, note the impressive silver collection from the decommissioned battleship *Florida*. Guests exit by way of a formal brick-walled English garden.

Next door to the mansion, partially hidden by heavy shrubbery, you can catch a glimpse of **The Grove**, an impressive brick antebellum home with a Doric portico constructed by Territorial Governor Richard Keith Call in 1825. The house remains in the hands of the Call family.

ADDITIONAL SIGHTS *1 day*

★★ **Museum of Florida History (M)** – *500 S. Bronough St. In the R.A. Gray building, two blocks west of Capitol Complex; entrance on basement level. Open year-round Mon–Fri 9am–4:30pm, Sat 10am–4:30pm, Sun & holidays noon–4:30pm. Closed Thanksgiving Day & Dec 25.* ✗ & *www.dos.state.fl.us/dhr/museum* ☎ *850-488-1484*. Occupying the ground floor of the state archives building, exhibits such as a re-created Confederate campsite and a 1926 Florida farmhouse kitchen recount the state's history from pre-historic times to the 20C. Of particular interest is a 12,000-year-old **mastodon skeleton** discovered in Wakulla Springs *(p 176)* in 1930. A replica citrus packing house (c.1920) illustrates the importance of the citrus industry to the state's economy, while panels of early photographs detail the contribution of the lumber industry. Highlighting the waterways display is a reproduction of the forward portion of the steamboat *Hiawatha*, which plied the Oklawaha River in the early 1900s.

Black Archives Research Center and Museum – *On the campus of Florida A&M University. Open year-round Mon–Fri 9am–4pm. Closed major holidays.* & ▣ ☎ *850-599-3020*. Housed in the Greek Revival Carnegie Library (1907), the eclectic group of artifacts and papers held here witness the black presence in southern, national and international history. Several small rooms, opened to the public in 1977, display a collection of items ranging from Zairean ivory carvings to a Ku Klux Klan robe. Among the museum archives are the original copy of the 1864 National Anti-Slavery Standard and a collection of rare recordings of famous black musicians.

★**Maclay Gardens** – *3540 Thomasville Rd. Gardens on left, .5mi north of Capitol Circle. Open year-round daily 8am–dusk. $3.25/vehicle.* ⛭ ☎ *850-487-4556.* Designed to "soothe the senses," this 28-acre garden was created by New York financier Alfred B. Maclay in 1923 and donated to the state of Florida by his widow 30 years later. Maclay planned his garden around winter and spring—the seasons he stayed here. In winter more than 100 varieties of **camellias** burst into bloom; in spring a spectacular display of azaleas, dogwood, wisteria, mountain laurel and magnolias festoon the grounds. Summer transforms the gardens into a cool tapestry in rich shades of green.

Resting atop a manicured lawn sloping down to Lake Hall, the single-story peach **Maclay House**, formerly a hunting lodge (c.1905), contains family furnishings and exhibits relating the evolution of garden design in Europe *(open Jan–Apr daily 9am–5pm; $3)*. South of the house, a formal flower garden boasts a 500ft-long allée with a reflecting pool that looks out over the lake. This surprise **view**, one of several in the gardens, was a popular device in 1920s garden design.

★**San Luis Archaeological and Historic Site** – *2020 W. Mission Rd. From downtown, take Tennessee St. west past Florida State University; turn right on White Dr. and right again on Mission Rd. Open year-round Mon–Fri 8am–4:30pm, Sat 10am–4:30pm, Sun noon–4:30pm. Closed major holidays.* ▣ *www.dos.state.fl.us/dhr/bar/sanluis* ☎ *850-487-3711.* This elevated site near fresh water and arable land was the location of the largest Spanish mission village (c.1656) and fort (c.1696) established by Franciscan friars as the western capital of their Florida mission network. Apalachee Indians, who were already living in the area, elected to combine forces with the Spaniards in an apparent attempt to consolidate strength against hostile enemies. Here the Spaniards and Apalachee lived together for the next 50 years. In its heyday in 1675, San Luis boasted a population of at least 1,400 and comprised a fort, an Apalachee council house, church, several Spanish-style residences and a large central plaza. Threatened by British attack, San Luis residents abandoned their village and fort in 1704, setting the complex afire as they fled.

Visit – *1.5hrs.* The **visitor center**, housed in a 1930s era home on the grounds, contains scale models of the Apalachee council house and fort. Other exhibits showcase bits of Majolica pottery, Spanish coins and Indian arrowheads found on the property. Also on the grounds are hiking trails and a laboratory where archaeological artifacts are cleaned and catalogued.

A reconstructed colonist's home, known as the Spanish House, is the site of living-history programs *(Tue–Sat 10am–2pm)*. A re-created blacksmith shop and tannery also host occasional demonstrations *(third Sat of each month)*. Reconstruction of the mission church (c.1680), now furnished with period antiques and artifacts, was completed in 1998, while work on the Apalachee council house (c.1660) is scheduled for completion in 1999. Later restoration efforts call for a replica Apalachee chief's house, priory and fort.

★**Tallahassee Museum of History and Natural Science** – 🎫 *3945 Museum Dr. Take Capitol Circle S.W. to Orange Ave., turn right on Rankin Ave.; continue .3 mi. to where Rankin dead-ends into Museum Dr. Open year-round Mon–Sat 9am–5pm, Sun 12:30pm–5pm. Closed major holidays.* $6. ⛭ ▣ *www.tallahasseemuseum.org* ☎ *850-575-8684.* This museum, set on 52 wooded acres near the airport, was created to acquaint visitors with North Florida history and wildlife. Follow the boardwalk through a cypress swamp to a **natural habitat zoo** featuring indigenous animals such as eagles, river otters, white-tailed deer and Florida panthers. Also on the grounds, **Big Bend Farm** comprises a 19C Cracker farmhouse, church and schoolhouse, which were relocated to this site.

Near the visitor center sits **Bellevue**, the modest Tallahassee home of Catherine Murat, widow of Prince Achille Murat. This nephew of Napoleon Bonaparte came to America after his family's downfall in Europe in the early 19C. He eventually established a plantation near Tallahassee, where he met and married Catherine Daingerfield Willis, great-grandniece of George Washington. After Murat's death, Catherine purchased the vernacular log house (1841) constructed with raw board walls and a high, beamed ceiling typical of Tallahassee frontier architecture. The residence was moved to the museum in 1967.

★**Canopy Roads** – *Driving guide available from visitor center (first floor of new Capitol building; p 172)* Shaded by an airy vault of moss-draped live oak branches, five specially designated historic roads—Old St. Augustine, Old Bainbridge, Miccosukee, Meridian and Centerville—fan out from Tallahassee. During the 1980s, as development encroached, preservationists became concerned about the future of these thoroughfares. Consequently, they are now protected from development by county ordinance. Although most of the roads still maintain their rural Old South character, part of the bordering landholdings have been sold off to developers, and local traffic has increased.

© Robert Holmes

Canopy Road

★ **Old St. Augustine Road** — The oldest of the canopy roads dates back to the 1600s when, known as the Royal Road, it linked St. Augustine with the missions in Leon County. During the British occupation, it was called King's Highway. Later it was renamed Bellamy road, because Leon County landholder John Bellamy's slaves were used in the 1820s to rebuild and extend the highway to Pensacola. Today Old St. Augustine contains cool stretches of dense canopy from Capitol Circle to Williams Road.

Old Bainbridge Road (Route 361) — Originally a Native American trail, Old Bainbridge also served as a major thoroughfare for Leon County's early Spanish inhabitants. A Spanish mission once occupied the plot that now forms the right-of-way where Old Bainbridge crosses I-10; several Spanish *rancheros* were also located along this stretch of road.

★ **Miccosukee Road (Route 146)** — In the 1700s, this former footpath led to Miccosukee, an Indian village located in the same spot as its modern namesake. In the 1850s, plantation owners carted bales of cotton on this road to markets in Tallahassee. Today vast acres of plantation woodland still line picturesque Miccosukee Road.

Meridian Road (Route 155) — This route runs due north from its starting point at the **prime meridian line** from which all land surveys in the state of Florida were conducted *(corner of Meridian Rd. and Bloxham St.)* beginning in 1824. Although the road starts in the city, the canopied portion doesn't begin until the route crosses I-10. From there, Meridian leads to US-319 in Grady County, Georgia, terminating near Pebble Hill Plantation *(p 177).*

Centerville Road (Route 151) — Thought to have been established in the 1820s as an avenue linking the numerous area plantations to the capital city, Centerville Road also begins in Tallahassee, but the canopied portion is limited to the section east of Capitol Circle. From there it winds along a shaded 17mi course, passing through the tiny community of Chemonie Crossing and ending at Miccosukee. On the way, the **Old Pisgah United Methodist Church** *(Old Pisgah Church Rd., 7.6mi north of Capitol Circle)*, a simple white wooden structure built in 1858, exemplifies early frontier church design.

EXCURSIONS *Map p 159*

★★ **Wakulla Springs State Park** — *3hrs. 16mi south in Wakulla Springs. Take Rte. 61/319 south from Capitol Circle; follow left fork and continue 8mi on Rte. 61; turn left on Rte. 267. Entrance on right. Open year-round daily 8am–dusk. $3.25/vehicle. All boat tours depart from dock. River Cruise Wildlife Tour: daily 9am–4:30pm; round-trip 45min; commentary; $4.50. Glass-Bottom Boat Cruise (water conditions permitting): daily 9am–4:30pm; round-trip 45min; commentary; $4.50.* ✗ ⚹ 🅿 ☎ *850-224-5950.* Set amid lush vegetation in rural Wakulla County, one of the world's largest and deepest springs forms the centerpiece of this 2,900-acre park. Reputed to have been discovered by Spanish explorer Ponce de León around 1521, the spring was home to paleo-Indians over 10,000 years ago. In 1935 Ed Ball, heir to the du Pont fortune and owner of sizable timber interests in north Florida, purchased the spring and its surrounding acreage. After Ball's death in the early 1980s, the property was acquired by the State of Florida and opened as a state park in 1986.

Known by indigenous peoples as "mysterious water," this underground spring pumps some 400,000 gallons of crystal-clear water per minute into the Wakulla River. The source of the spring's waters, which maintain a constant year-round temperature of 70°F, remains a secret. Although divers have plumbed to depths of 360ft, the spring's source has never been reached.

To cruise this river is to travel back in time. Longleaf pine, beech and cypress trees dripping with Spanish moss surround the river; alligators, turtles and a wealth of waterbirds call its shores home. This primeval atmosphere provided the jungle setting for a number of films, including *Tarzan* movies (late 1930s to early 1940s), *Creature from the Black Lagoon* (1954) and *Airport '77*.

On the banks of the river, a stucco Mission-style guest lodge (c.1937) features a hand-painted cypress ceiling, imported Spanish tiles and Tennessee marble floors in the lobby. Nature trails within the park wind through a variety of plant communities, including old-growth floodplain swamps and longleaf pine forests.

© Robert Holmes

Turtles Sunning at Wakulla Springs State Park

★★**Pebble Hill Plantation** – *2hrs. 20mi north in Thomasville, Georgia. Take Thomasville Rd. (US-319) north 20mi to Pebble Hill entrance on left. Visit by guided tour (1hr) only, Oct–Labor Day Tue–Sat 10am–5pm, Sun 1pm–5pm. Closed Jan 1, Thanksgiving Day & Dec 24-25. $7.* &. ▣ *www.webvista.com/ tlh/sghtsee/pebble/* ☎ *912-226-2344.* Venerable live oaks shade the lane that winds up to the graceful white-brick manor house on this 3,000-acre plantation. Located just 20mi north of Tallahassee, Pebble Hill is one of 71 existing antebellum estates situated in a 300,000-acre area around the Florida/Georgia border—the greatest concentration of original plantations in the US. The majority of these sites are now private estates; Pebble Hill remains the only one open to the public.

Purchased by Ohio industrialist Howard Hanna in 1896, Pebble Hill was a working farm owned by Hanna's granddaughter Elisabeth (Miss Pansy) Ireland Poe. The original house (1827) was redesigned and enlarged in the 1850s and virtually rebuilt in 1936 by Abram Garfield (son of President James Garfield) after most of the original structure burned to the ground. The 1936 house, far grander than the one that had preceded it, is an elegant two-story structure distinguished by a large front portico anchored by slender square columns and decorative second-floor wooden balustrades. Prior to the blaze, Garfield had added the impressive twin gatehouses and four buildings in the stable complex. Pebble Hill remained in the Hanna family until Miss Pansy died in 1978. For many years, the plantation was a private retreat for wealthy northerners who came south during the winter to hunt quail; the site was opened to the public in 1983.

Visit – A free-standing mahogany staircase dominates the foyer of this 40-room mansion. English wallpaper, Hanna family antiques and a collection of 33 early **Audubon prints** thought to have been purchased in England number among the treasures found here. Filled with overstuffed furniture grouped around a central fireplace, the comfortable, informal **Drawing Room** at the east entrance connects to the house by way of a fern-filled, glassed-in loggia. The room's focal point is a large wraparound mural by Palm Beach artist J. Clinton Shepherd depicting wildlife native to the region. Outside, a formal garden with brick walkways connects beds of azaleas, camellias and annuals.

The **ticket house** and photographic exhibits detailing the family's and home's history are in the plantation's former cow barn, which once housed a prize Jersey herd. All of the barns and stables, handsome red-brick and green-shuttered buildings, are modeled after designs by Thomas Jefferson. Among the 17 outbuildings are a bathhouse built to resemble Noah's ark, a log cabin school where plantation children were tutored, and a guest cottage.

Returning to Tallahassee, the most scenic route is via Meridian Road *(Rte. 155; Exit Pebble Hill and turn right on US-319; go 4.7mi. south and turn right on Meridian Rd.)*, one of Leon County's designated canopy roads *(p 175)*. The route passes the privately owned inn **Susina** *(1420 Meridian Rd.)*, an antebellum plantation house built by Thomasville architect John Wind, who also designed an earlier version of Pebble Hill.

St. Marks Lighthouse and National Wildlife Refuge – *2hrs. 23mi south in Newport. Take Rte. 363 south to Wakulla and turn left on Rte. 267; continue to US-98 and turn left. Follow US-98 3mi and turn right on Rte. 59 to park entrance. Open year-round daily dawn–dusk. Closed major holidays. $4/vehicle.* & 🅿 ☎ *850-925-6121.* This 40mi, 67,000-acre parcel encompasses one of Florida's oldest lighthouses, a nature museum, wildlife preserve and recreation area. The **visitor center** *(open year-round Mon–Fri 8:15am–4pm, weekends 10am–5pm)* introduces visitors to the refuge via a video *(15min)* and several shadowbox exhibits detailing the area's history and wildlife. Constructed in 1829 from limestone bricks plucked from the ruins of nearby San Marcos de Apalache, the **lighthouse** *(7mi south of nature center)*, remains in use today. A wooden observation tower next to the light affords excellent opportunities for watching some of the park's 300 species of birds and the Monarch butterflies who migrate here in late October.

San Marcos de Apalache – *1.5hrs. 26mi south in St. Marks. Take Rte. 363 to St. Marks. Turn right on Old Fort Rd. and follow to end.* Located at the confluence of the Wakulla and St. Marks Rivers a few miles from the Gulf of Mexico, San Marcos de Apalache is the site of several early Spanish forts and later English and Confederate ramparts. Although no major battles were fought here, San Marcos was always considered a key military site because of its location. The first fort (c.1679), built of lime-coated wood to resemble stone, was burned and looted by pirates in 1682. Thirty-six years later, the Spanish constructed a second wooden fort here; they began work on a third—this one stone—in 1739. Occupation of the stronghold vacillated between the British and Spanish until 1821, when Florida became a US territory. In 1857 a federal marine hospital was constructed on the site using stones from the Spanish bombproof—the most secure part of the fort, where soldiers sought refuge during attack. During the Civil War, Confederate soldiers claimed and refurbished San Marcos, renaming it Fort Ward. After a four-year blockade by Union gunboats, the Confederate Army surrendered the fort in 1865.

Today a windowless concrete **museum**, built on the hospital's foundation, contains exhibits detailing the site's history *(open year-round Thu–Mon 9am–5pm; closed major holidays; $1; ☎ 850-925-6216)*. A self-guided walking tour *(pamphlet available in the museum)* leads visitors along the banks of the Wakulla River past the limestone outlines of the fort's north and west walls and the Spanish bombproof, as well as around the large, wooded hill that served as a powder magazine for Confederate soldiers.

Forest Capital State Museum – *1hr. 50mi southeast in Perry. Take US-27/Apalachee Pkwy. south to Perry (US-27 becomes US-19/98 in Perry). From Perry center, follow US-19/98 south 1mi to museum entrance on right at 204 Forest Park Dr. Open year-round Thu–Mon 9am–5pm. Closed Jan 1, Thanksgiving Day, Dec 25. $1.* & 🅿 ☎ *850-584-3227.* Exhibits in this small museum, devoted to Florida's forests, recount the early days of the state's lumber and turpentine industries. The latter industry thrived, providing resin for the US Navy, until lumber became a more valuable wood commodity in the 1920s. On the grounds is a reconstructed log **Cracker homestead**, a fine example of an early dogtrot *(p 27)* house. The homestead and outbuildings illustrate how the state's settlers would have lived in the 1860s.

Before planning your trip to Florida, be sure to consult:
   • *the Map of Principal Sights pp 2-3.*
   • *the suggested automobile tours presented on pp 4-5.*

South Florida

Aerial View of Miami Beach – Bill Staley, Tony Stone Images

Florida's most heavily developed strip extends along the Atlantic in a 70mi-long megalopolis from Miami to West Palm Beach. Called the Gold Coast, this region packs in some of the state's most valuable real estate, from the multimillion-dollar compounds of Palm Beach to the high-rise condos of Miami Beach. Here in the urban backdrop to America's sandbox, people drive fast, work hard, and take the big business of tourism seriously. The majority of South Florida's residents live on a swath of land some five to ten miles wide; just to the west lie the nearly unpopulated expanses of the EVERGLADES.

Before the arrival of the first European explorers, South Florida was inhabited by Tequesta Indians. These hunter-gatherers subsisted on a diet of fish, clams, manatee and turtle meat, and flour made from the roots of the coontie, a palm-like tropical plant that grew wild throughout the region.

During his initial explorations in 1513, Ponce de León sailed into Biscayne Bay, but there was no real effort to colonize Indian territory until Pedro Menéndez de Avilés turned his sights to South Florida—ideally situated to control the Florida Straits—after founding ST. AUGUSTINE in 1565. After failing to establish a permanent settlement and mission here in 1567, the Europeans retreated.

The area became an established tourist mecca in the 1890s when **Henry Flagler** tamed the frontier with his famous **Florida East Coast Railway**, extending the line from St. Augustine to Palm Beach and then to Miami and the KEYS. In-between towns like Fort Lauderdale and Boca Raton, already settled by vegetable and fruit farmers, did not attain full resort status until the 1920s. Synonymous with warm sunshine and fresh oranges, southeast Florida has throughout this century attracted hordes of visitors from points north to its year-round warm weather, clear blue water and elegant resorts.

Whether your tastes take you to the posh shops of Palm Beach's Worth Avenue *(p 233)*, to the art museums of West Palm Beach, to Miami Beach's bright parade of world-class Art Deco architecture, to Fort Lauderdale's famous beach, or to Miami's cultural melting pot of eateries, festivals and languages, South Florida promises to keep you entertained.

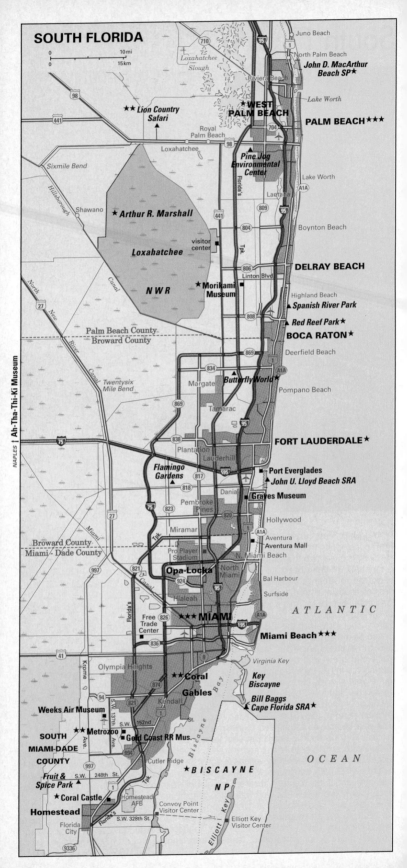

SOUTH FLORIDA

0   10mi

0   15km

710

Juno Beach

Loxahatchee Slough

North Palm Beach

95

John D. MacArthur Beach SP ★

98

★★ **Lion Country Safari**

Riviera Beach

WEST PALM BEACH ★★

704

PALM BEACH ★★★

Royal Palm Beach

Loxahatchee

98

Lake Worth

Pine Jog Environmental Center

Lake Worth

441

Sixmile Bend

809

Lantana

A1A

Shawano

804

Boynton Beach

★ **Arthur R. Marshall**

95

441

Tpk.

806

DELRAY BEACH

Loxahatchee

visitor center

Linton Blvd.

N W R

★ **Morikami Museum**

Highland Beach

▲ **Spanish River Park**

808

Red Reef Park ★

Palm Beach County
Broward County

BOCA RATON ★

869

Deerfield Beach

North New River Canal

Twentysix Mile Bend

834

Butterfly World ★

Margate

Pompano Beach

75

869

Tamarac

838

FORT LAUDERDALE ★

Plantation

Lauderhill

95

Flamingo Gardens

817

505

Port Everglades

818

▲ **John U. Lloyd Beach SRA**

Dania

Graves Museum

75

823

Pembroke Pines

820

Hollywood

27

Miramar

A1A

Aventura

Broward County
Miami-Dade County

Pro Player Stadium

821

Aventura Mall

Tpk.

997

924

N. Miami Beach

Opa-Locka

95

N. Miami

Bal Harbour

Hialeah

Surfside

Florida's

826

Free Trade Center

ATLANTIC

★★★ **MIAMI**

195

A1A

836

Miami Beach ★★★

41

9

Virginia Key

Olympia Heights

874

★★ **Coral Gables**

Key Biscayne

821

Kendall

Bill Baggs Cape Florida SRA ★

Weeks Air Museum

94

S.W. 137th

152nd

St.

Biscayne Bay

★★ **Metrozoo**

821

Gold Coast RR Mus.

SOUTH MIAMI-DADE COUNTY

S.W. Ave.

994

S.W. 248th St.

OCEAN

997

Cutler Ridge

Fruit & Spice Park ▲

★ **BISCAYNE**

★ **Coral Castle**

Krome Ave.

1

N P

Homestead

Homestead AFB

Convoy Point Visitor Center

Florida City

Florida's

S.W. 328th St.

Elliott Key

Elliott Key Visitor Center

9336

NAPLES ↑ **Ah-Tha-Thi-Ki Museum**

BOCA RATON★

Situated halfway between Fort Lauderdale and West Palm Beach, sun-soaked Boca Raton has catered to the well-heeled for more than 70 years. This clean, prosperous community, whose 2mi stretch of public beaches is warmed by Gulf Stream waters flowing only 200 yards offshore, still attracts monied visitors.

Historical Notes

Meager Beginnings – Prehistoric Indians were the first to recognize the area's natural enticements, building villages by the coastal marshes and lagoons. By the end of the 18C, they were gone, victims of white men's diseases and British slave raiders. For the next century, the place remained largely untouched, dangerous offshore reefs forbidding much exploration. But in the latter part of the 19C, settlers began penetrating the area's dense subtropical wilderness.

In 1884 Captain Tom Rickards of Missouri bought 50 acres of land adjacent to Lake Boca Ratone, as this bulge in the present Intracoastal Waterway was then called. Early mapmakers mistook the area for a similar site near Miami's Biscayne Bay and called it by the same Spanish name, *Boca Ratone* (popularly translated as "mouth of the rat"). A few years later, Rickards moved his farming operations here after freezes devastated his crops in the northern part of the state. He and his son built a house out of timbers from shipwrecks, and began clearing land and planting it with pineapples and citrus trees. After being hired by the Florida East Coast Railway as a surveyor and land developer, Rickards drew up a plan for a farming town called Boca Raton and promoted the area to prospective buyers. By 1900, orchards and vegetable farms punctuated the palmetto forests.

Boom and Bust – Boca Raton might yet be a sleepy seaside hamlet if architect Addison Mizner had waited an extra year to turn his attention to it. In the early 1920s, while speculators were buying and selling chunks of Florida at ever-increasing speed and price, Boca Raton consisted of little more than a train depot and a few scattered homes. Then in 1925, Mizner's corporation bought lakeside acreage and began construction of a hotel that would draw hundreds of rich and famous visitors. With Mizner's signature, the open arcades and pastel pink walls of the Mediterranean Revival-style Cloister Inn (now Boca Raton Resort and Club; *p 183*) rose from the coastal swampland in just six months.

Not content with a mere hotel, the flamboyant architect envisioned an entire city with landscaped gardens and promenades, world-class theaters and a huge cathedral. Work on his grandiose plan, which called for developing 2mi of beachfront and 16,000 acres inland, was well underway when the Florida real-estate bubble burst. Investors shied away from Mizner, leaving many of his ideas on paper. As one longtime resident put it, "We woke up with a jolt, and gold dust underfoot became just plain Florida sand again." Even so, by the end of 1925 Mizner had sold $11 million worth of lots.

A devastating hurricane brought the 1926 summer season to a dramatic close. The Cloister Inn, however, weathered that storm and another two years later. It remains today a testament to Mizner's vision, as does **Camino Real**, a 160ft-wide avenue once divided by a canal on which gondolas ferried the Cloister's guests from the inn to the beach. Another surviving Mizner structure, the **Administration Building** *(2 E. Camino Real, at intersection of Dixie Hwy.)*, modeled after El Greco's home in Toledo, Spain, now houses a popular restaurant.

Silicon Beach – Boca Raton's crown-jewel hotel remained the town's lifeblood until the opening of Florida Atlantic University in the early 1960s. Tourism—which swells the city's population by 10 percent in the winter season—now has given way to high-tech industry as Boca's largest source of commercial revenue. More than a dozen major companies, including IBM and Sony, maintain operations here, supporting a flourishing young population that takes pride in its town's appearance and heritage. A city ordinance requires all new commercial buildings to meet the strict standards of Boca's architectural board. After decades of uninspired building, the Mediterranean style has returned with **Mizner Park** *(400 N. Federal Hwy., between Palmetto Park Rd. and Glades Rd.; open year-round Mon–Sat 10am–9pm, Sun noon–6pm; closed Dec 25; ✗ ৬ ☏ 561-362-0606)*, a pink-stucco shopping/office/apartment complex (1991) distinguished by its airy arcades, fountains and courtyards. Elsewhere, the town boasts well-kept parks, year-round professional theater, fine golfing and fishing, and winter polo matches.

SIGHTS *2 days. Map p 182.*

Boca Raton Museum of Art – *801 W. Palmetto Park Rd. Open year-round Tue–Fri 10am–4pm (Wed until 9pm), weekends noon–4pm. Closed major holidays. $3.* ৬ 🅿 ☏ *561-392-2500.* Expanding on a collection donated in 1989 by Dr. and Mrs. John J. Mayers, this museum contains three galleries for the display of temporary exhibitions and holdings from the permanent collection, which includes works by such modern masters as Matisse, Modigliani, Picasso, Warhol and Johns. African and pre-Columbian masks and statuary are also highlighted.

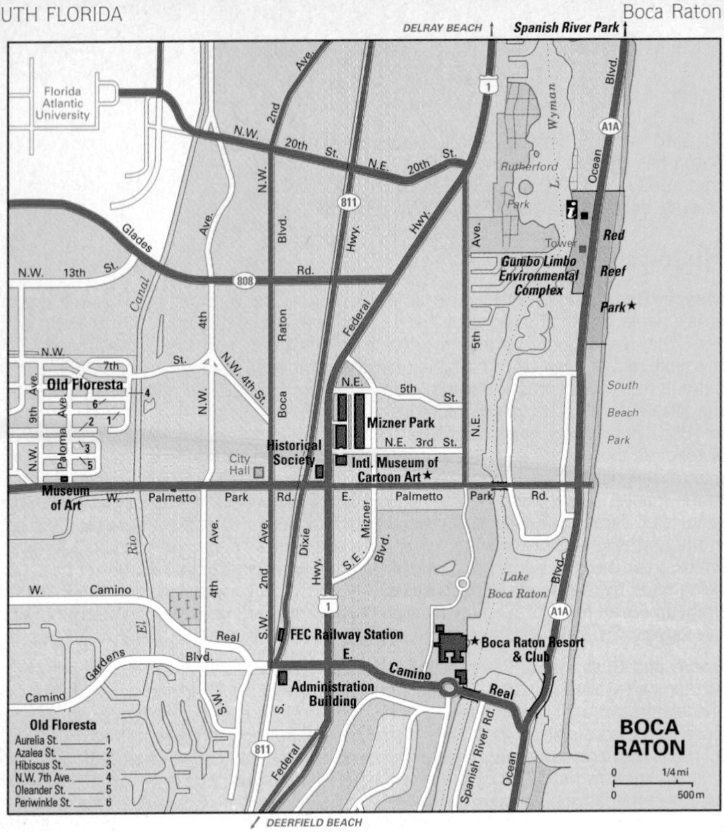

Old Floresta – *Adjacent to art museum; bounded by W. Palmetto Park Rd., Periwinkle St., N.W. 9th Ave. and N.W. 7th Ave.* Drive down Aurelia, Azalea, Hibiscus or Oleander Streets behind the Boca Raton Museum of Art for a glimpse at one of Boca's oldest neighborhoods. Designed by Addison Mizner for his executives in 1925, Old Floresta still boasts 29 original houses characterized by red barrel-tile roofs and light-colored stucco walls. Large palm and banyan trees shade these quiet, pleasant streets.

Boca Raton Historical Society – *70 N. Federal Hwy. Open Oct–May Mon–Fri 10am–4pm. Rest of the year Tue–Fri 10am–4pm. Closed Dec 25–Jan 2. ☎ 561-395-4154. Guided city tour (1hr 30min) departs from Royal Palm Plaza every Wed 9:30am. Commentary. Reservations required. $7.50. ☎ 561-395-6766.* Identifiable by its gilded dome, the elegant **Old Town Hall★** was originally designed by Addison Mizner as Boca Raton's first municipal edifice. Mizner began construction of the building in 1926, but after his financial collapse the project was scaled back and completed a year later by William E. Alsmeyer of Delray Beach. The finished building, fashioned with beams and paneling of pecky cypress (a porous wood resistant to termites) and pine floors, housed city officials and the fire and police departments until 1983. The first-floor library now contains archives, photographs and Mizner artifacts. A gift shop occupies the old fire bay, and the former mayor's office features a permanent time line of Boca's history.

★**International Museum of Cartoon Art** – Kids *201 Plaza Real. Open year-round Tue–Sat 10am–6pm, Sun noon–6pm. Closed Thanksgiving Day, Dec 25. $6. www.cartoon.org ☎ 561-391-2200.* At the south end of the stylish Mizner Park shopping complex stands this two-story, 50,000sq ft, Mediterranean Revival-style showplace. It opened its main exhibition floor only in March 1996; two years later its second floor was being prepared for additional displays. Only a small portion of the museum's archival collection—containing more than 160,000 original works on paper, and more than 1,000 hours of animated films—can be exhibited at any one time, however.

Here you'll find an original 19C newspaper tearsheet of Richard F. Outcault's "The Yellow Kid," generally regarded as the first comic strip, and the initial story board for Walt Disney's "Plane Crazy," which introduced Mickey Mouse predecessor Steamboat Willie. Displays on the right side of the main floor present comic strips, comic books, gag and editorial cartoons. On the left side of the floor are temporary exhibits, rotated four to six times a year. Also here is the **Hearst Cartoon Hall of Fame** (begun in 1975, it had 32 plaques through 1997). "Beetle Bailey" creator Mort Walker is regarded as the museum's founder.

FEC Railway Station – *747 S. Dixie Hwy. Not open to the public.* To enhance the town's appeal for guests arriving on the Florida East Coast Railway, Boca Raton Club owner Clarence Geist commissioned this graceful structure (1930) with its arched loggias, spiral columns and roof of interlocking sienna tiles. When passenger service was discontinued in 1963, the station rapidly fell victim to decay and vandalism. The local historical society rallied the community to save it, and—thanks to a donation from the Count and Countess deHoernle, whose name it bears—the station now enhances an otherwise bland commercial stretch. A 1930 steam locomotive and other railroad cars sit on special sidings outside the building.

★**Boca Raton Resort & Club** – *501 E. Camino Real.* ♿ ☎ *561-395-3000. Open only to hotel guests and club members. Visit by guided tour (1hr 30min) only, year-round Tue 1:30pm. $5. Reservations required through Boca Raton Historical Society* ☎ *561-395-6766.* The world-class hotel that put Boca Raton on the map began life as the Cloister Inn, a 100-room Mediterranean Revival-style inn completed in 1926. Architect Addison Mizner, fueled with his success in Palm Beach, pushed himself to a higher creative level than ever before, even forming his own corporation to finance the work. Though Mizner went bankrupt a year after the hotel opened, the Cloister Inn continued to attract well-heeled patrons as it still does today.

The original part of the hotel remains as the **east wing**★ *(right side of the palm-lined driveway leading to the hotel)*, decorated with pecky cypress beams and 15C Spanish furniture. On the wing's first floor, gilt columns and a soaring ceiling distinguish the Cathedral Dining Room. Note the scrupulous attention to ornamental detail throughout the grand lobby and other public areas.

Outside, espaliered bougainvillea climbs the wall beside Romanesque arches, while a loggia and cloister open onto a central courtyard whose fountains are accented with bright Spanish and Portuguese tiles. A 1929 addition—300 rooms in two wings—by the new owner, Indiana utilities millionaire Clarence Geist, created the hotel's present horseshoe shape while maintaining the graceful blend of Spanish, Italian and Moorish styles. Arthur Vining Davis, founder of the Arvida Company, bought the hotel in 1969 and added the 300ft pink tower. A beach club and golf-course villas bring the current room total to 960.

★**Red Reef Park** – *1400 N. Ocean Blvd. (A1A), 1 mi north of Palmetto Park Rd. Open year-round daily 8am–10pm. $8/vehicle, $10/vehicle weekends.* 🅿 ☎ *561-393-7974.* A densely vegetated dune, a boardwalk and a pleasant beach for swimming, fishing and snorkeling over an artificial reef occupy the east side of this 67-acre park. The west side contains the **Gumbo Limbo Environmental Complex** [Kids], a 20-acre swatch of tropical hammock preserved in its natural state. A small but inviting **visitor center** *(open year-round Mon–Sat 9am–4pm, Sun noon–4pm; closed Jan 1, Jul 4, Thanksgiving Day, Dec 25;* ♿ ☎ *561-338-1473)* displays live snakes, tree frogs, tanks of living corals and crustaceans, and a shell collection. Large outdoor saltwater tanks allow visitors an up-close look at anemones, urchins,

Boca Raton Resort & Club

loggerhead turtles (taken as fledglings for study by Florida Atlantic University students, and then released), and other local marine life. An informative boardwalk trail *(.3mi)* winds over a coastal dune, through a Sabal palm hammock and mangrove wetland, past strangler fig trees, paradise trees, and the red-bark gumbo-limbo. A 40ft observation tower clears the forest canopy, providing ocean views.

Spanish River Park – *3001 N. Ocean Blvd./A1A. Entrance on west side, just north of Gumbo Limbo Environmental Complex. Open year-round daily 8am–dusk. $8/vehicle, $10/vehicle weekends.*   ☎ *561-393-7815.* Taking its name from a shallow freshwater stream that coursed along its western edge before the creation of the Intracoastal Waterway, the park provides oceanfront as well as coastal woodlands recreation. A nature trail *(.25mi)* beside the lagoon provides a pleasant stroll through the forest, where the fall of tiny pinecones and needles sounds like a gentle rain. Along the trail, a 40ft observation tower offers a fenced-in view of the Intracoastal Waterway and perhaps a glimpse of local waterfowl.

DELRAY BEACH

Population 50,720
Map of Principal Sights p 3 – Map p 180
Tourist Information ☎ 561-278-0424

Sitting quietly between Fort Lauderdale and Palm Beach, this unassuming beachfront town eschews the glitz of its neighbors to the north and south, while proudly preserving the legacy of its American and Japanese settlers.

Historical Notes

Delray Beach originated as 160 acres of palmetto and scrub pine on a barrier island purchased by—and named for—William Linton, an itinerant Michigan postmaster who was later elected to the US Congress. After purchasing the land for $25 an acre, Linton sold five-acre plots to a handful of Michigan farmers who settled the isolated area in 1895. Two freezes in the late 1890s destroyed the pioneers' bean and tomato crops, prompting settlers to rename the town in 1901 (Linton became synonymous with failure) after the Detroit suburb of Delray. Five years later, Henry Flagler's Model Land Company brought in a group of Japanese farmers to Yamato *(p 185)*, a Japanese colony that occupied a tract of land west of Delray. This sparked the beginning of the area's thriving pineapple crop. Having begun as a market center for commercial agriculture, Delray blossomed into a winter resort during the 1930s. Today the low-key seaside city derives most of its revenue from automobile retail sales and tourism.

Stroll tree-lined **Atlantic Avenue**, the principal east-west artery that ends at the ocean, for a glimpse of the town's largest restored historic district *(between N.E. 4th and Swinton Aves.)* and its quaint shops. Some 150 yards off the south end of Delray's public beach, the wreck of the *S.S. Inchulva* sits in 25ft of water. In 1903 the English steamship went down in a hurricane while headed north to Newport News, Virginia.

SIGHTS *1 day*

Old School Square Cultural Arts Center – *51 N. Swinton Ave., at northeast corner of Atlantic Ave., 6 blocks west of Intracoastal Waterway.* Occupying a grassy, four-acre downtown city block, Old School Square is the heart of Delray's largest historic district and includes three former school buildings. **Crest Theater** (1925), formerly Delray High School, is used today for arts performances *(season Nov–Apr; for schedules and tickets ☎ 561-243-3183).* The adjoining **Gymnasium** (1926) houses a community hall that is available for social events, and a 1913 schoolhouse holds the site's centerpiece, the **Cornell Museum of History and Art** *(open Sept–May Tue–Sat 11am–4pm, Sun 1pm–4pm; rest of the year Tue–Sat 11am–4pm; closed major holidays; $3;*   ☎ *561-243-7198).* Refurbished in 1990, the museum sits on a shady, well-manicured lawn and features a large entry fountain. Named after two local benefactors, Harriet and George Cornell, the two-story structure contains three temporary exhibit rooms downstairs that display the work of national and regional artists. Two grand wooden staircases lead to the second floor, where the museum's collection of **military miniatures** is displayed in glass showcases with panoramas. An archives room also hosts exhibits that chronicle the city's history.

Cason Cottage Museum – *5 N.E. 1st St., across from north end of Old School Square. Open year-round Tue–Fri 10am–4pm. Closed major holidays. $2.*   ☎ *561-274-9578.* This frame vernacular cottage was built in 1915 of Dade County pine by Dr. J.R. Cason, Sr., a Methodist minister and the father of one of Delray's founders. The last remaining structure of a four-building family compound, the three-bedroom house was renovated in 1928 to include a sun porch, a porte cochere and a triple roof line. Forty double-hung windows surround the cottage, which is furnished with post-Victorian period pieces and decorated with historic photos of the city.

★**Morikami Museum & Japanese Gardens** – *4000 Morikami Park Rd. Take I-95 south to Linton Blvd. and go west 3.5mi; turn south on Jog Rd. and continue 1.5mi to park. Open year-round Tue–Sun 10am–5pm. Closed major holidays. $4.25.* ✕ ♿ ▣ *www.icsi.com/ics/morikami* ☎ *561-495-0233.* Started on a 200-acre parcel of pond-studded pine forest donated to Palm Beach County by prosperous pineapple farmer George Sukeji Morikami, this park and museum pay homage to Japanese culture. Morikami immigrated here from Japan in the early 1900s to join the Yamato Colony, a Japanese agricultural community on the southern edge of Delray. In the 1920s, when many of the settlers returned to their native country after selling their land during the Florida real-estate boom, Morikami remained and continued farming.

Visit – *2 hrs.* Begin at the white stucco **museum exhibition building**, whose oriental architectural overtones are accented inside by dark wood trim and shoji screens. Temporary exhibits here emphasize Japanese arts, crafts and changing lifestyles. In the Seishin-an Tea House adjacent to the lobby, visitors can watch an authentic Japanese **tea ceremony**★ in a *soan*-style tea hut *(third Sat of every month at noon, 1pm, 2pm & 3pm; $3/person).*

Tea Ceremony

The museum also houses a theater, a library and a multimedia resource center with touch-screen access to a wealth of information about Japanese culture.

A short drive (or lakeside walk) from the museum lies **Yamato-kan**★, inspired by a Japanese imperial villa. Enclosing a central pebble garden, the rooms include a bath and bedroom, both serenely furnished like a traditional Japanese home. Additional rooms hold interactive displays, as well as a permanent exhibition relating the story of Yamato Colony through photographs and artifacts. *In accordance with Japanese custom, visitors must remove their shoes before entering; paper slippers are provided.* A two-acre garden with a traditional koi pond, waterfall and **bonsai garden** surrounds the building. Nature trails thread the forested acreage, which is dotted with shady picnic areas.

The museum sponsors four **annual festivals:** the Japanese New Year *(first Sat following Jan 1)*; Hatsume Fair *(last weekend in Feb)*, celebrating the advent of spring; Children's Day *(last Sun in Apr)*; and Bon Festival *(mid-Aug)*, featuring Japanese folk music, dancing and a sunset lantern-floating ceremony.

EXCURSION

★**Arthur R. Marshall Loxahatchee National Wildlife Refuge** – *3 hrs. 12mi west of Delray Beach, on US-441. Take Rte. 806/Atlantic Ave. west to US-441; go north on US-441 3mi to refuge entrance. Open year-round daily 6am–dusk. $5/vehicle.* ▣ *www.fws.gov/~r4eao/nwrlxh.html* ☎ *561-734-8303.* Encompassing 145,000 acres of freshwater habitats unique to the Everglades, this refuge provides a home to more than 18,000 alligators and numerous species of birds and other wildlife, including the endangered snail kite and wood stork. The visitor center *(open mid-Oct–Apr Mon–Fri 9am–4pm, weekends & holidays 9am–4:30pm; rest of the year Wed–Fri 9am–4pm, weekends & holidays 9am–4:30pm)* contains fine dioramas and exhibits on local ecology. Just behind the center, a boardwalk *(.4 mi)* snakes back into a dark cypress swamp. Reptiles flourish here, as do a variety of ferns and colorful bromeliads and trees, some streaked with the blood-red baton rouge lichen. Another trail *(.8mi)* marked with interpretive signs circles a freshwater impoundment past an observation tower. Canoeists can take a 5.5mi loop trail through the refuge, which is surrounded by a 57mi-long canal and levee that stores water for area residents.

FORT LAUDERDALE★

Population 151,805
Map of Principal Sights p 3 – Map p 180
Tourist Information ☎ 954-765-4466

Straddling 300mi of natural and artificial waterways, the "Venice of America," as Greater Fort Lauderdale is known, has in recent decades undergone a remarkable transformation from a small Southern community to an international tourist destination. The largest city of sprawling Broward County, Fort Lauderdale lies a mere 23mi north of Miami and covers 30sq mi of territory, stretching from the glistening waters of the Atlantic Ocean to a ring of suburban communities encircling it.

Historical Notes

A Fort on the River – For 3,000 years the area's first residents, members of the migratory Tequesta tribe, lived along the river that still traverses the city's heart. Following the Spanish entry into Florida in the 16C, natives decreased in number until, by the late 1700s, the population of future Fort Lauderdale consisted only of the five-member Lewis family of white Bahamian immigrants.

By the early 1800s, additional squatters had created a small farming community along both banks of *Rio Nuevo*, as early Spanish visitors named the New River. Seminoles, who now occupied the territory, cohabited peacefully with the settlers until 1836, when Indians massacred the family of William Cooley, the settlement's leader, during the Second Seminole War. Fear of similar attacks caused the New River settlement's few white inhabitants to flee. Two years later, Major William Lauderdale and his detachment of volunteers built an army fort atop a series of Tequesta Indian mounds near the present intersection of Ninth Avenue and Fourth Court; the future city of Fort Lauderdale inherited the name of the fort's commanding officer.

Following the Second Seminole War, Fort Lauderdale's population remained limited to a few scattered families. By the century's final decade, however, fears of Indian attack had subsided, and several homesteaders, availing themselves of liberal federal land offers, returned to farm along the river. In 1892 work began on a paved road connecting Fort Lauderdale with Miami.

The City Grows – In 1896 Henry Flagler's Florida East Coast Railway entered Fort Lauderdale en route to Miami, catalyzing the development of a busy agricultural community. A sandy thoroughfare running perpendicular to the New River arose near the railroad tracks. Named for the family that possessed large parcels of land in the area, Brickell Avenue soon formed the hub of a small business community. Several modest wood-frame vernacular structures were erected along this street, although none remain standing.

By 1900, Fort Lauderdale's population had risen to 52 and the settlement began to exhibit many of the trappings of a developing community. In 1906 Florida Gov. **Napoleon Bonaparte Broward** (for whom the county is named) spearheaded a state-sponsored program of Everglades reclamation *(p 39)*, or drainage, beginning at the south fork of the New River. Land speculators suddenly appeared and purchased large amounts of reclaimed Everglades land, which they marketed aggressively in many parts of the country. When more than 3,000 investors descended on Fort Lauderdale in early 1911 to view land they had purchased sight-unseen, the community of fewer than 200 residents was overwhelmed. Immediately afterward (March 1911), Fort Lauderdale was incorporated as a town and the amenities sorely lacking up to that time were provided.

The city grew quickly as tourism took its place alongside real estate and agriculture as a major ingredient in the community's economic mix. As more people settled here, imaginative developers dredged and filled marshy waterfront areas east of downtown and created posh new neighborhoods. Their activity anticipated the great real-estate boom that engulfed Florida in the 1920s. As speculators poured into Fort Lauderdale, the community's population spiraled beyond 15,000, and handsome Mediterranean Revival subdivisions opened on both sides of the New River. The city's first skyscraper, the nine-story Sweet Building *(now One River Plaza, 305 S. Andrews Ave.)*, appeared in the mid-1920s, as did the **Bryan Arcade (A)** *(201 S. Andrews Ave.)*. Both buildings were designed in the Mediterranean Revival style, but have been greatly modified over time; the latter now sports an Art Deco facade.

In the aftermath of the twin blows of the economic bust and the hurricane that followed in 1926, Fort Lauderdale slipped into an economic depression. The city began to emerge from its doldrums in the late 1930s, when new hotels welcomed the growing legions of tourists on Lauderdale's beaches.

During World War II, Fort Lauderdale hosted thousands of servicemen who trained on the beach and at several local bases, including the Fort Lauderdale Naval Air Station. After the war, the city's growth accelerated as former farmland was rapidly transformed into developments, the largest being the Coral Ridge subdivision northeast of downtown. By the 1970s, Fort Lauderdale's population had reached 140,000 and the city was building a new downtown from the ground up. At the same time, it was acquiring an international reputation as a tourist haven. Lauderdale's famed **Strip**★ of beach, which stretches for 2mi along Atlantic Boulevard *(on A1A, from Sunrise Blvd. to Bahia Mar Yacht Basin)*, had become known in the 1950s not only for its beauty but as the destination for hundreds of thousands of college students—from all over the US—who flocked there each year during Spring Break. Fort Lauderdale reigned for over 30 years as the mecca of Spring Break bacchanalia—celebrated in the film *Where the Boys Are* (1960). In the mid-1980s, city officials began actively discouraging the legions of collegiate visitors from adopting local beaches as a springtime playground. Fort Lauderdale Beach is now quiescent, with families and older visitors making up its predominant elements.

Fort Lauderdale Today – Growth has declined slightly in recent decades because the post-war population surge (Fort Lauderdale counted just

© Bill Wisser

The Strip

18,000 residents in 1940) pushed development out to the borders. The modern city is a boater's paradise with more than 40,000 registered yachts, many of which are moored at the Radisson **Bahia Mar Yacht Basin** on the Atlantic Intracoastal Waterway. Created in the early postwar period, this facility is one of the largest of its kind in the entire nation.

Visitors from the US, Canada and Western Europe visit Fort Lauderdale in growing numbers. The city's flourishing tourist industry received a boost with the opening in 1991 of the $50 million Greater Fort Lauderdale/Broward County Convention Center, marked by a Kent Ullberg sculpture depicting sailfish and dolphins frolicking in a waterfall, on the northern edge of **Port Everglades**. This seaport, which contributes $3.5 billion annually to the economy of Broward County, handles more than 16 million tons of cargo each year, placing it second among Florida's busiest ports. It also ranks as the world's second largest cruise port (Miami is first) with more than two million people annually leaving its shores for Caribbean ports of call.

The Strip, which fell into a state of seediness in recent decades, has been enlivened by an ambitious beach redevelopment program that has attracted new businesses and added a $26 million beachfront promenade. Having shed its image as the capital of springtime frivolty, Fort Lauderdale, with its diversified economy—tourism generates $3.1 billion annually—and growing cultural offerings, now ranks among America's most attractive and liveable mid-size cities.

DOWNTOWN *1 day. Map p 189.*

Fort Lauderdale's downtown has undergone a dramatic face-lift in the last 10 years with the building of Blockbuster Video's international headquarters and the creation of the **Arts and Sciences District**. This district—bounded by E. Broward Boulevard on the north, the New River on the south, and S.E. Third and S.W. Seventh Avenues on the east and west, respectively—encompasses the Museum of Art, the Museum of Discovery and Science and the Broward Center for the Performing Arts *(201 S.W. 5th Ave.; ☎ 462-0222)*. The latter, a contemporary complex on the river's north bank, brings world-class performances to the city. The Center anchors the western terminus of **Riverwalk**, a tree-lined bricked esplanade that stretches along the north and south banks of the New River. Just east of downtown, trendy **Las Olas Boulevard** boasts a wide variety of shops, galleries and outdoor cafes *(between S.E. 6th and 11th Aves.)*.

★**Stranahan House** – *335 S.E. 6th Ave., .2mi south of Las Olas Blvd. just above the New River Tunnel. Open Sept–May Wed–Sat 10am–4pm, Sun 1pm–4pm. Closed major holidays. $5.* ▢ *www.goriverwalk.com/stranahan* ☎ *954-524-4736.*

Practical information... Area Code: 954

Getting There – Fort Lauderdale/Hollywood International Airport (FLL): 4mi south of city; information ☎ 359-1200. Transportation to downtown: Airport Express shuttle *($6)* ☎ 561-8888; taxi *($12)* and hotel courtesy shuttles. Rental car agencies *(p 323)* located at airport. Train service to Palm Beach and Miami by Tri-Rail ☎ 728-8445. Amtrak **train** station: 200 S.W. 21st Terr. ☎ 800-872-7245. Greyhound/Trailways **bus** station: 515 N.E. 3rd St. ☎ 800-231-2222.

Getting Around – Local **bus service**: Broward County Mass Transit (BCT) *($1; transfers 15¢)* route information ☎ 357-8400. **Downtown shuttle** (free) between Courthouse and BCT Terminal *(year-round Mon–Fri 7:30am–6pm, every 15min)* and the Lunchtime Express on Las Olas *(year-round Mon–Fri 11:30am–2:30pm; every 10min)* ☎ 761-3543. **Water taxi** along Intracoastal Waterway and New River *(year-round daily 10am–1:30am; one-way $7, round-trip $13; day pass $15)* ☎ 467-6677. Metered **parking** *(25¢/hr)* along Andrews Ave. and Las Olas Blvd., and along 3rd and 4th Aves.

Visitor Information – **Greater Fort Lauderdale Convention and Visitors Bureau**, 1850 Eller Dr., Suite 303, Fort Lauderdale FL 33316 *(open year-round Mon–Fri 8:30am–5pm)* ☎ 765-4466 or 800-227-8669 (US and Canada). **Greater Fort Lauderdale Chamber of Commerce**, 512 N.E. 3rd Ave., Fort Lauderdale FL 33301 *(open year-round Mon–Fri 8:30am–5pm)* ☎ 462-6000. *These organizations provide additional information regarding shopping, entertainment, festivals (p 318) and recreation.*

Accommodations – *(p 324)* Area vacation planner including lodging directory available (free) from Greater Fort Lauderdale Convention and Visitors Bureau *(above)*. Accommodations range from luxury hotels and spa resorts ($150 and up) to moderate inns and motels ($75-$125) and superior small lodgings ($35–$90). Youth hostel ($12) ☎ 568-1615. Campgrounds and RV parks available. *Rates quoted are average prices per night for a double room and are subject to seasonal variations.*

Entertainment – Consult the arts and entertainment section of the *Sun Sentinel* (Friday) and *Travelhost* magazine, or the 24hr hotline ☎ 357-5700, for schedules of cultural events. Broward Center for the Performing Arts ☎ 462-0222; Sunrise Musical Theater ☎ 741-7300. For tickets: **Ticketmaster** ☎ 523-3309.

Sports and Recreation – Boating, windsurfing, snorkeling, diving and sunbathing at area beaches. For information on recreation and area parks ☎ 563-PARK. **Cruise ships** depart from Port Everglades. **Fishing** piers: Fisherman's Wharf ☎ 943-1488; Anglin's Fishing Pier ☎ 491-9403. Carolina **Golf** Club ☎ 753-4000 and Jacaranda Golf Club ☎ 472-5836 welcome non-members. **Shopping**: downtown on Las Olas Blvd., Galleria Mall, Sunrise Blvd.; Swap Shop, 3291 W. Sunrise Blvd. (shopping and entertainment) ☎ 791-7927; Sawgrass Mills, 12801 W. Sunrise Blvd. (outlet mall) ☎ 846-2350.

Airy and elegant, the two-story frame house skirted by wide verandahs is Broward County's oldest building, and its most popular historical site. It was built on the banks of the New River in 1901 by **Frank Stranahan**, the area's first permanent white settler, who came to the area in 1893 from Ohio to operate a ferry on the New River.

This graceful example of Florida pioneer architecture is located on the site of the trading post Stranahan originally set up to service settlers and Seminoles. In 1906, with the help of Edwin King, a local ship's carpenter, Stranahan converted the 2,000sq ft structure into a home for himself and his new wife, Ivy Cromartie. By 1915 the Stranahans had added bay windows, a fireplace, kitchen, electricity, indoor plumbing and a water tower, solidifying the couple's high-ranking social status. Frank committed suicide in 1929, reportedly as a result of a depression that followed his bank's failure. After his death Ivy moved into the attic and leased the bottom floor as a restaurant and the second floor as a boarding house in order to make ends meet. She remained in the house until her death in 1971. In the early 1980s the home was restored to its 1915 appearance and furnished with period pieces, several of which belonged to the Stranahans. The interior boasts lovely double-beaded wall paneling expertly crafted from Dade County pine.

★**Fort Lauderdale Museum of Art** – *One E. Las Olas Blvd. Open year-round Tue–Sat 10am–5pm (Fri until 8pm), Sun noon–5pm. Closed major holidays. $6.* &. ▣ ☎ *954-525-5500.* Edward Larrabee Barnes designed this three-story white structure (1986), on a prominent corner near the New River, as part of the city's downtown revitalization. Best known for its 1,200-piece collection of **CoBrA art**★★—

the largest assemblage outside Europe—the museum comprises over 5,400 pieces ranging from a comprehensive collection of paintings by American Impressionist William Glackens to works by Pop artist Andy Warhol.

Four ground-floor galleries focus on traveling shows. On the second floor, a large gallery *(northeast corner)* features a rotating group of statues, oils, gouaches and ceramics crafted by CoBrA artists. Born in Paris in 1948, the CoBrA movement consisted of Expressionists from **Co**penhagen, **Br**ussels and **A**msterdam who drew their inspiration from folk art and children's drawings. Pierre Alechinsky, Christian Dotremont, Karel Appel and Carl-Henning Pedersen are among the movement's best-known artists. Leading to the gallery, two glass boxes encase pan-African masks, deities and ceremonial headgear. The remainder of this floor is given over to temporary exhibits showcasing pieces of the permanent collection as well as thematic shows.

Fort Lauderdale Historical Society Museum (M¹) – *219 S.W. 2nd Ave. Open year-round Tue–Fri 10am–4pm. Closed Jan 1, Jul 4, Dec 25. $2.* & ☎ *954-463-4431.* Displays in this small facility chronicle the city's past from its founding to the present day. Changing exhibits focus on specific aspects of local history. The historical society also operates a research library and bookstore here.

The museum now forms part of a **Historic Village Complex** *(bounded by S.W. 2nd St., N.W. 1st Ave., Broward Blvd. and the New River)*, containing several vernacular early 20C structures. Here you will find the 1904 **Bryan Homes** *(301 and 303 N.W. New River Dr.)*, which have been connected and converted into Reed's River House restaurant, and the 1905 **New River Inn** *(231 S.W. 2nd Ave.; not open to the public)*. All three properties were owned by the Bryan family, who numbered among the city's first settlers. Broward County's oldest hotel, the New River Inn was constructed using hollow concrete blocks made with local sand by Fort Lauderdale's first builder, Edwin King. The Dade County pine **King-Cromartie House** *(229 S.W. 2nd Ave.)*, built in 1907 on New River Drive, was moved via river barge to its present site in 1971. *Guided walking tours (2hrs) of the complex available; reservations required. For schedules and departure points, contact the museum* ☎ *954-463-4431.*

★★ Museum of Discovery and Science – 🅺🆂 *401 S.W. 2nd St., 1 block south of Broward Blvd. Open year-round Mon–Sat 10am–5pm, Sun noon–6pm. Closed Dec 25. $6; $12.50 combo ticket (for museum and IMAX theater).* & 🅿($3) *www.mods.org* ☎ *954-467-6637.* Opened in 1992, this slick $30 million facility draws visitors of all ages. The three-story museum acquaints visitors with a variety of scientific fields ranging from ecology to physics—beginning with the fantastic

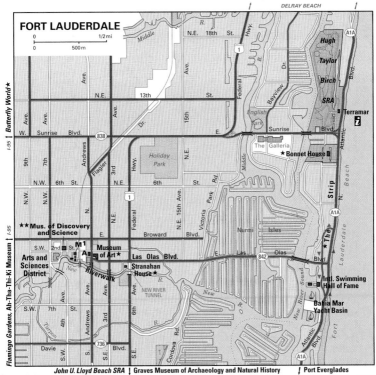

John U. Lloyd Beach SRA ┃ Graves Museum of Archaeology and Natural History ┃ Port Everglades

gravity clock just in front of the entrance. Florida Ecoscapes dominate the first floor: live trees and native plants form the setting for examples of local flora and fauna, including a colorful coral reef, an underground cave and a walk-in beehive. An adjacent gallery offers a series of interactive exhibits about anatomy, genetics and the human body.

On the second floor a new exhibit, Gizmo City, gives visitors a chance to play virtual volleyball and surf the Internet. Other highlights include the **Manned Maneuvering Unit** ride and the **Space Flight Simulator**, which re-creates a trip to the moon. The museum also features a changing selection of exhibitions from science centers around the US. Downstairs, an IMAX theater shows a variety of films *(The Rolling Stones, Antarctica, Blue Planet)* on a five-story-high screen *(year-round; call for show times; $9; ☎ 954-463-IMAX)*. A well-stocked gift shop flanks the entrance.

ADDITIONAL SIGHTS

International Swimming Hall of Fame – *1 Hall of Fame Dr., off A1A. Open year-round daily 9am–7pm. Closed Thanksgiving Day & Dec 25. $3.* ♿ ☎ *954-462-6536.* This museum and aquatic complex, built in 1965 and updated with a $13 million renovation in 1990, centers around two 10-lane, 50m Olympic pools, which host international, national and regional swimming, diving and water-polo competitions. Above the gift shop, a 10,000sq ft **exhibition hall** is dedicated to the sports of swimming, diving, water polo and synchronized swimming. Descriptive panels, photographs and memorabilia illustrate the history of each sport and its inclusion in the Olympics. Visitors can access biographies of famous international aquatic athletes on a touch screen. The adjoining Huizenga Theater offers short videos on water safety and other topics.

Hugh Taylor Birch State Recreation Area – *3109 E. Sunrise Blvd. and A1A. Open year-round daily 8am–dusk. $3.25/vehicle.* △ ♿ **P** ☎ *954-564-4521.* The original property on which the park lies was purchased for $1 per acre by Chicago attorney Hugh Taylor Birch, who came south in 1893 in search of a tranquil respite from city life. Donated for use as a state park in 1942, the 180-acre site rests on a barrier island between the Atlantic Ocean and the Intracoastal Waterway. Ringed today by urban development, the park extends along 1.5mi of beachfront and includes a lagoon system, mangrove swamps and hardwood hammocks. Birch's former home, Terramar (c.1940), now houses the **Terramar Visitor Center** *(open year-round weekends & holidays 10am–5pm).*

★**Bonnet House** – *900 N. Birch Rd. Visit by guided tour (1hr 15min) only, mid-Sept–mid-Aug Wed–Fri 10am–2pm, weekends noon–3pm. $9.* **P** *www. bonnethouse.com* ☎ *954-563-5393.* Nestled into a 35-acre wooded oasis in the midst of modern Fort Lauderdale, this two-story coral rock and Dade County pine house reflects the talent and imagination of its architect, Chicago muralist **Frederic Clay Bartlett** (1873-1953). The land on which the house is built was a wedding present to Bartlett and his first wife, Helen, from her father, Hugh Taylor Birch *(above)*, who owned 3mi of oceanfront property (A1A now separates the estate from the beach). Avid art collectors, the Bartletts purchased an impressive group of paintings in their travels. After Helen died suddenly of cancer in 1925, Frederic donated 24 works by post-Impressionist masters, including Georges Seurat's *A Sunday On La Grande Jatte*, to the Art Institute of Chicago in his wife's memory *(see Michelin Green Guide to Chicago)*.

Six years later, Bartlett married Evelyn Fortune Lilly. An artist in her own right, Evelyn encouraged her husband to add touches of whimsy, such as an aviary, the marine mural on the ceiling of the south loggia, and the fanciful shell inlay in the north loggia, to their winter residence. After Frederic's death, Evelyn continued to winter here. Having no heirs, she deeded the property to the Florida Trust for Historic Preservation in 1983.

Visit – *1.5hrs.* A peaceful lagoon rimmed with stately Royal palms fronts Bartlett's 1920 interpretation of a plantation house with its wrought-iron balustrades from New Orleans—a design that he intended as a reaction against the craze for Mediterranean Revival architecture that Addison Mizner *(p 228)* was perpetuating at the time up the coast in Palm Beach. Named for the yellow Bonnet lilies that still bloom at the south end of the lagoon, the 30-room structure contains the family's eclectic collection of furnishings and objets d'art. The **music room** showcases an 1871 square Steinway piano and a delicately carved marble bust of *The Veiled Lady* by Italian sculptor Giuseppe Croff. Evelyn's realistic portraits and still-life paintings hang in the former guest wing.

The first building on the estate, Bartlett's **studio**, with its high beamed ceiling and two-story north window, displays his works as well as some of those that he collected. Also on the grounds are the tiny, round shell museum and the adjoining orchid house, where multicolored examples of Evelyn's favorite flower grow.

EXCURSIONS *Map p 180*

John U. Lloyd Beach State Recreation Area – *2hrs. 4mi south in Dania. 1mi north of intersection of Dania Beach Blvd. and A1A at 6503 N. Ocean Dr. Open year-round daily 8am–dusk. $4/vehicle.* ✗ & 🄿 ☎ *954-923-2833.* Named after the man who was Broward County's District Attorney for more than 30 years, this 251-acre park provides a haven from the urban sprawl that surrounds it. Affording great views, uncrowded beaches and quiet forests, this microcosm of South Florida flora and fauna occupies the northern end of a narrow, elongated barrier island within view of Port Everglades. An 11,500ft-long **beach** is dotted with shaded picnic sites and sea-turtle nesting areas, and extends northward to a paved fishing jetty. Whiskey Creek, a mangrove-lined tidal waterway, divides the park along its length and harbors manatees and abundant bird life. A hardwood forest and man-made wetland fill the park's interior. A self-guided walk *(45min)* traverses the hammock.

Graves Museum of Archaeology and Natural History – *2hrs. 6mi south in Dania. From Las Olas Blvd., take US-1 south to museum entrance on S.E. 4th Terrace (.5mi south of Stirling Rd.). Open year-round Tue–Sat 10am–6pm, Sun 1pm–5pm. Closed Jan 1, Thanksgiving Day, Dec 25. $6.* & 🄿 *www.gravesmuseum.org* ☎ *954-925-7770.* Exhibits in this two-story, peach-colored building chronicle a range of archaeological periods including the days of ancient Egypt and Florida's early history and geology. The first gallery contains a large collection of minerals, featuring an 8ft 7in-long **quartz crystal** weighing 6,600 pounds, as well as a delicate assemblage of Florida fossil shells. In a connecting hallway, three life-size dioramas trace the development of Florida's first peoples. Guarded by a giant statue of Neptune, the dimly lit **Maritime Gallery** simulates an underwater environment, showcasing artifacts recovered from shipwrecks. Here visitors learn about the early exploration of Florida's coast and the techniques used in underwater archaeology.
Exhibits on South America highlight Peruvian and Columbian pottery, sculpture and jewelry; note the extensive collection of **miniature vessels** dating from AD 1100-1450. Marking the center of another gallery is a Turkish Mugla house, its characteristic sitting room furnished with plush rugs and richly colored pillows. A replica of King Tut's tomb heralds the Ancient Egyptian gallery. Under development is a new African exhibit using masks, beadwork and wall hangings to show the evolution of society from prehistory through colonial times to the present day.

★ **Butterfly World** – 🄺🄸🄳🅂 *1.5hrs. 10mi north in Coconut Creek. Take I-95 to Sample Rd.; continue west 4mi to 3600 W. Sample Rd.; enter at Tradewinds Park, on left. Open year-round Mon–Sat 9am–5pm, Sun 1pm–5pm. Closed Thanksgiving Day & Dec 25. $10.95* ✗ & 🄿 *www.butterflyworld.com* ☎ *954-977-4400.* Tucked away in a county recreational park, Butterfly World offers a pleasant walk through a screened-in aviary landscaped with waterfalls and bright blooms to resemble a tropical rain forest. Inside, some 2,000 rainbow-colored butterflies flit around, vying with the flowers in beauty. Outside the aviary, a rose garden and vine-covered arbor surround a small pond, attracting local species of the order Lepidoptera. A small pavilion here contains mounted specimens of exotic insects and butterflies from around the world.

Young Visitors Enjoy Butterfly World

© Barry Barker/Odyssey/Chicago

191

Flamingo Gardens – *3hrs. 16.5mi west in Davie. Take I-595 west to Flamingo Rd.; continue 3mi south to entrance on left at 3750 Flamingo Rd. Open daily Oct–May 9:30am–5:30pm. Rest of the year Tue–Sun 9:30am–5:30pm. $10.* ✕ ⌗ ⓟ ☎ *954-473-2955.* Lush tropical plantings now grace the grounds of the former citrus plantation owned by Floyd and Jane Wray. After Floyd's death in 1959, Jane set up a foundation to develop botanical gardens here in memory of her late husband. Today paved paths traverse a mosaic of tropical plants and a narrated tram tour *(30min; $2)* takes visitors through a wetlands area and part of the original citrus grove. The Wrays' original home, furnished with period pieces, operates as a museum *(open year-round daily 11am–5pm)*. Displays of alligators, crocodiles and birds of prey, a walk-through aviary and daily wildlife encounters *(12:30pm, 1:30pm & 2:30pm)* add to the fun.

Ah-Tha-Thi-Ki Museum – *3hrs. 65mi west of Fort Lauderdale via I-75. Take I-75 west to Rte. 833 (Exit 14); turn north 17mi to Big Cypress Seminole Indian Reservation. Open year-round Tue–Sun 9am–5pm. $6.* ⌗ ⓟ ☎ *954-792-0745.* The name of this $12 million museum, opened in August 1997 by the Seminole Indians, means "a place to learn, a place to remember." Upon arrival, visitors view a 17min orientation movie on the Seminoles' 300-year history in Florida. The 5,000sq ft exhibit hall presents a series of dioramas and displays illustrating tribal customs and beliefs, including such artifacts as traditional jewelry, clothing, weapons and musical instruments—some on loan from the Smithsonian Institution. Students of culture can learn more about the Seminoles through interactive computer technology; there's also a reference library and a folklore theater. Outside the museum building, signs along a 1.5mi boardwalk identify native medicinal and other plants. About halfway along its route stands a "living village" of chickee homes where members of the 2,000-strong Seminole tribe can be seen cooking and creating such traditional crafts as wood carvings, handmade dolls and basketry. Ritual ceremonies and dancing may be performed on special occasions *(call ahead for information)*.

MIAMI★★★

Population 365,127
Map of Principal Sights p 3 – Map p 195
Tourist Information ☎ 305-539-3060 or 800-283-2707 (US & Canada)

Renowned for its tantalizing tropical landscape of blue sky, aqua waters and fabulous white beaches, Miami is one of the most popular resort destinations in the US. Each year some nine million visitors from around the world pour into the city that the late resident author and conservationist Marjory Stoneman Douglas characterized as "the most maddening, stimulating, life-encouraging city in the world." In this winter playground they enjoy golf, tennis, yachting, deep-sea fishing, scuba diving, a lively nightlife and a seemingly inexhaustible supply of sunshine. And owing to its key position on the Florida Straits near the southeast tip of the state, Miami boasts the largest cruise-ship port in the US, serving some 3.5 million visitors who pass through annually on their way to and from the Caribbean.

Geographical Notes

Greater Miami embraces all of Miami-Dade County along with numerous islands, including Miami Beach, a long, narrow barrier island located 2.5mi off the mainland between Biscayne Bay and the Atlantic Ocean. Primarily flat, the topography averages only 10ft above sea level, with a narrow limestone ridge (5mi across at its widest point) running north-south along the coast. Mangrove swamps and hardwood hammocks that once bordered the ridge are now gone, but the region still boasts lush vegetation such as bougainvillea, banyan trees, poincianas and palms. Until the early 20C, the EVERGLADES were an unbroken wilderness in this region, stretching almost to Biscayne Bay. The Glades met the limestone ridge near the modern intersection of N.W. 32nd Avenue and 18th Terrace, creating a waterfall that in turn formed the headwaters of the 4mi-long Miami River. In 1909 the falls were cut off from the main body of the river when the man-made Miami River Canal was dredged in order to drain water from the Everglades.

To the east of downtown lies 39mi-long Biscayne Bay. Seven causeways link the mainland to Miami Beach, while an eighth, Rickenbacker Causeway, brings auto traffic to Virginia Key and Key Biscayne, situated to the south.

Size and Population – Sprawling along the coast, the 2,400sq mi Miami metropolitan area—stretching from Aventura, at the north border of Miami-Dade County, south to Homestead—is actually a collection of 27 municipalities that lend the city a complex persona at once urban and small-town. The actual City of Miami consists of the 1.5sq mi downtown district at the mouth of the river as well as several other communities that are annexed to the city but retain strong characters of their own. Among these are Coconut Grove and Coral Gables. Most of the county comprises densely populated business and residential sections, but southern Miami-Dade County remains largely agricultural.

In 1995 the population of Miami-Dade County reached just over two million people, with nearly one-fifth of them living in the City of Miami—making it Florida's largest in terms of population. Of the total county headcount, 20.5 percent was African American, 30.3 percent was Caucasian (and other), and 49.2 percent was Latin. As a result, distinct ethnic communities have also sprung up, most notably Little Havana, just west of downtown; Little Haiti, west of Biscayne Boulevard below 79th Street; and the African-American neighborhoods of Overtown, Liberty City and Brownsville. Even as this ethnic diversity has led to tense confrontations, the mix is precisely what makes Miami so interesting.

Historical Notes

Early Explorers – When Pedro Menéndez de Avilés came ashore here in October 1566, he found he had been preceded by a group of ragged mutineers who had been put off a ship sailing from the Spanish fort of San Matéo near present-day JACKSONVILLE. The mutineers had established friendly relations with the Indians, and in return for amnesty agreed to remain and help Menéndez establish a permanent settlement. In 1567 about 30 additional Spanish colonists, led by a Jesuit priest, arrived to found a Catholic mission. At first the mission prospered, but within a year relations with the Indians deteriorated. After a soldier killed a Tequesta elder, Indians retaliated by murdering four soldiers and subsequently drove the remaining Europeans out. During the next century and a half, the Tequesta population was drastically reduced by disease and by wars with the Creek Indians. When Florida became a British Colony in 1763 at the end of the French and Indian War, the remaining Tequestas accompanied the retreating Spanish to Cuba.

Pirates, Wreckers, and Pioneers – Cut off by the Everglades, South Florida attracted few settlers in the next century. Of those, most made their livings as wreckers, salvaging spoils from ships that ran aground on the treacherous reefs of the Florida Straits. Some operated legitimately; others were pirates. Legend has it that the most notorious of these buccaneers, known as Black Caesar (he was said to be an African prince who escaped from a wrecked slave ship), purposely sent navigators off course by lighting decoy fires on shore. It was then a simple matter to plunder stranded vessels of everything from gold doubloons to casks of rum. The area between lower Biscayne Bay and the Atlantic Ocean is still known as Caesar's Creek.

In 1808 John Egan, a salvager from the Bahamas, petitioned the Spanish government in Cuba for one of the land grants in South Florida and received 100 acres at the mouth of the Miami River. By the mid-1830s a handful of pioneers had settled in the area, then dominated by the 2,500-acre sugarcane plantation of Richard Fitzpatrick, which incorporated Egan's original holdings. In 1836, however, these early settlements were obliterated by Indians in the early stages of the Second Seminole War. As a result of the increasing Indian threat, the US Government established a military encampment called **Fort Dallas** on the former Fitzpatrick plantation on the north side of the river in 1838. When the Second Seminole War ended in 1842, Fitzpatrick sold his former plantation to his nephew, William English, who rebuilt on the site of the abandoned fort and platted a town on the south side of the river. His name for the new town, Miami, is thought to derive from an Indian word meaning "sweet water." (The Indians first used the name *Mayami* for Lake Okeechobee; in the 19C it was applied to the Miami River, and ultimately to the city.)

In 1855 Fort Dallas reopened during the third Seminole War. When the fort closed for the final time in 1858, only a few scattered pioneers were established here. Early settlers earned a living milling coontie starch, the baking staple first used by the Tequestas. Known as "Florida arrowroot," coontie was used in puddings, breads and cakes, and was sold by the barrel in Key West. Its manufacture remained a local industry throughout the 19C. Wrecking also thrived, now legitimized through formal contracts between salvage companies and underwriters.

The Mother of Miami – By the late 19C, **William and Mary Brickell** and **Julia Tuttle** were the two major landholders in the area. Brickell, a native of Steubenville, Ohio, bought part of the William English tract on the south side of the Miami River in 1870 and opened a store. He traded mostly with the Seminoles, who came by canoe. By 1880 the Brickell family owned all of the prime bayfront land south to Coconut Grove.

Meanwhile, Julia Tuttle, a widow from Cleveland, had purchased 40 acres on the north side of the river in 1891. Her campaign to put the fledgling town on the map soon earned her the title "Mother of Miami." Failing to convince Henry Plant *(p 279)* to bring his railroad this far south, Mrs. Tuttle shifted her efforts to **Henry Flagler**, whose Florida East Coast Railway (FEC) extension to St. Augustine had already transformed that town into a booming resort. The turning point came with the devastating freezes of 1894-95. This series of cold snaps decimated citrus groves in central and north Florida, but did not touch the south. To prove it, the story goes, Tuttle sent Flagler a bunch of orange blossoms that had continued to flower in the tropical climate despite the frost farther north.

Flagler was convinced. In exchange for riparian rights and half of Tuttle's land, the entrepreneur laid out streets, supplied the town with water and electricity, financed a channel across the bay and donated land for the first community buildings. In April 1896, the first train chugged into the village of 300 citizens, which was incorporated three months later (by then a boomtown with a population nearing 800). The following year the grand **Royal Palm Hotel** opened on the old Fort Dallas site, complete with swimming pool, elevators and a park landscaped with hundreds of coconut palms. Designed to attract tourists to the city that advertised itself as "America's sun porch," the five-story, yellow clapboard building contained 350 guest rooms. Unfortunately, Flagler's hotel fell victim to the 1926 hurricane and was demolished several years later.

Prior to the founding of Miami, independent "pre-railroad" communities had sprouted up elsewhere in the area. Among the most significant were Coconut Grove, south of Miami, and Lemon City, around N.E. 61st Street, a bustling commercial port in its own right. In 1904 Flagler extended the FEC tracks into South Miami-Dade, spawning a string of railroad towns, including Goulds, Princeton and Homestead (near the end of the line), and opening up this rural farm belt to a national market for the fruits and vegetables grown there.

Black communities in Coconut Grove, Lemon City and downtown Miami also thrived. By 1920 Bahamian and American blacks accounted for one-third of the population. Some 5,000 lived in the so-called Colored Town laid out by Tuttle and Flagler west of the railroad tracks in the area of N.W. 6th and 12th Streets. Many prospered as businessmen, doctors and tradesmen.

Boom, Bust and Recovery – Miami enjoyed its heyday in the years following World War I, the famed era of movie stars, luxury hotels and unprecedented real-estate development. By the 1920s, land was selling so fast that citrus and vegetable growers in the area began posting "not for sale" signs. On the average, the City of Miami issued 10 real-estate licenses a day. In most cases, only a 10 percent deposit, or "binder," was required to hold a lot. Since it was legal to sell before the balance was due, property often changed hands sight-unseen many times in a single day—with the addition of an inflated profit to each new sale.

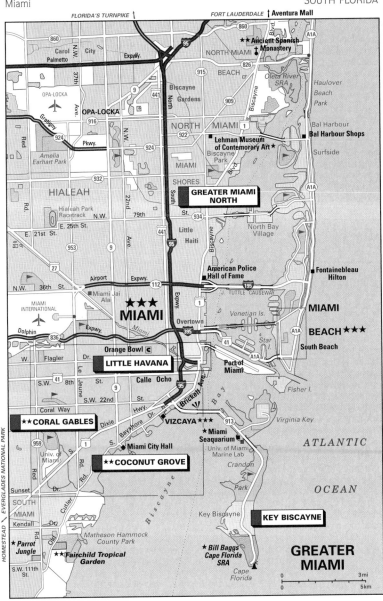

While growth corresponded directly to the development of the FEC and the federal highway system, a handful of brilliant visionaries earn the real credit for creating the pastel boomtowns that put Miami on the map as the "Sunshrine" of America. With its tropical climate and exotic foliage, South Florida was so unfamiliar that it might as well have been a foreign destination. Deliberately capitalizing on the air of fantasy, a number of developers lured buyers with the promise of something new and different: Carl Fisher's Miami Beach; George Merrick's planned Mediterranean paradise, Coral Gables, complete with man-made canals and costumed gondoliers imported from Italy; and the North Miami-Dade developments of Hialeah and Miami Springs, created by James Bright and Glen Curtiss beginning in the early 1920s.

Whole towns were created from the ground up. The stranger the idea, the better the publicity. Curtiss' 1926 design for **Opa-locka**, north of the present-day Miami International Airport, for example, featured some 100 Arabian-style buildings (some still standing) inspired by *The One Thousand and One Tales from the Arabian Nights*.

The mid-1920s marked the beginning of the end. Anti-Florida propaganda and tax investigations had already put a damper on investment by 1925, when a Miami cargo embargo—forced by a backlog of unloaded steamship and railroad freight—severely affected the state's economy. To make matters worse, a freighter capsized and blocked the channel for three weeks in 1926. In September of that year, a deadly hurricane swept in and dealt the final blow. Killing more than 100 people, the violent storm devastated tropical landscaping, damaged nearly every building downtown and ruined several businesses. As the economy faltered, banks closed and sidewalks led to nowhere in unfinished subdivisions.

While Florida's troubles may have preceded the 1929 crash, the state's economy was also among the first in the country to revive. Ironically, Prohibition helped. Eager for tourists, officials generally turned a blind eye not only to illegal gambling but also to rumrunners who smuggled so much liquor into South Florida from the Bahamas that Miami was dubbed the "leakiest spot in America." In 1931 the state legalized pari-mutuel betting. By the 1940s, however, organized crime dominated the gambling scene, with the S & G (Stop and Go) syndicate controlling dozens of bookies operating mainly out of Miami Beach hotels.

Tourists from the North poured in. Even the Indians got into the act, opening Seminole villages in the Everglades to visitors, who were lured in with such spectacles as alligator wrestling. Joining the northern visitors were thousands of Latin American travelers arriving by sea plane at the Pan American Air Terminal opened in Coconut Grove in 1934. During the 1930s, the Federal Works Project also generated jobs in the area, as buildings and parks were financed under the government program— among them the Miami Beach Post Office and Liberty Square, the first public housing project for blacks in Florida.

Miami Goes To War – "Grimly, earnestly and willingly, Miami assumed the mantle of a community at war," reported the *Miami Herald* in 1941. To save South Florida from another depression, officials lobbied the government to use Miami and Miami Beach as major training centers. Accordingly, the city doffed its fun-loving facade and took on the role of war camp: 147 chic hotels in Miami Beach were transformed into military barracks; the area's beaches and golf courses became drill fields and parade grounds. Expensive restaurants and elite social clubs were employed as mess halls. In 1942 the US Navy moved its Gulf Sea Frontier headquarters from Key West to the Alfred I. du Pont Building in Miami to monitor German submarine activity in the Florida Straits. Also that year, the Sub-Chaser School opened at the Port of Miami, where more than 50,000 Navy recruits were trained.

At the end of the war servicemen flowed into the city to take advantage of inexpensive housing—available for no money down—and educational opportunities offered by the University of Miami under the G.I. Bill. During the war, the Army, Navy and Marines had all run flying schools in the area and the air industry continued to burgeon here. Miami International Airport was established at the original Pan Am base at N.W. 36th Street, where World War I flying ace **Eddie Rickenbacker** had helped start Eastern Airlines several years earlier.

Growing Pains – The relative calm of the Eisenhower years ended abruptly with the 1959 Communist revolution in Cuba. The proximity of Miami to that Caribbean country and its similar climate made the American city a logical destination for exiles fleeing Fidel Castro's new government. In 1961, 1,180 US-trained Freedom Fighters were taken prisoner in Cuba after the failed invasion at the Bay of Pigs. By 1962 the US promised Nikita Khrushchev not to invade the island in return for the removal of Russian missile bases discovered there. Some 100,000 refugees already living in Miami now faced an indefinite stay. Beginning in 1965, a series of airlifts bringing families from Cuba to Miami increased the Cuban refugee population to 400,000, creating an exile community here that is said to be more like Havana than Havana itself.

For the most part, Miamians embraced the exiles, who were predominantly educated and hardworking. Tensions mounted, however, when more jobs started going to Cubans than to locals; black workers in particular felt displaced. As immigrants from Central and South America also poured in, the city became predominantly Latin. The intensity of growing anti-Hispanic sentiment was underlined in 1980 when the city voted to rescind a 1973 bilingual ordinance. The socioeconomic climate further deteriorated when the 1980 Mariel boatlift from Cuba dumped some 125,000 refugees, including criminals released from Cuban prisons, onto Miami streets.

That same year, a violent riot broke out in Liberty City when four white policemen were acquitted by an all-white jury in the beating death of a black insurance salesman. The three-day clash left 19 dead and caused more than $50 million in damages. Much of the Anglo population began to flee, prompting an oft-quoted bumper-sticker slogan: "Will the last American leaving Miami please bring the flag?"

By the mid-1980s, the national recession had hit Miami hard. The newest downtown office tower, One Biscayne Boulevard, went bankrupt, banks foreclosed on unfinished condos, shopping malls stood half-rented and the new billion-dollar Metrorail ran virtually empty. For a time it appeared the only people profiting in the faded resort were the "Cocaine Cowboys," reportedly generating $10 billion a year in illegal drug smuggling.

Modern Multicultural Metropolis – It seems only fitting in this city of fantasy and drama that a popular television show helped spark the most recent comeback. The resounding success of *Miami Vice* (1984-1989), which starred Don Johnson and Philip Michael Thomas, not only embedded exotic visions of glass block, pink stucco, neon and palm trees firmly in the national consciousness, but also managed to give Miami's seamy underside an edge of alluring intrigue. A more tangible economic boost came from a new **Free Trade Center** established in the early 1980s near the airport, along with an increasing number of US companies with Latin American trade locating their headquarters in Coral Gables. The 34,000-seat convention center in Miami Beach (host to both the Democratic and Republican national conventions in 1972) attracts international trade shows throughout the year. The city is also known as the site of the annual **Orange Bowl Parade** *(held on New Year's Eve)* and home to four major professional sports teams.

Downtown, innovative office towers designed by Miami's stellar architectural firm, Arquitectonica International, compose the dramatic city skyline, while the elegant Miami Dade Cultural center has done much to polish Miami's cultural image. The **Port of Miami**, the world's busiest cruise harbor, contributed $7 billion to the city's economy in 1993-94. In addition to being a shipping hub for agricultural produce, the port serves a total of eight cruise lines and boasts an annual passenger count nearing three million. Despite the income generated by the port and by commercial fishing and shell-fishing, however, Miami counts tourism as its top industry.

Unfortunately, it is not the city's many assets that have put Miami in national headlines in recent years. In the early 1990s, the city became the focus of public attention when a rash of violent highway murders occurred as robbers preyed on tourists in rental cars. In August 1992, **Hurricane Andrew**, one of the most devastating natural disasters in American history, blasted Greater Miami and caused an estimated $30 billion in damage. Andrew hit South Miami-Dade County the hardest.

Fall 1994 marked a new influx of refugees preceding the return of Haiti's President Jean-Bertrand Aristide to power at the end of the year. Around the same time, Fidel Castro sanctioned the emigration of Cuban citizens, presumably to force negotiations on the US trade embargo. In just a few weeks, thousands of refugees fled Havana on makeshift rafts. In the meantime, thousands more were detained at the US naval base in Guantanamo (on the eastern tip of Cuba), as well as in Panama. The refusal by US officials to let the refugees—many of them children—travel on to America provoked heated demonstrations and highly vocal rebukes from Miami's Cuban exile community. In 1994 President Clinton ended America's open-door policy and set a quota on the number of Cubans immigrating to the US.

No doubt, Miami will continue to struggle with its multifaceted image as it continues to reinvent itself. The city, however, has never pretended to be a simple place. "If you want sustained stability," former Florida Gov. Bob Graham once said, "don't come to Miami. But if dealing with change is a challenge, Miami is for you."

DOWNTOWN *Map p 201*

A vibrant 1.5sq mi quarter surrounded on three sides by the warm waters of Biscayne Bay and the Miami River, Miami's downtown exudes the bustling atmosphere of a Latin city. Here retailers purveying electronic goods, jewelry, clothing and fragrances in Spanish and Portuguese draw visitors from Cuba, Puerto Rico and Latin America. The site of the city's first wooden commercial structures now features a dense array of government and office buildings in a host of architectural styles including Neoclassical, Art Deco, Mediterranean Revival and the stark contemporary design of the skyscrapers that illuminate Miami's night skyline.

Historical Notes – The small commercial area built by Henry Flagler was incorporated as the City of Miami in July 1896 (1996 marked the city's centennial). Shortly thereafter, the intersection surrounding Avenue D and 12 Street (renamed Miami Avenue and Flagler Street, respectively, in 1920 when the present street system was introduced by Josiah Chaille) emerged as the hub of the business district, as well as one of the city's first upscale residential areas. On Christmas night 1896, a fire devoured most of the small downtown. Vulnerable frontier buildings were quickly replaced with new masonry structures that adhered to a vernacular style of architecture. The downtown's best example of vernacular storefront architecture is the 1914 **Chaille Block** *(Miami Ave. between N.W. 4th and N.W. 5th Sts.)*, which was recently incorporated into the facade of the new federal prison.

By World War I, Miami's downtown had exceeded its original borders and a bustling port was operating along the bayfront. New hotels and stores incorporated open walkways beneath a second-floor verandah, an architectural style clearly suited to the subtropics. Several such structures remain, notably the 1912 **Waddell Building** *(24-36 N. Miami Ave.)*.

Florida's real-estate boom of the mid-1920s resulted in the emergence of the city's first skyline along Biscayne Boulevard. Following the bust of Miami's real-estate market and the hurricane that devastated the south Florida coast in 1926, new construction screeched to a halt in downtown Miami for a decade.

It was not until the late 1960s that this area reached its apex as a retailing, business and entertainment district. In recent years, the revivified quarter has welcomed a large cluster of contemporary high-rise hotels and office buildings, including **International Place** (aka CenTrust Tower; 1985, I.M. Pei & Partners), a 47-story tiered tower *(100 S.E. 1st St.)* lit nightly by colored lights, and the 55-story **First Union Financial Center** (1984, Edward Bassett, Skidmore, Owings & Merrill), the tallest building in Florida *(200 S. Biscayne Blvd.)*. The spread of downtown south of the Miami

Getting There

By Air – **Miami International Airport** (MIA): 7mi northwest of downtown; international and domestic flights; ☎ 876-7000. Multilingual Information Service, Concourse B, D and G *(open daily 11am–10pm)*, Concourse E *(open daily year-round)*. Transportation to downtown: SuperShuttle *($9)* ☎ 871-8210, taxi *($15-$18)*, Metrobus and hotel courtesy shuttles. Rental car agencies *(p 323)* located near airport.

By Train and Bus – Amtrak **train** station: 8303 N.W. 37th Ave., information ☎ 835-1221; reservations ☎ 800-872-7245. Greyhound/Trailways **bus:** Miami International Airport; 4111 N.W. 27th St. and 700 Biscayne Blvd.; Miami Beach: 7101 Harding Ave. For reservations ☎ 800-231-2222.

Getting Around

By Public Transportation – Miami-Dade Transit Agency operates a public transit system connecting Greater Miami and beaches via Metrorail, Metromover and buses. **Metrorail** trains serve downtown Miami extending northwest to Hialeah and south to Kendall *(daily 6am–midnight; every 20min, every 5min during peak hours; $1.25 each way, exact change only; free transfers to Metromover)*. **Metromover** elevated rail system links the Brickell Ave. and Omni areas, and loops around downtown *(daily 6am–midnight, every 2min; 25¢)*. Metrorail connections at Government Center and Brickell stations, with nearby public parking *($2/day, free on weekends)*. **Metrobus** operates county-wide *(Mon–Fri 4:30am–2am, weekend hours vary; $1.25 each way, exact change only; bus-to-rail transfers 25¢)*. Schedules and route information: ☎ 638-6700. Disabled visitors ☎ 263-5406.

Tri-Rail provides **commuter rail** service between West Palm Beach and Greater Miami connecting to Metrorail *(daily 5am–10:30pm except Thanksgiving Day & Dec 25; $3.50-$9.25 round-trip depending on zones traveled)*. For schedules and route information www.tri-rail.com ☎ 728-8445.

By Car – Miami is laid out on a grid: the intersection of Flagler St. and Miami Ave. divides the city into four quadrants: southwest, northwest, southeast and northeast. Avenues and courts run north-south; streets and terraces run east-west. Speed limit within city: 25mph unless otherwise posted. Signs with the orange "Follow the Sun" symbol *(right)* direct visitors to major tourist destinations (maps available at airport and from car rental agencies). Downtown metered **parking:** $1/hr. Parking lots and garages average 75¢-$1 for first hour, 50¢ each additional half hour. For information, call Miami Parking System *(Mon–Fri 7:30am–5:30pm)* ☎ 373-6789.

By Taxi – Metro Taxi ☎ 888-8888; Flamingo Taxi ☎ 885-7000; Yellow Cab ☎ 444-4444. **Water Taxi** shuttle services downtown area and Biscayne Bay *(departs Bayside Marina year-round daily 11am–11pm; every 25-30min; one-way $3.50, round-trip $6)*. Also operates Miami Beach run *(same hours; one-way $7, round-trip $12)* ☎ 954-467-6677.

General Information

Visitor Information – **Greater Miami Convention and Visitors Bureau**, 701 Brickell Ave., Suite 2700, Miami FL 33131 *(open year-round Mon–Fri 8:30am–5pm)* ☎ 539-3000 or 800-283-2707 (US and Canada). **Miami Beach Visitor Information Center**, 1920 Meridian Ave., Miami Beach FL 33139 *(open year-round Mon–Fri 9am–6pm, weekends 10am–4pm)* ☎ 672-1270. *These organizations provide additional information regarding shopping, entertainment, festivals (p 318) and recreation.*

Accommodations – *(p 324)* Area visitors' guide including lodging directory available (free) from the Greater Miami Convention and Visitors Bureau *(above)*. **Reservation service:** Greater Miami Hotel Assn. ☎ 531-3553 or 800-531-3553 (US). Central Reservation Service ☎ 274-6832 or 800-950-0232 (US and Canada) operates 24hr courtesy phones at airport. Accommodations range from downtown hotels ($125-$175), luxury beachfront hotels ($200 and up) to economy motels ($50-$100). Miami Beach International **Youth Hostel** ($13-$45) ☎ 534-2988. *Rates quoted are average prices per night for a double room and are subject to seasonal variations.*

Local Press – Daily news: *Miami Herald;* entertainment section *Weekend* (Friday). Spanish editions: *El Nuevo Herald* and *Diario Las Americas.* Periodicals: *Miami Beach Post* (twice weekly); *Miami New Times, Travelhost* and *Welcome* (weekly); *Citizen News* (monthly).

Foreign Exchange Office – *(p 321)* Thomas Cook *(Mon–Fri 9am–5pm, Sat 10am–2pm)* ☎ 381-9252; Miami International Airport Concourse E, 2nd floor *(open daily year-round)* ☎ 876-0040.

Sightseeing – For sightseeing tours, consult the *Greater Miami & the Beaches Vacation Planner* available from the Greater Miami Convention and Visitors Bureau. Daily cruises around Greater Miami and Fort Lauderdale operate from Bayside Marina and the docks at 24th St. and Collins Ave. Miami Beach Art Deco Historic District **walking and bike tours** *(p 223)*. Dr. Paul George's Historic Tours—including Little Havana—are sponsored by The Historical Museum of Southern Florida *(Oct–Jun; boat tours, dinner in Coral Gables, gallery tours and walking tours);* for schedules ☎ 375-1625.

Shopping – **Downtown:** Omni International Mall and shopping district, Bayside Marketplace *(p 201)*, Fashion District. **Coconut Grove:** CocoWalk *(p 212)*, Streets of Mayfair *(p 212)*. **Miami Beach:** Lincoln Road Mall *(p 226)*. **North Miami Beach:** Bal Harbour Shops. **South Miami-Dade:** Dadeland Mall.

Entertainment – Consult the arts and entertainment section of local newspapers *(above)* for schedules of cultural events and addresses of theaters and concert halls. To purchase tickets, contact the box office or **Ticketmaster** ☎ 358-5885.

Venue	Performances	Tickets ☎
Miami-Dade County Auditorium	Florida Grand Opera, Concert Association of Florida, visiting ensembles	358-5885
Colony Theater	Ballet Flamenco La Rosa, Off-Broadway, theater, dance, comedy, concerts, film festivals	674-1026
Jackie Gleason Theater	Miami City Ballet, touring shows and concerts	358-5885
Gusman Center for the Performing Arts	Florida Philharmonic Orchestra, Miami International Film Festival, concerts and plays by touring companies	372-0925
Coconut Grove Playhouse	Plays	442-4000

Sports and Recreation – **Tennis** courts are plentiful; some area hotels offer tennis instructions and clinics. For further information contact Miami-Dade Park and Recreation Department ☎ 755-7800. Public **golf** courses: Miami Springs Golf Course ☎ 882-1918; Normandy Shores Golf Course ☎ 868-6502; Key Biscayne Golf Course ☎ 361-9129.

Spectator Sports: Thoroughbred racing at Calder Race Course, 21001 N.W. 27th Ave. *(year-round Thu–Mon 12:30pm)*, www.calderracecourse.com ☎ 625-1311; Hialeah Park, 2200 E. 4th Ave. *(simulcast races year-round; live racing mid-Mar–late May)*, www.hialeahpark.com ☎ 885-8000; Gulfstream Park, 901 S. Federal Hwy., Hallandale *(Jan–mid-Mar; Wed–Mon)*, www.gulfstreampark.com ☎ 931-7223.

Greyhound racing at Flagler Greyhound Track, 401 N.W. 38th Court *(year-round daily)* ☎ 649-3000. **Miami Jai Alai** , 3500 N.W. 37th Ave at N.W. 36th St. *(Mon, Wed–Sat 7pm)*, www.decoweb.com/jai-alai ☎ 633-6400. **Miami Dolphins** (NFL) ☎ 620-2578; **University of Miami Hurricanes** sporting events ☎ 284-2263; **Miami Heat** (NBA) ☎ 577-4328; **Florida Marlins** (MLB) ☎ 626-7400, **Florida Panthers** (NHL) ☎ 768-1900. Purchase tickets for major sporting events at the box office or through Ticketmaster *(above)*.

Useful Numbers   ☎

Police/Ambulance/Fire	911
Police (non-emergency)	579-6111
Beach Patrol, City of Miami Beach	673-7711
Dental Referral (24hrs)	667-3647
24-hour Pharmacy: Walgreens, 12295 Biscayne Blvd.	893-6860
Main Post Office, 2200 N.W. 72nd Ave.	639-4280
Weather (recorded)	229-4522
Hurricane Information	229-4470

© Bill Wisser

Metromover at International Place

River along Brickell Avenue *(p 202)* has resulted in the emergence of that area—once lined with the homes of Miami's richest citizens—as an international financial district containing numerous Latin American and Caribbean banks and law firms. Miami currently boasts 76 international bank offices, as well as some 250 multinational corporations.

Sights *1/2 day*

★ **Miami-Dade Cultural Center** – *101 W. Flagler St. Open year-round Mon–Sat 9am–6pm (Thu until 9pm), Sun 1pm–5pm. Closed major holidays.* ♿ 🅿 ☏ *305-375-1896.* A complex of three Mediterranean Revival buildings—the Miami Art Museum, The Historical Museum of Southern Florida and the fortress-like Miami-Dade Public Library—the center rests atop an elevated 33,000sq ft tiled plaza that illustrates architect Philip Johnson's design for a cultural oasis above the busy downtown streets.

★ **Miami Art Museum (A)** – *Open year-round Tue–Fri 10am–5pm (Thu 9pm), weekends noon–5pm. Closed major holidays. $5.* ♿ 🅿 ☏ *305-375-3000.* Dedicated to presenting international art of the post-World War II era, with an emphasis on art of the Americas, the Center stages 10 major shows a year in its two levels of gallery spaces and auditorium. The permanent collection, a small selection of which is displayed on a rotating basis, includes 50 works by such noted contemporary artists as Christo, Alexander Calder, Max Ernst, Jasper Johns, Robert Rauschenberg and Rufino Tamayo. Exhibitions of new work change four times a year; from December 1998 to March 1999, for instance, the museum will host a George Segal retrospective. Raymond Duchamp-Villon's black marble sculpture *Cheval Majeur* stands near the museum's entrance.

★★ **The Historical Museum of Southern Florida (B)** – *Open year-round Mon–Sat 10am–5pm (Thu 9pm), Sun noon–5pm. Closed Jan 1, Thanksgiving Day, Dec 25. $5.* ♿ 🅿 ☏ *305-375-1492.* The Historical Association of Southern Florida and its museum represent the region's most important historical organization and facility. Housed on the museum's second floor, the permanent exhibit **"Tropical Dreams: A People's History of South Florida"** recounts the area's colorful past. The wealth of artifacts and mixed-media presentations include an early Tequesta Indian settlement, treasures from sunken Spanish galleons, a Conch house from the heyday of Key West's sponge trade and a 1923 trolley car. The first floor contains a gallery for temporary exhibits focusing on Miami history and folklife, and a research library with an extensive collection of books, maps and historical photographs.

US Federal Courthouse – *301 N. Miami Ave. Open year-round Mon–Fri 9am–4:30. Closed holidays.* ♿ 🅿 ☏ *305-536-4548.* Designed in 1931 by Phineas Paist and Harold D. Steward as a courthouse and post office, this three-story keystone Neo-classical gem now serves only the former function. Denman Fink's mural, *Law Guides Florida's Progress* (1940), a whimsical look at the wide array of peoples and occupations in the Sunshine State, decorates the central courtroom on the second floor. The building also contains a lovely Moorish courtyard.

Alfred I. du Pont Building – *169 E. Flagler St.* This Depression Moderne edifice (1939, Marsh and Saxelbye) was built as the headquarters of the Florida National Bank, which was controlled at the time by the du Pont family. On the exterior, 16 stories of polished limestone rise above the first level of black granite. During World War II, the US Navy appropriated a portion of this building for its local offices. After the war, the structure reestablished itself as one of downtown's most prominent professional addresses. Today it houses the offices of Capital Bank.

Claude and Mildred Pepper Bayfront Park – *Biscayne Blvd. between N.E. 4th and S.E. 2nd Sts.* Known locally as Bayfront Park, the 32-acre greensward was dredged from bay bottom in the mid-1920s. A popular venue for many decades, the park fell deserted in the 1970s as people moved out to the suburbs and city officials stopped using the site for public concerts and other events.

Isamu Noguchi, famed Japanese landscape architect, planned the park's $30 million face-lift in the late 1980s. Noguchi's design incorporates (from south to north) his sculptures—the *Challenger* Memorial **(1)** and *Slide Mantra* **(2)** for children—as well as a prominent fountain, a broad bayside promenade, a laser light tower **(3)** and a large amphitheater. These elements have helped restore the park's popularity.

★**Bayside Marketplace** – *401 Biscayne Blvd. Open year-round daily. Events* ☎ *305-377-4091.* Connected to the north side of Bayfront Park via sidewalk, an ambitious example of The Rouse Company's festival marketplaces sits on the northeastern edge of downtown Miami overlooking the turquoise waters of Biscayne Bay. Geographically separated from the downtown retail sector, Bayside and its profusion of boutiques, eateries and entertainment sprawls over 235,000sq ft of space. The complex, composed of several buildings connected by plazas and open-air walkways, was completed in 1987 at a cost of $68 million ($17 million in additional improvements were added in 1992). The lower level teems with vendors hawking ethnic wares and local souvenirs; the upper level is devoted to mainstream chain stores. Distinguishable from the waterfront by the giant yellow guitar atop the resident Hard Rock Cafe, Bayside Marketplace lures visitors with its beguiling ambiance and vibrant nightlife.

Pleasure and deep-sea fishing cruises are available on a wide variety of vessels berthed near Bayside's northern pavilion.

Miami News/Freedom Tower – *600 Biscayne Blvd.* One of Miami-Dade County's most striking buildings, the Miami News/Freedom Tower sits on the desolate northern edge of downtown. Designed by the famed New York architectural firm of Schultze and Weaver, whose credits also include the Biltmore *(p 206)* in Coral Gables and the Breakers *(p 229)* in Palm Beach, the Spanish Renaissance Revival building consists of a three-story base that buttresses a slim 12-story tower. At the top of the tower is a cupola inspired by the 16C Giralda Tower in Seville, Spain. The 1925 structure housed the *Miami News*, the city's first newspaper, for more than 30 years before it was transformed into a federal processing center for Cuban refugees in 1962. As a symbol of liberation for the Cuban community, it was renamed "Freedom Tower." After the federal government closed the center in the mid-1970s, it stood vacant for several years and fell into disrepair. In the late 1980s, the tower was restored to its original splendor. In 1997 it was purchased by the family of exiled Cuban revolutionary leader Jorge Mas Canosa, with plans to eventually build a museum of Cuban refugee history and culture here.

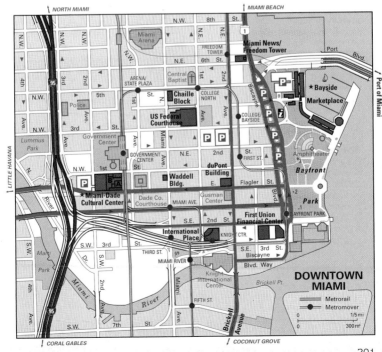

Brickell Avenue – Named for a wealthy pioneering family *(p 194)* who owned and developed a swath of desirable bayfront land south of the Miami River in the early 20C, Brickell Avenue is a broad, four-lane street—divided by a tree-shaded median—that parallels the contours of nearby Biscayne Bay for its entire 2mi length south of downtown. The avenue follows an old Indian trail that ran from the present-day site of Coconut Grove to the south side of the Miami River. The Brickell family designated this throughfare as the showcase for their lush, hand-some subdivisions. By the early 1900s, elegant estates began to spring up along the street, leading to its sobriquet "Millionaires' Row." Artist Louis Comfort Tiffany, Miami Beach developer Carl Fisher and politician William Jennings Bryan were among the most prominent residents of the neighborhood; Chicago entrepreneur James Deering erected his palatial Villa Vizcaya *(p 211)* at its southern end.

In the 1970s and 1980s, high-rise condominiums and modern office buildings began to replace the mansions. Soon an international financial center had emerged along Miami's new "Wall Street." During this period, several signature residential high-rises appeared, including **The Palace** *(no. 1541)*, recognizable by the striking stepped wing emanating from its east side; **The Imperial** *(no. 1627)*, with its red veneer, small, square windows and sloping roof; and **The Atlantis** *(no. 2025)*, whose much-photographed "skycourt" consists of a 37ft-square hole punched out of its central massing. This open-air cube contains a winding staircase and a live palm tree. Each of these structures was designed by Arquitectonica International, a local firm famous for its innovative, quirky designs and stunning use of color. Sitting between The Palace and The Imperial is the 28-story **Villa Regina** *(no. 1581)*, a condominium notable for its vivid color scheme, a product of the imaginative palette of Israeli artist Yacov Agam.

LITTLE HAVANA *Map pp 208-209*

Immediately east of downtown, a 3.3sq mi section of Miami bounded by the Miami River (east), S.W. 37th Avenue (west), N.W. Seventh Street (north) and Coral Way (south) represents one of the city's most lively and exotic neighborhoods. **Calle Ocho**, or Eighth Street—Little Havana's main thoroughfare—vibrates with a spirited street life where pungent tobacco and heady Cuban coffee scent the air, and English is rarely spoken. Here sidewalk vendors hawk a wide variety of wares and ubiquitous stand-up *cafeterias* dispense tiny cups of dense black *café cubano*. A bewildering variety of small businesses, including the tiny botanicas that sell religious para-phernalia for practitioners of *Santería*, a form of voodoo, cater to a Latin clientele.

A Haven for Refugees – Since the 1960s, the name Little Havana has been applied to several contiguous Miami neighborhoods whose destinies changed dramatically after Cubans fleeing the Castro regime began pouring into the area in 1959. Little Havana has remained a magnet for refugees from a variety of Spanish-speaking nations.

The district was a piney wilderness resting on an oolite limestone ridge when Miami incorporated as a city in 1896. In the early 20C, the smart suburbs of Riverside and Shenandoah spread west from the Miami River, occupying land that once con-tained fruit groves. By the late 1920s and early '30s, a large number of Eastern Europeans moved into the quarter, reaching their peak population in the early 1950s. Thereafter many of the developments' residents relocated to more remote suburbs and the old neighborhood declined.

By the mid-1950s, Hispanics occupied the quarter, paving the way for the subse-quent Cuban influx that reached flood proportions after the US commenced its "Freedom Flights" *(p 196)* in 1965. The large concentration of Cubans in the old neighborhood prompted its sobriquet, "Little Havana." Southwest Eighth Street, alternately known as Highway 41 and Tamiami Trail (so called because it connects Tampa to Miami), became the district's most important commercial thoroughfare.

Spanish Accents – Densely populated Little Havana is a poor community with a preponderance of young, struggling families and elderly residents. Although many Nicaraguans count among the 100,000 Hispanics who call Little Havana home, the sector remains the political nerve center of the influential Cuban exile colony. Refugees still seek sanctuary here, where virtually everyone speaks Spanish and housing—although limited—is inexpensive.

Cuban history is remembered in places such as **José Martí Park** *(351 S.W. 4th St.)*. Named for the apostle of Cuban independence (José Martí, 1853-1895), the park overlooks the western bank of the Miami River.

One of the quarter's most famous landmarks is the **Orange Bowl** *(1501 N.W. 3rd St.)*, a sports arena in the northern sector that was built in increments and com-pleted in 1979. Many college and professional football games have been played in the venerable stadium.

Each year on the second Sunday in March, Little Havana hosts the most popular of all Hispanic-oriented events, the **Calle Ocho Open House**. This gala street party, the culmination of a week-long Lenten festival known as Carnaval Miami, attracts in excess of one million revelers to a 2mi-long portion of Eighth Street.

Sights *1/2 day*

Visit the following sights beginning at S.W. 32nd Ave. and S.W. 8th St., and work your way east. Note that at S.W. 26th Ave., Calle Ocho becomes a one-way thoroughfare heading east. Metered parking is available on both sides of S.W. 8th St.

Woodlawn Park Cemetery – *3260 S.W. 8th St.* Miami's largest and one of its oldest (1913) burial spots, Woodlawn Park is the final resting place for thousands of Cuban refugees. The somber black marble wall commemorates the "Unknown Cuban Freedom Fighter" killed in the Bay of Pigs invasion. Two former exiled Cuban presidents, as well as Anastasio Somoza, longtime dictator of Nicaragua, are interred here.

Latin Quarter – So designated by the City of Miami in the late 1970s to promote the district as a tourist attraction, the Latin Quarter stretches along Calle Ocho between S.W. 17th and S.W. 12th Avenues. (The north-south portion of the quarter reaches from N.W. First to S.W. Ninth Streets.) Here quaint street lamps rise above red-brick sidewalks set with stars bearing the names of an international array of prominent Hispanic entertainers, including Julio Iglesias and Gloria Estefan.

Máximo Gómez Park – *Southeast corner of S.W. 15th Ave.* For a glimpse of local color drop by this tiny plaza, named for the Dominican Republic-born Chief of the Cuban Liberating Army and known locally as Domino Park. As they have been doing since the early 1960s, Cubans, primarily elderly men, assemble here daily for spirited games of dominoes (introduced to the hemisphere by the Spanish), chess, cards and checkers.

Cuban Memorial Plaza (A) – *In the median of S.W. 13th Ave./Cuban Memorial Blvd. and S.W. 8th St.* A hexagonal marble monument topped by a flickering eternal torch decorates this small square. Created in 1971 to honor those members of Brigade 2506 who lost their lives in the aborted invasion of Cuba in April 1961, the plaza now serves as a rallying point for political demonstrations.

Teatro Martí – *420 S.W. 8th Ave., at southwest corner of S.W. 4th St.* Several blocks southwest of the Miami River Inn *(p 204)* is Teatro Martí, one of Little Havana's oldest (founded in 1963) and the most important of the quarter's four theaters for film and live presentations. The theater is housed in the Riverside Commercial Building, built by the Ku Klux Klan as its headquarters in 1926.

① Versailles Restaurant

Map p 208. 3555 S.W. 8th St. ✗ ♿ 🅿 ☎ *305-444-0240.* Near the western perimeter of Little Havana lies the Versailles Restaurant, one of the quarter's most prominent attractions. In this large eatery you can enjoy café cubano from a stand-up counter inside or outside. Amid a swirl of fast-paced conversations, hearty Cuban sandwiches and heaping plates of food from a magazine-size menu are served inside the main dining room. Specialties include *ropa vieja* (shredded beef in a tomato-based sauce), *plátanos verdes* (fried green plantains), and desserts such as flan, a type of custard akin to *crème caramel.*

② Nicaragua Bakery

Map p 209. 1169 S.W. 8th St. ✗ ☎ *305-285-0239.* One of the most successful Nicaraguan businesses in Little Havana lies two blocks east of Memorial Plaza. Sample delicacies such as *tres leches* (three-milks cake), *torta des pasas* (raisin cake) and *torta de mantequilla* (butter cake) along with a steaming demi-tasse of *café cubano.*

③ El Crédito Cigar Factory

Map p 209. 1106 S.W. 8th St. ☎ *305-858-4162.* In 1969 the El Crédito company, which began in Havana in 1907, opened in Miami. The largest hand-rolled cigar factory in Miami-Dade County now produces more than one million cigars annually. Descendants of the founding Carillo family still own and operate the business, which claims Bill Cosby and Robert Goulet among its customers. Visitors can watch the cigar-making process through glass windows looking into the factory.

Templo Adventista del Septimo Dia (B) – *862 S.W. 4th St. at corner of 9th Ave.* Built in 1925 by the Seventh Day Adventist Church, this stucco structure exemplifies Mission-style architecture erected by the Spanish in many parts of their colonial empire. Today the congregation is largely Nicaraguan.

Dominoes Game at Máximo Gómez Park

© Robert Frerck/Odyssey/Chicago

Warner House – *111 S.W. 5th Ave.* This Neoclassical mansion was built in 1912 by the Warner family, who lived there and also used it as a venue for a successful floral business. Fully restored, it now houses the Miami-Dade County Historic Preservation Division, among other occupants.

Located one block east of Warner House, the **Miami River Inn (C)** *(118 S.W. South River Dr.)*, comprises several restored early 20C buildings that now function as a bed-and-breakfast inn.

★★CORAL GABLES *Map p 208*

Grandest and most successful of South Florida's boomtime developments, Coral Gables covers a 12.5sq mi area just southwest of downtown Miami and counts nearly 41,000 residents. The area is bounded roughly by S.W. 57th Avenue (Red Road) on the west, S.W. 37th Avenue (Douglas Road) on the east, S.W. Eighth Street (US-41) on the north and S.W. 72nd Street (Sunset Drive) on the south, and embraces a 6mi bayside stretch running south along Old Cutler Road. While largely residential, this city within a city also boasts a thriving center of international commerce, the University of Miami campus, three golf courses and some of the area's finest Mediterranean Revival architecture and mature tropical landscaping.

The City Beautiful – In 1899 Congregational minister Solomon Merrick moved to South Florida from Massachusetts with his wife Althea and their five children. There the Reverend Merrick purchased 160 acres for $1,100 in hopes of growing oranges, avocados and grapefruit. After Solomon died 13 years later, his oldest son, George, managed the grove, which prospered under his supervision and yielded one of the largest grapefruit crops in South Florida.

By 1921 **George Merrick** (1886-1942) had purchased 3,000 acres of undeveloped scrubland around the family groves to form the nucleus of a model suburb southwest of Miami. He dreamed of a comprehensively planned community in which buildings, streets, public plazas and utilities—discreetly out of sight—were all deliberately conceived together as part of a unified whole. Broad boulevards, formal entrances, sculpture and park-like landscaping more typically associated with European cities were important components of the scheme. Introduced to America at the 1893 World's Columbian Exposition in Chicago, such amenities were integral to the influential "City Beautiful" movement that swept the country in the decades following the Exposition.

To create "Miami's Master Suburb," Merrick assembled a team of top engineers, planners and designers. Among them were accomplished landscape architect **Frank Button**, artist **Denman Fink** (Merrick's uncle), and architects **H. George Fink**, **Phineas Paist** and **Walter DeGarmo**, the first registered architect in Florida. While early buildings were constructed of coral rock, most were eventually made of cheaper concrete, "aged" with special paint treatments. The prevailing style was **Mediterranean Revival**, a popular early 20C design featuring elements such as clay roof tiles, small towers, wrought ironwork, breezy courtyards and loggias. Borrowing heavily from both Spanish and Italian architecture, Merrick's Mediterranean Revival buildings exhibited, in his own words, "a combination of what seemed best in each (style), with an added touch of gaiety to suit the Florida mood."

Beginning in 1925, several small thematic villages designed to reflect the architecture of China, Italy, South Africa, France and the antebellum South added an exotic theatrical touch to Merrick's fantasy city. To maintain quality and uniformity of design, all new construction, including paint color, was subject to a review board. Extensive landscaping undertaken by a staff of 130 gardeners included some 100,000 flowering hibiscus, oleanders, poincianas and thousands of mature coconut palms designed to create an established look for the community.

Years in advance of official zoning laws, Merrick segregated business, manufacturing and public services into specific areas. Street lighting and fire alarms ensured safety. Luxury hotels, an exotic swimming pool *(p 207)*, a country club and playing fields offered recreational and social diversion. Churches and schools—including the first buildings of the University of Miami—met religious and educational needs.

Selling The Dream – Merrick's real genius lay in promotion. Budgeting $5 million for marketing alone, he opened sales offices in Atlanta and Chicago, operated a fleet of 86 buses to haul in prospective buyers, and managed a sales force of 3,000. Hawkers included **Edward "Doc" Dammers**, salesman extraordinaire and the city's first mayor, who sold lots from a horse-drawn wagon euphemistically dubbed a "mobile sales unit." Deliberately geared to all incomes, houses ranged from $4,000 bungalows to $75,000 mansions. In turn, a brilliantly devised series of canals (linking the landlocked community to Biscayne Bay) enabled Merrick to advertise 40mi of waterfront property—the "Miami Riviera"—in his development. By 1924 $7 million worth of lots in the new community had been sold. The next year Merrick's development received its charter, becoming the City of Coral Gables. Sales and construction screeched to a halt with the 1926 land bust, but the city revived after World War II. The original small-scale character of the downtown has since given way to high-rise development. In recent years, however, a new wave of restoration and strict historic preservation ordinances have promoted a revival of Mediterranean architecture, and today Coral Gables remains one of the most desirable residential enclaves in Greater Miami.

Sights *1 day*

To visit downtown, park on Miracle Mile (Coral Way) or Ponce de Leon Blvd. (metered parking) and walk. Giralda Ave. between Ponce de Leon Blvd. and Galiano St. is notable for its trendy restaurants; specialty shops on Aragon Ave. are also worth exploring. Apart from downtown, sights in Coral Gables are best reached by car; begin on Coral Way. Note that street names in the residential sections of Coral Gables are painted on white-washed concrete markers; look for them on corners, low to the ground. A free Coral Gables driving-tour map is available at the City Hall (405 Biltmore Way) information desk.

Coral Way – This busy thoroughfare is the main east-west artery in downtown Coral Gables. The four-block section between Douglas and LeJeune Roads has been renamed **Miracle Mile** (really a half-mile). Shops ranging from discount stores to chic bridal boutiques improve in quality as you move west. Fronted by Corinthian columns, the two-story, coral-colored 1926 **Colonnade Building** *(no. 169)* features a baroque, Spanish-inspired arched entrance topped by spires. Merrick built this imposing structure to house his sales offices. In later incarnations it served as a training center for World War II pilots and as real-estate offices; a bank now occupies the building. Walk inside to view the marble interior of the 75ft-high **rotunda**, connected to the Omni Colonnade Hotel tower built just north of the Colonnade Building in 1985.

Miracle Mile terminates at **City Hall** *(405 Biltmore Way)*. Designed by Phineas Paist and Denman Fink, this coral-rock monument topped by a three-tiered tower cost $200,000 to build in 1927. The curved, colonnaded front bay is slightly skewed so the building aligns with angled Biltmore Way.

Coral Gables Merrick House – *907 Coral Way. Visit by guided tour (45min) only, year-round Wed & Sun 1pm–4pm. Closed holidays. Grounds are open daily year-round. $2. & ▣ ☎ 305-460-5361.* George Merrick's two-story boyhood home was added to the modest frame cabin that Merrick's father built on the site c.1899. Designed by Merrick's mother, Althea, the house adapts Colonial New England architecture to the area's subtropical climate and indigenous oolite limestone (coral rock) and Dade County pine. The homestead—and later Merrick's planned community—was named for the structure's distinctive gabled roof. In 1976 the City of Coral Gables acquired the house and restored it. The interior is appointed with period and Merrick family furnishings, including the Baldwin grand player piano owned by Althea Merrick; surrounding gardens contain trees from the family's original plantation.

Houses along Coral Way between Toledo and Madrid Streets represent a variety of interpretations of the area's Mediterranean Revival architecture. Three doors west of Coral Gables Merrick House is **Poinciana Place** *(937 Coral Way)*, the home George Merrick built in 1916 for his new wife. Coral Gables' first mayor, Edward "Doc" Dammers, originally lived at 1141 Coral Way. Architect H. George Fink designed the one-story, rock **Casa Azul** *(1254 Coral Way)*, distinguishable by its blue glazed-tile roof, for himself in 1924.

Venetian Pool

★★The Biltmore Hotel – *1200 Anastasia Ave. Guided tour (30min), year-round Sun 1:30pm, 2:30pm & 3:30pm.* ✗ ⚹ ▣ *www.biltmorehotel.com* ☏ *305-445-1926.* Recently restored and reopened, the Biltmore was inaugurated in 1926 as South Florida's premier winter resort. This massive tile-roofed "wedding cake" boasted a Mediterranean Revival design by the prestigious New York architectural firm of Schultze and Weaver (designers of the Waldorf-Astoria Hotel in New York City) and formed the centerpiece of Coral Gables' 1,600-acre "Country Club Section." The 300ft-high tower with triple cupola—inspired by the 16C Giralda tower of the Cathedral of Seville, Spain—can be seen from miles around.

Remarkably, the 275-room extravaganza went up in just 11 months. The cost was $10 million; $1 million alone was spent on decorating the **lobby★** with custom-loomed carpets, Italian marble and Spanish tiles. In addition to a clubhouse modeled after an Italian Renaissance palazzo, there were two 18-hole golf courses, miles of bridle paths, 20 tennis courts, a polo field and a 1.25-million-gallon **pool**. While guests preferring freshwater frolicked here, Italian gondoliers ferried saltwater bathers down a canal to the beach on nearby Biscayne Bay.

In its heyday, the Biltmore attracted Hollywood stars such as Bing Crosby, Judy Garland and Ginger Rogers, as well as welcoming well-heeled Northerners who checked in for the entire winter season. (For their convenience, prominent brokerage firms interspersed branch offices among the beauty parlors and shops set around the central open-air courtyard.) After the crash, the Biltmore fell on hard times and from 1942 to 1968 served as a hospital, first for the Army, then for the Veterans' Administration. Ceilings were dropped, windows blocked and the marvelous pool filled with concrete.

Visit – *30min.* Two separate restoration efforts—one completed in 1987, the other in 1992—restored not only the pool but also elegant ballrooms and the second-story lobby, with travertine marble columns running the length of the room. Hand-painted with gold stars, the 45ft-high groined and vaulted ceiling was refurbished by 35 ecclesiastical restorers. Its former glory fully reclaimed, the hotel is now the setting for elegant weddings, fashion photography and major motion pictures.

Directly opposite the hotel is the 1924 **Coral Gables Congregational Church** *(3010 DeSoto Blvd.),* built on land donated by George Merrick in memory of his father, Solomon Merrick, a Congregational minister who served at Plymouth Church in Coconut Grove. With its arcaded loggias, arched bell tower and ornate baroque entry, the yellow-stucco building is an excellent example of Spanish Colonial architecture and was the first church in Florida to be named to the National Register of Historic Places *(open year-round daily by appointment only;* ⚹ ▣ ☏ *305-448-7421).*

★★Venetian Pool – *2701 DeSoto Blvd. Open Jun–Aug daily Mon–Fri 11am–7:30pm, weekends & holidays 10am–4:30pm. Rest of the year Tue–Sun 10am–4:30pm. $5.* ✗ ⚹ ▣ ☏ *305-460-5356.* A limestone quarry that supplied building materials for

© Robert Holmes

the area's early homes formed the base of this whimsical municipal pool. Working in tandem in 1922, artist Denman Fink and architect Phineas Paist concocted a fanciful design incorporating a casino, towers, striped light poles (inspired by those lining Venice's Grand Canal) and footbridges that crossed the free-form swimming area. The pool is drained each night and refilled with water from underground artesian wells. Today the renovated Venetian Pool, ornamented with waterfalls and pocked with rock caves, provides a unique recreational venue for Coral Gables residents and visitors.

Entrances – Designed to set Coral Gables apart from surrounding areas, grand drive-through entrances also welcomed visitors with suitable pomp—much in the spirit of the triumphal arches of Spanish cities like Seville and Toledo. Only four of eight planned entries were built. The 1922 **Granada Entrance** *(Granada Blvd. and Tamiami Tr.)* was the first. Of rough-cut coral rock, this 300ft-long gateway boasts a 40ft-high arch and flanking pergolas. **Commercial Entrance** *(Alhambra Circle, Madeira Ave. and Douglas Rd.)*, completed in 1923, is dominated by a 600ft curved coral-rock wall and archway marking the approach to the business section of the Gables. Costing nearly $1 million, the 1925 **Douglas Entrance** *(Tamiami Tr. and Douglas Rd.)*, called *La Puerta del Sol* (Gate of the Sun), was designed with a series of arcades and complexes to suggest a Spanish town square. Smaller than originally planned, it nevertheless included a 90ft clock tower, grand arch,

© Bill Wisser

Coral Gables Congregational Church

207

shops, galleries, apartments and a lavish ballroom. (Renovated, it now houses offices.) Equally elaborate is the **Country Club Prado Entrance** *(Country Club Prado and Tamiami Tr.)*. This 1927 gateway of stuccoed concrete occupies a 240ft length of grassy median at the end of a tree-shaded boulevard. Recalling an Italian Renaissance garden, the symmetrical layout incorporates 20 masonry pillars topped with classical urns and pedestal fountains at both ends of a reflecting pool.

Plazas – Intended to break the predictable grid of house lots, 14 plazas were also created for Coral Gables. Many served as European-style traffic circles, highlighted by fountains, such as the elaborate tiered pedestal supporting an obelisk at **DeSoto Plaza** *(Sevilla Ave. and Granada and DeSoto Blvds.)*.

Another notable landscape feature is the Coral Gables **Water Tower** *(Alhambra Circle, Ferdinand St. and Greenway Ct.)*. Disguised as a lighthouse, this decorative landmark was actually a utility, providing water to the city until 1931. The tower has recently been restored to its original color and design.

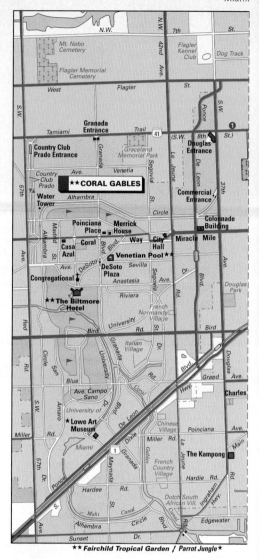

★★ *Fairchild Tropical Garden* / *Parrot Jungle* ★

★**Lowe Art Museum** – *1301 Stanford Dr., on University of Miami campus. Take US-1 (S. Dixie Hwy.) south to Stanford Dr.; turn right on Stanford and pass under Metrorail; museum is 2nd building on right. Open year-round Tue–Wed & Fri–Sat 10am–5pm, Thu noon–7pm, Sun noon–5pm. Closed Jan 1 & Dec 25. $5. & ⛨ www.lowemuseum.org ☎ 305-284-3535.* Named for Joe and Emily Lowe, wealthy New Yorkers who donated the funds for the building, the Lowe Art Museum was initiated by a group of Miami citizens who wanted to create a local space where traveling exhibits could be displayed. The museum, which opened in 1952, now showcases a permanent collection of some 8,000 works. Housed in a high-ceilinged one-story structure, expanded in 1996 to 36,000sq ft, this diverse assemblage highlights objects from the pre-Columbian and Greco-Roman periods, Renaissance and Baroque paintings, European masters and 19C-20C American paintings, Native American textiles and jewelry, and African and Asian art. Eight annual special exhibitions complement the permanent collection.

Begin to the left of the spacious, glass-fronted lobby in the Bermont Hall, which contains Picasso pottery and American paintings. Pass through a Greco-Roman Antiquities gallery to the Kress Collection of **Renaissance and Baroque art** to see works (14C-17C) by Tintoretto, della Robbia, Guardi, Isenbrandt and Jordaens. The Beaux Arts Gallery features 19C-20C European and American works; exhibits are rotated twice a year, but always include examples from the museum's important collections of Frank Stella and Roy Lichenstein paintings.

NORTH MIAMI | MIAMI BEACH |

DOWNTOWN

PORT OF MIAMI

Orange Bowl

N.W. 5th | St.

Warner House

Latin

LITTLE HAVANA

Marti Park

Quarter

Teatro Marti

Calle Ocho

Máximo Gómez Park

Woodlawn Park Cemetery

Shenandoah

Shenandoah Park

M I A M I

The Palace

Villa Regina

The Imperial

Brickell

The Atlantis

Silver Bluff Estates

The Pines

TOLL

RICKENBACKER CAUSEWAY

KEY BISCAYNE

Museum of Science & Planetarium

VIZCAYA ★★★

Ermita de la Caridad

Sister Banks

**COCONUT GROVE

Deering Channel

Grove Island

Kennedy Park

B i s c a y n e

★ Coconut Grove Village

Fuller Street

Commodore Plaza

Miami City Hall

Dinner Key

Ave. ♦ Playhouse

B a y

★★ The Barnacle SHS

★ Plymouth Congregational

Dinner Key Channel

LITTLE HAVANA
CORAL GABLES
AND
COCONUT GROVE

Metrorail with station

0   1 mi
0   1 km

Four Way Channel

Sunrise Harbor

Off a central garden, several smaller galleries include masks, sculpture, ceramics and beadwork from Africa, Asia and the Americas. A fine **Native American collection** of textiles, baskets and pottery from the Southeast, Southwest and Northwest cultural areas occupies the Barton Gallery. The Green Galleries and other exhibition halls at the rear of the museum showcase contemporary art and other changing exhibits.

★★ **Fairchild Tropical Garden** – *Map p 195. 10901 Old Cutler Rd., 10mi south of downtown. Open year-round daily 9:30am–4:30pm; tram tours (40min) Mon–Fri 10am–3pm on the hour, weekends 10am–4pm on the hour. Closed Dec 25. $8.* ✕ 🚻 🅿 *www.ftg.org* ✆ *305-667-1651.* Set on 83 well-tended acres studded with a series of 12 man-made lakes, the largest botanical garden in the continental US boasts more than 2,500 species of plants and trees from around the world. The gardens, named for plant explorer David Fairchild, opened in 1938. Plants here are grouped together by families and arranged in spaces that vary dramatically from narrow allées to open beds. A tram tour *(45min)* takes visitors past a sampling of the garden's flora, including 500 species of **palms** and a group of rare **cycads**, a species that dates from the Cretaceous period some 100 million years ago. Tropical vegetation is maintained in a steamy greenhouse; a separate garden nurtures endangered botanical species. The new **Gate House Museum of Plant Exploration**, housed in a limestone cottage built in 1939 by the Civilian Conservation Corps, holds interpretive displays that tell the story of botanists (including Fairchild himself) who comb the earth seeking unusual plants. Fairchild's own private estate, **The Kampong** *(p 214),* can be visited in nearby Coconut Grove.

★**Parrot Jungle and Gardens** – 🚻 *Map p 195. 11000 S.W. 57th Ave. Open year-round daily 9:30am–6pm. $12.95.* ✗ ♿ 🅿 *www.parrotjungle.com* ☎ *305-666-7834.* A rainbow of vivid-colored macaws perched inside the entrance greets visitors to this first-generation Miami tourist attraction, which opened its doors in 1936. The site is home to more than 1,100 exotic birds, including some 80 pink flamingos that frequent **Flamingo Lake**. Within the park, a path winds through lush tropical gardens and a walk-through aviary, past banana trees, orchids, bromeliads and a banyan tree that shades nearly an acre of land. In the amphitheater, trained macaws and cockatoos perform such feats as riding a bicycle across a tightrope and roller skating *(trained-bird shows and wildlife shows are presented 4 times daily; consult schedule for show times).*

Before the end of 2000, Parrot Jungle plans to move to a lush new site on Watson Island, in Biscayne Bay east of downtown Miami via US-41 (MacArthur Causeway). Blueprints for the new 18-acre, $47-million park include an Everglades exhibit, a children's petting zoo, baby bird and plant nurseries, a 500-seat theater, two amphitheaters, jungle trails and aviaries.

★★COCONUT GROVE *Map pp 208-209*

Lush foliage and venerable banyan trees enhance the tropical feeling of this picturesque village stretching 4mi south of Rickenbacker Causeway along Biscayne Bay. The oldest community in the Miami area and home to some 19,000 people, Coconut Grove retains a strong sense of history in its quiet residential neighborhoods, where many of the vine-covered bungalows and Mediterranean-style estates date to the early 20C. By contrast, trendy bars and cafes make the downtown one of Miami's hippest entertainment spots. Pulsing with activity at night and on weekends, the Grove is also widely known for its Saturday farmers' market and colorful fairs occurring throughout the year. Among the most notable are the **Arts Festival** *(late February)*; the **Goombay Festival** *(early June)*, a celebration of Bahamian culture; and the **King Mango Strut** *(late December)*, a zany parade.

Historical Notes – Cocoanut Grove (spelled with an "a" until 1919) owes its name to Horace Porter, a Connecticut doctor who dreamed of starting a coconut plantation here in 1873. Although Porter gave up and left after a year, remnants of his grove (two palm trees) and the post office he christened still remained when Ralph Middleton Munroe *(p 214)* arrived in 1877. Among the Grove's most prominent settlers, Munroe was captivated by the beauty of the area and tirelessly promoted the tropical paradise. In 1882 he helped friends Charles and Isabella Peacock open a hotel in what is now Peacock Park. Called Bay View House (later Peacock Inn), the fashionable hostelry established a sense of social cachet in the village and was instrumental in attracting many winter visitors who returned to build houses of their own.

By 1890 Cocoanut Grove had become the largest town on the south Florida mainland, boasting the first school, library and yacht club (founded by "Commodore" Ralph Munroe) in the region. On the west side of town a sizable black Bahamian community took root. These settlers supported themselves by salvaging shipwrecks, manufacturing coontie starch, and working in the local construction and service industries. By the early 20C, estates on the eastern and southern bayfront had become a prime winter address for society figures and affluent industrialists like James Deering *(p 211)*. In the 1920s and '30s, artists, academics and writers—including Robert Frost—affiliated with the Winter Institute of Literature at the University of Miami were in turn drawn to the intellectual community that had thrived in the village since its earliest days. Leading lights such as Alexander Graham Bell and Charles Lindbergh were frequent visitors. In 1917 the Grove also became home to one of the first naval air stations in the US, established on **Dinner Key**, a small island attached to the mainland by landfill. As the site of the seaplane base for Pan American Airways in the 1930s, Dinner Key contributed greatly to Miami's growth as an international city.

Although Coconut Grove was annexed by the City of Miami in the summer of 1925, the village never lost its independent character and bohemian flair. After a decline in the 1950s, the Grove resurfaced as an artistic community with the 1963 inauguration of the annual **Coconut Grove Arts Festival**, a three-day event that now attracts more than half a million visitors each winter. An influx of hippies in the 1960s was succeeded by a crop of yuppies in the 1970s. In the next decades, high-rise luxury hotels and apartment buildings surfaced along South Bayshore Drive. Completed in 1987, the $14 million, city-operated **Dinner Key Marina** further altered the waterfront with some 600 boat slips complete with electricity, telephone and cable-television hookups. A preservation movement that actively opposes development reflects a continued effort to maintain the distinctive identity of this historic community.

Sights *2 days*

To fully enjoy this area, reserve a day to see Vizcaya and the nearby Miami Museum of Science and Space Transit Planetarium, and a second day to explore Coconut Grove proper. To shop in the village and tour The Barnacle, park on Grand Ave. or Main Hwy. (metered parking) and walk. Other sites are best visited by car.

© Paul Rocheleau

Bayside View of Vizcaya

★★★**Vizcaya** – *3251 S. Miami Ave. Open year-round daily 9:30am–5pm, gardens until 5:30pm. Closed Dec 25. $10.* ✗ & ⬛ ☎ *305-250-9133.* Overlooking the calm, blue waters of Biscayne Bay, this ornate Italian Renaissance-style villa and formal gardens embody the fantasy winter retreat of their builder, **James Deering**. This 35 acre estate was raised from a Florida hardwood hammock in 1916, the culmination of a collaboration between Deering, decorator Paul Chalfin and architect F. Burrall Hoffman, Jr.

The Man Behind the Mansion – The second son of William Deering, developer of the Deering harvester machine, James (1859-1925) joined the family's Illinois-based farm machinery business after graduating from Northwestern University and the Massachusetts Institute of Technology. When his company merged with McCormick Harvester Company in 1902, Deering became vice-president of the newly formed International Harvester Company, a position he held until he retired 17 years later. Like so many of the Sunshine State's illustrious snowbirds, ill health first brought Deering to Florida. Deering's doctors advised him to seek out a warm winter climate to combat the symptoms of his severe anemia, which they were unable to treat. After ruling out Egypt, the French Riviera and the South Seas, among other salubrious climes, Deering chose Miami as the site of his winter home. Both Deering's parents and his older brother, Charles, owned property in the area.

Evolution of a Palace – In 1912 Deering purchased 180 acres of Miami shoreline and set about planning his house. Craving privacy, Deering envisioned a "homey" cottage on the banks of Biscayne Bay. His decorator and art advisor, **Paul Chalfin**, had grander ideas. A graduate of the Ecole des Beaux-Arts in Paris and former curator at the Boston Museum of Fine Arts, Chalfin accompanied Deering to Europe, where the two men combed old European castles and Italian villas for treasures to fill the house—which had yet to be built. Guided by Chalfin, Deering purchased paintings, sculpture, furniture, tapestries, antique ceilings, wrought-iron gates and a host of other objets d'art. By the time they returned, Deering had amassed such a collection that he realized his house would have to be designed to fit its furnishings instead of the other way around.

For this job, Chalfin hired New York architect **F. Burrall Hoffman, Jr.** Inspired by 15C and 16C villas in the Venetian countryside, Hoffman's design resulted in a triumphal merging of Italian Renaissance style with Florida's tropical landscape. Rooms opened onto a central courtyard designed to catch cool bay breezes. Deering's

Vizcaya (a Basque word meaning "elevated place") required 1,000 workers, $15 million and over two years to complete. On Christmas Day 1916, Deering moved into his new 70-room mansion. "When I started to build a house," he later wrote, "I did not expect to have anything so large ... or costly as it has turned out to be." Deering, who never married, lived at Vizcaya until his death in 1925. The following year, the house and gardens were badly ravaged by the legendary 1926 hurricane (p 195).

The Deering family hired Chalfin in 1934 to renovate the damaged house and replant the gardens in preparation for opening the house to the public as a museum. But public interest in Vizcaya waned, and in 1945 the family sold 130 acres to the Catholic Church to build a hospital complex. Deering's estate remained in the hands of his heirs—his brother's children—until 1952, when Dade County purchased the villa and its remaining 35 acres for $1 million.

Visit – 2hrs. Guided tour (45min) covers first-floor rooms. After the tour, visitors are free to visit the second-floor rooms and stroll through the gardens. Architect Hoffman crafted Vizcaya to resemble a 16C Italian Renaissance villa. Two floors of rooms surround a central courtyard (now roofed to protect the priceless art within from heat and humidity). An airy loggia follows three sides of the ground floor; second-floor rooms open onto galleries overlooking the courtyard.

The 34 rooms that are open to the public incorporate elements of four major styles: Renaissance, Baroque, Rococo and Neoclassical. Rooms remain true to Chalfin's designs—each is set like a stage for a period drama. The Neoclassical **Entrance Hall** contains hand-blocked c.1814 wallpaper from the Paris workshop of Joseph Dufour. Three pairs of 1C AD Roman marble columns adorn the **Renaissance Hall**. The walls and ceiling of the Italian Rococo **Music Room** are covered with canvas panels hand-painted with a fanciful marine theme. Looking out over the gardens, the **Tea Room★** is actually an enclosed loggia, featuring a 17C Nubian marble mantelpiece and a modeled ceiling with Neoclassical motifs. The room's stained-glass wall displays Vizcaya's emblematic sea horse and caravel.

Reclusive Deering lived in a suite of rooms on the second floor. His elegant sitting room and bedroom incorporate elements from the Neoclassical and Adam styles. Also of note is the second-floor **Dining Room**, whose walls are covered by murals of nautical theme.

The **East Loggia**, with its striking colored-marble floor, opens out onto the terrace that fronts Biscayne Bay. Just off the terrace sits the **Stone Barge★**, an ornamental Venetian-style breakwater where Deering once tied his luxurious 80ft yacht, Nepenthe. The barge is embellished with sculpture by A. Sterling Calder (father of renowned 20C sculptor Alexander Calder) and bordered by striped replicas of Venetian gondola poles.

More than 10 acres of formal **gardens★★★** flank the south side of the house. Colombian-born architect Diego Suarez planned the fan-shaped Italian hill garden with its curvilinear parterres. Here tropical plants replace their European counterparts (i.e., clipped jasmine hedges substitute for traditional boxwood). The garden's central axis draws the eye up a water stairway to a two-room baroque **Casino**, or garden house, set on an artificial hill. Semicircular pools and domed stone gazebos define the garden's east-west axis.

4 Streets of Mayfair

Map p 209. Grand Ave. between Virginia and Mary Sts. ✗ ▯ ☎ 305-448-1700. The hip restaurant Planet Hollywood anchors the corner of this complex, a colorful array of high-end shops, restaurants and movie theaters that occupies an entire block on Grand Avenue. The vine-draped, pink and white concrete extravaganza was designed in 1979 by Grove architect Kenneth Treister (whose work includes the Holocaust Memorial in Miami Beach and originally housed boutiques reportedly used to launder South American drug money. Be sure to explore the interior courtyard (enter from Virginia St.), reminiscent of the style of architect Antonio Gaudi in Barcelona. Treister adorned this courtyard with lush greenery, multilevel walkways, tiled fountains and striking copper bird sculptures.

5 CocoWalk

Map p 209. 3015 Grand Ave. on the west side of Virginia St. ✗ ☎ 305-444-0777. Opened in 1991, the U-shaped ensemble of bars, chain stores, clubs and movie theaters embraces an open plaza with a central cupola-topped pavilion. Pink stucco and three levels of loggias and balconies give the mall a cheerful tropical air. To catch up on all the local sports gossip, try Legends All Pro Sports Bar and Cafe, a popular watering hole once owned by Miami Dolphins' quarterback Dan Marino.

The farm section of the estate is located across South Miami Avenue from the villa. Residences for members of Vizcaya's managerial staff were located here, as were stables, a dairy and poultry house. Some of the Farm Village buildings are currently being restored and will eventually be added to the museum complex.

Miami Museum of Science & Space Transit Planetarium – *3280 S. Miami Ave., across from Vizcaya. Open year-round daily 10am–6pm. Closed Thanksgiving Day & Dec 25. $10. Fri & Sat laser shows 9pm, 10pm, 11pm & midnight. $6.* ⚼ ▣ *www.miamisci.org* ☎ *305-854-4247.* More than 150 exhibits at the museum allow visitors to touch objects, wave wands, ride bikes and dig for fossils while learning about everything from gravity and light refraction to muscle flexibility and mastodon teeth. It's all geared toward young minds, though adults will find much to amuse them as well. Housed in a Mediterranean-style building decorated with arches and barrel tiles, the museum also features ever-changing temporary exhibits. Out back, the Wildlife Center—which doubles as a rehabilitation facility for birds of prey—also displays wood storks, common and endangered tortoises, and startlingly big pythons and boa constrictors. The adjacent planetarium offers astronomy and laser shows, including popular rock 'n roll laser concerts on weekend nights. *Observatory is free to visitors on Sat and Sun evenings.*

Having recently entered a partnership with the Smithsonian Institution, the museum foresees building a $100 million Science Center of the Americas, six times the size of the existing facility. An optimistic timetable for groundbreaking is 2003, as no suitable site has yet been determined.

Miami City Hall – *3500 Pan American Dr. (off S. Bayshore Dr.). Open year-round Mon–Fri 8am–5pm. Closed major holidays.* Located on Dinner Key, this two-story Streamline Moderne gem with a flat roof and glass-block windows was designed in 1933 as the seaplane terminal for Pan American Airways. (Note the roofline frieze of winged globes, rising suns and eagles.) In the peak years of the late 1930s, flights left for 32 foreign countries and some 50,000 passengers per year passed through, making this the largest international port of entry in the US. (Charles Lindbergh was one of the early pilots.) The terminal originally featured a second-story restaurant and promenade deck. Watching the spectacle of large flying clipper ships taking off and landing in Biscayne Bay—tended by ground crews clad in bathing suits—was a popular weekend pastime. The last flight left Dinner Key in 1945 and the building has served as the City Hall since 1954.

★**Coconut Grove Village** – Centered around the intersection of Grand Ave. and Main Hwy. Once a sleepy village with a single grocery store, the downtown has undergone several transformations in recent decades. Galleries, coffeehouses and head shops abounded in the 1960s, replaced in the '70s by tony boutiques stocked with Gucci handbags. Today sidewalk cafes and hip swimwear shops cater primarily to the under-40 crowd, attracting local students, professionals and tourists alike. Cultural offbeats are now a relatively rare sight, but don't be surprised to encounter occasional gangs of leather-clad bikers roaring through the village on weekends.

© Bill Wisser

CocoWalk

Shopping in the Grove offers something for everyone. A mélange of high-end shops and boutiques appealing to "Generation X" clientele fill **Streets of Mayfair** and **CocoWalk**. Cafés line **Commodore Plaza** and the north end of Main Highway, while interesting book and clothing shops are tucked into **Fuller Street**.

At the south end of town is the 1926 **Coconut Grove Playhouse** *(3500 Main Hwy.)*. Twisted columns flank the Moorish-style entry of the substantial three-story corner building, originally a movie house. After a brief stint as a training center for World War II Air Force pilots, the enterprise reopened as a legitimate theater with the US premiere of Samuel Beckett's play *Waiting for Godot* in 1956. Current offerings in the 1,100-seat theater and more intimate cabaret room include experimental dramas as well as Broadway-bound musicals and plays. *For information on performances, call ☎ 305-442-2662.*

★★**The Barnacle State Historic Site** – *3485 Main Hwy. Open year-round Fri–Sun 9am–4pm. Interior of house by guided tour (1hr) only, 10am, 11:30am, 1pm & 2:30pm. Closed Thanksgiving Day & Dec 25. $1. ☎ 305-448-9445.* This five-acre bayfront site preserves one of the last patches of tropical hardwood hammock in Coconut Grove, along with the 1891 home of **Ralph Middleton Munroe**. An accomplished sailor and yacht designer, Munroe ran a profitable oystering business in Staten Island, New York. He first came to the Grove in 1877 on a sailing trip and returned four years later hoping the warm climate would improve the health of his ailing wife, Eva. Although Eva died in Florida, Munroe became attached to the area and by 1882 was engaged in several enterprises here, including sponge planting, pineapple canning and shipwreck salvage. In 1886 he purchased a 40 acre tract of property for $400 and a sailboat valued at another $400. To frame his new house, Munroe used lumber salvaged from a shipwreck, cut it to size in his own sawmill and treated it with crude oil to deter termites. Nicknamed The Barnacle for its octagonal center that tapers to a small open-air vent, the five-room, hip-roofed structure features a Bahamian design well-suited to the Grove's tropical climate. A verandah covers two sides of the square structure, providing shade and catching prevailing breezes; the cupola atop the hipped roof draws hot air up through the central octagonal room inside.

In 1908 Munroe, who had remarried, enlarged the single-story house to accommodate his growing family by jacking it up and adding a new ground floor in concrete underneath. Virtually unchanged since Munroe's day, the house remained in the family until the 1970s and still contains the original furnishings. The 1926 **boathouse**, showcasing Munroe's shipbuilding tools, is also open to visitors. Moored just offshore is a replica of the *Egret*, a shallow-draft sailboat called a sharpie, ideal for navigating the bay waters. A talented boat designer, Munroe designed the original 28ft *Egret* himself.

Charles Avenue – Once called Evangelist Street for its many churches, this quiet road runs west through the oldest black community on mainland Florida. Known as Kebo, the area was settled in the 1880s by Bahamians who came north by way of Key West. These pioneers helped northern settlers cultivate tropical greenery in the village and brought many of the seeds for the soursops, sugar apples and Barbados cherries that thrive here today. The avenue is notable for its early 20C **shotgun houses** *(p 27)*. A drive west to the corner of Douglas Road brings you to one of the first cemeteries in South Florida, used since 1906. Note the unusual two-headed images on the Bahamian gravestones.

Further down Douglas Road, just south of Main Highway, is **The Kampong** *(4013 Douglas Rd.; visit by appointment only; 1st Sun of each month; $10; ☎ 305-442-7169)*, botanist David Fairchild's private estate and garden. Fairchild first introduced soybeans and many exotic fruits to North American soil; the original plantings are in this garden.

★**Plymouth Congregational Church** – 3429 Devon Rd. Visit by appointment only. Open Sun for church service only. ♿ 🅿 ☎ *305-444-6521.* This 1917 Spanish Colonial-style church was modeled after a 16C mission in Mexico, recalled by the broad facade with symmetrical bell towers flanking a curving roof parapet. Of local oolitic limestone, the building and massive cloister walls were reportedly built by a single Spanish mason using nothing more than a hatchet and a plumb line. The walnut door (c.1600) is thought to be from a monastery in the Pyrenees mountains. Tucked into the charming banyan-shaded grounds are a small meditation garden, a rose garden and a tropical cloister garden.

Moved from its original site near the Peacock Inn, the one-room **schoolhouse** at the north end of the property dates back to 1887 *(open by appointment only)*. Built of lumber from a salvaged shipwreck, it initially housed a Sunday school run by Isabella Peacock. In 1889 it became the first public school in what is now Miami-Dade County. The bell is original.

KEY BISCAYNE *Map p 195*

Locals enjoy the 7mi-long barrier island, located 2mi south of downtown Miami, as a haven for water sports and bicycling and as an upscale residential neighborhood. First named Santa Marta by Ponce de León in 1513, Key Biscayne caught the public's attention when President Richard Nixon bought a vacation home here in the 1970s. It is now an affluent community boasting luxury accommodations, fine restaurants and some of the state's prettiest beaches.

Historical Notes – In 1825 the Cape Florida Lighthouse was erected at the tip of the key to guide ships safely through the Florida Channel. After Seminole Indians attacked the lighthouse in 1836 during the Second Seminole War, the key was used as a military encampment while the area's few settlers fled to safety. In the early 1900s, Dr. William J. Matheson developed the land by dredging a yacht basin and planting thousands of coconut trees.

In 1947 the Rickenbacker Causeway opened with a then-pricey 25-cent toll *(now $1)* and linked Miami to the island across Biscayne Bay. The old bridge is now used as a fishing pier and sits beside a taller, arching span built to accommodate the key's burgeoning population and the bay's increasing boat traffic. In the 1960s Key Biscayne experienced a construction surge and high-rises sprang up next to the working-class residential neighborhoods that dotted the island. Property prices soared in the next decade as buyers realized the island's exclusivity.

Today residents of Key Biscayne—now an independent city from Miami—enjoy a slow pace bolstered by a small but thriving commercial center. The southern end is ceded to two popular beachfront parks, Crandon and Bill Baggs, both lauded for the beauty of their **beaches**. Strands on either side of the roadway heading east are favorite haunts of windsurfers and jet skiers. Head west on the causeway toward Miami for spectacular **views★** of downtown and its commercial carotid, Brickell Avenue *(p 202)*.

Sights *1/2 day*

★**Miami Seaquarium** – Kids *4400 Rickenbacker Causeway, 5mi east of the Key Biscayne toll booth. Open year-round daily 9:30am–6pm. $19.95.* ✗ 🅿 *www.miamiseaquarium.com* ☎ *305-361-5705.* In its late 1950s heyday, this 37-acre marine-life park served as the set for the TV series *Flipper* and home to its star, the world's most photogenic dolphin. Today, a regular schedule of shows with an educational subtext are offered daily *(see park brochure for show times)*. Lolita, the five-ton star of the **killer whale show**, draws the largest crowds with her graceful leaps, accompanied by several dolphin friends. Nearby, visitors can watch fish and sharks being hand-fed by divers in a reef tank. The main building provides two viewing levels for a peek at some 10,000 varieties of aquatic life. At the back of the park, sharks swim in an open-air channel that is crossed by several bridges; neighboring **Lost Islands Wildlife Habitat** features endangered reptiles, mammals and birds. The world's first controlled manatee breeding program—a joint effort with the University of Miami marine lab next door—also takes place here.

A proposed $70 million expansion has thus far been thwarted by citizens of Key Biscayne, who maintain that additional traffic on the Rickenbacker Causeway—their lifeline to the mainland—would cause undue hardship for residents.

★**Bill Baggs Cape Florida State Recreation Area** – *1200 S. Crandon Blvd., 7mi from the toll booth entrance to the key. Open year-round daily 8am–dusk. $4/vehicle.* ⚠ ✗ 🅿 ☎ *305-361-5811.* A mile of Biscayne Bay beachfront attracts locals to this secluded 900-acre park on the south end of Key Biscayne, which affords a view of downtown Miami. Designated a state park in 1966, the recreation area owes its name to the newspaper editor of the now-defunct Miami News who encouraged the land's preservation. The original red-brick, 95ft-high **Cape Florida Lighthouse** set on the southeastern tip of Key Biscayne was constructed in 1825; today tours of the keeper's quarters and kitchen follow presentation of a 14min video *(visit by 1hr guided tour only—arrive 30min early; Thu–Mon 10am & 1pm; $2)*. During the Seminole Wars in 1836, Indians set fire to the structure, killing the lightkeeper's assistant. Engineers rebuilt the tower and raised it 30ft in 1846. The light was destroyed again in 1861—this time by Confederate sympathizers. Relit after the war, the beacon operated until 1878 when it was replaced by the iron Fowey Rock Lighthouse set in the reef some 7mi southeast of Cape Florida.

Now fully restored after damage from Hurricane Andrew in 1992, the Cape Florida light again shines its beacon to sea as a navigational aid. The hardwood hammock bordering the beach has been replanted with such native species as sea grape trees and wax myrtle. A bicycle trail loops through the park, and a new 1.5mi nature trail weaves through an adjacent 63-acre resurrected wetland.

GREATER MIAMI NORTH *Map p 195*

Homesteaders settled the area now stretching north of present-day Miami Shores to the county line above Golden Beach during the late 19C, when small stations such as Arch Creek and Buena Vista began popping up along the new Florida East Coast Railway. The district consisted primarily of farms and citrus groves until a period of rapid residential development during the boom years of the 1920s. At this time, several planned subdivisions, including Morningside, El Portal and Miami Shores, were developed as theme communities, often featuring Spanish or Mediterranean Revival-style architecture. Some had added attractions: the development of Fulford-by-the-Sea, for example, boasted the Fulford Speedway, which offered a $30,000 purse for its inaugural—and only—race in 1925. (Unfortunately, the track was destroyed by the 1926 hurricane and never rebuilt.) Many of the other new North Miami communities stood unfinished after the bottom fell out of the real-estate market the same year.

Today Greater Miami North is largely residential, a mix of luxury apartment houses, modern suburban developments and remnants of the older, established neighborhoods from bygone boom days. The fashionable district of Aventura, just north of the Lehman Causeway, comprises luxury resorts and the upscale **Aventura Mall**, containing fine shops and department stores.

Sights *1 day*

★**Joan Lehman Museum of Contemporary Art** – *770 N.E. 125th St., North Miami. Open year-round Tue–Sat 11am–5pm, Sun noon–5pm. Closed major holidays. $4. ♿ 🅿 ☎ 305-893-6211.* Architect Charles Gwathmey combined cubes and cylinders in designing the simple but elegant 23,000sq ft building on palm-studded grounds within the North Miami civic complex. Changing exhibits feature artists like French sculptor Annette Messager, Brazilian performance artist Tunga and American pop artist Keith Haring, whose work is much more recognizable than their names. As yet the permanent collection, including Jasper Johns, Roy Lichtenstein, Claes Oldenburg, Robert Rauschenberg, Julian Schnabel and others, is not on display. Lehman—wife of Congressman Bill Lehman and a sculptor in her own right—was the leading financial sponsor of the museum, which opened in 1996.

★★**Ancient Spanish Monastery** – *16711 W. Dixie Hwy., North Miami Beach. Take Biscayne Blvd. (US-1) north to N. Miami Beach Blvd. Turn left, then right on W. Dixie Hwy. Open year-round Mon–Sat 10am–4pm, Sun noon–4pm. Closed major holidays. $4.50. ♿ 🅿 ☎ 305-945-1461.* Nestled on the woodsy site of a former nursery in North Miami Beach, the Cloisters of St. Bernard of Clairvaux provides a unique look at a 12C monastery. Known locally as the Ancient Spanish Monastery, this superb example of early Gothic architecture stood in Sacramenia, a small community in the Spanish province of Segovia, from the time of its completion in 1141 until it was disassembled and moved to the US nearly eight centuries later.

A Building Out of Time – Built under the auspices of King Alphonso VII of Castille and Leon, the monastery was initially named the "Monastery of Our Lady, Queen of Angels." When Bernard de Clairvaux, the influential leader of the Cistercian Monks, was canonized in 1174, the monastery was renamed in his honor. Cistercian Monks ran the complex for nearly 700 years before the Spanish government cut off financial support.

The Cloisters languished as a granary and stable until 1925, when **William Randolph Hearst**, a wealthy American newspaperman and collector extraordinaire, purchased the monastery and its outbuildings for $500,000. Hearst planned to reconstruct his "greatest art treasure" on the grounds of San Simeon, his lavish California estate (*see Michelin Green Guide to California*). Accordingly workers dismantled the buildings stone by stone, numbering each one for identification. Pieces were then painstakingly wrapped in hay, and placed in 10,751 wooden crates before being shipped to the US.

When the shipment arrived, however, the US Department of Agriculture quarantined it because hoof-and-mouth disease had broken out in Segovia. Each crate was opened and the protective hay—considered a potential carrier of the disease—was burned. When workers repacked the stones, they neglected to place them in the original numbered boxes before shipping them to a warehouse in New York City.

The stones remained packed away for more than a quarter of a century while Hearst turned his attention elsewhere. Following the publisher's death in 1951, the stones were purchased by two South Florida developers who hoped to reconstruct the cloisters as a tourist attraction.

Giant Jigsaw Puzzle – In 1952 the boxes reached North Miami Beach, where the assemblers learned that the stones were not in their original boxes. Thus began work on the "world's largest jigsaw puzzle." It took 23 men 90 days just to open the packing cases. Then the 36,000 stones—weighing from 50 to 3,000 pounds—were spread over the 20-acre site. Allan Carswell, a renowned stone mason, was hired to supervise the arduous process of fitting the stones together, using photographs that Hearst had taken of the intact monastery. Nineteen months and $1.5 million later, the reconstructed cloisters opened in 1954.

Unfortunately, the monastery's appeal as a tourist attraction fell short of its owners' expectations. They sold the Cloisters in 1964 to the Episcopal Diocese of South Florida, who opened the St. Bernard Mission Church in the complex. In the early 1970s, the diocese, unable to meet the rising expenses of maintaining the building, faced the prospect of selling the property until Robert Pentland, a devout Episcopalian and monied benefactor of many Episcopal churches, purchased the structure and presented it to the parish of St. Bernard de Clairvaux, whose members still worship here.

Visit – *1hr.* Visitors enter the complex through a 200-pound wrought-iron gate crowned with the Latin inscription meaning "These Sacred Cistercian Walls." A lush garden filled with colorful subtropical plants fills the space beside the cloisters. On the garden's southern perimeter stands the entrance to a long cloister. The top of its portal is adorned with the figure of Mary, the mother of Christ, encircled by angels. A series of ribbed arches form the cloister's vault; tile now covers the floors that once consisted of small stones.

The **Chapel of St. Bernard de Clairvaux**, which served as the monks' refectory, occupies the first corridor of the cloister; the small iron bell at the entrance once called the brothers to meals. Above the altar, two circular stained-glass windows, depicting scenes from the Book of Revelation written by St. John, are as old as the monastery. They represent two of only three known **telescopic windows**★ in existence (so-named for the three rings of receding frames that encase the windows, creating a telescopic effect). In the middle of the complex stands a **Prayer Well** composed of elements of an AD 1C Roman temple.

A life-size statue of King Alfonso VIII stands at the end of the first corridor; diagonally across the courtyard is a statue of his grandfather, King Alfonso VII. Both sculptures first stood in the adjoining church. Located midway along the second corridor, the **Chapter House** formed part of the original monastery. Monks gathered here to receive their work assignments, study or hold choir practice. The medieval pink-limestone, Gothic-style altar (at the corner past the Chapter House) was carved in Cannes, France. Ten corbels along the Cloister walls—part of Hearst's art collection—portray shields of 12C Segovia noble and royal families who pledged their allegiance to both the Catholic Church and the Spanish king.

American Police Hall of Fame and Museum – *3801 Biscayne Blvd. Open year-round daily 10am–5:30pm. Closed Dec 25. $6.* ♿ 🅿 ☎ *305-573-0070.* This former FBI building is recognizable by the police patrol car mounted on its facade. On the main level, a marble **memorial** bears the names of more than 3,500 police officers slain in the line of duty. The upper level contains a hodgepodge of artifacts related to law enforcement, including a "you-solve-it" crime scene, electric chair and jail cell replicas.

SOUTH MIAMI-DADE COUNTY *Map p 180*

Isolated by the marshy fringes of the Everglades, the southern portion of Miami-Dade County (below Coral Reef Drive) was among the last parts of Florida to be settled and remains a separate community in both spirit and appearance. While the fast-growing region has its share of tract housing and new shopping malls, its rural western section is still dominated by produce farms, lime groves and tropical plant nurseries, preserving a distinctive small-town feel virtually nonexistent elsewhere in the Miami area. Despite the ravages left by Hurricane Andrew in 1992, agriculture and tourism continue as the top industries.

Winter's Salad Bowl – Lured by the frost-free climate, pioneers began arriving in the area after the great freezes of 1894-95 decimated commercial citrus groves farther north in the state. Development came with the southern expansion of the Florida East Coast Railway from Miami in the early 1900s. As workers laid out the rails, camps of portable buildings were taken down and put up again with each section of completed track. Homestead, now the largest city in South Miami-Dade, was named in 1904 when flat railcars full of building materials labeled "homestead country" arrived at the end of the line.

The region's fertile soil, produced by draining the swampy glades, proved ideal for beans, tomatoes, avocados and other cash crops. Railside towns such as Cutler and Princeton were soon serving as shipping depots for produce, and by the 1950s South Miami-Dade—known widely as "Winter's Salad Bowl"—was one of the top vegetable-producing areas in the US.

Its agricultural economy was devastated in August 1992, when Hurricane Andrew raged into the county packing winds up to 175mph. Cutting an 8mi-wide path, the storm spent its full fury in and around Homestead, leaving 175,000 people homeless and more than one million without power. Some 60,000 houses were destroyed and four trailer parks were reduced to tangled piles of scrap metal. In some areas, terrain was so changed that people got lost in their own neighborhoods. Recovery was aided by the $7.9 billion Hurricane Relief Bill, the largest federal disaster package of loans and grants in US history. While some small tourist sites were lost, many others have reopened, and most commercial nurseries are back in business as well. Funds also have provided a face-lift to **Homestead's Old Downtown** *(38mi southwest of downtown Miami)*, the historic business district where recently restored early-20C storefronts lining Krome Avenue recapture the original character of this former railroad town.

Field of Young Carrots

Larry Lefever/Grant Heilman Photography

■ **Hurricane Andrew:**

Debris generated by Hurricane Andrew would make a mound 200 stories high—more than enough to fill the Orange Bowl stadium in Miami.

Sights *2 days*

★★**Miami Metrozoo** – 〔Kids〕 *12400 S.W. 152nd St. 18mi from downtown Miami. Take Florida's Turnpike south to Exit 16. Go west on S.W. 152nd St. and follow signs to zoo. Open year-round daily 9:30am–5:30pm (admission gates close at 4pm). Guided tram ride (45min) tours the zoo and offers a behind-the-scenes glimpse of hatcheries and breeding pens. $8. ✕ ♿ 🅿 ☎ 305-251-0400.* The best way to see the zoo is to wander at your own pace along the 3mi loop trail that winds through the park, replanted with hundreds of palm trees and flowering shrubs after Hurricane Andrew ravaged the site. An elevated monorail also makes regular runs around the grounds, offering its riders a bird's-eye view of the animal habitats.

Occupying 290 acres of landscaped park, this popular cageless zoo specializes in tropical species adaptable to South Florida's hot climate. Some 900 reptiles, birds and mammals—primarily from Asia, Africa and Australia—are showcased. Camouflaged moats and other inconspicuous barriers separate zoo visitors from the animals, who roam freely in natural habitats.

© Stephen Frink

Bengal Tiger at Metrozoo

Among the highlights are an affectionate band of **lowland gorillas** (a walk-in viewing cave permits a close-up look) and a group of stunning **Bengal tigers**, whose habitat features a replica of Cambodia's 13C Angkor Wat ruins. Elephant rides, feedings and wildlife shows occur throughout the day *(check brochure for times)*. **PAWS**, a children's petting zoo, is also a popular attraction.

Gold Coast Railroad Museum – *12450 S.W. 152nd St., across the road from Metrozoo. Open year-round Mon–Fri 11am–3pm, Sat 11am–4pm. Closed major holidays. $5.* 🅿 *www.elink.net/goldcoast* ☎ *305-253-0063.* A self-guided tour of this museum's grounds reveals numerous historic, renovated railroad cars, including the *California Zephyr* and a diesel locomotive formerly owned by the National Aeronautics and Space Administration (NASA). A highlight is the Pullman car *Ferdinand Magellan*, used by Presidents Franklin Roosevelt, Harry Truman, Dwight Eisenhower, Ronald Reagan and George Bush. The interior of one car displays a collection of train parts and related memorabilia. On weekends, visitors can ride on historic diesel or steam locomotives.

★**Coral Castle** – *28655 S. Dixie Hwy., 30mi south of Miami (2mi north of Homestead). Open year-round daily 9am–6pm. Closed Dec 25. $7.75.* ♿ 🅿 *www.netrunner.net/~coralroc/coralrok.html* ☎ *305-248-6344.* Shrouded with an air of mystery concerning its construction, this three-acre mansion and monolithic sculpture garden was crafted of more than 1,100 tons of coral rock (oolitic limestone). Ed Leedskalnin, a tenacious 5ft-tall, 110-pound, Latvian immigrant, took 20 years to create the sculptures, reportedly without using any mechanical equipment. After his fiancée jilted him in 1913, Leedskalnin left Latvia for the US. He eventually ended up in South Florida, hoping that the climate would alleviate respiratory problems he was having. In 1918 the broken-hearted jack-of-all-trades bought one acre of land near Florida City for $12 and began carving a castle encircled by an 800-ton wall in tribute to his lost love. In order to escape the invasion of a new subdivision in his neighborhood, reclusive Leedskalnin moved the carvings a distance of 10mi to their present site in 1936. Coral Castle has been listed on the National Register of Historic Places since 1984.
Be sure to see the movable **Nine-Ton Gate**; Polaris Telescope, a 25ft-high, 30-ton rock telescope aimed toward the North Star; the 20ft-long Florida Table, carved in the shape of the state and surrounded by 10,000-pound coral rock chairs; and the two-story tower where Leedskalnin lived in spartan quarters upstairs and labored with crude tools in the room below.

★**Biscayne National Park** – *East end of N. Canal Dr. (S.W. 328th St.), Homestead. 38mi south of downtown Miami. Take Florida Turnpike south to Exit 2 (Campbell Dr.). Drive east to Kingman Road, then south to S.W. 328th St. (N. Canal Dr.). Turn east again and travel 6mi to Convoy Point Visitor Center: open year-round daily 8:30am–5pm. Closed Dec 25. Park grounds open year-round daily 8am–5:30pm. Closed Dec 25.* ⚠ ♿ 🅿 *www.nps.gov/bisc* ☎ *305-230-7275.* The largest marine park in the US, Biscayne National Park was established in 1980 to help protect a 275sq mi area of coastal wetlands, mangrove shorelines, coral reefs

219

and a string of 32 small barrier islands (keys) threatened by increasing commercial boat traffic and freshwater outflow from Everglades drainage canals. About 95 percent of the park is located in the aqua seas of the Atlantic Ocean and Biscayne Bay. The protected waters stretch 26mi south from Key Biscayne to Card Sound near Key Largo, running between the coastline and the underwater continental shelf.

Star attractions are the **reefs★★★**, located about 10mi offshore. Here warm Gulf Stream currents nurture some 50 species of living coral that create a hospitable environment for loggerhead turtles, spiny lobsters, sponges and crabs. An array of flamboyant tropical fish, including the brilliant rock beauty and parrot fish, also put on a spectacular show of color in the crystal-clear water.

Biscayne's new **visitor center** (1997) features life-size dioramas of the park's habitat areas and their denizens. Three different videos—a general overview, a park history and a look at the effects of 1992's Hurricane Andrew—are presented in a theater. Interpretive exhibits are displayed along a short bayside walking trail from which fishing is permitted. Canoe rentals are available for bay excursions. A dive shop offers scuba and snorkeling rentals for visitors venturing to the Atlantic reefs, which are accessible only by boat.

Weather permitting, park-sponsored reef trips leave daily from the Convoy Point Visitor Center. The morning tour (daily 10am; round-trip 3hrs; $19.95) is aboard a glass-bottom boat. An afternoon trip (daily 1:30pm; round-trip 3-4hrs; $27.95) takes snorkelers on a swimming adventure (bring a swimsuit and towel; gear and snorkeling vests are provided.) Scuba divers may also arrange excursions (Mon–Fri 9am, weekends 8:30am; round-trip 4hrs). Reservations suggested for all boat excursions; Biscayne National Underwater Park Inc. www.nps.gov/bisc ☎ 305-230-1100. In winter (when mosquitoes are less numerous), boat transportation is offered with reservations to Elliott Key, 7mi offshore. Camping and nature walks are available on the island. To bird-watch or explore estuaries along the main coast, you can rent a canoe at the Convoy Point Visitor Center.

Weeks Air Museum – *14710 S.W. 128th St. (at Kendall-Tamiami Airport). 19mi southwest of downtown Miami. Open year-round daily 10am–5pm. Closed Thanksgiving Day & Dec 25. $5.95.* ♿ 🅿 *www.weeksairmuseum.com ☎ 305-233-5197.* Featuring the private collection of Florida aerobatic pilot Kermit Weeks, this small but comprehensive museum showcased some 25 aircraft—from the earliest days of flight through World War II—until Hurricane Andrew flattened the hangar housing the exhibits in 1992. The storm shattered several planes and blew two rare bombers (a B-17 and a B-23) more than a mile away. Brand-new quarters in the same location are now open, complete with a dramatic photo display of the storm ruins. About 15 planes, among them a TBM Avenger Torpedo Bomber, a Tiger Cat and the world's only surviving Dual Control TP-40, are currently displayed. Other hurricane-damaged planes, including a Curtiss Falcon and a Douglas A-26C Invader, are still under repair. Several videos explore aviation history.

Fruit & Spice Park – *24801 S.W. 248th St. at S.W. 187th Ave. in Homestead. 27mi southwest of downtown Miami. Open year-round daily 10am-5pm. Closed Jan 1, Thanksgiving Day, Dec 25. $3.50.* ♿ 🅿 *☎ 305-247-5727.* Opened in 1944, this unusual tropical park rebounded from Hurricane Andrew with a flourish. Hundreds of varieties of exotic fruit and nut trees, vegetables, herbs and spices have been replanted in geographical theme areas across its 32 acres, with mango and avocado orchards among the most interesting groves. There also are such striking specimens as the Panama candle tree, named for its long yellow fruit. Future plans call for creation of rice paddies and a small lake circled by a motorized tram. An interesting gift shop offers an array of delicacies, including canned jackfruit, lychee, sugarcane and palm nuts. Workshops on tropical plants and edible oddities are offered weekly.

MIAMI BEACH ★★★

Population 94,540
Map of Principal Sights p 3 – Map p 224
Tourist Information ☎ 305-672-1270

Touted as one of the country's great tropical paradises, Miami Beach is justifiably famed for its fabulous palm-studded shoreline, eccentric architecture and colorful locals, including elderly Jews, young Cubans, aspiring actors, gays and yuppies alike. Built on dreams and speculation, this is an island in perpetual transition, where the atmosphere can shift from shabby to chic in a single block. Despite stubborn pockets of poverty, many faded neighborhoods are staging comebacks. The rejuvenated Art Deco Historic District, with its fashionable clubs and boutiques, draws its share of both domestic and international visitors.

Geographical Notes

A separate community from Miami, the City of Miami Beach occupies a narrow barrier island (7mi long and 1.5mi wide) 2.5mi off the mainland, along with 16 islets scattered in Biscayne Bay. Dredging and land-fill have reconfigured the main island, where mangrove swamps once covered the entire area west of present-day Washington Avenue. Fisher Island, located at the southern tip, was created in 1905 when the Government Cut shipping channel sliced through to link Biscayne Bay with the Atlantic. The famous **South Beach** area *(below 23rd St.)* and **Art Deco District** are reached directly by MacArthur Causeway, which passes the exclusive residential neighborhoods on man-made Star, Palm and Hibiscus Islands, and offers a great view of the enormous cruise ships that dock in the Port of Miami.

Historical Notes

Taming the Swamp – Although occupied by Tequesta Indians in the distant past, the inhospitable, mangrove-tangled spit of land that would become Miami Beach had no permanent settlers until the late 19C. In 1882 **Henry Lum**, a former nurseryman originally from Pennsylvania, purchased the land south of present-day 11th Street from the State of Florida in hopes of starting a coconut plantation. New Jersey investors Ezra Osborn and Elnathan Field followed suit, snapping up all the coastal acreage to the north between Key Biscayne and JUPITER. Although they planted hundreds of thousands of coconut palms, swamps and mosquitoes ultimately drove all three men to abandon their ventures.

The first tourists arrived with the railroad. To get them to the beach, Richard M. Smith, a Connecticut schooner captain who had moved to Miami in 1900, erected a two-story pavilion at the southern edge of today's Ocean Beach and started a ferry service in 1907 to transport sunbathers across Biscayne Bay. A couple of years later, Yankee businessmen Avery Smith and James Warr purchased Smith's pavilion. They renovated it, added a pier and boardwalk, and thus Fairy Land—as they called their enterprise—became Miami Beach's first resort.

In 1912 New Jersey horticulturist **John C. Collins** (whose 1907 endeavor to cultivate avocados on land north of Lum's had proved successful) formed the Miami Beach Improvement Company to raise capital for a trans-bay bridge. When funds ran short, yet another entrepreneur, **Carl Fisher**—an Indiana automobile magnate who built the Indianapolis Speedway in 1909 to help promote the auto industry—stepped in with a $50,000 loan. In return Fisher received 200 acres from the ocean to the bay south of the 2.5mi Collins Bridge (now the Venetian Causeway).

Hoping to capitalize on the flurry of tourism and development sparked by Collins' bridge, two Miami bank presidents, brothers **John and James Lummus** (who had bought the land once occupied by Lum's failed coconut plantation) founded the Ocean Beach Realty Company in 1912 and laid out their first subdivision. As their cash began to dwindle the following year, Fisher stepped in and helped finance the brothers' effort to dredge their bayfront property. In return for Fisher's loan, the Lummus brothers gave him a large parcel of their Ocean Beach property. With this, Fisher founded his own realty company.

The Lummus subdivision offered small lots and modest bungalows to anyone who was "white, law-abiding and could afford the down payment." By contrast, Fisher's tract (north of present-day Lincoln Road) was sold off to wealthy buyers. Restrictive covenants on the 400ft-deep oceanfront lots stipulated that lots be sold only to "Caucasians," and required a large down payment to discourage short-term speculators. A consummate promoter, Fisher ensured a steady stream of sunseekers to his tropical paradise by financing a paved road from Chicago to Miami; his famed **Dixie Highway** opened to great fanfare in 1915. That same year, Collins, Fisher and the Lummuses merged their companies and soon afterwards incorporated their land as the City of Miami Beach.

A Place in the Sun – "Had there been no Carl Fisher," Will Rogers once quipped, "Florida would be known today as the Turpentine State. ... But Carl drained off all the water moccasins ... and replaced them with hotels and New York prices." Indeed, after World War I. Fisher joined forces with Collins and a frenzy of publicity and building ensued. In the dead of winter, a Times Square billboard taunted shivering New Yorkers with the message: "It's June in Miami." Dozens of prominent industrialist families took up residence in sprawling Mediterranean Revival-style estates. By 1921 five luxury hotels provided lodging for those who could afford it. By day polo grounds, golf courses and tennis courts offered diversion. At night locals flocked to the gambling and bootleg liquor operations hidden in the back rooms of nightclubs, hoping to catch a glimpse of **Al Capone**, the notorious Chicago gangster who bought a house on Palm Island in 1928.

The end followed the crash. By 1930 Fisher's now-relatively-worthless land was tied up in large estates. However, most of South Beach was selling briskly to Jewish businessmen from small northern cities who were able to profit with these modest investments despite the Depression. The area boomed again in the late 1930s owing to a resurgence of tourism. In 1936 alone, some 36 hotels and 110 apartment houses were built in the new Art Deco style *(p 29)* in South Miami Beach.

By 1947, 50 percent of the permanent residents in Miami Beach were Jewish. Around that time, gangsters began buying up estates north of 23rd Street, breaking the zoning code in order to build big hotels. Miami's "Gold Coast" strip enjoyed its heyday in the 1950s and '60s, when hotels like the famous Fontainebleau *(p 227)* flourished, then slipped into an economic decline that left many faded resorts in its wake.

★★★ART DECO HISTORIC DISTRICT *Map p 224*

Listed on the National Register of Historic Places in 1979, this enclave of small-scale Art Deco hotels and apartment houses dating from the late 1920s to the early 1940s amounts to the largest concentration of architecture of its kind in the world. The official district measures about one square mile and is roughly bounded by the Atlantic Ocean on the east, Lenox Avenue on the west, Sixth Street on the south and Dade Boulevard along the Collins Canal to the north. People-watching is a prime pastime here in SoBe (local slang for South Beach), now a magnet for fashion models, designers and assorted glitterati. The real stars, however, are the buildings themselves.

Marlin Hotel, Collins Avenue

Architectural Heritage – One of the few resorts in the US open to Jews, South Beach was fully developed by 1940. After World War II, soldiers who had been stationed in South Beach hotels returned with their families. As new investment focused on north Miami Beach, the south grew increasingly shabby and economic decline was firmly entrenched by the 1960s. In 1966, however, a retrospective of the International Exposition of Modern Decorative and Industrial Arts held in Paris in 1925 sparked a renewed interest in the Art Deco style. (The term "Art Deco" was coined at this time.)

A decade later, Barbara Baer Capitman and Leonard Horowitz, two local design professionals, formed the **Miami Design Preservation League** to identify significant architecture in Miami Beach. The area's ensuing 1979 designation as a National Register Historic District was remarkable in that the roughly 800 Art Deco buildings included were only about 40 years old—and not of an age typically considered historic. Following the 1980 Mariel boatlift, when hundreds of Cuban prisoners were shunted off to South Beach, much of the established Jewish population fled and the Art Deco buildings—regarded as tacky and outdated—began to crumble.

Fueled by the efforts of Capitman and Horowitz, preservation of the Deco District began in earnest in the 1980s and continues to this day. Because National Register listing does not prevent demolition, several exceptional buildings have been lost to new development. Exterior changes and paint colors of new construction are, however, subject to approval by a local review board. The current trend for bright tropical hues is somewhat controversial, as the original Art Deco buildings were painted white and trimmed in primary colors.

Roots of Art Deco Style – The Art Deco Historic District is especially remarkable for its continuity of architectural scale and style. This occurred because South Beach of the 1930s was redeveloped rapidly over a short period by a relatively small group of like-minded designers—most notably architects **L. Murray Dixon**, **Henry Hohauser**, **Albert Anis**, **Robert Swartburg** and **Roy France**. Although the majority of structures in the district illustrate Art Deco designs, about a third were built in the Mediterranean Revival style. The 1930 **Casa Casuarina** *(1114 Ocean Dr.)*—renovated as the grand palazzo-style home of the late clothing designer Gianni Versace—is one of the best remaining examples.

Derived from the minimalist **International Style** *(p 29)* that originated in post-World War I Europe, Art Deco used decorative stylized elements to embellish simple, massive forms. Reveling in its own sun-washed locale, Miami Deco went a step further, incorporating flamingos, herons, palm trees and other evocative tropical motifs into exuberant door grills, bas-relief plaques, murals and etched windows of frosted glass. The timing of these joyful designs—accented with neon and brightly colored trim—was ideal. Concrete-block buildings were relatively cheap to construct and allowed the new South Beach designers (many of whom were trained as engineers) to experiment with machine-age design.

Many Art Deco buildings in the Historic District, exemplified by the 1937 **Leslie** hotel *(1244 Ocean Dr.)* and the 1939 **Imperial** *(650 Ocean Dr.)*, tend to have an angular look, with symmetrical, stepped-back facades and strong vertical banding and bas-relief decoration. The 11-story St. Moritz *(1565 Collins Ave.)*, designed by Roy France in 1939, stretches upward with a soaring tower that houses elevators and mechanical works.

In contrast to the angularity of these Deco structures, the later **Streamline Moderne style** *(p 29)* featured aerodynamic imagery; horizontal racing stripes and wraparound corners reflected a fascination with speed and motion fostered by contemporary advances in transportation and industrial design. In an unabashed imitation of an ocean liner, for example, a building might gain portholes, periscope-like air ducts and tubular railings, as seen in the 1930s **Beach Patrol Station** *(1001 Ocean Dr.)* designed by Robert Taylor. The patrol station now forms the rear facade of the **Oceanfront Auditorium**, which was added in the 1950s.

Sights *1 day*

South Beach is best navigated by foot. Parking is by meter (quarters only) with a strictly enforced 2hr limit. The Miami Design Preservation League (MDPL) offers walking tours that depart from the Art Deco Welcome Center (in Oceanfront Auditorium), 1001 Ocean Dr. (year-round Thu 6:30pm & Sat 10:30am; 1hr 30min; $10; ☎ 305-672-2014). MDPL bike tours depart from Miami Beach Bicycle Center, 601 5th St. (year-round on 1st & 3rd Sun of each month 10:30am; 1hr 30min; $10 & $5 bike rental; reservations required ☎ 305-674-0150 or 305-672-2014). An annual **Art Deco Weekend**, *featuring special programs and lectures, is held in South Beach in January.*

★★ **Ocean Drive** – Along this lively north-south boulevard bordering the Atlantic Ocean beats the heart of the SoBe scene. By day locals and tourists nosh at shaded sidewalk cafes, while scantily clad youths streak by on in-line skates and willowy models pose for fashion shoots. At night vivid neon signs beckon revelers to some of Miami's hottest bars and dance clubs. Across the street lies fabulous **Ocean Beach**⩡⩡,

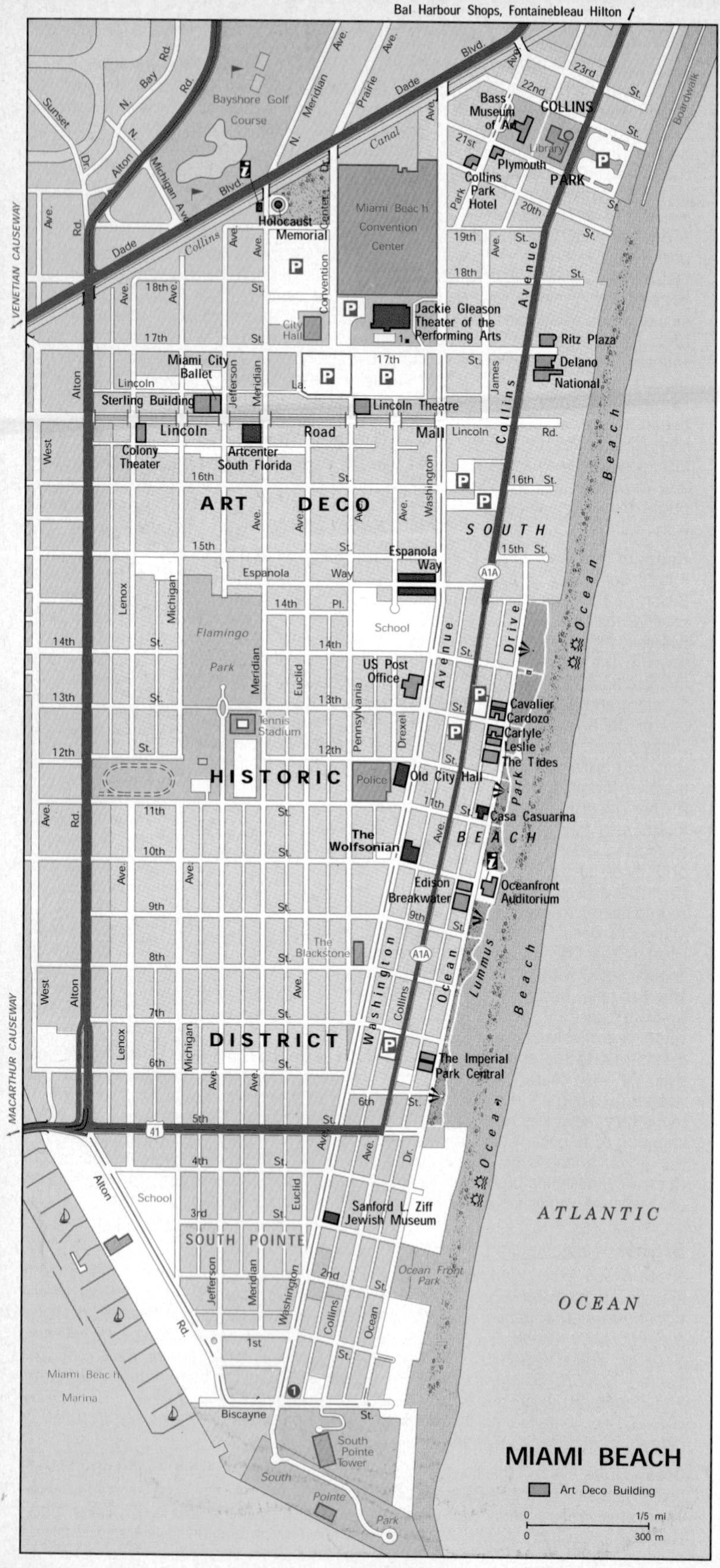

Bal Harbour Shops, Fontainebleau Hilton

Bayshore Golf Course

Bass Museum of Art

COLLINS

Plymouth

Collins Park Hotel

PARK

Holocaust Memorial

Miami Beach Convention Center

Jackie Gleason Theater of the Performing Arts

City Hall

Ritz Plaza

Delano

National

Miami City Ballet

Sterling Building

Lincoln Theatre

Lincoln Road Mall

Colony Theater

Artcenter South Florida

ART DECO

SOUTH

Espanola Way

School

US Post Office

Flamingo Park

Tennis Stadium

HISTORIC

Police

Old City Hall

Cavalier
Cardozo
Carlyle
Leslie
The Tides

Casa Casuarina

The Wolfsonian

BEACH

Edison
Breakwater

Oceanfront Auditorium

The Blackstone

DISTRICT

The Imperial
Park Central

VENETIAN CAUSEWAY

MACARTHUR CAUSEWAY

Sanford L. Ziff Jewish Museum

ATLANTIC

OCEAN

SOUTH POINTE

School

Ocean Front Park

Miami Beach Marina

Biscayne

South Pointe Tower

South Pointe Park

Lummus Beach

Ocean Beach

MIAMI BEACH

Art Deco Building

0   1/5 mi
0   300 m

refurbished and widened as part of a multimillion-dollar city project in 1982. **Lummus Park**, a magnet for teenage skaters and elderly dog-walkers alike, runs along the beach from 1st to 15th Streets. Located in the park is the nautically inspired Oceanfront Auditorium, which houses the **Art Deco Welcome Center** *(p 223)*, a tiny information center *(1001 Ocean Dr., ☎ 305-531-3484)* stocked with books and souvenirs.

The park offers a great **view**★ of Ocean Drive and its pastel parade of Art Deco hotels. The seven-story, blue-tinted **Park Central** *(no. 640)*, designed by Henry Hohauser in 1937, displays the characteristic symmetrical facade with vertical banding, steel corner windows (designed to maximize breezes in pre-air-conditioning days) and shaded central entrance. Notable for its horizontal racing stripes and futuristic double-faced tower, the yellow-and-blue-painted **Breakwater** *(no. 940)* shares a pool with the 1935 **Edison**. This Hohauser build-

Cafes Along Ocean Drive

© Robert Holmes

ing *(no. 960)* designed with a ground-floor arcade, arched windows and three-story twisted colonnette, recalls the area's earlier Mediterranean Revival architecture.

Among the first hotels to be restored in South Beach were a now-famous quartet: the **Leslie** (1937, Albert Anis) at no. 1244; the **Carlyle** (1941, Kiehnel and Elliott) at no. 1250; the **Cardozo** (1939, Henry Hohauser) at no. 1300, now owned by singer Gloria Estefan; and the **Cavalier** (1936, Roy France) next door at no. 1320. Among the newest to be renovated is **The Tides** (1936, L. Murray Dixon) at no. 1220, owned by music-industry impresario Chris Blackwell (who also owns the Leslie). This 11-story hotel is the largest on Ocean Drive.

Sanford L. Ziff Jewish Museum of Florida – *301 Washington Ave. Open year-round Tue–Sun 10am–5pm. Closed Jewish holidays. $5. & www.jewishmuseum.com ☎ 305-672-5044.* Housed in the restored, copper-domed Beth Jacob Orthodox Synagogue designed in 1936 by Henry Hohauser, this unique cultural institution opened in 1995 to display art and artifacts relating to more than 230 years of Jewish history in the Sunshine State. A 10-year comprehensive study of Jews in Florida led to more than 10,000 artifacts, photographs and mementos being combined in the MOSAIC exhibit, which became the museum's core collection in 1996. In addition, temporary exhibits relating different aspects of the Jewish experience in Florida rotate three times a year.

Light streams into the large domed room through eight colorful stained-glass windows. At the eastern end of the room stands a marble ark, crowned by a carved Torah supported by lions. A continuously running video *(18min)* illustrates the struggles and achievements encountered by Jews since they first landed on the Florida coast with Ponce de León to escape persecution in Spain.

★★**The Wolfsonian** – *1001 Washington Ave. Open year-round Tue–Sat 11am–6pm (Thu 9pm), Sun noon–5pm. Closed major holidays. $5. & ☎ 305-531-1001.* The seven-story Washington Storage Company building (1927, Robertson and Patterson), distinguished by an elaborate gold-colored Moorish relief facade of cast concrete, once stored clothing and furniture during summer months, when most apartments were vacant. Now owned and operated by Florida International University, it houses a museum and research center that oversees the Mitchell Wolfson Collection: more than 70,000 pieces of American and European (mainly British, German, Italian and Dutch) art and design dating from 1885 to 1945. These include rare books, graphics, political and propaganda artworks, architectural models, sculpture, glass, ceramics and furniture.

Joe's Stone Crab

Map p 224. 227 Biscayne St. Open mid-Oct–mid-May daily 5pm–10pm (Fri & Sat 11pm), Tue & Wed 11:30am–2pm. No reservations accepted. ♿ ✗ ♿ 🅿 ☎ *305-673-0365.* One of South Beach's best-known restaurants, Joe's has been a legend since 1913 when founder Joe Weiss began serving the succulent rust-colored crustaceans whose claws contain meat that rivals lobster for sweetness. Caught mainly off Florida's Gulf coast between October and May, stone crabs possess the ability to grow new claws within 12 to 18 months (fishermen take only the claws, since they contain the crab's only edible meat). Since the restaurant is as popular with locals as it is with visitors, expect to wait in long lines for dinner.

A **fountain** made from a fabulous glazed terra-cotta window grille from a 1929 movie theater dominates the lobby. The fifth floor is devoted to the permanent collection; about 300 works are displayed at any one time, illustrating how design has been used to help people adjust to the modern world. Focal points include design reform movements, urbanism, industrial design, transportation, world's fairs, advertising and political propaganda. Temporary exhibits occupy the sixth and seventh floors. The lower floors are given over to museum administration and student study areas.

Washington Avenue – A busy commercial thoroughfare encompassing chic restaurants and trendy dance clubs as well as ethnic markets and Cuban coffee shops, Washington Avenue features several public buildings of note. The grand, eight-story, Mediterranean-inspired **Old City Hall** (no. 1130) was designed by Martin Luther Hampton in 1927, before the Deco wave swept Miami Beach. The **US Post Office** (no. 1300) dates from 1939. Stripped of exterior ornament, the building displays the angular lines, glass-block window treatment and somewhat harsh overall modernist look widely adopted for Works Project Administration (WPA) structures of the 1930s—a style sometimes called Depression Moderne. Lined with cast brass lockboxes, the central **rotunda** boasts a 1940 mural by Charles Hardman depicting vignettes from Florida history.

Planned as an artists' colony in the 1920s, **Espanola Way★** *(between Washington and Drexel Aves.)* breathes fresh air into an otherwise shabby area. This gas-lit enclave, with its movie backdrop ensemble of Mediterranean Revival buildings decorated in coral-colored stucco and hand-painted tiles, features cozy courtyards, pink sidewalks and chic boutiques offering such apparel as sequined bikinis.

Lincoln Road Mall – *On Lincoln Rd. between Washington Ave. and Alton Rd. A tram runs regularly throughout the day.* This pedestrian-only enclave features shops, galleries, trendy restaurants and a central planted mall with quirky tiled fountains and coral rock pools. Lincoln Road is the oldest commercial street on the island, laid out in 1915 by Carl Fisher *(p 221)*, who promoted the link between his bayfront hotels and oceanside estates as the "Fifth Avenue of the South." The area has staged a second comeback since it was relandscaped and closed to traffic by Morris Lapidus (architect of the Fontainebleau Hotel) in the 1960s, and then deserted in the 1970s. After a $16-million face-lift, its latest transition is nearly complete. Shops—specializing in antiques, jewelry, books and designer clothing—and galleries improve in quality as you go west of Drexel Avenue. *(Most shops don't open until noon.)*

Originally a cinema, the 1935 Deco **Lincoln Theatre** *(nos. 555-541)* now hosts the New World Symphony, composed of promising music school graduates. A full season of concerts is offered from October to May *(for schedule ☎ 305-673-3331)*. Visitors are welcome at the **Artcenter South Florida** *(nos. 800-810)*, an intriguing warren of exhibit areas and studio spaces for some 100 photographers, ceramic artists, painters, jewelry designers and printmakers. *(Other Artcenter buildings are at 924 Lincoln Rd., 1035-43 Lincoln Rd., 1655-59 Lenox Ave. and 1632 Pennsylvania Ave.)* Virtually across the street from the Artcenter, members of the **Miami City Ballet** *(no. 905)* practice their pliés and pas-de-deuxs behind huge glass windows at the corner of Jefferson Avenue *(passers-by can pause and watch between August and March, 10am–5pm)*. The two-story **Sterling Building** *(no. 927)* dominates the streetfront with an undulating wall of tile-studded stucco and glass block. Across the mall at the corner of Lenox Avenue, the refurbished 1934 **Colony Theater** *(no. 1040)* presents plays, concerts and cultural programs *(for schedule ☎ 305-674-1026)*.

Jackie Gleason Theater of the Performing Arts – *1700 Washington Ave. For performance information ☎ 305-673-7300.* This confection of peach-colored concrete and glass block (1951, Pancoast, Hohauser and Dixon) was remodeled by

Morris Lapidus in 1976, and originally hosted comedian Jackie Gleason's popular television series from 1964 to 1970. The 3,000-seat theater now stages Broadway shows and ballets. Look for Roy Lichtenstein's red-and-white-striped **Mermaid (1)** on the south lawn *(fronting 17th St.)*. Set into plaques on the adjacent yard, cement footprints of such celebrities as Chita Rivera, Julie Andrews and *Miami Vice* star Don Johnson form the Walk of the Stars.

★**Holocaust Memorial** – *Nos. 1933-1945 Meridian Ave. Open year-round daily 9am–9pm.* ♿ 🅿 ☎ *305-538-1663.* Set in and around a tranquil lily pond, this haunting memorial (dedicated in 1990) to victims of the Holocaust leads visitors through a circular plaza of pale pink Jerusalem stone designed as a series of quiet outdoor passages and arbors. Names inscribed on the walls are a simple but chilling reminder of lives lost to the Nazis during World War II. The centerpiece is Kenneth Treister's *Sculpture of Love and Anguish*, which comprises several bronze vignettes and a giant 42ft-high outstretched arm symbolizing the last reach of a dying person. Miami artist and architect Treister also designed the Streets of Mayfair shopping complex in Coconut Grove.

Collins Park – *Between 21st and 22nd Aves. next to the ocean.* The area around Collins Park is the site of the first lots sold by John Collins *(p 221)* to finance his bridge project in 1912. Modernist hotels replaced older buildings in the 1930s. The marvelous futuristic tower fin on the restored **Plymouth** *(336 21st St.)*, designed by Anton Skislewicz in 1940, characterizes designs inspired by the space-age pylon featured at the 1939 World's Fair. The lobby mural by Ramon Chatov shows scantily clothed figures cavorting on the beach. (The Plymouth is now the residential home of the New World Symphony.) A grassy plaza and rounded glass-block entrance front the **Collins Park Hotel** *(2000 Park Ave.).* Designed in 1939 by Henry Hohauser, this marvel combines Art Deco zigzag motifs with the curving walls and portholes characteristic of the Moderne style.

★**Bass Museum of Art** – *2121 Park Ave. Open year-round Tue–Sat 10am–5pm, Sun 1pm-5pm. Closed major holidays. $7.* ♿ *www.ci.miami-beach.fl.us/culture/bass* ☎ *305-673-7530.* This landmark Art Deco structure (1930, Russell Pancoast) of oolitic limestone decorated with Mayan motifs was designed as the centerpiece of a nine-acre park given to the city in 1920 by developer John Collins. Originally used as both a library and art center, the building was renamed in 1964 when Austrian-born New York entrepreneur and philanthropist John Bass donated his art collection to the city of Miami Beach. Two first-floor galleries display fine European paintings, furnishings, altarpieces and other works spanning the 14C to 20C. Several masters are represented, including Peter Paul Rubens and Sandro Botticelli. Three upstairs galleries are devoted to temporary exhibits (in early 1999, Maxim Kantor and Roy Lichtenstein).

Two 19C tapestries by Louis-Marie Baader will flank the foyer when the first phase of a major expansion is completed in 1999. The expansion—directed by Japanese architect Arata Isozaki—will more than double the museum's size to 37,000sq ft, adding new gallery space as well as classrooms, an auditorium, a courtyard and a cafe.

★**Collins Avenue** – Although Collins Avenue is now one of the main traffic arteries in Miami Beach, it originally knew a more affluent lifestyle, catering to pedestrians with juice bars and small boutiques. Between 16th and 23rd Streets, hotels climb to 10 stories, the maximum height allowed; below 16th they may rise higher. Among the stars from the 1940s are the **National** *(no. 1677)* by Roy France; Robert Swartburg's **Delano** *(no. 1685)*, renovated in 1995 but still recognizable by its finned spaceship tower; and the **Ritz Plaza** *(no. 1701)* by L. Murray Dixon. With their squared, stepped-back facades and quirky central towers, these local landmarks resemble a trio of oversized party-goers dressed in giant overcoats and jaunty hats. For the best view, walk west two blocks on 17th Street and look east.

Driving north on Collins you will encounter a 13,000sq ft **mural** *(at 44th St.)* bearing the trompe l'œil image of a triumphal arch framing the **Fontainebleau Hilton** Resort and Towers, by noted muralist Richard Haas. The real Fontainebleau is just around the corner *(no. 4441)* on the 20-acre site of the former Harvey Firestone estate. This 1,200-room extravaganza (1954) is the work of Morris Lapidus, a set designer-turned-architect who dubbed it "modern French Château Style." The hotel fronts a beachside boardwalk (monitored by beach-patrol joggers) stretching 24 blocks from 23rd to 47th Streets.

To the north and west lie the exclusive residential areas of Middle Beach and Bal Harbour Village, a complex of high-rise condos and resorts. **Bal Harbour Shops** *(no. 9700)* is a mecca of high-fashion stores and boutiques including Tiffany & Company, Louis Vuitton, Cartier and Neiman Marcus.

PALM BEACH ★★★

Population 9,637
Map of Principal Sights p 3 – Map p 180
Tourist Information ☎ 561-575-4636

Occupying the northern part of a 16mi-long subtropical barrier island, this strip of real estate harbors one of the highest concentrations of multimillion-dollar mansions in the world. Though it has been a refuge for the rich for more than a century, Palm Beach attracts streams of tourists—particularly in winter—who venture across one of the bridges from the mainland to sample fine restaurants, stay in world-class hotels, shop along Worth Avenue and ogle the elegant estates bordering the ocean.

Historical Notes

From Coconuts to Palms – When a Spanish schooner aptly named *La Providencia* wrecked off this coast in 1879, the area's few settlers happily inherited a windfall cargo of coconuts. They planted the spoils and met with surprising success: a flourishing grove of some 20,000 coconut palms. This lush, tropical-looking shoreline caught the eye of Henry M. Flagler as he was scouting out a site for a new resort town. In Palm Beach Flagler claimed to have found "a veritable Paradise."

In the 1890s, Palm Beach had its first taste of the kind of development that would characterize the area for decades to come. Flagler's Royal Poinciana Hotel, now gone, opened in 1894 (the year his railroad came to town) with 540 rooms and the claim that it was the world's largest wooden structure. Only 17 guests occupied the hotel on its grand opening, but Flagler continued to believe he could entice travelers to the wilds of Florida, and he soon was proved right. More than any other person, Flagler was responsible for the development of southern Florida at the turn of the century. A New York Herald reporter wrote in 1903: "The Aladdin of Florida, Mr. Flagler rubbed his bank account and Palm Beach sprang into being." Flagler's indelible mark on the town is most apparent in two buildings: The Breakers hotel and Whitehall, his former Palm Beach home.

High Society Architecture – The next phase of growth owes much to the aquaintance of two men: Paris Singer, son of the sewing-machine magnate, and architect **Addison Mizner** (1872-1933). They met in Palm Beach, where both men had come in 1918 to convalesce. Singer's interest in architecture and Mizner's wit and bonhomie made for a quick friendship, and soon Singer was financing Mizner's bold ideas. Born into a prominent California family, Mizner at age 16 had traveled to Central America, where his father was serving as a diplomat. He later attended classes at the University of Salamanca in Spain and, though he never earned a degree, he began trading on his big talent and personality. His early exposure to Spanish culture showed in the country homes he designed in New York, where he practiced for 14 years before coming to Palm Beach. By the time Mizner and Singer went to work, Palm Beach was already a posh resort for the wealthy. Thus when their first project, a veteran's hospital, failed to attract enough patients, they simply converted the building in 1918 into the exclusive Everglades Club *(p 233)*, of which Singer was the sole owner. Mizner was then hired by the reigning social queen, Eva Stotesbury (wife of Philadelphia banker Edward Stotesbury), to build a lavish 32-room mansion. This and similar commissions for palatial homes occupied Mizner—now Florida's foremost society architect—throughout the early 1920s, until he began his projects in BOCA RATON.

Mizner and other Palm Beach architects took their inspiration from Spanish colonial manor houses and Italian Renaissance villas and palaces, developing or importing the necessary craftsmen, ceramic kilns and materials. To create an antique feeling, Mizner purposely chipped stone carvings, blackened ceilings with soot, and punctured furniture with fake wormholes. His style—broadly known as Mediterranean Revival *(p 28)* and characterized by pastel pink stucco walls, red-tile roofs and breezy loggias with fanciful embellishments—is now considered authentic Palm Beach style and is still imitated by modern architects.

The spectacular building boom of the late 1910s and early '20s left the town utterly changed. Early wooden seaside cottages and hotels were replaced by baronial mansions, giving Palm Beach its present look. Known as the "winter Newport" (for the Rhode Island retreat of the rich and famous), Palm Beach boasted restaurants, shops, clubs, hotels and villas, all tailored to the tastes of the wealthiest people on both sides of the Atlantic—the Vanderbilts, the Rockefellers, the Duke and Duchess of Windsor. When Florida real-estate speculation caved in on itself and the Depression gripped the country in the late 1920s, Palm Beach society continued to enjoy a luxurious lifestyle: the rich merely became less ostentatious.

Bastion of Elegance – While World War II brought air bases and new construction to the mainland of Palm Beach County, it also brought German U-boats to the coast. At least 12 Allied ships were torpedoed off the coast of Florida in 1942, including several oil tankers that exploded within sight of Palm Beach. Residents responded with fundraisers and other volunteer activities as well as nighttime blackouts to impede the Germans from spotting US ships.

After the war, Palm Beach society became less formal and the season extended well beyond winter, with many residents making permanent homes on the island. Among the elite who own property here today are Donald Trump, Ivana Trump, Estée Lauder and Jimmy Buffett. Today Palm Beach remains a picture-perfect island of palm-lined thoroughfares, immaculately clean streets and opulent homes where the only signs of activity are the perpetually busy gardeners. Visitors to this elegant small city will find shopkeepers and restauranteurs congenial, prices high and architectural beauty widespread.

DRIVING TOUR *1 day. 7.5mi. Map p 230.*

Start at Southern Blvd. and Ocean Blvd. (A1A) and head north. The speed limit is 35mph, though most people go slower.

This drive begins along the Atlantic, offering expansive **views**★★ of the ocean on the right and large, elegant homes on the left. The first mansion, partially hidden by walls and a massive gate, is **Mar-a-Lago** (1927, Joseph Urban and Marion Syms Wyeth), so-named ("sea to lake") because it extends from the Atlantic to Lake Worth. Widely considered the grandest residence in Palm Beach, this 188-room Moorish fantasy, built for cereal heiress Marjorie Merriweather Post, has been owned in recent years by Donald Trump; it is now a private social club.

Drive north 2.6mi on Ocean Blvd. and turn left at dead-end on Barton Ave. Park beside church on Barton Ave. or on Via Bethesda, one street to the north.

★★**The Episcopal Church of Bethesda-by-the-Sea** – *141 S. County Rd. Open year-round daily 8am–5pm. Closed major holidays.* ♿ 🅿 ☎ *561-655-4554.* Built in the Gothic Revival style in 1927, this graceful Episcopal church is actually the third church with the same name, replacing two earlier buildings outgrown by the population's size and prominence. The present structure of cast stone, designed by Hiss and Weeks of New York, features a prominent bell tower and several notable ornamentations, including sculptures of the four Evangelists standing in niches in the main entrance archway.

Inside, the nave sweeps upward to wooden rafters and forward to a dazzling blue stained-glass window above the altar. Called the **Te Deum Window**, the three lancets *(from left to right)* depict the apostles St. Peter and St. Paul, the risen Christ, and martyred saints Stephen and Catherine. Carried on three different ships, the glass made a precarious journey from England across a submarine-infested ocean in 1940. The white limestone reredos at the high altar shows, in the left panel, Jesus healing the paralytic at the pool of Bethesda. In the south transept hangs a 17C **Madonna and Child** by Spanish painter Esteban Murillo and a suspended model ship. The nautical motif continues in the north aisle windows, which portray biblical sea scenes.

A cloister to the left of the entrance leads to a courtyard and then to the **Cluett Memorial Gardens**, a lovely small formal garden with fountains, a gazebo and cruciform parterres.

Continue .3mi north on County Rd.

★★**The Breakers** – *1 S. County Rd. Visit by guided tour (1hr) only, year-round Wed 3pm; meet in main lobby. $10. Reservations suggested.* ✗ ♿ ☎ *561-655-6611 or 800-273-2537.* When Henry Flagler's famous hotel burned for the second time in 1925 (reportedly started by a curling iron left plugged in by the wife of Chicago's future mayor, Richard J. Daley), his heirs decided not to rebuild with wood. Instead they put up $6 million, hired the best architects, imported 75 artisans from Italy, and employed 1,200 craftsmen to construct a palatial hotel. Eleven and a half months later, the new Breakers was complete.

In the hotel's early days, formal attire—tuxedos, long gowns and a profusion of glittering jewelry—was *de rigueur* seven nights a week. Back then guests were expected to wear hat, gloves, coat and tie just to ride the carriage over to the beach where, as local historian Jim Ponce says, "you put on almost as much as you took off." An employee was posted to check that ladies' bathing stockings were dark enough. Many people chose to simply sit in a grandstand listening to the orchestra and watching the action on the beach.

The present grand hotel roughly follows an H-shaped layout and features twin two-tiered belvedere towers with open arches, a colonnaded porte cochere and exterior relief panels. The lobby runs the entire 200ft length of the center section (the cross in the "H") with an 18ft vaulted ceiling. From the lobby extends a lush courtyard with fountains and a sunken garden. The **Mediterranean Ballroom** boasts a striking hand-painted ceiling; this room is often used for charity balls, some with tickets priced as high as $650 (the hotel prides itself on raising several million dollars for charity annually). From the walls of another room, now used mostly for meetings and conventions, hang 15C and 16C **Flemish tapestries**. Behind the lobby, the Florentine Dining Room extends half the length of a football field; above one section of the room, a domed ceiling is painted with frescoes and Italian pastoral scenes.

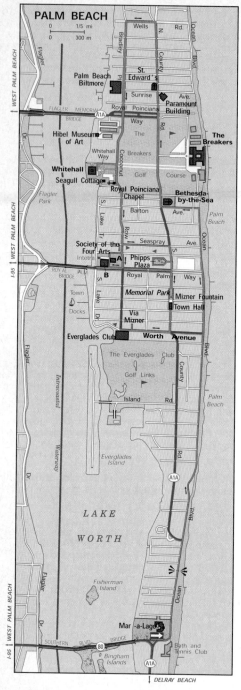

Modern facilities in this 572-room hotel include two 18-hole golf courses, 21 tennis courts, a half-mile of beachfront, pool, health club, water sports, croquet, shuffleboard, a shopping arcade and five restaurants.

Continue .3mi north to the southeast corner of Sunrise Ave.

Paramount Building – *139 N. County Rd.* This yellow building with green awnings, distinguished by its central entranceway and tall pointed arch, dates from 1927 when it opened as a 1,028-seat movie palace. Joseph Urban, set designer for the Ziegfield Follies and architect to Austrian Emperor Franz Josef, designed the theater, reportedly drawing the plans on a tablecloth in a Manhattan restaurant. Live performers included Charlie Chaplin, W.C. Fields and Glenn Miller. Women patrons wore so much jewelry that the semi-circle of box seats was dubbed the "diamond horseshoe," and season tickets sold for as much as $1,000 apiece. Closed in 1980, the building changed hands several times and the theater has been replaced by galleries, shops and offices.

Cross N. County Rd.

★**Saint Edward's Church** – *144 N. County Rd. Open year-round Mon–Fri 7am–4pm, Sat 7am–7pm, Sun & holidays 6:30am–1pm.* ♿ 🅿 ☎ *561-832-0400.* Distinguished by elaborate decoration inside and out, this Roman Catholic church (1927) features a baroque entrance of cast stone, a belfry and a red-tile roof. In the narthex, spiral marble pillars and carved wooden gates lead into a vast sanctuary vaulted with a hand-painted and mounted coffered ceiling that soars 65ft. The main altar, dedicated to the Sacred Heart, was carved from a single piece of Carrera marble and measures 28ft by 15ft. Eight clerestory windows on either side of the nave represent scenes from the life of the Virgin Mary. Cloister windows on the north depict eight parables, those on the south eight miracles. Other windows were donated by such illustrious patrons as the Hearsts and the Kennedys, who worshipped here in the early 1960s.

Continue north .6mi on County Rd. and turn left onto Wells Rd. and left again on Bradley Pl.

Seven blocks down on the right stands the **Palm Beach Biltmore** (*Bradley Pl. and Sunrise Ave.*), a 1927 resort hotel that closed in 1970. Purchased that year by insurance tycoon John D. MacArthur (*p 236*) for $1.5 million and sold seven years later for $5.3 million, the building now houses luxury condominiums.

Proceed two blocks farther south across Royal Poinciana Way and turn right into Royal Poinciana Plaza.

Hibel Museum of Art – *150 Royal Poinciana Plaza (rear of plaza). Open year-round Tue–Sat 10am–5pm, Sun 1pm–5pm. Closed Jan 1, Thanksgiving Day, Dec 25.* ⚹ ☎ *561-833-6870.* This attractive repository contains more than 1,000 works by American artist Edna Hibel. The museum opened in 1977, the project of art patrons Clayton and Ethelbelle Craig, who were deeply moved by the love of humanity displayed in Hibel's work. Born in 1917, Hibel began painting at age 10 and sold a painting to the Boston Museum of Fine Arts *(see Michelin Green Guide to New England)* at age 23. Since then Hibel, who lives and works in Palm Beach County, has exhibited her work around the world. On display are her sensitive paintings, stone lithographs, sculptures and porcelains, many of which reflect a mother-and-child motif.

Continue south on Cocoanut Row (the continuation of Bradley Pl.) and take the first right onto Whitehall Way.

★★Henry M. Flagler Museum (Whitehall) – *Whitehall Way. Open year-round Tue–Sat 10am–5pm, Sun noon–5pm. Closed Jan 1, Thanksgiving Day, Dec 25. $7.* ▣ *www.flagler.org* ☎ *561-655-2833.* Florida railroad magnate and Standard Oil partner **Henry Morrison Flagler** built this 55-room Gilded Age mansion overlooking Lake Worth in 1901 as a wedding gift for his third wife, Mary Lily Kenan. Flagler's first wife, Mary Harkness, died of a respiratory illness in 1881; his second wife, Mary's nurse, Ida Alice Shourds, was committed to an asylum in 1897 when she announced her engagement to the Czar of Russia, with whom she communicated by Ouija board. The 71-year-old Flagler used his influence to bend state laws so that he could obtain a divorce and marry 34-year-old Kenan of North Carolina. The marriage caused an irrevocable split between Flagler and his son.

Determined to give his young bride a proper welcome into the family, Flagler decided to build the greatest house on the island. He hired prominent architects John M. Carrère and Thomas Hastings, designers of the New York Public Library. They built Whitehall in just 18 months at a cost of $2.5 million.

After Flagler's death in 1913 the house closed, reopening as the Whitehall Hotel in 1925 with the ungainly addition of a 12-story tower on the lake side. When the hotel failed in 1959, Jean Flagler Mathews, Henry's granddaughter, saved the family home from demolition by turning it into a historic house museum.

Visit – *2hrs.* The mansion, designed by Carrère and Hastings, has been restored to its Flagler-era appearance with many of the original furnishings. A formally land-scaped walkway leads to a two-story verandah that spans the front of the house; lower wings on either side create the illusion of great length. **Marble Hall**, a 110ft-by-40ft imitation of a Roman villa's atrium decorated in seven different shades of polished marble, dazzles the eye with its opulent appointments: Louis XIV gold armchairs covered in silk velvet; a massive marble-top table; a 9ft rosewood clock; and the masterful oval ceiling mural by Italian artist Benvenuti, entitled *Crowning of Knowledge*, in homage to formal education (of which Flagler received little).

Louis XVI Salon, Whitehall

231

Just off the entrance hall to the south, the Italian Renaissance Library displays the original red-velvet wall covering. Next door, the **Louis XIV Music Room** reflects the interests of Mary Lily Flagler, who enjoyed singing. The 24-rank organ was played regularly by the resident organist in this chamber hung with Baccarat chandeliers and paintings by such 18C masters as Gainsborough and Romney.

The **Ballroom** features gilt mirrors, crystal chandeliers, damask draperies and bronze fixtures hung with crystal grapes, pears and Florida bananas. In the Elizabethan Breakfast Room, guests were expected to arrive promptly at 9am. The adjoining **Francis I Dining Room**, with its carved walnut woodwork and coffered plaster ceiling, saw a procession of royalty, wealth and fame with names such as Rockefeller, Astor and Vanderbilt. After dinner, ladies withdrew to the elegant **Louis XVI Salon**.

The second floor contains the Rococo-style **Master Suite** dressed in yellow watered silk damask, Mrs. Flagler's sitting room, and 14 guest suites, each decorated in a different style.

In the central outdoor courtyard, arched loggias define the north and south walls, while in the middle a marble Venus poses above four lecherous satyrs. Flagler's private railroad car, "Rambler," stands on the south lawn. Visitors may walk through the car to see its sumptuous sleeping berths and kitchen area.

Sitting on a serene lawn, two structures counterpoint the grandeur of Whitehall. The gray wood non-denominational **Royal Poinciana Chapel** *(60 Cocoanut Row, just south of the Flagler Museum; visit by appointment only;* ♿ ☎ *561-655-4212)* was built by Flagler in 1896 for use by guests at his Royal Poinciana Hotel. Moved to Whitehall's grounds when Cocoanut Row was installed, the church features a Classical clapboard facade topped by a square carillon tower and set with Georgian arched windows. Behind the chapel stands the oldest extant house in Palm Beach, **Seagull Cottage** *(not open to the public)*. In 1893 Flagler bought this Queen Anne-style cottage, built by Denver railroad entrepreneur Robert McCormick in 1886, and used it as his winter home until the completion of Whitehall. It now serves as the chapel's parish house.

Drive south .7mi and turn right on Royal Palm Way; take first right into Four Arts Plaza.

★**The Society of the Four Arts** – *Four Arts Plaza.* Organized in 1936 to foster an appreciation for art, music, literature and drama, The Society of the Four Arts retained the services of Swiss architect Maurice Fatio to design an appropriate building. Fatio's elegantly restrained Italianate edifice now houses the **Gioconda and Joseph King Library★ (A)** *(east end of mall)*, containing more than 40,000 volumes for community use *(open Nov–Apr Mon–Fri 10am–5pm, Sat 9am–1pm; rest of the year Mon–Fri 10am–5pm;* ♿ 🅿 *www.fourarts.org* ☎ *561-655-2766)*. The walls of the entrance loggia display canvas murals of the four arts for which the society was named. The walkway and entrance floor are made of coquina rock cut from the Florida seacoast.

In the late 1940s the society began looking for additional space for a gallery and theater. Across the street to the west stood a vacant building that Addison Mizner and his assistant, Lester Liesler, had designed in 1928. Originally a nightclub known for its asymmetrical features, this handsome structure caught the eye of prominent architect John Volk, who suggested that the society purchase it. In 1947 he went to work, transforming halls into galleries, enclosing the courtyard, converting the bar into executive offices, and creating a 716-seat theater. The resulting **Esther B. O'Keeffe Gallery Building (B)** provides space for exhibitions, films, lectures and concerts *(open Dec–mid-Apr Mon–Sat 10am–5pm, Sun 2pm–5pm; closed major holidays; $3; films $3; concerts $20-$25;* ♿ 🅿 ☎ *561-655-7226)*.

At the west end of the grassy, palm-lined mall behind the gallery stands Isamu Noguchi's compelling pyramid, *Intetra*. Adjoining the library, intimate **gardens★** feature a Chinese rock garden, a rose garden and tranquil, fern-rimmed pools.

At the entrance to the adjoining **Philip Hulitar Sculpture Garden**, Edward Hoffman's bronze, *Reaching*, gracefully evokes the mother-and-child bond. Named for the noted dress designer, this lovely greensward boasts sculpture by renowned 20C artists, among them Henry Mitchell and Anna Hyatt Huntington *(open Nov–Apr Mon–Fri 10am–5pm, Sat 9am–1pm; rest of the year Mon–Fri 10am–5pm; closed major holidays;* ♿ 🅿 ☎ *561-655-7226)*.

Cross Four Arts Plaza (north) and turn right on Seaview Ave. Take first left on Cocoanut Row, then right on Seaspray and right on County Rd. Make second right into Phipps Plaza.

Phipps Plaza – *On N. County Rd. between Seaview Ave. and Royal Palm Way.* Planned by affluent resident socialite John S. Phipps, this peaceful old-world cul-de-sac is a smooth mix of residential and commercial properties. The leading Florida architects of the 1920s—Addison Mizner, Maurice Fatio and Marion Syms Wyeth—contributed to the streetscape, which blends Mediterranean and Bermudan styles. Distinctive features include belfries and walls covered with tiles taken from old buildings in Cuba, ornate iron gates, winding staircases and a densely planted central park of ficus and yucca, frangipani and golden shower trees. Phipps Plaza became the town's first designated historic district in 1979.

Turn right on County Rd. and continue 3 blocks south.

Town Hall – *360 S. County Rd., between Australian and Chilian Aves. Open year-round Mon–Fri 8:30am–5pm.* ♿ ☎ *561-838-5400.* Designed by Harvey and Clarke in 1924, this attractive building originally consisted of two separate edifices joined by a courtyard. Architect John Volk connected the two in 1965 to provide more office space for a growing city. Beige stucco walls rise to a barrel-tile roof crowned by an enclosed bell tower. On the north side of Town Hall, **Mizner Fountain** splashes into three basins upheld by heroic rearing horses. Addison Mizner designed the fountain and surrounding **Memorial Park**, an oasis in the middle of busy County Road, which features cut coral-stone pavement and plantings that flank the narrow pool leading from the fountain.

Continue two blocks south of Town Hall and turn right on Worth Ave.

★★**Worth Avenue** – *Between Ocean Blvd. and Cocoanut Row.* The East Coast's answer to Rodeo Drive in Beverly Hills, California, this charming street acts as a magnet for well-heeled tourists and residents, as well as the merely curious, who come to eat, shop, browse and ogle the merchandise. Though named for a colonel in the Seminole Wars, the avenue really measures worth in simple terms: money. Here the island's palmiest boutiques stand shoulder to shoulder and read like names from a shopper's Who's Who: Cartier, Ralph Lauren, Liz Claiborne, Charles Jourdan, Saks Fifth Avenue. In between are galleries, eateries and specialty shops, such as the one that sells only leaden toy soldiers.

Worth Avenue's mélange of styles succeeds in creating a picturesque street with a decidedly European flair. Addison Mizner designed many of the connecting two-story villas along the street in 1924, as well as the delightful *vias*, or alleyways, that thread off the main road into charming little courtyards of tile-work fountains and hanging flower baskets. Among these, **Via Mizner**★ stands out for its labyrinthine passages and pastel walls of yellow, pink and aqua. Mizner's own four-story apartment dominates the skyline here. At the west end of the street stands his first Florida commission, the three-story **Everglades Club** *(no. 356)*—an exclusive gathering place that started life as a convalescent home for veterans of World War I. Its design blends features of Venetian, Spanish and Moorish architecture.

In spite of Worth Avenue's high-toned commercialism, visitors can buy a reasonably priced meal at a courtyard restaurant or simply stroll the bougainvillea-studded sidewalks and watch the people: chic women bejeweled and gloved, men in straw boaters stepping from convertible BMWs, slim models showing off the latest fashions, shoppers burdened with precious purchases.

WEST PALM BEACH★

Population 79,305
Map of Principal Sights p 3 – Map p 180
Tourist Information ☎ 561-833-3711

A West Palm Beach resident, referring to the gulf in wealth and social status between the Palm Beaches, once observed that "Lake Worth is the largest body of water in the world." Hugging the inland side of the lake, this center of commerce and industry remains, at least to some degree, in the shadow of its glamorous parent, PALM BEACH. Although West Palm Beach has outstripped the resort island in size, population and skyline, outsiders still tend to view it as little more than a commercial suburb. Nevertheless, the city offers its own attractions, including one of Florida's finest art museums.

Historical Notes

Humble Origins – West Palm Beach first attracted workers who came to build the grand hotels on Palm Beach. In 1893, under the direction of Henry Flagler, the area's premier developer, surveyors laid out a town site and named streets in alphabetical order—Althea, Banyan, Clematis, Datura, etc. In keeping with Flagler's intention of reserving the island for tourists and the mainland for commerce, West Palm Beach played the rough-and-tumble laborer to Palm Beach's uppercrust gentleman, with Banyan Street becoming known for its saloons, gambling dens and brothels. While vice flourished, many civic organizations—churches, public utilities and schools—brought cohesiveness to the community. By 1909 West Palm Beach attained the county seat and propelled itself into a booming era of construction. As ritzy hotels and houses were blossoming across the lake, West Palm Beach began sprouting a commercial skyline, the construction of which lasted through the building period of the 1980s.

A Modern Cityscape – Along **Flagler Drive** high-rise banks and office buildings contrast with such Palm Beach landmarks as The Breakers and Whitehall visible across Lake Worth. Bikers and joggers take advantage of the drive's landscaped promenade, which provides fine **views**★ of the sparkling lake and its marina. The **Old Northwood**

Flagler Drive

neighborhood *(bounded by Flagler Dr. and Broadway Ave., 25th and 36th Sts.)* contains a number of Spanish-style homes dating from the 1920s, some designed by late Palm Beach architect John Volk. Generally the more expensive and attractive houses are closest to the water; poorer homes lie between Dixie Highway and Australian Avenue.

In addition to its commercial and banking concerns, West Palm Beach serves as the area's transportation hub: an international airport and the restored Mediterranean Revival **Seaboard Air Line Railway Station** *(201 S. Tamarind Ave.)*, built in 1925 by Harvey and Clarke, service the city's burgeoning population. Two major thoroughfares (US-1 and I-95) cut through West Palm Beach, and Florida's Turnpike runs just west.

SIGHTS *2 days. Map p 235.*

★★**Norton Museum of Art** – *1451 S. Olive Ave. Open mid-Nov–Apr Mon–Sat 10am–5pm, Sun 1pm–5pm. Rest of the year Tue–Sat 10am–5pm, Sun 1pm–5pm. Closed Jan 1, July 4, Thanksgiving Day, Dec 25. $5.* ✕ ⑃ ▣ *www.norton.org* ☎ *561-832-5196.* Founded in 1941 by steel tycoon **Ralph H. Norton** (1875-1953), this gallery boasts a wonderful spectrum of some 4,000 pieces. In its permanent holdings, special emphasis is placed on 19C–20C American and European works and Chinese art from 1700 BC to the early 1900s. Born to wealthy parents, Norton gained his appreciation of fine art by attending the Chautauqua series of lectures and concerts held in summer near his Chicago home, and by traveling to Europe with his mother. Although he began studying music, he also completed a course in a manual training school. After college he became a tool and machine designer with Acme Steel Goods Company. Norton began collecting art in 1921, buying, as he put it, "some original oil paintings for decorative purposes." Soon afterwards, collectors' mania struck. He began educating himself by attending art show openings in Chicago, New York and Pittsburgh, and slowly amassed a formidable collection.

In 1939 the semi-retired Norton, who wintered with his wife in West Palm Beach, offered his art collection to The Society of the Four Arts *(p 232)* in nearby Palm Beach. When they delayed making a decision, he purchased a city block near his house and commissioned the Norton Museum to "preserve for the future the beautiful things of the past." Marion Sims Wyeth, co-architect of Mar-a-Lago *(p 229)*, designed the original museum, a modest white building along classical lines, trimmed with Alabama limestone. When the gallery opened in 1941, the collection numbered just over 100 paintings. Over the years, the accumulation of Norton's purchases and third-party gifts have resulted in one of the finest collections of its size in the US.

Visit – *3hrs.* An expansion, completed in 1997, more than doubled the museum's size to 77,500sq ft. Architect Chad Floyd (Centerbrook Architects) remained faithful to Wyeth's original design while giving special attention to South Florida's unique climate- and humidity-control issues. The museum gardens were relandscaped; the number of galleries was increased from 9 to 19; an education wing, cafe and visitor parking were added.

The permanent collection includes a group of **French Impressionist** and **Postimpressionist** paintings by such notables as Cézanne, Matisse, Monet, Renoir, Gauguin and Picasso. Gauguin's *Agony In The Garden* (1889), a self-portrait of the artist as Christ, and Picasso's *The Red Foulard* number among the best-known works. **Twentieth-century American art** forms another significant part of the permanent holdings. Works by Davis, Hopper, Marin, O'Keeffe, Rauschenberg, Warhol and Pollock figure prominently.

The museum's renowned **Chinese collection★** comprises archaic jade tomb carvings (c.1500-500 BC) and ritual bronzes from the Shang (1527-500 BC) and Early Eastern Chou (7C-6C BC) Dynasties. Ceramics and Buddhist sculpture, some from as early as the Shang period, round out this collection.

Between 10 and 14 traveling exhibitions rotate through the museum each year. A series of music and educational programs is also presented.

Ann Norton Sculpture Gardens – *253 Barcelona Rd., north corner of Flagler Dr. Open mid-Oct–mid-Jun Tue–Sat 10am–4pm. Closed major holidays. $3.* 🅿 ☎ *561-832-5328.* This former residence of gallery founder Ralph Norton has been converted to a display grounds for his second wife's sculpture. **Ann Weaver Norton** (1905-1982) came to the area in 1942 as the Norton School of Art's first instructor in sculpture. She married Ralph Norton in 1948, a year after the death of his first wife. The two-story house (1925) was remodeled in the mid-1930s by Marion Sims Wyeth, who added the wrought-iron balcony and first-floor bay

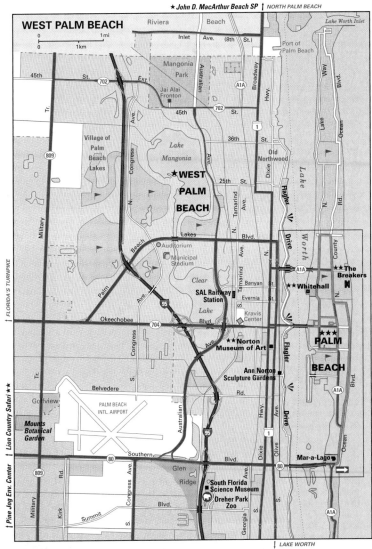

windows. The house now contains more than 100 of Ann Norton's sculptures and hosts frequent shows of local artists' work. In the garden, a walking trail leads past nine of Norton's monumental brick and granite **abstract megaliths**, designed to suggest Tibetan shrines, mythical beasts and totemic figures. An outstanding collection of palms—some 300 trees representing over 200 varieties—also graces the property.

Palm Beach Zoo at Dreher Park – **Kids** *1301 Summit Blvd., just east of I-95, accessible from Southern Blvd. or Forest Hill Blvd. exits. Open year-round daily 9am–5pm. $6. ✕⅋ ▣ www.bestzoo.org ☎ 561-533-0887.* Set on 23 acres adjacent to I-95, this small zoo is home to more than 400 animals representing 128 different species. Outstanding among the 22 endangered and threatened species are the white Bengal tiger, Florida panther and golden lion tamarin. None of the animals displayed here were captured in the wild—some were borrowed from other zoos, some were donated, and others were placed here by wildlife officials. A short boardwalk nature trail *(.25mi)* leads through lush tropical foliage.

South Florida Science Museum – **Kids** *4801 Dreher Trail North, just north of the zoo. Open year-round daily 10am–5pm (Fri 10pm). Closed Thanksgiving Day & Dec 25. $5 (additional $2 for planetarium shows, $4-$6 extra for laser light shows). ⅋ ▣ www.sfsm.org ☎ 561-832-1988.* A mastodon skeleton in the front hall greets visitors to this single-story museum. Found in central Palm Beach County in 1967 by a work crew, most of the original mastodon bones were destroyed or looted, but enough remained for paleontologists to reconstruct the entire creature. At some of the 28 different interactive exhibits visitors can test their senses, create frozen shadows and learn about electricity. A native plant center and aquarium room explore local flora and fauna; another room is dedicated to temporary exhibits. The observatory, planetarium and laser shows are perennial favorites.

Pine Jog Environmental Center – *6301 Summit Blvd., 5mi west of I-95 on north side just before Summit dead-ends into Jog Rd. Trails open year-round Mon–Fri 9am–5pm. ▣ ☎ 561-686-6600.* The Atlantic Ocean retreated from this area 10,000 years ago, leaving behind a marsh that has gradually evolved into a dry sandy flatland. Owned by Henry Flagler at the turn of the century, this 150-acre tract was designated a wildlife sanctuary that in 1970 became associated with Florida Atlantic University. Through school programs, nature walks and interpretive displays, the center seeks to promote awareness of the changes wrought by man and nature on the Florida wilderness.

Mounts Botanical Garden – *531 N. Military Trail. Open year-round Mon–Sat 8:30am–4:30pm, Sun & holidays 1pm–5pm. Closed Jan 1, Thanksgiving Day, Dec 25. ⅋ ▣ www.mounts.org ☎ 561-233-1749.* Though low-flying planes from the nearby airport mar its tranquillity, this 14-acre garden does lure visitors to meander down paths by rose beds, herbs, desert plantings, palms and a central pond and fountain. A Xeriscape (dry landscape) area offers tips on water-saving gardening. Started in 1954 by county extension agent Marvin Mounts, the site maintains an educational outreach program for local gardeners.

EXCURSIONS *Map p 180*

★**John D. MacArthur Beach State Park** – *2hrs. 9mi north of Palm Beach, on Singer Island. Take US-1 north 4mi to Riviera Beach; turn right on Rte. 708 (Heron Blvd.), which becomes A1A. Follow A1A north 5mi to park entrance. Open year-round daily 8am–dusk. $3.25/vehicle. Nature center offers ranger-led nature walks (Jan–Apr Wed–Mon 10am, rest of the year Fri–Sun 10am). Evening turtle walks (p 299) in June & July by reservation only. ⅋ ☎ 561-624-6952.* Named for the eccentric insurance baron who donated a portion of his valuable property on Singer Island, this natural haven encompasses 760 acres of mangrove estuary and pristine beach. Bordered by high-rise apartment buildings and hotels, the park reigns as the most productive estuary in a county that has lost more than 85 percent of its estuarine wetlands to development in the last few decades.

The weathered wood **nature center** contains excellent exhibits, and a video *(15min)* explains the ecosystem of a barrier island *(open year-round Wed–Mon 9am–5pm; ⅋ ☎ 407-624-6952).* Just outside, the Butterfly Garden Trail offers a peaceful stroll among native flowers and the butterflies they attract; beside the parking lot, the Satinleaf Trail *(.5mi)* loops through a hardwood forest that supports tropical trees such as the mastic and strangler fig.

A 1,600ft wooden bridge across Lake Worth Cove *(accessible by foot or tram)* provides wonderful **views**★ of the mangrove estuary and its birdlife—150 species, mainly waterfowl but also songbirds and raptors, have been identified here. A dense coastal hammock anchors the east end of the bridge, where vistors may continue on to a wide beach littered only with brown sargassum. Undeveloped Munyon Island (formerly the site of a resort hotel; now part of the park) is accessible only by boat.

★★Lion Country Safari – 🄺🄸🄳🄼 *1/2 day. 16mi west of I-95 on Southern Blvd. (Rte. 80); turn right at sign and continue 2mi to entrance. Open year-round daily 9:30am–4:30pm. $14.95.* △ 🍴 & 🅿 *www.lioncountrysafari.com* ☎ *561-793-1084. Visit begins with a drive of the 8mi road that loops through the park. Visitors are requested to remain in their cars with windows rolled up. Convertibles are not allowed; air-conditioned sedans are available for rent. Motorists may drive the loop and pull over as often as they like for views and photographs, but are cautioned to stay in their cars at all times. Admission price includes a guide booklet, which provides information about the animals.*

Billing itself as North America's first cageless zoo, this 500-acre, drive-through game preserve opened in 1967. The road loops through five simulated African, Asian and North American habitats, taking visitors past more than 1,300 animals of 131 different species. Drawing some 500,000 visitors a year, the safari ranks as one of the area's most popular attractions.

The first section, **Lake Nakaru**, features such exotics as the lowland tapir from South America, the white-handed gibbon and the Australian emu. The **Great Plains** area includes a variety of cattle species, bison and water buffalo among them. Lions roam the **Gorongosa Reserve**, separated from other animals who represent their natural prey. Though easily visible, lions are apt to be asleep. On the **Serengeti Plain** visitors can spot waterbuck, wildebeest, eland and the African ostrich. The world's largest bird, the ostrich has a reputation for pecking at windshields. African elephants, an endangered species, live within a large enclosure in this section. Finally, the **Wankie National Park** holds giraffes, zebras, rhinoceroses and chimpanzees. One of the continent's most successful chimp populations inhabit several little islands, each family segregated from the others because they cannot swim. Several generations, led by a dominant male, inhabit each island, which is furnished with wooden platforms and vine-like ropes.

An amusement park near the entrance offers boat and carousel rides, animal demonstrations, miniature golf, a petting zoo and a short nature trail.

Southwest Coast

Stretching 120mi along the Gulf of Mexico from Bradenton down to Naples, southwest Florida presents a mirror image of the state's Atlantic coast, but in softer tones. As on the east coast, major highways trace the shoreline, linking cities of gleaming white high-rises that face the sea; but this side enjoys a calmer pace, smaller cities and waters that lap more gently on the shore. And on this coast the sun sets into the sea in a pageant of colors.

Though Ponce de León and other 16C Spanish explorers sailed along this shore, they concentrated their attentions for the most part on Tampa Bay and left the southwest coast to the Calusa Indians. White settlement, which commenced in the mid-1800s, proceeded in fits and starts until the turn of the century, when development solidified into a leisurely pace. While TAMPA and the east coast were booming with railroads and buildings, the southwest remained agricultural. Fishing villages and a handful of scattered tourist hotels attracted those with a penchant for adventure and the resources to make an excursion by boat. By the late 1920s, though, the area was coming into its own: **John Ringling** (p 254), who had begun developing some of the islands near Sarasota, started wintering his famous circus here in 1927, the same year the Seaboard Air Line Railway finally reached Naples.

Charting a steady course of progress up to the present, Southwest Florida now faces many of the same dilemmas looming in other parts of the state. Most of its coast is already developed to capacity, and a largely sophisticated and environmentally aware population is working to control the rampant growth of past decades. Large tracts of land on Sanibel and other barrier islands have been preserved for shorebirds and other wildlife; citizens are realizing the need for long-term planning in an area where tourism ranks as the top industry and the beach is its greatest asset. Recent beach replenishment projects—with sand pumped up from offshore or trucked in from elsewhere—have taken place in Naples, Venice, Bonita Beach, Marco Island, Longboat Key and Captiva Island.

For tourists the Southwest Coast continues to hold many charms. From the cultural enticements of Sarasota and the sparkling beaches and excellent resorts of the barrier islands, to the fossilized sharks' teeth buried in Venice's sands and the fashionable shops and restaurants in Naples, this diverse region offers visitors a corner of paradise.

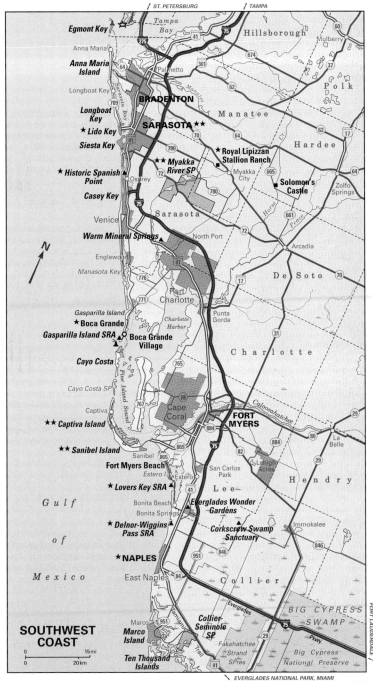

SOUTHWEST COAST

0   15mi
0   20km

BOCA GRANDE★

Map of Principal Sights p 3 – Map p 239
Tourist Information ☎ 941-964-0568

This charming village of sun-splashed houses and quaint, pastel-colored shops perches at the southern end of 7mi-long **Gasparilla Island**, separated from the mainland by a 2mi toll bridge and causeway. Spanish for "big mouth," Boca Grande refers to the pass that opens to Charlotte Harbor, one of the state's deepest natural inlets. Visitors will find here an unhurried island with natural beauty to rival the more well-known Sanibel and Captiva Islands to the south.

Making a good living from the sea, the Calusa Indians knew of Gasparilla's charms more than 1,000 years ago. By the late 1870s, Cuban and Spanish fishermen had established a fishing ranch on the north end of the island. With the discovery of phosphate on the nearby mainland in 1885, port Boca Grande became a worldwide shipping center. The completion of the Northern Railroad in 1907 facilitated the transport of phosphate, and also created an avenue south for wealthy northerners.

Already known as a **tarpon-fishing** mecca, Boca Grande soon grew into an actual town with streets, a post office and the stately 1912 **Gasparilla Inn** *(500 Palm Ave.)*, which continues to welcome guests. Today vacationers seek respite on the island's lovely peaceful beaches and fishermen continue to cast their lines in the waters of Boca Grande Pass in hopes of netting *Tarpon atlanticus*—which can weigh as much as 300 pounds apiece.

SIGHTS *1/2 day*

Boca Grande Village – *Located on the south end of Gasparilla Island; follow Gasparilla Rd. south to Park St.* This charming hamlet merits a couple of hours to wander through its quaint shops, sample its restaurants, and stroll past the handful of restored early 20C buildings that make up its center. Planted in 1914, stout trees form a dark tunnel over locally famous **Banyan Street**; the white-frame 1910 **United Methodist Church** *(Gilchrist Ave. and Third St.)* still holds Sunday services. The railroad quit running here when the causeway opened in 1958, but the old **depot** *(Park Ave. and Fourth St.)* was restored in the 1970s into a plaza of shops, offices and a restaurant. Around the corner on Third Street, the former **San Marco Theatre** (1926) now holds a restaurant and yet more shops.

Gasparilla Island State Recreation Area – *On the southern end of island; follow Gulf Blvd. south of village. Open year-round daily 8am–dusk. $2/vehicle.* ☎ *941-964-0375.* Five separate parking lots allow access to the sparkling white beach here. At the southern tip of the island, a picnic area surrounds the two-story, white-frame **Boca Grande Lighthouse** *(follow Gulf Blvd. south to Belcher Rd.)*. Built in 1890, the beacon served as a navigational aid at the mouth of Charlotte Harbor until 1966. Relit in 1986, the tower is still undergoing restoration *(open last Sat of every month 10am–4pm; contribution requested)*. From here you can see Cayo Costa *(below)* across breezy Boca Grande Pass, and the twin green tanks of Boca's oil-transfer station, where great tankers off-load oil destined for Fort Myers and other points.

EXCURSIONS

Cayo Costa – *1 day. Description p 254. Accessible by boat only. Ferry service operates year-round daily 10:30am, return at 3pm. 15min one-way. Reservations required. Tram service from dock to Cayo Costa State Park. $25 round-trip. Boat charter service offered ($65/hr).* ♿ ▣ *Boca Grande Charters* ☎ *941-964-1100.*

Cabbage Key – *1 day. Description p 254. Accessible by boat only. Ferry service operates year-round daily 10:30am, return at 3pm. 30min one-way. Reservations required. $25 round-trip. Boat charter service offered ($65/hr).* ♿ ▣ *Boca Grande Charters* ☎ *941-964-1100.*

BRADENTON

Population 47,219
Map of Principal Sights p 3 – Map p 259
Tourist Information ☎ 941-729-9177

Set on the banks of the Manatee River 11mi north of Sarasota and bisected by US-41, Bradenton exudes a more commercial air than its southern neighbor. A relaxed pace lies to the west at low-key Bradenton Beach on Anna Maria Island and in the folksy 19C fishing village of Cortez.

Historical Notes

For more than 500 years the local Indians farmed and fished this region with no thought of the Europeans to come. Early conquistador Pánfilo de Narváez left little permanent imprint here. Then in 1539 an armada of nine galleons, spearheaded by **Hernando de Soto**, appeared in Tampa Bay and disgorged more than 600 soldiers for the start of a 4,000mi inland odyssey. The probable landing site was the south shore of the Manatee River, just northwest of present-day Bradenton. De Soto's four-year journey marked the first massive exploration of North America, and the DeSoto National Memorial *(below)* commemorates his landing.

Another 300 years passed before the first wave of permanent white settlers discovered what is now Bradenton. Among the pioneers were **Hector and Joseph Braden**, wealthy brothers from Tallahassee who moved south in the early 1840s and together purchased more than 1,000 acres of land. Here Joseph built a two-story "castle" of tabby with walls some 20in thick to ward off Indian attacks. Its crumbling, fenced-in ruins stand today in a retirement community *(Braden Castle Rd., north end of 27th St. E.)*. Another Tallahassee native, **Major Robert Gamble** *(p 242)* moved to this area in 1842, to begin planting sugarcane on the plantation he started nearby.

After recovering from the economic losses of the Civil War, the Bradenton area experienced a steady rise to prosperity. Following the establishment of the town's first post office in 1878, there began a period of building that lasted to the Depression years. After World War II, more businesses sprang to life to service the well-established tomato and citrus farms in the surrounding county. Boat manufacturing and tourism round out today's economic profile, with a large working-class community creating the need for inexpensive housing and modern urban conveniences.

Don't be discouraged by the sprawling gridwork of streets and highways that presents a generic assemblage of retail and service outlets in contrast to Sarasota, Bradenton's well-heeled and art-conscious neighbor to the south. A handful of historic and natural sites here prove well worth the short drive up from Sarasota or down from TAMPA.

SIGHTS   *1 day. Map pp 258-259.*

South Florida Museum, Bishop Planetarium and Parker Manatee Aquarium – *201 10th St. W. Open Jan–Apr & Jul, Mon–Sat 10am–5pm, Sun noon–5pm. Rest of the year Tue–Sat 10am–5pm, Sun noon–5pm. Closed Jan 1, Thanksgiving Day, Dec 25. $7.50.* ▣ *www.manatee-cc.com/planets* ☎ *941-746-4131.* Dedicated in 1946 to interpreting the cultural and natural history of Manatee County and Florida, this museum complex—a full city block in size—boasts two floors filled with artifacts from prehistory to the space age. The first floor contains fine exhibits on Indians and an extensive collection of fossils, shells and minerals. On the second floor, you'll find pioneer rooms, a maritime history exhibit and a medical wing with life-size dioramas. The back of the museum opens onto a courtyard surrounded by replicas of Hernando de Soto's 16C Spanish home, a chapel and a manor house. The mainstay of the **Parker Manatee Aquarium** 🄺🄸🄳🅂 *(2nd floor)* is a middle-aged manatee named Snooty, who celebrated his 50th birthday in 1998. Five months prior, he was joined in his pool by a four-year-old manatee named Newton *(manatee demos daily 12:30pm, 2pm & 3:30pm)*.

The **Bishop Space-Transit Planetarium**, meanwhile, offers state-of-the-art star and laser shows *(astronomy shows Tue–Sun 1pm & 4pm; weekend star show 7:30pm; $3; matinee laser shows daily 2:30pm, evening show hours vary)* and access to a formal astronomical observatory.

Manatee Village Historical Park – *604 15th St. E. at Manatee Ave. Open Sept–June Mon–Fri 9am–4:30pm, Sun 1:30pm–4:30pm. Rest of the year Mon–Fri 9am–4:30pm. Closed major holidays. Contribution requested.* ♿ ▣ ☎ *941-741-4075.* Sandwiched between Route 64 and a residential neighborhood, this collection of 10 turn-of-the-century structures depicts pioneer life in Manatee County. Highlights include a 1903 general store, a 1912 "Cracker Gothic-style" settler's house with period furnishings, the county's first courthouse (1860), a spacious wooden church from 1887, a 1908 one-room schoolhouse and a reconstructed early 1900s barn.

De Soto National Memorial Park – *De Soto Point, at north end of 75th St. W. Open year-round daily 9am–5pm. Closed Jan 1, Thanksgiving Day, Dec 25.* ♿ ▣ ☎ *941-792-0458.* Honoring Hernando de Soto's 1539 thrust into North America, this site serves as a reminder of the paradox of early exploration. In his 4,000mi quest for gold and glory, de Soto and his army of 600 men heroically

❶ Mixon Fruit Farms

Map p 259. 2712 26th Ave. E. Open Nov–Apr Mon–Sat 8:30am–5:30pm. ♿ ☎ *941-748-5829.* Set amid 350 acres of lush groves, this popular citrus outlet began life in 1939 as a roadside fruit stand. Visitors may stand on an observation platform and enjoy the hustle and bustle of the plant: Six hundred oranges per minute ride the conveyor belts toward a quality-control room where workers separate the good fruit from the bad. Select oranges continue on into crates for shipping or end up in the juicing room. Free samples of juice and sections of grapefruit, orange and tangerine are available in the sizable gift shop.

Pier at Anna Maria Island

endured terrible marches through nearly impenetrable wilderness, while leaving a legacy of cruelty and disease to the native population. The expedition, which likely started from here (according to descriptions from journal entries), ultimately cost de Soto his life. Informative exhibits, a 22min film and a .5mi nature walk recapture the culture clash of 16C Spain in America. From late December to early April, costumed park rangers demonstrate the use of the harquebus, the crossbow and other antique weapons in a replica Spanish camp.

Anna Maria Island – *West of Bradenton via Rte. 64.* Though heavily developed like most of the large barrier islands in the area, Anna Maria is worth the drive for the parks on its north and south ends. Starting with the north, **Anna Maria Bayfront Park** *(northeast end of Pine Ave. at Bay Blvd.)* holds a 1,000ft stretch of shoreline running just north of the City Pier. Built in 1911, the pier extends 678ft into Tampa Bay and tempts visitors with a no-frills oyster bar.

Just south of the Route 684 causeway, **Bradenton Beach** is a quaint seaside hamlet composed of lovely beaches framed by low-rise motels, shops and ice-cream parlors. At the island's southwest end, attractive **Coquina Beach**⌂ provides picnic tables, ample free parking, a snack bar, playground and a wide expanse of white sand and inviting Gulf water.

For a look at one of Florida's few remaining early fishing villages, drive east across the causeway to **Cortez** *(south of Cortez Rd./Rte. 684 at 119th St.)*. This Manatee County Historic District contains a good sampling of vernacular structures built with local materials.

EXCURSIONS

★**Gamble Plantation State Historic Site** – *2hrs. 6mi north in Ellenton. Take US-41 north across Manatee River to US-301 and turn right (east); then left on 36th St./Ellenton Gillette Rd. Turn right on Patten Ave. to plantation at no. 3708. Visit by guided tour (45min) only, year-round Thu–Mon 8am–5pm. Closed Jan 1, Thanksgiving Day, Dec 25. $3.* ☎ 941-723-4536. The 1850 Greek Revival-style Gamble House represents the last vestige of the many sugarcane plantations established in southern Florida after the area opened to settlers at the end of the Second Seminole War in 1842. Major Robert Gamble came here from Tallahassee in hopes of recouping some of the money his family had lost when the capital's banks failed in 1839. Amassing some 3,500 acres on the Manatee River, Gamble used slave labor to build his columned 10-room house, constructed of plastered tabby bricks (made from local oyster shells and lime). The plantation was successful for several years before falling sugar prices drove down Gamble's profits and forced him to sell his property in the late 1850s. During the Civil War, the plantation served as a supply depot for rebel troops. After the fall of the Confederacy, Judah P. Benjamin, Secretary of State to Jefferson Davis, hid here while awaiting safe passage to England. Over the next 48 years, the house changed hands several times and was eventually abandoned.

Visit – Visitors can tour the restored house, where knowledgeable guides recount plantation life and the history of the residence and its occupants. The dwelling's second story boasts a sprawling verandah supported by columns on three sides.

From this vantage point, you can see across the yard to stone memorials honoring veterans of the Confederacy and World War I. The grounds also include a small **visitor center** *(same hours as Gamble Plantation;* ♿ *)* with exhibits on Florida plantation life. Nearby is the Patten House (1895), a wood-frame farmhouse built by the son of the plantation's later owner. The former Patten residence now serves as headquarters for the United Daughters of the Confederacy, who spearheaded the site's restoration in 1925.

Egmont Key *– 1/2 day. Accessible by boat only. Open year-round daily dawn–dusk. No facilities.* ♿ ☏ *813-893-2627. Sightseeing cruise departs from Cortez (southeast end of Cortez Rd./Rte. 684 bridge) year-round Tue, Thu & Sun 1pm–5pm. 1hr each way; 2hrs on island. Commentary. Reservations required. $15.* ✗ ▣ *Cortez Fleet* ☏ *941-794-1223.* Now a peaceful national wildlife sanctuary of shorebirds and gopher turtles, Egmont has known busier times. Positioned at the entrance to Tampa Bay, the key was an ideal place for a lighthouse in the early days of shipping. The 87ft structure dates back to 1848 and was rebuilt after devastating storms in 1848 and 1852. Seminoles were imprisoned on Egmont Key in 1854 on their way to reservations out west. In anticipation of the Spanish-American War, a fort was built on the island; although it never saw action, **Fort Dade** included 70 buildings and held 300 people. Ruins of the fort's concrete bunkers and gun emplacements jut from the island's north tip. Besides a tour of the fort, visitors to Egmont Key can enjoy an afternoon of swimming, snorkeling and shelling.

Solomon's Castle *– 1.5hrs. 40mi east of I-75 in Ona. Take Rte. 64 (Exit 42) east 30mi to Rte. 665. Turn right (south) and go about 9mi to Solomon Rd.; turn left and follow signs. Visit by guided tour (30min) only, Oct–Jun Tue–Sun 11am–4pm. Closed Thanksgiving Day & Dec 25. $7.50.* ✗ ♿ ▣ *www.roadsideamerica.com-/attract/FLONAcastle.html* ☏ *941-494-6077.* Sculptor Howard Solomon believes that "to have a house like everyone else's is to show a lack of imagination." Accordingly, he built his 12,000sq ft home in the 1970s to resemble a medieval castle, complete with turrets, stained glass and a drawbridge. Wacky and impressive, the castle and its 300 pieces of original sculpture were made entirely from discarded materials. The castle's siding, for example, incorporates shiny aluminum printing plates from a local newspaper. Visitors take a pun-filled 25min tour of the interior. A 60ft replica Spanish galleon, handmade by Solomon, contains a restaurant. Also on location are picnic tables, a gift shop and a nature trail that meanders along Horse Creek.

FORT MYERS

Population 45,917

Map of Principal Sights p 3 – Map p 245

Tourist Information ☏ 941-768-3633 or 800-533-4753 (US & Canada)

A city of royal palms and tropical flowers, Fort Myers curves along the shore of the gentle Caloosahatchee River. Though development in recent decades has sprawled the urban area out past I-75 and into the jam-packed adjoining communities of North Fort Myers and Cape Coral, a renewed downtown offers restaurants, historic houses and a scenic waterfront. Just south on Estero Island, **Fort Myers Beach** is the center of the local sun-and-fun scene.

Historical Notes

When relations between whites and Indians flared up again after the Second Seminole War, Fort Myers was established on the site of an earlier fort. From 1850 to 1859 the post served the interests of local settlers. When the Indian disputes were finally resolved the fort closed, only to reopen a few years later as a Union outpost during the Civil War. By the 1880s, area cattle ranches and pineapple plantations were thriving, and fishermen were gleaning a reliable harvest from the local waters. In 1885 Fort Myers incorporated, elected a mayor and received a visitor who would become the town's most important citizen.

Newly widowed and in poor health, inventor **Thomas Alva Edison** (1847-1931) traveled from New Jersey to Florida in the mid-1880s to look for a winter home in which to recuperate. He liked what he saw along the river in Fort Myers, bought a 14-acre estate and set up shop. His laboratory and botanical gardens became the proving ground for devices we take for granted today. Here he perfected such inventions as the incandescent light bulb, the phonograph, the moving-picture camera and projector and the storage battery, in addition to working on new projects. An active member of the community, Edison imported royal palms from Cuba in the early 1900s to line his property along **McGregor Boulevard**. The city took up where Edison left off, and now some 14mi of the city's signature avenue are edged with stately palms.

The publicity that followed America's most famous inventor gave a tangential boost to Fort Myers; by the 1920s building boom, the city was off and running. Subject to the urban decay that followed the suburban growth of the 1950s, the downtown area along First Street is slowly coming back to life with businesses and restaurants. Like most of southwest Florida, the economy of Fort Myers balances today on three legs: tourism, construction and agriculture.

SIGHTS 2 days.
Map p 245.

★★ **Edison and Ford Winter Estates** – *2350 McGregor Blvd. Open year-round Mon–Sat 9am–5pm, Sun noon–5pm. Closed Thanksgiving Day & Dec 25. $10.* & ▣ *www.edison-ford-estate.com* ☎ *941-334-7419.* Situated on the Caloosahatchee River, this complex holds the winter homes and tropical gardens of inventor Thomas Edison and auto-maker **Henry Ford** (1863-1947). Edison bought his property in 1885 and designed two connecting cottages—one for his family and the other for his business partner, Ezra Gilliland. Among the first prefabricated homes in the country, the houses were constructed of lumber cut in

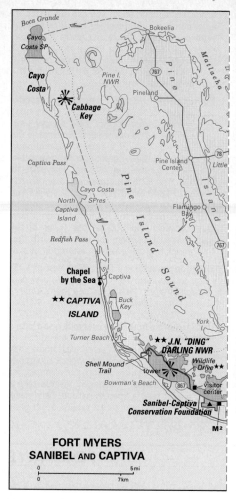

**FORT MYERS
SANIBEL AND CAPTIVA**

Maine and shipped down in four schooners. Shortly afterward, Edison had a disagreement with his partner and did not vacation in Fort Myers for 14 years, during which time Gilliland sold Edison the smaller house. In 1901 the inventor returned and began using the additional structure—connected to his by a latticed breezeway—as a guest cottage.

While attending a company conference in 1896, Edison met a young man named Henry Ford. Edison encouraged Ford, who was then working in the Edison Illuminating Company in Detroit, to follow his dream of building cars. The two men became friends, and in 1916 Ford bought a house on an adjacent piece of land to be near his mentor. The two comrades went on camping trips in the Everglades and shared many lively, thought-provoking conversations, though Ford was very private and Edison nearly deaf. After Edison died in 1931, Ford never again wintered in Fort Myers, saying he could not bear to be there without his friend. Today Edison's home and the adjacent winter cottage of his billionaire buddy Ford draw hundreds of thousands of visitors a year.

★ **Edison's Home** – The star attraction here, Edison's spacious house, "Seminole Lodge," nestles in an Eden of tropical flowers and trees, odd hybrids and towering bamboo—all part of the botanical gardens the inventor used for his experiments. Tours wend along garden paths and enter the double house (as the two connected structures are called), immediately inviting with its 14ft verandahs furnished with wicker chairs and porch swings. French doors provide cross-ventilation and give access to the dining, living and other rooms. All are appointed as nearly as possible the way Edison's second wife, Mina Miller Edison, left them when she died in 1947.

Ford's Home – Ford bought the "Mangoes" (1911), a relatively modest cottage, for $20,000 in 1916. The two-story frame house is furnished with reproductions in the Ford fashion—English walnut chairs and table, Belgian tablecloths, Wedgwood

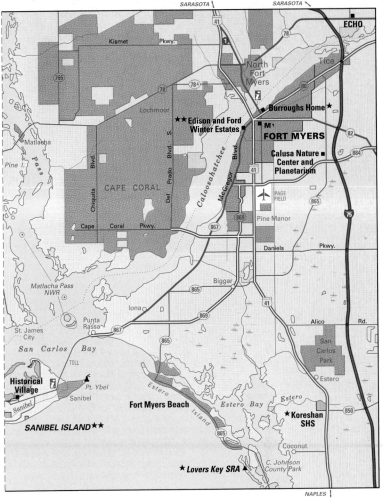

china. Tours take in the pantry, kitchen, dining room and living room. Outside, a garage houses vintage Ford automobiles. A paved path connects the properties, curving by the river where Ford and Edison used to fish.

Edison Laboratory and Museum – Outfitted with a multitude of test tubes and glass beakers, Edison's lab served as a testing ground for the inventor's experiments—including his work on domestic rubber production, which sadly met with little commercial success. One difficult project, the storage battery, drove Edison to 9,000 failed experiments, which he optimistically referred to as, "9,000 things we won't have to do again." After 41,000 additional tests, the battery was finally ready for patenting and marketing.

Adjacent **Edison Museum**★ boasts six rooms filled with thousands of items, including more than 200 Edison phonographs—his favorite invention. Positioned at the end of the house tour, this museum documenting the life's work of one of the country's greatest geniuses is almost overwhelming in its scope.

A final highlight stands just outside the laboratory: The **banyan tree** that tire magnate Harvey Firestone brought back from India for Edison in 1925 has grown to measure some 400ft around its myriad trunks, and ranks as the state's largest banyan.

★**Burroughs Home** – 2505 1st St. at Fowler St. Visit by guided tour (30min) only, Dec–Apr Tue–Fri 11am–3pm. $3. Free parking at Sheraton Hotel (one block south on 1st St.). ☎ 941-332-6125. This handsome 1901 Georgian Revival house was built by a Montana land and cattle baron and purchased in 1918 by Midwestern banker and cattleman Nelson T. Burroughs. His daughter bequeathed the house to the City of Fort Myers in 1978. Royal palms and other lush plantings grace the lawn of the two-story house, and a wraparound porch collects cool river breezes. Once the city's largest residence, the house features Florida pine floors, a mahogany fireplace, a winding staircase and original furnishings. On engaging

Edison's Laboratory

30min tours, costumed docents play the roles of the Burroughs' sisters, transporting visitors back to the turn of the century, when the family entertained such local leading lights as the Thomas Edisons and the Henry Fords.

Fort Myers Historical Museum (M¹) – *2300 Peck St., at Jackson St. Open year-round Tue–Sat 9am–4pm. Closed major holidays. $4. & ⚿ ☎ 941-332-5955.* Housed in a 1924 railroad depot, a summary of local history offers exhibits on the Calusa and Seminole Indians, Spanish explorers and white settlers. Among the indoor displays are a saber-toothed cat skeleton found in central Florida (only some of the bones are original), a model of Fort Myers in 1850, and collections of Carnival glass and Depression glass (inexpensive colored glass made between 1929 and 1941, now considered a collector's item). Outside stands the **Esperanza**, an 84ft private railcar—the longest and one of the last built by George Pullman. Visitors may walk through the 1930s car and observe the luxurious stateroom fitted with Cuban mahogany and brass, ice-cooled air-conditioning ducts, call buttons for summoning the porter, and tiny kitchen for preparing large meals. On the other side of the museum sits a replica of a vernacular Cracker house.

① Shell Factory

Map p 245. 2787 US-41, north of Littleton Rd. In North Fort Myers. Open year-round daily 9am-5pm. & ☎ 941-995-2141. If you're tired of sifting through piles of shells on Sanibel and Captiva Islands *(p 250)*, this is the easy way out. Bins of shells from 53 countries fill the 65,000sq ft of warehouse space, along with shell jewelry, shell lamps and a multitude of other souvenirs. Just inside the entrance, glass cases hold a collection of labeled seashells from around the world.

Calusa Nature Center and Planetarium – 🔟 *3450 Ortiz Ave. Open year-round Mon–Sat 9am–5pm, Sun 11am–5pm. $4. & ⚿ ☎ 941-275-3435.* This facility offers a pleasant diversion for children and adults. Live turtles, fish and snakes head the indoor exhibits; outside stands an aviary for injured raptors, while a separate enclosure holds a bobcat. Three miles of interpretive boardwalk trails weave through hammocks of pine and cypress frequented by raccoons, otters, lizards and other animals. At the end of one trail stands a replica of a Seminole village and an exhibit detailing an earlier people, the Calusa. Also on the grounds is the **planetarium**, which presents star and laser shows *(same hours as above; laser light shows Fri; $3 all seats; ☎ 941-275-3183).*

EXCURSIONS

ECHO – *2hrs. 10mi east in N. Fort Myers. Take I-75 north to Exit 26; (Rte. 78 East/Bayshore Rd.); continue 1mi east on Rte. 78 to 17430 Durrance Rd. Visit by guided tour (1hr) only, Tue, Fri & Sat 10am. Closed major holidays. ⚿ www.xc.org/echo ☎ 941-543-3246.* Dedicated to helping people feed themselves, the Educational Concerns for Hunger Organization was founded in the 1970s to help farmers in Haiti. It now serves as a laboratory of farming techniques for the Third World. The 12.5-acre site bustles with activity as volunteers and employees tend the urban roof garden, tropical fruit trees, desert greenhouse, tire garden and rainforest greenhouse. On tours, visitors learn how ideas developed here help feed people all over the globe. ECHO's seed bank and informational network connect gardeners, missionaries and farmers throughout the world. Also on location are special breeds of animals, a research library and gift shop.

★**Koreshan State Historic Site** – *2hrs. 16mi south in Estero; Take US-41 south; turn right on Corkscrew Rd. and follow it to park. Open year-round daily 8am–dusk. $3.25/vehicle.* ⚠ 🅿 ☎ *941-992-0311.* This 305-acre site preserves 12 buildings remaining from a turn-of-the-century religious settlement whose adherents believed that the earth was a hollow sphere and the universe existed inside it. The community was founded along the Estero River in 1893 by New York physician Cyrus Teed. Calling himself "Koresh" (Hebrew for Cyrus), Teed, with the help of his followers, began building their "New Jerusalem," which they believed would eventually accommodate 10 million people. Though industrious and devout, the religious order, which numbered 250 members at its peak, began to decline after the 1908 death of Teed (who believed himself immortal). Furthermore, a vow of celibacy virtually ensured the group's extinction. The final four members deeded part of their land to the state of Florida in 1961. A self-guided tour through the grand art hall, planetary court, founder's house and other buildings provides a fascinating glimpse into an earnest but dead-end social experiment in the Florida wilderness.

★**Lovers Key State Recreation Area** – *1/2 day. 30mi south on Lovers Key; parking on Black Island. Take US-41 south to junction of Rte. 865; turn right on Rte. 865 (which becomes Estero Blvd.) and continue 8mi to park entrance on west side at 8700 Estero Blvd. Open year-round daily 8am–dusk. $2/vehicle.* ♿ 🅿 *www.dep.state.fl.us/parks* ☎ *941-463-4588.* Occupying a gorgeous stretch of undeveloped barrier island, Lovers Key encompasses 434 acres of tidal lagoon and canal, mangrove estuary and white-sand beach. Among the prolific wildlife to be spotted are roseate spoonbills, egrets, bottle-nosed dolphins and endangered West Indian manatees. A boardwalk to the beach crosses two peaceful lagoons where fishermen cast for trout, redfish and snook.

NAPLES★

Population 19,777
Map of Principal Sights p 3 – Map p 239
Tourist Information ☎ 941-262-6141 or 800-605-7878 (US)

Highlighting the southwest end of Florida, Naples marks the edge of civilization, basking on the shore just west of Big Cypress Swamp *(p 45)* and north of the EVER-GLADES. In little more than 100 years, this city has grown from a fishing hamlet to an outpost of culture and fashion—a small-scale PALM BEACH.

Historical Notes

Impressed by the area's dazzling beaches and subtropical foliage, Walter S. Haldeman, owner of the *Louisville Courier-Journal*, created the Naples Town Improvement Company in 1887. It is thought that the city's name derives from early comparisons of its location and aspect to that of Naples, Italy. Within a few years Haldeman's company had built the Naples Hotel and the Pier, and houses began to appear in the vicinity. Unfortunately, the company overextended itself; property sales never gained much momentum, and Haldeman's fledgling company soon went belly-up.

The town, accessible only by boat or ox cart, began attracting a few well-to-do families and reclusive millionaires who started erecting impressive estates along the beach, hidden from the road by lush landscaping. Real prosperity for Naples had to wait until the 1920s, with the arrival of the railroad and the completion of the Tamiami Trail in 1928—the latter financed largely by local landowner Barron G. Collier *(p 250)*, a wealthy Memphis businessman for whom the county is named. Today Collier County remains the richest county in Florida: The average annual personal income, in 1995, was $47,628.

Many modern vacationers choose to venture out into the wilderness on an Everglades excursion, or to sample the archipelago to the south known as the **Ten Thousand Islands** *(p 45)*. At this chain's northern extreme, **Marco Island** offers a resort lifestyle on one end and an old Florida maritime village called Goodland on the other. Naples occupies visitors with a wealth of fine restaurants and hotels, upscale shops, the 1,200-seat Philharmonic Center for the Arts, more than 40 golf courses and 9mi of beautiful sun-drenched beaches.

View of Marina from Gulf Shore Boulevard

© David R. Frazier

SIGHTS

1 day. Map p 249.

Naples Area Tourism Bureau (895 5th Ave S.; open mid-Dec–mid-Apr Mon–Fri 9am–5pm, weekends 10am–3pm; rest of the year Mon–Fri 9am–5pm, Sat 10am–3pm; closed major holidays; www.naples-online.com ☎ 941-262-6141) and Golden Gate Visitors' Center (3847 Tollgate Blvd.; open year-round Mon–Fri 9am–5pm, weekends 10am–2pm; closed major holidays; ☎ 941-352-0508) dispense information on dining, accommodations, cruises and other activities.

★Scenic Drive *– 6mi. Begin on Mooring Line Dr., north of downtown (off US-41). Follow Mooring Line south as it becomes Gulf Shore Blvd.; turn left on 19th Ave. where Gulf Shore ends and go 1 block to Gordon Dr.; turn right on Gordon and follow to dead-end at Gordon Pass.* Driving south on Gulf Shore Boulevard, you pass the finest homes in Naples, with the larger and more modern houses sprouting along the last 2.5mi of Gordon Drive. One block west of Gulf Shore Boulevard, the **Naples Pier** *(at 12th Ave. S.)* harkens to Naples' earliest days, when vacationers disembarked at this point. Built in 1888, the 600ft wooden pier now serves as a point-of-entry only for the many fish reeled in by sportsmen.

★Old Naples – *5th Ave. S. and 3rd St. S.* The historic downtown area offers chic shops and restaurants on palm-lined streets, as well as shaded courtyards perfect for sipping tea or coffee. Galleries along **Third Street South**, particularly near Broad Avenue, sell original paintings, sculpture, prints and glass objects. For other shops, stroll down **Fifth Avenue South** between Third and Ninth Streets.

Across Fifth Avenue stands the Mediterranean-style **Naples Depot** *(1051 5th Ave. S.)*, built in 1927 as the southern terminus of Seaboard Air Line Railway's west coast line. The building served as a depot until 1971; it now holds offices, temporary art exhibits, and a display of railroad memorabilia. A caboose and boxcar beside the depot contain shops.

 Tin City

Map p 249. East end of 5th Ave. S. Open year-round Mon–Sat 10am–9pm, Sun noon–6pm. Restaurant hours vary. ✕. A cluster of shops and restaurants resides along the harbor in a tin-roofed emporium that functioned as an oyster-processing plant in the 1920s. Some 40 stores here offer items ranging from scrimshaw to Hawaiian shirts.

Palm Cottage – *137 12th Ave. S. Visit by guided tour (30min) only, Oct–May Mon–Fri 1pm–3:30pm. Rest of the year tour hours vary. Closed major holidays. $5. க ☎ 941-261-8164.* Town founder Walter Haldeman built this pleasant house for a friend in 1895. Constructed of tabby mortar (burnt seashells), the simple green-and-white cottage features a gabled roof and a wide screened porch. Palm Cottage and another nearby Haldeman house rank as the oldest existing residences in Naples. Later Palm Cottage owners entertained such luminaries as Gary Cooper, Hedy Lamarr and Robert Montgomery here. In 1979 the Collier County Historical Society purchased the house as its headquarters. Tours of the two-story structure outline the area's history.

★Lowdermilk Park – *1405 Gulf Shore Blvd. N. Open year-round daily dawn–dusk.* This beachfront park, with its tidy landscaping and well-patrolled parking area, shows neat and orderly Naples at its best. A groomed volleyball court, clean picnic area and snack bar, and pristine 1,000ft beach attract strollers, sunbathers and windsurfers. Only the non-native, red-splotch-faced Muscovy ducks seem to be out of place.

Teddy Bear Museum – 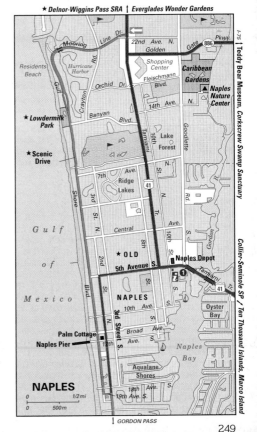 *2511 Pine Ridge Rd. at intersection of Pine Ridge and Airport-Pulling Rds. Open Dec–Apr Mon, Wed–Sat 10am–5pm, Sun 1pm–5pm. Rest of the year Wed–Sat 10am–5pm, Sun 1pm–5pm. Closed major holidays. $6. &. P www.teddymuseum.com ☎ 941-598-2711.* In this unusual museum, opened in 1990, you'll see more than 2,500 endearing bears. Special display areas showcase antique bears (dating back to 1903), designer bears, international bears and a "libeary." Poohs, Paddingtons, grizzlies, soldier and sailor bears, Victorian bears, boardroom bears, and hosts of tiny dollhouse miniatures manifest the infinite variety of the time-honored teddy.

Caribbean Gardens – *1590 Goodlette-Frank Rd. (just south of Golden Gate Pkwy.). Open year-round daily 9:30am–5:30pm. Closed Easter Sunday, Thanksgiving Day, Dec 25. $13.95. ⚔ &. P www.caribbeangardens.com ☎ 941-262-5409.* Exotic trees and animals inhabit the 52-acre garden park that began as a botanical collection in 1919. When the original owner died in 1929, the gardens grew wild for more than 20 years until a new owner took over and opened them to the public. Visitors stroll among such trees as gumbo-limbo, jacaranda and Hong Kong orchid while viewing alligators, clouded leopards, tigers and birds. High point of the gardens, a **boat ride** in an island-dotted pond gives visitors a close look at agile primates, including the white-handed gibbon whose whooping call is audible throughout the park *(daily; first departure 10am, last departure 4:30pm; round-trip 20min; included in admission)*. A petting zoo, animal lectures and shows add to the fun.

Naples Nature Center – *1450 Merrihue Dr., off 14th Ave. N. (adjacent to Caribbean Gardens). Open Jan–Mar Mon–Sat 9am–4:30pm, Sun 1pm–5pm. Rest of the year Mon–Sat 9am–4:30pm. $5. &. P www.conservancy.org ☎ 941-262-0304.* A modern educational facility, this 15-acre preserve boasts hands-on displays, video presentations, live snakes and other exhibits on southwest Florida's various ecosystems. Outside, a boardwalk trail loops through a mangrove swamp and past a wildlife rehabilitation center, where injured pelicans and other birds take therapeutic swims. Free 45min boat rides on the Gordon River are offered, and canoes and kayaks are available for rent.

★ **Delnor-Wiggins Pass State Recreation Area** – *West end of Bluebill Ave., off US-41. Open year-round daily 8am–dusk. $4/vehicle. &. P ☎ 941-597-6196.* If you want a break from crowded Lowdermilk Park and Vanderbilt Beach, Delnor-Wiggins is the place to go. Punctuating the heavily developed shoreline north of Naples, this delightful park offers more than a mile of unspoiled beach backed by sea grapes, sea oats, cabbage palms and mangroves. Through Wiggins Pass, at the park's north end, the Cocohatchee River finds its outlet to the sea. Also at this end, a 30ft observation tower clears the jungle canopy to provide glimpses of the Gulf of Mexico and its backwaters.

EXCURSIONS

Map p 239

Collier-Seminole State Park – *2hrs. 17mi southeast on US-41. Open year-round daily 8am–dusk. $3.25/vehicle. ⚠ &. P ☎ 941-394-3397.* Poised on the northwestern edge of the Everglades, this 6,423-acre preserve boasts a wide diversity of plants and wildlife. For an introduction to the park's flora and fauna, stop by the visitor center. Tennessee advertising magnate **Barron Collier**, who owned 1 million acres of royal palm hammock in the area, chose a chunk of his holdings to donate towards a national park in the 1940s. The federal government declined his offer, so in 1947 the state of Florida created its own park. Rare royal palms flourish in this tropical hammock, and mangrove and cypress swamps, salt marshes and pine flatwoods create an unusually variegated landscape. A 6.5mi trail offers hikers occasional glimpses of such rare species as wood stork, bald eagle, black bear and Florida panther. The boardwalk nature trail *(.9mi)* loops to a viewing platform where wading birds and alligators cohabit in the tall grasses of a quiet salt marsh. A concessionaire offers boat tours on the scenic Blackwater River *(depart from concession stand year-round daily 9:30am–4pm; round-trip 1hr; commentary; $8.50;* & 🅿 *Collier-Seminole State Park Boat Tours* ☎ *941-642-8898)*.

On the way in, notice the monstrous **walking dredge** on display just off the road *(on right)*. Used in the 1920s to construct the Tamiami Trail that stretches from Tampa to Miami, this specialized machine trudged through countless miles of soupy swamp and mud-thick glades.

Everglades Wonder Gardens – 🎏 *1hr. 14mi north in Bonita Springs. Take US-41 north and turn right (east) on Old US-41; Wonder Gardens entrance is 1mi north of Bonita Beach Rd. Open year-round daily 9am–5pm. Closed Dec 25. $9.* & 🅿 ☎ *941-992-2591.* Reminiscent of bygone Florida tourism, this 60-year-old attraction exhibits more than 2,000 species of plants and animals from Florida, Asia, and Central and South America. Included are crocodiles, snakes, snapping turtles, flamingoes and peacocks, housed in 1930s animal enclosures. Near the ticket booth is an indoor display of animal bones and preserved specimens, the latter including shark and horse embryos. Daily tours and animal feedings are also offered here.

Corkscrew Swamp Sanctuary – *2hrs. 30mi northeast of Naples. Take US-41 north 9mi to Rte. 846/Immokalee Rd.; turn right (east) on Rte. 846 and continue 18mi. Turn left on Sanctuary Rd. and follow it to park entrance. Open Dec–Apr daily 7am–5pm. Rest of the year daily 8am–5pm. $7.* & 🅿 *www.audubon.org* ☎ *941-348-9151.* Off the beaten path but well worth the visit, the country's largest stand of virgin cypress occupies this 11,000-acre tract owned by the National Audubon Society. A 2mi boardwalk trail begins in pine flatwoods and snakes through dense saw palmetto to a cypress swamp marked by soaring 500-year-old bald cypress trees. Visitors to this primitive landscape may see alligators, endangered wood storks, tropical orchids and swamp lilies. *Mosquito repellent recommended.*

SANIBEL AND CAPTIVA ISLANDS★★

Population 5,584 (Sanibel City)
Map of Principal Sights p 3 – Map pp 250-251
Tourist Information ☎ 941-472-1080

Long known as a paradise for shelling, these popular barrier islands, connected by causeways to each other and to the mainland, form a 20mi arc into the Gulf of Mexico 23mi southwest of downtown Fort Myers. Though the winter season brings a steady stream of traffic, the pockets of tranquillity and beauty that exist on these islands merit the drive over.

Historical Notes

Spanish navigators who first discovered Sanibel and Captiva in the 16C never settled here, leaving the islands to the Calusa Indians. Sometime during the next 200 years, the Spanish labeled the islands *Puerto de Nivel del Sur* ("port of the south plain") and *Boca del Cautivo* ("captives' entrance"). Over the years these names became corrupted to Sanibel and Captiva. Pirate lore maintains that buccaneers kept the loveliest of women prisoners on the smaller northern isle, hence its name. Since many of these legends are inextricably tangled with early 20C real-estate hype, the more likely original captive was a Spaniard named Juan Ortiz, kidnapped by the Calusa in 1528. Pioneers attempted to settle Sanibel as early as 1833, but the lack of a mainland port to market their produce forced them to give up. By 1889 lighthouse keepers and homesteaders composed the island's population of 100 people. Development proceeded slowly all the way up to 1963 when the causeway was built, at which time the floodgates opened to tourism. During the 1964-65 season, 110,000 vehicles crossed the bridge; in 1995 that number exceeded three million. When construction of the causeway looked inevitable, conservation groups rallied to protect their island from unchecked development. One noteworthy result of their efforts, the J.N. "Ding" Darling National Wildlife Refuge, preserves more than one-third of Sanibel's total acreage and provides a haven for native species.

PRACTICAL INFORMATION .... Area Code: 941

Getting There – **Southwest Florida International Airport** (RSW): in Fort Myers, 26mi east of islands; international and domestic flights; information ☏ 768-4383. Transportation to Sanibel/Captiva: airport shuttle *($37-$56)*, for reservations ☏ 466-3236 or 800-566-0007; taxi *($20)*. Visitor booth in baggage claim area *(open daily 9am–6pm)* ☏ 768-4374. Rental car agencies *(p 323)* located at airport and in Fort Myers. Nearest Amtrak **train** station is in Tampa, with Greyhound/Trailways **bus** connection to Fort Myers ☏ 800-872-7245 or ☏ 800-231-2222. **Major access roads**: I-75, US-41 and Route 869 south to Sanibel Causeway; $3 toll in-bound.

Getting Around – Adventures in Paradise Trolley narrated sightseeing tour of Sanibel and Captiva departs from 21 different boarding stations in Sanibel *(Mon–Fri 10am–noon; $15; 2hrs)* ☏ 472-8443. Sanibel taxi: ☏ 472-4160; Sanibel Limo Service: ☏ 472-8888. Enterprise Rent-a-Car provides a rental car drop-off service for Sanibel from its Fort Myers Beach location ☏ 454-0770 or 888-FLA-RENT. No public transportation available on the islands. Best way to get around is by bicycle on the islands' 25mi of bike paths. **Bicycle rental shops**: Bike Route ☏ 472-1955; Finnimore's Cycle Shop ☏ 472-5577; Island Moped ☏ 472-5248; Jim's Bicycle Shop ☏ 472-1296.

Visitor Information – **Lee County Visitor and Convention Bureau**, 2180 W. First St., Fort Myers FL 33901 *(open Mon–Fri 8am–5pm)* ☏ 338-3500 or 800-237-6444 (US and Canada); **Sanibel-Captiva Islands Chamber of Commerce**, 1159 Causeway Rd., Sanibel FL 33957 *(open Mon–Sat 9am–7pm, Sun 10am–5pm)*. www.sanibel-captiva.org ☏ 472-1080. *These organizations provide additional information regarding shopping, entertainment, festivals (p 318), sports and recreation.*

Accommodations – *(p 324)* Area visitors' guide including lodging directory available (free) from Lee County Visitor and Convention Bureau *(above)*. Advance reservations are strongly suggested in season (Dec–Apr) and during Jul–Aug. Accommodations range from hotels and resorts ($150-$300) to inns and motels ($100-$200) and small guest houses ($40-$75) within easy walking distance to beaches. Weekly and monthly rentals of condominiums and apartments available through local rental and real-estate agencies. **Camping**: Periwinkle Trailer Park (tents and RVs) ☏472-1433.
Camping is permitted only in specified campgrounds. Cayo Costa State Park *(p 254)* accessible by boat only: hiking, shelling, camping, bicycle rental; for cabin reservations Barrier Island GEO Park ☏964-0375. *Rates quoted are average prices per night for a double room and are subject to seasonal variations.*

Sports and Recreation – Most **beaches** have public access and restrooms. Parking at Sanibel beaches *(7am–7pm; 75¢/hr, free other times)*; at Captiva beaches parking is free. Driving on beaches is prohibited. Water sports include swimming, boating, sailing, canoeing, saltwater and freshwater fishing *(p 331)*. The islands are accessible by Intracoastal Waterway. Major **bike** path runs from Lighthouse Point to Blind Pass at western end of island. **Nature tours** (canoe/kayak) and fishing excursions, boat and bicycle rentals in J.N. "Ding" Darling National Wildlife Refuge *(p 253)*: Tarpon Bay Recreation ☏ 472-8900. Nature and sunset **cruises**: Captiva Cruises *(daily 4pm–5:30pm & sunset; $17.50)* ☏ 472-5300. **Snorkeling** and dolphin-watching excursions: Captain Bob's Shelling & Dolphin Watch *(daily excursions; 5hrs; $50; reservations required)* ☏ 472-0982. For shelling cruises, see *p 253*. **Golf**: Beachview Golf Club ☏ 472-2626; Dunes Golf & Tennis Club ☏ 472-2535; both clubs allow non-members.

Entertainment – Consult the *Sunny Day Guide* and Sanibel-Captiva Islands Chamber of Commerce publication available locally (free) for schedules of activities, dining and local events. Pirate Playhouse: theater and plays (Nov–May) ☏ 472-0006; Old Schoolhouse Theater: musicals (Dec–Apr) and light theater (summer) ☏ 472-6862.

The main thoroughfares (Periwinkle Way and Sanibel-Captiva Road) today pass tony boutique-and-restaurant complexes on Sanibel's south end, then traverse a long stretch of bayside wilderness before crossing to Captiva for the 3.5mi drive to the end. Traffic moves at a leisurely pace. Though occasionally affording a view of the sea, the road mostly tunnels through the dense greenery shielding tasteful resorts and expensive houses.

A. Blake Gardner

A Shellseeker's Paradise

SIGHTS

1 day. Map pp 250-251.

Bailey-Matthews Shell Museum (M²) – *3075 Sanibel-Captiva Rd. Open year-round Tue–Sun 10am–4pm. Closed major holidays. $5.* & 🅿 ☎ *941-395-2233.* A must for conchologists, this attractive stucco building—opened in 1995—houses a reference collection of some two million shells. In the main exhibit hall, displays range from the geographic location of shells worldwide to the variety of mollusks that can be found on Sanibel and Captiva Islands. The role of shells in tribal art, medicine and as a food source is also explored.

Sanibel Historical Village and Museum – *950 Dunlop Rd., off Periwinkle Way in the government complex. Visit by guided tour (1hr) only, Dec–Apr Wed–Sat 10am–4pm, Sun 1pm–4pm. Rest of the year Wed–Sat 10am–4pm. $2.* & 🅿 ☎ *941-472-4648.* Set up as a pioneer village, the local history museum features a 1913 Cracker house with a dining room, parlor and kitchen furnished to depict early island life. Additional rooms contain fossil and shell displays, Spanish shipwreck artifacts and 2,000-year-old remains of the Calusa Indian culture. Other buildings on the site include a tea room, the 1926 Sanibel post office and Bailey's General Store. This general store, which functioned as the hub of the community until the early 1960s, was moved here in 1993 from its original site near the causeway.

Sanibel-Captiva Conservation Foundation – *3333 Sanibel-Captiva Rd. (1mi southeast of J.N. "Ding" Darling Refuge entrance). Open late Nov–Easter Mon–Sat 8:30am–4pm. Rest of the year Mon–Fri 8:30am– 3pm. Closed major holidays. $3.* 🅿 *www.sccf.org* ☎ *941-472-2329.* This 247-acre site centers around a nature center containing a touch tank and informative displays on wetlands ecology. Out

■ **Shelling: Favored Island Pastime**

Calico Scallop

Dubbed *Costa de Caroeles* ("Coast of Seashells") by 16C Spanish explorers, Sanibel and Captiva beaches continue to harvest a staggering number and variety of colorful shells. The islands' unusual east-west orientation intersects with the junction of gulf currents, acting as a natural catchment for the more than 200 species of mollusks that inhabit the Gulf of Mexico's shallow continental shelf.

Fighting Conch

One of the more popular pastimes here is the "Sanibel stoop," the bent-over posture assumed by serious conchologists, or shell collectors. For best finds, arrive an hour before low tide; tides are especially low at new and full moons. Two days after a northwesterly wind is when you'll discover the largest assortment churned up on the beach from deep waters. Common among the myriad shells found here are calico scallops, kitten's paws, turkey wings, lightning whelks, fighting

Coquina Clam

Lion's Paw Scallop

Flame Auger

front is a native plant nursery; behind the center, nearly 5mi of boardwalk trails wind through a humid forest. One walk *(.3mi)* leads to a 30ft observation tower that provides fine **views** of the Sanibel River, the forest canopy, and possibly a pair of roosting ospreys or other birds. The foundation, which owns 1,000 acres in the barrier islands, works to preserve natural resources; its programs include land acquisition, habitat management, environmental education, landscaping for wildlife and sea-turtle research.

★★**J.N. "Ding" Darling National Wildlife Refuge** – *1 Wildlife Dr., off Sanibel-Captiva Rd. Open Nov–Apr Sat–Thu 9am–5pm. Rest of the year Sat–Thu 9am–4pm. Closed major holidays.* ♿ ▣ *www.dingdarling.org.* ☎ *941-472-1100.* A showcase of barrier island wildlife abounds here in canals, bogs, inlets, mangrove swamps and upland forests. Begin at the **visitor center**, where you can acquaint yourself with the 5,404-acre refuge and its natural history through displays and videos. Jay Norwood Darling, for whom the refuge is named, owned a cottage on Captiva, and for 25 years—until his death in 1962 at age 86—he championed conservation causes on the islands. Best known as a Pulitzer Prize-winning political cartoonist, Darling also directed the US Biological Survey under President Franklin Roosevelt. An average of 500 cars a day enter the refuge, many motorists choosing to take the one-way, unpaved **Wildlife Drive**★★ *(5mi),* which offers virtually guaranteed sightings of water-birds and other animals, including the ubiquitous alligator *(gates open year-round Sat–Thu 1hr after sunrise, close one half-hour before sunset; speed limit 15mph; $5/vehicle, exact change required).*

A 20ft observation tower *(on left, about halfway along the drive)* allows wonderful **views** of herons, egrets, roseate spoonbills, ospreys and many others. For best bird-watching, visit near dawn or sunset and at low tide, when the mud flats are exposed. Near the end of the drive, the **Shell Mound Trail** *(.3mi; parking on left)* loops through lush vegetation over an ancient Calusa shell mound.

Those who want a closer look at local flora and fauna can hike the refuge's 4mi of interpretive trails, or paddle the 6mi of marked canoe courses. *Canoes, bicycles and fishing equipment are available for rent in the refuge. Guided canoe and kayak excursions depart from north end of Tarpon Bay Rd. year-round daily; round-trip 2hrs; reservations required; $20. Tram tours depart from Tarpon Bay Feb–Mar (rest of the year from visitor center) Sat–Thu; round-trip 2hrs; commentary; $8.* ♿ ▣ *For all tour schedules, contact Tarpon Bay Recreation* ☎ *941-472-8900.*

Sanibel Lighthouse – *Point Ybel, east tip of Sanibel Island. Not open to the public.* Bureaucratic snafus kept Sanibel in the dark for more than 50 years from the time islanders first petitioned for a lighthouse. Finally erected in 1884, the 98ft iron-work beacon still guides mariners. The light and keeper's quarters *(not open to public),* listed on the National Register of Historic Places, are the oldest buildings on Sanibel. The lighthouse stands between parking areas that provide access to a bayside fishing pier and beach.

Chapel by the Sea –*Take Sanibel-Captiva Rd. to north end of Captiva; turn left on Wiles Dr. and follow to end; turn left into church parking lot. Open for Sunday services only.* Built as a county school in 1901, this tiny, simple white clapboard church offers quiet respite from sun and sea. The building was purchased by the Methodists in 1921 as a mission church, but owing to a scarcity of local followers the chapel gradually became interdenominational. An adjacent **cemetery**, holding the remains of many early settlers, skirts the beach under a canopy of Sabal palm, sea grape and gumbo-limbo trees.

conchs and tiny coquina clams. Rare finds include the prized brown-speckled junonia, lion's paw and Scotch bonnet. *Taking live shellfish, sand dollars, sea stars and sea urchins is prohibited by state law; violators are subject to a $500 fine and 60 days in jail for a first offense. Local Sanibel ordinances prohibit taking any live shells.* Lovely Bowman's Beach *(3mi north of Ding Darling Refuge entrance; turn left on Bowman's Beach Rd.; parking 7am–7pm 75¢/hr)* and Turner Beach *(at Blind Pass between the islands; limited parking)* are popular starting places for beginning shellers. For those wishing to venture a bit farther afield, a number of **shelling excursions** are available: Captain Bob's Shelling & Dolphin Watch cruises depart from Punta Rassa Boat Ramp *(year-round daily; round-trip 5hrs; $50; reservations required* ☎ *472-0982);* Fuery's Shelling Charters depart from 'Tween Waters Marina on Captiva Island *(year-round daily; round-trip 3hrs; $37–$40; advance reservations required* ☎ *472-1015);* another cruise departs from Bayside Marina, on the north end of Captiva *(year-round daily 9am & 1pm; round-trip 3hrs; $35; reservations required* ☎ *472-7611).*

Junonia

Kitten's Paw

Lightning Whelk

Shark's Eye Moon Snail

EXCURSIONS

Cayo Costa – *1 day. Accessible by boat only. Departs from McCarthy's Marina Nov–May Tue–Sat 10am, returns from Cayo Costa 4pm. One-way 1hr 30min. Reservations required. $35.* ▣ *Captiva Cruises www.captivacruises.com* ☎ *941-472-5300*. Used as a quarantine station for tall ships in the early 1800s, Cayo Costa (Spanish for "key by the coast") is now owned by the state park department. Thus protected from development, the 1,600-acre island maintains its pre-European appearance, dense with palmetto brush and pine forests. **Cayo Costa State Park** occupies the north part of the island *(open year-round daily 8am–dusk; $2; guided tours offered every 3rd Sat of the month, call for schedule; △ ☎ 941-964-0375)*. Visitors may hike or bike the 5mi of developed inland trails, or stroll the deserted shell-strewn beach and watch pelicans and dolphins at play. In summer, loggerhead turtles *(p 298)* come to the island's shores to lay their eggs.

Cabbage Key – *1 day. Accessible by boat only. Departs from South Seas Plantation on Captiva year-round daily 10:30am, return from Cabbage Key 3:30pm. One-way 1hr 15min. Commentary. Reservations required. $27.50.* ▣ *Captiva Cruises www.captivacruises.com* ☎ *941-472-5300*. To visit this tiny island in Pine Island Sound is to travel back to the earliest days of Florida tourism. Its dominant building is the weathered **Cabbage Key Inn** (1938), built on a Calusa Indian shell mound as a winter residence for the son of mystery writer Mary Roberts Rinehart. In the early 1940s, a subsequent owner turned the house into an inn. Some 25,000 dollar bills, signed by patrons, hang from the ceiling of the restaurant, which serves good, simple fare. In this unpretentious setting, occasional celebrities—actors Katherine Hepburn and Arnold Schwarzenegger, singer Jimmy Buffett—blend in with other tourists and fishermen. After lunch, you can take a half-mile nature trail through a dense understory of mangroves, strangler figs and sea grapes. A 30ft water tower provides a **view** of the surrounding islands.

SARASOTA★★

Population 50,891
Map of Principal Sights p 3 – Map p 259
Tourist Information ☎ 941-957-1877 or 800-522-9799 (US & Canada)

Lying on the Gulf coast just south of Bradenton, Sarasota offers one of Florida's best-balanced menus of attractions. Here you'll find the official art museum of Florida, a host of cultural and sports activities, two shopping districts that rival the swankest in PALM BEACH, restaurants catering to all palates and budgets, and a 35mi stretch of beach unsurpassed anywhere on the Gulf. Into one medium-sized city Sarasota combines the kind of variety found in much bigger urban areas. It pleases the eye with an appealing downtown, attractively landscaped neighborhoods, and spanking clean sidewalks and streets.

Historical Notes

Scottish Origins – Just old enough to look and feel established, the town has a short history. The bulk of the area's pioneers began arriving in the late 1860s, enticed by free land offered to homesteaders by the federal government. In 1885 a boatload of Scottish settlers landed here and, though disappointed to find only a sand trail through the woods and a few scattered buildings, quickly set about clearing roads and building a community. After the Spanish-American War at the end of the 19C, many soldiers stationed in the area settled here, resulting in a 42 percent jump in population in only 10 years.

In 1902 the town elected its first mayor, John Hamilton Gillespie. Son of a Scottish nobleman, Gillespie built one of the country's first golf courses in Sarasota, thus introducing a sport that now is played on 46 area courses. Gillespie's original course, located near the current Sarasota County Courthouse, is long gone, but a pleasant park *(7th St. and Gillespie Ave.)* still bears his name. The mayor also established a list of ordinances prohibiting profanity, animal abuse and prostitution. Included in the laws were guidelines for tourists: those with money were welcome, those with "no visible means of support" were considered vagrants.

The Circus Comes To Town – Another influential city father, **John Ringling**, bought a house in Sarasota in 1912. For several years, Ringling kept a low profile in the community, spending much of his time traveling with his famous **Ringling Bros. and Barnum & Bailey Circus**. Then in 1917 he founded a local real-estate development company and for the next 10 years poured much of his time, money and energy into the area. He even served for a while as president of the chamber of commerce. Thanks to Ringling, the barrier islands that were once his personal property are now linked by causeway to the mainland.

In 1927 Ringling moved the circus' winter headquarters from Bridgeport, Connecticut, to Sarasota, providing a much-needed injection to the local economy in the wake of the Florida land bust. Visitors paid 25 cents to watch circus rehearsals, with the proceeds going to the Salvation Army. That same year, Ringling and his wife began construction of a grand Italian Renaissance-style residence and museum *(p 256)* to house their growing collection of paintings. Ringling expressed his gratitude to the citizens of Sarasota at a dinner honoring him shortly before the museum's opening: "Any little thing that I have done from time to time, I have been most happy to do, because this is my home town and I love Sarasota better than any other place on earth."

A City For All Ages – The local population boomed again in the late 1940s as young couples in search of a temperate climate and inexpensive housing began swelling the population of southwest Florida. Developers turned huge tracts of scrub and wetland into single-family subdivisions, and Arthur Vining Davis' Arvida Corporation changed Lido, St. Armands, Longboat and other keys into bastions of high-toned homes, shops and resorts. Though middle-class senior citizens from the Midwest have formed the backbone of these keys since the 1950s, the last few years have witnessed a shift toward younger, wealthier residents with more expensive tastes.

On the mainland, efforts to save existing structures such as the 10-story, Mediterranean-style 1927 John Ringling Towers hotel *(US-41 and 2nd St.)* are giving the city a greater sense of permanence and tradition. Neighborhoods like **Indian Beach**, just south of the Ringling Museum, showcase older homes (some on the National Register of Historic Places) in styles ranging from Mediterranean Revival to simple Craftsman bungalows.

In addition to tourism, Sarasota's economy rides on information systems and health care, as well as a substantial finance business to provide for the area's many monied retirees. Visitors are attracted to the city's natural beauty and its many cultural offerings. The Ringling complex, the adjacent **Florida State University Center for the Performing Arts** and the distinctive purple shell-shaped **Van Wezel Performing Arts Hall** cover the cultural spectrum, presenting the best in art, music, dance and theater. Other entertainment options include the Sarasota Ballet, the Sarasota Opera Association, the Florida West Coast Symphony, and a number of small theaters and several annual film festivals. Baseball enthusiasts can watch the Pittsburgh Pirates play spring exhibition games in the area. Opportunities for water sports, tennis and golf also abound.

Practical information .... Area Code: 941

Getting There – **Sarasota Bradenton International Airport** (SRQ): 3mi north of city; information ☎ 359-5200. Transportation to downtown: Westcoast Limo ☎ 355-9645, 24hr reservations required *($12)*; and taxi *($8)*. Rental car agencies *(p 323)* at airport. **Amtrak** bus connection to Tampa leaves from Burger King at 5748 Clark Rd. and I-75 ☎ 800-872-7245. Greyhound/Trailways **bus** station: 6th St. & Rte. 301 ☎ 800-231-2222.

Getting Around – Local **bus service:** Sarasota County Area Transit *(Mon–Sat 5:30am–7pm; 50¢)*; for bus schedule and route information ☎ 951-5851. Downtown metered parking *(25¢/hr)* and free on-street parking is available.

Visitor Information – **Sarasota Convention and Visitors Bureau,** 665 N. US-41, Sarasota FL 34236 (open *year-round Mon–Sat 9am–5pm)* ☎ 957-1877 or 800-522-9799 (US & Canada). *This organization provides additional information regarding shopping, entertainment, festivals (p 318) and recreation.*

Accommodations – *(p 324)* Area visitors' guide including lodging directory available (free) from Sarasota Convention and Visitors Bureau *(above)*. Accommodations range from luxury hotels and resorts ($150-$300) to moderate motels *($55-$100)* and bed-and-breakfast inns ($75-$150). *Rates quoted are average prices per night for a double room and are subject to seasonal variations.*

Entertainment – Consult the arts and entertainment section of the *Sarasota Herald-Tribune* (Friday) for schedules of cultural events or INFOline ☎ 953-4636. Van Wezel Performing Arts Hall ☎ 953-3366; Florida State University Center for the Performing Arts ☎ 351-8000; Sarasota Opera House ☎ 953-7030.

Sports & Recreation – **Golf:** Forest Lake Country Club ☎ 922-1312; Bobby Jones Golf Club ☎ 365-4653. **Sailing** charters *($35-$50/person)* and sunset cruises *($20)* Enterprise ☎ 951-1833; sailboat (reservations required) and jet-ski rentals O'Leary's Sarasota Sailing School ☎ 953-7505. **Shopping:** Sarasota Quay *(p 258)* ☎ 957-0120; St. Armands Circle *(p 259)* ☎ 388-1554; Sarasota Outlet Center, Exit 40 off I-75 North; Gulf Coast Factory Shops, Ellenton, Exit 43 off I-75 North.

THE MAINLAND *2 1/2 days. Map p 259.*

Sarasota's museums and many of its other sights are concentrated along US-41 north of downtown. Begin your exploration with the Ringling Museum and work your way south to the Downtown Art District.

★★**John and Mable Ringling Museum of Art** – *5401 Bayshore Rd. Tickets include admission to Ringling Museum, Cà d'Zan, and Circus Museum. Allow 1 day. Open year-round daily 10am–5:30pm. Closed Jan 1, Thanksgiving Day, Dec 25. $9.* ✗ ♿ 🅿 ☎ *941-359-5700.* A treasury of European culture, this museum stands as the artistic triumph of southwest Florida. Complemented by magnificent architecture, the Ringling concentrates on paintings of the late Renaissance and Baroque periods (1550-1750), including significant works by Rubens, Van Dyck, Velazquez and Poussin. In fact, the **Baroque Collection**★ is considered one of the finest in the US. The 66-acre landscaped complex holds the art gallery, Ringling's mansion, a gallery of circus memorabilia, the Historic Asolo Theater, and Mrs. Ringling's rose garden. A gift of John Ringling to the state in 1936, the site was designated in 1946 as the official art museum of Florida.

The Showman's Art – John Ringling (1866-1936), one of the founding partners of the Ringling Bros. and Barnum & Bailey Circus, first visited Sarasota in 1911, lured by reports from land speculators. The following year, he bought property north of Sarasota and built a winter home. He and his beloved wife, Mable, lived primarily in New York City at that time, and traveled abroad several times a year looking for new acts for the show. During these trips they began buying paintings, turning their passion for fine art into a dedicated connoisseurship. By the 1920s they had amassed hundreds of objets d'art, including the world's largest private collection of works by Baroque master **Peter Paul Rubens** (1577-1640).

The Ringlings soon envisioned plans for a palatial repository for their holdings. They hired architect John H. Phillips, previously known for his design work, and construction of the art museum began in 1927. Two years later, just before the museum's opening, Mable died. Ringling's fortunes declined from then until his own death, seven years later. The museum complex is his gift to Sarasota, a legacy to his adopted state. Ringling's museum is the Greatest Show on Earth in formal attire. Where Ringling was quiet, his museum is flamboyant. The majestic entrance shouts its Italian-villa influence with three soaring arches crowned by a balustrade upon which stand four larger-than-life figures representing music, sculpture, architecture and painting. Of the paintings inside, a journalist in 1928 wrote: "The gift of showmanship, the energy, the vitality, the enthusiasm that have made the circus thrilling are excellent qualifications for the man who would meet the old masters on familiar terms." The museum, which opened to the public in March 1930, now welcomes more than 300,000 visitors a year.

★★**Art Galleries** – *1hr guided museum tour starts in the Rubens Gallery (gallery 2).* More than 10,000 objects (the majority acquired after Ringling's death), including 1,000 paintings, 2,500 prints and drawings, and 1,500 decorative art objects are exhibited here. Inside and out, the building displays an abundance of architectural flourishes: friezes, medallions, cartouches, wall fountains, inlaid marble mosaics and other ornaments that Ringling found in his travels. These elements accentuate—and sometimes overshadow—the paintings.

Abraham and Melchizedek (c. 1625) by Peter Paul Rubens

256

A wing of 11 rooms, the **North Galleries** *(galleries 1-11)* offer a broad survey of late Medieval through early Baroque art of Italy and northern Europe, with emphasis on 16C and 17C Italian works. The **Rubens Gallery★** consists of four huge paintings (each about 15ft tall) executed by Rubens and his assistants around 1625. Part of a series called *The Triumph of the Eucharist*, the paintings were commissioned by Hapsburg Archduchess Isabella Clara Eugenia as patterns for tapestries, which to this day hang in a Carmelite convent in Madrid. The series originally included 11 paintings, although four of them were destroyed in a 1731 fire in the Arch-duchess' palace in Brussels. Ringling bought four in 1925; the museum acquired a fifth (which hangs in gallery 21) in 1980. These paintings, with their brilliant colors, their dramatic scenes and their breathtaking size, manifest the appeal that the Baroque period had for Ringling. The room itself occupies a vast chamber with clerestory windows more than 30ft above the floor; the floor is of teak bought by Ringling in South America.

Continuing through this wing, you'll find numerous other Baroque masterpieces, as well as fine examples from the Middle Ages and Renaissance. Among the many outstanding pieces are: Rubens' *Portrait of the Archduke Ferdinand* (1635), Lucas Cranach the Elder's visually sumptuous *Cardinal Albrecht of Brandenburg as St. Jerome* (1526), Piero di Cosimo's *Building of a Palace* (1515-20) and Francesco del Cairo's mysterious *Judith with the Head of Holofernes* (c.1630).

A graceful central **Courtyard★** extends 350ft out from a marble-paved bridge linking the two wings. From the bridge you can behold the formal plantings and sculp-ture in the elegant garden, which is lined by parallel vaulted loggias. More than 90 columns support the loggias, some of which date back to the 11C. On the other side of the bridge stretches a lovely view of Sarasota Bay.

The **South Galleries** *(galleries 12-21)* present a survey of 17C-19C European and 18C-19C American art. Found here are major works by Poussin, Vouet, Van Dyck, Jordaens and Tiepolo. Adjacent to the gift shop *(in gallery 12)*, the **West Galleries** display changing exhibits of contemporary art and house an educational area called "inner space." A nod to the museum's circus background may be seen in two American works acquired in the mid-1970s. Reginald Marsh's playful *Wonderland Circus; Sideshow, Coney Island* (1930) and Robert Henri's sensuous *Salomé* (1909) both depict early 20C performers in costume, the latter bearing the same name as Ringling's mother. Galleries 19 and 20 showcase the **decorative arts**. Furnished in the styles of Louis XV and Louis XIV respectively, these rooms were purchased from the New York City mansion of Mrs. William Backhouse Astor. Such painted panels, gilt moldings, Chinese fans and rococo medallions are typical of the inte-riors favored by American aristocrats in the late 19C.

★★**Cà d'Zan** – *Same hours as museum.* A paved pathway leads from the museum to Ringling's sprawling, extravagant Venetian-style palace overlooking Sarasota Bay. Ringling built the Cà d'Zan (Venetian dialect meaning "House of John") as a winter residence in 1926. The mansion, with its stucco walls and red-tiled roof, its bal-conies and grand turret, incorporates Italian and French Renaissance, Venetian Gothic, Baroque and modern architectural elements. The west side, facing the water, glows amber in late afternoon as the sun lights up its terra-cotta walls. Inside, note the 30ft-high **court room** with painted cypress beams, the stained glass in the **tap room**, Ringling's eight-piece mahogany bedroom suite and his Siena marble bathtub. Be sure to walk out on the **marble terrace** for a sweeping **view** of Sarasota Bay. Ceiling panels in the **ballroom**, depicting dance costumes from various nations, were painted by Willy Pogany, set designer for the New York Ziegfeld Follies. Peeling wallpaper in this room testifies to many years of damage by the elements; a five-year, multimillion-dollar restoration project is currently underway.

Circus Museum – 🅺🅸🅳🆂 *Same hours as museum.* Though not part of Ringling's original plan, this building was added as a tribute to the circus king in 1948. Ringling himself did not collect circus artifacts, but the gallery exhibits items from his era. Circus posters and photographs, antique circus wagons and calliopes, and a hodge-podge of other memorabilia depict the old days of the big top. Though somewhat static for an exhibition on the circus, the dimly lit museum features worthwhile displays on tiny actor Tom Thumb and famed clown Emmett Kelly, as well as a mechanized miniature circus.

Cars and Music Museum of Sarasota – *5500 N. US-41; across the street from Ringling Museum. Open year-round daily 9am–6pm. $9. Closed Dec 25.* ♿ 🅿 ☏ *941-355-6228.* This 50-year-old attraction boasts antique cars, musical instru-ments and arcade games. Over 50 classic and antique automobiles occupy one wing. The haphazard arrangement includes such makes as Rolls Royce, Mercedes and Pierce Arrow. Highlighting the collection are five cars owned by circus magnate John Ringling. In the **music room** tour guides demonstrate the still-wonderful sounds of antique street organs, hurdy-gurdies, and others in a collection claiming more than 1,000 instruments *(visit by 30min guided tour only, every hour on the hour)*. Bring dimes and quarters for the old-fashioned arcade and pinball games; player pianos and mannequin shows evoke seaside amusements of the past.

Gulf Coast World of Science – Kids *8251 15th St. E., in Airport Mall opposite Bradenton/Sarasota Airport. Open year-round Tue–Sat 10am–5pm, Sun 1pm–5pm. Closed major holidays. $3.* ⚐ 🅿 ☏ *941-359-9975.* This hands-on facility offers good educational fun for young children. Equipped with the standard gear—giant bubble-maker, echo tube, plasma ball, frozen-shadow booth—the museum also features a Rube Goldbergesque pedaling machine with flywheels, lights, gears and chains. In a reptile petting area, brave youngsters may handle a king snake (with assistance). The unique Take-apart Table gives children the opportunity to disassemble stereo equipment and computer components.

Sarasota Jungle Gardens – Kids *3701 Bay Shore Rd. Open year-round daily 9am–5pm. Reptile shows 10am, noon, 2pm & 4pm; bird shows 10:30am & 12:30pm, 2:30pm, 4:30pm. Closed Dec 25. $9.* 🍴⚐🅿☏ *941-355-5305.* Envisioning an exotic botanical garden, local newspaperman David Lindsay bought a 10-acre tract of swampland in the early

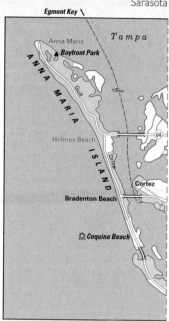

1930s, drained it and planted tropical trees and flowers imported from around the world. Open to the public since 1940, Sarasota Jungle Gardens exhibits thousands of native and non-native plants and scores of animals. Brick paths wind through a dense jungle of coconut palms, viburnum, rubber trees and other plants. Bridges cross lakes and lagoons loud with the calls of flamingos and the rushing of waterfalls. An enchanting wonderland for children, the gardens also include a petting zoo and playground.

★**Downtown Art District** – *Palm Ave. and Main St.* Along these two streets beats the heart of downtown Sarasota. Locals and tourists alike promenade past the many art galleries, antique shops, small theaters and fashionable restaurants. Lunchtime finds the sidewalks particularly busy with employees from area banks and other businesses. One notable building, the red-tiled 1926 **Sarasota Opera House** *(one block north of Main St. on Pineapple Ave.),* once hosted vaudeville acts and minstrel shows; Will Rogers, Elvis Presley and other big names performed there. A few blocks south lies **Sarasota Quay** *(on US-41 at Fruitville Rd.),* an attractive bayfront park heralded by white arches and planted with oleander and palms. For a quiet diversion from the bustle of downtown, stroll the Quay's boat docks and watch the shorebirds. At night restaurants and nightclubs pick up the pace.

★**Marie Selby Botanical Gardens** – *811 S. Palm Ave. Open year-round daily 10am–5pm. Closed Dec 25. $8.* ⚐🅿 *www.selby.org* ☏ *941-366-5730.* Occupying an nine-acre peninsula on the downtown waterfront, these lovely gardens display more than 20,000 tropical plants, including 6,000 orchids. The **tropical display house**★, just beyond the entrance, is widely known for its **epiphytes** (plants that grow on other plants and take their nourishment from the air and rainfall), which include a large collection of colorful orchids and bromeliads. A paved path outside circles 20 garden areas, including the cycad collection (a class of plants that date from the age of dinosaurs), the cactus and succulent garden, the shady banyan grove and a native plant community. Here an elevated walkway takes visitors along a lush grove of palms and bamboo, past a mangrove swamp, to an idyllic **view** of Sarasota Bay, framed by a spreading pipal fig tree, known to Buddhists as the *bodhi* tree, or tree of enlightenment.

The **Museum of Botany and the Arts**, at the north end of the garden, was built as a private residence in 1935 and now hosts temporary exhibits of painting and photography with a botanical theme. Nearby you'll find the tropical food and medicinal plant gardens, as well as the butterfly garden and learning center.

BARRIER ISLANDS *1 day. Map above.*

Flung out north and south along Sarasota's Gulf coast lie several idyllic barrier islands, connected to the mainland by causeways. To the north, **Longboat Key** is a resort island, offering vacation condos and a wide variety of hotel accommodations along its 10mi of glittering sand. Tennis is the game of choice on Longboat Key, headquarters of the US Professional Tennis Association. Directly across the causeway

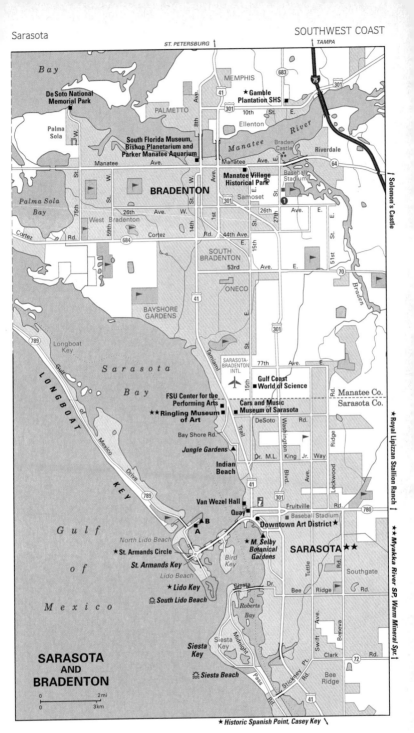

★ Historic Spanish Point, Casey Key ➘

from downtown Sarasota lie fashionable St. Armands Key and the pleasant beach parks of Lido Key. To the south stretch the white high rises of Siesta Key and, finally, tiny residential **Casey Key**, its pastel houses tucked amid lush foliage.

St. Armands Key – *Located across the John Ringling Causeway from downtown Sarasota.* Named after its first homesteader, French farmer Charles St. Armand, this key began as a mangrove island rumored to have been won by John Ringling in a poker game. The majority of its 132 acres is covered by Sarasota's most famous shopping district, **St. Armands Circle★**, which owes its existence to John Ringling's vision and devotion to his wife. As Ringling explained it: "Now Mable won't have to go to Palm Beach to shop." Strategically positioned at the end of the John Ringling Causeway, the circle and the streets that radiate from it encompass more

Jack Elka

Sarasota

than 160 specialty shops, galleries, restaurants and businesses. The circle's hub is an oasis of palms, bougainvillea and hibiscus; around its edge, bronze plaques honor great circus performers of the past.

★**Lido Key** – *Just west of St. Armands Key on Ringling Causeway.* Some of the area's most prestigious real estate lies on this J-shaped barrier island, developed by John Ringling in the late 1920s. Ringling built roads and canals with the help of his circus elephants who transported timber for the causeways. A year after the key opened to the public, the Depression slowed business and the barrier islands lay quiet until the 1950s. Now posh hotels, condominiums and homes share the narrow island with popular Lido Beach, pine-fringed North Lido Beach and lovely **South Lido Beach**⌂, flanked by an expanse of mangroves on its bay side *(1.8mi south of St. Armands Circle; open year-round daily 9am–dusk,* 🅿*)*.

Mote Marine Aquarium (A) – 🄺🄸🄳🅂 *1600 Ken Thompson Pkwy., on northern tip of Lido Key (2.2mi north of St. Armands Circle). Open year-round daily 10am–5pm. Closed Easter Sunday, Thanksgiving Day, Dec 25. $8.* ✗ ᴋ 🅿 *www.mote.org* ☎ *941-388-2451.* Dedicated to enlightening the public about the world beneath the sea, the fine little facility features a score of aquariums holding sea turtles, skates, moray eels and other denizens of Sarasota Bay and the Gulf of Mexico. One perennial favorite, the 135,000gal shark tank, offers both above- and below-water viewing areas. A 30ft touch tank allows visitors a chance to handle living sea creatures. Known for its research efforts with sharks and environmental pollutants, the Mote also operates a visitor center adjacent to its research lab and a marine mammal center across the street.

Pelican Man's Bird Sanctuary (B) – *Adjacent to Mote Marine Aquarium. Open year-round daily 10am–5pm. Closed Jan 1, Thanksgiving Day, Dec 25. Contribution requested.* ᴋ 🅿 *www.pelicanman.com* ☎ *941-388-4444.* Stroll the boardwalk here past 30 pens that house birds too disabled to return to the wild. This sanctuary rescues more than 7,000 injured birds a year, among them night herons, brown pelicans, crows, ospreys, owls and double-crested cormorants. Volunteers provide information about the birds, many of which were injured by fishing lines or automobiles. Recipient of one of President Bush's Thousand Points of Light Awards, the sanctuary's founder, Dale Shields (a.k.a. "Pelican Man"), is often on hand to answer questions.

Siesta Key – *6mi southwest of Sarasota. From downtown, take US-41 south to Siesta Dr. (Rte. 758); go west on Siesta Dr. 1mi to Siesta Key.* This popular barrier island, with its clutch of white, high-rise condominiums, is highly regarded for its soft white-sand beaches. Analyzed by Harvard geologists, the fine-grained sand is millions of years old and 99 percent pure quartz (with no shell or coral content), resulting in a talcum-soft texture. **Siesta Beach**⌂ sports 2,400ft of sparkling shoreline and a seaside pavilion with a snack bar, souvenir shop and rental stand *(Beach Rd., 1mi southeast of Ocean Blvd.; open May–Jan Mon–Fri 9am–5pm; rest of the year Mon–Fri 9am–5pm Sat 9am–1pm;* ᴋ 🅿*)*.

EXCURSIONS *Map p 239*

★**Historic Spanish Point** – *2.5hrs. 8mi south in Osprey, via US-41. Open year-round Mon–Sat 9am–5pm, Sun noon–5pm. Buildings are accessible by guided tour (2hrs) only. Mon–Sat 10am, 11am, 1pm & 2pm Sun 12:30pm, 1:15pm, 2pm & 2:30pm. Closed Jan 1, Easter Sunday, Thanksgiving Day, Dec 25. $5.* 🅿 ☎ *941-966-5214.* Jutting into scenic Little Sarasota Bay, this peaceful 30-acre site illuminates the lives of prehistoric Indians and early pioneers. Tours follow a gravel path through a landscape varying from mangrove estuary to live oak forest to formal garden (after the tour, visitors are free to stroll the grounds on their own). The path winds past a burial mound, a packing house, an 1894 chapel and graveyard, and a fascinating archeology dig within a 15ft-high shell midden. Called **Window to the Past**★, the exhibit features a Plexiglas wall that allows visitors to actually see the shells, bones and shards in the midden, while video footage and other displays explain the sleuth work of archaeologists. Other high points along the way include three pioneer cottages and the restored gardens of former Chicago socialite Bertha Honoré Palmer, Sarasota County's leading lady in the early 1900s.

★★**Myakka River State Park** – *1/2 day. 14mi east in Myakka via Rte. 72 (Clark Rd.). Open year-round daily 8am–dusk. $4/vehicle.* △ ✕ ♿ ▣ *www.myakka. sarasota.fl.us* ☎ *941-361-6511.* One of the oldest and largest of Florida's parks, this 28,875-acre parcel stretches along the primeval Myakka River—protected by the state as a designated Wild and Scenic River—for 12mi and encompasses a wide variety of animal and plant communities. Deer and bobcat favor the palm hammocks, pine flatwoods and dry prairies, while alligators and numerous species of wading birds inhabit Upper Myakka Lake and its grassy marshes. Hiking trails traverse the park, as does a flat road perfect for bicycling. The highly popular **tram and airboat tours**★ give visitors a close-up look at native flora and fauna *(depart from boat basin Jan–Jun daily 10am–2:30pm, rest of the year daily 10am–1pm; no tours Dec 25; round-trip 1hr; commentary; $7;* ♿ ▣ *Myakka Wildlife Tours, Inc.* ☎ *941-365-0100).* Concessionaire at the boat basin sells fishing, camping and picnicking supplies and rents boats, bicycles and canoes.

★**Royal Lipizzan Stallion Ranch** – 🄺🄸🄳 *2.5hrs. 23mi east in Myakka City. Take Fruitville Rd. (Rte. 780) east 17.5mi to Verna Rd. Turn left and continue 1.1mi to Singletary Rd. Turn right and go 4.3mi to ranch (entrance on left) at 32755 Singletary Rd. Open Nov–Apr daily 9am–5pm. Performances Thu & Fri 3pm, Sat 10am. Contribution requested.* ♿ ▣ ☎ *941-322-1501.* Bred from strains of Arabian and Andalusian stallions, the so-called "aristocrats of the horse world" perform amazing feats that originated more than 300 years ago as battle maneuvers. Guests watch a free 90min outdoor training session hosted by affable, Austrian-born Colonel Ottomar Herrmann. Noble Lipizzans execute difficult leaps and kicks, including the famous capriole, in which the horse jumps up and kicks his hind legs out horizontal to the ground. These winter sessions prepare the troupe for a rigorous annual US tour. *Arrive early to get choice seats.*

Warm Mineral Springs – *1/2 day. 30mi southeast in Warm Mineral Springs. Take I-75 south to Exit 34; go 5mi south to US-41. Turn left on US-41 and continue 2.5mi to Ortiz Blvd.; turn left on Ortiz and follow 1mi to springs' entrance on right. Open year-round daily 9am–5pm. $7.* ✕ ♿ ▣ ☎ *941-426-1692.* Indians knew of the warm mineral springs here for perhaps 10,000 years before an English hunter discovered the area in 1874. Yet it was not until the 1930s that the springs were developed for tourists. Billed today as a resort, Warm Mineral Springs retains the flavor of a latter-day Florida spa. Palms and lawn chairs fringe the 2.5-acre, spring-fed lake, set in a trim carpet of grass. A mostly senior clientele takes to the soothing 87°F waters and enjoys such treatments as massage, whirlpool and acupuncture.

Space Coast

Shuttle *Atlantis* Liftoff, June 27, 1995 – NASA

Spanning some 40mi from Titusville down to Melbourne, this region experienced phenomenal growth after the birth of the space program in the late 1950s. The edge of Brevard County and its overlapping barrier islands, separated by lagoons known as the Indian River and the Banana River, are home to the thousands of people employed in the space industry, either at the Kennedy Space Center or in nearby electronics and computer companies. By contrast, the north part of the Space Coast holds one of the state's largest wilderness areas—the nearly 200,000 combined acres of Canaveral National Seashore and Merritt Island National Wildlife Refuge.

One of the earliest settlers here, Captain Douglas Dummitt, acquired land on Merritt Island in 1843. In this period just after the Second Seminole War, the Armed Occupation Act offered 160 acres to anyone who would stay for at least five years. In a jungly landscape known as Mosquito County, Dummitt began a commercial orange grove that would blossom into Florida's largest 25 years later. Here he developed his famous Indian River Oranges, which he would wrap in Spanish moss and pack in barrels for shipment by dugout to ST. AUGUSTINE. Schooners relayed the delicious cargo to ports as far north as Boston. So widespread grew the fame of these oranges that czars of Russia sent ships here for them. About six million bushels are still shipped worldwide annually.

Up to World War II, most area residents made a living by fishing or raising cattle or citrus fruits. Today the space and defense industries generate the majority of the area's revenue. The service industry is second, with tourism bringing in some $650 million a year.

KENNEDY SPACE CENTER★★★

Map of Principal Sights p 3 – Map p 267
Tourist Information ☎ 407-452-2121

Protruding from Florida's Atlantic coast, this barrier island of orange groves, tidal flats and pristine beaches is home to the nation's space program. Here the world's most sophisticated technology emerges from Florida's largest east-coast wilderness. Every US rocket—from the one that carried the Explorer I satellite in 1958 to modern space shuttles—has blasted off from Merritt Island or adjoining Cape Canaveral. Opened to the public in 1966, the **Kennedy Space Center Visitor Complex** ranks as the fourth largest attraction in Florida. More than three million visitors tour the facility each year.

Historical Notes

The Race for Space – Rocket launches from the beginning of the American space program up to 1964 took place exclusively at Cape Canaveral Air Force Station (called Cape Kennedy from 1963-73), located on the spit of land extending southeast from Merritt Island. The Cape had been in use by the US Air Force since 1950 as the test site for long-range guided missiles. Though both the Soviet Union and the US announced their intention in 1955 of launching artificial satellites, the Soviets took the first steps with the deployment of two Sputnik satellites in late 1957. The following year, the US launched its first satellite. In October 1958, the National Aeronautics and Space Administration (NASA) was created; its mission was the exploration of space.

Activity on the Cape accelerated after President John F. Kennedy's challenge to the nation in May 1961 "to achieve the goal, before the decade is out, of landing a man on the moon and returning him safely to Earth." The press soon declared a "space race" between the two Cold War superpowers, and NASA began buying up land on Merritt Island for its main launch facility.

In 1963 NASA handed the US Fish and Wildlife Service management of the 95 percent of Merritt Island not needed for its own operations. With the creation of the Merritt Island National Wildlife Refuge in 1963 and the Canaveral National Seashore in 1975, the area has become a haven for migratory waterfowl and other animals. When the space program began gearing up, the government leased resident citrus growers' land on the north part of Merritt Island, where orange groves continue to flourish.

To the Moon and Beyond – The Mercury and Gemini missions (1961-66) accomplished several feats that captured the attention of the nation. Alan Shepard's 15min ride in the cramped nose of a Redstone rocket in 1961 made him the first American in space. Early in 1962, John Glenn became the first US astronaut to orbit the earth. In 1965 Edward White walked in space, another first.

The new Apollo program stalled for a year and a half after White and fellow astronauts Gus Grissom and Roger Chaffee died in a fire on the launchpad during a 1967 test of *Apollo 1*. Following this first NASA disaster, manned missions were halted until *Apollo 7* was launched in October 1968. On July 20, 1969, Neil Armstrong and Buzz Aldrin walked on the moon; in a mere eight years NASA had met Kennedy's challenge. After launching Skylab, the first US space station, and conducting experiments from orbit in 1973-74, the Apollo series concluded in a joint mission with a Soviet Soyuz spacecraft in 1975. NASA's answer to a reduction in funding in the late 1970s was a fleet of reusable space shuttles, which have been the centerpiece of the space program since the maiden voyage of *Columbia* in 1981. Able to carry a crew of seven who could conduct experiments, repair satellites and deliver commercial payloads, the shuttle (though without the glamorous goal of the Apollo program) proved highly useful and versatile, thus justifying the continuation of manned space ventures.

The 1986 explosion of *Challenger*, killing the entire crew of seven, again concentrated national attention on NASA and underscored the lack of focus that the space program faced in the decade after the historic moon missions. More than two and a half years elapsed before the next shuttle launch. Though the flawed Hubble Space Telescope unleashed a storm of criticism, NASA regained its prestige with the spectacular in-space repair job of the telescope in December 1993.

NASA's primary goal by the millennium is to establish an **International Space Station**. A combined effort of the US, Russia, Canada, Japan and the 14 member nations of the European Space Agency, the space station will require 38 shuttle trips to carry and assemble sections to its fixed orbit 250mi above the earth. As many as eight astronauts could work in the station for up to six months. NASA's long-range plans call for a permanent lunar research base and a manned mission to Mars.

VISIT *1 1/2 days*

Bus Tours – *Kennedy Space Center Tour departs year-round daily every 15min, first tour 9:30am, last tour 2hrs before dusk. 2-4hrs. $14; $19 combination ticket includes IMAX movie. Cape Canaveral Tour schedule varies; call for availability ☎ 407-452-2121. 2hrs. $14. Commentary on board both tours. Special operations or imminent shuttle launches may alter tour itineraries. ⅙.* The **Kennedy Space Center Tour★★**, the more popular of the two, takes visitors around the space shuttle

When to Go

The Space Coast region enjoys a mild climate with an average annual temperature of 73°F. Highs during the summer months reach into the mid-80s with frequent afternoon thunderstorms. Main tourist season for the area: October through May.

Getting There

By Air – **Melbourne International Airport** (MLB): 35mi south of Kennedy Space Center; international, domestic and commuter flights; information ☎ 723-6227. Transportation to Kennedy Space Center: Melbourne Airport taxi *($85)* ☎ 724-1600. Rental car agencies *(p 323)* located at airport and on US-1. Space Coast visitor information booth adjacent to baggage claim area ☎ 952-4589.

Orlando International Airport (MCO): 37mi west of Kennedy Space Center; international, domestic and commuter flights; information ☎ 825-2001. Regularly scheduled shuttle to Cocoa Beach leaves from Level 1 *(every two hours daily 9am–7pm; $18-$20 one-way)*. For reservations, call Cocoa Beach Shuttle ☎ 784-3831.

By Car – Kennedy Space Center is located roughly in the middle of Florida's east coast, in a region often referred to as the Space Coast. The area can be reached in about an hour's drive from most central Florida locations via Route 528 (Beeline Expressway). Sample distances from Cocoa Beach: Orlando 51mi; Jacksonville 156mi; Miami 187mi.

From Interstate I-95, exit on Route 407 East; take Route 405 (NASA Parkway) east across causeway and follow signs. Kennedy Space Center is located 6mi east of US-1 on NASA Parkway. Free parking.

By Train or Bus – Nearest Amtrak **train** station is in Sanford (48mi northwest of Kennedy Space Center) ☎ 323-4800 or 800-872-7245. Greyhound/Trailways **bus** station: 302 Main St., Cocoa ☎ 800-231-2222. Local bus service: Space Coast Area Transit ☎ 633-1878. Cocoa Beach Shuttle from area hotels to Kennedy Space Center *(pick-up 9am; return 3pm; $45/two people)* ☎ 784-3831.

General Information

Accommodations – *(p 324)* A wide range of hotels, motels, condominiums and campgrounds are available in Titusville, Cocoa Beach, Cocoa and Melbourne. Some offer shuttle bus service to the Kennedy Space Center. For information, contact **Florida's Space Coast Office of Tourism**, 8810 Astronaut Blvd., Cape Canaveral FL 32920 ☎ 868-1126; **Titusville Area Chamber of Commerce**, 2000 S. Washington Ave., Titusville FL 32780 ☎ 267-3036; or **Cocoa Beach Area Chamber of Commerce**, 400 Fortenberry Rd., Merritt Island FL 32952 ☎ 459-2200. *These organizations provide additional information regarding shopping, entertainment, festivals (p 318) and recreation.*

Reservations for accommodations during space shuttle launches should be made well in advance. Reservation service: ☎ 800-USA-1969. Daily room rates range from $55-$175. Numerous campgrounds and RV parks offer full-service amenities, fishing and other recreational facilities. *Rates quoted are average prices per night for a double room and are subject to seasonal variations.*

Roving "Spaceman" at Kennedy Space Center Visitor Center

Visitor Information – *NASA Kennedy Space Center Visitor Complex: open year-round daily 9am–dusk. Closed Dec 25 and certain launch days.* ✗ ♿ ▣ *www.kscvisitor.com* ☎ *452-2121.* Kennedy Space Center (KSC) is busiest between June and August and on holidays. Weekends are less crowded. Begin your visit at Spaceport Central; here, multilingual staff provide information about the Space Center and area attractions. Arrive early and buy tour and movie tickets right away to ensure your first choices; the ticket pavilion is located right behind Spaceport Central. Taking pictures is permitted; free cameras are available at the Information Counter. All exhibits are free. Two restaurants (The Lunch Pad and the Orbit Cafeteria) are located at the visitor complex. Area hotel reservations can be made from the information booth located at the visitor complex (☎ 455-1309). Wheelchairs and strollers are available free of charge. Call ahead for on-site kennel reservations (free). For bus tour information, see p 263. Group tours in foreign languages are available by advance reservation; individual visitors should inquire at guest services in Spaceport Central about foreign language tours on day of visit. A costumed "Spaceman" roams the complex from 10:30am–5:30pm for picture-taking opportunities. At **IMAX 1 & 2**, movies *(admission $7.50)* are shown several times a day in two different IMAX theaters. **IMAX 1**: *The Dream Is Alive (daily 9:30am, 10:20am, noon, 12:50pm, 1:40pm, 3:20pm, 4:10pm, 6:00pm, & 7pm)* and *Mission to Mir (daily 11:10am, 2:30pm & 5pm).* **IMAX 2**: *offers 12 show times for* 3-D movie *L5: First City In Space (daily beginning at 10am; last show at 7:10pm).* Schedules may vary with season. The exhibit Launch Processing is also located at IMAX 1 & 2.

> ### ■ Shuttle Facts:
>
> Each of the solid rocket boosters on the space shuttle contains more than one million pounds of propellant; the external tank is loaded with 500,000 gallons of liquid oxygen and liquid hydrogen. Once launched, a space shuttle in low orbit around the earth flies at about 17,500mph.

To View a Shuttle Launch – To obtain a launch schedule, write to Florida's Space Coast Office of Tourism *(p 264)*; schedules are published twice a year. To request complimentary vehicle passes for viewing a launch, write three months in advance to: NASA Visitor Services, Mail Code: PA-Pass, Kennedy Space Center FL 32899. Launch viewing tickets go on sale approximately five days prior to launch date and must be purchased in person at the KSC Visitor Complex Ticket Pavilion *(open year-round daily 9am–5pm; $10).* For updated launch information, call ☎ 867-4636, or toll-free ☎ 800-KSC-INFO (Florida only).

If you are unable to reserve a spot at KSC to watch a launch, we suggest the following alternative sites. Be sure to arrive early and make sure you have an unobstructed view to the east.

- Along Canaveral National Seashore.
- Along Route 402, north of Complex 39 *(map p 267)* in Merritt Island National Wildlife Refuge *(parts of refuge may be closed due to launch activities).*
- Along the Indian River on US-1 in Titusville between Route 528 and Route 402 *(the city permits roadside parking up to 24hrs before launch time).*
- Jetty Park *(east end of Jetty Dr.; map p 267).*
- Or rent a hotel room on the beach for a great vantage point.

Sports and Recreation – Melbourne Greyhound Park *(Mon–Sat noon & 6:30pm; Sun noon)* ☎ 259-9800. Airboat rides on St. Johns River at Camp Holly *(depart year-round daily 9am–dusk; round-trip 35min; $9.35;* ☎ *723-2179),* and Lone Cabbage Fish Camp *(depart year-round daily 10am–dusk; round-trip 30min; $12;* ♿ ☎ *632-4199).* For information on other recreational activities, call the visitor organizations *(p 264).* Florida Marlins **baseball spring training** *(Mar)* in Melbourne ☎ 407-633-9200. **Cruises:** Carnival Cruise Lines (☎ 800-327-9501), Disney Cruise Line (☎ 407-566-7000) and Premier Cruise Lines (☎ 800-327-7113) depart for the Caribbean from Port Canaveral.

Useful numbers ☎

Lost and Found	449-4323
First Aid	867-2776

Vehicle Assembly Building and Launch Complex 39

facilities. Though the architecture is an uninspiring mix of industrial bulk and launchpad scaffolding, visitors are entertained with a recital of amazing technological facts.

Buses first pass the cubical, 525ft-high **Vehicle Assembly Building** (VAB) where the shuttle is assembled. As the third largest building in the world, the VAB could hold 3.75 Empire State Buildings. Once ready, the space shuttle inches to the pad at 1mph on the six-million-pound Crawler Transporter. At **Launch Complex 39**, visitors can climb an observation gantry and, perhaps, see a shuttle awaiting launch from another nearby complex. Shown here are a short film and exhibit on the launch procedure, a presentation that does not omit NASA's disasters.

An excellent movie about the *Apollo 11* mission and a close-up inspection of a 363ft *Saturn V* moon rocket highlight a stop at the **Apollo/Saturn V Center**. Built of stages destined for canceled Apollo missions, the Saturn V is one of three such rockets in the world. Tours of the center include a stirring multimedia review of the Apollo series and displays of original lunar-excursion and command-service modules.

Newest addition to the Red Tour is the **International Space Station Center**, where visitors learn about the venture that is driving the space industry into the 21C. In June 1998, the first of 38 flights from the US and Russia carried into orbit component parts for the construction of the International Space Station, a permanent orbiting scientific laboratory scheduled for completion in 2003. Eighteen countries on four continents are involved in the project. Exhibits include a movie about the station and mock-ups of its various elements, including living quarters and working space. An enclosed catwalk offers a bird's-eye view of the factory floor where module components are being processed.

Concentrating on space-flight history, the less frequent **Cape Canaveral Tour** begins with a scenic 11mi drive out to Cape Canaveral. On the way, visitors can glimpse shuttle facilities and the ships that salvage rocket boosters. A simulated launch is staged in the actual Mission Control Building used for the Mercury program, while visitors stand in the press gallery. Launch site of the first US satellite, the **Air Force Space Museum**, a 30min stop, offers an impressive array of rockets and historical artifacts *(open year-round Mon–Fri 10am–2pm, weekends 10am–4pm; museum can be closed due to operational requirements without prior notice;* ♿ ☎ *407-853-3245).*

★**Gallery of Space Flight** – *Left of ticket pavilion. Open 9am–dusk.* This cornucopia of space gear highlights the 1960s and '70s. Included are the Apollo spacecraft that docked with a Soviet Soyuz in 1975, a Gemini capsule that orbited the earth in 1966, and a piece of moon rock. Spacesuits and full-scale mock-ups of a Lunar Rover and a Soviet Soyuz spacecraft complete the exhibits.

Outside the museum *(west side)*, the **Rocket Garden** displays eight rockets, as well as gigantic tracking antennae and the access arm through which the *Apollo 11* crew entered their space capsule before liftoff.

IMAX 1 & 2 – *Directly behind the ticket pavilion.* Two IMAX theaters present compelling films in 70mm format throughout the day. Projected on screens more than five stories high, three **films**★—*The Dream Is Alive, Mission to Mir* and (in 3-D) *L5: First City in Space*—include stunning footage shot from space. Seat-rumbling, six-channel digital stereo adds to the realistic effect *(for film schedules, see p 265).*

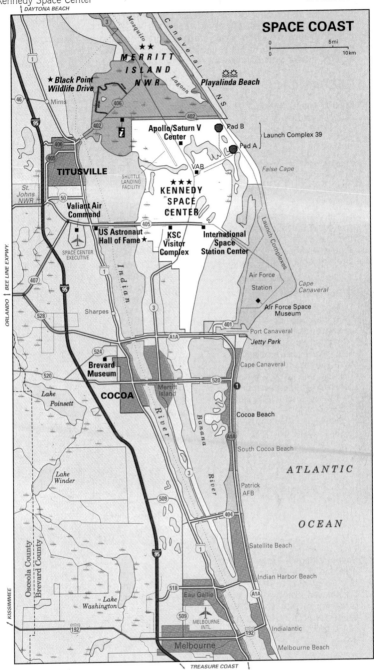

A gallery of space-related art includes paintings and sculptures, and an exhibit called Spinoffs from Space demonstrates the benefits of space exploration for such fields as medicine and sports.

Behind the IMAX theaters, the **Astronauts Memorial** is a moving tribute to astronauts who have made the ultimate sacrifice. Computers keep the black granite monolith tilted to the sun so that the names, engraved on panels equipped with a reflective surface, will be projected on the clouds *(names are easiest to see in the sky at sunset; weather conditions may affect visibility)*.

Just to the right of the memorial, a full-scale replica of the **Space Shuttle** *Explorer* offers visitors an idea of the relative roominess of modern space vehicles compared with the claustrophobic dimensions of pioneering spacecraft.

Also in the visitor complex, the **Spaceport Theater**, separate from the IMAX, offers a pair of films: *Boy From Mars* and *Apollo 13: Houston, We Have a Problem*. In other buildings are a 45min audiovisual program on satellites, exhibits and videos on a robotic mission to Mars, and a "Near Earth-Asteroid Rendezvous." There's also a **Center for Space Education** and a children's play dome.

EXCURSION

★★**Merritt Island National Wildlife Refuge** – *1/2 day. 4mi east of Titusville on Rte. 402. Description p 270.*

COCOA

Population 18,279
Map of Principal Sights p 3 – Map p 267
Tourist Information ☎ 407-459-2200

This small coastal town might have grown faster if developer Henry Flagler, angry that he could not purchase the Plaza Hotel, had not torn out the railroad spur line serving that grand Cocoa establishment. But Cocoa had an independent spirit. One of its pioneers and premier citizens, Albert Taylor, moved here in 1886 and helped found the Brevard County State Bank—the only bank between Titusville and Key West at the time. Today the town, boosted over the last few decades by the space industry, sprawls along the Indian River yet maintains a modest population.

Due east of Cocoa across the Merritt Island Causeway (Route 520) lies the unpretentious burg of **Cocoa Beach**, where water sports and spaceflight merit nearly equal importance. Several surfing competitions are held here, and informal beach activity abounds, particularly near the 800ft Cocoa Beach Pier *(Meade Ave., off A1A)*, which offers open-air bars and live music. At the southeast corner of Port Canaveral lies **Jetty Park**, highly popular as a winter home for serious campers and also a good spot for watching rockets arc across the Atlantic *(p 265)*. Just south of town, the missile display outside Patrick Air Force Base *(5.5mi south of Cocoa Beach on west side of A1A)* serves as another reminder of the significance of high-tech aviation to the area.

> **① Ron Jon Surf Shop**
>
> *Map p 267. 4151 N. Atlantic Ave.* ♿ ☎ *407-799-8888.* It's hard to miss this gaudy two-story Art Deco surfwear palace, which has ranked as a Cocoa Beach institution since 1963. If it's related to the beach or water sports, you'll find it here: surfboards, in-line skates, boogie boards, beachwear, bathing suits, sunglasses, surfboard wax, flip-flops and the requisite plethora of T-shirts. A "must" visit for restless kids on a rainy—or sunny—day.

SIGHTS *3 hrs*

★**Cocoa Village** – *South of Rte. 520 at Brevard Ave.* Brochure of the village is available at the Brevard Museum of History and Natural Science *(below)* ☎ *407-632-1830.* For a relaxing afternoon, walk through this charming four-block, brick-paved historic district of cafes and boutiques shaded by old trees. Here, the three-story 1924 **Cocoa Village Playhouse** *(300 Brevard Ave.)*, once a venue for vaudeville acts, continues to stage a wide range of performances *(for schedules, call ☎ 407-636-5050)*.

Porcher House – *434 Delannoy Ave. Open year-round Mon–Fri 9am–5pm;* ♿ ▣ *www.cocoafl.org* ☎ *407-639-3500.* Home to wealthy citrus growers Edward and Byrnina Porcher, the white-columned residence was built in 1916 of local coquina rock. The house was once a social center for the town's elite. Mrs. Porcher's love of bridge remains evident on the front patio, where playing-card symbols are carved into coquina blocks. After the Depression, the house was leased as a restaurant and boarding house. Eventually the state restored the structure, which now houses city offices on the second floor; the first floor is furnished with period pieces.

Brevard Museum of History and Natural Science – *2201 Michigan Ave. Open Oct–May Mon–Sat 10am–4pm, Sun 1pm–4pm. Rest of the year Mon–Sat 10am–4pm. Closed major holidays. $5.* ♿ ▣ *www5.palmnet.net/~brevardmuseum* ☎ *407-632-1830.* Situated in a quiet neighborhood on the north side of Brevard Community College, this modest museum features a fascinating live-bee exhibit and a quick rundown of area history with emphasis on 19C pioneers. Temporary exhibits are also presented on a regular basis.

TITUSVILLE

Population 41,543
Map of Principal Sights p 3 – Map p 267
Tourist Information ☎ 407-267-3036

Founded in 1873, the county seat is named for Colonel Henry Titus, a blockade runner for the Confederacy who settled here after the Civil War and built Titus House Hotel. Once a shipping point for oranges, Titusville now ties its fortunes primarily to Kennedy Space Center, which lies across the Indian River and employs some 60 percent of the local work force. The vital artery from Merritt Island to the mainland, Highway 405, is often congested with commuter and visitor traffic.

SIGHTS *2 hrs*

★**U.S. Astronaut Hall of Fame** – *Southeast quadrant of intersection of US-1 and Rte. 405. Open year-round daily 9am–6pm. Closed Dec 25. $13.95.* ✗ ♿ 🅿 *www.astronauts.org* ☎ *407-269-6101*. Honoring the first 44 US astronauts, the Hall details the accomplishments of the Mercury, Gemini and Apollo heroes in individual displays that feature not only mission gear, but also such personal items as Jim Lovell's Eagle Scout badge and Buzz Aldrin's junior-high report card. It adjoins the Astronaut Core museum, where audiovisual and computer displays, artifacts and memorabilia, a Mercury spacecraft and the Apollo 14 lunar-command module document the history of the nation's space program.
Two 10min films are shown continually: *To Explore* links the triumphs of the earliest New World adventurers to the space pioneers of present and future, while *Shuttle to Tomorrow*, shown in a space-shuttle replica outside the building, envisions future commercial space flight. In the interactive Astronaut Adventure room, visitors experience astronaut training regimens in the likes of a centrifuge machine (used for G-force training) and a shuttle-landing simulator. The museum is run by the nonprofit Mercury 7 Foundation and the US Space Camp Foundation, the latter offering year-round camp sessions in an adjoining building.

American Space Firsts

- US launched its first earth satellite, *Explorer 1*, on January 31, 1958.
- The first American in space was Alan B. Shepard, Jr., who completed a 15-minute suborbital flight aboard *Freedom 7* on May 5, 1961.
- On February 20, 1962, John Glenn, Jr., became the first American to orbit the earth.
- Virgil Grissom and John Young made the first US two-man flight on March 23, 1965. Their space capsule, *Gemini 3*, was the first manned craft to change its orbital path.
- Gemini 4 astronaut Edward White was the first American to walk in space. On June 3, 1965, White took a 21-minute "stroll" outside his craft.
- Frank Borman, James Lovell and William Anders completed the first manned orbits of the moon during the Apollo 8 mission of October 11, 1968.
- During the Apollo 11 mission—the first manned moon launch—Neil Armstrong became the first man to walk on the moon on July 20, 1969.
- *Apollo 18* initiated the first cooperative international space flight on July 15, 1975. During this historic mission, crew members Vance Brand, Thomas Stafford and Donald Slayton linked their spacecraft with the USSR *Soyuz 19*.
- On April 12, 1981, the era of reusable spacecraft was inaugurated with the first space shuttle launch from Cape Canaveral.

Valiant Air Command Warbird Museum – *6600 Tico Rd. (at Space Center Executive Airport, off Rte. 405, .5mi west of US-1). Open year-round daily 10am–6pm. Closed Jan 1, Thanksgiving Day, Dec 25. $6.* ♿ 🅿 ☎ *407-268-1941*. This building displays aviation memorabilia from World War I, World War II, Korea, Vietnam and Operation Desert Storm. Examples of enemy paraphernalia—a Japanese pilot's outfit, a captured swastika—and a small exhibit on women in aviation are displayed inside the building. Airplane buffs will appreciate the adjoining hangar filled with wartime aircraft. Outside the hangar sits a C-47 troop transport that took part in the D-Day invasion of Normandy. Visitors may walk through this plane.

EXCURSION

★★Merritt Island National Wildlife Refuge – *1/2 day. 4mi east on Rte. 402. Open year-round daily dawn–dusk. Closed 24hrs prior to space shuttle launches.* &♿ 🅿 *www.nbbd.godo.minwr* ☎ *407-861-0667. Roads closed south of Haulover Canal during shuttle launches.* On 140,000 acres owned by NASA, the refuge provides habitat to more than 500 animal species, including such endangered and threatened animals as the southern bald eagle, the manatee and the loggerhead sea turtle. In addition, 1,530 acres are devoted to citrus groves, some of which existed before NASA bought the land in the early 1960s. Areas open to the public *(north of Rte. 402)* offer an idea of how the Florida coast looked before the incursion of man. The **Visitor Information Center** *(on Rte. 402, 3mi east of Rte. 406)* contains informative displays on wildlife in the surrounding marshes, hardwood hammocks and pine flatwoods *(open Nov–Mar Mon–Fri 8am–4:30pm, weekends 9am–5pm; rest of the year Mon–Fri 8am–4:30pm, Sat 9am–5pm;* &♿ 🅿*).*

⌂⌂**Playalinda Beach** – *6mi east of visitor center. No drinking water, showers or lifeguards. Clothing optional at north end.* Four miles of gorgeous unspoiled beach lies here with not a high rise in sight—except for the Vehicle Assembly Building and the two shuttle launchpads on the southern horizon. Advanced technology seems incidental here, where pelicans skim the surf and sea oats bend in gentle breezes. The beach is part of **Canaveral National Seashore**, which extends 22mi north to Apollo Beach *(accessible from A1A; open May–Oct daily 6am–8pm; rest of the year daily 6am–6pm; closed Jan 1 & Dec 25; reservations required for turtle walks (p 298) and canoe tours; $5/vehicle;* &♿ 🅿 *www.nbbd.com/godo/cns* ☎ *407-267-1110).*

★Black Point Wildlife Drive – *Entrance 2mi west of visitor center, off Rte. 406. Stop at visitor center for self-guided driving-tour brochure. Bring binoculars.* This 7mi one-lane dirt road *(30-45min)* traverses a dike built in the 1950s to control mosquitoes. Here you'll be treated to close-up views of waterbirds and a chance to compare the different habitats associated with a shallow-water impoundment and a natural marsh. A short trail leads to an observation tower about halfway along, and several turn-outs provide places to study wildlife.

Merritt Island National Wildlife Refuge

Tampa Bay Area

Tampa Skyline from Bayshore Boulevard – © S. McVicker

Blessed with perennially fine weather and a resplendent waterfront setting, Florida's second-largest metropolitan area has carved a niche for itself as the state's west-coast capital, a destination for business travelers and vacationers alike. Tampa Bay—the state's largest open-water estuary—opens mouth-like onto the Gulf of Mexico, its two densely populated centers linked by three causeway bridges. On the east side of the bay sits Tampa and its soaring skyscrapers, while to the west lies the Pinellas Peninsula, site of St. Petersburg and such easygoing beach towns as Treasure Island and Clearwater. Just north, Tarpon Springs adds international flair, supporting a community of Greek sponge divers.

Tampa Bay was a favorite landing site for gold-seeking Spanish explorers in the early 1500s. **Juan Ponce de León, Hernando de Soto** and **Pánfilo de Narváez** all sought glory and wealth in their expeditions around this wide natural harbor. After encountering hostile natives and equally inhospitable territory, the Europeans abandoned the area for nearly three centuries. By the 1820s, a few settlers and fishermen had made tentative homes here, with an ambition that more closely mirrored that of the natives—eking a livelihood from the sea. Unfortunately, whites and Indians came to distrust each other, and Fort Brooke was erected in 1824 to help maintain local law and order.

In the early 1880s, financier **Henry Plant** assured Tampa's future importance by connecting it via railroad to the east coast and building luxury hotels along the line. Tampa soon established a reputation as the world's cigar-manufacturing center and a significant port for the shipment of cattle, phosphate and citrus. In the meantime, St. Petersburg and other towns across the bay became known for their healthy climate, good fishing and fine beach resorts.

Today, despite the growing pains associated with any swelling metropolitan area, increasing numbers of retirees and young professionals continue to bolster the population of Hillsborough and Pinellas counties. Tampa now ranks as the 11th leading port in the US, trading in shrimp, phosphate and agricultural products. Nearby, the resort-laden beach strand from St. Petersburg Beach up to Clearwater rates as west Florida's most popular. From the modern cityscape of downtown Tampa, to the attractively landscaped waterfront in St. Petersburg, to the timeless allure of the Gulf's white-sand beaches, the Tampa Bay area epitomizes Florida on the move.

CLEARWATER

Population 100,132
Map of Principal Sights p 3 – Map p 273
Tourist Information ☎ 813-461-0011

Consisting primarily of a 4mi stretch of Gulf coast barrier island, Clearwater is Tampa's beach. This popular resort, located 22mi west of Tampa, attracts 1.3 million visitors each year to its wide, pearly sand beaches and calm, sparkling waters.

Historical Notes

The area's early inhabitants discovered bubbling clear springs percolating along Clearwater's shores. Presumably these springs were also a welcome sight to Spanish explorer Pánfilo de Narváez, who sailed through Johns Pass and landed near present-day Clearwater with 400 soldiers in 1528—92 years before the Pilgrims landed at Plymouth Rock.

In the mid-1830s the first white settlers appeared, including Odet Philippe, a French surgeon who built his home where lovely Philippe Park *(p 273)* now stands in Safety Harbor. More settlers followed after the federal government passed a law that opened the territory to homesteaders willing to bear arms against the Indians. In 1841 the US built Fort Harrison on the bluffs overlooking Clearwater Harbor. The following year, land occupied by the fort and much of what is now downtown Clearwater was granted to James Stephens, the area's first homesteader.

The commercial center began to develop in the late 19C after Henry Plant extended his railroad through the city and built the elegant Belleview Hotel (now Belleview Mido Resort in Bellair) nearby. The c.1898 pink frame **Louis Ducros House** *(1324 S. Ft. Harrison Ave.)*, ornamented with Gothic Revival fretwork, survives as one of the few remaining structures from that period. Down the street, the Neoclassical **Pinellas County Courthouse** *(324 S. Ft. Harrison Ave.)* was hastily built in 1917 in an attempt to steal the county seat from neighboring St. Petersburg. The hefty, brick **South Ward School** *(610 S. Ft. Harrison Ave.)*, which dates back to 1906, is the county's oldest school to operate continually in one building.

Connected to downtown by Memorial Causeway, **Clearwater Beach**⌂ began as Tate's Island. Its namesake, Ernest Tate, bought the entire 200-acre parcel for $1.25 an acre in 1896. He resold it a few years later for $450, and the beach eventually developed into a resort community. Vacationers—who contribute the largest amount of revenue to the city—still cavort on its powdery sand. Although you pass through a dense commercial strip to get to the shore, once you reach it you'll find a low-key resort town that appeals to families, couples and seniors alike.

SIGHTS *1/2 day*

★**Sand Key Park** – 1060 Gulf Blvd. Open year-round daily 7am–dusk. ⓑ ☎ 813-595-7677. Located on 65 pristine acres on a spit jutting into the Gulf of Mexico, Sand Key provides a respite from the development that crowds Clearwater Beach. This land passed through a succession of owners, including US Steel and the City of Clearwater, before Pinellas County finally bought it and opened the park in 1984. Edged with sea oats and sea grape trees, a wide, sugary sand beach forms the centerpiece of the park.

Clearwater Marine Aquarium – 🄺🄸🄳🅂 *249 Windward Passage, Clearwater Beach. Open year-round Mon–Fri 9am–5pm, Sat 9am–4pm, Sun 11am–4pm, holidays 9am–2pm. Closed major holidays. $6.75.* ⓑ 🄿 *www.flaoutdoors.com/wildlife* ☎ *813-441-1790.* This private, nonprofit research facility is dedicated to public education and the rescue, rehabilitation and release of injured or sick marine mammals, otters and sea turtles. A 55,000gal mangrove seagrass tank *(second floor)* offers visitors a close-up view of the estuary environment. A variety of sea turtles, dolphins, sharks and stingrays are also on display.

EXCURSIONS

Safety Harbor Museum – *30min. 7mi east in Safety Harbor. Take Gulf-To-Bay Blvd./Rte. 60 east to Bayshore Blvd. (last left before crossing Campbell Causeway); turn left (north) on Bayshore. Museum is on left at 329 Bayshore Blvd. S. Open year-round Tue–Fri 10am–4pm, weekends 1pm–4pm. Closed major holidays & last 2 weeks of Aug. $2.* ⓑ 🄿 ☎ *813-726-1668.* Perched on an Indian shell mound overlooking Tampa Bay, the museum offers a lovely setting for picnics as well as an informative look at archaeology and local history. Colorful displays sketch the area's importance as an ancient native settlement and trace its development up to the 20C. Fossils, projectile points, prehistoric tools and pottery tell the story of the Tocobaga Indians (200 BC to AD 1700) who inhabited Florida's west coast. Additional exhibits focus on turn-of-the-century Safety Harbor and the local natural mineral spring. Visitors can sample these healing waters nearby at **Safety Harbor Resort and Spa** *(105 N. Bayshore Dr., ☎ 813-726-1161 or 800-237-0155).*

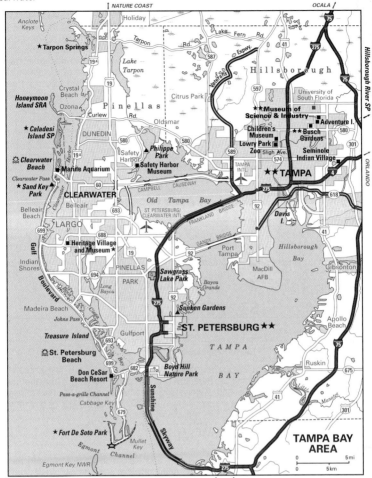

Philippe Park – *1hr. 8mi east in Safety Harbor. Take Gulf-To-Bay Blvd./Rte. 60 east to Bayshore Blvd. (last left before crossing Campbell Causeway); turn left (north) on Bayshore, which becomes Philippe Pkwy. Continue north to entrance of park at 2525 Philippe Pkwy. Open year-round daily 7am–dusk.* 🚻 🅿 ☎ *813-464-3347.* Named for the Frenchman who founded Safety Harbor in 1823 *(p 272)* and reputedly planted the area's first citrus groves, this county park occupies 122 acres of huge oak trees, sweeping green lawns and water views. The Tocobaga Indians, the last aboriginal culture to exist on Florida's central west coast, left a legacy of massive ceremonial mounds in the park. The **temple mound** *(turn left into the first parking area; mound is by the water, marked with a sign)* was the seat of the principal village of Tocobaga. When the site was excavated, archaeologists found pottery shards, bones, tools and 16C European artifacts (some of which are displayed at Safety Harbor Museum).

★ **Heritage Village & Museum** – Kids *2hrs. 8mi south in Largo. Take US-19A south to Ulmerton Rd. Turn right on Ulmerton and follow to 125th St. Turn left; follow signs to village on left at 11909 125th St. N. Open year-round Tue–Sat 10am–4pm, Sun 1pm–4pm. Closed major holidays.* 🅿 ☎ *813-582-2123.* More than 20 of the county's earliest structures are displayed at this 21-acre historical village and museum that re-creates turn-of-the-century living. The oldest one, Cracker-style **McMullen-Coachman Log House**, was completed in 1852. Set in a pine forest threaded by brick walkways, the complex resembles a pioneer community, complete with a replica one-room schoolhouse, an early church, private homes and a train depot. Also on the grounds, the modest two-story **Plant-Sumner House** was built by Henry Plant in 1896 for his foreman's family. Its simple decor contrasts with the Victorian **Seven Gables House** (1907) that sits nearby. This rambling yellow structure with white gingerbread trim originally served as a bayside winter retreat for a wealthy Illinois family *(visit by 20min guided tour only)*.

★**Caladesi Island State Park** – *1/2 day. 9mi north on Caladesi Island. Accessible only by boat. Open year-round daily 8am–dusk. $3.25.* ✗ ♿ ☎ *813-469-5918. Ferry departs from Honeymoon Island (below) year-round daily 10am–4:30pm. Commentary. $6.* ♿ 🅿 ☎ *813-469-5942.* Situated in the Gulf of Mexico off the coast of Dunedin, Caladesi Island offers a sparkling white-sand beach○○—framed by undulating grasses—that in 1998 *USA Today* ranked as one of the nation's top five beaches. Benefiting from an inaccessible location that failed to attract developers, the 600-acre island survives with its native flora and fauna intact. Along more than 2mi of lovely beach, visitors may swim, fish, picnic, shell, stroll or explore the nature trail *(2.5mi)* that cuts through the island's interior.

Honeymoon Island State Recreation Area – *1/2 day. 9mi north in Dunedin. Take US-19A north to Dunedin, (road becomes Broadway Bayshore Blvd.). Turn left on Dunedin Causeway Blvd./Rte. 586. Follow causeway to park. Open year-round daily 8am–dusk. $4/vehicle.* 🅿 *www.dep.state.fl.us/parks* ☎ *813-469-5942.* In 1921 a fierce hurricane sundered this barrier island from its southern half, now called Caladesi Island *(above)*. A causeway from Dunedin now connects the mainland to the 385-acre park, which features a rocky beach and 208 species of plants. Once known as Hog Island (for a successful hog farm that operated on its shores), Honeymoon Island owes it present moniker to a New York developer who built 50 thatched-roof "honeymoon cottages" here in 1939. One of the last virgin slash-pine forests still standing in south Florida lies along the island's northern loop trail.

★**Tarpon Springs** – *1/2 day. 13mi north of Clearwater via US-19A. Description p 290.*

ST. PETERSBURG★★

Population 235,988
Map of Principal Sights p 3 – Map p 273
Tourist Information ☎ 813-464-7200

Lying on the west side of Tampa Bay and linked to its sister city's fast-paced commerce by three bridges, sunny St. Petersburg is Tampa on holiday. A thriving mix of young professionals, retirees and sun-seeking vacationers enjoy St. Pete's relaxed lifestyle, its first-rate museums, its sparkling Gulf beaches (10mi west of downtown), and its almost perpetually clear skies and warm weather.

Historical Notes

Conquest of Paradise – Pánfilo de Narváez and Hernando de Soto landed on the Pinellas Peninsula (from the Spanish for "point of pines") in the early 16C, but did scarcely more in their search for gold than harass the natives. Until the 19C the area remained little-known except to pirates and fishermen; thick mangrove swamps, bloodthirsty mosquitoes and the newly arrived Seminoles discouraged all but the pluckiest adventurers from exploring Tampa Bay.

With the establishment of Fort Brooke *(p 279)* in 1824 at present-day Tampa, homesteaders began trickling in to try their luck at growing citrus fruits and vegetables. In the 1840s Antonio Maximo Hernández set up a rustic fishing camp on the tip of the peninsula, now called Maximo Point. Other fishermen and settlers soon followed, some lured by tales of the salubrious Espirito Santo springs at Safety Harbor, discovered long before by de Soto.

One of those who moved to the area for his health in the late 1870s was Detroit native **John C. Williams**, a retired Union general who purchased 1,600 waterfront acres. In 1885, an American Medical Association journal proposed that a "health city" be founded on the Pinellas Peninsula. The combination of warm climate, fresh air and good beaches made the Tampa/St. Petersburg area a leading candidate. Although the spa city never came into being, the peninsula's fame caught the attention of Russian speculator **Peter Demens**, who in 1888 brought his Orange Belt Railroad to John Williams' farm. Legend has it that Demens beat Williams in a lottery and earned the right to name the new city for his hometown in Russia. Williams laid out the city's first streets on his property and named the first hotel the Detroit.

Around the turn of the century, this once-sleepy community began attracting increasingly large numbers of vacationers, enticed by the area's hospitable climate. By the beginning of World War I, another railroad connected St. Pete to Tampa, and development of the beaches had started. It was around this time that the city's waterfront park system—still a showpiece today—was created. The Florida land boom of the 1920s elevated St. Petersburg to resort status, with 3,000 hotel rooms and a population of 60,000. Two world-class resorts were built during this decade: the Vinoy Park *(p 276)* downtown, and the Don CeSar *(p 279)* on the beach.

Recovering quickly from the Depression, St. Pete erected more hotels to cater to monied tourists, and more permanent residents began moving here. The 1950s and '60s witnessed greater urban sprawl and the addition of a few skyscrapers.

A Modern City – Today St. Petersburg ranks as Florida's fourth most populous city, right behind Tampa, with tourism-related businesses employing the most people in Pinellas County and generating $1.9 billion in annual revenues. Downtown smoothly blends old and new styles of architecture; Art Deco and Mediterranean harmonize with contemporary styles. Seven miles of handsomely landscaped waterfront parks attract visitors to the bayside to stroll the Pier, take in the art museums and nearby galleries, and bask in the sun at the expansive municipal marina. The St. Petersburg Yacht Club, established more than 90 years ago, has hosted numerous international regattas. A 30min drive away, **Gulf Boulevard** runs from St. Petersburg Beach up to Clearwater, the most popular strand on Florida's Gulf coast.

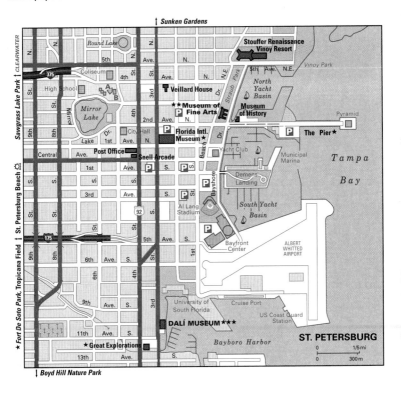

DOWNTOWN *1 1/2 days. Map above.*

The original downtown laid out by John Williams and Peter Demens in 1888 extended from Seventh Avenue South to Fifth Avenue North, and from about Ninth Street to the bay; each street was 100ft wide. Population remained under 2,000 and development lagged until 1900, when word of St. Pete's healthy climate and good fishing began to spread.

A number of attractive structures from the ensuing building boom remain. Moorish-style 1926 **Snell Arcade** *(405 Central Ave.),* boasting crenellated turrets and fanciful embellishments, is considered the city's best example of 1920s office architecture. One-half block north, an interior passageway leads to the open-air, Mediterranean Revival-style **Post Office** *(400 1st Ave. N.)* built in 1917. St. Petersburg Public High School, erected in 1919 in the Mediterranean style, sits just off lovely Mirror Lake *(709 Mirror Lake Dr.).* The 1924 Coliseum *(535 4th Ave. N.)* continues to draw crowds for frequent tea dances and sock hops. Across the street, St. Petersburg Shuffleboard Club **(A)**, the largest in the world, dates back to 1924; adjacent St. Petersburg Lawn Bowling Club **(B)** began in 1926, making it one of the country's oldest. **Veillard House** *(262 4th Ave. N.),* built of rusticated stone block in 1910 for one of the city's pioneers, exemplifies a fine blend of Queen Anne and Bungalow styles.

Immediately west of downtown is **Tropicana Field** *(1 Tropicana Dr.; entrance off 10th St. S. at 3rd Ave. S.),* a 45,360-seat baseball stadium where the Tampa Bay Devil Rays play their home games. A 16-month, $85 million, 319,000sq ft expansion and renovation of a pre-existing facility led to this modern domed stadium's completion for the major-league team's inaugural 1998 season. The dimensions of the field, which guarantees a constant 72° temperature, were designed by a Yale University professor who took into account such factors as latitude, humidity, air flow and atmospheric pressure within the dome.

© Kevin Shields

The Pier

★**Florida International Museum** – *100 2ⁿᵈ St. N. Open for special exhibitions daily 9am–6pm. For schedule ☎ 813-822-3693. "Empires of Mystery: The Incas, The Andes and Lost Civilizations" exhibition on view from late Oct 1998. $13.95.* ✗ ᶳ *Advance ticket purchase www.floridamuseum.org ☎ 800-777-9882.* Located in the heart of downtown, St. Pete's slick new international cultural center was designed to host grand-scale traveling exhibitions from prestigious institutions around the world. A $4 million face-lift completed in 1995 modernized the 1948 structure—a former department store—with 20,000sq ft of exhibit space. Although it holds no permanent collection, the museum showcases at least one grand-scale exhibition from the world's leading art institutions each year. The opening show, "Treasures of the Czars," gathered over 270 lavish objets d'art from the Romanov dynasty (1613-1917) lent by the Kremlin Museums in Moscow. Other important shows have included "Splendors of Ancient Egypt," "Alexander The Great" and "Titanic: The Exhibition." The museum's fifth show, "Empires of Mystery: The Incas, The Andes and Lost Civilizations," opening in October 1998, promises hundreds of artifacts from more than 30 ancient Peruvian cultures.

The Stouffer Renaissance Vinoy Resort – *501 Beach Dr. N.E.* ✗ ᶳ *☎ 813-894-1000.* A fanciful pink observation tower marks this sumptuous Mediterranean Revival resort, considered one of the crown jewels of St. Petersburg architecture. Developed in 1925 by Pennsylvania oilman Aymer Vinoy Laughner, the hotel—then called the Vinoy Park—functioned as the social center of town, attracting the rich and famous for nearly two decades. During World War II, members of the Army Air Corps were housed here. In the 1970s the Vinoy fell on hard times—rooms rented for only $7 a night, and volleyball was played in the grand ballroom—and it closed in 1974. Reopened in 1992 after a $93 million restoration, the hotel today boasts a glazed-tile lobby, stenciled pecky cypress beams and frescoed ceilings, as well as a championship tennis facility and golf course.

★**The Pier** – *East end of 2nd Ave. N.E. Open year-round Mon–Thu 10am–9pm, Fri & Sat 10am–10pm, Sun 11am–7pm.* ✗ ᶳ 🅿 *www.stpete-pier.com ☎ 813-821-6164. Valet parking available at the pyramid; pay parking lots and some free parking along the pier. Free trolley rides from Pier to parking lots and to local museums.* Opened in 1973, the Pier and its modernistic upside-down pyramid juts a half-mile into Tampa Bay. The popular five-story structure contains an **Information Center** *(open Mon–Sat 10am–8pm, Sun 11am–6pm)* and restaurants and shops on the first level, an aquarium on the second level, and a restaurant and observation deck on the top. Along the Pier you'll find fishing platforms, jet-ski and sailboat rentals, and a miniature golf course.

St. Petersburg Museum of History – *335 2nd Ave. N.E. Open year-round Mon–Sat 10am–5pm, Sun 1pm–5pm. Closed Jan 1, Thanksgiving Day, Dec 25. $4.* ᶳ *☎ 813-894-1052.* Set at the foot of the Pier, this museum contains a replica of the six-cylinder Benoist airboat that made the world's first commercial flight *(p 280)*. In 1914 Tony Jannus flew the mayor of St. Petersburg in such a plane to Tampa, 21mi northeast. Displays in the Timeline Gallery chronicle the area's history from mastodons to tourists, and include a dugout cypress canoe, a simulated 1870 general store and a replica Orange Belt Railway depot.

★★Museum of Fine Arts – *255 Beach Dr. N.E. Open year-round Tue–Sat 10am–5pm, Sun 1pm–5pm. Closed Jan 1, Thanksgiving Day, Dec 25. $6.* ♿ 🅿 *www.fine-arts.org* ☎ *813-896-2667.* Housed in an attractive Palladian-style building designed by John Volk, this museum presents an impressive range of masterpieces from around the world. The museum opened in 1965 on land donated by the city.

Visit – *3hrs.* All 20 galleries here are located on one floor. Starting to the left of the marble-floored Great Hall, the Acheson Gallery displays some of the museum's most notable **Impressionist** treasures—works by Cézanne, Renoir, Monet and others. Just off the Acheson Gallery, the Poynter Gallery holds a remarkable trove of early **Asian sculpture**, including an intricate Jaina shrine (c.1600) from India.

Continuing clockwise around the museum, you will encounter pre-Columbian art *(Gallery 6)* in juxtaposition with modern American paintings *(Gallery 5)*. In the latter room hang works by John Sloan, George Bellows and Georgia O'Keeffe. O'Keeffe's glorious *Poppy* (1927) is considered one the most valued paintings in the entire collection. Galleries 1 through 4 offer fine examples of art from ancient Greece, the Renaissance, 18C Europe and 19C America. The back (east side) of the museum showcases two pleasant shady gardens, from which you can access the concert and lecture auditorium. Italian bronzes from the 19C grace the south garden, which opens onto the museum's south wing where traveling exhibitions are often shown. Of special note is the luminous collection of **Steuben glass★** in Gallery 16. Each hand-finished crystal sculpture in this darkened room is spotlighted to enhance its diamond-perfect facets.

★★★Salvador Dalí Museum – *1000 3rd St. S. Open year-round Mon–Sat 9:30am–5:30pm (Thu 8pm), Sun noon–5:30pm. Closed Thanksgiving Day & Dec 25. $8.* ♿ 🅿 *www.daliweb.com* ☎ *813-823-3767.* The world's most comprehensive collection of works by the late Spanish surrealist **Salvador Dalí** (1904-1989) resides in this single-story beige building located on resplendent Bayboro Harbor (just south of the Port of St. Petersburg). Searching for a repository for their vast Dalí holdings, Cleveland industrialist A. Reynolds Morse and his wife Eleanor picked this former warehouse on the waterfront. Though Denver, Colorado, and Austin, Texas, had been front-runners for the enormous collection, officials in St. Petersburg enticed the Morses to consider their city. The couple liked what they saw, particularly this nondescript building, formerly used for storing marine-research equipment, beside a yacht harbor. "We don't need a building to make any Dalínian Statement," Morse said. "What goes inside has plenty to say." The museum opened in 1982 after a $2 million face-lift financed by the state of Florida. It has since become one of Florida's most popular art museums.

A Flamboyant Career – Born and raised in a Catalonian farming village near Barcelona, Dalí began painting at a young age. He attended the San Fernando Academy of Fine Arts in Madrid and held his first one-man show in Barcelona in 1925 at the age of 21. In 1929 he moved to France, where he joined the Paris Surrealists Group led by writer André Breton. Also in that year, he met Gala Eluard, his future

The Disintegration of the Persistence of Memory (1952-54) by Salvador Dalí

wife and inspiration for much of his work. Surrealists eschewed convention and believed instead in the omnipotence of dreams and the suspension of conscious thought. Dalí soon became one of the movement's brash leaders, painting fantastic subjects in obsessive detail and declaring, "The difference between me and the Surrealists is that I *am* Surrealism." By 1940 however, Dalí had broken with the group and announced his intention to return to "Classical" painting, as embodied in the High Renaissance works of Raphael.

Dalí continued executing his detailed symbolic and trompe l'œil effects in 18 masterworks—huge canvases dealing with historical, scientific or religious themes. By the time of his death he had become as famous for his trademark handlebar mustache and publicity stunts, which often involved wild animals, as for his artistry.

Salvador Dalí Museum, Inc.

Visit – *2hrs*. Five galleries here display pieces from the museum's collection of 94 oil paintings, more than 100 watercolors and drawings, and 1,300 graphics, sculptures, photographs and objets d'art. The first gallery contains a permanent retrospective of oil paintings arranged in chronological order, starting to the left of the entrance with Dalí's childhood works (1914) and ending with his masterworks. Early paintings, such as *Girl's Back* (1926), *Girl with Curls* (1926) and various self-portraits, demonstrate young Dalí's talent and show the strong influence of masters from the 17C Flemish to the Impressionists and Cubists.

Between 1929 and 1940, Dalí experimented with Surrealism, often attenuating figures—as in *Archeological Reminiscence of Millet's Angelus* (1933-35) emphasize his obsession with time, death and sex. On the south wall hang four of Dalí's **masterworks★★**, each of which took at least a year to complete. These tremendous canvases, measuring about 13ft by 10ft, were painted between 1948 and 1970. Two smaller masterworks, *Nature Morte Vivante* and *Velazquez Painting the Infanta Margarita with the Lights and Shadows of His Own Glory*, are displayed in other galleries in the museum.

★**Great Explorations** – 🄺🄸🄳 *1120 4th St. S. Open year-round Mon–Sat 10am–5pm, Sun noon–5pm. Closed Jan 1, Thanksgiving Day, Dec 25. $5.* ♿ 🅿 ☎ *813-821-8885.* Located across Third Street from the Dalí Museum, this state-of-the-art science museum offers 15,500sq ft of hands-on activities in six sections. Visitors may crawl through a pitch-black 90ft tunnel, measure their strength and flexibility, play a synthesizer and create dancing silhouettes and works of art.

ADDITIONAL SIGHTS *1/2 day. Map p 273.*

Sunken Gardens – *1825 4th St. N. Open year-round daily 9:30am–5pm. $14.* ♿ 🅿 ☎ *813-896-3186. Visitors enter the gardens through a large gift shop that includes a wax museum of Biblical figures and an antique gallery.* Dating back to 1935, Sunken Gardens ranks as one of the area's oldest attractions, mixing kitsch with real beauty. A small lake was drained here in 1903 and planted with 50,000 examples of endemic and exotic flora. Footpaths wind through five lush acres of tropical foliage and flowering shrubs, past cages of rare birds and animals. Trained parrots and alligators are featured in daily shows *(parrot shows at noon, 2pm & 4pm; alligator shows at 11:15am, 1:15pm, 3:15pm & 4:30pm)*.

Boyd Hill Nature Park – *1101 Country Club Way S. Entrance just west of 9th St. S. (Martin Luther King St.), adjacent to public library. Open Nov–Mar daily 9am–5pm. Rest of the year daily 9am–5pm (Tue & Thu until 8pm). Closed Thanksgiving Day & Dec 25. $1. Tram tour daily 1pm; $1.* ♿ 🅿 ☎ *813-893-7326.* The 245-acre preserve contains more than 3mi of trails and boardwalks through hardwood hammocks and pine flatwoods and along willow marshes past Lake Maggiore. Dammed in 1940, this tidal estuary supports a wide variety of birdlife. A small nature center offers interpretive displays.

Sawgrass Lake Park – *7400 25th St. N. Open year-round daily 7am–dusk.* ♿ ☎ *813-527-3814. Entrance at end of 25th St., through a residential area.* Nearly 300 species of waterfowl and other animals inhabit this 400-acre wildlife sanctuary. Two miles of elevated boardwalk and footpaths lead through a red-maple swamp and a hammock of oaks, cabbage palms and hickories. A wooden observation platform at the lake provides an excellent perch for bird-watching; an environmental education center *(same hours as park)* features a turtle tank, live snakes and other displays. The county park also acts as a water-control site to protect surrounding communities from flooding.

ST. PETERSBURG BEACH *1/2 day. Map p 273.*

A resort town of 9,200 residents, St. Petersburg Beach anchors the southern end of Gulf Boulevard, which stretches 18mi north to Clearwater. Though not a scenic drive, the highway does pass many beach access points sandwiched between motels and condominiums. The **beach**≜ itself offers clean, white sand and gentle Gulf waters. *(Public access areas have metered parking; 50¢/hr.)* Just north, **Treasure Island** features wide, uncrowded shores. *Snack bars and restrooms are available, as well as rental umbrellas, rafts and cabanas.*

Don CeSar Beach Resort and Spa – *3400 Gulf Blvd.* ☎ *813-360-1881.* Built in 1928 for $1.5 million, this landmark pink Belgian concrete-and-stucco palace mixes Moorish and Mediterranean elements. It was the crowning achievement of realtor and developer Thomas Rowe. Orphaned at four and sent to Ireland to live with his grandfather, Rowe returned to the US at age 18. He moved to Florida for his health in his 40s, bought an 80-acre tract and began building. The resulting 10 story hotel immediately attracted the nation's glitterati: F. Scott Fitzgerald, Franklin Roosevelt and the New York Yankees baseball team numbered among the hotel's guests in the 1920s and '30s. Used as a hospital during World War II, "The Don" went through decades of neglect until reopening in 1973. The interior features high arched windows, Italian crystal chandeliers, Carrara marble fountains and foyers, and floors covered with terra-cotta and Cuban tile.

EXCURSION

★**Fort De Soto Park** – *2hrs. 8mi south of St. Petersburg Beach on Mullet Key. Take Rte. 682 east and turn right on Rte. 679 (Pinellas Bayway). The park headquarters (stop for information) is 6.5mi south; fort is 2mi farther west. Open year-round daily dawn–dusk.* ⚠ ✕ ⛗ 🅿 ☎ *813-866-2484.* Robert E. Lee was one of four US Army engineers who in 1849 recommended a military installation for this V-shaped string of islands at the mouth of Tampa Bay. Several years later the Union took his advice, setting up a blockade on Mullet and Egmont keys. Construction of the fort began during the Spanish-American War in 1898, but the conflict was so short-lived that the fort never saw action. The only shots fired were for practice, and mosquitoes posed the biggest threat to soldiers. Decommissioned in 1923, the fort remains on view behind a 30ft earthwork on the beach.

Visitors can view shot rooms and powder magazines—with concrete walls 8-20ft thick—and walk atop the ruins. From here you can see the **Sunshine Skyway** (named for its yellow suspension cables), which connects Pinellas and Manatee Counties. Other activities in this 900-acre park, located only a 15-minute-drive away from the heavily urbanized Suncoast strip, include hiking, fishing and swimming on quiet **beaches** rated in 1998 among the top 10 in the US.

TAMPA★★

Population 285,206
Map of Principal Sights p 3 – Map p 273
Tourist Information ☎ 813-223-2752 or 800-448-2672 (US & Canada)

Florida's third largest city is both port and resort. Its subtropical climate and location on the transparent blue waters of Tampa Bay make Tampa a year-round recreational paradise that draws sun-seekers and business people alike. Visitors here can choose from a host of attractions ranging from the Latin accents of Ybor City to the thrill rides of Busch Gardens and the deep-sea denizens of the new Florida Aquarium.

Historical Notes

Exploration and Settlement – Native artifacts found in the area have been dated to thousands of years BC. By the 16C the area was occupied by members of the Calusa and Timucua tribes, who subsisted on shellfish and game. Pánfilo de Narváez is generally credited with being the first Spanish explorer to see Tampa Bay. On Good Friday 1528, de Narváez sailed into Johns Pass and landed near what is now Clearwater, marching north to modern TALLAHASSEE. When the expedition's supplies failed, de Narváez died in the wild. A few of his crew survived, including the voyage's treasurer, Alvar Núñez Cabeza de Vaca, who described Tampa Bay as "the best port in the world." In 1539 Hernando de Soto also landed briefly but continued west, never to return.

In the early 19C, Cuban and Spanish fishermen built a small village called Spanishtown Creek, coexisting peacefully with Indian neighbors in an area that now defines the Hyde Park neighborhood west of downtown. When Florida became a territory of the US in 1821, the government established an Army post near Spanishtown Creek, which Colonel George Mercer Brooke and his troops occupied in 1824.

A massive hurricane hit in 1848, causing serious flooding and submerging the area across the bay that would later become St. Petersburg. Tampa rebuilt, but the storm's effects wiped out Pinellas' first settlement and it was years before a new attempt was made. By 1880 Fort Brooke had closed and Tampa's only links to the outside world were slow boats, stagecoaches and oxcarts that clattered along the sandy trails.

Development Rides the Rails – It was then that visionary tycoon **Henry Bradley Plant** (1819-1899) chose Tampa over CEDAR KEY as the port for a new railroad that would connect Florida with the eastern seaboard and the west. Born to middle-class Connecticut farming parents, Plant left home at age 18 to be a jack-of-all-trades aboard a Yankee steamboat. This experience led him to a position with the Adams Express Company, which shipped parcels by boat and later by railroad. When his wife's failing health forced him to spend several months near Jacksonville, Florida, in 1853, Plant became manager of the company's southern region. At the onset of the Civil War in 1861, Plant organized the Southern Express Company. Beginning with the purchase of two railroads at postwar foreclosure sales, Plant built a multimillion-dollar transportation empire that eventually included 14 railway companies and several steamship lines, and stretched from Jamaica to Boston and as far west as New Orleans and St. Louis. A number of grand hotels complemented Plant's transportation network. One of these properties was the Tampa Bay Hotel (p 282), which he began building on the banks of the Hillsborough River, west of downtown; its minarets are now city landmarks.

Railroad transportation and a flourishing port assured Tampa's growth by attracting new businesses and commercial developers who would forever change the face of the city. One such entrepreneur was **Vicente Martínez-Ybor** (p 285), who relocated his cigar business to Tampa from Key West in 1886. Ybor bought land east of downtown, where he built a factory that, after a year, produced 900,000 cigars a month. Other cigar makers soon relocated to Tampa and Spanish, Italian and Cuban workers flocked to the factories. Their community is now Tampa's historic Spanish neighborhood, Ybor City. As Tampa's famous cigars sold across the country and legions of the nation's wealthiest and most influential people vacationed at the luxurious Tampa Bay Hotel, the city forever left its past as a parochial backwater. By the turn of the century, Tampa was exporting

Cigar Box Art

Courtesy Tampa Historical Society

citrus fruit, cattle, vegetables and phosphate fertilizer on the railroads. When Plant used his influence to have the city declared a port of embarkation for US troops fighting the Spanish-American War, Tampa enjoyed international press attention. Supply trains carried food, ammunition and equipment to soldiers in Tampa; boats left the city docks piled high with goods to be shipped to Cuba. Troops camped just outside the city limits, eating at the Tampa Bay Hotel and spending their money here, much to the delight of local merchants.

Although there was a booming community across Tampa Bay in St. Petersburg, no bridge connected the two cities until 1924. The journey required a day of travel by boat, a situation that pilot Tony Jannus (p 276) thought unnecessary. He made history when he carried the first airline passenger across the bay on his Benoist airboat during a 23min flight, thus launching the world's first commercial airline. Ten years later, transportation expert George S. Gandy built a toll bridge finally linking Tampa with St. Pete.

Growing Pains – Tampa's population had swollen to nearly 38,000 by 1920. Another major hurricane disabled the city the following year, leaving Bayshore Boulevard, the 7.2mi signature roadway, under 20ft of water. Again the city rebuilt and continued to grow, hitting its peak during the Roaring Twenties' real-estate boom. Tampa developer D.P. Davis paid $3.5 million for dredgers to turn the bay bottom into a speculator's dream. Before any mud had even been pumped, Davis had already recouped his expenses, promoting **Davis Islands** as "a veritable Venice at one's door." Streets outside his office were jammed with investors snapping up hundreds of lots in the first few days of offering. Though the islands never became a Venice, they were and still are considered one of Tampa's most prestigious residential areas.

Sadly, the land boom could not last, and Tampa's economy failed even before the New York Stock Exchange crashed In October 1929. The 1930s brought the Depression, a new airport on Davis Island and the founding of the University of Tampa, which moved into the vacant Tampa Bay Hotel in 1933. In 1935 Tampa suffered yet another hurricane, the Labor Day monster that killed hundreds in South Florida before raking the Gulf Coast with its fury. A political storm was also brewing, with gangsters and gambling kingpins accused of corrupting city government. A spell of election outrages finally spawned a reform movement led by the city's newspaper editors.

Growth continued in the 1950s with the opening of MacDill Air Force Base, which has employed thousands of service people and continues to be an important source of revenue for the city. In 1958 the state selected a parcel in North Tampa as the site of the new University of South Florida. The 1,700-acre campus now has a student body of 35,000.

Tampa Today – Tampa's modern economy rests on tourism, health/biomedical and high-technology industries, business and financial services, agriculture, aquaculture, international trade, and phosphate mining and export. Tourism is the area's third largest employer, generating 40,000 full-time jobs a year and pumping $1.7 billion into the economy.

Downtown Tampa is in the midst of a transformation, with plans underway for a $144 million arena for the Tampa Bay Lightning hockey team and the $300 million **Garrison Seaport Center**. The latter includes the new $84 million Florida Aquarium and two cruise terminals, which city officials hope will bring more than half a million passengers a year into the former warehouse district east of downtown. Tampa's revived economy continues to attract new businesses, residents and visitors; city leaders are banking on these factors to propel Tampa into a new chapter of prosperity in the 21C.

PRACTICAL INFORMATION .... Area Code: 813

Getting There

By Air – Tampa International Airport (TPA): 5mi west of city center; information ☎ 870-8700. Transportation to downtown: The Limo *($13)* ☎ 572-1111, taxi *($11)* and hotel courtesy shuttles. Rental car agencies *(p 323)* located at airport.

By Train and Bus – Amtrak train station: 601 N. Nebraska Ave. ☎ 800-872-7245. Greyhound/Trailways bus station: 610 Polk St. ☎ 800-231-2222.

Getting Around

By Public Transportation – Local bus service: HARTline Transit System *($1.15)*. For bus schedules and route information ☎ 254-4278. **Tampa-Ybor Trolley** *(daily 7:30am–5:30pm, every 15min; 25¢)*. **PeopleMover** monorail: between Old Fort Brooke parking garage and Harbour Island *(daily 24hrs; 25¢ one-way)*. **Water taxi** *(daily; $5 round-trip, regular stops at several downtown locations)*. Tampa Town Ferry ☎ 253-3076.

By Car – Limited on-street parking; public parking garages *($1/hr)*.

By Taxi – United Cab ☎ 253-2424; Yellow Cab ☎ 253-0121.

General Information

Visitor Information – Tampa/Hillsborough Convention and Visitors Association, 400 N. Tampa St., Suite 1010, Tampa, FL 33602; Visitor Information Center, corner of Ashley and Madison Sts. *(open Mon–Sat 9am–5pm)* www.thcva.com ☎ 223-2752. **Tampa Bay Visitor Information Center**, 3601 E. Busch Blvd. *(open Mon–Sat 9am–6pm, Sun 9am–2pm)* ☎ 985-3601. *These organizations provide additional information regarding shopping, entertainment, festivals (p 318) and recreation.*

Accommodations – *(p 324)* Area visitors' guide including lodging directory available (free) from Tampa/Hillsborough Convention and Visitors Association *(above)*. Reservation service: ☎ 800-44-TAMPA (US and Canada). Accommodations range from luxury hotels and resorts ($120-$350) to budget motels ($45-$90) and bed-and-breakfast inns ($80-$150). *Rates quoted are average prices per night for a double room and are subject to seasonal variations.*

Local Press – Daily news: *The Tampa Tribune*; entertainment section, *Friday Extra. Travelhost, The Weekly Planet* and *See Tampa* (available free at hotels and restaurants) are handy guides to arts, entertainment and sports.

Foreign Exchange Office – *(p 321)* Nations Bank, 400 N. Ashley Dr., ☎ 224-5756.

Shopping – Old Hyde Park Village *(p 285)*, W. Swann Ave. at Dakota St. ☎ 251-3500; Ybor Square *(p 287)*, 1901 N. 13th St. ☎ 247-4497; Floriland Flea & Farmer's Market, 9309 N. Florida Ave. *(open Sat–Sun 9am–5pm)* ☎ 932-4319.

Entertainment – Consult the arts and entertainment section in the local newspaper *(above)* for schedule of cultural events and addresses of principal theaters and concert halls. Tampa Bay Performing Arts Center ☎ 229-7827. For arts and sporting events tickets: **Ticketmaster** ☎ 287-8844.

Sports and Recreation – Football: Tampa Bay Buccaneers ☎ 879-BUCS. Baseball: Tampa Bay Devil Rays (St. Petersburg) www.devilray.com ☎ 825-3120 **Hockey**: Tampa Bay Lightning ☎ 229-BOLT. **Soccer**: Tampa Bay Mutiny ☎ 288-0096. **Thoroughbred racing**: Tampa Bay Downs ☎ 855-4401. Public **golf courses**: Babe Zaharias ☎ 631-4375; Rocky Point Golf ☎ 673-4316.

Useful Numbers   ☎

Police/Ambulance/Fire	911
Traveler's Aid	273-5936
24-hour Pharmacy: Walgreen's, 2782 Henderson St.	877-3360
Weather (recorded)	645-2323

DOWNTOWN *1 day. Map below.*

Where a nondescript cluster of outdated commercial buildings hunkered 15 years ago, now rise the proud and glimmering towers of glass and steel that characterize the city's modern face. The best of early Tampa's architecture survived the wrecking ball and stands today in the shadow of 30- to 40-story skyscrapers; the elegant 1915 Beaux Arts-style **City Hall** *(Kennedy Blvd. and Florida Ave.)*, for example, nestles among the city's tallest buildings. Along with monumental edifices, the development boom of the mid-1980s included such ground-level improvements as the Franklin Street Mall—a pedestrians-only brick avenue, adorned with plantings and fountains, and lined with stores extending from Cass to Washington Streets—and the ubiquitous sculptures and artworks that grace many public spaces. *Art in Public Places brochures are available at the Tampa/Hillsborough Convention and Visitors Association, p 281).*

Across the Beneficial Boulevard bridge from downtown, Harbour Island is a former railroad terminus that arose when Hillsborough Bay was dredged in 1908. By the 1970s the island had degenerated into a 178-acre abandoned railway yard, which it remained until a $1 billion development project in the mid-1980s transformed Harbour Island into an upscale complex of condominiums, shops, restaurants and a hotel. Today the complex has been converted into commercial office space.

*★**Henry B. Plant Museum** – 401 W. Kennedy Blvd. Open Jan–Nov Tue–Sat 10am–4pm, Sun noon–4pm. Dec daily 1pm–8pm. Closed Jan 1, Thanksgiving Day, Dec 24-25. $3 ($6 in Dec). ⚄ ♿ ▣ ☎ 813-254-1891.* Facing the smooth brow of the Hillsborough River and a gleaming clutch of downtown skyscrapers, the exotic silver minarets and gold crescents atop the former **Tampa Bay Hotel★★** have been synonymous with Tampa since the hotel's lavish opening in 1891. Today a section of the red-brick hotel has been preserved as a museum; the rest of the building houses University of Tampa offices and classrooms.

In 1890 Tampa was a grimy backwater of only 5,532 souls before the hotel's architectural splendor and luxurious accommodations put the city on the map. Like his rival and former business partner, Henry Flagler, Yankee railroad magnate Henry Bradley Plant built the Tampa Bay Hotel in an effort to fortify his transportation empire, which connected Tampa with the north and west parts of the state.

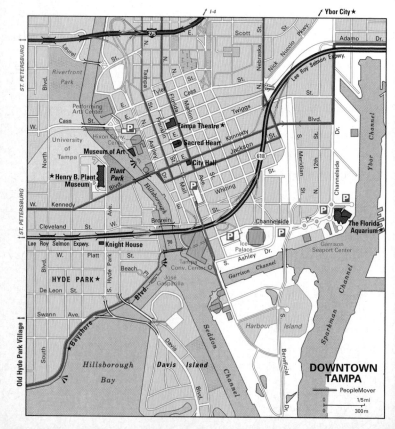

DOWNTOWN
TAMPA

PeopleMover

The hotel rose on a flat peninsula of citrus groves and dense woods, bounded by Hillsborough and Tampa bays; it required two years and an astounding $2.5 million to construct. Designed by New York architect John A. Wood, the five-story structure contains 500 rooms and sits upon six acres. The architect chose the then-popular Moorish Revival style, which echoed Florida's long history as a Spanish possession. Its sensational effect attracted more than 4,000 wealthy visitors a year.

Plant and his second wife, Margaret, spent another $500,000 as they traveled the world in 1889 on a buying spree for the new hotel. They scoured Europe and Asia, filling 80 railcars with fine antiques, sculpture, paintings, furniture and carpets. Some of those pieces can still be seen in the museum's permanent collection.

Tampa Bay Hotel

© Paul Rocheleau

For years Plant's hotel—the second in Florida to have an elevator, steam heat, electric lights, telephones, running water and private baths for each suite—was the centerpiece of Tampa's social life, hosting a flurry of balls and civic events. Such world-renowned performers as French actress Sarah Bernhardt and Russian ballerina Anna Pavlova entertained audiences in the hotel's casino. In 1898 the hotel earned international fame when Plant used his influence to have Tampa declared a port of embarkation for US Army troops during the Spanish-American War.

In 1899 Plant died of a heart attack and his hotel began to decline. Six years later, the City of Tampa bought the building, practically stealing it for $125,000; it closed as a hotel in 1930. The University of Tampa leased the building in 1933 and the city set aside the south wing of the first floor as a municipal museum.

Visit – *1.5hrs. A 14min video in the room next to the gift shop introduces the hotel.* The lush lawn of **Plant Park**, carved from the original hotel grounds, sets off the building's fanciful white wood **fretwork**. Wide verandahs along the front and back sides, and three chrysanthemum windows on the uppermost story above the portico, add to the air of Victorian grandeur that embraces this structure.

Inside the museum, visitors glimpse what life was like for Plant's fortunate guests, who included such luminaries as Thomas Edison, Theodore Roosevelt and Babe Ruth. Long, dignified corridors decorated with rich fabrics are brightened by the gleam of brass and gilt. Massive wooden doors open onto rooms where lace draperies cascade from 11ft-high keyhole-shaped, beveled-glass windows. The hotel's most authentic chamber, the **Reading and Writing Room**, still contains most of its original furnishings and has been restored to its 1891 color scheme. Crowned with an elaborate carved mantel and a huge mirror, a fireplace occupies the north end of the room; the hotel's chairs—ebonized wood with mother-of-pearl inlay— sit against the walls near a matching writing desk. Other displays include a typical guest bedroom outfitted with Eastlake furniture and original electric light fixtures, a solarium overlooking Plant Park, and Plant's own suite.

Among the museum's collections are an assortment of Wedgwood pieces, hand-carved Venetian mirrors, and a length of vivid red carpet woven with a lion pattern. Plant is said to have purchased 30,000 yards of the carpet "for a song" after Queen Victoria refused to tread upon it owing to the design's close resemblance to the symbol of the British Empire.

The rest of the hotel, now **Plant Hall**, houses University of Tampa offices and classrooms *(open year-round Mon–Fri 8am–7pm, weekends 10am–7pm; closed Jan 1 & Dec 24-31;* ☐ ☎ *813-254-1891).* Although the architecture is spectacular, the interior has not been restored. Note domed Fletcher Lounge *(northernmost end of ground floor),* which served as the hotel's main dining room, and the Grand Salon *(just off the lobby),* where guests once gathered to socialize.

★**Bayshore Boulevard** – Skirting the shore from the Hillsborough River to MacDill Air Force Base, this scenic drive provides some of the finest **views**★ of Hillsborough Bay and the downtown skyline, and it sweeps past one of Tampa's oldest neighborhoods. Along the water's edge runs a landscaped sidewalk frequented by

cyclists, skaters and pedestrians. Starting at the north end, Bayshore passes the three-masted schooner *José Gasparilla (opposite Beach Pl.)*, named for legendary pirate José Gaspar, who once terrorized settlers along the Gulf coast. Each February the city stages the **Gasparilla Festival**, a month-long celebration of Tampa's past.
The boulevard rims the Hyde Park district *(p 285)* and continues south, where it swerves inland at Ballast Point, bypassing a small park and fishing pier. The road ends at MacDill Air Force Base, which served as the command center for Operation Desert Storm in 1991.

★**The Florida Aquarium** – 🅺🅸🅳🆂 *701 Channelside Dr. at Garrison Seaport Center. Open year-round daily 9:30am–5pm. $10.95.* ✕ ♿ 🅿($3) *www.sptimes.com/aquarium* ☎ 813-273-4000. Beneath a signature green glass dome composed of more than 1,100 panels, Tampa's aquatic-life facility harbors over one million gallons of fresh- and saltwater. Opened in 1995, it is unique in its focus solely on Florida ecosystems. The 152,000sq ft aquarium provides a home to 5,300 animals and plants representing 600 native species.

Visit – *2hrs. Information desk located on ground level.* Viewing galleries are neatly laid out in a self-guided tour of four aquatic communities. In the first, **Wetlands**, visitors enter a humid zone of cypress swamps and bogs, mangrove forests and saw grass marshes. Eight different habitats display a great variety of animals, among them freshwater gar, bass, white ibis, snakes and great horned owls. Each habitat occupies a fairly small area and, as in the wild, blends seamlessly into the next. Notice the water overhead—as well as on each side—in the springs exhibit; and be sure to spend some time observing the mischievous river otters at play.
The ecosystems comprising **Bays and Beaches** include bay bottoms, with graceful stingrays and bottom-dwelling guitarfish; bridges, which host a fascinating community of barnacles and fish; and beaches, whose sandy miniature offers above- and below-water viewing accompanied by the sounds of calling gulls and hissing surf. Both "Wetlands" and "Bays and Beaches" include small demonstration laboratories within the galleries, and throughout the aquarium, exhibits pose and answer interesting questions: How are beaches created? Do fish sleep? What fish change sex?
In the popular **Coral Reef**★, visitors explore a world where colorful butterfly fish dart through forests of staghorn coral and sharks lurk in dark grottoes. One large room contains a tri-panel transparent wall 14ft high and 43ft wide for the display of 1,500 tropical fish of 60 species. The 12in-thick acrylic wall holds back a half-million gallons of water and allows for a more accurate view than glass. Three times a day *(11am, 1pm & 3pm)*, a diver enters the tank to conduct a tour of the reef, which is composed of amazingly life-like artificial coral. In a working lab across the room, you can talk to aquarium biologists and use interactive computers to explore reef life.
Offshore★ presents the wonders of deep-sea marine life. A fine shark exhibit is its primary feature. Several species of shark share a large aquarium tank; numerous displays, including a cross-section of shark anatomy, describe the primeval creatures' behaviors and lifestyles. In other tanks, beautiful, ghostly moon jellyfish glide, and a tangle of sargassum grass shelters and nourishes offshore fish and a variety of invertebrates.
Continuous videos on marine life are shown in a main-floor theater. A short elevator ride takes you to a roof-top garden where you can overlook the artificial reef and glimpse the Port of Tampa, Florida's largest port by tonnage. From this vantage point at the confluence of Ybor and Garrison Channels, you can see the great tankers that carry cement, asphalt and petroleum products.

★**Tampa Theatre** – *711 Franklin St. Visit by guided tour (1hr) only, year-round twice/month.* ♿ *For schedule and reservations* ☎ *813-274-8981*. This grand 1926 movie palace, described as an "Andalusian bonbon" by one historian, boasts iron entrance gates, a glazed-tile lobby and a wonderfully fanciful interior blending Byzantine, Italian Renaissance, Greek Revival and other styles. Dramatic facades embellished with statuary and spiralling pillars vie for attention with an ornate proscenium arch and the overhead star display and cloud machine. The 1,446-seat theater presents a year-round program of art and foreign films, concerts and various special events.

Tampa Museum of Art – *600 N. Ashley Dr. Open year-round Mon–Sat 10am–5pm (Wed 9pm), Sun 1pm–5pm. Closed major holidays. $5.* ♿ *www.tampamuseumofart.org* ☎ *813-274-8130*. Highlights from the permanent collection of this small museum include the **Classical World Gallery**, which features more than 400 Greek and southern Italian antiquities. Marble sculptures, grave altars, bronze figurines and an outstanding collection of colorfully painted **Greek vases**★ offer insight into the origins of Western civilization. Also permanently on display are modern works of sculpture in the Terrace Gallery, overlooking the Hillsborough River. Among the artists represented are Robert Rauschenberg, Jo Davidson and C. Paul Jennewein. About half of the museum's exhibit space is devoted to temporary exhibitions, including the work of established and emerging Florida artists.

Just beside the museum, visitors will find a shady courtyard with fountains and benches, and a stairway leading to an amphitheater that provides a **view** of the striking minarets of the University of Tampa across the river.

Sacred Heart Catholic Church – *Southeast corner of Florida Ave. at Twiggs St. Open year-round Mon–Fri 7am–3pm, Sat 8am–5:30pm.* & *For schedule of organ concerts* ☎ *813-229-1595.* Dedicated in 1905, this massive Romanesque stone structure features a triple-arch entrance with carved oak doors and pews, columns of Tennessee marble, brilliant stained-glass windows and a painted 14-story dome soaring above the main altar. The church was restored in 1977 after water rot and termite damage left the dome in danger of collapse.

★**Hyde Park** – *North and south of Swann Ave. between South Crosstown Expressway (Rte. 618) and Bayshore Blvd. Driving tour pamphlets may be obtained from the Tampa/Hillsborough Convention and Visitors Association (p 285).* This district originated in the late 18C as a clutch of Cuban fishing villages and palmetto huts called Spanishtown Creek. In 1886 O.H. Platt bought and subdivided 20 acres, naming the tract for his Illinois hometown. Tampa's wealthiest families built homes here in a wide range of architectural styles. Today Queen Annes and Colonial Revivals elbow Mediterranean Revivals and eclectic bungalows. Carefully pruned yards are shaded by overhanging live oaks draped with Spanish moss. Some of the finest houses lie south of Swann between Rome Avenue and South Boulevard.

Tampa's most fashionable shopping district, **Old Hyde Park Village**, lines South Dakota and Snow Avenues south of Swann Avenue. This 10-year-old development boasts 65 boutiques and restaurants as well as a movie theater.

Peter O. Knight House – *245 S. Hyde Park Ave. Open year-round by appointment. Closed major holidays.* 🅿 ☎ *813-259-1111.* Constructed in 1890 as a honeymoon cottage by Colonel Knight, one of Tampa's early business leaders, the house is currently headquarters for the Tampa Historical Society. Exhibits in several small rooms explain the city's cigar industry, Tampa Bay's Victorian era, the role of women in Tampa, and area shipbuilding. The Historical Society also maintains a photo archive and library here.

★YBOR CITY *1/2 day. Map p 286.*

The heart of Tampa's Cuban population once beat within this 1sq mi historic district, now a thriving neighborhood. Latin accents remain, even now that Ybor City has been resuscitated into a trendy spot for shopping, restaurants and nightlife.

Cigar Capital of the World – When labor union pressures in KEY WEST forced cigar manufacturer **Vicente Martínez Ybor** (pronounced "EE-bore") to find a new site for his operations, he chose a mosquito-infested plot of wilderness adjoining the young city of Tampa. The new railroad, shipping port and warm climate made this location ideal for his intentions. On 40 acres purchased in 1885 from the Tampa Board

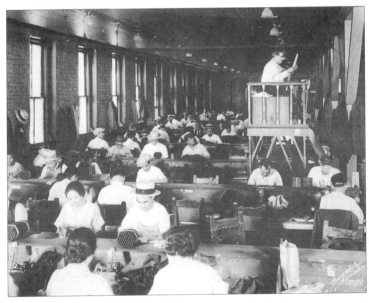

Lectore Reads to Workers at Cuesta Rey Factory (1929)

Florida State Archives

285

of Trade, Ybor began building his plant and supporting city. Ybor's cigar factory opened in 1886 and soon became the largest in the world, employing over 4,000 people. By the turn of the century, cigars fired Tampa's main industry with some 150 factories producing more than 100 million hand-rolled cigars a year. The city teemed with a lively mix of optimistic young laborers—a work force composed mostly of Cuban, Spanish, Italian and German immigrants. Spanish was the language spoken in the factory, where *lectores* read newspapers and poetry aloud to rooms full of busy workers. Shops, restaurants, mutual-aid societies and social clubs sprang into being to serve the growing population.

In the late 1800s, Ybor City became a base of operations for the Cuban revolution. During the Spanish-American War, the US Army stationed troops here, among them Col. Teddy Roosevelt and his Rough Riders. A year after Cuba won its independence in 1898, Ybor City saw the first wave of labor strikes and unrest, as fresh immigrants—fueled by the socialist doctrines preached in their home countries—clashed with conservative Tampa business leaders.

The advent of machine-rolled cigars, the increasing popularity of cigarettes, and the beginning of the Depression spelled doom for the cigar industry in Ybor City. As factories closed and families moved out, the whole town began a gradual postwar decline. Many old houses, factories and businesses were demolished during a period of urban renewal in the 1960s.

Back to Boomtown – The past decade has ushered in a resurgence of interest in Ybor City. Buildings have been renovated and historical elements spruced up as cobblestone streets, Old World street lamps and wrought-iron balconies have been installed. Since the early 1990s more than 100 businesses have moved into the area, and city officials are renovating historic structures to make room for future commerce. Now produced by machine, local cigars generate $150 million in annual sales revenue.

Increasing numbers of visitors have been drawn to Ybor City since 1990, when it was designated one of Florida's three National Historic Landmark Districts (along with ST.AUGUSTINE and PENSACOLA). In addition to tourists, Tampa's younger set has rediscovered the quarter's charm. Off-beat galleries, chic retail shops, nightclubs and ethnic restaurants line Seventh Avenue, the main thoroughfare since Ybor City's inception. On Thursday, Friday and Saturday nights throughout the year, the avenue takes on a Mardi Gras atmosphere, as police block traffic between 13th and 20th Streets and turn Seventh into a pedestrian promenade. Crowds spill onto the street from dozens of bars boasting all manner of live music.

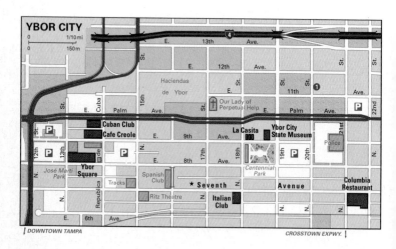

Sights *Map above*

1.6mi from downtown Tampa. Ybor City Chamber of Commerce operates a visitors welcome center at 1800 E. 9th Ave. ☎ *813-248-3712.*

★**Seventh Avenue** – A walk along this avenue reveals some of the district's more interesting architecture. **Columbia Restaurant** *(no. 2117)*, a landmark since 1905, is justly praised for its colorful exterior **tilework**. The three-story Neoclassical **Italian Club** *(at 18th St.)*, distinguished by its tripartite facade, has served as a center of cultural enrichment, education and financial aid to local Italians since 1894; the present structure dates from 1918. Tracks/El Goya *(no. 1430)*, now an alternative dance club, occupies the building that held the city's first restaurant. The Mediterranean-style establishment achieved notoriety in 1890 when the Rough Riders (the 1st Regiment of US Cavalry Volunteers, organized by Teddy Roosevelt during the Spanish-American War) trotted into the restaurant on horseback.

Two blocks off Seventh Avenue sits the yellow brick **Cuban Club** *(2010 Avenida Republica de Cuba at 14th St.)*, which dates from 1917. In its heyday, the club offered its members a ballroom, library, gym, theater and medical clinic. Today the building houses a Health Maintenance Organization (HMO) and also sponsors social events.

The nearby two-story brick **Cafe Creole** *(1320-1330 E. 9th Ave.)*, with its graceful arches, gained fame as El Pasaje, or the Cherokee Club, a rowdy hotel and restaurant that opened in 1888 and welcomed Cuban revolutionary José Martí, Teddy Roosevelt, President Grover Cleveland, Sir Winston Churchill and many Florida governors in its heyday.

Ybor City State Museum – *1818 9th Ave. Open year-round daily 9am–5pm. Closed Thanksgiving Day & Dec 25. $2.* ♿ ☎ *813-247-6323. Museum personnel lead guided tours through the historic district, starting at Ybor Square.* Housed in the 1923 yellow-brick Ferlita Bakery building, this museum outlines the development of Ybor City from frontier village to boomtown to urban wasteland. Exhibits include photographs, cigar-making tools, two commercial bread ovens and tobacco-box artwork. Guided tours of adjacent **La Casita** (1895) provide a glimpse of a typical turn-of-the-century cigar-maker's shotgun *(p 27)* cottage *(visit by 20min guided tour only, year-round daily 10am–3pm)*.

> **① Ybor City Brewing Company**
>
> *Map p 286. 2205 N. 20th St. (at 11th Ave.). Visit by guided tour (45min) only, year-round Tue–Sat 11am–3pm. $2.* ♿ ☎ *813-242-9222.* The area's first microbrewery began operation in November 1994 after a $3 million renovation of a 100-year-old cigar factory. The three-story, 36,000sq ft building now turns out 15,000 barrels of home brew a year, including the locally popular Ybor Gold, a frothy German lager; Calusa Wheat, a golden tropical ale; and Ybor Brown Ale, an Old English-style ale. Tours of the sweet-smelling facility explain the multistep brewing process and end with a sampling of the company's products.

Ybor Square – *1911 N. 13th St. Open year-round Mon–Thu 10am–6pm, Fri & Sat 10am–9pm, Sun noon–5:30pm.* ♿ ☎ *813-247-4497.* Built in 1886 by Vicente Ybor, this three-story, red-brick building once housed Ybor City's oldest and largest hand-rolled cigar factory, the Martínez Ybor Cigar Factory. The remodeled complex, consisting of two three-story factories and a two-story warehouse with courtyard, now houses specialty shops and eateries, as well as a 50-year-old cigar company. From the front steps of the building, José Martí, hero of the Cuban revolution, once rallied his countrymen.

A small park across Eighth Avenue *(corner of 13th St. and E. 8th Ave.)* honors Martí. The park marks the original site of the home of the Pedroso family, Cubans who sheltered Martí from Spanish loyalists.

NORTH TAMPA *2 days. Map p 273.*

★★**Busch Gardens Tampa Bay** – 🧒 *1 day. 3000 E. Busch Blvd. Open year-round daily 9am–6pm. Extended hours on selected holidays. $38.95; children 3-9 $32.95; $10.95 next-day return ticket and annual passes available* ✗ ♿ *($5)* ▥ *www.BuschGardens.org* ☎ *813-987-5082. Trams take visitors from the parking lot to the park entrance; be sure to note the section and row in which you park.* In 1959 the local Busch family built a brewery on a parcel of land just south of the University of South Florida. Later that year, August A. Busch, Jr., who served as president and chairman of Anheuser-Busch, Inc. from 1946 to 1975, opened a bird sanctuary and garden on the brewery grounds. Within three years it was attracting thousands of visitors. Since then, Busch Gardens has become the queen of Tampa attractions: an internationally famous zoo and park with a turn-of-the-century-Africa theme. More than 3,000 animals roam 300 acres of tropical flowering gardens. Roller coasters and rides, trams and trains, and music and shows add to the entertainment.

Visit – *1 day. Busch Gardens Tampa Bay is divided into 10 sections. Move in a clockwise direction for most efficient viewing, and arrive early to avoid long lines; parking areas open at 8:30am. Most popular months to visit are December, and March through August; busiest days are Friday–Sunday. When purchasing a ticket, you'll receive a Busch Gardens park map and guide that lists times and locations for performances and other entertainment. The daily entertainment schedule is also posted in Morocco, the first land you encounter upon entering the park. The Guest Relations window is located near the main entrance; staff there will exchange foreign currency at no charge.*

Thrill rides (such as the roller coasters Montu, Kumba, Python and Scorpion, and water rides Tanganyika Tidal Wave, Stanley Falls and Congo River Rapids) tend to be the most popular; head for these first. Note that participation on some rides is restricted by guest height, size and physical condition. Visitors may not bring coolers, food or drink into the park; a variety of eateries are scattered around the grounds. First Aid is available in the infirmaries next to the Festhaus in Timbuktu and in the Crown Colony's Skyride and Monorail Station.

Morocco – A mosaic-tiled palace and a bustling marketplace recall the romance and mystery of this section's North African inspiration. Visitors here are treated to a 35min ice show that celebrates a century of Hollywood filmmaking. Here you will also find a bakery, an open-air dining room, and two theaters presenting musical and dance revues.

Bird Gardens – Busch's original interest, the bird gardens now feature 198 exotic species. Their highlight is the new **Lory Landing** aviary, a rainforest setting in which parrots, lorikeets, hornbills and other brightly colored tropical birds fly freely. You also may attend an unusual Bird Show featuring trained raptors and parrots, many of which fly free above the audience. Keepers explain how the birds live in the wild and detail efforts to preserve endangered species. The theme area also includes a Flamingo Island and a koala display. Adjacent is Land of the Dragons, a play area for young children named for the nearby pen for Komodo dragons.

Stanleyville – Built to resemble an African village, the area includes the Stanley Falls Log Flume and the Tanganyika Tidal Wave, a ride that creates a huge splash as it careens down a 55ft drop. Orangutan and warthog exhibits, orchid garden and hands-on reptile exhibit complete the attractions here. Stanleyville Theatre and Zambezi Pavilion feature live entertainment.

The Congo – Here you'll find several of the Southeast's most gut-wrenching roller coasters, including **Kumba**, one of the largest and fastest steel coasters in the Southeast, which hits 60mph and zooms riders through seven inversions. It joins the Python, a 1,200ft-long coaster with two 360-degree loops, and Congo River Rapids, a water ride. For the younger set there are the Ubanga-Banga bumper cars. At Claw Island, rare Bengal tigers live in a landscape remarkably similar to their native jungle habitat.

Timbuktu – In this replica of a desert trading center, you'll find the Scorpion roller coaster that drops 62ft into a 360-degree loop; and the Dolphin Theatre, starring leaping dolphins and a comical California sea lion. Skill and arcade games line the aisles in the shopping bazaar/midway, and live shows are presented on the Festhaus stage.

Nairobi – This section of the park features an outstanding variety of animals, including **Myombe Reserve**, a three-acre gorilla and chimpanzee habitat where guests can observe these primates up-close through a glass window. Asian elephants, tortoises, a petting zoo and animal nursery are also located here. In an incongruous nod to Anheuser-Busch tradition, the international Show Jumping Hall of Fame shares space in a reptile house with snakes and lizards. From the Nairobi station, the steam-powered Trans-Veldt Railroad carries visitors around the theme park in open coaches.

© Janice Travia/Tony Stone Images

The Python Roller Coaster

Crown Colony – Victorian-style Crown Colony House hospitality center is the focal point of this part of the park. It overlooks zebras, hippos and ostriches that roam the nearby Serengeti Plain. Adjacent are the **skyride** and **monorail** stations, as well as stables of Anheuser-Busch's famous Clydesdale horses.

Edge of Africa – Busch Gardens' newest theme area comprises a short trek past habitat areas for such animals as baboons, hippos, lions, hyenas and meerkats. Introduced on video at an "Encampment Welcome Center" by noted animal handler Jack Hanna, it enables observers to get as close to large animals as acrylic panes will allow.

Serengeti Plain – From antelopes to zebras, more than 500 large African animals roam freely in herds on the 80-acre grassy savannah. You'll see ostriches, rhinos, giraffes, zebras and more. For viewing, you can take the monorail, skyride or train, but the flat-bed truck tours offered by **Serengeti Safari** *($20)* enable guests to get even more up-close and personal.

Egypt – The easternmost area of Busch Gardens features nearly seven acres of rides, including **Montu**, a spine-tingling inverted roller coaster, as well as a replica of King Tut's tomb, eateries and shopping bazaars centering around ancient Egypt. Its newest attraction is **Akbar's Adventure Tours**, a simulated journey with a second-rate tour guide (as played on video by actor Martin Short) through a bustling casbah, around the pyramids and into a haunted tomb.

Should you need a break from the heat, try **Adventure Island Waterpark**, another Busch attraction across the street that features water rides for patrons of every age *(4500 E. Bougainvillea Ave.; open mid-Feb–early Apr daily 10am–5pm; weekends Labor Day–late Oct 10am–5pm. Rest of the year hours vary. $22.95; children 3-9 $20.95; $8 next-day return ticket and annual passes available. ✗ P [3] www.adventureisland.com ☎ 813-987-5660).*

★★ **Museum of Science & Industry** – Kids *4801 E. Fowler Ave. Open year-round daily 9am, holidays 10am; closing times vary. $12. ✗ ♿ P www.tampatrib.com/mosi ☎ 813-987-6100.* This quintessential hands-on science museum received a $35 million face-lift in 1995 with the addition of a starkly modern four-story, aluminum-clad wing designed by Arizona architect Antoine Predock. Connected to the original museum by a bridge, the new west wing tripled the museum's size to 201,700sq ft, making it one of the largest science centers in the Southeast. Some 450 permanent exhibits address subjects from butterflies to nuclear fusion. These are complemented by several special exhibits each year, and a county library on the first floor offering high-tech computer games and access to the Internet.

West Wing – The museum's main entrance is now in the new building. One gallery on the ground level is reserved for traveling exhibits; the main exhibit area is housed on the second floor, where the 350-seat **IMAX Dome Theatre** presents changing films on an 82ft-high screen. Across from the theater, **Our Place on the Planet** explores Florida's unique flora, fauna and geography in the context of an ordinary backyard. Among the highlights are a 27ft-long topographic floor map and a crawl-through simulation of a gopher tortoise hole. In **The Amazing You** exhibit on the third floor, visitors examine health and the human body. See how muscles move on a bicycle-riding skeleton, and learn about nutrition at the Food for Thought Cafe. Also on this level, Our Place in the Universe focuses on past and future space exploration. A causeway leads to the 47-acre **Back Woods**, whose features include two short nature trails (one of them paved), a gopher tortoise habitat and several acres of wetlands.

East Wing – A restaurant, museum store and toddler's play area occupy the ground level of the original building. Displays on the second floor address a variety of general science topics, including gems and minerals, weather, electricity and lightning, and nuclear physics. Here visitors can experience a hurricane chamber, play energy pinball, help excavate a fossilized whale, and wander through a rooftop butterfly garden. The **Saunders Planetarium** dominates the third floor; behind it, **LabWorks Theater** stages live experiments *(see museum schedule for planetarium and theater show times)*. The rest of the third level is devoted to the science of communications, including the GTE Challenger Learning Center.

Lowry Park Zoological Garden – Kids *7530 N. Boulevard. Open year-round daily 9:30am–5pm. Closed Thanksgiving Day & Dec 25. $7.50 ✗ ♿ www.aza.org ☎ 813-932-8552.* A family entertainment value, the 24-acre zoo contains natural habitats for 1,600 animals, including endangered species such as the Florida panther and Sumatran tiger. West Indian manatees frolic in the **Pepsi Manatee and Aquatic Center**, where large underwater viewing tanks put visitors nose-to-nose with these gentle giants. The center also operates a manatee emergency rescue clinic.

Children's Museum of Tampa – Kids *7550 N. Boulevard. Open year-round Mon–Fri 9am–4pm, Sat 10am–5pm, Sun 1pm–5pm. Closed major holidays. $4. ♿ P ☎ 813-935-8441.* Kids will want to spend a couple of hours trying out the costumes, puppets and computers at this hands-on museum located just down the street from the zoo. Outside, **Safety Village**, a pint-size version of Tampa complete with a city hall, supermarket, bank and hospital, provides lessons in traffic safety. Streets feature kid-size stoplights and marked lanes, where visitors are welcome to ride bikes and tricycles. Children can enter many of the miniature structures to experiment with interactive exhibits.

Seminole Indian Village – *5221 N. Orient Rd. Enter through the gift shop. Open Apr–late Oct Mon–Sat 9am–5pm, Sun 10am–4pm. Rest of the year Mon–Sat 10am–6pm, Sun 10am–4pm. Closed Thanksgiving Day & Dec 25. $3.50.* ⚐ ▣ ☎ *813-620-3077.* This family-run site features thatch houses and ceremonial structures found in an actual native village. A guide explains Indian costumes and customs before finishing at the museum, built in the shape of an eight-sided star representing the eight clans of the Seminole Nation. Built over sacred burial ground, the museum displays a variety of artifacts including jewelry, arrowheads, baskets and clothing. (The village is not affiliated with the Seminole bingo parlor adjacent to it.)

EXCURSION

Hillsborough River State Park – *1/2 day. 20mi northeast in Thonotosassa. From downtown, take I-4 east 6mi to US-301 north (Exit 6); Follow this 14mi to park entrance on left at 15402 US-301 N. Open year-round daily 8am–dusk. $3.25/vehicle.* ▲ ▣ *www.edp.state.fl.us/parks/index.html* ☎ *813-987-6771.* Tampa's largest park covers nearly 3,000 acres of marshes, cypress swamps and pine flatwoods. Centerpiece of the park, the Hillsborough River cuts through outcroppings of Suwannee limestone and creates a series of Class II rapids. Eight miles of marked trails, some with interpretive plaques, course along the river and through hammocks of magnolia, Sabal palm, hickory and live oak. *Bring mosquito repellent in summer months.*

Across US-301 sits a reconstruction of **Fort Foster**, which served as a supply depot from 1837-38 during the Second Seminole War *(visit by 1hr guided tour only, Nov–Mar weekends every hour 10am–3pm; $2;* ▣ ☎ *813-987-6771.)* General Zachary Taylor commanded the fort briefly in 1838. Soldiers in period uniforms interpret life in the rustic wooden fort. Tours begin just north of the ranger station at a small museum that displays Seminole War artifacts.

TARPON SPRINGS★

Population 18,660
Map of Principal Sights p 3 – Map p 273
Tourist Information ☎ 813-937-6109

A surprising taste of the Mediterranean flavors this small town on Florida's west coast. Best known as a commercial sponging center, Tarpon Springs derives much of its character from a strong, close-knit Greek community, which fans out from the sponge docks on the Anclote River, an estuary of the Gulf of Mexico.

Historical Notes

From Spa to Sponges – The first settlers arrived in 1876. According to one story, they named the area Tarpon Springs in the mistaken belief that the mullet spawning in the mineral spring at the head of the bayou were tarpon. By the next decade, the town had developed as a fashionable winter resort and health spa. Visitors arrived at the bayou dock by steamer from CEDAR KEY, or by the Orange Belt Railroad, which delivered passengers from New York in only 36 hours. Many of these wealthy 19C "snowbirds" built Victorian homes and bungalows around the graceful "Golden Crescent" that surrounds **Spring Bayou**.

Beginning in 1905, hundreds of expert sponge divers—the majority of whom hailed from the Dodecanese Islands near Crete—immigrated from Greece. Usurping the Key West sponge business, Tarpon Springs' industry peaked in the 1930s with a fleet of some 200 commercial sponge boats. By the late 1940s, a local blight, the American preference for synthetic sponges, and growing Mediterranean competition for the natural sponge business decimated the Florida market. In 1986 however, the Soviet nuclear-reactor disaster in Chernobyl wiped out the Mediterranean beds, and Tarpon Springs revived to become the largest natural sponge market in the world—with annual revenues amounting to $7 million.

Old World Atmosphere – Today Greek culture maintains a tangible presence in Tarpon Springs. The longest-standing example is the **Festival of Epiphany**, celebrated here each January since the early 1900s. To commemorate the baptism of Christ at the River Jordan, a colorful contingent of children, acolytes and church dignitaries parades around Spring Bayou after a noontime Blessing of the Waters at the

St. Nicholas Greek Orthodox Cathedral *(below)*. The highlight occurs when the Archbishop tosses a wooden cross into the water for local youths to retrieve; the one who does so is blessed with good fortune for the coming year. Following this ritual, festivities include Greek dancing and music accompanied by mouth-watering Mediterranean food.

SIGHTS *1/2 day*

★**Dodecanese Boulevard** – *North of Tarpon Ave., off N. Pinellas Ave. US-19A.* Running parallel to the Anclote River, this lively waterfront thoroughfare forms the commercial spine of the Greek community. While sidewalk vendors cater primarily to tourists who busily poke through bins of sponges and curios from the sea, the colorful family-run cafes and bakeries draw as many locals as out-of-towners to sample honey-soaked baklava and other Greek specialties that scent the air. Be sure to explore the side streets behind the boulevard, where the atmosphere recalls the residents' homeland.

© Justine Hill

Sponge-Fishing Boat

Housed in a former sponge factory at the east end of Dodecanese Boulevard is the **Spongeorama Exhibit Center** *(no. 510; open year-round daily 10am–5pm; closed Thanksgiving Day & Dec 25;* ✗&☎ *813-943-9509)*, a dockside complex consisting of shops, a small museum and theater *(30min film)*. Just up the street, working shrimp and sponge boats are tied up at the main dock. Here a **cruise**★ aboard one of the traditional sponging vessels *(departs from sponge docks year-round daily 10am–5pm; does not operate Jan 6, Easter Sunday, Dec 25 and during inclement weather; round-trip 30min; commentary; $5;* 🅿 *[$2] St. Nicholas Boat Line ☎ 813-942-6425)* offers a demonstration of sponge harvesting *(p 292)*. Across the street, the former **Sponge Exchange** *(no. 735)* now houses specialty shops and displays an early 20C sponge-diving boat in the plaza. The **Coral Seas Aquarium** *(no. 852, west end of sponge docks)* features a touch-tank swimming with stingrays and baby sand sharks *(open year-round daily 10am–5pm; closed Thanksgiving Day & Dec 25; $4.75;* &🅿☎ *813-938-5378)*.

St. Nicholas Greek Orthodox Cathedral – *36 N. Pinellas Ave. Open year-round Mon–Sat 9am–4pm, Sun & holidays 1:30pm–4pm. Contribution requested.* &🅿 ☎ *813-937-3540.* Crowned by a three-story central **rotunda** and soaring corner bell tower, this Byzantine Revival-style church of buff-colored brick was built in 1943 to accommodate the town's rapidly growing Greek Orthodox population. The interior boasts a majestic **dome** resting on four arches, inspired by the great dome of the 6C Church of Hagia Sophia in Constantinople (Istanbul). Twenty-three stained-glass windows, imported chandeliers of Czech glass and a high altar carved from Greek marble ornament the sanctuary. Murals of various saints and apostles were painted in the dome by religious artist George Saclarides.

The cathedral is the site of one of the most elaborate Epiphany rituals *(above)* in the US. In addition, thousands of pilgrims come here each year to view the small glass-framed icon of St. Nicholas, patron saint of sailors, the poor and children. Inexplicably, the icon (displayed in the narthex) began "weeping" droplets of water in 1970. The presumed miracle was last repeated in 1973.

Unitarian Universalist Church – *57 Read St., at corner of Grand Blvd. Visit by guided tour (30min) only, Oct–May Tue–Sun 2pm–5pm. Contribution requested.* ⚿ ▯ ☎ *813-937-4682.* The 1909 masonry edifice dominated by a crenellated tower showcases 11 **paintings★** by **George Inness, Jr.** (1854-1926). Inness, son of the famous American landscape painter, was a seasonal resident of Tarpon Springs. Characterized by vivid "living greens," dramatic shading and perspective, the works include a landscape of Spring Bayou and two religious canvases—fruits of Inness' studies with the renowned French landscape painters of the Barbizon School near Paris—that were awarded medals in the Louvre.

Shrine of St. Michael Taxiarchis – *113 Hope St. Open Nov–Mar daily 6:30am–6pm. Rest of the year daily 6:30am–7:30pm.* ⚿ ☎ *813-937-4942.* Filled with hundreds of silver icons, this tiny shrine offers an interesting glimpse into the close-knit Greek Orthodox community of Tarpon Springs. The shrine was built in 1941 by Marie Tsalichis out of gratitude to St. Michael Taxiarchis, whom Marie believed had cured her son of a brain tumor. Thousands of worshippers have since come to light candles, hold services and pray for miracles.

Fred Howard Park – *Sunset Dr., .5mi west of Tarpon Springs. Open year-round daily 7am–dusk.* ⚿ ▯ ☎ *813-937-4938.* A palm-shaded causeway leads out to this lovely island park, which features a pristine crescent of white-sand beach and an expansive view of the Gulf of Mexico. In addition to offering sunbathing and swimming, it is a favorite fishing and jogging spot.

Sponge Diving: A Time-Honored Trade

A primitive aquatic animal with no brain or nervous system, the natural sponge (phylum Porifera) can be found in all seas but prefers shallow, temperate waters. Living in colonies at depths ranging from several feet to 28,000ft, sponges attach to stationary objects, such as rocks and coral, on the sea floor. In shallow water these animals can be collected from a boat using a long-handled metal hook; in deeper water, divers must walk along the bottom (sponges can be harvested from depths up to 150ft) and hook the sponges by hand, walking at a 45-degree angle against the current. Attached by air hose to their boat, Tarpon Springs divers use the same type of rubberized suit, round copper helmet and iron boots introduced by the first crew of Greek spongers who arrived in 1905. Altogether, this equipment weighs 172 pounds.

After the sponges are gathered, they are cleaned and dried. The part of the sponge that consumers use is actually the animal's skeleton, which is composed of a fine meshwork of fibrous spongin—a material related to horn—that can absorb 25 times its weight in water. While there are more than 4,500 known species of natural sponges, only four with any commercial value live in the Gulf of Mexico: wool (best grade, used for car and bath sponges), yellow (household sponges), wire (packing and insulation) and grass (cosmetic sponges), in that order of quality. You will find all these for sale in Tarpon Springs, along with decorative finger sponges and loofahs—actually a land-growing member of the cucumber family.

Treasure Coast

Jupiter Inlet Lighthouse – © Barbara Brady Conn (f/STOP PICTURES)

The stretch of Florida's east coast between Jupiter in north Palm Beach County and the city of Melbourne, 100mi north, has earned the moniker "Treasure Coast" because millions of dollars worth of sunken booty has been recovered from its offshore waters. Today the area also counts lovely barrier-island beaches, nature centers, parks and museums among its riches.

In late July 1715 a fleet of Spanish galleons, laden with treasure, was driven by a hurricane onto the reefs off Florida's east coast. Eleven of these 12 ships went down beyond the barrier islands extending from St. Lucie Inlet to Sebastian Inlet. Two such treasure fleets were sent every year by Spain on a sweep of the silver and gold mines in Mexico and South America. The return route threaded the Caribbean islands, then followed the Gulf Stream up the Florida coastline.

About 700 people died in the 1715 wrecks, but of more concern to the Spanish government was the freight valued at 14 million pesos. The 1,500 survivors set up camp on the shore opposite Sebastian and, with the help of local Ais Indians, began salvaging the sunken treasure. Though most was recovered, much of the booty was soon looted by British pirates and spirited away to Jamaica. So dependent was Spain and the rest of Europe on these regular injections of precious metals and gems that an economic depression resulted from this loss.

Modern treasure hunters have determined that the galleons carried treasure not reported on ship manifests. A great deal of such undeclared cargo has been found off this coast in recent decades with the use of sophisticated technology. Pieces of eight (17C Spanish pesos) and other artifacts still occasionally wash ashore after storms churn up the ocean waters.

Settlement of the area did not occur until the late 19C, when orange and pineapple growers established permanent communities. Along with tourism, the citrus industry continues to be an economic linchpin of this relatively uncongested section of Florida's east coast.

FORT PIERCE

Population 36,876
Map of Principal Sights p 3 – Map p 296
Tourist Information ☎ 561-462-1535 or 800-344-8443 (US & Canada)

Located 55mi north of WEST PALM BEACH, this mid-sized coastal town exists on two shores: the cluttered business district that lies along the west side of the Intracoastal Waterway, and the tranquil beaches on nearby Hutchinson Island.

Historical Notes

Fort Pierce takes its name from the fortification built here in 1838 during the Second Seminole War by Benjamin Kendrick Pierce, brother of the 14th US President. When the war ended in 1842, Congress offered 160 acres to anybody with the stamina to live in the area for five years. Though Indians, mosquitoes and wild animals scared away those with less fortitude, enough pioneers settled near the abandoned fort to start a town. Fearing another Indian uprising, the Army built Fort Capron, just north of Fort Pierce at present-day St. Lucie, in 1850. For many years the Capron Trail, linking forts from here to Tampa, was the only road connecting the east and west coasts of the peninsula.

In 1901 Fort Pierce, with a population of 300, incorporated and blossomed into a center for cattle and citrus. Its beaches soon became a favored vacation spot for several US Presidents, in particular William Howard Taft. Fort Pierce revived its role as a military outpost when it became a training base for the Navy's special amphibious teams during World War II. Cattle ranches and citrus and vegetable farms continue to prosper in the region, employing about 10 percent of the work force. Barrier-island beaches make retail and service industries economic mainstays by attracting vacationers and second-home owners. The area has also proved profitable for aquatic research. **Harbor Branch Oceanographic Institution** *(5600 Old Dixie Hwy. Visit by 1hr 30min guided tour only, year-round daily 10am, noon & 2pm; closed major holidays; $6;* ▣ *www.hboi.edu ☎ 561-465-2400)*, started in 1971, has grown to enjoy international prominence.

From the old downtown, **Indian River Drive** *(speed limit 35mph)* travels 16mi south to Jensen Beach, offering fine views of the river and the hulking twin containers of the St. Lucie nuclear power station.

SIGHTS *1 day*

★**UDT-SEAL Museum** – *3300 N. A1A, in Pepper Park (1mi north of Fort Pierce Inlet State Recreation Area). Open Jan–Apr Mon–Sat 10am–4pm, Sun noon–4pm. Rest of the year Tue–Sat 10am–4pm, Sun noon–4pm. Closed major holidays. $3.25.* ✕ ⅋ ▣ ☎ *561-595-5845.* Exhibits here vividly outline the history of the Navy SEALs (Sea, Air and Land), the elite commando units that evolved from the Underwater Demolition Teams and became famous for assisting astronauts after splashdowns. Better known as frogmen, these teams originated here in 1943 when the Navy began preparing special forces for the D-Day invasion. The museum's first section details action seen by frogmen in World War II. Another more popular exhibit relates recent events. Displays include an eerie, life-size diorama of a Viet Cong sharpening punji sticks while one of "the men with green faces," as the Viet Cong called them, emerges from the forest. In an adjoining audiovisual room, a series of films on SEAL operations runs continually.

Outside the museum, stone and metal spikes stuck into the ground represent obstacles frogmen had to remove to prepare beaches for large-scale invasions. Grounds also display boats from World War II and the Vietnam War.

Fort Pierce Inlet State Recreation Area – *905 Shorewinds Dr. off A1A, south tip of North Hutchinson Island. Open year-round daily 8am–dusk. $3.25/vehicle.* ▣ ☎ *561-468-3985.* Lying on the north side of Fort Pierce Inlet, a scenic park preserves 340 acres of beachfront and maritime hammock. Navy frogmen trained on these beaches for the D-Day invasion of Europe, giving to one headland the name Dynamite Point. The park now is a peaceful place to surf and swim, or to picnic by the inlet and watch pleasure craft ply the aquamarine waters. A trail *(.5mi)* off the parking lot loops through a forest of live oaks, strangler figs, cabbage palms and sea grapes. Leading to the beach, four boardwalks protect the fragile dune environment and safeguard feet from sandspurs and nettles. Anglers cast for snapper, snook and other fish.

Jack Island State Preserve, a separate, 958-acre section of the park *(1.5mi north on A1A, west side of road)*, is accessible by a 300ft concrete footbridge. Actually a peninsula in the Indian River, the mangrove-covered refuge provides a nursery site for young marine animals. Raccoons, otters, ospreys, herons and other animals also make homes here. A 4.3mi trail circles the island, and a shorter one *(1mi)* leads to a 15ft observation tower offering a panoramic view of the Indian River. Other trails traverse impoundment dikes constructed to control mosquitoes.

★**St. Lucie County Historical Museum** – *414 Seaway Dr. Open year-round Tue–Sat 10am–4pm, Sun noon–4pm. Closed major holidays. $3.* ✗ ⌖ 🄿 ☎ *561-462-1795.* Housed in a replica of the town's Florida East Coast Railway station, this museum renders the essence of Treasure Coast history. Exhibits start with artifacts from the Ais Indians, who occupied the area more than 2,000 years ago. The Galleon Room chronicles the 1715 treasure fleet that sank near here. The early 19C is explored in exhibits on Seminole Indians and US Army soldiers. Turn-of-the-century storefronts and offices depict pioneer life, and an outstanding collection of glass-plate photographs (1890-1920) adds realism to the displays.
The adjacent **Gardner House** (1907), a restored frame Victorian, provides a peek at life during pioneer times *(visit by 20min guided tour only, same hours as museum)*. The cruciform layout and 12ft ceilings helped ventilate the house, and heart pine walls repelled termites. Outside, a garage displays farm equipment and a restored 1919 fire engine. Cannons and an anchor from the 1715 Spanish galleon *Urca de Lima*, whose ruins lie in 10ft of water off Pepper Park, decorate the lawn.

Energy Encounter – 🄺🄸🄳 *6501 S. A1A at Florida Power & Light Company, Jensen Beach. Entrance at Gate B on north side of plant. Open year-round Sun–Fri 10am–4pm. Closed major holidays.* ⌖ 🄿 ☎ *561-468-4111.* A perfect rainy-day activity for children, the facility offers hands-on displays that explore the worlds of electricity, nuclear power, energy conservation and environmental protection. Several presentations explain safety precautions, a comfort to visitors who stand only a few hundred feet from the plant's tremendous nuclear reactors. Manatees are occasionally spotted in the warm waters outside the plant. A 1 mi boardwalk nature trail traverses part of Turtle Beach.

HUTCHINSON ISLAND★

Map of Principal Sights p 3 – Map p 296
Tourist Information ☎ 561-334-3444

Upon receiving a Spanish land grant in 1807, James A. Hutchinson moved his farming operations from the mainland to this 22mi-long spit of land to avoid the local Indians who had been raiding his crops and stealing his slaves and cattle. His descendants found the island's bears and wildcats as detrimental to crops and livestock as were the Indians. Through the first half of the 20C, the island stayed an uncrowded jungly strand framed by broad beaches and the pellucid Indian River.
Today condominiums, golf courses, high-rise hotels and beach cottages cover much of the island's south end to cater to a mix of visitors and part- and full-time residents. Despite this development, long, unhurried beaches remain, enticing northerners who swell the winter population to nearly 20,000 — twice its normal size. On the west side of the Jensen Beach Causeway, two local artists have carved lithe sea creatures from the stumps of dead Australian pines.

SIGHTS *1/2 day*

★**Elliott Museum** – *825 N.E. Ocean Blvd., on east side of Stuart Causeway (A1A). Open year-round daily 10am–4pm. Closed major holidays. $6.* ⌖ 🄿 ☎ *561-225-1961.* Housed in a brick building flanked by two pink-painted wings, this repository holds an overwhelming collection of Victoriana. Harmon Elliott established the museum in memory of his inventor father, **Sterling Elliott** (1852-1922), whom Thomas Edison proclaimed "a genius."
Thirty-eight display areas, each packed with objects, document the early 1900s with such themes as miniature circuses, guns, railroads, Victorian mourning attire and dolls. Separate rooms re-create a period ice-cream parlor, general store, black-smith shop and Victorian parlor. Also on exhibit are several of Elliott's clever inventions, including his knot-tying machine and 100 of his 118 US patent docu-ments. One whole wing at the back of the museum is devoted to antique and classic automobiles.

Coastal Science Center – *890 N.E. Ocean Blvd., across from Elliott Museum. Open year-round Mon–Sat 10am–5pm. Closed major holidays. $3.50.* ♿ 🅿 *www.gate.net/~fos/fos.htm* ☎ *561-225-0505.* Located on 40 acres of land that runs from A1A at Stuart Beach to the Indian River, this research marine-life rehabilitation facility is operated by the Florida Oceanographic Society. A slick new marine-education center invites visitors to learn about the area's varied marine life through display panels, aquariums, touch tanks and computer games. One and a quarter miles of trail, much of it boardwalk, explore coastal hardwood hammocks and a mangrove marsh. An observation deck is planned.

★**Gilbert's Bar House of Refuge** – *301 S.E. MacArthur Blvd., 1.5mi south of A1A. Open year-round daily 10am–4pm. Closed major holidays. $4.* ♿ 🅿 ☎ *561-225-1875.* In 1875 the US Treasury Department erected 10 "houses of refuge" along the Florida coast to aid shipwrecked sailors. Though its namesake pirate and sandbar have long since disappeared, the sole surviving restored house of refuge

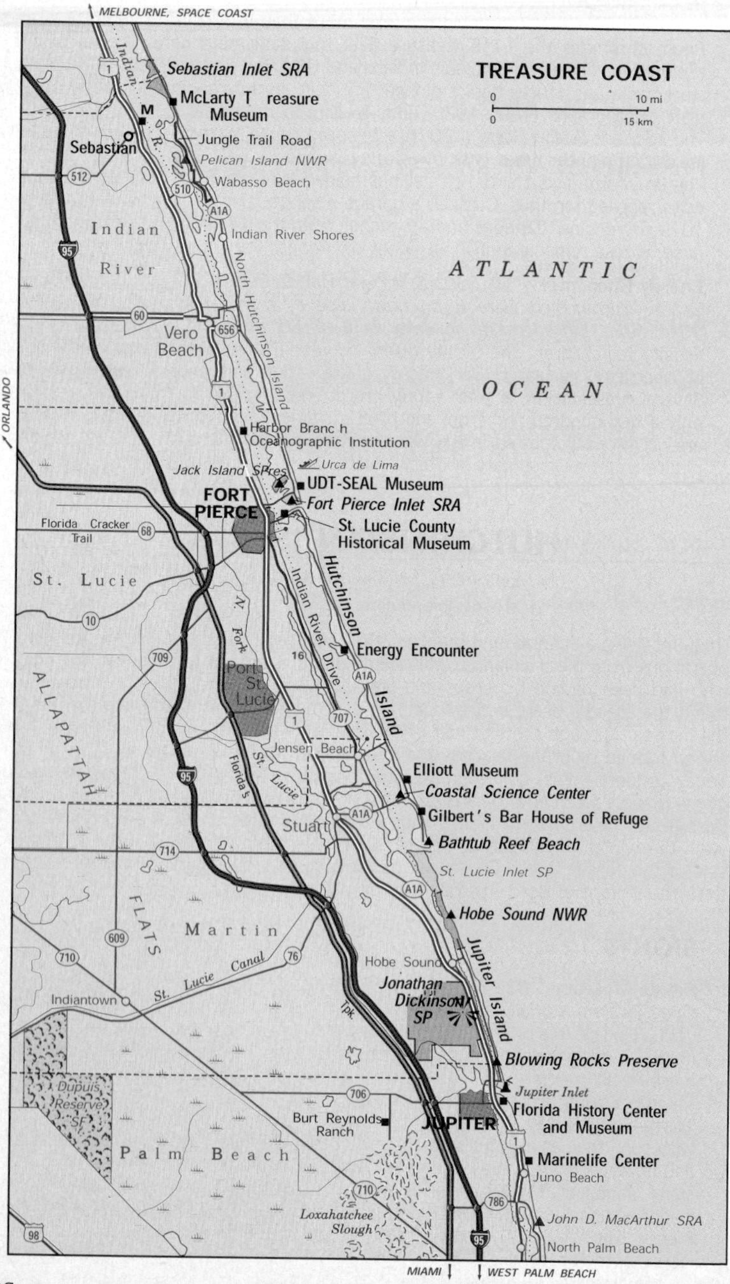

still stands atop a calcareous sandstone outcrop overlooking the ocean. Thirty-four rescues took place here from 1875 to World War II, when the Coast Guard turned the structure into a patrol base to guard against attack by German submarines. The boathouse displays antique lifesaving equipment and other marine artifacts; four rooms open to the public in the green wood-frame main house contain a number of treasures, including a model ship collection.

Bathtub Reef Beach – Kids *On MacArthur Blvd., 2.3mi south of A1A. Open year-round daily dawn–dusk.* &. Families with small children favor this county park, named for its shallow wading area created by an offshore reef. Constructed not by coral but by small, tube-building worms, the reef covers about 85 acres and renders the surf calm and shallow for nearly 300ft. Indigenous fauna include groupers, spider crabs, octopi and sea urchins.

JUPITER

Population 27,586
Map of Principal Sights p 3 – Map p 296
Tourist Information ☎ 561-746-7111

Seated on the north end of the Palm Beach County coast, Jupiter offers a respite from the high energy of the Palm Beaches, yet development in recent years has placed this sprawling town firmly within the megalopolis that extends south to FORT LAUDERDALE and MIAMI.

Historical Notes

Although the area now welcomes tourists—who provide the county's major source of revenue—the first European visitors met with a less-than-gracious reception. When early settler Jonathan Dickinson's *(p 298)* ship wrecked off the coast of Jupiter Island in 1696, local Indians held members of his party captive for several months until they managed to escape. Over the next two centuries the number of natives was reduced by disease and war while white settlers began trickling in. General Thomas Jesup established a fort here in 1838 during the Seminole Wars. Fifty years later, the first train—dubbed the Celestial Railway because of its stops at Jupiter, Neptune, Venus, Mars and Juno—steamed through town. By 1895 Flagler's Florida East Coast Railway had replaced the narrow-gauge Celestial, and construction began on the Intracoastal Waterway. Jupiter grew slowly the first part of this century, its development overshadowed by Palm Beach, its chic neighbor to the south.

No longer just a city of vacation homes, Jupiter is now a thriving blend of businesses, upscale resorts, and golf and yachting communities. The 2,300-acre Abacoa development near I-95 has attracted a Florida Atlantic University honors campus and a spring-training stadium for the St. Louis Cardinals and Montreal Expos baseball teams; under construction are 6,000 new homes, parks and a golf course. The area's wide public beaches and numerous reefs attract snorkelers and surfers, as well as thousands of sea turtles who make an annual pilgrimage to nest on these shores each summer *(p 298)*.

Photographs and memorabilia from the acting career of the city's most famous son, Burt Reynolds, are displayed at the **Burt Reynolds Ranch** Kids *(16133 Jupiter Farms Rd.; open year-round daily 10am–5pm; closed major holidays. $1* ✗&🅿 ☎ *561-747-5390)*. In mid-1998, however, the Reynolds Ranch was up for sale, its future uncertain. And the popular Jupiter Theatre *(100 E. Indiantown Rd.)*, which Reynolds founded and which has presented such celebrities as Tony Bennett, Carol Channing and Rich Little, had been closed.

SIGHTS *1 day*

Marinelife Center of Juno Beach – Kids *14200 US-1, Loggerhead Park, .25mi north of Donald Ross Rd. Open year-round Tue–Sat 10am–4pm, Sun noon–3pm.* &🅿 ☎ *561-627-8280. Turtle walks offered in summer (p 299)*. This small, low-key operation dedicated to rehabilitation, research and education started in 1983 as one woman's quest to help the area's sea turtles survive the perils of heavy beachfront development. Exhibit space feels cramped and makeshift compared to bigger-budget facilities, but this center makes up for its shortcomings with its large spirit. Scores of turtle shells, snakeskins, fish teeth, mandibles and coral are displayed in two small rooms inside the center. Knowledgeable volunteers explain how weak or injured turtles, housed in large tanks outside, are cared for until they are large enough—or well enough—to be released back into the sea.

Florida History Center and Museum – *805 N. US-1, in Burt Reynolds Park. Open year-round Tue–Fri 10am–5pm, weekends noon–5pm. Closed major holidays. $5.* &🅿 ☎ *561-747-6639*. Exhibits in this modern, wood structure provide a good introduction to local maritime history. Here you'll find a Seminole dugout canoe,

Spanish earthenware and pioneer fashions, as well as stories and artifacts regarding some of the area's more colorful residents: hermit pioneer "Trapper" Nelson, actor Burt Reynolds and singer Perry Como. A new outdoor Seminole living-history village gives visitors insight into native culture. Traveling exhibits are presented regularly.

DuBois House – *DuBois Rd., in DuBois Park. Open year-round Wed noon–4pm. $3. 🅿 ☎ 561-747-6639.* This Cracker-style house overlooking picturesque Jupiter Inlet dates from 1898 and was built on a Jeaga Indian shell mound. Two front rooms and a bedroom, furnished with family and period pieces, provide a glimpse into Florida pioneer life. Family descendant and historian Bessie DuBois still lives in the neighborhood.

Jupiter Inlet Lighthouse – *US-1 and Rte. 707, west side of Jupiter Inlet Bridge, in Jupiter Lighthouse Park. Visit by guided tour (1hr) only, year-round Sun–Wed 10am–3:15pm. Closed major holidays. $5. 🅿 ☎ 561-747-8380.* George Meade, commander of the Union forces at Gettysburg, designed this bright red beacon, which reigns as the county's oldest surviving structure. Southern sympathizers took out the lantern in 1861, a year after it was first lit, fearing that it illuminated their blockade runners. Since 1866 though, the lighthouse has not missed a night of operation. Standing 105ft tall, it beams a signal visible 18mi out to sea. Informed docents at the small visitor center wear colorful hoopskirts and bonnets. Inside the oil house, interpretive exhibits relate local history. Visitors may climb the 105 steps to the top of the lighthouse tower for a birds-eye **view** of the surrounding area.

EXCURSION

★**Jonathan Dickinson State Park** – *3hrs. 7mi north of Rte. 706 on US-1. Open year-round daily 8am–dusk. $3.25/vehicle. ▲ 🅿. ☎ 561-546-2771.* English Quaker merchant Jonathan Dickinson found this area inhospitable when his barkentine, *Reformation*, wrecked on the nearby coast in 1696. Threatened, beaten and starved by the resident Indians, his group of 25 Quakers—bound from Jamaica

Katie Deits/© CAMERA GRAPHICS

■ Sea Turtles

Large air-breathing reptiles of the families Dermochelyidae and Cheloniidae, sea turtles inhabit all but the coldest of the earth's oceans. Five of the world's eight species of sea turtles frequent Florida waters; all are endangered, except the loggerhead (*Caretta caretta*), which is threatened. Atlantic green turtles (*Chelonia mydas*), leatherbacks and an occasional hawksbill (*Eretmochelys imbricata*) nest along the Atlantic coast of Florida between Cape Canaveral and Palm Beach. Loggerheads nest along both the Atlantic and Gulf coasts; the Kemps Ridley turtle is predominantly found in Gulf of Mexico waters.

The largest marine turtle, the leatherback (*Dermochelys coriacea*), can weigh as much as 1,300 pounds and grow to be 7ft long. The smallest, the Kemps Ridley (*Lepidochelys kempii*), measures 30in long and averages 100 pounds. Sea turtles can dive to depths of more than 3,000ft and can swim great distances, thanks to their low streamlined shell and powerful front flippers.

The longest sea turtle migration ever recorded was accomplished by a leatherback tagged in Surinam,

to Pennsylvania—finally escaped, only to struggle 240mi up the coast to
ST. AUGUSTINE. His record of their travails provided one of the first written accounts
of the southeastern Indians.

This 11,500-acre tract of land and river contains the largest piece of sand-pine
scrub in southeast Florida and shelters alligators, manatees, gopher tortoises, bald
eagles, scrub jays and sandhill cranes, among other unusual species. Sand-pine
scrub, a rare desert-like environment of evergreen oaks and saw palmetto, covers
about 20 percent of the park's acreage.

Visitors may walk the **Hobe Mountain Trail** *(.5mi)* to a high sand ridge topped by a
50ft wooden observation tower that provides a panoramic **view** of the flatlands, the
Intracoastal Waterway, Jupiter Island, and beyond to the Atlantic. Here, from deep
in the park, the landscape appears remarkably unspoiled by development. A 44-
passenger tour boat plies the Loxahatchee—designated a National Wild and Scenic
River—through primeval wilderness *(departs from boat dock in park year-round
Wed–Sun 9am, 11am, 1pm, & 3pm; round-trip 2hrs; commentary; $10;* 🅿 ☎ *561-
746-1466).*

JUPITER ISLAND *1/2 day*

This scenic 16mi-long slice of once-submerged sandbar, now separated from the
mainland by the Intracoastal Waterway, has for decades harbored winter homes
for wealthy families. In recent years, professional athletes, including golfers Lee
Trevino and Greg Norman and Miami Dolphins quarterback Dan Marino, have
bought property here. Houses mostly occupy one- and two-acre parcels, keeping
population density low and real-estate value high. A well-groomed hush hangs
over this exclusive island, and the narrow road offers few stopping places or beach
access points; bicyclists, pedestrians and motorists all proceed at a slow and
measured pace.

★ **Blowing Rocks Preserve** – *S. Beach Rd., 1.8mi north of Jupiter Inlet. Open year-
round daily 9am–5pm. $3.* 🅿 ☎ *561-744-6668. Guided walks (45min) year-round
Thu 2pm & Sun 11am; field trips Nov–Feb, reservations required; turtle walks are*

South America. The turtle was found four months later in Ghana, Africa—over
4,000mi away. Scientists believe these reptiles navigate by means of their highly
developed sense of smell and by magnetically sensitive particles in their brain that
act as a natural compass.

Every two or three years, the turtles mate offshore and the female crawls up on
the beach after dark to dig a nest. Here she will lay a clutch of up to 150 ping-
pong-ball-size eggs. Female sea turtles find their way back to the same beaches
year after year; when young turtles mature, they will likely return to the beach on
which they were hatched to make their own nests. During nesting season (April
to October), a single female will come ashore several times, laying from 300 to
800 eggs.

Hatchlings incubate for 54 to 57 days. After emerging from their eggs, the babies
instinctively move away from the shadows and seek the brightest horizon. Glaring
lights of beachfront condominiums and houses confuse the young turtles, who
often head in the wrong direction, thus decreasing their chances of survival.

At many beach access points, signs caution visitors to avoid turtle nesting sites
and to keep lights off the beach at night during nesting season, or risk up to a
$20,000 fine. It's a federal offense to touch or even to disturb a sea turtle.

During June and July, the following local organizations sponsor guided "turtle
walks" on a regular basis to known nesting sites along the coast. Lucky groups
may see nesting females or even tiny hatchlings. Led by a naturalist or park
ranger, the walks take place after dark and can last several hours. *Bring
mosquito repellent. Make reservations well in advance of your trip, as these
popular walks tend to fill up quickly. Call sites by mid-April for information and
reservations.*

Hobe Sound Nature Center	☎ 561-546-2067
Florida Power and Light Company	☎ 800-552-8440
Marinelife Center of Juno Beach	☎ 561-627-8280
Merritt Island National Wildlife Refuge	☎ 407-867-4077
Blowing Rocks Preserve/The Nature Conservancy	☎ 561-744-6668
Sea Turtle Preservation Society	☎ 407-676-1701
Sebastian Inlet State Recreation Area	☎ 407-984-4852
Canaveral National Seashore	☎ 904-428-3384

offered in summer (p 299). Run by the Nature Conservancy, the 73-acre refuge possesses the largest limestone outcropping on the Atlantic coast. Extending for nearly a mile along the beach, this unique rock formation contains fissures that become waterspouts during very high tides, creating dramatic plumes up to 60ft high and giving the preserve its name. West Indian manatees, great blue herons, ospreys, brown pelicans, sea turtles and other animals feed and nest among the site's four plant communities: mangrove swamp, tropical hammock, coastal strand and beach dune. Since 1985, 60,000 native plants have been replanted and non-native species removed; as a result, 12 native animal species have returned. Tall sea-grape thickets hedge the path that runs more than a mile along the dune. A wooden pavilion beside the parking lot displays panels describing the preserve's flora, fauna and geography.

Hobe Sound National Wildlife Refuge – *2.5mi north of Bridge Rd. (entrance a dead-end of Beach Rd.). Open year-round daily dawn–dusk. $5/vehicle* ☐ *www.fws.gov/r4eao/nwrhbs.html* ☎ *561-546-6141*. At the north end of Jupiter Island, 700 acres of wild, unpublicized coastal habitat provide a refuge for the area's diverse animal and plant life. Refuge-sponsored turtle walks *(p 299)* begin at the **Hobe Sound Nature Center** on the mainland *(east side of US-1, 2.3mi south of Bridge Rd.)*. This separate section of the refuge comprises 229 acres of sand pine scrub along Hobe Sound and features an informative half-mile nature walk *(open year-round Mon–Fri 9am–3pm; closed major holidays; contribution requested;* ☎ *561-546-2067)*.

SEBASTIAN

Population 13,014
Map of Principal Sights p 3 – Map p 296
Tourist Information ☎ 561-589-5969

In the late 1800s when riverboats steamed up and down the Indian River, this small town was a fishing and trading center. Locals twice tried to open an inlet to the sea (1886 and 1915), but sand from storms and erosion filled it in. Jetties were built in 1923 to create a permanent inlet. Scenic **Jungle Trail Road** *(runs 5mi from Old Winterbeach Rd. to A1A)* tunnels through a forest of live oak and pine along the eastern shore of the Indian River. Passing orange groves and palm stands, the old road offers a glimpse of pioneer Florida. *After hard rains, parts of this sandy road may be washed out.*

SIGHTS *1/2 day*

★**Mel Fisher's Treasure Museum** (M) – *1322 US-1. Open year-round Mon–Sat 10am–5pm, Sun noon–5pm. Closed Jan 1, Easter Sunday, Thanksgiving Day, Dec 25. $5.* ☐ ☎ *561-589-9875*. Dioramas, exhibits and artifacts here recount the search for remains of the 1715 Spanish fleet *(p 293)*. The most popular display area, the **gold room**, boasts plates, chains, crucifixes and rings, all exquisitely crafted

Artifacts From Mel Fisher's Treasure Museum

Dylan Kibler/Mel Fisher Maritime Heritage Society

from Peruvian gold and Mexican silver. A film *(28min)* provides a good introduction to the treasures housed here. A host of recovered artifacts is available for purchase in the gift shop.

McLarty Treasure Museum – *13180 N. A1A. Open year-round daily 10am–4:30pm. $1.* 🔲 ☎ *561-589-2147.* Built on the site of the 1715 survivors' camp *(p 293),* this small museum focuses on marine archaeology and searching for the ill-fated Spanish fleet. Displays include early instruments used to explore the ocean floor and items recovered from the Spanish wrecks. In the auditorium, two different slide shows depict the natural history of the inlet *(15min)* and chronicle treasure hunting off the coast *(20min).*

Sebastian Inlet State Recreation Area – *On A1A, 1mi north of McLarty Museum. Open daily year-round. $3.25/vehicle.* ⚠ 🔲 ☎ *407-984-4852.* The picturesque 587-acre park spans both north and south sides of the inlet. In addition to the usual water sports, the area offers excellent shrimping, clamming, snorkeling, scuba diving and surfing. Several major surfing meets are held here annually. Drive over the bridge for a good **view** of Sebastian Inlet and its tiny islands.

The Bahamas

Cable Beach, Nassau – Cosmo Condina, Tony Stone Images

Just 55mi off the southeast coast of Florida, this archipelago of coral islands is sprinkled across 100,000sq mi of the Caribbean. The name Bahama derives from the Spanish *baha mar*, meaning shallow sea, an apt description of the reef-strewn, turquoise waters surrounding these 700-plus islands and islets, of which only about 20 are inhabited. More than 3.5 million visitors annually—many of whom arrive via cruise ship—are drawn to this tropical setting, most coming to Nassau or Freeport The Bahamas' less-developed **Out Islands** (also called the Family Islands) are also gaining popularity, particularly among sailing, fishing, snorkeling, diving and birding enthusiasts. They boast pristine beaches and residents who are easygoing and friendly. Now serviced by commercial airlines and ships, the Out Islands include Acklins, Andros, Bimini, Cat, Crooked, Eleuthera, Long, Mayaguana, Ragged and San Salvador islands; the Abacos, Berry, Exuma and Inagua groups; and Rum Cay. One of the longest **coral reefs★★★** in the world extends 140mi along the eastern edge of Andros, largest island in the chain. A part of the British Empire since the 17C, the Bahamas are now an independent member of the British Commonwealth.

NEW PROVIDENCE ISLAND★

Population 172,196 (including Paradise Island; 1990)
Maps p 304 & pp 308-309
Tourist Information ☎ 242-322-7500

As the governmental and commercial center of the Bahamas, New Providence teems with activity. Only 22mi long and 7mi across at its widest point, New Providence is one of the smaller islands in the Bahamas, yet it claims more than 60 percent of the country's total population. The island's historic heart, Nassau, still retains a traditional British flavor, while modern resorts rise nearby.

Historical Notes

A Providential Place – Lucayan Indians had occupied the Bahamas for more than 500 years when **Christopher Columbus** arrived in the Caribbean in 1492. Scholars long believed that Columbus's first New World landfall was on San Salvador Island at the east edge of the Bahamas, but recent research has led to speculation that he may

have landed on nearby Samana Cay instead. In any case, the land of the Bahamas was little touched by the Spanish. The same could not be said for the people. The Lucayans, enslaved by the Spanish to work mines on Hispaniola, were virtually extinct within 25 years of Columbus' arrival, victims of disease and poor treatment.

With the disappearance of the Lucayans, the Bahamas remained virtually unpopulated until the early 17C, when the Eleutherian Adventurers appeared on the scene. This band of Puritans had fled to Bermuda to escape persecution, and from there to the Caribbean. Shipwrecked off present-day Eleuthera, they established a short-lived settlement there. The group's leader, **William Sayles**, later met with better success when he discovered a fine natural harbor on another, smaller island to the west. In 1666 the Puritans established themselves on Sayles' Island. Grateful for this second chance, they rechristened the island New Providence.

The Age of Empire – At the end of the 17C, the British began to exercise control over the island when Proprietary Governor Nicholas Trott arrived. He renamed the existing settlement of Charlestown in honor of the Prince of Orange-Nassau (who would eventually reign as William III) and built Fort Nassau in 1697 on the present site of the British Colonial Beach Resort *(p 307)*. The settlement and its harbor soon became a center for British privateers involved in plundering Spanish and French ships in the Caribbean and for wreckers salvaging vessels that had gone down on the treacherous offshore reefs.

In the early 18C, the island's first Royal Governor, **Woodes Rogers**, transformed the rundown, garbage-strewn town of Nassau into a "civilized place," and introduced a gridded street plan. He was also instrumental in bringing an end to piracy and in convening the first General Assembly in 1729. In the 1780s the modestly prospering island witnessed a new influx of refugees as American Loyalists (those who pledged allegiance to the British Crown) fleeing the Revolution resettled here. In 1782 the Spanish overran New Providence and occupied it for about a year before being driven out by a Loyalist militia.

Many of the Americans had brought slaves with them when they resettled on New Providence, in hopes of establishing cotton plantations. Finding the soil too poor to sustain that kind of agriculture, a number of Loyalists returned to America. They left, however, several legacies: an impressive array of English Georgian homes, two large new forts and an expanded black population. In 1838 the blacks they left behind became free men when Britain abolished all slavery within its empire. Though free,

303

the black population of New Providence existed in a distinctly segregated society, living "over the hill" in interior enclaves such as Fox Hill, Adelaide, Gambier, and Grants, Bain and Delancey Towns.

American events continued to affect Bahamian prospects throughout the 19C and 20C. During the Civil War, a flurry of commerce gripped the island when locals and Southern sympathizers used the area as a base from which to run Northern blockades of Confederate ports.

In the 1920s American Prohibition brought further prosperity as local **rumrunners** became involved in smuggling liquor to mainland bootleggers, and American gangsters and gamblers flocked to Nassau. Interest in tourism outlasted the end of Prohibition in the 1930s, resulting in the development of Cable Beach *(p 311)* as a resort area.

A Separate Peace – In the 1960s the island's black population grew increasingly resentful of the continued domination of politics and business by the white "Bay Street Boys," as members of the ruling United Bahamian Party were known. In 1967 the country elected its first black Prime Minister, **Lynden Pindling**. During the same period, tourism increasingly came to dominate the economy, as the large high-rise resorts of Paradise Island shot up, adding their modern luster to such traditional island hostelries as the mid-18C Graycliff, the now-defunct 1861 Royal Victoria, and the turn-of-the-century British Colonial.

On July 10, 1973, the Bahamas peacefully gained their independence from Britain, with Nassau remaining the capital. Today roughly 55 percent of visitors to the Bahamas spend time here. Nassau also ranks as a regular port-of-call for some 30 cruise ships, which deliver about a million visitors to its shores annually.

★★ NASSAU

Long the center of the island's tourism, Nassau's historic heart beats along 25 blocks of the harbor front bordered by Bay Street on the north, Hill Street on the south, Elizabeth Avenue to the east, and West Street to the west. All aspects of the city's checkered past are reflected in the tenor of this district—from its founding by Puritans over 300 years ago to its days as a rough bailiwick of buccaneers through the eras of British Loyalists and American rumrunners, and finally into its current role as the Bahamas' banking center and a popular haven for sunseekers. Along Bay Street, countless duty-free shops cater to cruise-ship passengers, while quieter side streets shade classic pink-and-white Bahamian Colonial structures. Vestiges of formal British tradition prevail in the workings of the national government at Parliament Square and Government House.

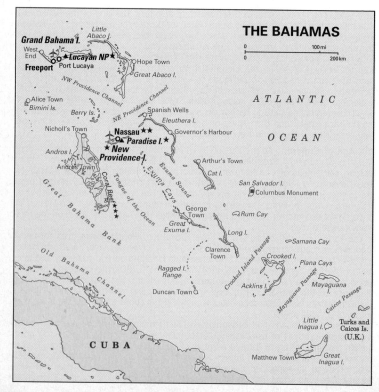

PRACTICAL INFORMATION .... Area Code: 242

When to Go

Weather in the Bahamas is pleasant throughout the year. High season runs from mid-December through mid-April; hotel reservations should be made well in advance. During the winter months (Nov–Feb) temperatures average 72°F/22°C, while southern trade winds keep the islands comfortable during the summer months when temperatures average 80°F/27°C. In the rainy season (Jun–Oct) showers are frequent but brief.

Planning your Trip – Citizens of the US and Canada entering the Bahamas are required to present proof of citizenship (passport or birth certificate and photo ID) and a return ticket. Limit of stay: 8 months. Visitors from other countries should check with the Embassy of the Bahamas in their country before traveling. **Bahamas Tourist Office in Florida:** 19495 Biscayne Blvd., Suite 809, Aventura FL 33180 ☎ 305-932-0051 or 800-327-7678 (US).

Getting There

By Air – Major US and international airlines fly into **Nassau International Airport** and **Freeport International Airport**. Visitor Information booths: ☎ 377-6806 (Nassau); ☎ 352-6909 (Freeport). Transportation from airports by taxi: Nassau International Airport to Cable Beach *($12)*; to Paradise Island *($23)*; to downtown *($18)*; Freeport International Airport to downtown *($5.50)*. Bahamasair (☎ *352-8341*) provides regular service from Nassau to most of the Out Islands. Rental car agencies *(p 323)* are located at the airports and in downtown Nassau and Freeport.

By Boat – Cruise ships departing from Miami dock at Nassau; some make stops in Freeport. Another way to island-hop is to take the mail boat *(operating year-round; for schedules and fares contact the Ministry of Tourism or Dock Master's office, Potter's Cay Dock ☎ 393-1064)*.

Getting Around

By Car and Taxi – Foremost to remember, vehicles are driven **on the left** side of the street. Scooters *($28–$40/day)* and bicycles *($15–$20/day)* can be rented throughout the islands. Both scooter driver and passenger must wear helmets. Unless otherwise posted, **speed limits** are generally 30mph outside city limits, 25mph within city, and 15mph in school zones. **Taxis:** Nassau ☎ 323-5111; Freeport ☎ 352-6666. Small buses called "jitneys" are the most economical way to get around the islands *(daily dawn–dusk; 75¢; exact change required)*. Maps are available at main bus stops.

General Information

Visitor Information – **Bahamas Ministry of Tourism**, PO Box N 3701, Market Plaza, Bay Street, Nassau ☎ 322-7500 provides information regarding accommodations, shopping, entertainment and recreation. Tourism hotline *(Mon–Fri 9am–5:30pm ☎ 326-4357; until 11:30pm ☎ 377-6833; hotline accessible in Bahamas only)*.

Accommodations – Lodgings in the Bahamas range from hotels and resorts ($95–$575), and family-run inns ($60–$200), to villas and apartment rentals (from $175/day for a one-bedroom). All hotels charge a 5% room tax. Some luxury hotels have casinos. *Rates quoted are average prices per night for a double room and are subject to seasonal variations.*

Foreign Exchange – The Bahamian dollar is equivalent to the US dollar. Numerous foreign banks have offices in Nassau and Freeport *(open Mon–Thu 9:30am–3pm, Fri 9:30am–5pm)*.

Sports and Recreation – Underwater expeditions to coral reefs include half-day of instruction and reef dive *(45min)*; all-day excursion to an Out Island *(two dives and beach picnic $135)*: Nassau Scuba Centre ☎ 362-1964. Half-day cruise *(daily 9am–12:30 & 12:30–4pm; $34)* or full-day cruise and beach barbecue *(daily; $55)*; snorkel gear and free pick-up at hotel included: Barefoot Sailing Cruises ☎ 393-0820.

Shopping: Bay Street, downtown Nassau; Hurricane Hole Plaza, Paradise Island; International Bazaar & Port Lucaya Marketplace, Freeport. There is no sales tax charged and all goods are available duty-free.

Useful numbers   ☎

Police/Fire	919
Directory Assistance	916
Weather	915

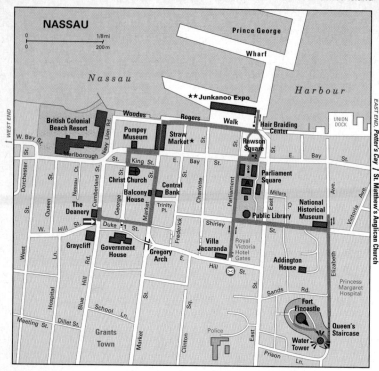

Old Town Walking Tour *1/2 day. Map above.*

Begin at the intersection of West Hill St. and Cumberland St. (which becomes Blue Hill Rd.).

Graycliff – *10 W. Hill Rd. (on corner of Cumberland St./Blue Hill Rd.).* One of the oldest hotels in the Bahamas, this dignified Georgian Colonial structure with its foot-thick limestone walls and two-story verandah is attributed by legend to Capt. John Howard Graysmith. The daring privateer of the schooner *Graywolf*, Graysmith is said to have built the house in the mid-18C on the site of Nassau's first Anglican church. By 1844 the building had become Nassau's first inn. During the American Civil War it served as a US Officer's Mess; in the mid-20C it eventually became the private home of the British peers Lord and Lady Dudley, who entertained many notable figures here, including the Duke and Duchess of Windsor and Sir Winston Churchill. Today Graycliff still operates as a fine inn and restaurant. The interior is furnished with early 20C pieces, including a Baccarat chandelier that graces the entrance hall. Outside, the cozy grounds abound in tropical foliage.

A half-block north on Cumberland Street stands **The Deanery** *(west side)*. Built at the turn of the 19C as a parsonage for Christ Church, this three-story stone building with its lattice timber gallery is considered the oldest extant residence in Nassau.

Cross Cumberland St. and walk briefly south; turn left (east) on Duke St.

Broad stone steps on the street's south side lead to Government House. A statue of **Christopher Columbus (1)**, situated about halfway up the staircase, looks out over the town.

Government House – *Corner of Blue Hill Rd. and Duke St. Not open for public tours.* The stately white-columned, pink mansion now crowning Mount Fitzwilliam was built in 1932, one in a succession of official residences of Governors General dating from the 1730s. In the 1940s the **Duke and Duchess of Windsor** occupied the building during the Duke's tenure as Governor General of the Bahamas. (The Duke had reigned briefly as Edward VIII before abdicating to marry American divorcee Wallis Simpson.) On alternate Saturdays, a public **Changing of the Guard** ceremony is held here, accompanied by music provided by the Royal Bahamas Police Force Band *(year-round, second Sat each month).* The Governor General also hosts a **public tea party** at Government House on the last Friday of every month *(Jan–Aug 4pm–5pm; reservations and proper attire required;* ☎ *242-326-5371).*

Continue east on Duke St. to the intersection with Market St.

Note the stone archway on the south end of the street. Known as **Gregory Arch**, it was built in the 1850s and served as an access point to Grant's Town, one of the traditionally black "over-the-hill" neighborhoods.

Turn left on Market St. and continue one block.

Small, aptly named **Balcony House** *(Market St. and Trinity Pl.; not open to the public)* is distinctive for its cantilevered balcony. Built of American cedar and over 200 years old, the house also features a staircase believed to have been part of a ship. Directly across Market Street, the **Central Bank of the Bahamas** devotes its public lobby area to changing exhibits of works by Bahamian and foreign artists.

Continue one block north on Market to King St. Turn left on King and walk west one block to George St.

Christ Church Cathedral – *George and King Sts. Open year-round Mon–Sat 7am–6pm, Sun 7am–7pm.* ⚹ ☎ *242-322-4186.* Established in 1670, Christ Church was the first Anglican church in the Bahamas. The current Gothic Revival edifice with its stone buttresses and timbered, trussed interior roof was constructed in 1840 and is the fifth church on the site; the two east bays were added subsequently. It was designated the cathedral of the diocese in 1861.

Turn right on George St. and walk one block north to Bay St.

The historical **British Colonial Beach Resort** now anchors the north end of East Bay Street, former site of Fort Nassau (1695-1899). At the turn of the century, railroad and hotel magnate Henry Flagler *(p 104)* built the spacious Hotel Colonial on this spot. When fire destroyed it in 1922, the government purchased the land and constructed a new hotel, later bought by Sir Harry Oakes *(p 311)* and renamed the British Colonial. Since 1988 the property has been part of the Best Western hotel chain.

Cross Bay St. to north side.

Pompey Museum – *Bay St., at George St. Open year-round Mon, Wed & Fri 10am–1pm & 2pm–4:30pm, Tue & Thu 10am–4:30pm, Sat 10am–1pm. Closed major holidays. $1.* ☎ *242-326-2566.* This museum devoted to the history and culture of the Bahamas occupies historic Vendue House, a well-proportioned two-story stone structure with arched bay windows. Built as a public market in the mid 18C, it served as the site of slave auctions. The current name, Pompey, derives from a rebel slave on the island of Exuma in the early 19C. Exhibits trace the hardships and brutality of slave life, and the coming of emancipation. A second-story gallery features a display of the **paintings★** of local folk artist **Amos Ferguson**. Videos on Ferguson and the history and cultural traditions of the Bahamas may be viewed on request.

Continue 1 block east on Bay St.

As you walk east on Bay Street, you'll pass numerous shops selling duty-free liquors, European crystals, gems, perfumes and other merchandise.

★Straw Market – *Bay St. across from Market St. Open year-round Mon–Sat 7am–6pm.* ⚹ ☎ *242-302-2049.* Famous throughout the Caribbean, Nassau's labyrinthine Straw Market consists of a warren of small stalls where vendors, most of them women by tradition, hawk a plethora of inexpensive straw goods, T-shirts, local wood carvings and other items designed to tempt tourists. Straw-plaiting and straw work have long been done by Bahamian women, particularly on the Out Islands. Haggling with the market's vendors over the price of goods is part of the fun here.

Walk through the market to its north, waterfront side.

Junkanoo Festival

Woodes Rogers Walk, named for the Bahamas first Royal Governor *(p 303)*, leads along the dock area to shady **Rawson Square**, which is flanked by more shops and the governmental Churchill Building. A bust of **Milo Butler (2)** (1906-1979), the first Governor General of the independent Bahamas (1973), stands at the south end of the square. Across from the north side of the square, an open-air plaza serves as the popular **hair-braiding center**, where Bahamian women negotiate with tourists to plait their hair into tiny braids, or cornrows. Behind lies the capacious dock area of **Prince George Wharf**. Large commercial cruise ships on tour through the Caribbean dock here—some only overnight—to allow their passengers to visit Nassau.

Walk north behind Rawson Square to Prince George Wharf.

★★Junkanoo Expo – *Entrance faces Prince George Wharf. Open year-round daily 9am–5pm. Closed major holidays. $2.* ☎ *242-356-2731.* This former customs warehouse displays the enormous, lavishly designed costumes that enliven the annual **Junkanoo** parades. A rich Afro-Bahamian mix of traditions, Nassau's famous Junkanoo celebration revolves around a night-long parade held on December 26 (Boxing Day in England) and again on New Year's Day. Tens of thousands of spectators gather to watch the revelry, which can be heard across the island. A handful of skilled craftsmen undertake the design and building of each major costume. Sculpted of cardboard and crepe paper, costumes are embellished with bright beads and sequins and often reflect cultural or political themes, sometimes even incorporating contemporary international personalities.

Winning costumes from each parade are added annually to the museum's collection and older pieces are retired. Some 30 elaborate costumes, including extra large and smaller ones, are on display. A video of past Junkanoo festivals adds the appropriate sounds and vitality to the exhibit hall.

Return to Rawson Square and cross to south side of Bay St.

Parliament Square – Governmental hub of the Bahamas, the square is centered around a **statue (3)** of a serenely young Queen Victoria. Three pink and white public buildings, built in the early 19C and modeled on the Tryon Palace in New Bern, North Carolina, flank the statue. The columned Southern Colonial structure in the middle serves as the **House of Assembly (A)**. Behind this edifice, more pink official buildings, including the stately, colonnaded **Supreme Court (B)** (1921), overlook the Garden of Remembrance, a palm-shaded greensward that commemorates Bahamians who lost their lives while fighting beside the British in World Wars I and II.

Walk south up Parliament St. and cross Shirley St.

Two gateposts on the east side of Parliament Street bear the insignia of the **Royal Victoria Hotel**, once the Bahamas' most fashionable hostelry. Built in the mid-19C, the elegant building played host to Confederate blockade runners and Prohibition-era rum-runners. Fire ravaged it in 1990 and Hurricane Andrew further devastated the ruins. Across Parliament Street, just below the intersection with East Hill Street, stands gracious **Villa Jacaranda** *(not open to the public)*, whose double galleries, shutters and stone exterior exemplify the Loyalist architectural tradition prevalent in Nassau in the mid-19C.

Walk one block north to Shirley St. and turn right (east).

The octagonal Nassau Public Library, on the south edge of Parliament Square *(corner of Parliament and Shirley Sts.)*, is topped by a third-floor wraparound gallery and belfry, whose bell once summoned members to openings of the House of Assembly. Originally constructed as a prison at the turn of the 18C, it became a public library in 1873 *(open year-round Mon–Thu 10am– 8pm, Fri 10am–5pm, Sat 10am–4pm;* ☎ *242-322-4907).*

From the library, continue east on Shirley St.

After passing the intersection *(left side)* of Millars Court, note the expansive lawn that sweeps upward to the mid-19C **Addington House**, formerly

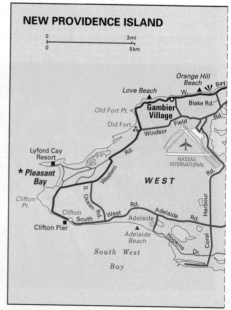

NEW PROVIDENCE ISLAND

0   3mi
0   5km

Orange Hill Beach
Love Beach
Old Fort Pt.
Gambier Village
Blake Rd.
Old Fort
Windsor
Field
NASSAU INTERNATIONAL
Lyford Cay Resort
Rd.
★ **Pleasant Bay**
Western
WEST
Rd.
Clifton Pt.
Clifton South
West
Ocean Rd.
Rd.
Adelaide
Adelaide
Rd.
Harbour
Clifton Pier
Adelaide Beach
Hopkins
Coral
Dr.
South West
Bay

the official residence of the Anglican Bishop of Nassau and the Bahamas.

Walk east on Shirley St. to the intersection with Elizabeth St. and turn left.

National Historical Museum/Bahamas Historical Society – *Northwest corner of Shirley and Elizabeth Sts. Open Sept–June Mon–Fri 10am–4pm, Sat 10am–noon. Closed major holidays. $1 www.bahamas. net.bs/history/bhs ☎ 242-322-4231.* Since 1976 this former hall of the Daughters of the Empire has been used by the Bahamas Historical Society to display Lucayan Indian stone tools, crockery and artifacts from the Loyalist period, old photographs and personal memorabilia.

Walk south one block up Elizabeth St.

Hewn into the rock of Bennet's Hill, the steep, 66-step **Queen's Staircase** occupies a surprisingly sylvan

Uniphoto Picture Agency

View of Fort Fincastle and Nassau Harbor

setting, next to a pleasant waterfall spilling over fern-draped rocks. The stairs were purportedly built by slaves in the 1790s to allow access to Fort Fincastle.

Fort Fincastle – *Located at the top of the Queen's Staircase. Open year-round daily 8am–5pm.* From its vantage atop the town's highest point (74ft), this small fort, shaped like a paddle wheeler, was built by Lord Dunmore in the 1790s. Though it never saw battle, the fort proved useful, serving as a lighthouse until 1817 and a signal beacon thereafter. Today the ramparts command a fine view of the waterfront and much of the island's interior.

The 126ft **Water Tower** adjacent to the fort was built in 1928 and is topped by a beacon light. No longer used as a water tower, it now houses an elevator that whisks visitors to an open-air observation deck with 360-degree **views**★ of the island's interior and its eastern shoreline *(50¢).*

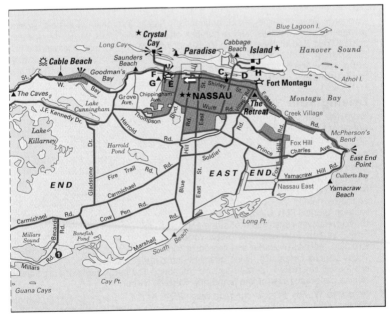

Additional Sights

St. Matthew's Anglican Church (C) – *Map p 309. Shirley St. west of Mackey St. Open year-round daily 9am–5pm.* & @ 242-323-8220. The oldest extant church structure (1802) in the Bahamas, the simple rectangular stone edifice with its Neo-classical detailing was originally referred to as the "eastern church," since it served parishioners on that side of town. A chancel, organ chamber and vestry room were added in 1887. The extensive cemetery surrounding the church contains headstones covering two centuries.

Potter's Cay (D) – *Map p 309. Just north of the intersection of E. Bay and Mackey Sts. Open year-round daily 7am–8pm.* & ▣. Located beneath the Paradise Island bridge, the stalls of this colorful marketplace feature an array of fresh fruits, vegetables and seafood. Island fishermen tie up at the dockside market to sell conch, lobster, grouper and other local specialties.

EAST END *2hrs. Map p 309.*

Threaded by Eastern Road and more densely populated than the West End, the island's East End is devoted to pleasant waterfront homes and the local community of Fox Hill, which holds its own festival, Fox Hill Day, every year on the first Tuesday of August. Rocky **Yamacraw Beach** curves below McPherson's Bend at the eastern tip of the island. The drive along Eastern Road skirts the shoreline framed by elegant homes and ends at **East End Point**, where a panoramic **view** encompasses cerulean waters and offshore cays.

Fort Montagu – *East end of E. Bay St. Interior not open to public. Grounds open year-round daily.* Commanding the east entrance to the harbor, the small stone battlement (1742) is the oldest extant fort on the island. It was the second fort to be constructed after Fort Nassau *(p 303)* and was intended to ward off possible attack by Spanish forces. A roadside beach on Montagu Bay stretches south from the fort.

The Retreat – *Village Rd., south of the intersection with Shirley St. and Eastern Rd. Open year-round Mon–Fri 9am–5pm. Closed holidays & week following Dec 25. $2.* ▣ *www.bahamas.net.bs/* @ 242-393-1317. This 11-acre botanical preserve is largely the work of Arthur and Margaret Langlois, who purchased the property in 1925. Finding that the land supported 11 kinds of palms, they set upon a 55-year endeavor of collecting other palm species worldwide and adding them to their gardens. Today the preserve features 92 genera of rare and exotic **palms★**, including species from Asia, Africa, Australia, and North and South America. Shaded paths also weave past such species as mahogany and cedar trees and orchids. In 1975 the Bahamas National Trust acquired the property; a modest but charming mid-19C Bahamian cottage on the grounds serves as the National Trust headquarters.

WEST END *1 day*

Two large lakes (Killarney and Cunningham), Nassau International Airport, several private resort complexes, and a number of commercial sites lie on the sparsely settled West End of New Providence Island. After West Bay Street leaves the historic district, it hugs the coastline along the West End, affording numerous **views** of the azure Atlantic. When the road reaches Clifton Point, it swings southeast and heads inland.

Driving Tour *3hrs. 16mi. Map pp 308-309.*

From the British Colonial Hotel, head west on W. Bay St. After .5mi take the unmarked road to the left at the sign for Bahamas Medical Arts Institute. Continue .3mi to the parking area for Fort Charlotte.

★**Fort Charlotte (E)** – *On Marcus Bethel Way. and West Bay St. behind Clifford Park. Open year-round daily 8am–4pm.* ▣ @ 242-325-9186. Built by Lord Dunmore between 1787 and 1796 during the American Loyalist period, the island's largest fortress complex actually comprises three forts: the original eastern portion, Fort Charlotte, named for George III's queen; the middle section, Fort Stanley; and the western works, Fort D'Arcy. Occupying a hill overlooking the town and harbor, the fortress was constructed of stone and armed with some 40 guns. "Dunmore's Folly," as Fort Charlotte was called, owing to the awesome expense of its construction, never saw battle and ceased to function in a military capacity in 1891. Today various casemates, living quarters and parapets are open to the public, as is a loosely re-created "pirate's torture chamber." The battlements of Fort Stanley offer a panoramic **view** of the island and western harbor.

Return to W. Bay St. and continue west .25mi to the entrance to Crystal Cay on right.

Angelfish

Susan Blanchet/Dembinsky Photo Assoc.

★ **Crystal Cay** – *1mi west of downtown Nassau. A .6mi access road leads across Arawak Cay (where local vendors sell conch shells, crafts, fish and produce) to the island's parking area; from here shuttle buses ferry visitors over the arcing, one-lane bridge to the island. Open Jan–Apr Mon–Sat 9am–5pm. Rest of the year Mon–Sat 9am–5:30pm. $16.* ✕ ♿ 🅿 ☎ *242-328-1036.* This commercial marine park covers the western side of 16-acre Crystal (formerly Silver) Cay. Its open-air and indoor wildlife tanks, set amid tropical vegetation, include a wraparound reef tank inhabited by local marine life; pools housing stingrays, sharks and turtles; and the Marine Garden aquarium, where wall cases contain bright tropical fish. The island's landmark tower allows you to descend below sea level to an **underwater observatory★**, where you can observe fish and other sea creatures on the surrounding coral reef. An observation deck atop the tower affords **views** toward Paradise Island and Cable Beach. Visitors can snorkel in the roped-off area near the tower *(equipment can be rented on-site).*

From Crystal Cay, turn right on W. Bay St. Take immediate left on Chippingham Ave. and continue .1mi. Parking lot on left.

Nassau Botanic Gardens (F) – *Chippingham Ave., just south of W. Bay St. Open year-round Mon–Fri 8am–4pm, weekends 9am–4pm. Closed major holidays. $1.* 🅿 ☎ *242-323-5975.* The wives of British colonial officials established this as a five-acre coronation garden honoring the crowning of George VI in 1937. Now owned by the government and encompassing 26 acres—12 of them in public gardens—the site features terraced beds, a sunken garden occupying a former rock quarry, and a lovely palm allée. Exotic tropical and subtropical species represent the southern Caribbean, India and Africa.

Continue .2mi south on Chippingham Ave. Turn right at sign for zoo.

Ardastra Gardens and Zoo (G) – *Off Chippingham Ave., just west of Botanic Gardens. Open year-round daily 9am–5pm. Closed Dec 25. $10.* ✕ ♿ ☎ *242-323-5806.* A 5.5-acre commercial animal park, Ardastra comprises a series of small cages set amid lush vegetation. Fifty-nine animal species are represented, including tropical birds, monkeys and reptiles. A troupe of some 30 marching Bahamian flamingos (the national bird) performs several times daily. The term Ardastra derives from the Latin *per ardua ad astra* ("through endeavor to the stars"), the name given the gardens by Hedley Edwards, a Jamaican horticulturist who began them as a private endeavor in 1937. The Latin phrase also serves as the motto of the Royal Air Force.

Return to W. Bay St., turn left and continue west .5 mi.

Following the curve of the shoreline, you will pass **Saunders Beach,** a narrow but popular roadside beach with views out to Crystal and Long Cays. After rounding Brown's Point, the road bends south along **Goodman's Bay,** another roadside beach. A sweeping view here scans the high rises of Cable Beach.

⌂ **Cable Beach** – Sometimes called the Bahamian Riviera, Cable Beach rises in a gleam of towering hotels and casinos that virtually wall off the beach itself. In 1892 a telegraph cable was laid between this point and JUPITER, Florida, providing the first such communication between the Bahamas and the North American mainland and giving the beach its name. Pineapples were cultivated along this stretch of the island until the 1920s, when Americans began building fine vacation homes here. Sir Harry Oakes, a Canadian entrepreneur, began developing Cable Beach as a major resort—complete with casino—

Cable Beach Resort

© Ping Amranand/Uniphoto Picture Agency

in the 1930s. The area remains a mix of tourist facilities along its eastern half and upscale private homes to the north. A lovely stand of casuarina trees overarches portions of the road through the residential section.

Continue west on W. Bay Street.

After crossing the Sandyport Bridge, the road returns to the water's edge. A private pink home hugging a point *(.8mi beyond the bridge)* is recognizable as one of the settings from the James Bond movie *Thunderball*. After .6mi, look to the left for **The Caves**, a limestone labyrinth once used by Lucayan Indians and now home to a colony of bats. Beyond this the road curves past long, narrow **Orange Hill Beach**. At the intersection of West Bay Street and Blake Road *(.2mi farther on)*, notice the *Ficus benjamina* tree in the intersection's grassy triangle. US President John Fitzgerald Kennedy planted the tree in 1962 in commemoration of his meeting on the island with the prime ministers of Canada and Britain.

Continue west 2mi past Blake Rd.

Gambier Village – This hamlet ranks as the oldest settlement on the island. Liberated Africans, freed from Caribbean slave ships by the Royal Navy, established Gambier Village as a farming community shortly after 1807. Recently it has become a tourist destination with the development of Compass Point, a resort identifiable by its small but vividly colored oceanfront cottages. Beyond Compass Point, the road passes the fine homes of **Love Beach** for 3.5mi before reaching the entrance gates to exclusive **Lyford Cay**, a private resort *(not open to the public)* frequented by such stars as Sean Connery, Sidney Poitier and Mick Jagger.

From Lyford Cay continue south 2.5mi. Turn right at turnoff for Pleasant Bay, marked by a sign for Atlantis Submarines.

★**Pleasant Bay** – A lovely crescent beach with easy public access edges the southern half of the small protected bay here, culminating in Clifton Point. The bay's northern half fronts the exclusive homes of Lyford Cay. The dock was used as a set in one of the *Jaws* movies and now serves as a starting point for submarine excursions to the offshore reef.

Return to the main road and continue south 1mi.

Freighters exporting rum from the nearby Bacardi Distillery and importing such commodities as gasoline dock at **Clifton Pier** at the western tip of the island.

① Bacardi Distillery

Map p 309. Southwest side of New Providence on Bacardi Rd. off Carmichael Rd. No public tours available. A major corporate hub for Bacardi & Co., Ltd., this plant occupies 40 acres and employs 130 people. Five rums, a vodka and a liqueur are produced here; about 95 percent of the total product is shipped to European markets via tankers that tie up at nearby Clifton Pier. A hospitality center located on the grounds offers visitors complimentary drinks and information on the company's history and facilities *(open year-round Mon–Thu 9:30am–4pm, Fri 9:30am–3pm; closed major holidays; ♿ ☏ 809-362-1412).*

PARADISE ISLAND★

Map p 309

Tourist Information ☎ 242-322-7500

Now a mega-resort complex, the 826-acre island (5.5mi long and .6mi at its widest) on the north side of Nassau Harbour was for centuries known as Hog Island—reportedly so-named by Nicholas Trott (p 303) after his father's estate in Hog Bay, Bermuda. Sand beaches lining the island's north shore have drawn crowds since the end of the 19C, when entrepreneurs operated public "bathing houses" here to serve beachgoers. Two casinos also were constructed during this period. Unlike the present-day Paradise Island casino, these early versions offered dining, dancing, billiards and bowling.

Historical Notes

Early in this century, wealthy Americans established a winter colony of vacation homes on the island, but its quiet tenor remained unchanged until 1959, when American grocery-store heir and philanthropist Huntington Hartford bought a large parcel of the island from Swedish financier Dr. Axel Wenner-Gren. Determined to develop its resort potential, Hartford successfully petitioned the government to change the name of the island to Paradise in 1962. He went on to open the small, exclusive Ocean Club hotel, a golf course and horse stables, and to complete the quarter-mile-long Versailles Gardens that Wenner-Gren had begun. Though Hartford's endeavors failed financially, they did succeed in establishing the tourist potential of Paradise Island.

In 1967 the current arcing bridge—1,500ft long and 70ft at its pinnacle—was built, connecting the island to Nassau. During the same period the large Paradise Island Hotel and Casino opened, as did the Yoga Retreat, a far different type of guest establishment constructed on land bequeathed to Swami Vishnu Devananda. In the following decade, a half-dozen major resort complexes sprang to life, including a Club Med on the western end of the island.

The recent history of Paradise Island, however, has been changeable. Paradise Island Resort and Casino, once owned by Merv Griffin's Resorts International, met with financial problems in the early 1990s. Sun International Investments, Ltd., a South Africa-based firm, purchased these properties in 1994 and opened an ambitious $250 million resort and casino called Atlantis, Paradise Island, in December of that year. In addition to Atlantis' 14-acre waterscape, Paradise Island offers a mix of hotels, pristine beaches and remnants of its past.

SIGHTS 1hr. Map p 309.

A water taxi ($2) runs year-round between the island and Nassau (times vary, depending on demand). The Paradise Island Bridge charges an incoming fee of 25¢/pedestrians and $2/rental cars and taxis.

The Cloisters (H) – *On Paradise Island Dr., east of Casino Dr. at Cloisters Dr. Open daily year-round.* An unlikely vision of medieval piety, the columned stone Cloisters crown a rise overlooking Nassau Harbour. The structure, once part of a c.14C Augustinian monastery in Montréjeau, France, was disassembled and shipped to Florida in the 1920s by newspaper magnate William Randolph Hearst. Huntington Hartford purchased the still-crated structure from Hearst and had it reassembled on this location in 1962. *Silence*, the marble statue in the Cloister's center, is the work of contemporary American sculptor Dick Reid.

Across Paradise Island Drive from the Cloisters, the seven-tiered gardens of Wenner-Gren's **Versailles (J)** lead down to a private swimming pool for guests at the elegant Ocean Club, refurbished in 1994 to reflect its 1960s style.

Paradise Island's north shore is rimmed with stunning white-sand **beaches**≙≙. While all beaches on the island are considered public below the low-water mark, access to many is difficult. **Cabbage Beach** *(between the Radisson Grand and Sunrise properties)* offers easy public access.

GRAND BAHAMA ISLAND

Population 40,898 (1990)

Map p 304

Tourist Information ☎ 242-352-6909 or 800-448-3386 (US)

The second most visited island in the Bahamas archipelago lies a mere 55mi east of Florida. Measuring 96mi long and 17mi at its widest, Grand Bahama is the fourth largest island in the chain. Its new towns of Freeport and Lucaya, established in the mid-20C, were specifically developed to attract tourists and commerce.

Historical Notes

A Free Port – Covered in pines for much of its history, Grand Bahama was first home to Lucayan Indians who inhabited the land prior to the Spanish arrival in the Caribbean. After their decimation, the island supported few inhabitants until the 1870s, when sponge fishermen settled here. During Prohibition the West End of the island became a major hub for rumrunners. That lucrative business ended with the repeal of Prohibition in the 1930s, and soon thereafter a blight destroyed Bahamian sponges.

A new boom began in 1944 when the Abaco Lumber Company relocated here, having exhausted the pine forests on Abaco Island. Four years later, **Wallace Groves**, an American entrepreneur living in the Bahamas, purchased the failing lumber company, modernized it and made it profitable. By the early 1950s the Abaco Lumber Company was one of the largest employers in the Bahamas, but Groves soon sold the lucrative business in order to pursue a grander scheme. In 1955 he entered into the **Hawksbill Agreement** with the Bahamian government, which allowed him to develop a free port on the island, where goods could be imported without heavy duty taxes being imposed. Grove's port initially attracted investors to the island, but the area's lack of amenities discouraged them.

Gambling on the Future – Persistent in his plan, Groves again approached the government. This time his Grand Bahama Port Authority was granted exclusive rights to license new businesses and develop the land. An impressive infrastructure for residential and resort areas was laid out, centering around the inland administrative area that was to become Freeport and the oceanside resort area of Lucaya. Though there was initial interest, particularly by Americans and Europeans, the island never developed as Groves had hoped. To bolster his failing investment, he applied for a gambling license and opened an impressive casino at the Lucayan Beach Hotel in 1963. Gambling rather than commerce became the lifeblood of the island.

Groves' infrastructure was developed to support half a million people, but only about 40,000 now live on Grand Bahama. The impressive network of roads, intended for residential areas, lead only into the pine barrens. Activity centers around a handful of resorts, two casinos and the shopping complexes of Freeport and Lucaya. A harbor on the island's southwest edge accommodates a host of cruise and cargo ships.

FREEPORT

Built as the administrative and commercial core of the island, the inland town of Freeport revolves around the business and governmental activities of **Churchill Square** *(intersection of E. Mall Dr. and Pioneers Way)*, the tourist activities at **International Square** *(intersection of W. Sunrise Hwy. and E. Mall Dr.)* and the extensive Bahamas Princess Resort and Casino complex that adjoins it. **Xanadu Beach**, adjacent to the Xanadu Hotel on the south shore of Freeport, offers a lovely stretch of white sand.

Along the island's west end, a string of small towns remains largely the domain of Bahamians, though the hamlet of West End itself, on the far tip of the island, holds a modest marina that attracts boaters and visitors.

Sights *1 day*

International Bazaar – *Intersection of W. Sunrise Hwy. and E. Mall Dr. Open year-round Mon–Sat 9:30am–5:30pm, Sun hours vary.* This maze of small shops, fronted by a landmark torii (a Japanese ceremonial gate), was designed by American special-effects artist Charles Perrin and completed in 1967. The architecture of the 90-some shops and eateries, as well as their themes and merchandise, reflect the motifs of 25 different countries. Peek behind the scenes at the Perfume Factory

Straw Market

(east rear of bazaar), where you can tour the facilities and mix your own personal fragrance *(open year-round Mon–Fri 10am–5:30pm; closed major holidays;* ☎ *242-352-9391)*; or watch jewelers at work at Paris in the Bahamas.

At a local **straw market** occupying a lot behind the bazaar, small stalls of vendors display T-shirts, African-inspired textile items and other souvenirs.

★**Rand Nature Centre** – *E. Settlers Way. Open year-round Mon–Fri 9am–4pm, Sat 9am–1pm. Closed Jan 1 & Dec 25. $5.* ▣ *www.bahamasnet.com/rand.html* ☎ *242-352-5438.* This 100-acre nature preserve was established in 1969 by Dorothy Rand in memory of her husband, James Henry Rand, an American inventor and founder of the Remington Rand Corporation. In the 1960s the Rands moved to the Bahamas, where Mr. Rand established a medical facility and was involved in philanthropic pursuits. Initially operated by Trustees of the Rand Corporation, the Nature Centre was given to the Bahamas National Trust in the early 1990s. A .4mi trail rambles through the Centre's varied native and introduced flora, with a rich display of orchids, pines and palms—and even a re-creation of a Lucayan village. At the trail's end a large pond provides habitat for flamingos, herons, egrets and other waterbirds.

LUCAYA AND EAST END

Comprising a small open-air mall of souvenir shops and restaurants overlooking Bell Channel Bay, **Port Lucaya** *(south end of Seahorse Rd.)* reigns as the center of activity here. Headquarters for the **Underwater Explorers Society** (UNEXSO), which runs commercial diving excursions, is located at the west end of the mall. Across Seahorse Road, several large hotels rise along popular **Lucayan Beach.** East of Port Lucaya, **Taino Beach**⚓ offers a quieter, less crowded beach experience (*from Port Lucaya, take Midshipman Rd. east to W. Beach Rd.).*
The virtually undeveloped 60mi stretch of island between Lucaya and McLean's Town on the far eastern tip is blessed with spectacular, deserted beaches along its southern edge. Grand Bahama Highway follows the coastline here, cutting through Lucayan National Park and through scrub pine forests that obstruct views of the ocean. The isolation of this area is broken only momentarily by the tiny hamlets of Free Town, High Rock, Pelican Point, Rocky Creek and, finally, McLean's Town.

Sights *1 day*

★★**Garden of the Groves** – *On Magellan Dr., northwest of the intersections of E. Sunrise Hwy. and Midshipman Rd. Open year-round Mon–Sat 9am–4pm, Sun 10am–4pm. Closed Dec 25. $7.95.* ✗ ⚹ ☎ *242-373-5668.* Georgette and Wallace Groves, Freeport's founders, developed this lovely, relaxing 12-acre botanical preserve in the early 1970s. Situated around a winding man-made lagoon, the site is landscaped with waterfalls, a hibiscus garden, a lush **fern gully**, a hanging garden of exotic potted plants, and walkways edged by crotons, firecracker, crown-of-thorn bushes and towering palms and citrus trees. A small, simple **chapel** overlooking the gardens replicates a Bahamian church that stood in the mid-century logging town of Pine Ridge.

★**Lucayan National Park** – *On Grand Bahama Hwy., 26mi east of Freeport. Open year-round daily 9am–4pm. $3* ▣ ☎ *242-352-5438.* Watered by Gold Rock Creek and straddling the Grand Bahama Highway, the diverse 42-acre tract is administered by the Bahamas National Trust. On the north side of the road, a park trail *(.3mi)* leads past two limestone caverns. The clear freshwater pool in **Ben's Cavern**★ supports a newly discovered centipede-like crustacean called *Speleonectes lucayensis*, and its ceiling serves as a summer nursery for migratory bats. In 1986 explorers found the skeletal remains of Lucayan Indians in **Burial Mound Cave**. Both grottoes are part of one of the most extensive underwater cave systems in the world.
On the south side of the park *(across the street from parking lot)*, a half-mile trail loops through a lush mangrove marsh, supporting a variety of birds, bromeliads and orchids, and leads to the oceanfront. Here the island's highest coastal dunes—13ft—are dotted by palms, casuarinas, sea grapes and other tropical vegetation. Beyond the dunes lies **Gold Rock Beach**⚓, named for the limestone formation that juts out of the sea offshore and takes on a golden hue at sunset.

The Dolphin Experience – *Departs from Underwater Explorers Society (UNEXSO) dock at Port Lucaya year-round daily 10am, 11:30am, 1pm & 2:30pm. Round-trip 2hrs. Commentary. Reservations required. $36.* ⚹ ▣ *www.dolphinexperience.com* ☎ *242-373-1250 or 800-992-3483 (US).* Participants take a 20min boat ride east along the coast to sheltered Sanctuary Bay, home of more than a dozen Atlantic bottlenose dolphins. After an introduction to dolphin behavior, guests are allowed to stand on a submerged platform and touch these docile marine mammals.

© Bill Wisser

Practical Information

Calendar of Events

Listed below is a selection of Florida's most popular annual events; some dates may vary from year to year. For detailed information, contact local tourism offices (numbers listed under individual entries) or VISIT FLORIDA ☎ 850-488-5607.

Date	Event/description	Location

Spring

Date	Event/description	Location
early Mar	**Marlboro Grand Prix** (auto racing)	Homestead
early Mar	**Carnaval Miami**	Miami
	Sanibel Shell Fair (shell exhibition, crafts)	Sanibel Island
	Bike Week	Daytona Beach
Mar–Apr	**Springtime Tallahassee** (festivals, parades, crafts)	Tallahassee
late Mar–Apr	**Festival of States** (parades, concerts, fireworks, crafts)	St. Petersburg
	Winter Equestrian Festival (equestrian competition)	Tampa
	Jazz Festival	Sarasota
	Bay Area Renaissance Festival	Largo
early Apr	**Bausch & Lomb WTA Championships** (tennis)	Amelia Island
Apr	**Seven-Mile Bridge Run**	Marathon
	Fun 'n Sun Festival (parades, concerts, crafts)	Clearwater
Apr–May	**SunFest**	West Palm Beach
May	**Florida Folk Festival**	White Springs
	Isle of Eight Flags Shrimp Festival	Fernandina Beach

Summer

Date	Event/description	Location
early June	**Billy Bowlegs Festival** ("Pirate invasion," treasure hunt)	Fort Walton Beach
	Goombay Festival	Coconut Grove
June	**Sarasota Music Festival**	Sarasota
	Fiesta of Five Flags (ethnic festival, street parades)	Pensacola
	Spanish Night Watch (music and pageantry of colonial times)	St. Augustine
July	**Hemingway Days**	Key West
late July–early Aug	**Florida International Festival** (music festival; held every other year)	Daytona Beach
Aug	**Shark's Tooth & Seafood Festival**	Venice

Fall

Date	Event/description	Location
Oct	**Clearwater Jazz Holiday**	Clearwater
mid-Oct	**Bicycle Festival**	Mount Dora
	Walt Disney World Oldsmobile Classic (golf tournament)	Orlando
late Oct	**Guavaween** (Latin-style Halloween)	Ybor City
	St. John's Seafood Festival	Madeira Beach
	Fantasy Fest (gay and lesbian festival)	Key West
early Nov	**Florida Seafood Festival**	Apalachicola
Nov	**Jacksonville Jazz Festival**	Jacksonville
	Florida Horse & Agricultural Festival	Tampa
	Micanopy Fall Festival (antique fair)	Micanopy

Winter

Date	Event/description	Location
Dec	**Winterfest Boat Parade**	Fort Lauderdale
late Dec	**King Mango Strut**	Coconut Grove
	Junkanoo	Nassau, Bahamas
	Indian Arts Festival, Miccosukee Indian Village	Everglades
Jan 1	**FedEx Orange Bowl** (college football)	Miami
	Gator Bowl (college football)	Jacksonville
	Outback Bowl (college football)	Tampa
	Florida Citrus Bowl (college football)	Orlando
Jan 6	**Festival of Epiphany**	Tarpon Springs
mid-Jan	**Art Deco Weekend** (street festival)	Miami Beach
	Winter Equestrian Festival (equestrian competition)	West Palm Beach

late Jan	**Rolex 24 Hours of Daytona** (sports car race) .... *Daytona Beach*
Feb	**Gasparilla Festival** (arts, sporting events, entertainment) .... *Tampa*
mid-Feb	**Florida State Fair** (livestock, rides, arts & crafts, entertainment) .... *Tampa*
	Miami International Boat Show .... *Miami*
	Daytona 500 (stock car race) .... *Daytona Beach*
late Feb	**Medieval Fair**, Ringling Museum of Art .... *Sarasota*
	Coconut Grove Arts Festival .... *Coconut Grove*
Feb–Mar	**Florida Strawberry Festival** .... *Plant City*

■ Consult individual entries for detailed practical information about the following areas and cities: Bahamas *(p 305)*, Everglades *(p 38)*, Fort Lauderdale *(p 188)*, Jacksonville *(pp 91)*, Keys *(pp 48-49)*, Key West *(p 58)*, Kennedy Space Center *(pp 264-265)*, Miami *(pp 198-199)*, Orlando *(p 124)*, Pensacola *(pp 163)*, Sanibel & Captiva Islands *(pp 251)*, Sarasota *(p 255)*, St. Augustine *(p 105)*, Tallahassee *(p 170)*, Tampa *(pp 281)* and Walt Disney World *(pp 135-136)*.

Planning Your Trip

Tourist Information – To request the *Florida Vacation Guide* (published annually) or a state map, contact VISIT FLORIDA, P.O. Box 1100, Tallahassee FL 32302 ☎ 850-488-5607 or 888-735-2872. Local tourist offices (telephone numbers listed under each entry) provide additional information free of charge regarding accommodations, shopping, entertainment, festivals and recreation. *Florida On the Go* books, giving information on lodging, attractions and shopping, and containing money-saving coupons, are distributed by many businesses and hotels.

Health Insurance – Before departing, check with your insurance company to ascertain if your medical insurance covers doctors' visits, medication and hospitalization while traveling. Prescription drugs should be properly identified and accompanied by a copy of the prescription. Companies offering travel insurance: Access America ☎ 800-284-8300; TravelEx ☎ 800-228-9792; The Travelers ☎ 800-243-3174. Physician referrals from a nationwide network are offered by HotelDocs (24hrs/day) ☎ 800-468-3537.

Disabled Travelers – *Wheelchair access to sights described in this guide is indicated in admission information by* &. Federal law requires that businesses provide access for the disabled, devices for the hearing impaired, and designated parking spaces. Many public buses are equipped with wheelchair lifts; many hotels have rooms designed for visitors with special needs. For information on support groups, consult the *Planning Guide for Travelers with Disabilities* published by the Office of the Physically Challenged, Governor's Office, Tallahassee FL 32399-0001 ☎ 850-488-4441.

Amtrak publishes a handy book, *Access Amtrak*. Passengers who will need assistance should give 24hr advance notice. Information ☎ 800-872-7245 and 800-523-6590 (TDD). Disabled riders are encouraged to notify Greyhound/Trailways 48hrs in advance by calling ☎ 800-752-4841 and 800-345-3109 (TDD). *Greyhound Travel Policies* is published annually for clients who require special assistance. Reservations for hand-controlled cars at rental companies should be made well in advance. For information about travel for individuals or groups, contact the Society for the Advancement of Travel for the Handicapped, 347 5th Ave., Suite 610, New York NY 10016 ☎ 212-447-7284.

Senior Citizens – Many hotels, attractions and restaurants offer discounts to visitors age 62 or older (proof of age may be required). For further information contact the American Association of Retired Persons (AARP), 601 E St. N.W., Washington, DC 20049 ☎ 202-434-2277.

When to go

In the Sunshine State most sights and attractions are open year-round, although peak seasons vary by region. High season in south Florida is during the winter (Oct–Apr) when many visitors escape colder climates. Daytime winter temperatures average 70°F/21°C, while in the Everglades and Keys daytime temperatures reach 73°F/23°C. North and central Florida enjoy the traditional four seasons: spring 67°F/20°C; summer 83°F/28°C; fall 69°F/20°C; and winter 55°F/13°C. January is usually the coldest month. Winter, when mosquitoes are tolerable and migratory birds are plentiful, is the best time to view wildlife in parks and reserves. Insect repellent is recommended year-round.

Although **summer** months are hot and humid throughout the state, sea breezes moderate temperatures along the coasts. Daytime temperatures average 88°F/31°C and do not vary much between the northern and southern regions. Daily afternoon showers are common between June and September.

Pleasant water temperatures foster swimming and other water sports year-round. Beaches are most crowded during school holidays, spring breaks and summer vacation periods. Reduced admissions to sights are generally available for senior citizens, students and children under 12.

Casual dress is accepted in most facilities. Better restaurants may request that men wear jackets, but rarely is a tie required. A hat will come in handy while standing in line, especially during the summer heat. Always protect yourself and wear a good sunscreen, even on a cloudy day. And don't forget to bring your sunglasses.

January	April	July	October
54°F/12°C	69°F/21°C	82°F/28°C	70°F/22°C
55°F/14°C	70°F/21°C	82°F/28°C	71°F/22°C
53°F/12°C	69°F/20°C	82°F/28°C	70°F/21°C
69°F/21°C	78°F/26°C	84°F/29°C	80°F/27°C
68°F/21°C	76°F/24°C	83°F/29°C	78°F/26°C
65°F/19°C	73°F/23°C	82°F/28°C	77°F/25°C
61°F/16°C	72°F/22°C	83°F/29°C	74°F/23°C
51°F/11°C	68°F/20°C	83°F/29°C	69°F/21°C
60°F/16°C	72°F/22°C	83°F/29°C	75°F/24°C
51°F/10°C	68°F/20°C	82°F/28°C	68°F/20°C
60°F/16°C	68°F/20°C	83°F/28°C	74°F/23°C

International Visitors

PLANNING THE TRIP

Visitors from outside the US can obtain information from VISIT FLORIDA *(p 7)*, which maintains offices in the countries listed below, or from the US embassy or consulate in their country of residence.

Florida Tourist Offices: ☎

Brazil	Alameda Ribeirao Preto 130, Sao Paulo SP 01414-901	11/283-4741
Canada	121 Bloor St. East, Suite 1003, Toronto ON M4W 3M5	416-928-3139
Germany	Schiller Str. 10, 60313 Frankfurt/Main 1	69/131-0091
Japan	204 Belvedere Kudan Bldg, Fujimi, Chiyoda-ku, Tokyo 102	3-5276-0260
United Kingdom	Roebuck House, Palace St., London SW1E 5BA	171-630-6602

Many foreign countries have consular offices in Miami *(for phone numbers, check the yellow pages of the telephone directory under Consulates).*

Entry Requirements – Citizens of countries participating in the Visa Waiver Pilot Program (VWPP) are not required to obtain a visa to enter the US for visits of less than 90 days. For a list of countries participating in VWPP, contact the US embassy or consulate in your country of residence. Citizens of non-participating countries must obtain a visa. Upon entry, non-resident foreign visitors must present a valid passport and round-trip transportation ticket. Canadian citizens are not required to present a passport, although identification and proof of citizenship may be requested (the best proof of citizenship is a passport, but a Canadian birth certificate and photo ID are usually acceptable). Inoculations are generally not required (contingent upon country of residence and countries recently visited). Check with the US embassy or consulate about entry regulations before traveling.

US Customs – Articles brought into the US must be declared at time of entry. Prohibited items: plant material, firearms and ammunition (if not intended for sporting purposes), meat or poultry products. For information about US Customs, contact the US embassy or consulate before departing. Visitors should also contact their country's customs service to determine reentry regulations.

Getting Around by Car – Foreign visitors are not required to obtain an International Driver's License to drive in the US. A valid license issued by the country of residence is sufficient. Rental cars *(p 323)* are usually equipped with automatic transmission. Rental rates are more economical when made before entering the US. Gasoline is sold by the gallon (1 gallon = 3.8 liters) and is less costly than in other countries. Road regulations in the US require that vehicles be driven on the right side of the road. Distances are posted in miles (1mi = 1.6km).

BASIC INFORMATION

Currency Exchange, Credit Cards & Travelers Checks – *p 326*. Some statewide banks (Barnett, First Union and SunTrust) exchange foreign currency at local offices. Most banks charge a fee for this service. Thomas Cook has exchange offices throughout Florida ☎ 800-287-7362. Most banks are members of the network of Automated Teller Machines (ATM). ATMs are located at airports, banks, train stations and some tourist attractions. Check with your bank before departing to obtain a Personal Identification Number (PIN); transaction fees may be charged to your account. Travelers checks are accepted at all commercial banks, in hotels, restaurants, stores and most theme parks.

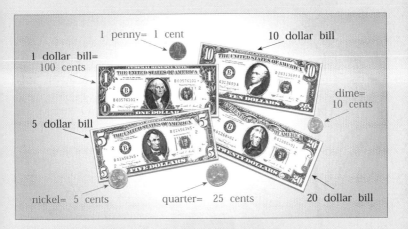

Electricity – Voltage in the US is 120 volts AC, 60 Hz. Foreign-made appliances may need AC adapters (available at specialty travel and electronics stores) and North American flat-blade plugs.

Emergencies – In all major US cities you can telephone the police, ambulance or fire service by dialing **911**. Another way to report an emergency is to dial **0** for operator.

Telephones/Telegrams – *p 327*. Instructions for using **public telephones** are listed on or near the telephone. A local call from a pay phone typically costs 25¢-35¢. Long-distance calling cards can be used at all public phones. To call other area codes, dial 1+area code+number. International calls: 011+country code+area code+number. Telephone numbers preceded by **800** or **888** are toll-free (no charge). Most hotels add a surcharge for local and long-distance calls. For further information dial "0" for operator assistance. Sending telegrams, cablegrams and wiring international currency and money orders are handled through Western Union (☎ 800-325-6000) and local International Telephone & Telegraph (ITT) offices.

Temperature and Measurement – In the US temperatures are measured in degrees Fahrenheit and measurements are expressed according to the US Customary System of weights and measures.

Equivalents

Degrees Fahrenheit	95°	86°	77°	68°	59°	50°	41°	32°	23°	14°
Degrees Celsius	35°	30°	25°	20°	15°	10°	5°	0°	-5°	-10°

1 inch = 2.54 centimeters	1 pound = 0.454 kilogram
1 mile = 1.609 kilometers	1 gallon = 3.785 liters
1 foot = 30.48 centimeters	1 quart = 0.946 liter

Time Zones – Most of Florida is on Eastern Standard Time (EST), 5hrs behind Greenwich Mean Time (GMT). The Panhandle region west of the Apalachicola River adheres to Central Standard Time (CST), 1hr behind EST. Daylight Saving Time (clocks are advanced 1hr) is in effect for most of the US from the first Sunday in April until the last Sunday in October.

For insight into Florida's history, economy, architecture and art,
consult the introduction chapter.

Getting There & Getting Around

Distances in Florida are relatively short; it only takes a couple of hours to travel between the east and west coasts (except in the northern part of the state). Even the stretch from the Panhandle to Miami can be driven in one day. Many towns are serviced by Amtrak. In some areas links are maintained with bus connections. Some of the more remote communities, especially along beaches, can only be reached by car.

By Air – Most US airlines offer direct and non-stop flights to Florida. For flight information, contact the airline directly. Nine major international airports—the largest are

Orlando/Orange County CVB

Miami, Orlando and Tampa International—offer service between Florida and Europe, Central and South America and the Caribbean. Smaller regional airports are usually accessible through commuter carriers.

Airports offer a variety of ground transportation: limousines, shuttle vans, taxis, public transportation and hotel courtesy shuttles. Some of these services (limousines and shuttles) require advance reservations.

By Train – The Amtrak rail network offers a variety of travel packages that combine rail, air and bus. Advance reservations are recommended to ensure lower fares—including non-refundable tickets—and availability of desired accommodations. Passengers can choose from first-class, coach and sleeping cars. On some routes, bi-level Superliner cars with glass ceilings allow a panoramic view. Smoking is not permitted on most trains. Information for passengers who require special assistance. *(p 319)*. Travelers from Canada should inquire with local travel agents regarding Amtrak/VIARail connections. **Explore America Pass** allows travel over any distance during 45 days (limited to three stops). **USA RailPass** (not available to US or Canadian citizens or legal residents) offers unlimited travel within Amtrak designated regions at discounted rates; 15- and 30-day passes available. Daily service is provided on the *Silver Star* (New York–Jacksonville–Miami), *Silver Palm* (New York–Tampa–Miami) and *Silver Meteor* (New York–Jacksonville–Miami). The *Sunset Limited* (Orlando–Los Angeles) makes the transcontinental trip three times weekly *(Tue, Thu & Sat; one-way $279/coach)*.

The **Auto Train** offers a relaxing alternative featuring first-class sleeping accommodations, a full-service restaurant, a glass-topped Sightseer Lounge and even a movie presentation—all included in the ticket price *(leaves Lorton, Virginia daily 4:30pm; arrives Sanford, Florida 9am)*. Only passengers with automobiles are permitted on the train. No cars accepted after 3:30pm. Check restrictions when making reservations. Amtrak and United Airlines offer a package allowing passengers to travel one way by train, and the other way by plane with three stops along the way. Air-Rail travel is also available from some points in Canada. For information: ☎ 800-321-8684.

Amtrak **Thruway Bus** Connections provide a link to motor coach service. Tickets must be purchased at Amtrak stations, travel agencies or by mail before boarding buses. For schedule and route information: ☎ 800-872-7245 (US only).

By Bus – Greyhound/Trailways offers access to most cities in Florida at a leisurely pace. Overall, bus fares are lower than other forms of transportation. **Ameripass** allows unlimited travel for 7, 15, 30 or 60 days. Advance reservations suggested. Information for disabled riders, *(p 319)*. Schedule and route information: ☎ 800-231-2222 (US only). Most communities have a Greyhound/Trailways bus station; in small towns the local post office or gas station often doubles as a stop. In the Keys along the Overseas Highway the bus stops at designated flag stops.

By Car – Florida has an extensive system of well-maintained major roads, some of which are designated limited-access highways that require a toll *(average toll 6¢/mi)*. Four major interstates traverse Florida: I-10 runs from Jacksonville to Pensacola; I-4 links Daytona

Beach and Tampa; I-75 cuts southwest across the state from Georgia; and I-95 travels the length of Florida's east coast, ending at Miami. Welcome centers that greet visitors with samples of free citrus juice are located on three of the interstates. Some centers are equipped with computer kiosks where you can access tourist information at the touch of a screen. Many rest areas offer picnic tables; most are open 24 hours and are patrolled by security officers at night. Watch for wildlife on roads in remote areas. Along highways and major urban thoroughfares, many gas stations stay open 24 hours. Most self-service gas stations do not offer car repair, although many sell standard maintenance items. Write for free maps to the convention & visitors bureaus of your destination or to VISIT FLORIDA (p 7). The **Florida Turnpike** (a toll road) branches off I-75 northwest of Orlando and slants southeastward across the state until it ends below Miami in Florida City ($14 for entire distance). Toll booths are manned, but for quick travel motorists should carry correct change. Call boxes placed at mile intervals allow travelers to phone for help. For further information: ☎ 800-749-7453.

Motoring Safety Tips:

- Do not stop if strangers try to flag your car down.
- Ask the concierge or hotel clerk what parts of the city should be avoided.
- If you carry a cellular phone, dial *FHP for the Florida Highway Patrol.
- Don't stop if your car is bumped from the rear; instead proceed to the nearest well-lit public area and contact the police.

Rental Cars — Most large rental companies have offices at major airports and downtown locations. Packages may offer unlimited mileage and discounted prices. If a vehicle is returned at a different location from where it was rented, drop-off charges may be incurred. Reservations are accepted through a toll-free service with a major credit card. Minimum age for rental is 21. A surcharge ($2.05/day) for persons up to age 25 is applied to all rentals in Florida. Be sure to check for proper insurance coverage, offered at extra charge. Liability is not automatically included in the terms of the lease. Aside from the national rental agencies listed below, there are local companies that offer reasonable rentals. See yellow pages of local directories for phone numbers.

Alamo	☎ 800-327-9633	Avis	☎ 800-331-1212
Budget	☎ 800-527-0700	Dollar	☎ 800-421-6868
Hertz	☎ 800-654-3131	Enterprise	☎ 800-325-8007
National	☎ 800-227-7368	Thrifty	☎ 800-331-4200

Recreational Vehicle (RV) Rentals — One-way motor-home rentals are offered from several locations in Florida. Some models accommodate up to eight people, and service can include free mileage and airport transfers. Make reservations 2-3 weeks in advance. In the summer months (Jun–Aug) and during holiday seasons, reservations should be made at least 4-6 weeks in advance. Cruise America RV Depot ☎ 602-464-7300 or 800-327-7778; Camptown RV Country, Homestead ☎ 305-258-1783.

Road Regulations and Insurance — The maximum speed limit on interstate highways is 70mph, 55mph on state highways, unless otherwise posted. Speed limits are generally 35mph within city limits, and average 25mph in residential areas. Right turns on red are allowed after coming to a complete stop, unless otherwise indicated. Florida law requires that headlights must be turned on when driving in fog and rain. Seat belts must be worn by driver and front-seat passengers. Children under 6 must ride in child safety seats (seats are offered by most car-rental agencies; indicate such a need when making reservations). The law requires motorists in both directions to bring their vehicles to a full stop when the warning signals on a school bus are activated. Parking spaces identified by ♿ are reserved for handicapped persons only. Anyone parking in these spaces without proper identification will be ticketed and/or their vehicle will be towed. Drivers are required to have personal injury protection and property liability insurance. Carry proof of insurance in the vehicle at all times. Apart from local authorities, motor clubs (membership required) offer road assistance: **American Automobile Association (AAA)** ☎ 800-222-4357; **Mobil Auto Club** ☎ 800-621-5581; **Shell Motorist Club** ☎ 800-852-0555.

In Case of Accident — If you are involved in an accident resulting in personal or property damage, you must notify the local police and remain at the scene until dismissed. If blocking traffic, vehicles should be moved as soon as possible.

Accommodations

Florida offers accommodations suited to every taste and pocketbook. Choose large hotels in major cities, luxury resorts along the coastlines and on secluded islands or roadside motels and hostels. Grand South Florida hotels like The Breakers *(p 229)*, The Biltmore *(p 206)* or the Boca Raton Resort and Club *(p 183)* have been lavishly restored and afford the visitor luxuries of a bygone era. Bed-and-breakfasts (B&Bs) are usually located in historic houses or private homes. Oceanfront condominiums and houses for relaxed family vacations can be rented by contacting individual resorts or local property management agencies. Campsites and RV parks offering pools, recreational facilities, tennis or golf are plentiful. Although Florida's weather permits visiting year-round, rates are lower in off-season: South Florida, popular in winter, offers lower rates from May to October; in the Panhandle and northern coastal areas, prices are lowest from December to February, with "shoulder" seasons in spring and fall. In most hotels children under 18 stay free when sharing a room with their parents. Many small hotel and motel rooms include efficiency kitchens. Almost all accommodations are air-conditioned. Typical amenities at hotels and motels include television, smoking/non-smoking rooms, restaurants and swimming pools. The more elegant hotels and resorts may also offer entertainment, gourmet dining, health clubs, private golf courses and tennis clubs. Hotel taxes and gratuities, which vary according to location, range from 6-15% and are not included in rates quoted. Contact the local tourist office to request free brochures that give details about accommodations. The Florida Hotel & Motel Association publishes the *Florida Accommodations Directory*, available from VISIT FLORIDA *(p 7)*. State-wide hotel **reservation service**: ☎ 800-847-4835.

© The Walt Disney Company

Disney's All Star Music Resort

Hotels/Motels – Most major hotel chains have properties throughout Florida *(for toll-free numbers check local phone directories)*. Accommodations range from luxury hotels ($200 and up) and superior hotels ($80–$200) to moderate motels ($50–$80). Rates vary greatly according to season and location and tend to be higher during holiday and peak seasons. Many hotels and motels offer packages, which can include meals, passes to local attractions, organized trips and theme and weekend specials. Advance reservations are recommended. Always advise the reservations clerk of late arrival; unless confirmed with a credit card, rooms may not be held after 5pm.

Bed-and-Breakfasts and Country Inns – Most B&Bs are privately owned and many are located in historic structures in residential sections of a city or in small towns and rural areas. Amenities include complimentary breakfast ranging from continental fare to a gourmet repast; some offer afternoon tea and the use of sitting rooms or garden areas where hosts and guests mingle. Most establishments are small and offer fewer than 10 rooms. Private baths are not always available, and often there is no phone in individual rooms. Smoking indoors may not be allowed. Reservations should be made well in advance, especially during holiday seasons; be sure to ask about minimum stay, cancellation and refund policies. Most establishments accept major credit cards. Rates vary seasonally but range from $55 in low season to $250 in high season for a double room per night. Rates may be higher when amenities such as hot tubs, private entrances and ocean views are offered.

Inn Route .... 281-499-1374 or 800-524-1880
PO Box 6187, Palm Harbor FL 34684 www.florida-inns.com
Bed & Breakfast Co. 305-661-3270
1205 Mariposa Ave. #233, Miami FL 33146

Resorts & Spas – Modern spas offer a variety of programs, from fitness, beauty and wellness, to weight management and stress relief, to relaxation and adventure vacations. Guests are pampered with European mud baths, daily massages, state-of-the-art fitness and exercise programs, cooking classes and nutritional counseling. Spas offer luxurious facilities in beautiful settings that can include championship golf courses, equestrian centers and even formal Italian gardens. Most offer packages for stays ranging from 2 to 10 nights, which include health and fitness programs, golf and tennis as well as relaxation and image enhancement. Most facilities have age restrictions. Most spas are informal, but check when making your reservations.
Prices range from $800/week in summer to $3,500/week during the winter season depending on choice of program (price per person, double occupancy). All meals, including special diets, use of facilities, tax, gratuities and airport transportation are usually included. Spa Finders, 91 Fifth Avenue, New York NY 10003. **Reservation service:** ☎ 800-255-7727.

Condominiums – Furnished apartments or houses are more cost-effective than hotels for families with children. Amenities include separate living quarters, fully equipped kitchen with dining area, several bedrooms and bathrooms, and laundry facilities. Most condos provide televisions, basic linens and maid service. Depending on location, properties often include sports and recreational facilities, patios and beach access. Most require a minimum stay of three nights or one week, especially during peak season. When making reservations, ask about cancellation penalties and refund policies. Chambers of commerce and convention and visitors bureaus have listings of local property management agencies that can assist with the selection. A variety of private accommodations can be arranged through Condo & Villa Authority, 305 N. Pontiac Trail, Walled Lake MI 48390 ☎ 800-831-5512 (US & Canada). For single-family vacation homes in Naples and the Orlando area, contact Florida Choice Vacation Home Rentals Inc. ☎ 800-847-2731 (US & Canada).

Hostels – Simple budget accommodations are offered at hostels in Clearwater Beach, Key West (p 58), Miami Beach (p 198), Kissimmee (p 124) and Melbourne Beach. Dormitory-style rooms average $14-$17/night for members; non-members pay an additional $3/night. Private rooms are available at additional charge; amenities include swimming pool (Kissimmee), air-conditioning, common living room, laundry facilities, self-service kitchen and dining room. Blankets and pillows are provided; linens can be rented. Reservations are suggested. The Kissimmee hostel offers a City Stay package starting at $58 (3 days/2 nights), which includes prepaid accommodation vouchers, breakfast and round-trip transportation to one area attraction. All hostels accept credit cards. **Hostelling International**, 733 15th St. N.W., Suite 840, Washington, DC 20005, www.hiayh.org. ☎ 202-783-6161. Reservations: ☎ 800-909-4776.

Camping – Campsites are located in national parks, state parks, national forests, along beaches and in private campgrounds. Many camping facilities are located in central Florida near theme park attractions. Most offer full utility hookups, lodges or cabins and recreational facilities. Florida's many rivers and lakes allow boat camping and usually include mooring facilities and marinas. Primitive camping is for the experienced camper only. Because there is a large population of unpleasant creatures in Florida (p 328), plan to sleep well-protected in the outdoors. Make sure your tent is waterproof; sudden thunderstorms can soak through quickly. Advance reservations are recommended, especially during holidays and school vacations.
A variety of camping facilities, from full-facility camping to cabins, resort lodges, boat camping and primitive camping, await the outdoor enthusiast in Florida's national and state parks. Some facilities are available on a first-come, first-served basis, while others require advance reservations; permits are required for certain campsites. Reservations for campsites are accepted up to 60 days in advance, cabin rentals up to one year in advance. Rates vary according to season and facilities: cabins ($20–$110/day), campsites ($8–$21). For reservations (Mon–Fri 8am–5pm) contact the park directly. For a free brochure listing all state park facilities, contact: Florida Department of Environmental Protection, Division of Recreation & Parks (p 7).

Campgrounds and Recreational Vehicle (RV) Parks – The Florida Association of RV Parks & Campgrounds publishes the annual *Florida Camping Directory*, which lists member sites and gives addresses and details on hookups, laundry facilities, pools, playgrounds, sporting facilities, freeway access and shopping. Parks are family oriented and open year-round. Most campgrounds offer daily, weekly or monthly occupancy for recreational vehicles. Prices range from $10-$60 for campsites and average $20-$25/night for RV. Reservations are recommended, especially for longer stays and in popular resort areas, including the Keys. For a free copy of the directory: 1340 Vickers

Dr., Tallahassee FL 32303-3041, www.floridacamping.com ☎ 850-562-7151. KOA Kampgrounds are located all across Florida; some resort properties offer pools, hot tubs, air-conditioned cabins, restaurants, boat ramps, deep-sea fishing and snorkeling. For a directory *(include $3 for shipping)*, write to KOA Kampgrounds, PO Box 30558, Billings MT 59114, www.koakampgrounds.com ☎ 406-248-7444.

General Information

Business Hours – In general, most businesses operate Monday–Friday 9am–5pm. Banking institutions are normally open Monday–Thursday 9am–4:30pm, Friday until 5pm or 6pm. Some banks may be open on Saturday morning. Most retail stores and specialty shops are open Monday–Saturday 10am–6pm (Thursday 9pm). Malls and shopping centers are usually open Monday–Saturday 10am–9pm, Sunday 10am–6pm.

Credit Cards – Automated Teller Machines (ATM) allow cash withdrawals using bankcards and major credit cards 24 hours a day. To inquire about ATM service and location in any city call: Cirrus ☎ 800-424-7787; Plus System ☎ 800-843-7587. To report a lost or stolen credit card, call: American Express ☎ 800-528-4800; Diners Club ☎ 800-234-6377; MasterCard ☎ 800-627-8372; Visa ☎ 800-336-8472; or your bank. Banks and almost all stores accept travelers checks with proper identification.

Liquor Laws – The legal drinking age is 21. Proof of age may be required. Most restaurants/bars do not serve liquor prior to 1pm on Sunday. Liquor is sold in liquor stores only, while beer and wine is available at grocery stores. Consuming liquor in public places and carrying an open liquor container in a moving vehicle is illegal.

Mail – First-class postage rates within the US: letter 32¢ (1oz), postcard 20¢. Overseas: letter 60¢ (.5oz), postcard 50¢. Most post offices are open Monday–Friday 9am–5pm, some are open Saturday 9am–noon. Establishments such as Mail Boxes Etc., *PAKMAIL* and Mail Express USA handle regular and overnight mail, packages, and offer fax and copy services *(see yellow pages of phone directory under Mailing Services)*.

Major Holidays – Banks and government offices are closed on the following legal holidays *(* many retail stores and restaurants remain open on these days)*:

January 1	**New Year's Day**
3rd Monday in January	**Martin Luther King, Jr.'s Birthday***
3rd Monday in February	**Presidents' Day***
Last Monday in May	**Memorial Day***
July 4	**Independence Day**
1st Monday in September	**Labor Day***
2nd Monday in October	**Columbus Day***
November 11	**Veterans Day***
4th Thursday in November	**Thanksgiving Day**
December 25	**Christmas Day**

Taxes and Tips – In Florida the sales tax is 6%. Some counties levy an additional local sales tax, and/or a 1-4% tourist tax. The hotel occupancy tax (p 324) and tax rate for rental cars (p 323) vary according to location. It is customary in restaurants to tip the server 15-20% of the bill. At hotels, porters should be given $1 per suitcase; maids $1 per day. Taxi drivers are usually tipped 15% of the fare.

Telephones/Telegrams – Public telephones are located in many public places, hotel lobbies, convenience stores and along major highways. **Emergencies** (police, fire, ambulance): dial 911. The cost of a local call from a pay phone is typically 25¢-35¢. Most hotels add a surcharge on all calls made from the hotel room. All public phones will accept long-distance calling cards. For area codes of major cities, consult the front pages of the local phone directory, or dial "0" for directory assistance. Unless otherwise indicated, telephone numbers listed in this guide that start with "800" or "888" are toll-free. Telegrams, cablegrams and money orders are handled through Western Union ☎ 800-325-6000.

Shopping

Florida is a shopper's paradise where the sophisticated, practical and curious shopper can indulge. Downtown areas in cities tempt travelers and residents alike with department stores, specialty shops, antique shops, galleries, restaurants and theaters. Worth Avenue (p 233) in Palm Beach attracts the most elegant patrons with its high-fashion boutiques and trendy art galleries set amid lush landscaping. Shops at Bal Harbour and Streets of Mayfair (p 212), Miami; St. Armands Circle (p 259), Sarasota; Galleria, Fort Lauderdale; and Park Avenue (p 152), Winter Park, all dazzle the most discriminating clientele.

Shopping venues such as large malls, flea markets and theme-park villages all await the adventurous buyer. Bargains galore (reductions up to 75%) can be found in **outlet malls**—Sawgrass Mills (over 200 stores), Fort Lauderdale; Belz Factory Outlet (150 stores), Orlando; and Bay Area Outlet Mall (70 stores), Clearwater—to name just a few. Most stores are reluctant to accept out-of-town checks.

Native American crafts such as hand-crafted dolls and beaded belts are sold at the Miccosukee and Seminole reservations in the Everglades (p 37). **Seashells** are offered in many souvenir shops, especially on Sanibel Island and along the Southwest Coast, where the best seashells can be found. The Shell Factory (p 246) near Fort Myers boasts the largest commercial assortment of shells. Natural sponges from the Gulf of Mexico can be selected at the waterfront in Tarpon Springs (p 290). Many of the local bait and tackle shops are a good source for sporting and fishing equipment. In historic Ybor City (p 285) near Tampa, fine hand-rolled cigars make a prized gift for the connoisseur. And don't overlook Downtown Disney Marketplace (p 143), which offers merchandise from around the world.

Agriculture is big business in the Sunshine State and farmers everywhere offer the fruits of their labor at local markets. Visit these **farmers' markets**, held most Saturday mornings in small towns and large city neighborhoods, to shop for produce, fresh fish, and flowers grown in nearby nurseries. Take some of Florida's sunshine with you and buy **citrus fruits**. Many growers have roadside stands and welcome travelers to the orange groves that line many roads. Fruit can be shipped anywhere in the continental US. Inquire about shipping costs; they can run higher than the merchandise.

Antique Shopping – A unique selection of antique shops can be found in north and central Florida. Micanopy (p 79) features a collection of antique shops clustered along Cholokka Blvd., as well as Smiley's Antique Mall. The hamlets of Havana and Quincy near Tallahassee are known for their small-town charm and abundance of antiques, art galleries and collectible shops. An assemblage of over 60 shops is located in the Munn Park Historic District (p 118) in Lakeland. Quaint craft and antique shops line Fifth Avenue and Donnelly Street in Mount Dora (p 79). The Wagon Wheel Flea Market, located in St. Petersburg, claims to be the world's largest flea market and is well worth a visit. Streets in south Tampa and Ybor City are lined with antique shops, art galleries and studios. Antique-car buffs will want to visit car shows in Daytona Beach (p 86) that feature swap meets (Mar & Nov) offering vintage car parts and accessories.

In his 1865 novel From the Earth to the Moon, *Jules Verne imagined Florida as the launch site for the first lunar expedition. Just over 100 years later, imagination and desire combined to accomplish the seemingly impossible.*

Nature & Safety

Fauna Great and Small – A multitude of creatures such as mosquitoes, chiggers, scorpions, lovebugs, fire ants, sand flies, cockroaches and other wildlife enjoy Florida's subtropical climate as much as most visitors do. When planning outdoor activities, be sure to take necessary precautions. **Mosquitoes** are unavoidable, especially from June to September—the rainy months when humidity is high. In coastal areas mosquitoes are active year-round. Insect repellent, available at supermarkets, pharmacies and most camping stores, is as important as wearing long-sleeved shirts and long pants. When camping, remember that smoke from a campfire is an effective mosquito deterrent. It is unlikely that visitors will encounter **alligators**; they tend to avoid people unless provoked. However, stay clear of a mother guarding her young and do not swim in remote lakes, especially during gator mating season (mid-April). When hiking do not bring your dog; alligators have been known to attack dogs, especially small ones. Florida law prohibits the feeding or molesting of alligators. Twenty-six species of **snakes** inhabit the Florida landscape. The poisonous ones *(p 46)* include several species of rattlesnakes and the coral snake. However, like most wildlife, they generally do not pose a threat to people unless provoked. Always wear appropriate footwear and look where you are walking.

When visiting a national wildlife refuge, state park or national forest, remember that while the disturbance of a single person may be small, the cumulative impact of a large number of visitors may be disastrous. "Take nothing but pictures; leave nothing but footprints" has been adopted as a slogan and is posted in many parks.

Tips for Visiting Public Lands:

■ Enjoy the native vegetation, but please leave it untouched.

■ Do not feed animals; they may become ill and die.

■ Keep your distance from wildlife.

■ Do not walk on sand dunes, but stay on boardwalks.

■ Do not litter.

■ Remember to pack out everything you pack in.

■ Learn to recognize and avoid poisonwood, poison sumac, manchineel *(p 15)*, poison oak and poison ivy; contact may require medical attention.

Hurricanes – The hurricane season usually lasts from June to November with the greatest activity generally from August to October. Hurricanes *(p 13)* begin as tropical depressions and are classified as hurricanes once winds reach 74mph. The National Hurricane Center in Coral Gables, Florida tracks all storms and issues advisories every six hours; stay tuned to radio and television. A hurricane **watch** is announced if a storm may threaten an area; a hurricane **warning** is issued if landfall is expected within 24 hours.

Hurricane Precautionary Measures:

▲ Check your car battery and fill up the gas tank.

▲ Make sure you have a battery-operated radio and extra batteries.

▲ Collect plenty of fresh water in containers and bathtubs.

▲ When staying in coastal areas familiarize yourself with evacuation routes.

▲ Stay indoors once the hurricane has struck.

▲ Be aware of storm surges in coastal regions.

▲ Most importantly, never take a hurricane lightly, and follow instructions issued by local authorities.

Thunderstorms and Lightning – Storms occur almost daily in the summer in Florida (June–Sept) and can pass quickly. Peak lightning season is July to August. Some thunderstorms *(p 13)* can be severe, featuring hail and dangerous lightning.

Storm Safety Tips:

▲ Take cover.

▲ Stay away from trees and metal objects.

▲ If riding in a vehicle, remain inside until the storm has passed.

▲ Avoid being in or near water.

▲ If in a boat, head for the nearest shore.

▲ Do not use electrical appliances, especially the telephone.

Beach and Water Safety – In the strong subtropical sun, visitors run the risk of sunburn, even in winter. Reflections from the white sand and water increases the sun's intensity. Use sunglasses to protect your eyes, wear a wide-brimmed hat and drink plenty of liquids. Apply sunscreen even on overcast days, since ultraviolet rays penetrate the cloud cover. Avoid strenuous exercise during midday.

Never swim alone and heed **red warning flags** that indicate dangerous swimming conditions such as riptides, strong underlying currents that pull swimmers seaward. Warning flags are posted every mile along public beaches: blue means calm waters; yellow indicates choppy waters. Most public beaches employ lifeguards seasonally. Take care when swimming at an unguarded beach. Children should be supervised at all times. Scuba diving and snorkeling should never be undertaken alone.

© Susan Russell

Stinging creatures such as jellyfish, Portuguese men-of-war and sea urchins inhabit shallow waters. Although most jellyfish stings produce little more than an itchy skin rash, some can cause painful swelling. Treating the affected area with papain-type meat tenderizer will give relief. Stingrays and Portuguese men-of-war can inflict a more serious sting; seek medical treatment immediately.

A good rule of thumb for any water-sports activity is to check with local authorities about conditions before setting out. If you rent a canoe or charter a small yacht, first familiarize yourself with the craft and obtain maps and the latest weather information. When going out on a boat, always advise someone of your itinerary. **Life jackets** must be worn when boating. Many equipment rental facilities also offer instruction; be sure to choose a reputable outfitter.

Sports & Recreation

Florida has three national parks, two national seashores, three national forests, two national monuments, and more than 150 state parks that preserve and protect the natural and cultural heritage. Recreational activities at most parks include: hiking, biking, fishing, swimming, snorkeling, boating, horseback riding and camping. Parks are most frequently visited from Memorial Day to Labor Day, although in south Florida they are busiest during the dry season (October–April) when viewing of wildlife and migratory birds is best. Strenuous activities should be limited to early morning or late afternoon. The *Florida Sports Vacation Guide* (Florida Sports Foundation, *p 7*) and *A Guide to Florida's Natural Habitats* (VISIT FLORIDA, *p 7*) are available free of charge.

National Parks, Seashores and Monuments – Florida has seven units administered by the National Park Service; entrance fees are charged only at Everglades National Park *($10/vehicle)*, Castillo de San Marcos National Monument *($4/person)* and the Fort Pickens section of Gulf Islands National Seashore *($4/vehicle)*. Prices are subject to change. All are at least partially accessible to people with disabilities. There is camping *(fees range from $8-$21)* at Everglades, Biscayne and Dry Tortugas national parks and Gulf Islands National Seashore *(☎ 800-365-2267 for reservations)*. Most visitor centers offer interpretive exhibits, slide presentations and maps. Picnic areas are provided at parks and seashores. In some cases, visitors can explore the surroundings on self-guided nature trails and participate in ranger-led hikes. Boat rentals may be available. Most park beaches do not have lifeguards. Pets are welcome if kept on a leash, but are not allowed in camping areas or on bathing beaches. For detailed information, contact the individual park or write to National Park Service, Atlanta Federal Center, 100 Alabama St. S.W., Atlanta GA 30303, www.nps.gov.com ☏ 404-562-3123.

State Parks – Visitors can choose from an ever-expanding state park system, including nature preserves and historic landmarks. Parks are open year-round 8am–dusk. Visitor centers, museums and historic sites may have different opening hours. Entrance fees: $3.25–$4/vehicle (up to 8 people), $1/person when entering on foot or by bicycle. Camping fees vary according to season and location (average $8–$21). To request a copy of the guide *Florida State Parks* (free), write to the Department of Environmental Protection, Division of Recreation and Parks *(p 7)*.

Biking – Because of the flat terrain, bicycling is popular throughout the state. The cooler months (October–May) are the best cycling "season" since summer temperatures and high humidity can make long rides a true challenge. Bicycles are not allowed on highways, limited-access highways, expressways or some bridges. The most pleasant cycling conditions are north of I-4, in central Florida near Gainesville and Ocala, north in the Live Oak area, and on trails and greenways that link local and state parks and national forests. Beach areas from Fernandina Beach *(p 99)* to Melbourne and on Captiva and Sanibel Islands *(p 250)* offer pleasant riding paths. For more information, contact area tourist offices and local bike rental shops.

Biking Safety Tips:
- ■ Obey all traffic laws and ride single file.
- ■ The law requires bicyclists under 16 to wear a helmet.
- ■ Do not travel at night.

Three bicycle tours of varying lengths—from a weekend to a six-day excursion with overnight stops in state parks—have been organized by the Florida Department of Environmental Protection. For bicycle trail guides, a touring information package, maps and *Florida Trails* guide contact: VISIT FLORIDA *(p 7)*. Bicycling tours: Outdoor Adventures ☏ 904-393-9030; Brooks Country Cycling Tours ☏ 212-874-5151. Other sources for information: State Bicycle Office, Florida Department of Transportation *(p 7)*; Rails-to-Trails, 2545 Blairstone Pines Dr., Tallahassee FL 32301 ☏ 850-942-2379.

Horseback Riding – Many state parks and forests offer miles of unpaved roads and trails for horseback riding. State parks that provide overnight camping for riders and horses are: Florida Caverns *(p 160)*, Jonathan Dickinson *(p 298)*, Little Manatee River, Myakka River *(p 261)* and O'Leno. Call the park office to inquire about staging areas, camping facilities and trail conditions. Regulations require proof of a recent negative Coggins test for all horses entering park areas. Riders are required to stay on designated trails. The *Florida Horse Trail Directory* is available from the Florida Department of Agriculture, Room 416, Mayo Building, Tallahassee FL 32399-0800 ☏ 850-488-

Courtesy Biltmore Hotel

9682. Contact local chambers of commerce or the Florida Department of Environmental Protection for additional information. Horseback riding is allowed on several beaches. Check with local authorities before setting out. Ride from Hutchinson Island *(p 295)* by way of Lake Okeechobee to Lovers Key *(p 247)* and stay in roadside hotels *(all inclusive 8-day excursion; Apr–May & Oct–Nov; $2,270–$2,450; advance reservations required)*. For further information, contact Royal Palm Tours, PO Box 60079, Fort Myers FL 33906-6079 ☏ 941-368-0760 or 800-296-0249 (US & Canada).

Golf – Ranked one of the nation's top golfing destinations, Florida boasts well over 1,100 golf courses, several designed by such legends as Jack Nicklaus and Arnold Palmer. Florida's balmy climate makes golf accessible year-round. Duffers can practice their driving and putting expertise at numerous public courses or watch professional golfers at one of the numerous tournaments that take place throughout the state. Many hotels and resorts include golf facilities, and some private courses allow non-members to play. Numerous courses offer golf clinics and private instruction. Make reservations well ahead of time; teeing off during midday means less-crowded fairways and lower humidity. Greens fees average $85 in winter, $40 in summer. For golf vacation packages that include accommodations at over 90 courses *(starting at $75/person per night, depending on season and location)* in Jacksonville, Fort Lauderdale, Fort Myers, Naples, Orlando and the Tampa Bay area, contact World of Golf, Inc. ☎ 407-884-8300 or 800-729-1400 (US). The publication, *Destination Florida Golf*, is available (free) from Florida Sports Foundation *(p 7)*.

Tee Times USA will make reservations (free) for tee times at more than 150 selected golf courses. Discount golf packages are available. Written confirmation and travel directions will be mailed. To request a brochure or to make reservations, contact Tee Times USA, PO Box 641, Flagler Beach FL 32136, www.teetimesusa.com ☎ 800-374-8633 (US & Canada). To request a copy of *Fairways in the Sunshine*, contact the Florida Sports Foundation.

Hiking – The best time to hike is from late fall to early spring when temperatures are cooler and humidity is lower. When hiking, stay on marked trails; taking shortcuts is dangerous and causes erosion. Obtain up-to-date weather forecasts; a sudden storm can flood trails in swampy areas. If hiking alone, notify someone of your destination and anticipated return time.

The USDA Forest Service and the Florida Trail Association maintain the **Florida National Scenic Trail**, which extends from the Gulf Islands National Seashore in northwestern Florida to the Big Cypress National Preserve in southwestern Florida. All trails are marked; camping is limited. Some segments of the trail may be closed during hunting season. Before setting out, check with the local managing authority or write to: US Forest Service, Greenways & Trails *(p 7)* or the Florida Trail Association, PO Box 13708, Gainesville FL 32604, www.florida-trail.org/~fta ☎ 352-378-8823 or 800-343-1882 (US).

The Florida Trail Association builds and maintains trails, provides its members *($25/year)* with trail maps and a bi-monthly newsletter *Footprint*, and offers activities such as backpacking and canoeing trips. Details on trails—entry points, descriptions, tips for hiking and backpacking—are described in the *Florida Hiking Trails* guide, available at bookstores or from the Florida Trail Association *(above)*. For *A Guide to Your National Scenic Trail*, contact the US Forest Service *(p 7)*.

Fishing and Hunting – The many rivers, lakes, ponds and wilderness waterways offer experienced and amateur anglers some of the best fishing waters in the US. Fishing enthusiasts do not have to rent expensive boats to enjoy a day of angling. Many coastal communities have public fishing piers where equipment can be rented from bait and tackle shops for a minimal fee. Fish camps along inland waterways offer boat and houseboat rentals and guided fishing trips for the whole family.

Miles of coastline on the Atlantic and Gulf of Mexico give the saltwater enthusiast the chance to catch over 70 pecies of fish. For the average fisherman there are many opportunities to engage in surf casting and bridge and pier fishing. A variety of boat-charter services can accommodate every level of expertise and budget. Many marinas rent boats ranging from canoes to pontoon boats. Most backcountry channels in the Gulf are unmarked, and it is wise to employ the services of a local guide who can lead you to the best fishing spots. Be sure to choose a licensed outfitter. For additional information on saltwater fishing, contact the Department of Environmental Protection, Office of Fisheries Management *(p 7)*.

Resident and non-resident anglers must have a freshwater and saltwater **fishing license**. Bait and tackle shops, marinas and sporting-goods stores issue licenses. To receive a copy of *Florida Fishing & Boating Guidebook* (free), contact the Florida Sports Foundation *(p 7)*.

Monroe County TDC

331

Many different types of game await the sportsmen in Florida's forests, grasslands and vast swamps. Rifles and shotguns may be brought into Florida for hunting and sporting purposes (no permit required). Hunting is permitted in Big Cypress National Preserve *(p 45)*, wildlife-management areas and most state and national forests. Whether fishing or hunting, sportsmen should be aware that native species of birds are protected by law, as are all endangered and threatened animals. For freshwater **fishing and hunting regulations**, bag limits, seasons and the *Florida Hunting Handbook* (free), contact Florida Game and Freshwater Fish Commission, 620 S. Meridian St., Tallahassee FL 32399-1600 ☎ 850-488-4676.

Deep-Sea Fishing – Many species can be found along the Florida Keys year-round offering the greatest variety of offshore game fishing. Large "party boats" can take up to 20 fishermen. Half-day trips are great for beginners, while full-day excursions are designed for the avid angler, allowing the captain to change locations, according to where the fish are biting. Most boats have a fishing license and knowledgeable crew. Prices range from $50–$250/person.

Charter boats specializing in deep-sea sport fishing will appeal to the experienced fisherman who is looking to reel in "the big one"—sailfish, dolphin, wahoo, tuna, kingfish and blue or white marlin. Charters are costly but include equipment, bait and fishing licenses. For further information, contact the **Florida Sport Fishing Information Line** ☎ 800-ASK-FISH.

Outdoor Adventures – A naturalist-guided expedition that explores the Everglades in a canoe or kayak is a **learning vacation** offered by Sea Kayak Georgia, P.O. Box 2747, Tybee Island GA 31328 ☎ 912-786-8732. Bird-watching tours in the Keys and Dry Tortugas are led by Victor Emanuel Nature Tours, Austin TX ☎ 800-328-8368 (US & Canada). North Florida's premier outfitter for backcountry and **wilderness excursions** offers kayaking on Durbin Creek, canoeing on the Suwannee River, **tubing** on the Ichetucknee River; for reservations contact Outdoor Adventures, Jacksonville FL ☎ 904-393-9030; for more on **hot-air ballooning** ☎ 904-399-2882. Sail to the Bahamas from Fort Lauderdale and **swim with the dolphins**; 8-9 day excursions by Natural Habitat, Boulder CO ☎ 800-543-8917 (US & Canada).

Cruises – A variety of cruise vacations catering to families and singles are available. Choose from a four-day sail to the Bahamas with ample time to explore the islands; a relaxing cruise to Mexico's Yucatan Peninsula or through the Panama Canal to Los Angeles; or a voyage to some out-of-the-way island that includes educational lectures and on-shore excursions. Most cruise lines offer air/sea packages and discounts for early bookings. Florida has seven ports that offer service year-round. The three largest are the Port of Miami, Port Everglades (Fort Lauderdale) and Port Tampa. Major cruise lines departing from these ports are Carnival, Cunard, Norwegian, Premier, Royal Caribbean (Miami); Celebrity, Crystal, Discovery, Holland America, Norwegian, Princess, Radisson, Royal Caribbean, Sea Escape, Seabourn (Fort Lauderdale); and Holland America and Carnival (Tampa). All ports provide free parking facilities and free shuttle service to nearby hotels. For up-to-date information, check with individual cruise lines or contact the National Association of Cruise-Only Agencies (☎ 305-663-5626) for a listing of organizations that specialize in cruise vacations.

Things to do with children

Theme parks are the number one attraction for the young and young-at-heart, offering not only great entertainment but also education. Many state parks and nature preserves offer entertainment for children, with nearby campsites that allow children to boat, fish, swim or play along sandy beaches. Miniature golf courses that entertain young and old alike abound in Florida. Local festivals *(p 318-319)* are loads of fun for youngsters. Many sites offer discounted admission fees to children under 12. When reserving a hotel, check whether it offers organized children's programs that may include sports activities, arts and crafts, beach outings, canoe trips and more. In this guide, sites that are of particular interest to children are indicated by **Kids**.

Additional Activities for Kids:

Kids Ride the Florida *FUN-TRAIN* and enjoy video games and experience virtual reality in the action-packed game car, play in a bi-level Space Shuttle, let clowns entertain kids of all ages, and view the Florida countryside from glass-domed cars. Trains travel between Hollywood & Kissimmee *($69.95; children 12 & under $49.95)* and Kissimmee & Tampa *($30; children $20)*. For schedules and reservations contact Florida *FUN-TRAIN*, 37000 N. 29 Ave., Suite 202, Hollywood FL 33020 ☎ 888-386-8722.

Kids Ride a go-kart in Port Orange: Go-Kart City ☎ 904-761-2882.

Kids Attend a spring practice *(p 000)* and have a baseball signed by your favorite player (have a pen ready).

Kids Take a waterfall plunge, tube down five stories or splash around in an ocean-like wave pool at Wet'n'Wild, Orlando *(open year-round daily; mid-June–Aug 9am–11pm; rest of the year opening hours vary)* ☎ 407-351-1800.

Kids Participate in the "If I Had a Hammer" program *(year-round; $5; reservations required)* sponsored by the Miami Children's Museum ☎ 305-663-8800.

Kids Experience a trip to the moon in the Space Flight simulator at the Museum of Discovery & Science, Fort Lauderdale *(p 189)*.

Spectator Sports

Most major metropolitan areas have **greyhound racing** tracks close by, while **jai alai** (p 34) facilities are located in Fort Lauderdale, Fort Pierce, Miami, Ocala and Orlando. Winter brings the best horses and riders to south Florida. Horse lovers can experience the thrill of **thoroughbred racing** at four tracks in the Greater Miami area and at Tampa Bay Downs. For a listing of pari-mutuel betting establishments, write to the Department of Business Regulations, 1940 Monroe St., Tallahassee FL 32399 ☎ 850-488-3211. Pompano Park hosts **harness racing** from October to June. West Palm Beach, Boca Raton and Vero Beach present **polo** matches from November to mid-April. For venues check local telephone directories or contact area tourist offices.

Motor sports – The Daytona International Speedway *(p 88)* is home to a number of racing events throughout the year including motorcycle and go-kart racing. Enthusiasts of automobile racing flock here from late January to mid-February when the Rolex 24 IMSA sports car race and the world-famous **Daytona 500** stock car race take place. Held every spring, Bike Week *(p 89)* is a city-wide celebration of motorcycles. Gator-Nationals, the largest drag-racing contest on the Atlantic Seaboard, takes place each March in Gainesville.

Professional Leagues

Team/League Association	City	Location	☎
Miami Dolphins *NFL*	Miami	*Pro Player Stadium*	305-620-2578
Miami Heat *NBA*	Miami	*Miami Arena*	305-577-4328
Florida Panthers *NHL*	Sunrise	*Broward County Arena*	305-768-1900
Florida Marlins *MLB*	Miami	*Pro Player Stadium*	305-626-7400
Jacksonville Jaguars *NFL*	Jacksonville	*Alltel Stadium*	904-633-2000
Orlando Magic *NBA*	Orlando	*Orlando Arena*	407-896-2442
Tampa Bay Buccaneers *NFL*	Tampa	*Tampa Stadium*	813-879-2827
Tampa Bay Lightning *NHL*	Tampa	*Ice Palace Arena*	813-229-2658
Tampa Bay Devil Rays *MLB*	St. Petersburg	*Tropicana Field*	813-825-3120

(for tickets contact the local Ticketmaster office)

Spring Training Camps – If it's spring, it must be baseball season, when some of the major-league **baseball** teams head for training camps in Florida. Warm-up practice starts in late February and "Grapefruit League" exhibition games are played daily through March. Practices are held between 10am–2pm and are free. Tickets for games range from $5–$10. Order tickets early by calling the stadium directly or the local Ticketmaster outlet. For a free schedule, write to Major League Baseball, 350 Park Ave., New York NY 10022. The magazine *Spring Training ($4.99)*, published annually in late January, gives team histories, schedules, ticket details, directions and accommodations. To order, contact Vanguard Publishing, PO Box 667, Chapel Hill NC 27514 ☎ 800-473-1656 (US & Canada). A *Spring Training Guide* is available (free) from the Florida Sports Foundation *(p 7)*.

Team	City	Location	☎
Atlanta Braves	Kissimmee	Disney's Wide World of Sports	407-939-1500
Baltimore Orioles	Fort Lauderdale	Fort Lauderdale Stadium	954-776-1921
Boston Red Sox	Fort Myers	City of Palms Park	941-334-4700
Cincinnati Reds	Sarasota	Ed Smith Stadium	941-954-4101
Cleveland Indians	Winter Haven	Chain of Lakes Stadium	941-293-3900
Detroit Tigers	Lakeland	Joker Marchant Stadium	941-686-7911
Florida Marlins	Melbourne	Space Coast Stadium	407-633-9200
Houston Astros	Kissimmee	Osceola County Stadium	407-933-6500
Kansas City Royals	Davenport	Baseball City Stadium	941-424-2500
Los Angeles Dodgers	Vero Beach	Holman Stadium	561-569-4900
Minnesota Twins	Fort Myers	Lee County Sports Complex	941-768-4266
Montreal Expos	Jupiter	Roger Dean Stadium	561-775-1818
New York Mets	Port St. Lucie	Thomas J. White Stadium	561-871-2115
New York Yankees	Tampa	Legends Field	813-879-2244
Philadelphia Phillies	Clearwater	Jack Russell Stadium	813-442-8496
Pittsburgh Pirates	Bradenton	McKechnie Field	941-748-4610
St. Louis Cardinals	Jupiter	Roger Dean Stadium	561-775-1818
Tampa Bay Devil Rays	St. Petersburg	Al Lang Stadium	813-825-3250
Texas Rangers	Port Charlotte	Charlotte County Stadium	941-625-9500
Toronto Blue Jays	Dunedin	Dunedin Stadium at Grant Field	813-733-0429

Water Sports

With hundreds of miles of prime coastline bordering the Atlantic and Gulf of Mexico, a multitude of water sports is available year-round to visitors of all ages. Inland lakes, rivers and springs complete the array of opportunities to **swim**, boat or simply enjoy the relaxing sound of rippling water. Although Florida's Atlantic coast is not known for its large waves, **surfing** is popular along Sebastian Inlet south of Melbourne, and around Jacksonville and Miami. Surfboards and sailboards can be rented locally. Check water conditions with lifeguards or local authorities before setting out to surf or windsurf.

Selected Beaches *(listed by region)*

	$	🏊 swim	✚ lifeguard	△ camping	🎣 fishing	🏄 surfing	🤿 scuba
Panhandle							
Grayton Beach SRA ☎ 850-231-4210	•	•		•	•	•	
Henderson Beach SRA ☎ 850-837-7550	•	•			•		
Johnson Beach, Gulf Islands National Seashore ☎ 850-492-0912	•	•	•		•		•
Panama City Beach ☎ 850-235-1159		•	•		•	•	
Pensacola Beach ☎ 850-932-1500	•	•	•		•		
Santa Rosa Island ☎ 850-934-2600	•	•			•	•	•
St. Andrews SRA ☎ 850-233-5140	•	•		•	•	•	•
St. George Island SP ☎ 850-927-2111	•	•		•	•		
St. Joseph Peninsula SP ☎ 850-227-1327	•	•		•	•		•
East Coast							
Amelia Island SRA ☎ 904-251-2320		•			•		
Anastasia SRA ☎ 904-461-2033	•	•		•	•	•	
Daytona Beach ☎ 904-239-6414		•	•		•	•	
Flagler Beach ☎ 904-517-2086	•	•		•	•	•	•
Fort Pierce Inlet SRA ☎ 561-468-3985	•	•	•		•	•	
St. Augustine Beach ☎ 904-829-1711	•	•	•		•	•	
Sebastian Inlet SRA ☎ 407-984-4852	•	•	•		•	•	•
Vero Beach ☎ 561-567-3491	•	•			•	•	
South Florida and the Keys							
Bahia Honda SP ☎ 305-872-2353	•	•		•	•		•
Bill Baggs Cape Florida SRA ☎ 305-361-5811	•	•	•		•		
Crandon Park ☎ 305-361-5421	•	•	•				
Fort Lauderdale Beach ☎ 954-765-4466	•	•	•		•	•	•
Haulover Beach ☎ 305-947-3525	•	•	•		•		
Hugh Taylor Birch SRA ☎ 954-564-4521	•	•	•		•		
J. D. MacArthur Beach SP ☎ 561-624-6952	•	•			•		•
J. U. Lloyd Beach SRA ☎ 954-923-2833	•	•	•		•		
John Pennekamp Coral Reef SP ☎ 305-451-1202	•	•		•	•		•
North Shore SRA ☎ 305-993-2032	•	•			•	•	•
Ocean Beach ☎ 305-672-1270	•	•	•			•	
Gulf Coast							
Coquina Beach ☎ 941-729-9177		•			•		
Clearwater Beach ☎ 813-461-0011	•	•	•				
Delnor-Wiggins Pass SRA ☎ 941-597-6196	•	•	•		•		
Gasparilla Island SRA ☎ 941-964-0375	•				•		
Longboat Key ☎ 941-383-2466		•			•		
Lovers Key SRA ☎ 941-463-4588	•	•			•		
St. Petersburg Beach ☎ 813-464-7200		•			•		
Sanibel Island Beaches ☎ 941-472-1080	•	•	•	•	•		•
Venice Beach ☎ 941-488-2236	•	•			•	•	

Symbols on the above chart indicate: $ admission/parking fee; 🏊 swimming; ✚ lifeguard (seasonally); △ camping; 🎣 fishing; 🏄 surfing; 🤿 scuba/snorkeling.

© Stephen Frink

Canoeing – The Florida Canoe Trail system includes close to 950mi of scenic waterways. Canoe trails on rivers and creeks let the outdoor enthusiast paddle along slow-flowing waters of the Santa Fe River, glide through swampy areas along the upper Suwannee River, or camp on a secluded riverbank. *Florida Recreational Canoe Trails* (free from the Office of Greenways & Trails, *p 7*) lists facilities, camping and local outfitters. You can also contact individual national parks, state parks or preserves for additional information on local canoe trails. Flat-water wilderness canoeing can be experienced along the Wilderness Waterway *(p 45)* in the Everglades.

Employ the services of a reputable outfitter to explore Florida's backwaters. Guides lead paddle adventures on the Peace River for the whole family that range from half-day canoe trips to overnight canoe camping outings. For a brochure, contact Canoe Outpost, 2816 N.W. County Rd. 661, Arcadia FL 34266 ☏ 941-494-1215. Kayak, paddle boats, tubes and canoe excursions can be arranged through Adventures Unlimited, Milton FL 32570; for reservations ☏ 904-623-6197. To request a copy of the canoeing & kayaking directory that lists member outfitters, contact the Office of Greenways & Trails *(p 7)*. For canoeing in the Ten Thousand Islands area *(p 45)*, contact Wilderness Inquiries, 1313 Fifth St. S.E., Box 84, Minneapolis MN 55414, www.wildernessinquiry.org ☏ 612-379-3858 or 800-728-0719 (US & Canada).

Canoeing Tips:

- ■ Law requires that each occupant wear a flotation device.
- ■ Take an extra paddle.
- ■ Get a map of canoeing routes and keep abreast of weather conditions.
- ■ Keep in mind that coastal rivers are affected by tides.
- ■ Rivers in north Florida run high in spring and summer; in central and south Florida rivers run high in summer and fall.
- ■ Avoid flooded rivers.
- ■ Carry drinking water, and always advise someone of your plans.

Scuba Diving and Snorkeling – Most popular areas are the Keys and south Florida, where hundreds of private dive shops offer a variety of diving trips. Most venues rent equipment and organize dive excursions. For a listing of dive shops in the upper Keys, contact the Key Largo Chamber of Commerce ☏ 305-451-1414. A Certified Diver's Card is required in order to scuba dive. Courses to obtain the necessary certification are offered by most diving shops. Choose an instructor who is certified by the Professional Association of Dive Instructors (PADI) or the National Association of Underwater Instructors (NAUI). For more information, see p 48.

Snorkelers and scuba divers can enjoy the living coral reef that lies off the Florida Keys *(p 51)*. If you feel more at ease staying close to the surface, snorkeling trips are available. Although waters are shallow, you should be a good swimmer. To get close to the reef without the heavy air tank, try **snuba**. Expeditions by Snuba Tours of Key Largo let you explore the reef connected to a 20ft breathing hose that is attached to an air tank secured to a raft on the surface *(1hr lesson; half-day excursion and guided dive; $110/person; ☏ 305-451-6391)*. Make advance reservations for all expeditions. A few precautions: wear lightweight shoes to protect against sharp rocks; don't wear shiny objects that will attract hungry fish; if you leave the boat, display a red-and-white "diver down" flag, and most importantly **never dive alone**. Seas are usually rougher in winter and can produce poor visibility on the reefs.

Index

G-H

I-J

K-L

M

Notes